Practical Microservices Architectural Patterns

Event-Based Java Microservices with Spring Boot and Spring Cloud

Binildas Christudas

Foreword by Guy Pardon, Allard Buijze and Schahram Dustdar

Apress®

Practical Microservices Architectural Patterns

Binildas Christudas
Trivandrum, Kerala, India

ISBN-13 (pbk): 978-1-4842-4500-2   ISBN-13 (electronic): 978-1-4842-4501-9
https://doi.org/10.1007/978-1-4842-4501-9

Managing Director, Apress Media LLC: Welmoed Spahr
Acquisitions Editor: Nikhil Karkal
Development Editor: Siddhi Chavan
Coordinating Editor: Divya Modi

Cover designed by eStudioCalamar

Cover image designed by Freepik (www.freepik.com)

Distributed to the book trade worldwide by Springer Science+Business Media New York, 233 Spring Street, 6th Floor, New York, NY 10013. Phone 1-800-SPRINGER, fax (201) 348-4505, e-mail orders-ny@springer-sbm.com, or visit www.springeronline.com. Apress Media, LLC is a California LLC and the sole member (owner) is Springer Science + Business Media Finance Inc (SSBM Finance Inc). SSBM Finance Inc is a **Delaware** corporation.

For information on translations, please e-mail rights@apress.com, or visit www.apress.com/rights-permissions.

Apress titles may be purchased in bulk for academic, corporate, or promotional use. eBook versions and licenses are also available for most titles. For more information, reference our Print and eBook Bulk Sales web page at www.apress.com/bulk-sales.

Any source code or other supplementary material referenced by the author in this book is available to readers on GitHub via the book's product page, located at www.apress.com/978-1-4842-4500-2. For more detailed information, please visit www.apress.com/source-code.

Printed on acid-free paper

To Sowmya, Ann, and Ria.

Table of Contents

About the Author

Binildas Christudas provides technical architecture consultancy for IT solutions. He has over 20 years of IT experience, mostly in Microsoft and Oracle technologies. Distributed computing and service-oriented integration are his main skills, with extensive hands-on experience in Java and C# programming. A well-known and highly sought-after thought leader, Binil has designed and built many highly scalable middle-tier and integration solutions for several top-notch clients including Fortune 500 companies. He has been employed by multiple IT consulting firms including Infosys and Tata Consultancy Services and currently works for IBS Software Private Limited as the Chief Architect. In his role as VP and Head of Technology, he leads technology and architecture strategies for IBS's product portfolio.

Binil is a Sun Certified Programmer (SCJP), Developer (SCJD), Business Component Developer (SCBCD), and Enterprise Architect (SCEA), Microsoft Certified Professional (MCP), and Open Group (TOGAF8) Certified Enterprise Architecture Practitioner. He is also a Licensed Zapthink Architect (LZA) in SOA. Binil has his B.Tech. in Mechanical Engineering from the College of Engineering, Trivandrum (CET) and MBA in Systems from the Institute of Management Kerala (IMK). Binil was the captain of the Kerala University Power Lifting team and was the national champion during his university studies. IBS has applied for his proposal titled "A Method and a System for Facilitating Multitenancy of Services" to be a patent with the USPTO. Binil can be contacted through www.linkedin.com/in/binildasca/ or www.facebook.com/binildas.christudas.

About the Technical Reviewer

 **Arun Prasanth** has 12 years of experience as a hands-on software architect involved in the architecture, design, coding, and implementation of Java/J2EE-based microservices architecture and service-oriented architecture. He is currently working as senior technical architect in IBS software services in Japan. Previously, he worked in the banking domain at Societe Generale Global Solutions.

Acknowledgments

A big thanks to Apress Media for having trust in me and giving me the opportunity to write this book. Nikhil Karkal and Divya Modi from Apress have been very helpful in making the process seamless and quick for me. I want to thank Siddhi Chavan for collaborating with me and providing detailed instructions on how to make the content even better. I also thank Matthew Moodie for providing the shape of this book through the initial chapters.

The tech-friendly workplace at IBS Software has been a boon for me. Many thanks to Mr. V. K. Mathews, Executive Chairman, IBS Group, for consistent motivation throughout my literary journey. I also need to thank Mr. Arun Hrishikesan, Chief Technology Officer, IBS, for his constant reminders and support for completing this book, especially in providing his broader views on technology areas, which has influenced the content and style of this book to a great extent.

I thank Dr. Schahram for the many hours of interactions where he shared his views on CAP theorem and its implications in practical software architectures.

Special thanks are due to Mr. Allard Buijze, CTO & Founder at AxonIQ, who extended all support in completing this book.

My note of thanks to Dr. Guy Pardon, PhD, Global Solutions Architect at Atomikos, for providing his insights into my book proposal and contents. Guy kept us honest, picking up technical errors and ambiguities. The complete weekend dedicated to making the chapters on transactions so detailed was invaluable, and I am so thankful.

Arun Prasanth made sure all the examples within this book were working as expected. I thank him for reviewing the code content and also for doing the technical review for the book.

Finally, special thanks to my wife, Sowmya Hubert, who knows how strong my passion for technology is and who never complains about the time I spend writing. I would like to thank my daughters, Ann S. Binil and Ria S. Binil, who were way too understanding and supportive over the last many months while I was locked away with my laptop instead of spending time with them. A huge thanks is due to my father, Christudas Y., and mother, Azhakamma J., for their selfless support, which helped me reach where I am today. Also my note of thanks to my in-laws, Hubert Daniel and Pamala Percis. Finally, thanks to my sister, Dr. Binitha, her husband, Dr. Segin Chandran, and their daughter, Aardra.

Foreword

This book you currently hold in your hands is clearly the result of many years of hands-on experience of a software engineer and architect. Binildas Christudas has written a comprehensive volume guiding software engineers and software architects through the jungle of conceptual decisions to be made in the realm of distributed systems architectures.

The chapters are structured in a logical manner so that the reader is guided through a set of important questions that need to be asked in all large-scale distributed systems projects. In particular, it deserves to be highlighted that the author spends a good amount of the book explaining in detail all questions software architects and software engineers need to ask before embarking on projects considering the use of microservices and architecting the transition from monolithic architectures towards microservices-based architectures. Furthermore, this book also discusses issues related to cloud deployments, which constitutes a significant aspect of such systems.

The set of exciting and advanced issues discussed in this book covers a range of topics from fundamentals of microservices to questions related to transactions, eventual consistency, cloud deployments, and CAP theorem-related issues.

This volume can serve as a guiding book on all matters related to microservices. It's a step-by-step manual on which questions to ask and subsequently which steps to take in order to implement microservices-based distributed systems.

Thank you.

Schahram Dustdar
Fellow, IEEE, & Head, Distributed Systems Group
TECHNISCHE UNIVERSITAT, WEIN (Vienna University of Technology)

The domain of software engineering is evolving rapidly. Enterprises are continuously challenged by newcomers in the market and by changes in legislation and customer expectations. Startups evolve quickly and are challenged to handle the increasing demand for their services when they become successful. These challenges require a thorough review of how we design and build software. The microservices architecture provides a good foundation for systems that face these demands.

However, microservices come with challenges of their own.

Binildas did a good job combining his extensive hands-on experience in software development with an open mind towards new techniques and architectural styles. Throughout this book, Binildas takes a practical approach to introducing different architectural patterns relevant for microservices systems, describing both well-established, common patterns as well as some emerging patterns, such as CQRS.

If you wish to embark on the microservices journey, this book is your travel guide.

Allard Buijze
CTO & Founder of AxonIQ
Creator of Axon Framework

Microservices are all the news these days, just like SOA was a few years ago. Some people say that microservices are just SOA done right. Instead of heavy WS-* standards, we now have REST. Instead of the ESB, we have a lightweight broker like ActiveMQ. What about transactions? In the following of industry giants like Amazon, we don't necessarily use (nor recommend) global ACID transactions that span all our microservices. Instead, it's all about BASE and Sagas these days.

BASE means: not a giant ACID transaction across all microservices (with one enormous commit), but instead multiple, smaller ACID transactions that ripple through the system - so it becomes consistent, eventually. Messaging is crucial for this.

Each of these smaller ACID transactions can be controlled with proven technologies like XA, so they are really ACID - even when things go wrong.

Unfortunately, BASE is all too often just a misleading excuse used by modern frameworks or technologies / platforms that lack XA support. The way BASE is implemented is key, and without XA it is very hard to do it right - unless you don't care about duplicate processing or lost messages.

Duplicates may give issues sooner or later and get addressed with ad-hoc fixes. Lost messages may never be detected at all except via data inconsistency in the longer term - where the root cause will be extremely hard to find. You can have issues with both at the consumer side, but also at the sender side.

A simple and safe way of doing BASE is shown in Figure 13-3 of Chapter 13. Unless you feel adventurous, I recommend that you stick to this kind of style. If you're in financial services, you'll probably appreciate the strong guarantee offered by XA, with additional code simplicity as a free bonus.

As Chapter 14 shows, it takes a lot of extra coding and testing to mimic the guarantees that come out of the box with XA transactions. Most of the tweaking in Chapter 14 goes well beyond my own comfort zone, but Binildas has done a great job of pointing out how much needs to be taken into account. It's not a walk in the park; far from it.

Advanced coding as with Sagas (Chapter 15) can introduce a different level of transactions where you give up isolation and have to cope with compensation yourself. At Atomikos, we have a somewhat similar model

called Try-Confirm/Cancel (TCC for short; see www.atomikos.com/Blog/
TCCForTransactionManagementAcrossMicroservices). The concept is great, although
many people we talked to don't like it very much because the burden of rollback lies with
them (compensation must be programmed).

Guy Pardon, PhD
Founder
atomikos.com

Introduction

We have been developing and deploying distributed applications for about two decades, and microservices lays down architectural principles and patterns using many shortfalls in developing, deploying, and maintaining distributed applications can be dealt with. Microservices, also known as the microservice architecture, is an architectural style that structures an application as a collection of loosely coupled, independently deployable services that are highly maintainable and testable and are organized around business capabilities. *Practical Microservices Architectural Patterns* is a practical introduction to writing microservices in Java using lightweight and common technologies like Spring Boot, Spring Cloud and Axon. I present the material in a way that will enable you to use what you learn right away. To that end, I include code samples for all main concepts and show you exactly how to build and execute them.

The book exposes many architectural complexities you will deal with when designing microservices, and it uses code samples in solving challenging scenarios. `Practical Microservices Architectural Patterns` is an architect's book first, but developers and technical managers can benefit from it too. I wrote it keeping in mind Java architects who want to build serious distributed server-side applications in general and microservices in particular. Focus is on what an architect should be aware of on aspects like event-based systems, transactional integrity, data consistency, and so on; developers too will find the exhaustive code useful in their everyday work. Working knowledge of Java, Spring, and a bit of HTTP is assumed to get the samples up and running quickly. If you do not have background in Java and Spring, still the utility build scripts and step-by-step instructions should help you. Further, even though the samples are in Java, all the architectural aspects and many of the chapters are not specific to Java, hence architects with any technology background dealing with distributed systems should benefit from this book.

The book introduces a complete microservices sample e-commerce application. The readers can straightaway use it as a template to start building their production systems. Of all the books available in the Java world, this is the first one exclusively demonstrating by simulation all success and failure scenarios of a two-phase commit transaction leveraging an XA transaction manager and two different XA transactional resources, with complete code. Having shown the XA transaction in detail, the book next covers with code, techniques available to attain (eventual) transactional integrity by confining ACID-style transactions to within partitions and domains to adopt what is called a BASE transaction across partitions and domains. The book has working samples for Saga, one of the most well-known patterns for BASE-style distributed transactions. The book also covers high availability, security, and performance of microservices. Many of the mantras depicted here are only available with experienced architects; they're not available elsewhere in the public domain, but they're now condensed in the form of this book.

CHAPTER 1

Distributed Computing Architecture Landscape

The technology landscape within any given enterprise of considerable size is often very complex, with aging legacy systems, fragmented by business verticals, internal departments, a supply chain, and so on. In some cases, enterprises have more than one system per business process, given that many enterprises have grown through mergers and acquisitions and thus kept multiple systems and also operate internationally and need to maintain links to different partners and service providers. As a result, the technology infrastructure is often described as "spaghetti architecture," with many-to-many direct dependencies between business systems, partner and supply chain systems, and other service providers.

Starting from the early computer era, we have been developing software to build the above mentioned systems. We evolved from the early punch cards to the next generation assembly languages and then to the era of FORTRAN and COBOL, which further got replaced with C, Smalltalk, and others, and then to C++, Java, and C#. The evolution continues. Architecture has to be adaptable to the programming paradigm, including to the programming language and tools of choice. Any software system of considerable functionality and size has to be built as an afterthought of a suitable software architecture. Sticking to a single or similar software architecture, we can build software systems for varied domains and functionality, but no one can build all kinds of systems adopting the same architecture. Thus, the architectural style of software systems must be adapted based on a plethora of considerations, including but not limited to

- Business domain

- Functionality and usage scenarios

- Non-functional requirements and usage environments

© Binildas Christudas 2019
B. Christudas, *Practical Microservices Architectural Patterns*, https://doi.org/10.1007/978-1-4842-4501-9_1

- Devices and channels used to interact with the systems

- Programming tools used to build the systems

- Infrastructure used to operate the systems

System Architectures

If we trace back, we have been happily and successfully building software systems using a variety of system architectures. Notable among them in the last few years are the following:

- Mainframe architecture

- Client-server architecture

- Three-tier architecture

- N-tier architecture

Let's look at some of the salient features of these architectures with the help of Figure 1-1.

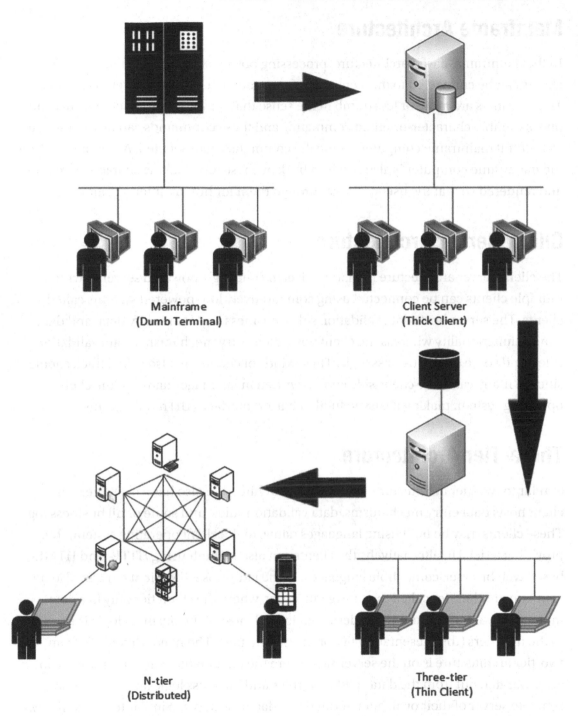

Figure 1-1. *Different forms of system architectures*

Mainframe Architecture

In the mainframe-based architecture, processing power is centralized and multiple clients can be connected to this central compute source using low-powered terminals. The terminals are more or less dumb in the sense that they are simple screens that can only assemble character-oriented commands and these commands can be then sent to the central mainframe computer, where the commands get executed. Any response from the mainframe computer is also received back by these terminals as character streams and rendered so that the user can read through them for human interpretation.

Client-Server Architecture

The client-server architecture is characterized by one high-powered server to which multiple clients can be connected using comparatively low-powered systems called clients. The server hosts data validation rules, business logic to modify data, and data storage functionality whereas the client hosts data entry mechanisms, data validation rules, and some or nil business logic. These kinds of clients are also called thick clients since in many cases the client-side code is written in languages native to the client operating system, making it easy to fulfil rich user interface (UI) requirements.

Three-Tier Architecture

Similar to two-tier architecture, the three-tier architecture also has a client tier. The client hosts data entry mechanisms, data validation rules, and some or nil business logic. These clients may be built using languages native to the client operating system, thus providing a rich UI; alternatively, the clients can also be built using HTTP- and HTML-based web browser-compatible languages. In the latter case, the client tier can also be split into another tier called the presentation tier, where the client tier only has data input, data validation, and UI rendering logic, and most of the business logic is moved to the next tiers (the presentation tier or the middle tier). The major difference from two-tier architecture is on the server side where the data management and storage logic are separated out from the data validation rules and business logic and are kept on a separate server of their own, often termed as a database server. Similar to that in the two-tier architecture, the data validation rules and business logic are retained in the middle-level server, often termed as the middle tier. As of the last few years, mobile devices also interface with the middle tier.

N-Tier Architecture

N-tier architecture can be viewed as an extended kind of three-tier architecture where there are multiple middle tier servers with their own database servers, and many of these middle tier servers are interconnected to leverage functionality reuse. The client tier can either directly connect to the middle tier or it can first connect to a presentation tier which in turn talks to the middle tier. Here again, clients in the client tier can be native thick clients or browser-based thin clients or any other variant of mobile client.

I will not explore further details of the above mentioned system architectures since it is assumed that you are knowledgeable in those aspects; otherwise you probably wouldn't be reading a book like this.

Network Architectures

While I covered system architectures of relevance in the previous section, equally important are the different topologies by which software systems can be interconnected so as to enable integration. Here again I will cover the broader classifications by which networks can be configured so as to enable systems to talk each other, with the help of Figure 1-2.

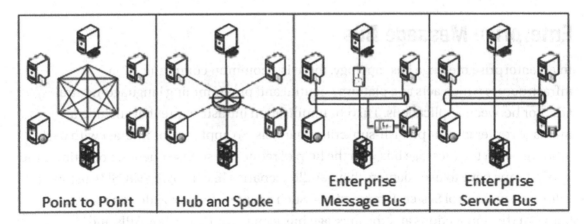

Figure 1-2. *Network integration topologies*

Point to Point

In point-to-point architecture, we define interconnections for a pair of applications. Thus we have two end points to be integrated. We can build protocol and/or format adaptors/transformers at one or either end. This is the easiest way to integrate, as long as the volume of integration is low. We normally use technology-specific APIs like FTP, IIOP, remoting, or batch interfaces to realize integration. Between any two integration points, there is tight coupling, since both ends have knowledge about their peers.

Hub and Spoke

Hub-and-spoke architecture is also called the **message broker** and provides a centralized hub (broker) to which all applications are connected. The distinguishing feature of the hub-and-spoke architecture is that each application connects with the central hub through lightweight connectors. The lightweight connectors facilitate application integration with minimum or no changes to the existing applications. Message transformation and routing takes place within the hub. Since the applications do not connect to other applications directly, they can be removed from the integration topology by plugging off from the hub. Since the hub is a central portion of this kind of topology, the hub is a single point of failure of the entire topology itself.

Enterprise Message Bus

In an enterprise message bus topology, there is a common communication infrastructure which acts as a platform-neutral and programming language-neutral adaptor between applications. This communication infrastructure may include a message router and/or publish-subscribe channels. So applications interact with each other through the message bus with the help of request-response queues. Sometimes the applications have to use adapters that handle scenarios like invoking CICS[1] (Customer Information Control System) transactions. Such adapters may provide connectivity between the applications and the message bus using proprietary bus APIs and application APIs.

---

[1]Customer Information Control System (CICS) is a family of mixed language application servers that provide online transaction management and connectivity for applications on IBM mainframe systems under z/OS and z/VSE.

Enterprise Service Bus (ESB)

The service bus approach to integration makes use of a technology solution to provide a bus for application integration. Different applications will not communicate directly with each other for integration; instead they communicate through this middleware service-oriented architecture (SOA) backbone. The most distinguishing feature of the ESB architecture is the distributed nature of the integration topology. Most ESB solutions are based on Web Services Description Language (WSDL) technologies, and they use Extensible Markup Language (XML) formats for message translation and transformation. Compared to an enterprise message bus, the ESB topology requires less adaptors, since interoperability is high due to the SOA nature of the interfaces.

Software Architectures

Having seen the system architectures and network architectures in general, let's now look at leveraging the notion of tiers and layers to bring modularity and manageability to software application architectures.

Application Tiers

Tiers generally provide distributed deployment capability for application concerns. Typical application tiers can be listed as follows:

- Client tier
- Presentation tier
- Business tier
- Integration tier
- Resources tier

The above list is not exhaustive. Again, I do not intend to explain these tiers in detail, but generally they enable us to group non-functional and technical capabilities and to provide varied operational abilities for these tiers during production deployments.

Application Layers

Layers help to separate concerns based on the single responsibility pattern. For example, there can be a controller layer which can provide a central entry point to the application tier where we can perform authentication and authorization checks, application entry logging, routing to right modules, and so on. Similarly, an ORM (object-relational mapping) layer may perform the required persistence services to transform application domain objects to storage schemas in a persistence disk and vice versa.

Each application tier can be logically separated out into one or more application layers.

The Application Architecture Landscape

If we look back a decade, we have been leveraging the n-tier or distributed way of building application architectures. Multiple applications can talk to each other since they are interconnected based on any of the above network topologies.

You will now concentrate on building a single such application. When I talk about a "single application," I am constraining that application as targeted to perform a set of related or grouped functionalities. An example is an e-commerce application that helps an enterprise to list products for selling purposes and helps its customers to pay and buy these products online with the help of a web browser. Similarly, a stock trading application is another application with a group of functionalities related to trading stocks. Typically we do not club these two applications together since they represent grouping two different sets of functionality. A CRM (customer-relationship management) application, a loyalty application, an airline booking application, and a taxi hiring application are few examples of different such applications.

There can be scenarios where two or more applications need to talk to each other or when we want to mash up functionality from two or more applications. For example, a holiday booking company's booking application may want to mash up services from the airline booking application of the selected airline and the taxi hiring application of the selected cab service provider mentioned above. These scenarios are outside the scope of a single application architecture but need to be considered at an application integration level. I do not intend to cover aspects like inter application integration or application mashups in the scope of our discussion. Instead, I want to concentrate on the architecture of a "single application," the size of which can vary from small to medium to large based on the volume of functionality we want to group together.

Since I mentioned an e-commerce application as good enough to be called a single application, I will use that analogy to discuss concepts and concerns in this book. You will look at the details of functionality of an e-commerce application in a different section, but for the time being you can assume that the e-commerce application is a right-sized application to help you understand almost every concern we want to discuss in this book.

Typical Application Architecture

Many modern applications used by enterprises today have been built using the n-tier architecture and object-oriented programming languages and are capable of being deployed using distributed technologies and infrastructure. The selection of appropriate layers and tiers enables deployment in a flexible manner to meet scalability requirements. Let's now look at a typical application architecture for an e-commerce application deployed in a distributed manner.

Figure 1-3 represents a typical application architecture. It is a three-tier application in the sense that the presentation tier is separated out from the business tier, and there is a third database tier too. The presentation tier is packaged as a `.war` file and encompasses all artifacts required to render the UI in a web browser. The business tier is packaged in a `.jar` format and contains most of the business functionality and business rules. You may also club the presentation tier and the business tier together and create an application artifact in an `.ear` format.

The presentation tier and the business tier can be deployed separately into their own set of dedicated server hardware configured either as a simple server farm or as a server cluster. A server farm is a set of server instances hosting application components in such a fashion that subsequent traffic from a single browser instance can be routed to any one instance irrespective of which server instance the previous request was routed to. Typically a load balancer sitting in front of the farm will distribute the traffic. Further, application components deployed in a server farm will typically be stateless, which means traffic from a single browser instance can be routed to any one instance irrespective of which server instance the previous request was routed to. In this manner, the requests are "not sticky," whereas in a server cluster, typically the server instances coordinate themselves with heartbeats and state replication. Here, the requests are sticky, which means requests from a single browser will always be routed to the same server instance in the cluster as long as that server instance is live. However, non-sticky requests can also be served by a cluster depending on how the cluster and load balancer is configured.

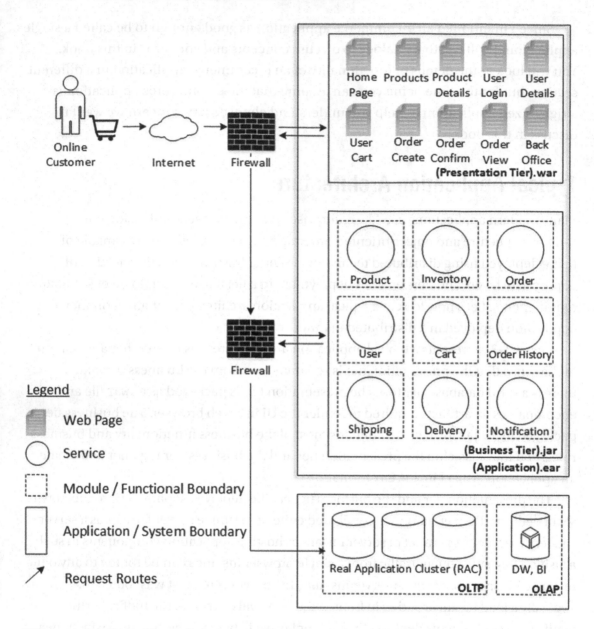

Figure 1-3. *Typical application architecture*

The database tier hosts the data management capability. It handles CRUD (Create, Read, Update, and Delete) requests and also takes care of data consistency functionality by coordinating concurrent CRUD requests appropriately.

Let's now look at the application in more detail. To be specific, assume that the presentation tier and the business tier are deployed separately, in which case the application tier hosts the business tier alone. Figure 1-3 denotes the application boundary, which is the business boundary itself. I talked about tiers and layers earlier, and equally important is dividing the application into multiple pieces, called modules. So, a module can be defined as a group of functionalities and components that are closely related and hence have a lot of "cohesion" between them. Multiple such modules that have the next level of "adhesion" between them make up the full application. Even though the module boundary is represented separately in the figure, in practice, such a differentiated separation may or may not exist in the physical software bundle. To be clear, when we design or build many such modules to get packaged into a single `.jar` or `.ear` file, there is nothing to prevent us from making requests from one module to another, and as the number of such dependencies increases, the adhesion between the modules increases. Hence, the boundary represented is just a virtual boundary that still allows chit-chattiness between modules. Typically, this chit-chattiness may be realized by in-process method invocations. The main realistic boundary in such an architecture is the application boundary itself and it is at this boundary we typically apply SOA (service-oriented architecture) and similar principles. If we want to deploy the modules into multiple processes, we may want to use suitable remoting methodologies for intermodule communications, but this can be possible only if we have designed the modules for this because it cannot be done as an afterthought.

Typical Deployment Architecture

As mentioned, we can club the presentation tier and the business tier together and create an application artifact in a `.ear` format for deployment, or they can be kept separate as `.war` and `.jar` files, which will allow a more flexible deployment where the presentation tier and the business tier are separated. If these two tiers are deployed together, it will allow for optimized intermodule communications by making local method calls. The reason to separate them is to allow differentiated scale-out deployments between these two tiers, and when we do that, a suitable remoting methodology has to be adopted to facilitate intertier communication. Generally we use Java RMI or more generic IIOP or more flexible protocols like HTTP for this intertier communication.

As shown in Figure 1-4, there can be one or more network layer firewalls positioned in front of these tiers to control the level of access to functionality to clients from known networks alone. It's the same case with the database tier. This means we will be able to apply configurations so as to allow only valid application-related calls from the Internet to the presentation tier, and then put more strict rules in front of the other tiers to allow calls to the business tiers only from known and valid IPs.

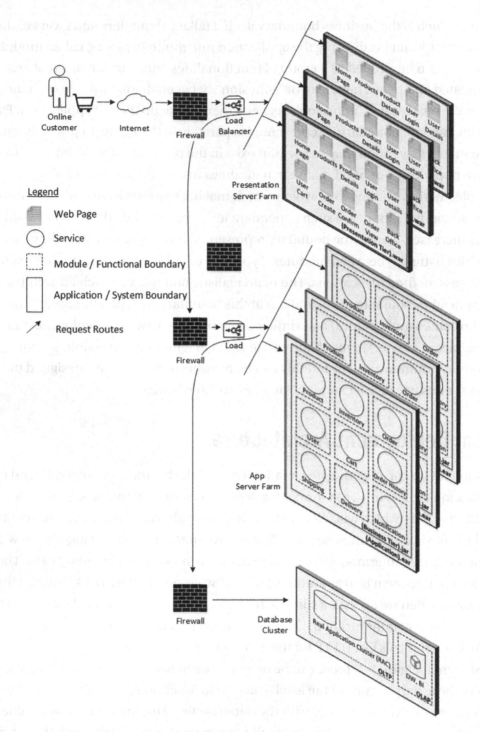

Figure 1-4. *Typical deployment architecture*

If the application services are designed to be stateless, by adopting a suitable deployment architecture we can address any increase in traffic volumes. Further, the level of scale out of the presentation tier is independent of the level of scale out of the business tier. A special note is required at the database tier. While the presentation tier is responsible for assembling contents for effective rendering of the UI, the business tier is responsible for effecting changes to the business data. The sole purpose of the database tier is to keep the state of the data accessible across user requests or across server restarts, that too in a consistent manner. So the database tier is the place for the single source of truth of data. And this puts limitations for scaling at the database tier. The scale out strategy for a database tier is to be different from that of the other tiers in the sense that concurrently modifiable data cannot be replicated just like that because then we need to address the requirement of reconciliation. Generally, the solution to the problem of database scale out and the associated problems of data consistency and data reconciliation are provided by database vendors, not by application architects. This same reason makes the technology stack at the database tier expensive compared to other tiers. Oracle RAC (Real Application Cluster) is one technology in this space. Equally important is another fact that even after these expensive solutions, the level of scale out achievable at the database tier is not comparable to that which can be achieved at other tiers since a database is always stateful, not stateless.

The Scalability Dilemma

You have seen the degree of scalability achievable following a well-designed application architecture. However, the technology landscape is evolving at a faster pace, and newer devices and access channels provide continuous pressure to the application architect in terms of increasing the scalability. This new trend is called "web scale," where the scalability of the application is limited by nothing but the Web itself. By web, we mean the network or the Internet helping unlimited users and devices get connected to the application and access the services.

Application State

How many of you don't like the javax.servlet.http.HttpSession API or the EJB (Enterprise Java Bean) deployment descriptor element called session-type, which can take a value of stateful? For readers unfamiliar with these APIs, here is a short description:

- **HttpSession:** A servlet container uses this interface to create a session between an HTTP client and an HTTP server. The session may persist for a specified time period, across more than one connection or page request from the user. A session instance usually corresponds to one user, who may visit a web site multiple times. The server can maintain a session in many ways, such as using cookies, URL rewriting, and an HttpSession object.

- **session-type:** This deployment descriptor element specifies the type of session bean as stateful or stateless. If it's marked as stateful, then the EJB instances are kept as dedicated for a particular user. This means the EJB instance cannot be pooled by the EJB container, since they are to remain dedicated for each user.

Both methods provide an easy means for the application architect to store user-specific data at the server side. Typical data to be stored in such ways are

- **Authentication and authorization flags:** Once a user has been authenticated by the server, a flag is kept in the presentation server to allow subsequent requests to bypass further authentication.

- **Shopping cart:** A shopping cart in an e-commerce application allows users to select items for eventual purchase. It allows customers to accumulate a list of items for purchase. Upon checkout, it calculates a total for the order, including shipping and handling (i.e., postage and packing) charges and the associated discounts and taxes as applicable. Until then it just keeps the order state temporarily only, and the above API methods are nice places to store such states.

But the downside of using these APIs is that, since the software component instances become user-specific, they cannot be shared for more than one user. In more technical terms, the instances become pinned resources and many times the load balancer instead of load balancing will send requests from a single user to the same server instance. This is not a good practice if we want to web scale.[2]

---

[2]Web-scale IT is defined as all the things happening at large cloud service firms, such as Google, Amazon, Netflix, and Facebook, that enables them to achieve extreme levels of agility and scalability by applying new processes and architectures (Gartner, 2013).

The Dependency Nightmare

The single responsibility pattern and principles of abstraction advocate building functionality in software using a modular approach. Functionalities that are closely related and similar are grouped together to form a software module. Any application of considerable size will have more than one module.

It is also common to have functionality in one module depend directly on functionality in another module within the same application. This dependency is often expressed in terms of method or service invocation across modules. Figure 1-5 shows a request from a user to create an e-commerce order. Once the request comes to the Order module, the module internally does a series of activities:

- Creates an Order entity and associated line items in the database

- Makes a call to the inventory database to deplete inventory

- If required, also invokes a call to the Order History module to make suitable entries

- Internally invokes the Notification module, which subsequently sends an order confirmation notification to the user

Often such intermodule calls are characterized by

- Synchronous Request Response style

- Binary dependency like Java interfaces, stubs, etc.

- Dependency on shared entities

When multiple teams or multiple people develop these modules separately, due to the nature of above intermodule calls, dependency exists across modules, people, and teams. Common libraries and common entities are to be shared. When something changes in a module, the associated libraries need to be updated and redistributed across people and teams so that they can still continue with the development of their individual modules.

Further, as discussed, due to these intermodule communications, it is not easy to further divide the application and deploy heterogeneously, if there is a need to do so.

The Application Monolith

If you closely observe Figure 1-4, you can understand how to scale the different tiers of an application. Since the application tier is designed as a single whole with intermodule communications as required, it is not easy to further divide the application and deploy heterogeneously. Then the question is, why do we ever want to deploy heterogeneously? Out of the different modules like Product, Order, and Shipping, many people might be browsing the product catalogue and the product details whereas only a percentage of these users will actually check out and buy, thus creating an order in the system. Further, we only want to ship orders that are actually paid and confirmed. So, the Product module needs to take more traffic and the Order module needs to handle comparatively less traffic. It would be good if we could deploy more instances of the Product module and fewer instances of the Order module to optimally utilize resources, but since the application tier is designed as a single whole, heterogeneous deployment is not straightforward.

Next, if we want to accommodate change requests in the software, whenever there is a change to be applied to some piece of code in the application, we want to upgrade the application as a whole. Downtime will be considerable, which will affect normal business operations.

Further, if there is a bug in the software or if there is some other defect that affects the running application, it is likely that the entire application is affected.

All of these downsides are in spite of the best architecture principles described earlier, and this is the side effect of the monolith architecture, since the application is one single, big block. See Figure 1-5.

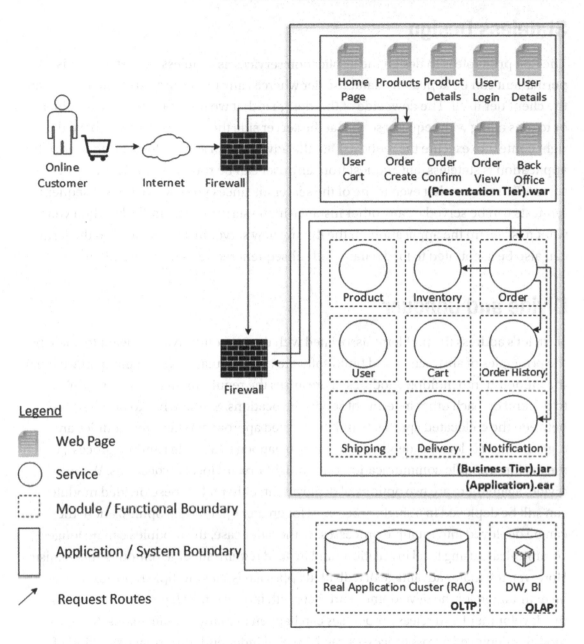

Figure 1-5. *Intermodule dependency*

The Scalable Architecture

Now let's look at few aspects of how to make the application architecture web scale.

Stateless Design

The first principle is to design the application services as stateless. Any state that is permanent can be kept at the database tier whereas any temporary state can be kept at the client tier itself. The downside of this design is that we may have to pass identifiers or tokens along with requests so that at the server side the components will have the right context to execute the requests. But the advantage of such a design is that since the application is stateless, any request from any user can be routed to any instance of the server. This means that even if one of the server instances goes down, the subsequent requests can be served by any other instance in the server farm. Similarly, when you want to scale up the application on the fly, any new server instance added to the farm can also be accounted to load balance all subsequent requests from any client.

Divide and Conquer

Next, let's address the problems associated with the monolith style. We want to abide by the principles of abstraction and build software in a modular way. The moment we break the monolith into multiple modules, there arises the requirement for these modules to depend on each other in terms of service invocations. So there has to be a trade-off between the collocated approach and the divided approach. When the modules are together and co-located, deployment can also happen to a single runtime process, which means intermodule communications are straightforward local invocations. When we divide, again there are two options of deployment: either all of these divided modules can still be deployed in a single process, or for greater operational optimization, they can be deployed into multiple processes. In the latter case, the modules can no longer communicate using local invocations and instead require suitable remoting mechanisms. However, the major advantage of a divided approach is that multiple repositories can be maintained for the development artifacts with indirect interdependency and also the development and release processes can happen in many parallel teams. Moreover, modules deployed across processes can be scaled independently, hence this kind of selective scaling will address optimize resources based on actual business needs, not based on constraints dictated due to not-so-well-thought-out architecture approaches.

Summary

This chapter concentrated on few major characteristics of distributed software architecture and its evolution from the early years of software to today. I offered a bird's eye view of the topics discussed, but the idea was to set the context and look at the different options existing. Towards the end, I touched upon the options for setting the software structure and its impact when we keep the modules together vs. when we separate them out. There are advantages and disadvantages in both of these approaches, but if the benefits we reap when we keep them separated is considerable, we then need to find out ways to manage the not-so-straightforward concerns surrounding manageability and the intermodule communication. I will briefly discuss these aspects in the next chapter. In the following chapters, you will see how all these theories can be put to practice with concrete code examples that you can build and run on your own inexpensive desktops or laptops.

CHAPTER 2

Introducing Microservices

The complexity of enterprise software systems increases with increase in the functionalities and features supported. As you saw in Chapter 1, every enterprise system today needs to transfer information seamlessly with many other systems, both internal and external to the organization. Traditionally we have been building software systems as a "modular monolith." By modular, we mean to say that they follow the principles of modules, layers, and tiers and hence there exists a logical modularity for elements within the software system. By monolith, we mean to say that the entire system is built with a specific scenario of deployment and operation in mind; most of the time, they are deployed as a single process or at the maximum they are distributed following the three-tier or n-tier architecture you saw in Chapter 1. But there ends the flexibility of deployment. Equally important is the process to be followed in getting such a system built in a multiteam or a distributed team organization.

In this chapter, you will look at few selected concerns enterprises face in building today's software applications. Once you understand these problems, you will then look at a new style of building software applications where you have increased flexibility in the build, deploy, or operations phases.

The Modular Monolith

I chose to call today's typical enterprise systems as modular monoliths, because they are characterized by many patterns and also not-so-obvious anti-patterns we have been religiously following while defining software architectures. Towards the end of this section, you will appreciate the reason why I use this phrase.

© Binildas Christudas 2019
B. Christudas, *Practical Microservices Architectural Patterns*, https://doi.org/10.1007/978-1-4842-4501-9_2

The Modular Organization

Since the days of structured programming languages, we have mastered the style of breaking software programs into smaller elements in terms of multiple files, include libraries, backing beans, and such, so that it is easy for a software developer to manage multiple files from within an integrated development environment (IDE) and still develop big applications, complex algorithms, and logic.

The next level of modularization is done at a module level or at a packaging level. A module is a collection of related functionalities organized together in the form of multiple program files, libraries, and so on, and which can be managed within the IDE with the help of a top-level build script. Thus one application can be composed of multiple such modules.

When we look at the next stage of the software life cycle where we build and package application, the concept of packages will come to play. Here we address the concerns of building the modules and making it manageable to distribute them to other environments, whether it is for the testing, staging, or production environments. Sometimes we also want to distribute software to third-party consumers in the form of libraries.

In the next stage of deployment, we may want to deploy the software packages into one or more computer process or computer runtimes. This is to address different runtime qualities of the system, usually defined in terms of non-functional requirements (NFR) and service level agreements (SLA).

Chapter 1 briefly touched upon the different options by which we can build distributed systems, and deploy and operate them in a flexible manner. Now the question is, how flexible they are? To answer this question, look at the typical application architecture shown in Figure 1-3 in Chapter 1. It consists of the presentation tier, the business tier, and the database tier. The majority of today's enterprise systems follow such an architecture, and systems with this kind of architectures will keep existing for few more years, at least till the end-of-life (EOL) for which they are built. What is wrong here? It is flexible to be deployed in a distributed fashion into its own tiers. But the flexibility ends there. So what additional flexibility would we require?

The Monolith Application

Before I attempt to answer the question asked in the previous section, let me define one main nomenclature and its interpretations, which we are going to follow in the rest of this book.

Figure 2-1 shows just the business tier from Figure 1-3. Typically this tier hosts most of the core logic or the business logic of the software system. Let's refer to this tier with the name application tier or services tier. This tier has a clear separation from the presentation tier, normally by a controller layer through which all service calls are routed. This tier may expose either a local interface or a remote interface. A local interface is sufficient if the presentation tier and the services tier are deployed in the same process whereas a remote interface like Java RMI, RMI-IIOP or .NET Remoting will be required if these two tiers are deployed in separate processes. In the service-oriented architecture (SOA) paradigm, a suitable SOA interface will replace plain remoting. SOAP over HTTP, REST, etc. are examples of such SOA-friendly interfaces.

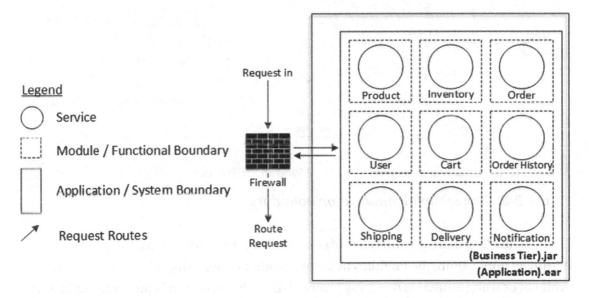

Figure 2-1. *The services tier*

Figure 2-1 shows that even though the modules or functional groups are separated from each other, the boundary is only logical and blurred (shown with dotted lines). This means there is no clear-cut separation between the modules. You may also note that it is typical for such architectures still to have an application boundary. But that application boundary is the boundary that encompasses all of its modules, hence we call it the "monolith." A monolith can live as a whole but struggles to exist if divided or separated out.

Monolith Application Boundary

Figure 2-2 depicts more than one monolith application. This is again typical for many existing enterprises where more than one application is required to meet the enterprise's various functionalities. Since applications in isolation cannot benefit much, they are interconnected at times.

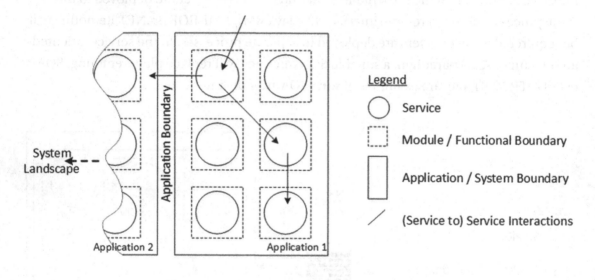

Monolith Architecture

Figure 2-2. *The monolith application boundary*

In Figure 2-2, there are two types of communications or interactions depicted. Within an application, the modules talk to each other either using a local invocation protocol or using a suitable remoting protocol. Equally important is the communication between applications. Typically enterprises use enterprise application integration (EAI) technologies to integrate between applications. The "Network Architectures" section in Chapter 1 discussed briefly how applications can integrate with each other. You might have noticed that most of the time application boundaries are clearly defined and separated, hence most of the time they are deployed out into separate processes or runtime. Due to this reason, they require a suitable remoting mechanism to talk to each other. Later advancements in SOA advocate using service-oriented integration (SOI) tools like ESB so that application integration can be done in a more flexible, seamless manner.

Monolith Intermodule Dependency

Modules within an application in a monolith architecture are tightly coupled. These modules talk to each other either using a local invocation protocol or a suitable remoting protocol. Most of the time these calls are synchronous in nature, which means every request transaction also expects a response or an exception back.

When all the modules of a monolith application are packaged and deployed together in the same process, local method invocation is the best option to communicate. In such a deployment, either the entire application is always up, or if there are any issues in any part of any module, the application can also go down in its entirety. If some of the modules are separated out and deployed into a different process, then the health of the process where we have deployed the separated modules will not affect the other dependent process. However, when we look at such a separately deployed module application from its entirety, if the separated modules are down for any reason, then the dependent modules can still be affected. This is because intermodule communication is defined as direct and synchronous method call dependencies, so if the called module does not respond or exist, the caller module will be affected. They either get blocked indefinitely or wait for some amount of time and then respond reporting error conditions. Figure 2-3 depicts this.

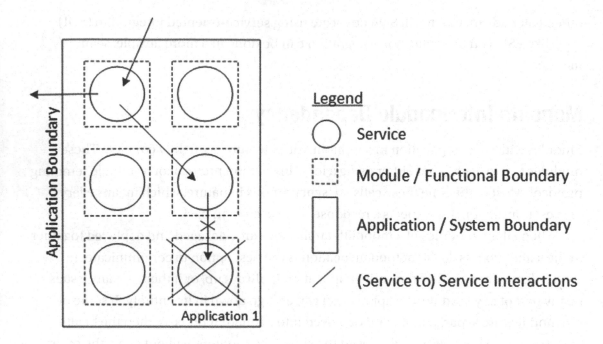

Intermodule Communication

Figure 2-3. *Monolith intermodule communication*

The Scalability Dilemma

Modern application architectures are horizontally scalable. By horizontal scalability, we mean more than one instance of the same functionality can be deployed into different processes, and traffic from clients to the same functionality can be served by any one among the server processes where there is duplicated functionality. Such topologies are called server farms. Ideally, requests from the same client (browser or mobile app) can also be routed to any instance of this server farm, irrespective of which server instance served the previous request from the same client.

Figure 2-1 depicts different modules of an e-commerce application. If you think about how a user typically interacts with an e-commerce application, the series of steps may go as follows:

1. Access the home page of the e-commerce application.

2. Browse through the product categories.

3. Select interested items and browse through the selected product details.

4. If interested, add the selected item to the cart.

5. Create a user profile or log in if you already have a user profile.

6. Pay and check out the item and confirm the order.

Typically you browse through many product categories and product details, and only add few to your cart. Even after adding items into the cart, the item can be deleted from the cart or the cart can be ignored or orphaned. Eventually, only a comparatively smaller percentage of the items added to cart will end up as a confirmed order in an e-commerce application.

In the "Typical Deployment Architecture" section in Chapter 1, you saw the option of the scale-out mechanism available for a typical monolith application. The relevant section of Figure 1-4 is replicated here as Figure 2-4 for further discussion.

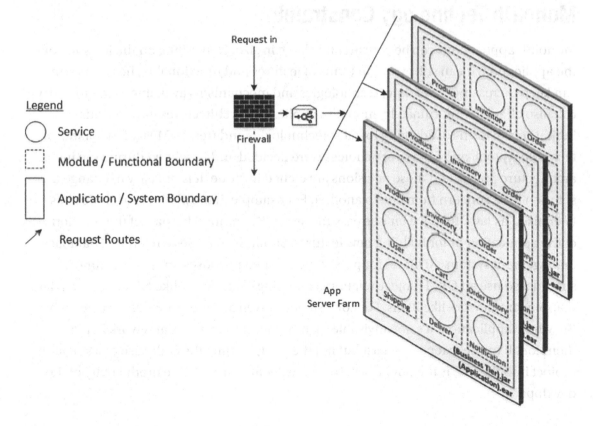

Figure 2-4. *Application tier scalability*

Since many logged in and anonymous (not logged in) users will be browsing through many product categories and product detail web pages, the application module serving those requests, the Product module, will be stressed more compared to the stress felt by the Order module. If the deployment architecture has to be flexible to address this varying requirement of scalability, we should be able to deploy more server instances hosting the Product module, whereas a lesser number of server processes will be required to host the Order module. Equally important is the need for deploying the Order module to server hardware of a higher grade of reliability compared to what is needed to deploy the Product module, since the cost of failure for an Order transaction is much higher compared to the cost of failure for a Product-related transaction. Due to all or many of the concerns discussed in previous sections, you know that separating the modules and deploying them based on the required operational qualities is not straightforward, since the application is architected as a monolith and permits only homogeneous deployment.

Monolith Technology Constraints

Monolith applications can be considerably large in size. Depending on the life span of the application, it can still evolve in terms of features and functionality, hence its size can keep increasing. Over time, technologies and mechanisms available in the industry can also change. Unfortunately, monolith application architectures have serious limitations in terms of adapting to latest technologies and trends. Most of the platform, technology, tool, and framework choices were decided and baselined during the initial architecture phase, and those decisions are etched in stone. It is not easy to change the solution for a concern from one to another. For example, if the platform of choice has been fixed as Java, then it won't be easy to use a .NET solution for part of the solution of the application or for building new features. Similarly, if it uses a relational database management system (RDBMS) for persistence related purposes, most of the time it should also use an ORM (object-relational mapping) framework like Hibernate or a data mapping framework like iBatis. For consistency as well as for economies of scale within the whole application, it's not advisable to introduce a new such framework in place of them for all future extensions. Last but not the least, loading the codebase of a single project into the IDE is memory intensive and will often impede the productivity of the developers.

Introducing Microservices

Microservices are a different approach to architecting software application. They attempt to address many modern application architecture challenges. We will look at the different architectural challenges we face today and set a base by which we can solve our issues and keep moving.

Before we delve deep, here's one more important nomenclature: the "service" in the context of a microservice.

In SOA, a service is a first-class business functionality that can be accessed by any clients using a standard access protocol over the network. SOA services are autonomous and typically idempotent and stateless. By autonomous, we mean the service by itself is self-sufficient in providing the functionality. By idempotent, we mean invoking the service more than once, knowingly or by error, will not have any side effect. To make it simple, a client can make the same request repeatedly while producing the same result. In other words, making multiple identical requests has the same effect as making a single request. By stateless, we mean we do not store any state on behalf of a specific client in the server, when the service is invoked (this was discussed in the "Stateless Design" section in Chapter 1).

You are yet to see what a microservice is, so to keep our current discussion moving, a microservice is analogous to an SOA service. Sometimes a collection of many such services that are functionally related can also be called by the term microservice. We will look at different meanings of this statement later.

Let's revisit few of the challenges we discussed with the monolith approach and see how to address them.

Independent Modules

The first and best distinguishable and observable characteristic I want to introduce to the monolith is to convert the monolith into a collection of discrete and independent modules. By making the modules independent, we want to bring all or most of the following flexibilities to the software paradigm:

- **Parallel development**: Each module can be source controlled as a separate repository, hence distributed teams can build these modules independently and in parallel.

- **Separated deployment**: Different from the single process deployment approach of the monolith, once the modules are independent, they should also be packaged, deployed, tested, and deployed into production into multiple runtime processes so that appropriate strategies can be adopted during deployment to address varying scalability, both at the software and hardware levels. This is especially important in a scenario like an e-commerce application where we want to deploy more server instances to host the Product module and less server processes for the Order module; similarly, we want to deploy Order modules into hardware and software stacks of greater reliability (which will cost more) compared to what is required to deploy the Product modules (where costs can be kept reasonably less by using commodity hardware).

Intermodule Communication

Most of the intermodule communications we have with existing systems are direct and synchronous method invocations. Even if we design these communications as idempotent and stateless, one of the side effects of such calls is that the called module has to be up and live to respond to the caller module, or exceptions and errors can occur. Even if we separate the different modules as independent and deploy them into multiple processes, this side effect still exists and propagates backwards in the call stack. The thread in the caller process making the request to the called process will wait until it gets a valid response with or without data, or until the called method raises an exception. This blocks the thread making the request in the caller process and renders the thread useless until the method call returns. So, not only is there a dependency to the called process, but resources in the caller process are also blocked, hence they cannot be multiplexed and reused.

There is, however, one advantage in this synchronous style of intermodule communication. The caller can take the next action after inspecting the response data send by the called process. Also, in a case where the called process doesn't return expected results, the caller can instantaneously hint that to the user or the client tier agent so as to leverage manual intervention for the next step.

The asynchronous or fire-and-forget style of intermodule communication can relieve the caller resources to be reusable instantaneously after making the call to the called process. Using a message queue between the caller process and the called process is one means of achieving this. But this also introduces extra complexity in the overall software architecture. Firstly, we need to deal with messaging infrastructure in our IT landscape. More important, the complexity of software design increases since we now also want to correlate the responses to a particular request, since they are no longer tied together using the compute thread's "wait and respond" primitive.

Asynchronous communication is a necessary evil.

With this background, let's now look into what improvisation you can do to the monolith to make it more modern and flexible.

The Microservices

You have looked at two main aspects in modernizing the monolith application architecture, They are

- Making the modules independent

- Redesigning the intermodule communications

Figure 2-5 depicts the two architecture modernizations we have discussed. You may want to spend some time observing the diagram in detail, since this is going to be the basic construct upon which you are going to build a lot more improvisations.

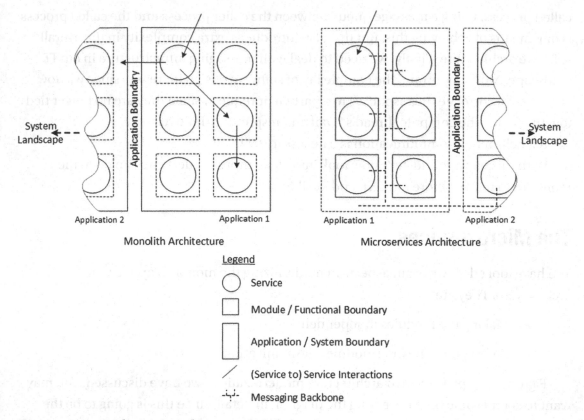

Monolith Architecture   **Microservices Architecture**

Legend

⭕ Service

▢ Module / Functional Boundary

▯ Application / System Boundary

╱ (Service to) Service Interactions

-⌐- Messaging Backbone

Figure 2-5. *Redesigning the monolith boundaries*

In the monolith style, each application is a different monolith, and they talk to each other as described in the "Monolith Intermodule Dependency" section earlier. Each application has a well-defined boundary that defines the bounded context of a functional grouping. In Figure 2-5, this is represented using thick rectangular boxes. If you look inside such an application, there are multiple modules. As discussed, these modules are logically separated, but due to the dependency in deployment as well as intermodule communication, the module boundary is not rigid; rather it's bloated. This is represented using dotted lined square boxes. Within such a module I have denoted a service. This can be a single service or a collection of functionally related services. They are represented using a circle. Note that a service can get an external request and a service can delegate requests to other services in another module or to other services in another application; all of this is shown using arrows.

When I want to introduce the new style of application architecture called the microservice, I inverse the boundaries, as shown in the right extreme of Figure 2-5. Here, each module or each distinguishable functional grouping is clearly separated from its peer. Each service or collection of services that are functionally related are grouped together logically and physically. In this diagram, this is represented by the square with thick lines, which is called a microservice. We will get into more details of it later, but for our discussion for the time being, such a microservice can be developed, source controlled, built, tested, distributed, and deployed independent of another microservice. If we want to map this to our monolith application, we can visualize a collection of such microservices can be called equivalent to our traditional monolith application. Just like different pieces or parts of our monolith application need to interact each other to realize the functionality built into it, in the microservices world too services internal to a microservice can talk to each other or services across microservices can talk to each other. When we adopt microservices, we do not want to ignore any or all of the principles of SOA. Going by that, we can use any standard SOA interface for the microservices to communicate with each other. Later you will see that in order to reap the true efficiency of microservices, you must adapt true SOA principles for the microservices architecture too.

The previous section on flexible "intermodule communication" pointed out that we can also use the asynchronous style of communication between modules, and the same can be done between microservices too. This gives us flexibility by reducing dependency and by breaking the request-response cycle so that we can address problems like what to do when the called microservice doesn't exist or is not responding. An appropriate message queue between microservices can help to achieve this, and such a message infrastructure is denoted by connecting microservices in Figure 2-5. Now comes the next important aspect: when microservices are interconnected in this manner, since the underlying message infrastructure blends seamlessly with the corporate IT infrastructure, theoretically microservices from any vertical or line of business are capable of exchanging information across each other, since all of them can be connected to the same corporate LAN. When this happens, the application boundary, which earlier used to be a well-defined, rigid boundary, now disappears. This is denoted using dotted lines between applications in Figure 2-5. In other words, the notion of applications that existed earlier as first-class bounded citizens in the enterprise software landscape gives space to microservices, and microservices now start to resemble many of the properties of those applications in terms of identity as first-class independent software building blocks.

You may also look at the formal definition of a microservice as provided by Wikipedia (https://en.wikipedia.org/wiki/Microservices).

> **Note**   "Microservices are a software development technique — a variant of the service-oriented architecture (SOA) architectural style that structures an application as a collection of loosely coupled services. In a microservice architecture, services are fine-grained and the protocols are lightweight. The benefit of decomposing an application into different smaller services is that it improves modularity. This makes the application easier to understand, develop, test, and become more resilient to architecture erosion. It parallelizes development by enabling small autonomous teams to develop, deploy, and scale their respective services independently. It also allows the architecture of an individual service to emerge through continuous refactoring."

Many of the aspects mentioned in this definition have been discussed in these first two chapters. You will now look into this definition from more perspectives and also much more in the next two chapters.

Summary

In this chapter, you looked at the state of traditional distributed or n-tier application architectures and explored a few shortcomings due to the monolithic nature of such architectures. There are many other advantages and disadvantages of the monolith architecture that have not been discussed yet, but such a discussion is not in scope since I just wanted to set the context to discuss the alternative way of doing things: using microservices. Now you know that when you switch your thoughts from the monolith to the microservice style, you need to inverse lot of concepts like the application boundary, intercommunications, etc. In the next chapter, you will revisit the microservice architecture in detail, relating the concept to real-world enterprise applications.

CHAPTER 3

Microservices in Depth

As you saw in Chapter 2, using microservices is an approach in architecting today's distributed software solutions. The software industry has gained experience in developing and deploying distributed applications over the past two decades, and microservices lay down architectural principles and patterns for dealing with many shortfalls in developing, deploying and maintaining distributed applications. We discussed the context and necessity for the microservices architecture in the previous two chapters and in this chapter we will look at it into more detail. I will again attempt to explain concepts in the context of a real-world application, the e-commerce application I introduced in Chapter 1. This will help you to quickly relate aspects to practical scenarios in your real-world experience.

You will explore the following aspects in this chapter:

- What the e-commerce architecture will look like in the microservices context

- The relationship between the classic tiered and layered approach in a microservices context

- The autonomous nature of microservices

- The relationship between microservices and traditional SOA and MOM

- The scalability and extensibility characteristics of the microservices architecture

© Binildas Christudas 2019
B. Christudas, *Practical Microservices Architectural Patterns*, https://doi.org/10.1007/978-1-4842-4501-9_3

Look and Feel of a Microservice

You just learned that, compared to a traditional monolith application, many characteristics and distinguishing features are inversed when talking about microservices. To better understand what this inversion is all about, let's look at a practical enterprise application scenario and understand the big picture first so that the fine-grained and most important details are easier to understand.

The E-Commerce Microservice

The "Typical Application Architecture" section in Chapter 1 introduced the e-commerce application. I explained how such applications are built following a traditional approach. Figure 1-3 in Chapter 1 depicted different tiers and a modular approach to managing software complexity. Even with the principles of tiers, layers, and modules, you saw that there's still the problem of undue dependency between modules, which impedes all stages in the software engineering life cycle. I will portray that monolith architecture in a slightly different style following the first principle of microservices introduced in Chapter 2.

Figure 3-1 shows what the architecture will look like if we redraw the traditional monolith-based architecture shown in Figure 1-3 in Chapter 1. Compared to the monolith architecture representation in Figure 1-3, I have softened the application boundary represented by the dotted and dashed line styles in the diagram. This is to emphasize the point that in the microservices architecture, it is not the application boundary that matters, it's the microservice boundary. The microservice boundary is shown with thick rectangles. There are many such microservices depicted in the diagram. In short, the single monolith application boundary represented in the traditional architecture has vanished and in that place, many microservices have popped up, and all of them have clear and concrete boundaries.

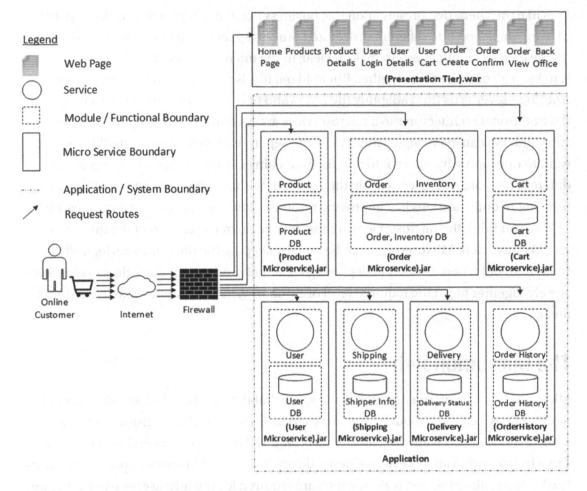

Figure 3-1. *E-commerce microservices architecture*

I have not introduced any new modules in this new architecture representation. Instead, retaining the already existing modules in the monolith architecture, I have considerably changed the structure of the software modules as well as the technology infrastructure. Let's look into this structural change in detail.

No Tier, Distributed

I discussed the three-tier and n-tier distributed architectures in the "System Architectures" section in Chapter 1. Going by that, it's not wrong to call the microservices architecture by the name "no tier, distributed." To make it clear, if you relook at the three-tier or n-Tier distributed architectures, within an application there are multiple tiers like the client tier, presentation tier, business tier, etc. These tiers are also capable of being deployed into different distributed process spaces. This is also inversed in the microservices architecture. To make it clear, in the microservices architecture, the aim is to keep all of these tiers together. But hold on, this is again not a hard-and-fast rule. Nothing prevents us from adapting the layers and tiers and other similar principles from the traditional architectures to a microservices architecture. All those good practices are still valid. We can even deploy these tiers into separate process spaces. But then, we may want to question why we want to do this. By keeping closely interacting pieces like the different tiers of a microservice together, perhaps within a single process itself, we can bring lot of optimizations like improving response time, reliable communications, etc.

We can think the microservices architecture again in the context of the three-tier architecture itself. Microservices can be built by keeping the different tiers logically separated, but when it comes to deploying for actual production, these tiers may be kept closely together to get the required level of autonomy. Let's look into what this autonomy means.

The Micromonolith

Microservices are micromonoliths in the sense that they are built by following layer and tier practices, but the boundary of a microservice should be clearly distinguishable and a microservice should encompass all that is required for that microservice to live and serve by itself without any external dependency. This is true in terms of physical artifacts like binaries, libraries, and scripts, which are required for the microservice to be up and running. This has to be also true in terms of any dependencies like container services or persistence services required during the runtime of the microservice. The physically bundled microservice artifact which when deployed to the runtime process has to exhibit complete autonomy in terms of its capability to provide its functionality. This is explained further in the next section.

Since we are organizing microservices as all-encompassing bundles with little or no external dependency, this provides certain advantages in terms of platform and technology choices. Any platform, technology, tool, or framework decision taken for a microservice shouldn't be a constraint for those of the other microservice. This provides freedom of choice of technology and architecture for teams across microservices. But at the same time, this autonomy also brings additional responsibility to the microservice; it has to own and manage all the resources necessary for its healthy existence, including the data and the database it requires to keep the state persistent. Data independency is typically managed by giving each microservice its own database (or even by giving each microservice its own schema in a shared database, but in that case, you should avoid all cross-schema operations). Typically, the presentation services required by a microservice are also enclosed within a microservice bundle. Figure 3-2 shows this for a single microservice, the Product microservice.

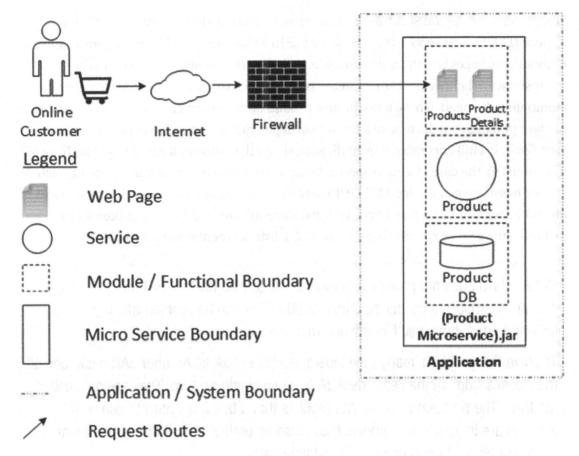

Figure 3-2. *A typical microservice*

Out of the various tiers, it is the business tier that does the core data massaging and processing work, and it is this tier where scalability issues often occur. With today's technology capability, especially using the **SPA** (**single-page applications**) web frameworks and caching frameworks, scaling the other tiers are comparatively straightforward. So for most of this discussion, we will be concentrating on the business tier when we talk about microservices. However, wherever required, we will also touch upon other tiers to present the complete picture. So, we want to represent the microservice shown in Figure 3-2, separating the presentation components apart, and that is what you saw in Figure 3-1. This will have some implications, but we will discuss them in a later section.

Understanding Self-Contained Microservices

Since microservices are SOA friendly (which we will discuss in the next section), they require HTTP server services to expose SOA or REST interfaces. While we deploy traditional monolith packages into the web-app folder of the HTTP container, in the case of a microservice, a lightweight HTTP listener is embedded within the microservice, thereby eliminating the need to have any external or standalone container or server requirement. In the Java paradigm, in the case of a traditional deployment, we used to deploy an `.ear` or a `.war` file into a full encompassing application server like JBoss or a web server like Tomcat. In contrast, in the case of a microservice there is no web server or `.war` file; instead, each service has its own embedded HTTP listener such as Jetty, Tomcat, or Undertow in a JAR file. While we build a microservice, the build stage will create this "executable fat JAR" file, including the service runtime such as the HTTP listener mentioned previously.

Note   Java does not provide a standard way to load nested JAR files (JAR files that are themselves contained within a JAR). This can be problematic if you are looking to distribute a self-contained microservice.

To solve this problem, many developers use "uber" JARs. An uber JAR packages all the classes from all the dependent JARs into a single archive. They are also called fat JARs. The problem with this approach is that it becomes hard to see which libraries are in your microservice. It can also be problematic if the same filename is used (but with different content) in multiple JARs.

The previous section indicated that microservices should encompass all of the physical artifacts like binaries, libraries, and scripts, required for the microservice to be up and running. In the traditional monolith deployment, we could place these kinds of dependencies in the `lib` folder of the application server. In the microservices world, executable jar files are a means to attain this. The structure of a typical executable jar file for the product microservice is shown in Listing 3-1.

Listing 3-1. Executable jar File Structure

```
product.jar
 |
 +-META-INF
 |  +-MANIFEST.MF
 +-org
 |  +-springframework
 |     +-boot
 |        +-loader
 |           +-<spring boot loader classes>
 +-BOOT-INF
    +-classes
    |  +-com
    |     +-acme
    |        +-ProductMain.class
    +-lib
       +-framework.jar
       +-log4j.jar
       +-jetty.jar
       +-. . .
```

In this manner, all required libraries as well as the required runtime services like HTTP, JMS, or AMQP are embedded within the executable jar file. In "Build and Package the Spring Boot Application" section in Chapter 7 you will code, build, package, and run an executable fat jar file.

Resemblance of Microservices to SOA

As discussed, multiple microservices make up an application. Microservices must be accessible from other microservices or from other components like the presentation components. For intermicroservice communication, a suitable interprocess communication mechanism is required, since most of the time microservices are deployed into separate processes. You shouldn't reinvent the wheel. You should adopt all the best practices you have been leveraging from the SOA bibles. Just like in SOA, in microservices too there are multiple options to expose services starting from high performance and binary level TCP-IP sockets to other remoting protocols like Java RMI, .NET Remoting, and RMI-IIOP to more web-friendly ones like SOAP or REST.

Figure 3-3 shows a redrawn e-commerce microservices architecture from Figure 3-1, highlighting few typical request flows. Assuming most of the presentation tier components can be cached by the browser once they are loaded initially from the presentation server, all subsequent hits can be directed to the services tier directly by the browser. This is what is shown in Figure 3-3 so that we concentrate on the microservices more. Keep in mind that even if we follow the typical presentation tier-based approach where all requests are always routed through the presentation server alone, the requests will hit the microservices next, which is nothing different from a request flow not passing through the presentation server. In Figure 3-3, assume that a request to confirm an order has hit the Order microservice. It will access its Order database and create the order. It should also make changes to the inventory database to deplete the inventory level by the amount we have ordered newly, by talking to the Inventory service. Assuming that there are other microservices like a Shipping microservice and an Order History microservice in the e-commerce application, the Order microservice will need to make requests to them as well while creating an order. The Shipping microservice will pack and ship the order whereas the Order History microservice will create an entry into the Order History database, which can be used for analytics purposes. In summary, microservices must be accessible from other microservices as well as from other components. So intermicroservice communication is a concern.

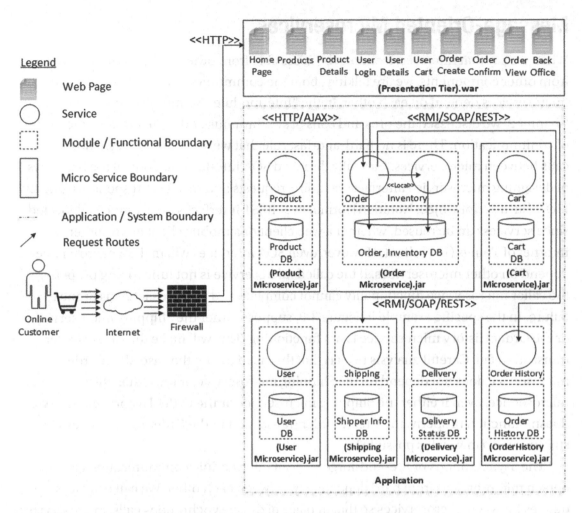

Figure 3-3. *Microservice communications are SOA friendly*

Careful observation of Figure 3-3 reveals another important concern in microservices architecture: the problem of maintaining data consistency across microservices. Since each microservice governs its own state and persistent data, and again since each microservice is typically deployed across its own process spaces, maintaining data consistency across microservices is going to be a challenge. Note the "Local" protocol marked as a communication mechanism between the Order and Inventory microservices; we will discuss it later in the "The ACID Within the BASE" section in Chapter 17.

Message-Oriented Microservices

When we say that microservices must be accessible from other microservices as well as from other components, we are talking about the communication mechanism by which microservices depend on each other. In the "Intermodule Communication" section in Chapter 2, we discussed the pros and cons of synchronous and asynchronous methods of communication. There is no hard-and-fast rule that we shouldn't use synchronous calls between microservices. Carefully designed SOA interfaces are one of the best ways of designing microservice interfaces. Sending requests and receiving responses using the JSON (Java Script Object Notation) format over REST interfaces is very much advocated since services can be reused, whether a web client or a mobile client or any other Internet of Things (IoT) client. However, even SOA interfaces will make a microservice depend on other microservices. If the called microservice is not functioning properly, the caller microservice functionality cannot complete and the transaction is prone to failure. In the specific example in Figure 3-3, suppose either the Shipping microservice or the Order History microservice is not functioning. This will make the Create Order transaction fail. Careful analysis reveals that this need not be the case. If the Order microservice does not depend on the Shipping microservice or the Order History microservice, even if either the Shipping microservice or the Order History microservice doesn't function properly, the Create Order transaction in the Order microservice can still succeed. How is this possible?

The asynchronous or fire-and-forget style of intermodule communication can detach microservices from hard dependency between each other. We can use message queues between microservices so that in place of direct synchronous calls, microservices can communicate sending messages through queue between them. In Figure 3-4, the architecture has been adjusted so as to bring a message queue system between microservices. The other SOA-based interfaces of the microservices have not been completely eliminated; they are retained but a message queue is also introduced. This is because any external component or service has to use the SOA interfaces of the e-commerce application or the e-commerce microservices. Along with that, any intermicroservice communication may be done using message queues. So, a request from the browser to confirm an order will hit the Order microservice using its SOA-based REST interface. The Order microservice will access its Order database and create the order. It should also make changes to the inventory database to deplete the inventory level by the amount just ordered.

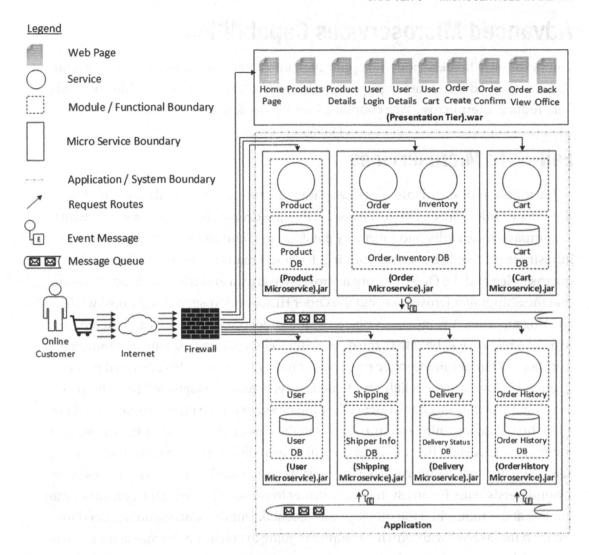

Figure 3-4. Event-based microservices

The Create Order transaction in the Order microservice will make entry in the order database, update the entry in the inventory database, and send messages to the message queue in an atomic manner. If any of these operations fail, the entire Create Order transaction will fail. If all of these operations succeed, the Create Order transaction will also succeed. Creating the order in the Order database and depleting the inventory in the Inventory database may be done within a single transaction. Here again let's leave that complexity for a detailed discussion later.

The message sent by the Order microservice to the queue while creating an order will then be picked up by the Shipping microservice and the Order History microservice.

Advanced Microservices Capabilities

You saw how to break a monolith application into a microservices-based architecture. You also learned about message queues in the microservices-based architecture, which help reduce intermicroservice coupling. Now let's look at the advantages.

Fail-Safe Microservices

In the message-oriented microservices paradigm, the only essential condition for the Create Order transaction to succeed is that the Create Order microservice (which encompasses the Order and Inventory database too) and its associated message queue infrastructure should be up and running. It doesn't matter whether the Shipping microservice and the Order History microservice are up and running or not. Assume that the Shipping microservice and the Order History microservice are down while creating an order. Any messages placed by the Order microservice as an outcome of order creation will be safe in the queue. Here again, we can assume that multiple instances of Order microservice can exist for redundancy and also clustered message queues will increase the reliability of queues. Persistent messages will be written to disk too as soon as they reach the queue. So if the message queue is persistent, even if one or all of the messaging infrastructure servers in the cluster go down after the Create Order transaction succeeds, the messages are still safe on disk. When we bring the queue up again, the message is still available for consumption. Durable queues keep messages around persistently for any suitable consumer to consume them, if the consumer was not live at the time when the message was reached. Durable queues do not need to concern themselves with which consumer is going to consume the messages at some point in the future. There is just one copy of a message that any consumer in the future can consume. Durable topics, however, are different because they must logically persist an instance of each suitable message for every durable consumer, since each durable consumer gets their own copy of the message. Thus, by judiciously combining the persistence and durability capability of queues or topics available within the messaging infrastructure, we can eliminate the dependency of the Order microservice from the Shipping microservice and the Order History microservice. At some later point in time when the Shipping microservice or the Order History microservice comes up again, they will consume the messages intended to be consumed by them and the rest of the functional flow will be continued by the respective microservices.

Scalable Microservices

In the "Scalability Dilemma" section in Chapter 2 we discussed that many logged in and anonymous users will browse through many product categories and product detail web pages, and the microservice serving those requests via the Product microservice will be stressed more compared to the stress felt by the Order microservice. This is because only a portion of the traffic due to browsing through the product category or the product detail web pages will finally get converted to a confirmed order transaction. So we need the capability to selectively scale the microservices of an application. We have already broken down the monolith e-commerce application into a microservices-based e-commerce application. The capability to selectively scale is a free offer we get with the microservices architecture. Figure 3-5 depicts exactly this.

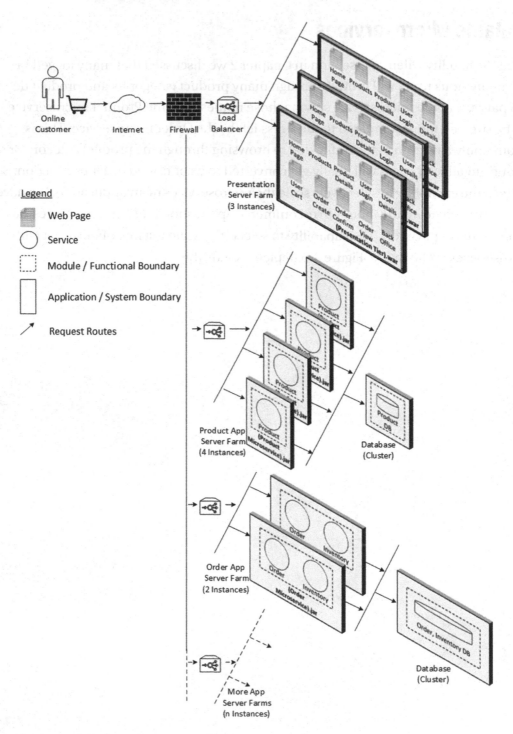

Figure 3-5. *Scaled-out microservices*

Figure 3-5 shows a typical microservices architecture deployed to scale selectively. This means the scalability of different parts of an application can be finely controlled and can be done independent of the other part. This is ultimate freedom.

Compared to the e-commerce microservices architecture shown in Figure 3-1, Figure 3-5 shows the database outside the microservice boundary. But in the "Microservices Are Self-Contained" section, I said that a microservice bounds all of its resources including the database. Isn't this a contradiction?

Take the case of the Product microservice in Figure 3-5. Four instances of the Product microservice are shown since we anticipate much more traffic in browsing product category and product details web pages compared to other parts of the application. But only a single Product database is shown and it is outside the boundary of the Product microservice. A product category or product details are a kind of master data for the e-commerce application. The database, once populated, is not going to change until we add a new product category or products or we retire an existing product category or product from the system. So the Product database is a "read" database. So, even if more than one instance of the Product microservice app server is going to connect to the single instance Product database, there won't be any data consistency issues to be addressed. Further, if we enable caching, then the hits coming to the Product database can be further reduced. In short, even though we have shown the Product microservice instances in a process separate from that of the Product database, you can visualize them to be an integral and single block. So the definition that a microservice bounds all of its resources including the database still holds good.

There are two instances of the Order microservices shown. Here again, the Order database is shown as outside the boundary of the Order microservice. The Order microservice is a shared database, and multiple instances of the Order microservice accessing a single instance of the Order database offer the complexity to address any possible data corruption. We can think of employing distributed locking of resources to address such shared data corruption issues. We will discuss more about this later but for the time being you can assume that even though the Order database is physically shown outside the boundary of the Order microservices, for every practical reasons it functions as an integrated whole of the Order microservice.

But what about the messaging infrastructure discussed in the "Message-Oriented Microservices" section? It was purposefully eliminated in Figure 3-5 to keep the complexity low. But now that you understand the basics of microservices scaling, I will introduce the message-oriented middleware to the microservices architecture so that the reference architecture is functionally complete.

Note that there are two microservices in Figure 3-6, out of the many microservices represented in Figure 3-1. This is again to keep the diagram comprehensible. You need to visualize that all of the identified microservices have to be appropriately scaled in the architecture shown in Figure 3-6.

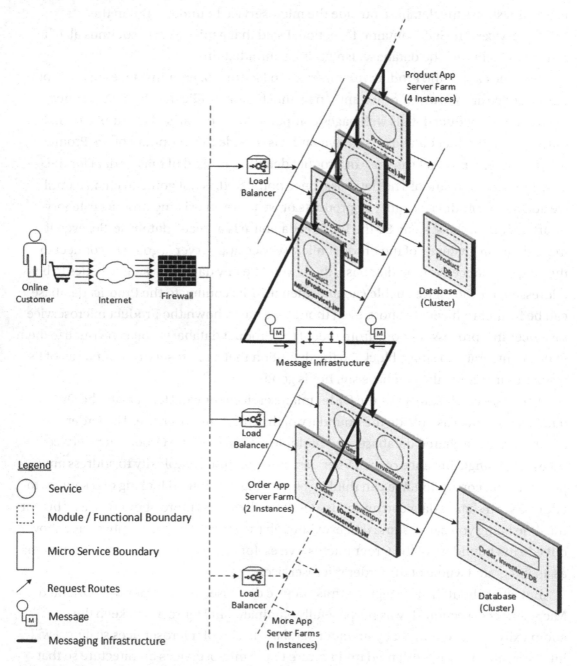

Figure 3-6. *Scaling message-oriented microservices*

As is depicted in Figure 3-6, any microservice will exchange information with any other microservice only in terms of messages over the messaging infrastructure. By leveraging the persistence and durable capability of queues or topics available within the messaging infrastructure, we can eliminate the direct dependency of a microservice to another dependent microservice. So if a few microservices are not available at the moment of a user transaction, still the business flow can proceed and complete at a later point in time when those microservices are brought back again.

Extensible Microservices

Most applications are built with a predicted end of life (EoL). Even if this EoL is too far in the future, applications keep evolving in terms of functional capability as well as non-functional capability. As a business expands and as new acquisitions and mergers happen, applications must be altered as well as extended. To extend or alter a monolith is more risky than to do it to microservices architecture. This is because, just like the manner by which we enabled selective scalability to microservices architecture, we can also extend or alter microservices selectively. This brings a lot of relief to application developers and the operations team.

I would like to borrow the "honeycomb analogy" used by Rajesh R. V. in his book "Spring Microservices" (Packt Publishing). Figure 3-7 shows my own representation.

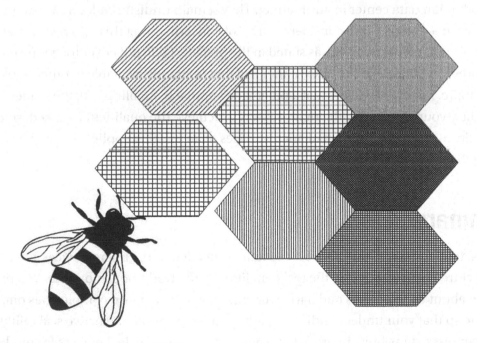

Figure 3-7. *Microservices: The honeycomb analogy*

Figure 3-7 represents how a bee builds a honeycomb. It starts by building the first cell and then keeps adding more and more cells to the honeycomb. So the honeycomb grows over a period of time. The materials used to build the different cells may not be the same; they differ based on what is available at the time of building of that cell. However, each new cell blends well with the overall honeycomb, and the honeycomb as a whole serves the functionality.

The microservices architecture follows a similar analogy. Since we have already broken down the application into many discrete pieces, we can start building one by one or a selected few alone first and quickly deploy them into production. This brings down the time to market considerably, and the business can start functioning at a reduced scale. For example, in our e-commerce application we can build the Product microservice first so that the product catalogue and the product details are accessible initially to provide an early web presence for the enterprise. We can add the Order, Shipping, and Delivery microservices to the application next so that a bare minimum e-commerce application is ready and functional for people to browse categories and do online orders. Maybe as a next step we can build more functionality like a Notification microservice to send e-mail and SMS-based notifications of order statuses as and when they change. The beauty of the microservices architecture is that as we keep adding more and more microservices to the application, we do not touch the existing microservices in the production data center in any manner. They remain undisturbed, serving traffic. Of course we need to take into consideration lot of concerns to get this into reality, but that is the only aim of this book. So, as stated in the preface, I will not cover too many basics or theories on microservices, since enough of that is already available in other books on the topic. Instead, I will present a pragmatic approach enabling you, the reader, to really dirty your hands with the right skillsets to achieve the qualities discussed; selecting scalability and the hot addition of microservices to an existing application are just few among them.

Summary

You just touched upon few practical capabilities needed in the microservices-based architecture if you want to get the real benefits over the traditional monolith. You have learned about the concerns and have been introduced to solution complexities one at a time so that your understanding is gradual and continuous. Selective scalability and seamless extensibility in production deployments are the deal makers for modern applications, which cannot stand any amount of downtime. You have seen how that is possible conceptually in this chapter. You will also see how to do this with actual code in later chapters. But before that, let's look at the bigger picture of where the microservices concept came from and why it matters to today's enterprises in the next chapter on microservices architecture.

CHAPTER 4

Microservices Architecture

After the initial three chapters, you now have set a solid knowledge base to distinguish between the microservices style of software architecture and the architecture of a traditional monolith. You learned the technique of breaking down the monolith into multiple small logical and physically separate groupings called microservices, thereby improving the scale out capability in a flexible manner. While in the traditional monolith schema of architecture you have one single, big application to manage, the same application when redesigned into a microservices architecture will be more than one single deployment and hence many more concerns like the intermicroservice communications, will pop up. You will explore the details of this new set of architectural concerns in this chapter. You will also explore a few relevant trends in the software paradigm that have compelled software architects to move away from traditional architectural styles.

You will learn in detail the following in this chapter:

- The digital context and the Mesh App and Service Architecture (MASA)

- Service granularity and where microservices fit in

- Domain-based partitioning for microservices

- The cloud native shift to address web scale scenarios

- The cloud architecture and services model, setting the environment for your deployment

- Virtualization and containers, and how they influence microservices

- The macro and micro architecture perspective of microservices

© Binildas Christudas 2019

B. Christudas, *Practical Microservices Architectural Patterns*, https://doi.org/10.1007/978-1-4842-4501-9_4

Architecture for Digital Business

We have evolved from the era of mainframes to desktops to laptops to mobile, and the evolution continues. The era of smartphones brought a hell of a lot of possibilities for how a mobile device can become the intimate companion of an individual. We have all skipped our lunches on some days either because of a meeting with our boss or customers extended endlessly or a family emergency. But how many of us can live for an hour without looking at the social apps or the chat apps on our mobile? Devices have started to become so intimate and essential, just like food, water, and air! This has brought new challenges for software developers. I'll explain more in this section.

The Digital Era

The human race is now in the era of digital business. Gartner offers the following definition of digital business:

> *Digital business is the creation of new business designs by blurring the digital and physical worlds.*

—Gartner

You can easily relate this definition to few real-world scenarios such as:

- You use Google Maps to lead you to your destinations by providing maps or driving directions.

- The Electronic Stability Program (ESP) in your cab improves your car's stability by detecting and reducing loss of traction (skidding) at unexpected times.

- People are starting to travel to space for recreational, leisure, or business purposes.

- Skinput provides an on-body finger input system that is always available, naturally portable, and minimally invasive.

- Bionics makes brain-computer, the next user interface (UI), a reality by which you can control artificial limbs.

- Biochip implants aids in medical administrations.

- A smart tag can tell you if your $200 bottle of scotch has been opened by someone else while you were away.

The list is endless. All each item on the list brings newer challenges for the software architect. A decade back, desktop browsers dominated at the client tier and we used them to access middle-tier services. The smartphone changed that by bringing microbrowsers and native apps to the list of client applications. Today we have the Internet of Things (IoT) and Web of Things (WoT), and this keeps evolving and changing the software architecture paradigm.

The Digital App

Digital business is taking microbrowsers and native apps to the next level by redefining what an app means. In the context of the digital era described in the previous section, the concept of the app is extended to any client software that can access back-end services, piercing the enterprise firewalls or otherwise. This client software can be executed in the embedded form or otherwise from any of the digital client devices mentioned earlier. Such client programs may not always follow the **WORA** (**Write Once, Run Anywhere**) principles; instead they are "fit for purpose" and act as the human's extension in the physical world. They can be activated autonomously, based on a human trigger, or based on a trigger from anything on the Internet in the IoT world. See Figure 4-1.

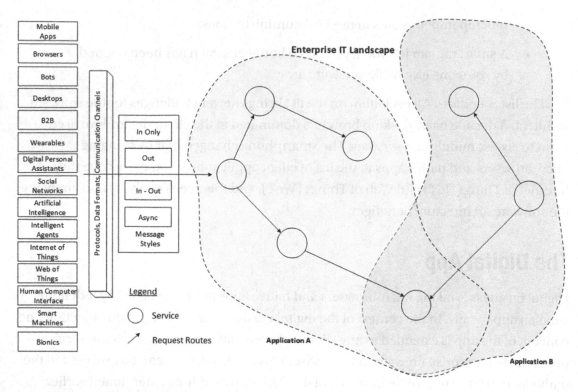

Figure 4-1. *The digital app context*

Requests from a digital app can travel through any medium of communication (like the Internet, microwaves, Bluetooth, e-mail, or even snail mail) and hit the enterprise's network perimeter. JSON-formatted data in a REST style is the popular method of data transport, but new developments are evolving in the context of IoT and WoT.

The Mesh App and Service Architecture

Gartner[1] provides the following definition for the MASA architecture:

> *The MASA (Mesh App and Service Architecture) is a multichannel solution architecture that supports multiple users in multiple roles using multiple devices and communicating over multiple networks to access application functionality. In this architecture, mobile apps, web apps, desktop apps,*

---

[1]Gartner, "An Introduction to How Software-Defined Application Services Enable the Apps and Services Architecture," www.gartner.com/doc/2924317/introduction-softwaredefined-application-services-enable, November 25, 2014.

and IoT apps link to a broad mesh of back-end services to create what users view as an application. The MASA enables users to have a continuous and ambient experience as they shift across these different channels.

—Gartner

As shown in Figure 4-1, when monolith services get replaced with microservices, traditional firewalls and routers are also replaced or enhanced with intelligent routers. which are software aware and software defined. They can be broadly called by the name service control gateways and it is through this intelligent layer that all APIs are exposed to the external world. The external world can include the digital apps as well as other microservices external to your application.

Figure 4-2 represents the MASA with the service control gateway included. You can also see the microservices grouped and named as Application 1 and Application 2. While microservices within an application communicate internally and directly, external calls to a microservice are always routed through a gateway. There's also the notion of common microservices. Access to common microservices or access to a microservice owned by other applications can also be controlled if routed through the gateway.

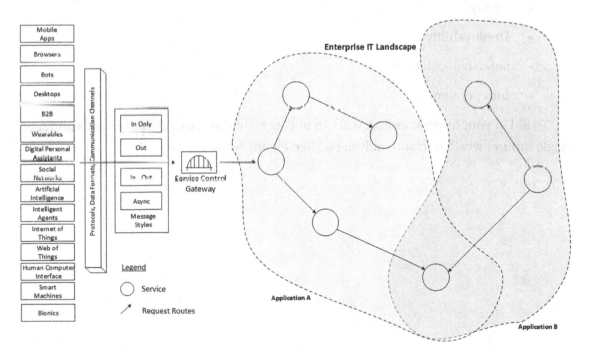

Figure 4-2. *The digital app context*

The Context for Microservices

Microservices are not a revolutionary new trend; instead, they are an evolution in the context of recent trends in the software computing landscape. Even before anyone first used the term microservices, many of you may have been following similar approaches in your enterprises. Componentization, service orientation, and SaaS (Software as a Service) are trends with principles similar to microservices. Miniaturization of these trends (components and services) are linked with recent trends like the public cloud and auto scale, so let's briefly look into this background to better understand microservices

Granularity of Services

You can classify services into different categories based on the granularity at which it is designed and built. Even though the term microservice implies small, the degree to which it is small compared to other services is often relative. In other words, the size is only an indicative characteristic; the more explicit characteristics listed below decide the granularity:

- Agility

- Deployability

- Selective scalability

- Independence

To aid in your understanding, you can bucket all of the above characteristics under a single umbrella called "cloud nativeness." See Figure 4-3.

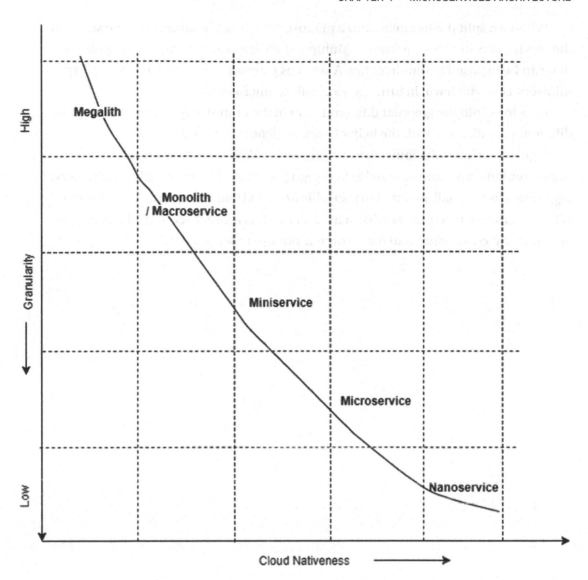

Figure 4-3. *Granularity of services*

As shown in Figure 4-3, when the granularity decreases, most of the qualities required for cloud nativeness increase.

If you relook at the monoliths, by following the best practices of SOA you can expose coarse grained or composite services. Such services expose the individual capability of a business domain. By exposing SOA interfaces, they support flexible enterprise application integration or what we call service-oriented integration. These services are classified under the term "miniservice" and they promote service reuse in terms of service composition. Miniservices are accessed by other miniservices or by the client tier.

When we split the monolith into a microservice-based architecture, the scope of the service gets limited to a feature. Multiple such features encompass a capability that can be exposed to the client tier. A services gateway can be provisioned to expose miniservices, which will in turn delegate calls to microservices.

Let's look into the granular differentiation in the granularity of services under a different classification with the help of a few indicative samples.

Figure 4-4 shows the indicative samples alone. While macroservices are implemented using conventional SOA design patterns and technologies, a miniservice aggregates functionality related to a specific domain (that is, an entity or resource). When compared to a microservice, a miniservice has a larger scope and relaxed architectural constraints, and it may or may not use independent data.

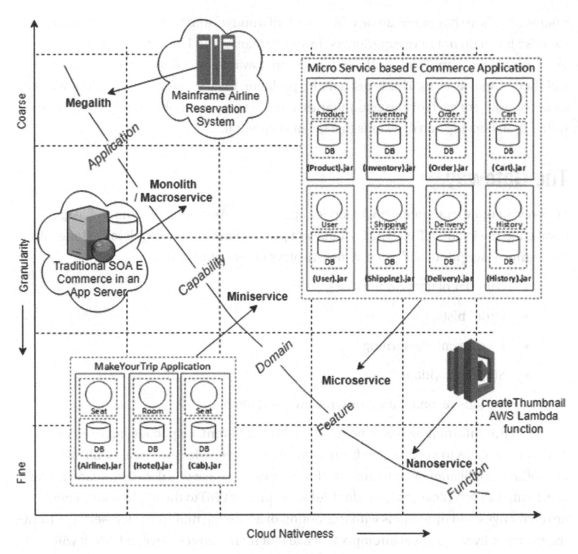

Figure 4-4. *Indicative samples for service granularity*

Again, the units of granularity marked in Figure 4-4 (Function > Feature > Domain > Capability > Application) are not hard-wired or fixed hard in the above granularity scale. Where you want to place your application architecture largely depends on many factors like type of application and the degree of cloud nativeness required. Placing the application architecture slightly towards the left or right is not the big aspect; instead, the rationale behind the place where you fix your architecture is based on the constraints, and the subsequent trade-offs matter. Dogmatic adherence to the microservices architecture can be a high-cost, disruptive, and often less predictable exercise if you do not have experienced in-house teams, and I have often seen enterprises create applications that adhere more towards the miniservices boundary but call them microservices. This is not a major problem. Instead, what is required is a clear understanding of each of these boundaries and then you can make judicious decisions rather than converge on decisions that occur accidentally.

The Gateway

Let's revisit our e-commerce microservice application. Assuming that the web page is displaying the Product Detail page, it doesn't just display the product details alone, like the name, description, and price; it also displays other details like

- Number of items in the cart

- Order history

- Low inventory warning

- Shipping options

- Various recommendations, reviews, and offers

All of this information has to be retrieved from different, respective microservices. The web page has to access them from respective microservices whereas while in a monolithic application architecture the browser can retrieve this data by making a single REST call (GET `api.acme.com/productdetails/productId`) to the application. There are challenges and limitations with this option of accessing multiple microservices from the browser. Even if a client attempts to make that many requests over a LAN, it will probably be too inefficient over the Internet and will face serious performance overhead, especially if the communication is over a mobile network. Also, if all the microservices don't expose web-friendly interfaces, which they are not mandated to expose, this can be another challenge. Further, extensions to or evolution of the application might necessitate splitting or merging existing microservices, which should be shielded from the APIs exposed publicly.

An API gateway can come to the rescue here. External-facing APIs can be coarse grained and can aggregate responses from multiple internal microservices and provide the aggregated response in a single go to the client device. Moreover, such external facing APIs can also do some kind of transformation based on the kind of client device that is asking the response. These kinds of value-adding features can be provided to the API gateway layer, thus making this layer intelligent compared to traditional firewalls or load balancers.

Domain-Centric Partition

Traditionally, we have been following the "one size fits all" approach for meeting non-functional requirements of an application. This is very true when it comes to scaling the application. A monolith can be scaled only uniformly for all of its functional or module boundaries, whereas the microservices principles advocate defining the boundaries based on business domains.

As is seen from Figure 4-5, in a technology-centric approach, the layers or tiers of an application can be scaled altogether. In the microservices approach, since each microservice's boundary is defined based on the business or functional domain, and since this boundary definition is also evident in the physical organization of the application, functions or domains can be scaled selectively. Such a selective approach in combating non-functional requirements also offers the flexibility of defining service-level agreements (like service uptime, etc.) against each microservice level.

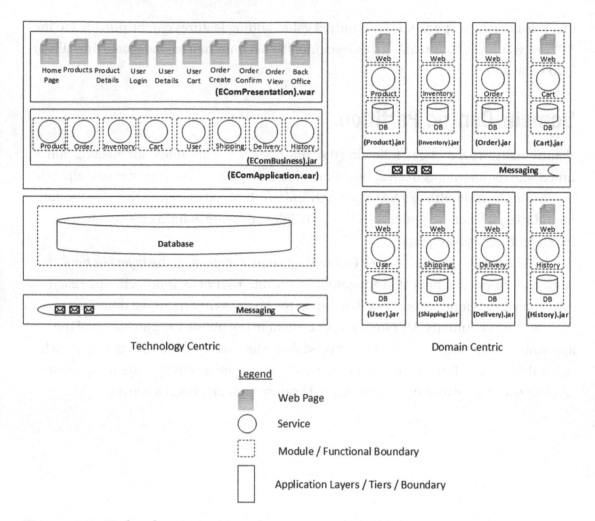

Figure 4-5. *Technology centric vs. domain centric*

In this e-commerce application context, while the Product, Inventory, Order, and Cart microservices must be highly and always available for non-disruptive business around the clock, 365 days a year, the auxiliary microservices like User, Shipping, Delivery, and Order History can be deployed for a lesser availability SLA. This is because, if the User microservice is down, a customer can still browse, add to the cart, and confirm the order by manually entering the address, e-mail, contact number, and other details along with the new order, without retrieving the previously saved user profile. Later, when the User microservice comes back up, the system can always associate this "anonymous order" to the customer profile that already exists in the system. A similar case exists with other modules, which you will examine in detail when you relook at the e-commerce application later.

The Cloud Native Shift

For ages we have been relying on dedicated infrastructures to address growing business demands, whether in a scale out or in a scale up philosophy. We add redundant and bigger pipes (Infinibands) for network connectivity, invest in engineered systems (Exalogic) to add compute power, and so on. Recent insights and incidents have opened the eyes of enterprise architects and they realize that these systems have limitations, and sooner than later they will be constrained by these limitations. The high throughputs provided by fiber optics or the high performance provided by in-memory computing all can provide exponential performance during the initial portions of a graph, but then will meet the limit, after which you get only little improvement even if you add more CPUs or bandwidth. Advancements in quantum computing and similar technologies will shift the plane, but again, businesses cannot wait until these technologies are commoditized and accessible at reasonable cost.

The public cloud is available today, which is of comparable and reasonable cost, if not cheaper. Cloud platform providers like Amazon and Azure provision commodity hardware in datacenters, which can be instantaneously provisioned as per your needs. When your business is faced with unpredicted hypergrowth or hyperscale requirements, the cloud is a reasonably right approach to keep your overall cost under control but at the same time provides the required agility. I do not intend to cover the features or characteristics of cloud computing or cloud service providers (CSP) here, but I surely want to discuss what cloud native means.

In an on-premises model, the availability policies and SLA management are in the hands of data center administrators. When you move to a public cloud model, such policies are transformed and abstracted to higher levels at your application stack. In the IaaS (Infrastructure as a Service) or PaaS (Platform as a Service) model provided by the CSPs, you have little control over the availability or storage policies, so you need better controls and tool provisioning at your application stack layer. Your software layer should by itself be geared to provide you hooks and controls for unprecedented scenarios. So in order for the applications to truly benefit from the advantages of CSPs, the applications should be smart enough in terms of recovering from failures, non-availability of resources, abrupt spikes in traffic, etc. Cloud native architecture speaks about the patterns and practices you need to adopt in building software applications for operating efficiently in a public cloud environment.

Web Scale Computing

Web-scale IT applies to designing, deploying, and managing infrastructure at any scale. Leveraging the capabilities of a web-scale IT, a business or enterprise can scale at massive levels. IT principles and practices are a priority when it comes to web-scale IT; of course cloud, microservices, and Dev Ops practices are to be named specifically. Companies like Google, Amazon, Facebook, and Netflix are to be mentioned here since by the mere nature of their business, their IT systems and practices fall in this category. Distributed Everything, fault tolerance, self-healing, and API-driven approaches are just few of the principles around web-scale computing.

The Indispensable Cloud

The cloud aims to provide distributed compute, storage, and network infrastructures in an autonomous manner at a comparatively reduced cost. A cloud-based architecture may be based on multiple models (i.e., IaaS, PaaS, and SaaS), and suitable provisioning can lead to a flexible environment for the customers. In the cloud, the customers can use the clouds' APIs to allocate the resources on demand and in near real time.

Cloud Architecture Model

The industry has divided the cloud architecture into four layers:

- **Hardware layer:** The hardware layer contains the physical resources of the cloud, such as CPUs, disks, and networks.

- **Infrastructure as a Service**: The IaaS layer abstracts physical resources using virtualization techniques, thus creating a pool of computing resources to be exposed as integrated resources to the layer above and to the end users. Features such as on-demand resource allocation happen at this layer.

- **Platform as a Service**: The PaaS layer provides application development tools and deployment environments in addition to the operation environment provided by the underlying IaaS, thus aiming to minimize the burden of deploying applications directly into virtual machines. Relational and No SQL storage, message queues, and mail servers are typical services made available at this layer by wrapping suitable frameworks.

- **Software as a Service**: At the top of everything lies the SaaS model, which can host enterprises' customized end user applications or hired third-party software, available as a network service, thus relieving the enterprise from the pains of managing and maintaining the various architectural layers of the cloud.

Figure 4-6 represents the various layers of the cloud architecture. Automatic scaling to achieve better performance and availability in an on-demand manner makes the cloud applications superior to applications deployed on premises.

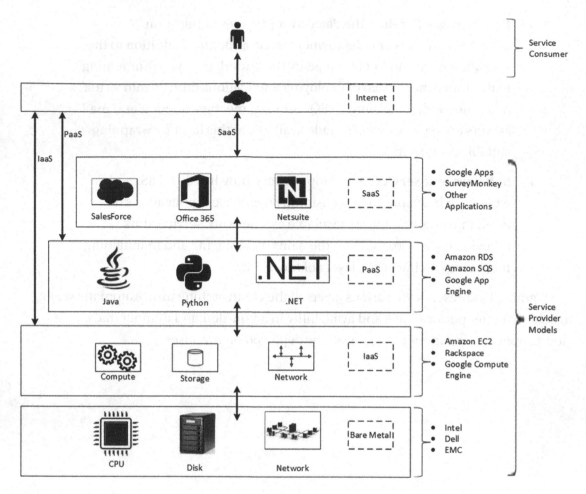

Figure 4-6. *Cloud architecture components*

Cloud Service Model

The cloud service model is based on the kind of control users may have over how the resources are being utilized. Figure 4-7 shows the different models.

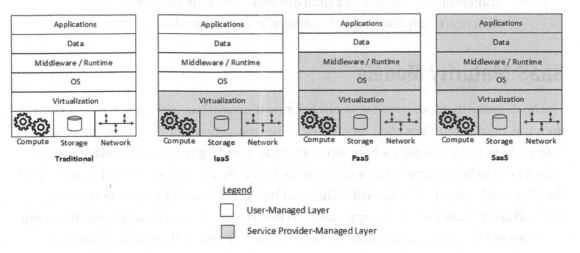

Figure 4-7. Cloud service models

Typically the cloud architecture itself can be mapped to the cloud service model. In the traditional service model, the user or the enterprise itself is responsible for managing the whole stack (e.g., hardware, data center facilities, software, and data) whereas in the cloud service model it varies as follows:

- **Infrastructure as a Service**: In the IaaS service model, the users request compute power, storage, network, and their associated resources alone and pay for what they use.

- **Platform as a Service**: In PaaS model, the users have zero control over the underlying infrastructure, such as CPU, network, and storage, as they are abstracted away below the platform. Instead, it allows application development platforms that allow the creation of applications with supported programming languages and related tools hosted in the cloud and accessed through an interface, mainly a browser. Many times the application runtime and middleware are also provided by the CSP, and the user develops, installs, manages, and operates the software application alone and its data.

- **Software as a Service**: This is the "forget everything" model where the user doesn't even own, manage, or operate the application. Applications are run on the cloud infrastructure and are accessible from various client devices. Limited user-configurations are available. Sometimes the same application instance serves the end users of more than one enterprise (tenant); such applications are called multi-tenant.

SaaS Maturity Models

The SaaS maturity model was coined by Microsoft[2] more than a decade ago, and since then this information has been mentioned by me many times during my discussions with architects. I will repeat it here, since an understanding is indispensable when we map it later to how microservices can be scaled for different levels. Figure 4-8 depicts the different levels of SaaS maturity. The term "tenant" is used here to denote an enterprise on whose behalf the application is hosted; the end users access services from these hosted instances of the applications. So, two different airlines or two different e-commerce enterprises are two different tenants. The different levels of SaaS maturity are as follows:

- **Level 1 – Ad Hoc/Custom**: At this level of SaaS maturity, each enterprise or tenant has its own custom-developed application. The source code of these applications is different, and the separate application instance is hosted either on premise or in a public cloud for each tenant.

- **Level 2 – Configurable**: At this level of SaaS maturity, there is only one code base. The code base is configurable separately for each tenant, and each separate application instance is hosted either on premise or in a public cloud for each tenant.

- **Level 3 – Configurable, Multi-Tenant Efficient**: At this level of SaaS maturity, there is only one code base. A single instance of this single code base is hosted either on premise or in a public cloud, which serves the end users of all tenants. The configuration of the code done while instantiating the application is in such a way that the

---

[2]"Architecture Strategies for Catching the Long Tail," Microsoft

runtime characteristics like features, functionalities, and look-and-feel are "adaptable" to a certain extent as per the wish of each tenant. Each customer's data is kept separate from that of other customers by employing suitable architecture-level partitions. But the limitation here is, if the number of tenants or the number of end users increases beyond a limit, it is difficult to scale beyond that point. Scalability can be managed to some extent by partitioning, but after a certain extent the application can be scaled only by moving it to more powerful servers (scaling up), until diminishing returns make it impossible to add more power cost-effectively.

- **Level 4 – Configurable, Multi-Tenant Efficient, and Scalable**: In Level 4 SaaS maturity, the capability to horizontally scale is added to Level 3. Multiple instances of app servers and DB servers can be added horizontally and load balancing routers can distribute load from users of multiple tenants to a pool of server instances in a round robin or equally distributed manner. While it is straightforward to scale out at the app server layer using app server farms, scaling at the DB layer is not that straightforward since it requires a database cluster, not a simple farm. You will learn more about this later when you look into the "write scalability" of data.

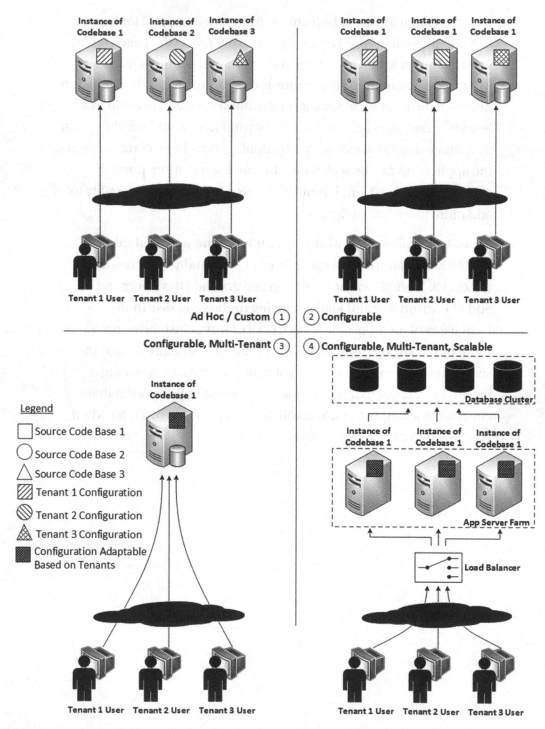

Figure 4-8. *SaaS maturity models*

Virtualization

Virtualization is a process of providing an abstract machine that uses device drivers targeting the abstract machine so as to provide virtual replication of hardware. Type 1 hypervisors[3] run on bare metal and most mid-end to high-end microprocessors can be virtualized. Server processors like Intel's Xeon and application processors like the Arm Cortex-A series are hardware with same capability. When virtualized, the VM (virtual machine) will run any software that runs on the bare metal hardware while providing isolation from the real hardware. See Figure 4-9.

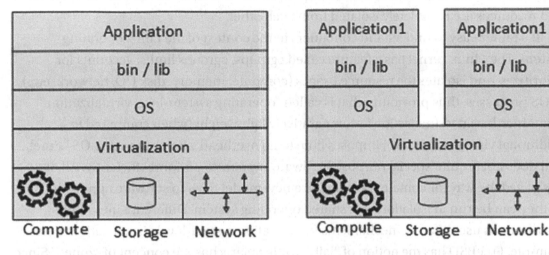

Figure 4-9. SaaS over abstract hardware

Instances of multiple applications or multiple instances of the same application can be run in a single hardware effectively by virtualization techniques.

Virtualized Servers vs. Containers

Containers provide a way to isolate applications and provide a virtual platform for applications to run on. The container's system requires an underlying operating system and this OS provides the basic services to all of the containerized applications

---

[3]Hypervisors are a way to manage VMs and Type 2 Hypervisors have an underlying operating system called the host OS.

using virtual-memory support for isolation. This is represented in Figure 4-10 in the Virtualization section. VMs have their own operating system using hardware VM support. The overhead of containers is comparatively lower than that of VMs and container systems typically target environments where hundreds or thousands of containers are in play. When you need to run multiple applications on multiple servers, virtualization may be the best option, whereas if you need to run many copies of a single application, containers offers compelling advantages. Let's look into the rationale behind this. Virtual machines package up the virtual hardware, a kernel (i.e. OS), and user space for each new VM. This provides the required level of isolation across applications, which is typically desirable if they are different applications so that concerns like security, data, and resources are completely isolated from each other.

It's rather easy to understand containers in the context of the Linux operating system. The Linux kernel has a feature called cgroups. cgroups limits, accounts for, prioritizes, and isolates the resource usages (compute, memory, disk I/O, network, etc.) of OS processes, thus providing what is called "operating system-level virtualization." Container-based virtualization is comparatively lightweight (when compared to traditional virtual machines), imposes little to no overhead, shares the same OS kernel, and does not require special purpose hardware support to perform efficiently. All of this has paved the way for containers to define a new model to wrap software applications so they can be run in isolation on a shared operating system. Different Linux/Unix distributions use different mechanisms for operating system-level virtualization. For example, FreeBSD has the notion of "jails" while Solaris has the concept of "zones." Since the technology used by containers to isolate the kernel is Linux-specific, containers can only run on Linux-based operating systems.

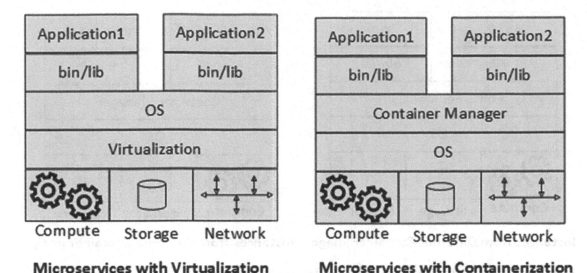

Figure 4-10. *Virtualization vs. containers*

Figure 4-10 shows how resources are shared in a container system. When you start two (or more) containers on the same host, using the same base image, the whole content of the base image will be shared. On the contrary, if you start multiple containers with different images, it may happen that these images may or may not share some common layers (bin, lib, etc.), depending on how each layer of the image was built.

Thus for each virtual machine the entire stack of components is running so that the operating system up to the application server and virtual hardware is emulated, including network components, CPUs, and memory. However, containers operate as completely isolated sandboxes with only the minimum required kernel alone of the operating system present for each container. The system resources of the underlying system are shared for containers so that the footprint is reduced, which means for the same hardware substantially more containers can be run than virtual machines. The sharing of resources in such a manner will decrease the overall footprint, which will also help to bring down the time required to bootstrap container instances as compared to instantiating the same app deployed in a VM system. This is the relevance of containers, especially in a cloud native environment where instantaneous auto scale is required. See Figure 4-11.

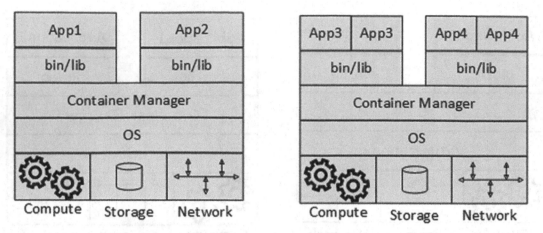

Instances from Different Container Image   Instances from the Same Container Image

Figure 4-11. *Container instances sharing resources*

Docker, which is now based on the Linux libcontainer, is a management system used to create, manage, and monitor containers in the Linux platform. Docker helps package an application on a laptop, which can then run unmodified on any public cloud, private cloud, or even bare metal, following the "build once, run anywhere" principle. The infrastructure footprint is minimal when compared to virtualization based on hypervisors such as VMWare or Hyper-V.

Red Hat favors Ansible, which is another container-management system. Kubernetes is another open source system for automating deployment, scaling, and management of containerized applications.

Docker is the most popular container provider system. Since it will run only on a Linux-based OS, if you have to set up Docker in Windows or Mac machines, you first need to start up a Linux VM using VirtualBox and then run the Docker containers inside this virtual machine.

Another feature when you move from a traditional monolith-based SaaS to a microservice-based SaaS, the so-called heavy middleware like Oracle Weblogic or IBM Websphere will get replaced by comparatively lighter runtimes, like Tomcat or Jetty. It is also common to have these runtimes configured to be run as embedded within the Java process so that the overall footprint is minimal.

The Architecture of Microservices

Microservices architecture (MSA) can be defined as a way of designing software applications with an aim to achieve agility of delivery, flexibility of deployment, and precision of scalability. There are a lot of associated benefits, and also a set of complexities you must deal with. Let's look at few of them and the bigger picture associated with them in this section.

Inversion of Architecture

In MSA, applications are composed of small, independently deployable processes communicating with each other using platform-agnostic and programming language-agnostic APIs and protocols. Each of these processes hosts application components that expose closely related business capabilities. Many such processes expose many such capabilities for an enterprise application. Thus in a MSA, a single capability or a single process or a single microservice alone may not be sufficient to represent an enterprise application of any considerable size.

In the monolith, it is one single (main) process that hosts the entire application package. Hence all or most of the following concerns within a monolith application are encompassed within the single process space itself:

- Service dependency management

- Service configuration management

- Service instrumentation

- Service SLA

- Service management and monitoring

In MSA, since there are many processes communicating with each other, all or most of the above concerns are not limited to a single process alone, unlike the scenario with a monolith. They are to be dealt with for all these coordinating processes and this means extra process complexities. And this is the next most distinguishable characteristic of a microservice, where the inner concerns of a single process of the earlier monolith are now exploded to the outside of many microservices. This is called the "Inversion of Architecture" (IoA).

The Inner Architecture Perspective

Since microservices are independent, autonomous, and self-encompassing packages deployable to their own process space, they are to be complete in terms of its own architecture. Figure 4-5 shows that microservices host their own presentation, business, and data components and also hosts their own messaging infrastructure. Hence all or most of the architectural concerns in terms of separation of concerns, layering, and interface-oriented design still exist and should be dealt with in the architecture of each and every microservice; this is the "inner architecture" of a microservice.

Gartner has four examples to explain the inner architecture of microservices:

- Simple/Scaled

- Complex/Scaled

- Externalized Persistence

- Command Query Responsibility Segregation

Figure 4-12 represents these example scenarios schematically. Let's cover these example scenarios with suitable analogies so that the concept is clear and so you understand the options available and the complexities involved.

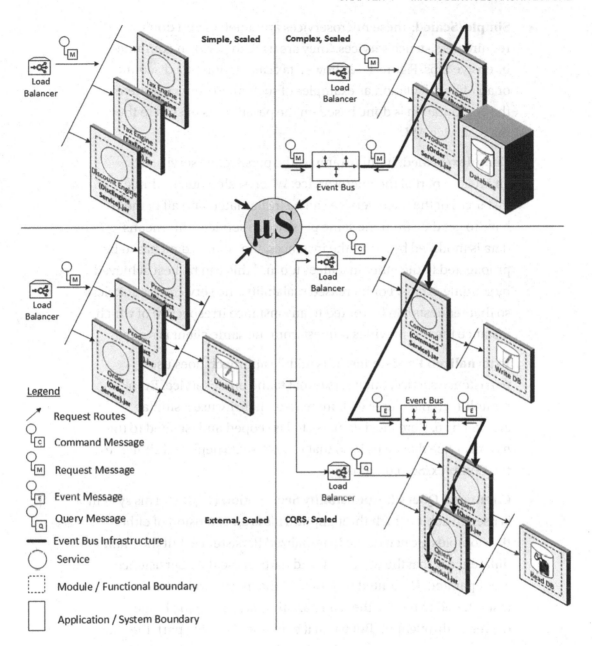

Figure 4-12. *Microservices inner architecture examples*

- **Simple/Scaled**: These microservices are stateless and don't require persistence services. They are used to perform compute-intensive jobs. Figure 4-12 shows a tax calculation or a discount or an offer calculation as examples of such microservices where the computation is done based on the parameters passed to the microservice API.

- **Complex/Scaled**: In this example, the persistence service is an integral part of the microservice. When scaled out, multiple instances of the microservice can be instantiated and all of them have to get data from the same persistence service. This means, if data is modified by any of the instances, the change data has to be propagated to the other instances too and this can be best achieved by sending events. For increased scalability, the services are stateless so that requests can be routed to any instance irrespective of which instance the just previous request from the same client is routed.

- **Externalized Persistence**: This middle approach does use a persistence service, but it is external to the microservice. Even monolith architectures with increased maturity use a similar architecture. Here the data persisted is scoped and isolated to the microservice that owns it, so that it can also be deployed similar to the Complex/Scaled topology.

- **Command Query Responsibility Segregation (CQRS)**: This system is used to achieve high throughput. This is an extension of either the Complex/Scaled or the Externalized Persistence, but the main difference is that the write and read parts of the data persistence are separated. Unlimited instances of the microservice can be instantiated to handle the read part, thus achieving the highest degree of throughput. But when it comes to the write part, the state changes must be propagated to the other instances of the read part and this can be best achieved again by sending events.

You will revisit the inner architecture again when I introduce the working e-commerce application in later chapters. For the purpose of brevity, I will use a simple notation to distinguish between the inner architecture and the outer architecture, shown in Figure 4-13. This notation will be followed in our further discussions.

Inner Architecture   **Outer Architecture**

Figure 4-13. *Microservices architecture notation*

The Outer Architecture Perspective

I mentioned that due to the Inversion of Architecture, many of the concerns that used to be solved at the inner architecture level of the monolith have now become the outer architecture concerns. Figure 4-14 attempts to show schematically the concerns we need to address at the outer architecture level of a microservice. Microservices interact with each other and this chattiness between process spaces increases the overall complexity. Concerns like fault tolerance, graceful retry, and alternate code execution are few among them and this necessitates strong management, monitoring, and control of microservices at its outer architecture level. The goal is to achieve agility of delivery, flexibility of deployment, and the precision of scalability in a microservices architecture. In order to do this, a new set of concerns must be addressed and this increases the complexity of microservices manyfold compared to that of a monolith.

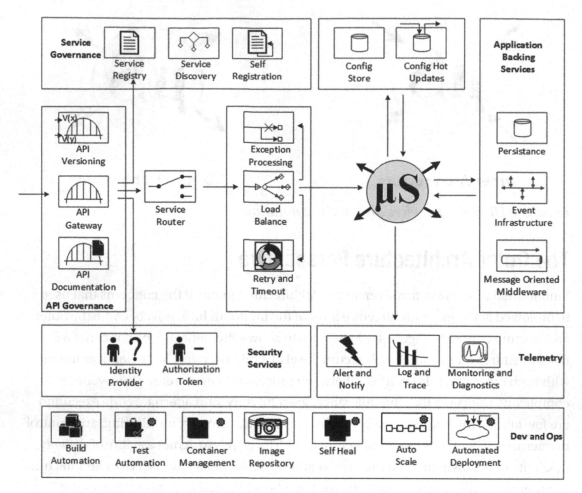

Figure 4-14. *Microservices outer architecture*

In a monolith, security can be easily controlled through a single controller whereas in a microservices architecture, since many services distributed in the network need to talk to each other to provide complete business capability, security is dispersed and has to be controlled at every microservice level. End-to-end logging and tracing is another aspect whose importance increases manyfold in the microservices architecture, since a call graph can span across many microservices. To aid seamless addition and retirement of microservice instances, dynamic service registration and discovery are required. Similarly, auto scale and auto deploy are new Dev Ops concerns to make the microservices cloud native and web scale.

The Big Picture of MASA

Having discussed the separation between the inner architecture and outer architecture concerns of microservices, it is time now to look at the big picture.

Figure 4-15 combines the inner architecture and the outer architecture of microservices to provide a view of a typical Mesh App and Services Architecture. Microservices interact with their environment and with other microservices, leveraging the outer architecture provisions, whereas each of the microservices' ability to scale selectively is built and managed using its inner architecture organization.

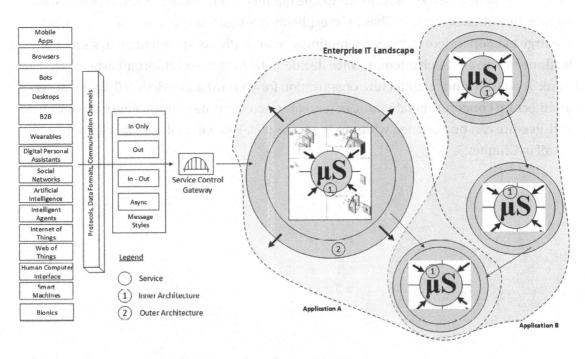

Figure 4-15. *The outer architecture of microservices*

Figure 4-15 shows only a few microservices. For any enterprise application of considerable size, this is not the case. There can be a number of microservices, starting at over a dozen and reaching the hundreds in number. Unlike how the name "microservices" sounds, microservices are not simple. They are far more complex than the traditional monolith, and in fact have all the complexities of the monolith. So, the decision to adopt microservices is to be taken with care. Microservices are not an option if the enterprise's development team doesn't have experienced guides. The scenario is changing as you read this book, since tool vendors and cloud providers are coming out with new offerings; once these offerings mature, they should hide a lot of the outer architecture complexities from developers.

Summary

In this chapter you looked at the forces that led to the evolution of microservices. The digital app, which connects humans with physical things, has necessitated this evolution. Inversion of Architecture is a normal outcome of this evolution, and the overall complexity of the software landscape has increased manyfold and is now visible outside to a microservice and has to be explicitly managed across microservices. While the urge to adopt microservices is tempting, a quantitative cost benefit analysis must be done before any such attempt. Once decided, the next most important aspect is to think about the inner architecture organization for your microservices. While the outer architecture concerns remain more or less same across context and scenarios, your inner architecture can be designed with varying trade-offs. You will look into this in more detail in Chapter 5.

CHAPTER 5

Essential Patterns for Microservices

Software architectures are comparatively easy to comprehend, especially if there is enough documentation on the subject. The hardship will emerge when you start implementing them to solve real-world problems. This is where architectural patterns will come to your rescue. If you understand the problem at hand and if you can reasonably attach this problem to a scenario similar to a problem you have already addressed, it's rather easy to follow an approach similar to what you adopted earlier. Architecture and design patterns help you to choose and adopt solutions to problems that are similar in nature. A pattern is a reusable solution to repetitive problems of a similar nature that occur in a particular context.

Having discussed the necessity of splitting monolith applications into multiple microservices, let's now take a pragmatic view of one of the major concerns any application architect will face in designing scalable application: scaling the write and read clusters of any application independently. You will look into this aspect in detail in this chapter. In doing so, you will also explore a powerful pattern that will help solve many concerns of a microservices architecture by adopting various flavors of it.

The concepts you are going to do a deep dive into in this chapter are as follows:

- The need to independently scale the read and write transactional capabilities of an architecture

- The CQRS pattern

- A metamodel for the CQRS pattern and more sample scenarios that will be explained in later chapters in the book

© Binildas Christudas 2019
B. Christudas, *Practical Microservices Architectural Patterns*, https://doi.org/10.1007/978-1-4842-4501-9_5

Orthogonal Scale Out of Services

If we put aside the other rationales behind the microservices architecture, one main requirement is to selectively scale out components or services within a single application. You know that in a monolith it is nearly impossible to easily split out components or services and then deploy them at a selected degree of scalability; however, this is one major advantage we get in adopting the microservices architecture. In previous chapters I discussed the need to instantiate more numbers of Product Catalogue and Product Details microservices as compared to the number of instances of the Order microservice required. A similar requirement is also relevant in scaling the transactions handling the state change and state view of application domains heterogeneously, so let's try to understand that in detail.

Write vs. Read Transactions

Any transaction originated through a B2B or a B2C channel, or for that matter through an IoT or Wearable channel, typically falls into one of the two categories of transactions:

- **Write transactions**: A write transaction will typically change the state of entities in the application. An e-commerce check out, a credit card payment, and a flight seat confirmation are first-class examples of a write transaction, since all of them change the state of entities, are usually kept in the server-side memory, and in many cases the state change also gets reflected in the backing persistent store as well as in any other counterpart B2B interfaces with which the application interfaces. Generally, write transactions are non-idempotent[1] unless they are designed with special care to behave differently. This means a credit card payment transaction, if it is intended to be executed once and if due to some reason it is executed twice (played once and replayed one more time) and if both these transactions are successful, then the payment will be processed twice, which may not be the desired outcome

---

[1]Idempotence is the property of certain operations in mathematics and computer science whereby they can be applied multiple times without changing the result beyond the initial application.

- **Read transactions**: A read transaction usually queries the existing
  state of an entity, either for view purposes or for caching purposes
  or as a part of another encompassing write transaction as an aid to a
  decision-making step. Whatever the case, typically a read transaction
  is idempotent. It will not alter the actual state of the entity either in
  the server-side memory or in the backing persistent store. Perhaps
  repeated read transactions can create or update the state of some
  related entities, like the corresponding audit or log entities; however,
  normally, if for some reason it is executed twice (played once and
  replayed one or more times) and if all of these transactions are
  successful, then there won't be any appreciable change in the state of
  the main entities involved in the transaction.

The Look-to-Book Challenge

I assume any of you reading this book have already have done online transactions,
especially in an e-commerce application. If so, you can appreciate the fact that it will
take more than one step, traversing through web pages, filling out forms, and so on,
before you actually do the confirmation for your first write transaction, which is creating
the order. To make it more clear, if you are shopping online for some retail item like an
electronic gadget, you follow these steps:

1. Type the URL for the home page.

2. Browse through the product categories and select the product of
   interest.

3. Retrieve the product details, including reviews, contents,
   and media.

4. Decide to purchase the item, add it to the shopping cart, and fill
   out payment information.

5. Click to confirm the purchase.

If you examine the minimum steps listed above, you can differentiate the last
transaction which is the actual confirm purchase transaction from the rest of the
transactions. While the confirm purchase transaction can be put under the write
transaction category, most of the other previous transactions listed above come under
the read transactions category.

Note   For every single write transaction, you do many more read transactions.

In the classic airline seat booking scenario, the ratio of reads to writes for every realized booked PNR comes in the range of 500 or even 1,000 or more. This is called look to book. When we say the look to book is 1,000 on average, this means is that for every write (book) transaction on behalf of a PNR created for a new booking, 1,000 or more read (look) transactions should have already hit the application. During peak season or during peak times of the week when sales are happening, this number can rise to the order of many thousands for a single booking! It is in this context, a microservice's selective scale out capability is relevant.

CQRS: Command Query Responsibility Segregation

The capability to selectively scale out is one of the advantages of microservices architecture, provided we design the microservice to have this characteristic. In the "Inner Architecture Perspective" section in Chapter 4, I discussed the various levels of maturity with which you can design your microservices architecture. I introduced the CQRS (Command Query Responsibility Segregation) pattern there, so let's look into the details of it at an architecture and design level. In the later part of this book you will see many samples and even a full-fledged application implemented using this pattern.

Traditional vs. CQRS-Based Software Systems

In traditional and monolith systems, both writes (updates to the entity) and reads (requests for viewing entity) are executed against the same set of entities in a single data repository. Usually these entities are a subset of the rows in one or more tables in a relational database such as MySQL or PostgreSQL. Figure 5-1 represents this design.

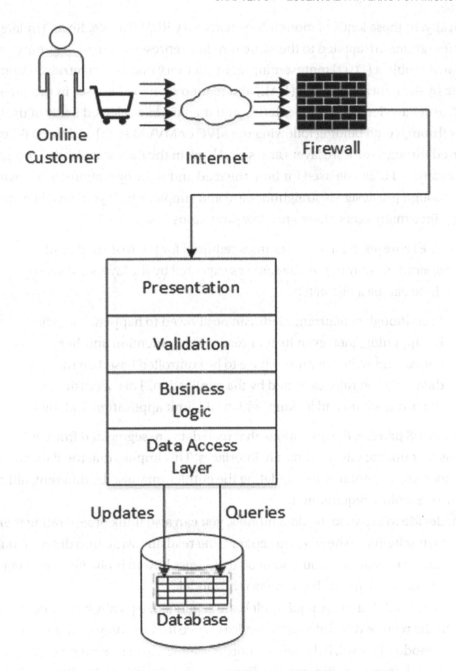

Figure 5-1. *Same schema for read and write transactions*

Typically, in these kinds of monolith systems, all CRUD (Create, Read, Update, and Delete) operations are applied to the same physical representation of the entity. In Java, a data transfer object (DTO) representing an in-memory instance is retrieved from the data store by the data access layer (DAL) and rendered on the browser in the client device. A user can view this representation and then update selected fields of the DTO (perhaps through data binding following the MVC or MVVM style) and the DTO is then transported through software layers and saved back in the data store by the DAL. Many times the same DTO can be used for both the read and write operations, as shown.

Even though the design is straightforward and simple, which you have been happily following since many years, there are a few limitations:

- The representation of the entities required for the write and read operations may not be the same as expected by the layers above, so there can be a mismatch.

- Even though concurrent reads can be allowed to happen, if a write is happening, then even further reads (not to mention another concurrent write operation) have to be controlled based on the data isolation rules expected by the application. This necessitates synchronization and locking, which will limit application scalability.

In the CQRS pattern, the operations that read data are segregated from the operations that update data by separate interfaces. This implies that the data models used for querying the entities and updating the entities may also be different, although this is not an absolute requirement.

If you decide to separate the data models, you can also think of separating them out into their own schemas. Whether you separate the read and write into different data models or different schemas, you also need to address how to replicate any changes happening in the write model back to the read model.

If the write models and the read models are separated, typically it is straightforward to scale out the read portion into many replicas, since they are only copies or views of the single write model. This will help you to address scaling out your read models to take care the look-to-book scenarios discussed earlier. In most cases, the scalability requirements for the write model are in a controlled manner compared to those of the read model. This means you may not want to scale out your write models to the same degree as your read models. However, write models may also want to scale out to more than one for reasons of backup, redundancy, and so on, which will also be discussed later.

All of this means that you have separate data models as well as data schemas for the read and write operations for the entities. Remember again, these two models or schemas are two aspects required for the same entity; just like when you look at a mirror, the mirror image of your face is analogous to the read model whereas your original face is analogous to the write model. You can feel pain if you slap yourself, whereas your mirror image can only "look" the pain; it can't "feel" the pain since it's analogous to the read model. Let's bring this improvement into the design from Figure 5-1; see Figure 5-2.

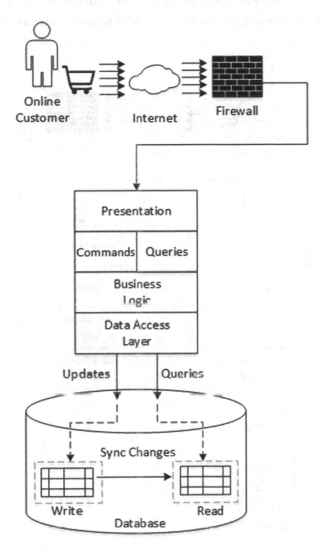

Figure 5-2. *Separate schemas for read and write transactions*

As stated, the read store can be a read-only replica of the write store, and the read and write stores may have a different data structure altogether. Once you bring this separation between the read and write store, change synchronization has to be done from the write store to the read store.

Once you separate the write part from your read part of the data store, the synchronization must be done irrespective of whether these read and write stores are physically in the same node or in two different nodes. Consequently, once the synchronization mechanism is in place, the next natural instinct is to separate out the read and write computations into their own separate nodes or processes, as shown in Figure 5-3.

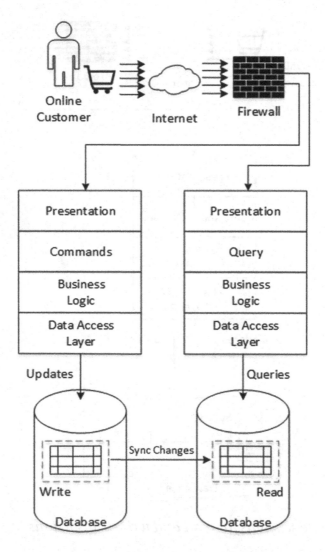

Figure 5-3. *Separate database nodes for read and write transactions*

The moment you separate out the read and write services into different physical nodes, you are in effect grabbing the extra lever of "scale out" to address the high look-to-book ratio mentioned earlier by instantiating more of the read services and keeping a single instance of the write service. See Figure 5-4.

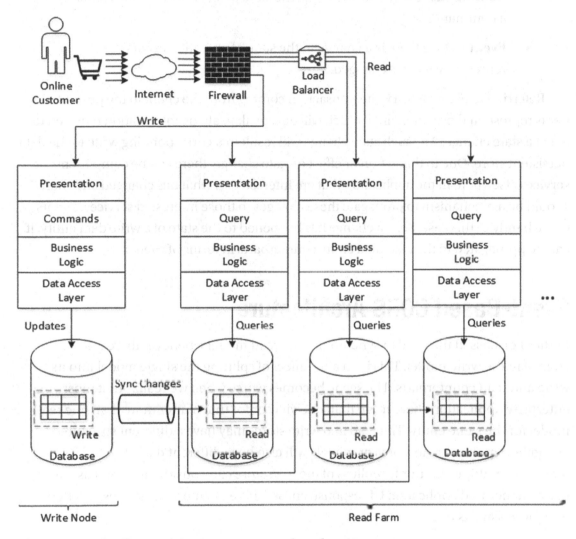

Figure 5-4. *Scale out using separate read and write processes*

The Nomenclature in CQRS

CQRS is based on the notion of two concepts, commands and events. Commands and events are explained as follows:

- **Commands**: The intent to change the state of an entity is modelled as a command.

- **Events**: Once there is a change in the state of an entity, events represent what has changed.

Referring to Figure 5-3, a write transaction coming from the client to the presentation tier is represented by commands, which will encapsulate all the information required to effect a state change. Any such state change will result in a corresponding write to the data persistent store. Due to this action or effect of state change, there can be components or services elsewhere in the application that are interested in what has changed and there should be a mechanism to propagate these changes to those interested services. Events come handy in this case. So, if a change has happened to the state of a write data entity, it can be propagated to the read data entity counterparts in terms of events.

Event-Based CQRS Architecture

Earlier I discussed the need to synchronize the read model whenever there is a change in the write model. This is an after-effect of splitting the single model into its write and read counterparts. The scene becomes worse when we realize that most enterprise applications have more than one view or for that matter more than one read model for the same entity. The read and write stores may have a different structure altogether; multiple read stores or models will also have different data structures so that using multiple read-only replicas of the read store can considerably increase query performance and application UI responsiveness. There are more intricacies so let's dig into these aspects next.

A Meta Model for Event-Based CQRS Design

You started this book by looking at the monolith model of application architecture and then you were introduced to microservices. You also looked at the associated increase in complexities, especially in the outer architecture between microservices. In this chapter, you are going to the next level of splitting the finest single entity, the microservice, into more than one to address the scalability requirement as well as the requirement for multiple views. With a preface that life is not going to be simple, let's discuss these details now.

Based on the knowledge gained so far from previous chapters and previous sections in this chapter, let's list a few intricacies of the CQRS architecture:

- An entity, if split and represented into more than one, has to be in sync.

- Entities and their views are to be scalable selectively

- Entities and their views may have more interacting parties and interested parties in future.

There are other requirements; however, for our discussion, the above list will suffice.

Let's conceptualize a meta model to address the concerns listed here. Figure 5-5 represents one such model.

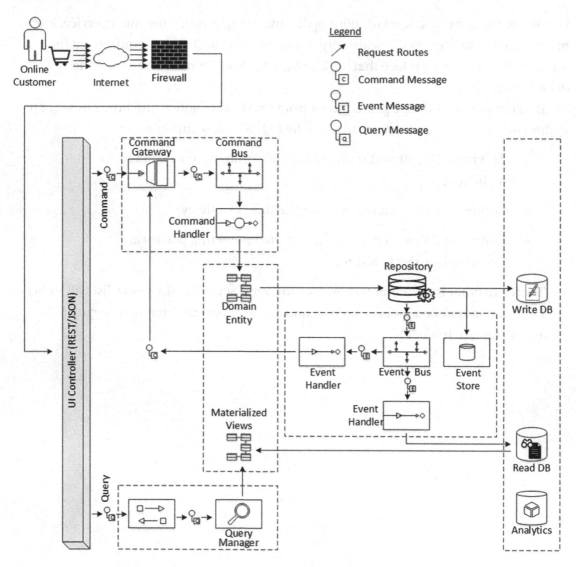

Figure 5-5. *A meta model for CQRS-based architecture*

This meta model is adopted from concepts implemented in the CQRS framework called Axon, the open source CQRS framework you will be using for the samples in this book, the details of which will be introduced later. Let's look at the major components abstracted out in the model here at a conceptual level; the detailed workings of the Axon framework are not required for the understanding of this chapter.

- **Controller**: A controller is typically a UI controller, which intercepts both the write and read transactions from the client.

- **Commands**: The intent to change the state of an entity is modelled as a command. A controller creates and emits commands in response to a write request from a client.

- **Command gateway**: A command gateway is a convenient interface that allows you to choose the command dispatching mechanism, especially by adopting a sync or async style.

- **Command handler**: A command handler responds to a specific type of command and executes business rules and logic based on the contents of the command. It retrieves domain entities and effects state change on them.

- **Domain entity**: Domain entities are aggregate entities modelled to represent the state of the components in the domain of interest. When the state of an aggregates changes, it results in the generation of a domain event.

- **Repository**: When provided with a unique identifier of an aggregate entity, a repository will have the role of looking up the aggregate instance and providing access to the aggregates. A repository can either store the state of the aggregate itself, in which case it can make use of a persistent store like a database, or it can use an event store to resurrect the state of an entity to any point in history, from all of the intermediate states it remembered earlier.

- **Event store**: Event stores usually store changes applied to an entity. By replaying the changes, it is possible to resurrect the state of an entity to any point in history. Event stores may also make use of a database to store state change audit trails.

- **Events**: Once there is a change in the state of an entity, events represents what has changed.

- **Event bus**: An event bus is a conduit for the events generated. Typically they are backed by a messaging topic so that you get the publish subscribe semantics over this conduit.

- **Event handler**: Event handlers receive events and handle them. Multiple event handlers can be subscribed to a particular event type. Some handlers may update data sources or the materialized views used for querying while others may send messages to external interfaces. An event handler may also create new commands.

- **Query**: A controller routes a read transaction to a query manager, which in turn executes the query on top of the specific materialized view of the entity.

Figure 5-5 illustrates a meta model of a CQRS-based architecture leveraging all or many of the actors described previously. The illustrated CQRS meta model also addresses few eventualities in the architecture, which are listed here:

- **Command-event-command cycle**: When the state of an aggregate changes due to a command, it results in the generation of a domain event. These events represent what changed and are injected into the event bus. Interested event handlers consume events and process accordingly. In some cases, the event processing creates new commands to be created and the cycle may repeat.

- The **event bus** exposes publish-subscribe semantics and so it is possible to attach more event handlers to the existing architecture non-intrusively to existing components. This provides for the extensibility of the application in future.

It is to be noted that a CQRS-based architecture doesn't mandate that you adopt a microservices architecture. Nor is a CQRS-based architecture mandatory to adopt a microservices-based architecture. Having said that, marrying these two will provide unique leverage for the software architect to scale the application with the ultimate flexibility.

Command Query Segregation Using Events

CQRS architecture may be utilized to better architect microservices-based systems. By doing a little fine tuning to the CQRS meta model, it is easy to segregate the read and write portions of your application entity into completely different techno-business domains. By techno, we mean to segregate into different process spaces, and by domain, we mean to segregate into different write and read transactional requirements of your business.

Figure 5-6 is an improvisation over the simple CQRS meta model illustrated in Figure 5-5. As you can see, all that is required to synchronize between the write and the read portions of the entity is the event bus. And you already saw that an event bus is typically a messaging backbone, leveraging a message topic. By suitably leveraging the persistence and durability qualities of the event bus, you can practically keep all read nodes in sync with the write node.

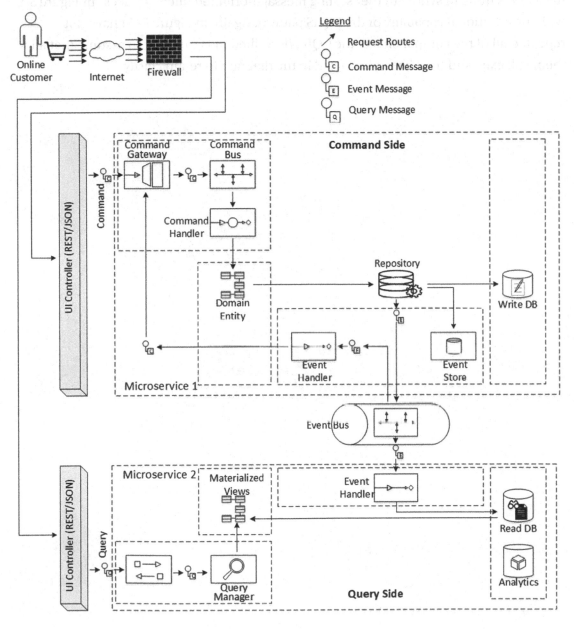

Figure 5-6. *A meta model for event-based CQRS architecture*

Scale Out for CQRS-Based Microservices

Refer to Figure 3-6, which shows the scaling message-oriented microservices. You can extend the same principles to scale out the Command and Query services of your CQRS-based microservices, and this is represented in Figure 5-7. This is just another view of the "scale out using separate read and write processes" represented in Figure 5-4; however, this view is more in sync with the "scaling message-oriented microservices" in Figure 3-6 with the additional capability of the CQRS pattern. Again, in Figure 5-7 I have not repeated all of the components of the CQRS described in Figure 5-6, so assume that all of them still exist and have been abstracted in the diagram to retain clarity.

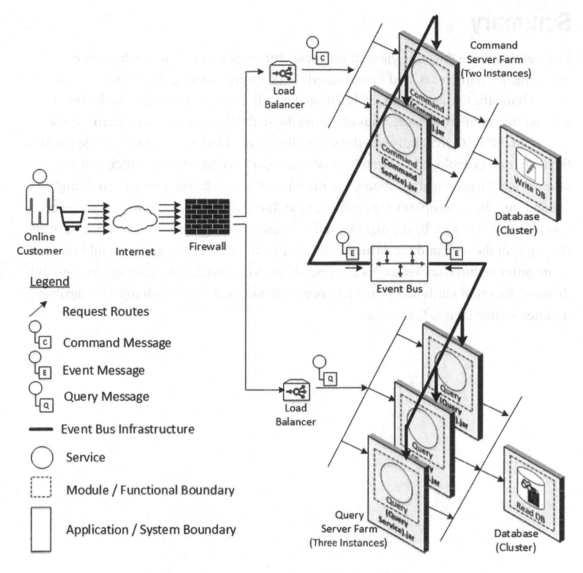

Figure 5-7. *A meta model for scaling out event-based CQRS architecture*

Careful observation of Figure 5-7 reveals another caveat: there are two instances of the Command service represented. While it's rather straightforward to maintain multiple instances of a read service, maintaining more than one instance of the same write service is non-trivial, since the entity with the same identity if accessed concurrently for modification across more than one instance can cause data consistency issues. You will explore this aspect in Chapter 16; until then, assume that you have one node of write service.

Summary

Maintaining more than one view for business entities is a technique we have been following for many years, and materialized views, caches, read replicas, and so on are all mechanisms to that end. CQRS is a more formalized pattern to improve the inner architecture of microservices, thus elevating the scalability options of a microservice manyfold. While CQRS addresses the scalability for the read part of the business entities, the write part is deployed separately to take care of data consistency, which will also take the lead in propagating changes to the entity state to all read parts. Even though the architecture is complex when compared to that of a simple microservice, the extra complexity will pay off by the exponential increase in the scalability of the microservice. Having split the read and the write part into separate microservices, you should now look at the outer architecture concerns between them in the synchronization of changes and the need for other kinds of intermicroservice communication in a reliable and flexible manner, so move on to Chapter 6.

Distributed Messaging

One of the most powerful mechanisms used in building enterprise grade software applications is messaging. Had we not invented messaging, all of the software applications around the globe would be like a complete workforce, needing to be working 24 x 7, 365 days a year without any room for downtime or failure. But in practice we know that every software application is prone downtime or failure; rather, every software application should be designed to have downtime or failure. Since enterprise applications don't live in isolation, instead they talk to each other in a distributed manner, what an application tried to talk to an application that is down? Messaging helps to gracefully accommodate unexpected downtime and failure of coordinating applications. In this chapter, you will look into a few messaging scenarios that will help you understand how these messaging functionalities play a vital role in distributed software architectures, especially in the context of microservices. Here again my intention is not to start from the basics of messaging or to get into all scenarios of messaging, which would be a book unto itself. Instead, I will show a few scenarios that are very critical in understanding the role of messaging in microservices architecture.

Messaging for Resiliency

Assuming that you are aware of the basic constructs in a messaging architecture, let's first look at some basics of how to bring resiliency to a messaging setup.

Message Persistence

Message persistence is a mechanism by which you can keep the messages delivered to a message broker in a persistent store. This will elevate the state of the messages on the wire or on main memory from a volatile state to a permanent safe state. This is very important in a microservices environment since coordinating microservices can come and go, fail or rejuvenate, etc.

105

© Binildas Christudas 2019

B. Christudas, *Practical Microservices Architectural Patterns*, https://doi.org/10.1007/978-1-4842-4501-9_6

Each service in a microservice ecosystem can only make one of its activities compliant to the consistency principle: either safely PUT the message into a message store or safely GET the message from a message store. A message broker sits between these two messaging primitives, and typically a message broker stores messages in its memory (RAM) and delivers messages again from its memory. But if a message broker fails, all messages stored in memory by that message broker are lost. This is undesirable. This is where message persistence comes into play. A message broker can be configured to be backed up by a suitable message persistence mechanism, typically a message-store on disk. Persisting messages to a message store on disk comes at a cost of performance, but it will increase the resiliency of the messaging architecture.

When two microservices want to connect to each other, they use a message channel where one microservice writes information to the channel and the other one reads that information from the channel. Thus the sending microservice doesn't just fling the information into the messaging system; instead, it adds the information to a particular message channel. A microservice receiving information doesn't just pick it up at random from the messaging system; instead, it retrieves the information from a particular message channel, from where it is intended to read from.

When using a message store, we can take advantage of the asynchronous nature of a messaging architecture. When a microservice sends a message to a channel, it sends a duplicate of the message to a special channel to be collected by the message store. The whole setup is shown in Figure 6-1.

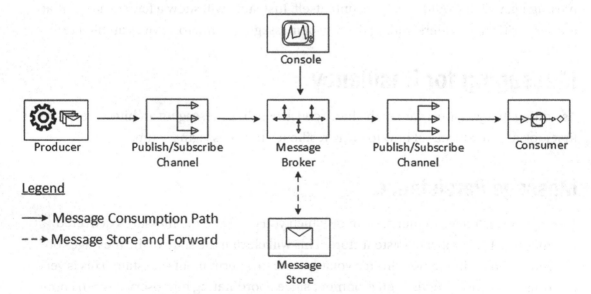

Figure 6-1. Simple publish subscribe with persistence

Design for Various Operational Characteristics of Microservices

One of the prime objectives in splitting the monolith into microservices is to bring complete independence for individual microservices in terms of architecture, technology, build, and operational constraints. This means microservices don't care if the other interacting microservices are up and running or not. Whether the dependent microservices are up and running or not, the independent microservice should be able to complete its operations and move forward. Let me bring clarity to my usage of "dependence" here since I started this paragraph talking about the ability to "bring complete independence for individual microservices" and then in the very next line I talk about their dependencies. Understand that in a distributed environment many or all of these microservices are dependent since they want to share information. Hence when I say "bring complete independence for individual microservices," what I mean is to change the style of dependency from direct to indirect, or in more technical terms, to prefer an asynchronous style in place of a synchronous style.

Using message brokers between microservices is a highly recommended approach to independence. Figure 6-2 shows a single message producer and two message consumers. Assume that they represent three different microservices and they are communicating through a message broker in an asynchronous manner. As you can agree, the moment the message producer publishes a message to the message channel, it can be sure that the message will be safe with the broker infrastructure and it can ignore the published message. When the time comes, interested subscribers can consume these messages from the message broker through their subscribed channel. It is not the business of the Producer microservice or the Consumer microservice to validate whether the other Consumer microservice has received the message or not. If the other microservice is up and running and is fast enough at consuming messages, it will receive the message from the message broker more or less instantaneously, thus responding with a performance grade more or less comparable to a synchronous style of communication between microservices. However, if that Consumer microservice is either too slow to consume or if that microservice is not up and running by the time the Producer published the messages, the message store may help by safely persisting the messages until the message has been consumed by all the registered, interested microservices.

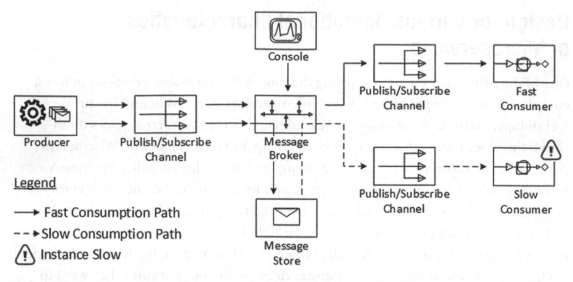

Figure 6-2. *Message persistence to balance operating characteristics*

A Chain Is As Strong As Its Weakest Link

This is extremely important in distributed applications especially when you expect application resiliency: a software application is only as resilient or available as its weakest resilient or available microservice or as the weakest component (link) in the entire infrastructure.

In Figure 6-2, the components of considerable significance are

- The Producer microservice

- The Consumer microservice

- The message broker

Of course there are other components in the architecture shown, but let's assume that those mechanisms to deal with their resiliency are known to us since we have been dealing with distributed systems for two or more decades.

We also acknowledge that the Producer and Consumer microservices also need to be resilient, but in this section we will look at the resilience of the message broker. The message broker is the central, single point of failure in the architecture shown in Figure 6-2. Figure 1-2 in Chapter 1 shows how to address this by adopting suitable network integration topologies. However, those basic topologies alone are not sufficient, so let's rearchitect the message broker infrastructure to avoid this single point of failure.

You may improve the scalability of your messaging system by adding multiple brokers to the system, thus providing redundancy. This will help you to escape the inherent resource limits or resiliency of a single broker deployed on a single machine. Message brokers can be combined into a cluster by adding network connectors between the brokers, which enables you to define broker networks with any arbitrary topology including but not limited to that shown in Figure 1-2 in Chapter 1. When microservices are linked together as a network, routes between microservices are created dynamically as they connect to and disconnect from the network. In other words, with the appropriate topology, a microservice can connect to any other microservice in the network and the network automatically routes messages from microservices attached at any other point in the network.

You should have at least one instance of the message broker in the cluster up and running if it has to take care of any PUT (publish) and GET (subscribe) primitives of the microservices, as depicted in the topology shown in Figure 6-3. One notable feature here is that even if the entire message broker cluster is down, the already persisted messages received from the microservices are safe and due for delivery. If and when at a later time one (or more) instances of the same message broker cluster comes up, it will be ready to deliver the delivery due messages. The same is true about the health of other microservices. If one of the Consumer microservice is down or not responding, the message due to be delivered to that Consumer microservice is safe with the broker and will not be purged or deleted until its delivery has happened eventually.

All of this brings absolute independence between microservices.

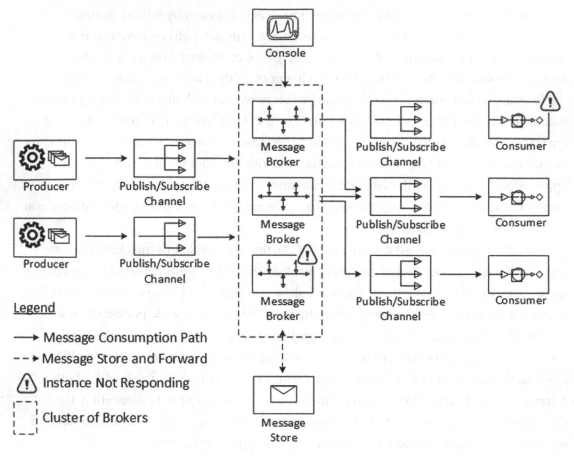

Figure 6-3. *Clustering message brokers for resiliency*

Synchronous vs. Asynchronous

Let's now look at two main styles of communication between microservices: synchronous and asynchronous communications.

Synchronous Interactions Between Microservices

The synchronous style of interaction between microservices is analogous to two people shaking hands. You extend your hand to shake your counterpart's hand, which is analogous to one microservice initiating the request. Your hand and henceforth your handshake will be received if and only if your counterpart is also awake and acknowledges that he or she is willing to shake hands with you and further attempts to respond to you by offering his or her hand, too. When that happens, your hand will be received by your counterpart and you will also feel your counterpart responding to you by clasping your hand to shake it. Similarly, the receiving microservice should be up and running and not too busy so that it can accept the request sent by the providing microservice within a reasonable timeframe (so that network timeouts won't hinder the process), process it, and send back a response, if any, instantaneously.

In the component world, especially when two components interact with one another within a single process, typically the synchronous style of request response cycle happens within a single thread of execution. The consumer component and the receiver component can share the same stack variables of the thread. Since all the request data and the temporary stack data are all available and shared within the single thread context, when the response data is received back by the consumer component from the producer component, the consumer can be sure that it has received the response corresponding to the request it fired towards the producer. This is shown in Figure 6-4.

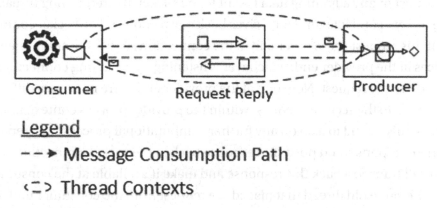

Legend
-- ► Message Consumption Path
‹‹⁻›› Thread Contexts

Figure 6-4. *Synchronous, in-process communication*

The scenario becomes slightly complex when the interacting components live in different process spaces. If components or microservices have to perform interprocess communication, which will be always be the norm in distributed enterprise applications, the processes must be interconnected using pipes (networks). Network sockets provide a fine abstraction for these pipes. Figure 6-5 depicts this scenario.

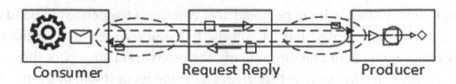

Legend

--→ Message Consumption Path

‹⊐› Thread Contexts

⟺ Socket Connection

Figure 6-5. *Synchronous interprocess communication*

An end-to-end request response cycle in such a scenario is tied together not directly, but indirectly. On the consumer side, the consumer process initiates a socket connection and a single thread within this process will send the request through the connection. Once the request or any adjoining data is sent to the socket, the requesting thread can do nothing but wait and idle until it receives back any response. The socket connection will pop out this request at the other end of the connection so that the components or microservices at the provider end, whichever is listening by accepting connections, will be able to receive the request. Note that at the provider end there must be a different thread dedicated to the received request within the provider process context, and it is the task of this thread to also do any further computational processing, prepare an appropriate response, and push the response back to the socket connection. The connection will transport back this response and make it available at the consumer end, from where the same old thread that placed the request from the consumer end, which was blocked and waiting to get a response from the pipe, will pick up the response; this completes a request response cycle. In short, in a synchronous style of interaction, coordinating threads will be blocked and must wait.

Figure 6-6 shows a more complex scenario where a component or a microservice instance in a single process has to respond to concurrent requests of the same type. When the same type of request comes, and once they are processed concurrently, now the dilemma for the producer is to return which response data to which requestor.

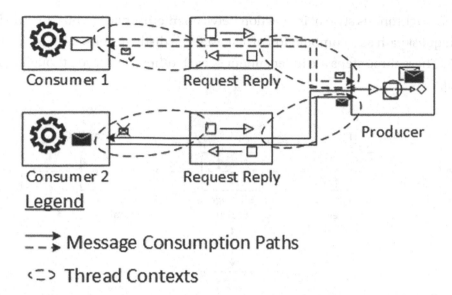

Figure 6-6. Synchronous, concurrent interprocess communication

In Figure 6-6, on the Producer side, requests from multiple consumers are getting processed concurrently: the white envelope request and the black envelope request. Consumer 2, sending the black envelope request, naturally expects a response to his message in a similar envelope, a black envelope response. If the Producer sends back a response intended to be sent to some other consumer, that is an error scenario, which is marked with a cross in the diagram. Fortunately, language primitives like threads, contexts, and sessions provide a nice abstraction to solve such puzzles without doing extra work from the developer side. In other words, concurrent requests are served by separate threads so each thread knows to which requester each response data must be returned.

So far so good, since we have been talking about synchronous communications. Let's now look at the asynchronous style.

Asynchronous Interactions Between Microservices

In Figure 6-1, you saw how a message broker can be introduced to make the interactions between components or microservices asynchronous. Let's look into further details of this kind of interaction.

In the asynchronous style of interaction between microservices, you can visualize a single Request path as a combination of at least three distinct steps, as depicted in Figure 6-7. These three steps are independent of each other steps, even though they are sequential.

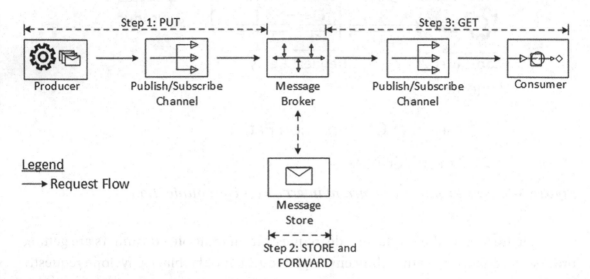

Figure 6-7. *Asynchronous request route*

1. The message Producer microservice creates a request message and publishes it into a message broker queue.

2. The message broker can either keep the request message in memory or in a persistent store or it can attempt to deliver it to a subscriber.

3. The message Consumer microservice, if interested in the above request message, can consume the message.

By introducing a suitable degree of redundancy to the different actors (producer, consumer, and broker), we can configure the application in such a way that even if one or more server instances hosting any of these components are down at any point in time, the request message is still safe (with at least any one of these actors) and will eventually be consumed once and only once by the consumer.

Another notable feature in Figure 6-7 is the reversal of the roles of Producer and Consumer as compared to Figure 6-6. This is because in the asynchronous world of messaging, whoever creates the message and publishes is termed the message producer and whoever consumes the message is termed message consumer (as compared to the synchronous SOA style interaction where whoever requests the service is termed the consumer and whoever provides the service is termed the provider).

The request path in Figure 6-7 must be completed by a response path with a response message too. This is shown in Figure 6-8. Here again, you need to visualize a single response path as a combination of at least three distinct steps, again consecutive.

4. The message consumer, after consuming the request message, performs any computations, creates a response, and publishes it to a message broker queue.

5. The message broker can either keep the response message in memory or in a persistent store or it can attempt to deliver it to a subscriber.

6. The previous message Producer microservice, if interested in the above response message, can consume the message.

I have purposefully stroked off the roles of Producer and Consumer in Figure 6-8 because in the truest sense of messaging, the component or microservice that creates the response and publishes it is called the producer and vice versa. But those terms are of less significance as long as you understand the concept discussed here.

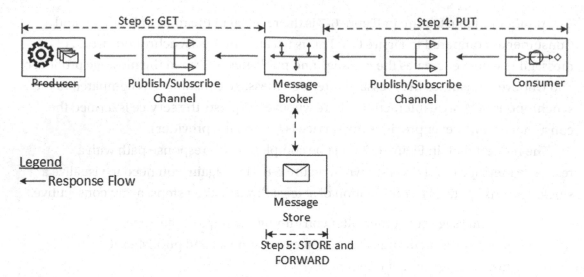

Figure 6-8. *Asynchronous response route*

Easier said than done! Now you need to closely relook at the above six steps. A single synchronous style of interaction between two microservices depicted in Figure 6-6 has been split into six different and independent steps. Each step doesn't have any dependency on its successor step or its predecessor step, provided there is a mechanism by which the state or data exchanged through these steps can be correlated. To make this clear, starting from the thread context or the stack variables in the place of the Producer code in Figure 6-7, there should be a way to connect back the response message consumed at the end of Step 6 to this. However, the reason for preferring the asynchronous style over the synchronous style is to release the threads to do other jobs, instead of waiting or idling for the responses. This means the original, initiator threads may no longer exist for taking the response and continuing the processing from there. Instead, the original or initiator piece of code that started the request should be kept paused, its original thread be released for reuse by some other context; this piece of code should be notified or called back when a response arrives, and the right response should be delivered to that piece of the program in the microservice.

Figure 6-9 represents a scenario where similar or different messages from same or different microservice or component are targeted to same or different microservice on the other end. Messages can be delivered concurrently, too. Make sure that, when the response arrives back, it is received by the right recipient. There are two mechanisms used by messaging architectures to deal with this situation:

- **Correlation identifier**: Using this method, we tie each reply message with a correlation identifier, a unique identifier that indicates which request message this reply is for. We can tag the message with this correlation identifier in the message header so that this can be controlled declaratively or with minimum intervention from the programmer side.

- **Return address**: The next method is to include a return address to the message that indicates where to send the reply message. By doing so, the replier microservice does not need to know where to send the reply; it can just ask the request itself. If different messages to the same replier microservice require replies to different places, the replier knows where to send the reply for each request. This encapsulates the knowledge of what channels to use for requests and replies within the Producer microservice so those decisions do not need to be hard coded within the replier. A return address is also put in the header of a message because it's not part of the payload being transmitted.

Figure 6-9 represents a reference set up of this.

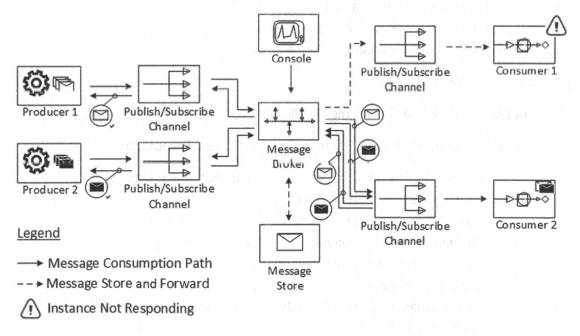

Figure 6-9. *Asynchronous, concurrent interprocess interaction*

Send and Receive Messages to a Single Node RabbitMQ Broker

You will now look at some code for sending messages to a RabbitMQ message broker and receiving the same using a listener to the broker. Refer to Appendix B to follow step-by-step instructions to install and bring up a RabbitMQ broker. The complete and running code samples for this exercise are kept in the folder named ch06-01, which is bundled along with the book.

RabbitMQ Message Sender

You need to make a connection to a RabbitMQ Message broker and send a message. For this, you can use the client package from RabbitMQ libraries. Listing 6-1 shows the steps involved in doing so.

Listing 6-1. RabbitMQ Message Sender (ch06\ch06-01\src\main\java\com\acme\ch06\ex01\Send.java)

```java
import com.rabbitmq.client.Channel;
import com.rabbitmq.client.Connection;
import com.rabbitmq.client.ConnectionFactory;

public class Send {

    private final static String QUEUE_NAME = "hello";

    public static void main(String[] argv) throws Exception{

        ConnectionFactory factory = new ConnectionFactory();
        factory.setHost("localhost");
        Connection connection = factory.newConnection();
        Channel channel = connection.createChannel();
        channel.queueDeclare(QUEUE_NAME, false, false, false, null);
        String message = "Hello World!";
        channel.basicPublish("", QUEUE_NAME, null, message.
        getBytes("UTF-8"));
        LOGGER.debug(" [!] Sent '" + message + "'");
```

```
        channel.close();
        connection.close();
    }
}
```

You create a connection to RabbitMQ message broker. RabbitMQ is an AMQP compliant broker and you use `com.rabbitmq.client.ConnectionFactory` to open a connection to the AMQP broker. `com.rabbitmq.client.ConnectionFactory` is a RabbitMQ library, but later you will see how to connect to a RabbitMQ broker using a non-RabbitMQ, AMQP alone client library. For RabbitMQ to accept client connections, it needs to bind to one or more interfaces and listen on protocol-specific ports. By default, RabbitMQ will listen on port 5672 on all available interfaces, but you can configure it using the `rabbit.tcp_listeners` config option if required. Alternatively, there are methods like `setHost(String host)` and `setPort(int port)` to configure the listening host, port, and so on. Also, you can assume that RabbitMQ is configured to allow connections using the default username of "guest" and the default password of "guest."

Next, you need to create a channel. By using a message channel, one application can write information to the channel and the other application can read that information from the channel. Now you must declare a queue to send the messages to, and once done, you can publish a message to the queue. Note that declaring a queue will create a new queue only if it doesn't exist already, hence the operation is idempotent. The `basicPublish` method in the channel expects message content in a byte array, so you can encode whatever you like here.

RabbitMQ Message Receiver

Listing 6-2 shows the code required to listen to a RabbitMQ Message broker to consume messages.

Listing 6-2. RabbitMQ Message Receiver (ch06\ch06-01\src\main\java\com\acme\ch06\ex01\Receive.java)

```
import com.rabbitmq.client.Channel;
import com.rabbitmq.client.Connection;
import com.rabbitmq.client.ConnectionFactory;
import com.rabbitmq.client.Consumer;
```

```java
import com.rabbitmq.client.DefaultConsumer;
import com.rabbitmq.client.Envelope;
import com.rabbitmq.client.AMQP;

public class Receive{

    private final static String QUEUE_NAME = "hello";

    public static void main(String[] argv) throws Exception{

        ConnectionFactory factory = new ConnectionFactory();
        factory.setHost("localhost");
        Connection connection = factory.newConnection();
        Channel channel = connection.createChannel();
        channel.queueDeclare(QUEUE_NAME, false, false, false, null);
        LOGGER.debug(" [!] Waiting for messages. To exit press CTRL+C");

        Consumer consumer = new DefaultConsumer(channel){

            @Override
            public void handleDelivery(String consumerTag,
                                       Envelope envelope, AMQP.
                                       BasicProperties
                                       properties, byte[] body)
                                       throws IOException {

                String message = new String(body, "UTF-8");
                LOGGER.debug(" [x] Received '" + message + "'");
            }
        };
        channel.basicConsume(QUEUE_NAME, true, consumer);
    }
}
```

Since a consumer is pushed messages from RabbitMQ when there are more messages in the broker for the channel, you need to keep it running to listen for messages and consume them as messages arrive at the broker. You use com.rabbitmq. client.Consumer as an application callback object to receive notifications and messages from a queue by subscription. You declare the queue here as well because if you start the consumer before the publisher, you want to make sure the queue exists on the broker end before you try to consume messages from it. Now you need to tell the broker to deliver the messages from the queue. Since the broker is expected to push the messages asynchronously, you provide a callback object that will buffer the messages until you're ready to use them. `com.rabbitmq.client.DefaultConsumer` comes in handy; it's a convenience class that provides a default implementation of `Consumer`.

Build and Run the RabbitMQ Sample

You will now build and run the code samples. Both Ant and Maven scripts are provided along with the code.

Maven Build

`ch06-01\pom.xml` contains the Maven scripts required to run the samples. Make sure the RabbitMQ broker is up and running.

You first build and bring up the consumer so that the consumer is ready to pick up messages (see Figure 6-10):

```
cd ch06-01
D:\binil\gold\pack03\ch06\ch06-01>listen
D:\binil\gold\pack03\ch06\ch06-01>mvn test -Plisten
```

```
cmd - Shortcut - listen                                           —    □   ×

D:\binil\gold\pack03\ch06\ch06-01>listen

D:\binil\gold\pack03\ch06\ch06-01>mvn test -Plisten
[INFO] Scanning for projects...
[INFO]
[INFO] ------------------------------------------------------------------
[INFO] Building Spring RabbitMQ AMQP 1.0-SNAPSHOT
[INFO] ------------------------------------------------------------------
[INFO] <<< exec-maven-plugin:1.1.1:java (default) < validate @ amqp-hello <<<
[INFO]
[INFO] --- exec-maven-plugin:1.1.1:java (default) @ amqp-hello ---
2018-12-11 21:34:37 INFO  com.acme.ch06.ex01.Receive.main:23 - Start
2018-12-11 21:34:37 DEBUG com.acme.ch06.ex01.Receive.main:29 -   [*] Waiting for
messages. To exit press CTRL+C
2018-12-11 21:34:37 INFO  com.acme.ch06.ex01.Receive.main:41 - End
2018-12-11 21:34:47 DEBUG com.acme.ch06.ex01.Receive$1.handleDelivery:37 -   [x]
Received 'Hello World!'
```

Figure 6-10. Maven building and running a RabbitMQ consumer

Next, you build and bring up the message producer. The producer publishes message to the broker so that the consumer can pick up messages (see Figure 6-11):

```
cd ch06-01
D:\binil\gold\pack03\ch06\ch06-01>send
D:\binil\gold\pack03\ch06\ch06-01>mvn test –Psend
```

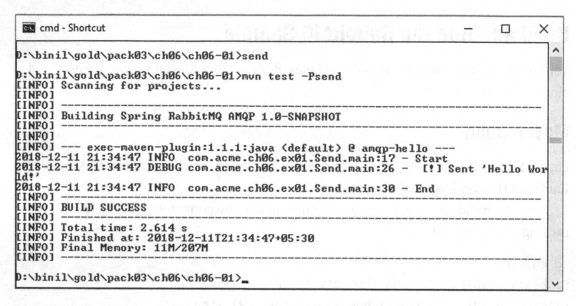

Figure 6-11. Maven building and running a RabbitMQ producer

Ant Build

ch06-01\build.xml contains the Ant scripts required to run the samples. Again, make sure the RabbitMQ broker is up and running.

You need to first build the sample. Execute the following commands:

```
cd ch06-01
D:\binil\gold\pack03\ch06\ch06-01>ant
```

Now bring up the consumer and have it ready to pick up messages. Execute the following command and see Figure 6-12:

```
D:\binil\gold\pack03\ch06\ch06-01>ant listen
```

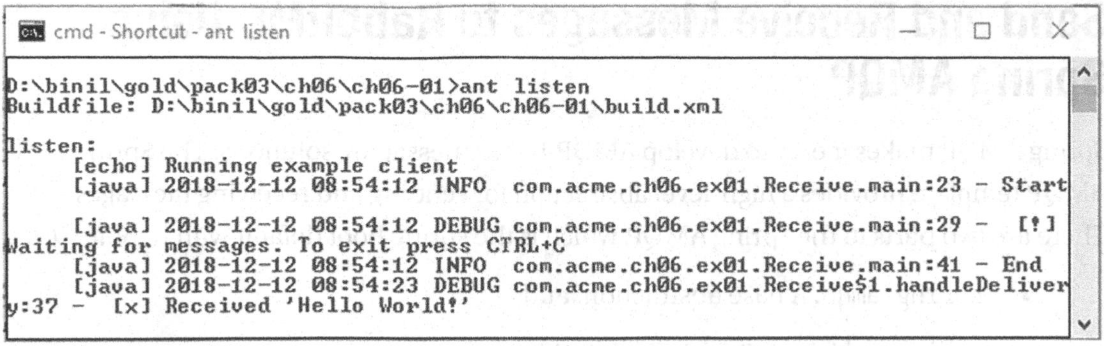
cmd - Shortcut - ant listen
D:\binil\gold\pack03\ch06\ch06-01>ant listen
Buildfile: D:\binil\gold\pack03\ch06\ch06-01\build.xml
listen:
[echo] Running example client
[java] 2018-12-12 08:54:12 INFO com.acme.ch06.ex01.Receive.main:23 - Start
[java] 2018-12-12 08:54:12 DEBUG com.acme.ch06.ex01.Receive.main:29 - [*]
Waiting for messages. To exit press CTRL+C
[java] 2018-12-12 08:54:12 INFO com.acme.ch06.ex01.Receive.main:41 - End
[java] 2018-12-12 08:54:23 DEBUG com.acme.ch06.ex01.Receive$1.handleDeliver
y:37 - [x] Received 'Hello World!'

Figure 6-12. *Ant building and running a RabbitMQ consumer*

Next, bring up the message producer. The producer publishes message to the broker so that the consumer can pick up messages. Execute the following commands in a different window and see Figure 6-13:

```
cd ch06-01
D:\binil\gold\pack03\ch06\ch06-01>ant send
```

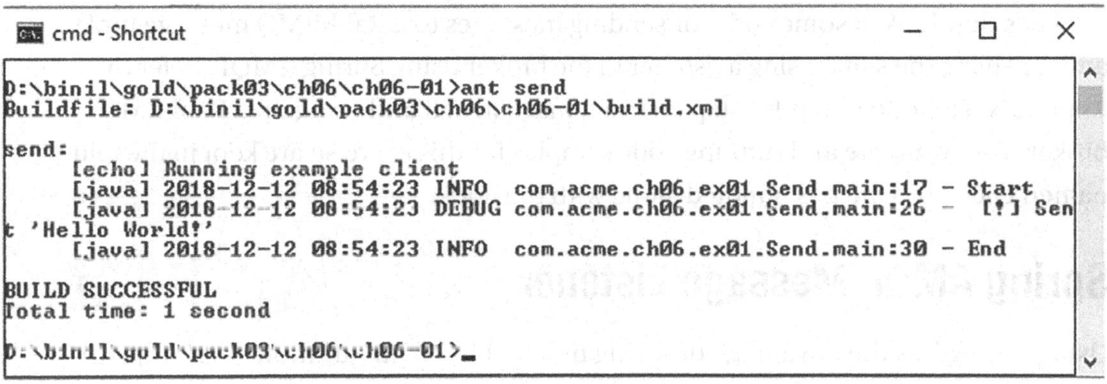
cmd - Shortcut
D:\binil\gold\pack03\ch06\ch06-01>ant send
Buildfile: D:\binil\gold\pack03\ch06\ch06-01\build.xml
send:
[echo] Running example client
[java] 2018-12-12 08:54:23 INFO com.acme.ch06.ex01.Send.main:17 - Start
[java] 2018-12-12 08:54:23 DEBUG com.acme.ch06.ex01.Send.main:26 - [*] Sen
t 'Hello World!'
[java] 2018-12-12 08:54:23 INFO com.acme.ch06.ex01.Send.main:30 - End
BUILD SUCCESSFUL
Total time: 1 second
D:\binil\gold\pack03\ch06\ch06-01>

Figure 6-13. *Ant building and running a RabbitMQ producer*

Send and Receive Messages to RabbitMQ Using Spring AMQP

Spring AMQP makes it easy to develop AMQP-based messaging solutions. The Spring AMQP template provides a high-level abstraction for sending and receiving messages. There are two parts to the Spring AMQP, which is the spring boot default with Rabbit MQ:

- `spring-amqp`: A base abstraction, and
- `spring-rabbit`: A RabbitMQ-specific implementation

The major features abstracted by Spring AMQP are

- A `Listener` container: For asynchronous processing of inbound messages
- A `RabbitTemplate`: A RabbitMQ-specific template for sending and receiving messages
- A Rabbit admin: Helpful in fast and automatic declaration of queues, exchanges, and bindings

Let's now look at some code for sending messages to a RabbitMQ message broker and receiving the same using a listener to the broker using Spring AMQP. Refer to Appendix B to follow step-by-step instructions to install and bring up a RabbitMQ broker. The complete and running code samples for this exercise are kept in the folder named `ch06-02`, which is bundled along with the book.

Spring AMQP Message Listener

Using Spring has the advantage of wiring much of the configurations in XML, and Listing 6-3 shows how to wire a message listener to the RabbitMQ broker.

Listing 6-3. Spring AMQP Listener Configuration (ch06\ch06-02\src\main\ resources\rabbit-listener-context.xml)

```
<?xml version="1.0" encoding="UTF-8" ?>
<beans >

    <rabbit:connection-factory id="connectionFactory" host="localhost"
        port="5672" username="guest" password="guest" />
```

```
<rabbit:admin connection-factory="connectionFactory" />
<rabbit:queue id="anonymousQueue" />

<rabbit:topic-exchange id="exchange" name="SAMPLE_EXCHANGE">
    <rabbit:bindings>
        <rabbit:binding queue="anonymousQueue"
            pattern=" my.routingkey.*"></rabbit:binding>
    </rabbit:bindings>
</rabbit:topic-exchange>

<bean id="listener" class="com.acme.ch06.ex02.Listener" />

<rabbit:listener-container id="myListenerContainer"
        connection-factory="connectionFactory">
    <rabbit:listener ref="listener" queues="anonymousQueue" />
</rabbit:listener-container>

</beans>
```

In Listing 6-3, you create an exchange and then bind the queue named anonymousQueue with my.routingkey.* to the SAMPLE_EXCHANGE. A binding is a bondage or "link" that you set up to bind a queue to an exchange. The routing key is a message attribute. The exchange, depending on the exchange type, might look at this key when deciding how to route the message to queues. The Listener class instantiated with bean id "listener" is shown in Listing 6-4.

Listing 6-4. Spring AMQP Listener Bean (ch06\ch06-02\src\main\java\com\acme\ch06\ex02\Listener.java)

```java
import org.springframework.amqp.core.Message;
import org.springframework.amqp.core.MessageListener;

public class Listener implements MessageListener {

    public void onMessage(Message message) {

        String messageBody= new String(message.getBody());
        LOGGER.debug("Listener received message-----> " + messageBody);
    }
}
```

The last step is to load the listener in the Spring context, which you do in Listing 6-5.

Listing 6-5. Spring AMQP Listener Container (ch06\ch06-02\src\main\java\ com\acme\ch06\ex02\ListenerContainer.java)

```java
import org.springframework.context.ApplicationContext;
import org.springframework.context.support.ClassPathXmlApplicationContext;

public class ListenerContainer {

    private static final String LISTENER_CONTEXT =
            "rabbit-listener-context.xml";

    public static void main(String[] args) {

        ApplicationContext context =
                        new ClassPathXmlApplicationContext(LISTENER_
                        CONTEXT);
        LOGGER.debug("Context successfully created from: "
                        + LISTENER_CONTEXT);
    }
}
```

The easiest way to bring all the required dependencies for your Maven build is to declare the snippet in Listing 6-6 into your build file, pom.xml.

Listing 6-6. Spring AMQP RabbitMQ Dependencies (ch06\ch06-02\pom.xml)

```xml
<dependency>
    <groupId>org.springframework.amqp</groupId>
    <artifactId>spring-rabbit</artifactId>
    <version>1.6.9.RELEASE</version>
</dependency>
```

Spring AMQP Message Producer

Here again you first create a rabbit connection factory with specified parameters. RabbitTemplate provides a convenient abstraction for sending and receiving messages, and Listing 6-7 shows the configuration.

Listing 6-7. Spring AMQP Sender Configuration (ch06\ch06-02\src\main\ resources\rabbit-sender-context.xml)

```
<beans ...>
    <rabbit:connection-factory id="connectionFactory" host="localhost"
        port="5672" username="guest" password="guest" />
    <rabbit:admin connection-factory="connectionFactory" />
    <rabbit:template id="sampleTemplate" connection-factory=
        "connectionFactory" exchange="SAMPLE_EXCHANGE"/>
</beans>
```

In Listing 6-8, you create a template of the bean defined in the previous Spring XML file and send few messages.

Listing 6-8. Spring AMQP Message Sender (ch06\ch06-02\src\main\java\com\ acme\ch06\ex02\Sender.java)

```
import org.springframework.amqp.core.AmqpTemplate;

public class Sender {

    private static final Logger LOGGER = LoggerFactory.getLogger
    (Sender.class);
    private static final String SENDER_CONTEXT = "rabbit-sender-
    context.xml";
    private static final String BEAN_NAME = "sampleTemplate";

    public static void main(String[] args) throws Exception {
```

```
            ApplicationContext context = new
                    ClassPathXmlApplicationContext(SENDER_CONTEXT);

        AmqpTemplate aTemplate =
                        (AmqpTemplate) context.getBean(BEAN_NAME);
        String message = null;
        for (int i = 0; i < 5; i++){
            message = "Message # " + (i + 1);
            aTemplate.convertAndSend("my.routingkey.3",
                                    message +" on "+ new Date());
            LOGGER.debug("Sender send message----->" + message);
        }

    }
}
```

Build and Run the Spring AMQP RabbitMQ Sample

You will now build and run the code samples. Both Ant and Maven scripts are provided along with the code.

ch06-02\pom.xml contains the Maven scripts required to run the samples. Make sure the RabbitMQ broker is up and running. You first build and bring up the consumer so that the consumer is ready to pick up messages. Execute the following commands and see Figure 6-14:

```
cd ch06-02
D:\binil\gold\pack03\ch06\ch06-02>listen
D:\binil\gold\pack03\ch06\ch06-02>mvn test -Plisten
```

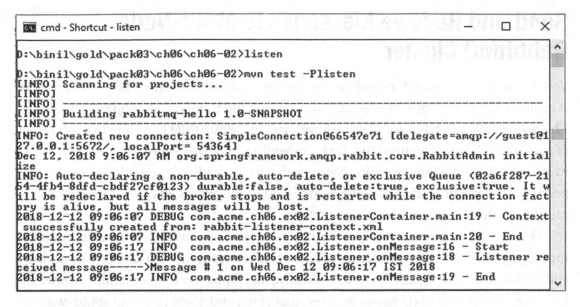

Figure 6-14. *Maven building and running a Spring AMQP consumer*

Next, bring up the message producer. The producer publishes a message to the broker so that the consumer can pick up the message. Execute the following commands in a different window and see Figure 6-15:

```
cd ch06-02
D:\binil\gold\pack03\ch06\ch06-02>send
D:\binil\gold\pack03\ch06\ch06-02>mvn test -Psend
```

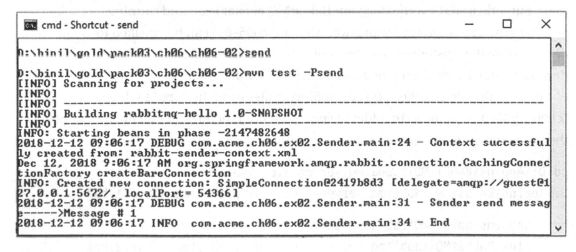

Figure 6-15. *Maven building and running a Spring AMQP producer*

Send and Receive Messages to Multi-Node RabbitMQ Cluster

You will now look at code for sending messages to a RabbitMQ cluster. Refer to Appendix B again to follow step-by-step instructions to install and bring up a RabbitMQ cluster. This section assumes that you already have a running RabbitMQ cluster with a minimum of two nodes. You further need to refer to Appendix C to follow step-by-step instructions to set up a TCP load balancer using Nginx so that traffic (rather, connections) from both consumer and producer can be multiplexed to at least one of the active nodes of a multinode cluster, if the other nodes are down.

This section is so important because in a microservices environment backed with a messaging infrastructure, the high availability of the messaging infrastructure by itself will decide the overall reliability of the infrastructure. You have seen that microservices instances can be coming (instantiated, restarted, etc.) and going (graceful shutdown, crashed, restarted, forcefully killed, etc.) in any order or at any pace in an enterprise production setup. Each of these microservice instances communicate with others through the messaging infrastructure or the event-based infrastructure by sending messages. So, when one microservice instance sends a message to the messaging infrastructure successfully, it assumes that the message will reach the receiver "eventually," as expected. The high availability of the messaging infrastructure must live up to this promise.

Assuming you have a multinode RabbitMQ cluster in high availability mode and you also have a TCP load balancer (Nginx configured as a TCP reverse proxy), you are all set to try out little trials to verify that your RabbitMQ cluster is up and running.

The sample you saw in the previous section (ch06-02) can be tweaked to demonstrate the cluster setup and is kept in folder ch06-03. You can follow a quick demonstration by executing the sample in the following order.

If you didn't do it earlier, copy the following files from the samples directory (ch06\ch06-03\) to the sbin folder of your RabbitMQ server, and execute the scripts in the following order in separate windows:

```
cd D:\Applns\RabbitMQ\rabbitmq_server-3.6.3\sbin
D:\Applns\RabbitMQ\rabbitmq_server-3.6.3\sbin>rabbitmq-server1.bat

cd D:\Applns\RabbitMQ\rabbitmq_server-3.6.3\sbin
D:\Applns\RabbitMQ\rabbitmq_server-3.6.3\sbin>rabbitmq-server2.bat
```

```
cd D:\Applns\RabbitMQ\rabbitmq_server-3.6.3\sbin
D:\Applns\RabbitMQ\rabbitmq_server-3.6.3\sbin>rabbitmq-cluster2.bat
```

The above will bring up a two-node RabbitMQ cluster. Note that you should give enough time for the above commands to finish so that the cluster formation is complete.

Now you can set up the TCP load balancer by executing the Nginx script. Refer to Appendix C to follow step-by-step instructions to configure Nginx as a TCP reverse proxy. After making the right entries in the Nginx configuration as shown in the sample file:

```
ch06\ch06-03\nginx.conf
```

Bring up the Nginx server like so:

```
cd D:\Applns\nginx\nginx-1.13.5
D:\Applns\nginx\nginx-1.13.5>nginx
```

When a message producer wants to send messages to a message consumer, it assumes that you're interested only in currently flowing messages, not in the old ones. Then whenever you connect to Rabbit, you need a fresh, empty queue; once you disconnect the consumer, the queue should be automatically deleted. To do this in RabbitMQ, you can create a queue with a random name or, even better, let the server choose a random queue name for you.

Giving a queue a name is important when you want to share the queue between message senders and message consumers. So both in

```
ch06\ch06-03\src\main\resources\rabbit-listener-context.xml
ch06\ch06-03\src\main\resources\rabbit-sender-context.xml
```

you define named queues as

```
<rabbit:queue id="otherAnon" name="remoting.queue"/>
```

There are numerous combinations by which you can configure RabbitMQ and also numerous sequences by which you can execute the sample programs to validate your RabbitMQ cluster. One combination is explained below.

Assuming your RabbitMQ instances are listening at ports 5672 and 5673, and your Nginx server is listening on TCP at port 5671, you can use the following configuration for both the message producer and the message consumer to connect to the cluster:

```
<rabbit:connection-factory id="connectionFactory" host="localhost"
port="5671" username="guest" password="guest" />
```

The rest of the configuration is similar to that explained in the example in the previous section. Now execute the following:

```
cd ch06-03
D:\binil\gold\pack03\ch06\ch06-03>mvn test -Psend
```

This will send a message to the RabbitMQ cluster. This will be confirmed on the message sender window with the following DEBUG message:

```
2017-06-12 19:50:59 DEBUG com.acme.ch06.ex03.Sender.main:32 - Sender send
message----->Message from Sender on Mon Jun 12 19:50:59 IST 2017
```

You may now want to inspect the RabbitMQ log files. Assuming rabbit1 and rabbit2 are the node names of the RabbitMQ server instances of your cluster, the logs are written to below files in my machine:

```
C:\Users\binil\AppData\Roaming\RabbitMQ\log\rabbit1.log
C:\Users\binil\AppData\Roaming\RabbitMQ\log\rabbit2.log
```

You should be able to see the following lines in the logs of any of the RabbitMQ instances of the cluster:

```
=INFO REPORT==== 12-Jun-2017::19:50:59 ===
accepting AMQP connection <0.1681.0> (127.0.0.1:54315 -> 127.0.0.1:5673)
```

```
=INFO REPORT==== 12-Jun-2017::19:50:59 ===
Mirrored queue 'remoting.queue' in vhost '/': Adding mirror on node
rabbit1@tiger: <33127.1408.0>
```

The above logs validate two aspects:

- The instance corresponding to this log file has accepted an AMQP connection from the message sender.

- Upon receiving the message from the message sender, the instance
  corresponding to this log file has mirrored the queue, which caused
  other instance of the RabbitMQ server in the cluster to receive the
  same message.

You may now bring up the message consumer:

```
cd ch06-03
D:\binil\gold\pack03\ch06\ch06-03>mvn test -Plisten
```

If everything goes fine, the listener will consume the previously sent message and this
can be confirmed on the message listener window with the following DEBUG message:

```
2017-06-12 19:56:58 DEBUG com.acme.ch06.ex03.Listener.onMessage:19 -
Listener received message-----> Message from Sender on Mon Jun 12 19:50:59
IST 2017
```

To attempt the next phase of testing your cluster, bring down the message consumer
by typing Ctrl+C in the message consumer window.

Next, send a new message to the cluster using the message producer. Inspect the
log files of both RabbbitMQ instances and find out which instance has consumed the
message. The instance that consumed the message will have an INFO REPORT similar to

```
accepting AMQP connection <0.3628.0> (127.0.0.1:54746 -> 127.0.0.1:5672)
```

Next, bring down the same instance that consumed the message by typing Ctrl+C
on the message consumer window. With the other instance of the cluster alone running,
bring up the message consumer. If everything goes fine, the listener will consume the
previously sent message. This validates that the cluster is working as intended and
messages received by one instance are getting mirrored to the other instance.

If a RabbitMQ cluster instance quits or crashes, it will forget the queues and
messages in that instance unless you tell it not to. Two things are required to make sure
that messages aren't lost:

- You need to mark both the queue and the messages as durable.

- You need to mark your messages as persistent by setting
  `MessageProperties`.

You may try out these and other options. I won't explain them here, since they are
not within the scope of this book.

Tying the Knots Between the Consumer and Producer

The very advantage of using a messaging infrastructure–making the message producer and message consumer flows disjoint–by itself can sometimes be a challenge for the application developer.

In a typical synchronous request response call by a client, the server can accept connections from the client in a single thread, process the request in that thread, and provide a response to the client in the same thread. However, connections and threads are scarce resources and you want to utilize them effectively. If the server-side processing is going to take a lot of time, or if the server thread is getting blocked in idling mode like waiting for I/O operations, blocking the thread is not desired. Instead, you want to design in such a way that the thread that accepted the connections is released to accept more connections and the processing and subsequent response to the client is handled in the background by different threads, that too just in time whenever the processing can proceed or just in time whenever the response is ready to be delivered back to the client. This is trivial to implement if you have one server and one client. The moment you have numerous clients all connecting to a server, also concurrently, if you release the thread that accepted the socket connection just after the connection is made but before the server provides a response back to the client, then later when the response is ready, it will pose a challenge to the server to correlate to which client all the responses are to be sent back.

Correlation ID

In the scenario presented above, you can create a callback queue for every request. But that's pretty inefficient. Fortunately there is a better way: by creating a single callback queue per client. But it raises a new issue; having received a response in that queue, it's not clear to which specific request from the same client the response belongs. That's where the `correlationId` property is used. You can set it to a unique value for every request. Later, when you receive a message in the callback queue, you'll look at this property, and based on it you'll be able to match a response with a request.

When you design a server handling request and response from multiple clients, make sure that you set the value of JMS Correlation ID on the response to the value of JMS Correlation ID on the request before sending the JMS response to the queue.

You can obtain the JMS Correlation ID when you receive a message using

```
String getJMSCorrelationID()
```

This method returns correlation ID values that provide specific message IDs or application-specific string values.

To set the JMS Correlation ID() when you send a message, type

```
void setJMSCorrelationID(String correlationID)
```

Let's look at a sample to understand this concept.

Code a Custom Network Server to Handle Concurrent Heavy Traffic

In this section, you will design and implement a network server listening using a TCP/IP server socket. Multiple clients or multiple threads from same client can open connections to this server and submit jobs; these clients or threads expect a response to the job back. You want the design to handle heavy traffic. Let's visit the architecture and control flow in the server. Figure 6-16 shows the architecture of the entire setup.

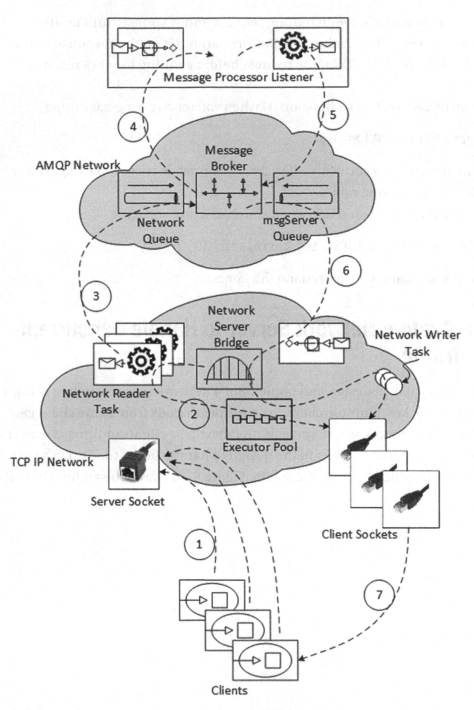

Figure 6-16. *Architecture to handle heavy traffic with optimized resources*

Two separate domains are shown here with names TCP IP Network and AMQP Network. To make it simple, assume that the client-to-server connections are handled within the TCP IP Network domain in a "pseudo synchronous"[1] manner whereas for the actual job execution, the job is submitted asynchronously to the AMQP network and the response is also received from the AMQP network asynchronously. Such an architecture makes sure that the TCP IP Network domain is not stressed by actually executing the job, hence connection management can be done efficiently. At the same time, submission of the job to the AMQP network domain is through message queues, so if the actual job processing within the AMQP network domain takes some time, additional jobs submitted to the queues are not lost but buffered so that the Message Processor Listener in the AMQP network domain can handle them at a later time.

You should have noted that while the handshake between the client and the network server is synchronous, the one between the network server in the TCP IP Network and the Message Processor Listener in the AMQP network domain happens to be asynchronous. Thus, the request and response flows between the network server and the message processor are disjointed and there is a need to correlate which response corresponds to which request so that the network server can channel it back to the right instance of client.

Note that the flows marked in dotted lines are passing through multiple components in some cases, and it is shown like that intentionally to depict that all of those components are involved in that particular flow. The complete and running code samples for this exercise are kept in the folder named ch06-04 bundled along with the book. Let's understand each component and the control flow in detail:

- **Client**: Multiple clients or multiple threads from a single client can connect to the server and submit a job. In this sample, you will just send a message in place of a heavy job.

- **Server Socket**: There is one instance of the server socket listening in a port known to clients so that clients can initiate connections.

---

[1]Pseudo synchronous because from a client perspective the connection is synchronous; however, the network server may use separate threads to handle request and response processing.

- **Client Sockets**: For each connection opened by a thread on the client side there is an instance of a client socket on the TCP IP Network side and messages are passed between server and client bidirectionally through the streams created out of this.

- **Network Server**: The primary job of the "main" method of this component is to accept connections, do any processing, and return responses back to clients. The design constraint is that the network server has to do all of this in an efficient manner. So, whenever a client connects to the network server, the server first accepts the connection and then creates a unique ID, which is used to correlate request and response flows. The corresponding client socket is indexed against this correlation ID and the server then gets a thread from the executor pool and asks the thread to handle the job for the client by assigning the job to a network reader task and providing the correlation ID. Once this much is done, the server is free and available to handle more clients.

- **Executor Pool**: The executor pool is a ThreadPoolExecutor that executes each submitted task using one of possibly several pooled threads.

- **Network Reader Task**: Whenever a client connects to the network server, a separate network reader task gets executed within a pooled thread. It will read message (or job) sent by client and submits it to the networkQueue for execution to the message processor.

- **Message Processor Listener**: The message processor listener is an AMQP listener. This is the place where the actual job processing happens. Once the job is complete, the message processor writes the result back to another queue, the msgServerQueue. While doing so, the message processor listener does its part of correlating the request and response by using the same correlation ID.

- **Network Writer Task**: While the main method of the network server handles connection management, the network server is also a message listener to receive the job results back from the msgServerQueue. Thus, for each result in msgServerQueue, there is a different instance of the message listener, and its job is to instantiate a new instance of the network writer task, hand over the result, and execute it again within a pooled thread.[2] The network writer task retrieves the correlation ID from the message and then retrieves the corresponding client socket to which this message is intended to be sent, and sends the message back to client.

This completes the architecture and the flow. We'll now look at the main code snippets. The complete end-to-end sequence of steps executed within a single request-response cycle is labelled from 1 to 7 in Figure 6-16.

The complete and running code samples for this exercise are kept in the folder named ch06-04, which is bundled along with the book.

The client uses a client task, as shown in Listing 6-9:

Listing 6-9. Client-Side Task (ch06\ch06-04\src\main\java\com\acme\ch06\ ex04\ClientSideTask.java)

```
public void execute(){

    Socket clientSocket = new Socket("localhost", 1100);

    dataOutputStream.writeUTF(MSG_SEED + id);
    dataOutputStream.flush();

    String fromServer = dataInputStream.readUTF();
    LOGGER.debug("Message Send to Server: " + MSG_SEED + id + ";
        Message Received back from Server: " + fromServer);
)
```

Here, the client opens a connection to the server and first writes a message to the stream of the socket. The client gets blocked and waits until it receives a message back. When it receives a message back, it logs both the message sent and received from the server so that you can validate that the client did in fact receive the response intended for itself.

---

[2]Note that threads from the single ThreadPoolExecutor are being pooled to execute both network reader tasks and network writer tasks, and this is an efficient way of consuming costly resources like threads, connections, and so on.

The network server in Listing 6-10 accepts connections and creates a unique ID that is used to correlate request and response flows. The client socket is indexed against this correlation ID and the server gets a thread from the executor pool and asks the thread to handle the job for the client by assigning the job to a network reader task and providing the correlation ID. The network server is also a message listener to receive the job results back from the msgServerQueue.

Listing 6-10. Network Server (ch06\ch06-04\src\main\java\com\acme\ch06\ex04\NetworkServer.java)

```java
public class NetworkServer implements MessageListener{

    private void listen(){

        serverSocket = new ServerSocket(1100);

        while(true){
            clientSocket = serverSocket.accept();

            correlationIdNew = getNextCorrelationId();
            addItem(correlationIdNew, clientSocket);
            networkReaderTask = new NetworkReaderTask(amqpTemplate,
                    correlationIdNew);
            executorPool.execute(new Worker(networkReaderTask));

        }
    }

    public void onMessage(Message message) {

        NetworkWriterTask networkWriterTask =
                        new NetworkWriterTask(message);
        executorPool.execute(new Worker(networkWriterTask));
    }

}
```

The network reader task in Listing 6-11 reads the message (or job) sent by the client and submits it to the networkQueue for execution to the message processor

Listing 6-11. Network Reader Task (ch06\ch06-04\src\main\java\com\acme\ ch06\ex04\NetworkReaderTask.java)

```java
private void receiveFromNetwrokAndSendMessage(){

    Socket clientSocket = NetworkServer.getItem(correlationId);
    inputStream = clientSocket.getInputStream();
    dataInputStream = new DataInputStream(inputStream);
    String fromClient = dataInputStream.readUTF();

    MessageProperties messageProperties = new MessageProperties();
    messageProperties.setCorrelationId(
        Long.toString(correlationId).getBytes());
    Message message = new Message(fromClient.getBytes(),
    messageProperties);
    amqpTemplate.send("my.routingkey.1", message);
}
```

Listing 6-12 shows the message processor where the job processing happens. Once the job is complete, the message processor writes the result back to another queue. While doing so, the message processor does its part of correlating the request and response by using the same correlation ID from the received message.

Listing 6-12. Message Processor (ch06\ch06-04\src\main\java\com\acme\ ch06\ex04\MessageProcessorListener.java)

```java
public void onMessage(Message message) {

    /* ASSUME THAT WE RECEIVED THE HEAVY JOB FOR EXECUTION HERE */
    String messageBody = new String(message.getBody());
    String correlationId = new        String(
        message.getMessageProperties().getCorrelationId());

    /* ASSUME THAT THE HEAVY JOB EXECUTION TAKES PLACE HERE */

    /* EXECUTE THE HEAVY JOB AND NOW WE CAN SEND THE
        PROCESSED RESPONSE BACK */
```

```
    MessageProperties messageProperties = new MessageProperties();
    messageProperties.setCorrelationId(correlationId.getBytes());
    Message messageToSend = new Message(messageBody.getBytes(),
        messageProperties);
    amqpTemplate.send("my.routingkey.1", messageToSend);
}
```

The network writer task code in Listing 6-13 retrieves the correlation ID from the message, retrieves the corresponding client socket to which this message is intended to be sent, and sends the message back to client

Listing 6-13. Network Writer Task (ch06\ch06-04\src\main\java\com\acme\ch06\ex04\NetworkWriterTask.java)

```
private void receiveMessageAndRespondToNetwork(){

    String messageBody = new String(message.getBody());
    String correlationId = new String(
        message.getMessageProperties().getCorrelationId());

    Socket clientSocket =
        NetworkServer.getItem(Long.parseLong(correlationId));
    NetworkServer.removeItem(Long.parseLong(correlationId));

    outputStream = clientSocket.getOutputStream();
    dataOutputStream = new DataOutputStream(outputStream);

    dataOutputStream.writeUTF(messageBody);
    dataOutputStream.flush();

}
```

Assuming your RabbitMQ cluster and Nginx load balancer are still up and running, you can execute the code by following these steps:

In one window, bring up the AMQP Broker:

```
cd ch06-04
D:\binil\gold\pack03\ch06\ch06-04>mvn test -Pmsg
```

In another window, bring up the network server:

```
cd ch06-04
D:\binil\gold\pack03\ch06\ch06-04>mvn test -Pnet
```

Now execute the client in third window (see Figure 6-17):

```
cd ch06-04
D:\binil\gold\pack03\ch06\ch06-04>mvn test -Psend
```

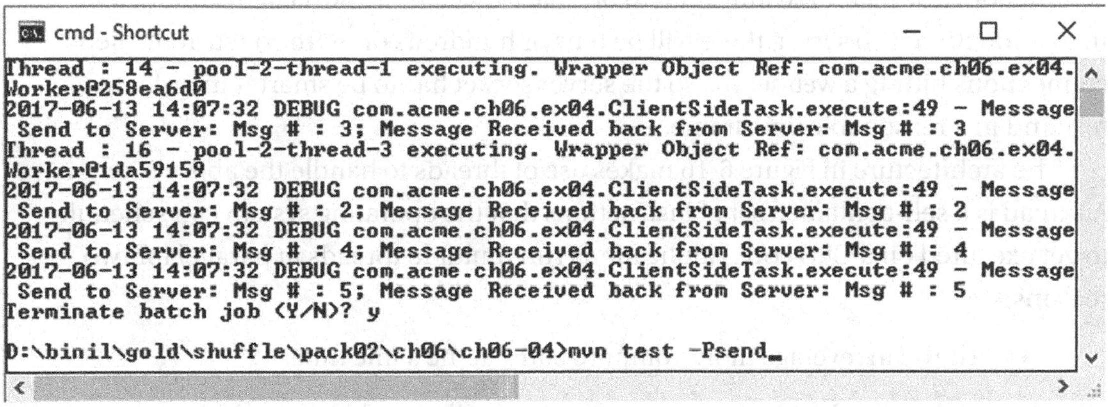

```
cmd - Shortcut                                              —    □    ✕
Thread : 14 - pool-2-thread-1 executing. Wrapper Object Ref: com.acme.ch06.ex04.
Worker@258ea6d0
2017-06-13 14:07:32 DEBUG com.acme.ch06.ex04.ClientSideTask.execute:49 - Message
 Send to Server: Msg # : 3; Message Received back from Server: Msg # : 3
Thread : 16 - pool-2-thread-3 executing. Wrapper Object Ref: com.acme.ch06.ex04.
Worker@1da59159
2017-06-13 14:07:32 DEBUG com.acme.ch06.ex04.ClientSideTask.execute:49 - Message
 Send to Server: Msg # : 2; Message Received back from Server: Msg # : 2
2017-06-13 14:07:32 DEBUG com.acme.ch06.ex04.ClientSideTask.execute:49 - Message
 Send to Server: Msg # : 4; Message Received back from Server: Msg # : 4
2017-06-13 14:07:32 DEBUG com.acme.ch06.ex04.ClientSideTask.execute:49 - Message
 Send to Server: Msg # : 5; Message Received back from Server: Msg # : 5
Terminate batch job (Y/N)? y

D:\binil\gold\shuffle\pack02\ch06\ch06-04>mvn test -Psend_
```

Figure 6-17.   *Client console*

Note the debug logged into the console, which validates that the client in fact received the response intended for it:

```
2017-06-13 14:07:32 DEBUG com.acme.ch06.ex04.ClientSideTask.execute:49 -
Message
 Send to Server: Msg # : 5; Message Received back from Server: Msg # : 5
```

The Simultaneous Exhibition Game

Go back to Figure 6-16. Let's discuss a little more in the context of resource sharing and resource utilization.

You might have observed the single server socket instance listening for client connections. It is this single server socket's duty to handle all incoming client connections. This is typical of many web servers existing today. A typical web server that produces relatively short content like a web page with text or an image will be 100KB in size for the response. Even though it will take only a fraction of a second to generate or retrieve this page, it can take as long as 10 seconds to transmit it to a client with a low bandwidth of 80 kbps (@ 10 KB/s). The issue of sending content to a slow client might be, to some extent, improved by increasing the size of the operating system kernel socket buffers; however, it's not a general solution to the problem. It can have undesirable side effects, requiring huge resources that will not scale linearly after a certain optimal point. In short, this single server socket cannot wait until all the processing, like I/O operations, happening within the client connection context are completed. If it keeps waiting until completion, it will take too long for it to be able to accept the next client connection. In a production web server, there will be tens or hundreds or more concurrent client connections hitting a web server, so the server socket has to be smarter in order to respond in a reasonable time frame.

The architecture in Figure 6-16 makes use of threads to handle the above scenario. A thread is a self-contained set of instructions that the operating system can schedule to get executed on a CPU core. Applications run multiple threads in parallel for two reasons:

- They can leverage more compute cores at the same time.

- They make it easy to do operations in parallel (in this example, to execute the code written within the client connection context).

However, threads also consume system resources. Each thread uses memory and other OS resources, and they need to be swapped on and off the cores by the process called context switching. Even though modern server processes can handle hundreds of active threads, performance starts degrading seriously once memory is exhausted or when a high I/O operation forces a large volume of context switches at the OS level. So, the creation of each thread has to be done with caution. Even if created, one optimization is to reuse threads. A thread pool can make this happen. Further, smart design can also allow these threads to be reused to execute a variety of tasks. In this example, threads from the same thread pool are used to execute the network reader tasks and the network writer tasks.

So, overall your network server is smartly implemented by using pooled threads, if not the smartest[3] possible manner. There is an analogy called "simultaneous exhibition or simultaneous display." This refers to a board game exhibition (commonly chess or Go)

---

[3]You could make the design smarter by using java.util.concurrent.Future, too.

where one player (typically of high rank, such as a grandmaster or dan-level player) plays multiple games at a time with a number of other players. The network server implemented here is similar to a grandmaster who can accept connections more or less concurrently and assign the associated computations to pooled threads, again more or less concurrently.

Message Correlation and Microservices

In microservices architecture, different pieces of the enterprise application are divided into multiple microservices and still they have to talk to each other. To get the real benefit of microservices, intermicroservice calls must be through a messaging infrastructure. This means the production ecosystem of an enterprise application with a microservices architecture will consist of many microservices, and many instances of these microservices, are interconnected with one or more messaging infrastructures. When you adopt an asynchronous style of communication between these instances, the main dilemma is how to effectively solve the routing of messaging between them. Previous sections in this chapter gave you a bird's eye view on the internal complexities involved in connecting microservices including the message correlation. If a developer has to do all of this wiring himself, it will bloat the code too much. You need a better way to handle this. I will introduce ways of handling this in Chapter 12 when I introduce the Axon framework (which will do this for you implicitly).

Summary

Messaging brings the power of detached processing to help enterprise applications deal with many real-world scenarios including downtime and failure. In this chapter, you looked at some of the powerful applications of messaging, including clustering and high availability. You also read through a few code samples, which showed the complexities involved if you hand-code cross-cutting concerns like message correlation, etc. By combining the multiple techniques discussed in this chapter, you'll be in a position to increase the reliability of your microservices infrastructure manyfold. You will see some of these messaging techniques applied in a different context in subsequent chapters since messaging is a core lever in the developer's toolset.

CHAPTER 7

Spring Boot

In the previous chapter, you looked at messaging. You used Spring to configure the message senders and listeners, and you did explicit wiring of beans and required infrastructure in Spring. So far, so good. Now how can you make aspects even simpler? You'll look at Spring Boot in this chapter, which makes use of an opinionated view of the Spring platform and many third-party Java libraries so that it is easy and straightforward to create stand-alone, production-grade, Spring-based applications that you can "just run." Since Boot follows many conventions and usage patterns followed by developers, which they have been leveraging while using Spring and other third-party libraries, most Spring Boot applications need very little Spring configuration. You will use Spring Boot to develop the few samples relevant to the discussion in this chapter. Again, the intention is not to cover Spring Boot in detail; that is outside the scope of this chapter. Readers familiar with Java or Spring should have no problem getting started by visiting the Spring Boot home page. I will spend time on very essential tools required for the discussion so that I don't deviate from the intention of this book, which is explaining practical microservices. However, by the time you start looking at the code samples in later chapters, you should be familiar with the basic building block code constructs.

You will learn the following in this chapter:

- How to use Spring Initializer to create a Boot project template

- How to use cURL to access a Boot sample for CRUD operations against MongoDB

- An HATEOAS and HAL introduction, and how to access data using `RestTemplate`

- How to developing an end-to-end Boot sample for performing CRUD operations against REST

© Binildas Christudas 2019
B. Christudas, *Practical Microservices Architectural Patterns*, https://doi.org/10.1007/978-1-4842-4501-9_7

Performing Data Operations Using Spring Boot and MongoDB

Polyglot persistence is a key aspect in the microservices architecture. While you still need ACID-compliant data stores with local and/or distributed transaction capabilities, careful analysis will reveal that majority of the data storage and retrieval operations don't need these rigid capabilities, which always come at a price. Today, many NoSQL databases are designed to operate over large clusters and can tackle very large volumes of data; they can also efficiently respond to read requests with traffic increasing exponentially, still performing more or less linearly. So, it is natural within a single application to address data store requirements addressing both kinds (SQL and NoSQL), and this is where polyglot persistence comes into play. In a microservice context, you may use multiple data storage technologies, chosen based upon the way data is used by individual microservices or components of a single large enterprise application. MongoDB is a best choice in scenarios when you need to store data in document format, so you'll look at a MongoDB sample over the rest of the chapters in this book.

You will implement a "Hello World" kind of Spring Boot application in this section. There is more than one way to start developing a Spring Boot application, and the main ways are

- Using the Spring Boot command line interface (CLI) as a command-line tool[1]

- Using IDEs such as Eclipse and Spring Tool Suite (STS) to provide Spring Boot support[2]

- Using the Spring Initializer project

You will follow the last method in this section.

---

[1]https://docs.spring.io/spring-boot/docs/current/reference/html/cli-using-the-cli.html

[2]www.eclipse.org/community/eclipse_newsletter/2018/february/springboot.php

Creating a Spring Boot Project Template Using the Spring Initializer

You will use the Spring Initializer to create a Spring Boot project here. The Spring Initializer is a drop-in replacement for the Eclipse-based Spring Tool Set (STS) project wizard and provides an online web UI to configure and generate different flavors of a Spring Boot project. Using the Spring Initializer, you can generate a project through the online interface, which can then be imported into any IDE.

The aim is to quickly develop an application that will help you to achieve the following:

- Get introduced to Spring Boot

- Get introduced to MongoDB

- Get introduced to basic CRUD operations using Spring Data

The Spring Initializer project is available at `http://start.spring.io`.

You need to fill in the details, such as whether it is a Maven project and whether you need to use Java for the Boot project and the Spring Boot version. Other details include group and artifact ID, as shown in Figure 7-1. Next, click Switch to go to the full version link under the Generate Project button. Here you can select MongoDB and Rest Repositories as the dependencies. You also need to make sure that the Java version is 8 and the package type is selected as JAR. Once the dependencies are selected, you may hit the Generate Project button. This will generate a Maven project. This project can be downloaded as a ZIP file into the default download directory of your browser.

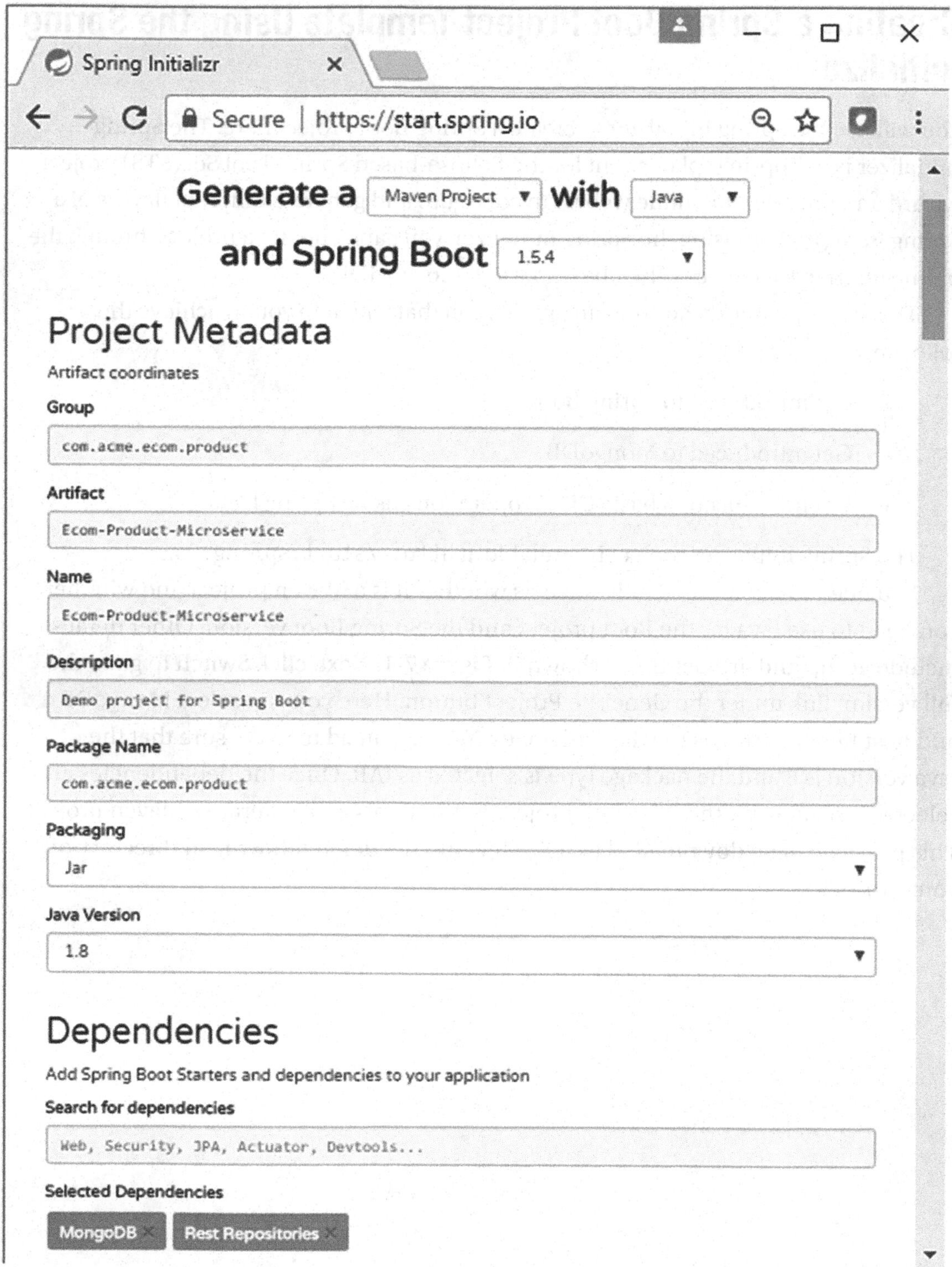

Figure 7-1. *Generating a Spring Boot template using the Spring Boot Initializer*

Spring Boot provides a set of Starter Poms or gradle build files that you can use to add required dependencies. Depending on the libraries in its classpath, Spring Boot will automatically configure the required classes by auto configuration. For example, to interact with a database, if there is a Spring Data library in the class path, it automatically sets up a connection to DB along with the required Data Source classes.

You can now unzip the file and save it to a directory of your choice in your file system. Again, a file path without any white spaces will save you from many unforeseen errors while you develop the application. You can now use your favorite IDE to continue application development.

1. If you use Eclipse, you may now go to the File menu and click Import.

2. Navigate to Maven ➤ Existing Maven Projects and click Next.

3. Click the Browse option next to Root Directory and select the folder you unzipped earlier.

4. Click the Finish button. This will load the generated Maven project into Eclipse Project Explorer.

Assuming you are familiar with Eclipse, I will not spend time or space explaining aspects of Eclipse here. Instead, let's look at the application development in detail.

First, look at the pom.xml that was autogenerated when you created the Spring Boot project. The main three elements are explained here.

Spring Boot Starter Parent

Typically your Maven pom.xml file will inherit from the spring-boot-starter-parent project and declare dependencies to one or more "starters." In Figure 7-1 you can see two such starters: MongoDB and Rest Repositories.

Listing 7-1 mentions your POM inheritance hierarchy, which is a Bill of Materials (BOM) to manage the different libraries and the versions required for a project.

Listing 7-1. Spring Boot Starter Parent (ch07\ch07-01\pom.xml)

```
<parent>
      <groupId>org.springframework.boot</groupId>
      <artifactId>spring-boot-starter-parent</artifactId>
      <version>1.5.4.RELEASE</version>
      <relativePath/>
</parent>
```

Spring Boot Dependencies

Next, if you can review the dependency section, you can see that the POM file mentions only three dependencies, as shown in Listing 7-2.

Listing 7-2. Spring Boot Dependencies

```
<dependencies>
      <dependency>
            <groupId>org.springframework.boot</groupId>
            <artifactId>spring-boot-starter-data-mongodb</artifactId>
      </dependency>
      <dependency>
            <groupId>org.springframework.boot</groupId>
            <artifactId>spring-boot-starter-data-rest</artifactId>
      </dependency>

      <dependency>
            <groupId>org.springframework.boot</groupId>
            <artifactId>spring-boot-starter-test</artifactId>
            <scope>test</scope>
      </dependency>
</dependencies>
```

These dependencies are explained next:

- `spring-boot-starter-data-mongodb`: The Spring Data MongoDB project helps you to integrate with the MongoDB document database. The main functional areas of Spring Data MongoDB are a POJO-centric model for interacting with a MongoDB Collection to do CRUD operations and easily write a repository-style data access layer.

- `spring-boot-starter-data-rest`: The Spring Data REST builds on top of Spring's MVC. Spring Data REST creates a collection of Spring MVC controllers and other beans required to provide a RESTful front end. These components then transitively link up to the Spring Data JPA backend. Using Spring Boot this is all autoconfigured for you.

- `spring-boot-starter-test`: This starter imports Spring Boot test modules, JUnit, AssertJ, Hamcrest, and a number of other useful libraries that will help you test the application.

Spring Boot Maven Plugin

Next, let's look at the Spring Boot Maven plugin. See Listing 7-3.

Listing 7-3. Spring Boot Maven Plugin

```
<build>
    <plugins>
        <plugin>
            <groupId>org.springframework.boot</groupId>
            <artifactId>spring-boot-maven-plugin</artifactId>
        </plugin>
    </plugins>
</build>
```

The Spring Boot Maven plugin in Listing 7-3 helps to create the single executable JAR. The single executable JAR is a self-contained executable JAR file that you can run in production.

In the "Microservices are Self-Contained" section in Chapter 3 you saw the requirement for self-contained and self-sufficient executable bundles. Java does not provide any standard way to load JAR files contained within a JAR file. Here you can use uber JARS. An uber JAR simply packages all classes from all JARs into a single archive. But this can sometimes run into problems when different versions of the same libraries are required or if the file names are same. So Spring Boot takes a different approach by nesting JARs directly, and the Spring Boot Maven plugin does all the plumbing required.

Design and Code the Domain Entities

For the sake of the sample in this section, you will keep the domain entity very simple. Your entity is a typical product that can be listed in an e-commerce site. Multiple products fall into a product category, so on the site you can first show product categories and an online user can explore or browse through the product categories to see all products available under the selected category. Figure 7-2 shows the design for your domain entity. This is a basic design that will help you manage product category vs. product relationship to meet the requirement of listing all products available under the selected product category.

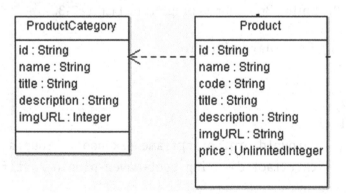

Figure 7-2. *Product/product category domain model*

Listing 7-4 shows the code required to do this.

Listing 7-4. Product/Product Category Domain Model (ch07\ch07-01\src\main\java\com\acme\ch07\ex01\product\model\Product.java)

```java
public class Product {

    @Id
    private String id;
    private String name;
    private String code;;
    private String title;
    private String description;
    private String imgUrl;
    private Double price;
    private String productCategoryName;
}

public class ProductCategory {

    @Id
    private String id;
    private String name;
    private String title;
    private String description;
    private String imgUrl;
}
```

Listing 7-4 also reveals an id object that is configured to be automatically generated so you don't have to deal with it manually.

Code the Repositories

The repository is an interface and it allows you to perform various operations involving Product and ProductCategory objects. It gets these operations by extending the MongoRepository interface defined in the Spring MongoDB project API. Basic functionalities provided by MongoRepository are

- Support for generic CRUD operations on a repository for a specific type

- Methods to retrieve entities using the pagination and sorting abstraction

See Listing 7-5.

Listing 7-5. Product and ProductCategory Mongo Repositories (ch07\ch07-01\src\main\java\com\acme\ch07\ex01\product\repository\ProductRepository.java)

```java
@RepositoryRestResource(collectionResourceRel = "products", path = "products")
public interface ProductRepository extends MongoRepository<Product, String> {

    public List<Product> findByProductCategoryName(
            @Param("productCategory") String  productCatagoryName);

}

@RepositoryRestResource(collectionResourceRel = "categories",
    path = "categories")
public interface ProductCategoryRepository extends
    MongoRepository<ProductCategory, String> {

}
```

You have defined here a custom query to retrieve a list of `Product` objects based on the `Category`. You can define more abstract utility methods to the above repository interfaces so that you will get their implementations free, but I have limited them as shown in Listing 7-5 to serve your purpose. At runtime, Spring Data REST will create implementations of the above interface automatically. Then it will use the `@RepositoryRestResource` annotation to direct Spring MVC to create RESTful endpoints at `/products` and `/categories`.

Code the Boot Application Executable

You can modify the `EcomProductMicroserviceApplication.java` file if required. Listing 7-6 shows the default code generated earlier. This is a simple Java class with a `main()` method so that it can be run as a standalone Java application with an embedded Tomcat servlet container as the HTTP runtime.

Listing 7-6. Spring Boot Application (ch07\ch07-01\src\main\java\com\acme\ ch07\ex01\product\EcomProductMicroserviceApplication.java)

```
@SpringBootApplication
public class EcomProductMicroserviceApplication {

    public static void main(String[] args) {
        SpringApplication.run(EcomProductMicroserviceApplication.class,
            args);
    }
}
```

While the `main()` method uses Spring Boot's `SpringApplication.run()` method to launch an application, Spring Boot internally spins up Spring Data JPA to create concrete implementation classes of the `ProductRepository` and `ProductCategoryRepository` and configure it to integrate to the back-end database using JPA.

Build and Package the Spring Boot Application

The Spring Boot style is to build and package the example by creating a completely self contained executable JAR file that you can run in production. As explained the "Microservices Are Self-Contained" section in Chapter 3, executable JARs are also called fat JARs and are archives that contain your compiled classes along with all of the other JAR dependencies that your code needs to run, which gets resolved when you interpret your POM dependency.

`ch07-01\pom.xml` contains the Maven scripts required to build run the samples. Make sure MongoDB is up and running. You may want to refer to Appendix A to get started with MongoDB.

You will first build and package the executables into a single JAR file:

```
cd ch07-01
D:\binil\gold\pack03\ch07\ch07-01>build
D:\binil\gold\pack03\ch07\ch07-01>mvn clean package -Dmaven.test.skip=true
```

This will generate the executable JAR in the target folder. One caveat is that when you execute the above Maven scripts, it will also execute the test cases by default, so you disabled it by skipping.

You may want to note the following two files, which you can use to customize many runtime parameters, which have been kept blank in the samples folder in your case:

```
ch07-01\src\main\resources\application.properties
ch07-01\src\test\resources\test.properties
```

Also, to fast-track your development cycle, when you want to just compile all Java files including your test classes, you may use the following command:

```
cd ch07-01
ch07-01>mvn clean test-compile
```

If you want to package your executable artifacts but do not want to build or execute your test classes, you may use the following command:

```
cd ch07-01
ch07-01>mvn clean package -Dmaven.test.skip=true
```

Run and Test the Spring Boot Application

In the Windows command prompt where the mongo shell is connected to a running mongod instance, you may want to first clean up any required collections:

```
> show collections
product
productCategory
> db.productCategory.drop()
true
> db.product.drop()
true
> show collections
>
```

You can now run the Spring Boot application in more than one way. The straightforward way is to execute the JAR file via the following commands:

```
cd ch07-01
D:\binil\gold\pack03\ch07\ch07-01>run
D:\binil\gold\pack03\ch07\ch07-01>rem java -jar .\target\Ecom-Product-
Microservice-0.0.1-SNAPSHOT.jar
D:\binil\gold\pack03\ch07\ch07-01>mvn spring-boot:run
```

Once the application is up, it will have created the required collections in the mongodb:

```
> show collections
product
productCategory
>
```

You can now test the application. You can use any REST client you wish. You may use the cURL tool to quickly execute commands against the server. Refer to Appendix D to get an overview on how to execute commands using cURL. You can now find what the server has to offer; see Listing 7-7.

Listing 7-7. GET HTTP Request Using cURL

```
$ curl http://localhost:8080
{
    "_links": {
        "categories": {
            "href": "http://localhost:8080/categories{?page,size,sort}",
            "templated": true
        },
        "products": {
            "href": "http://localhost:8080/products{?page,size,sort}",
            "templated": true
        },
```

```
        "profile": {
            "href": "http://localhost:8080/profile"
        }
    }
}
```

Refer to Appendix D to view a more exhaustive set of cURL commands that will be handy throughout the rest of this book. Figure 7-3 shows how to use cURL in a Unix-based environment to invoke basic REST operations.

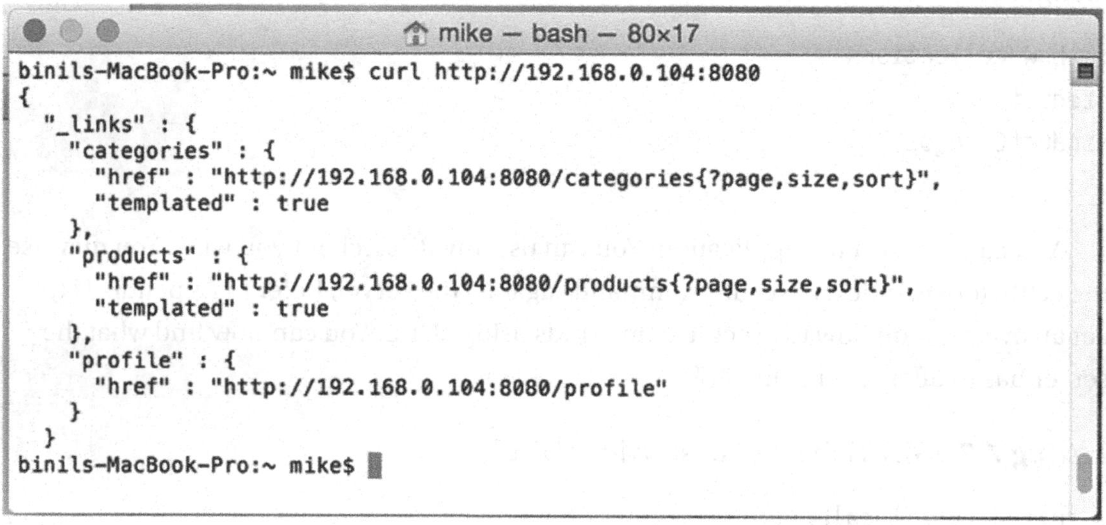

```
binils-MacBook-Pro:~ mike$ curl http://192.168.0.104:8080
{
  "_links" : {
    "categories" : {
      "href" : "http://192.168.0.104:8080/categories{?page,size,sort}",
      "templated" : true
    },
    "products" : {
      "href" : "http://192.168.0.104:8080/products{?page,size,sort}",
      "templated" : true
    },
    "profile" : {
      "href" : "http://192.168.0.104:8080/profile"
    }
  }
}
binils-MacBook-Pro:~ mike$
```

Figure 7-3. *GET HTTP request using cURL*

Listing 7-7 shows a products link located at `http://localhost:8080/products`. It has a few options such as `?page`, `?size`, and `?sort`. There are other links, which you may retrieve and understand.

Spring Data REST uses the Hypertext Application Language (HAL) format for JSON output. It is flexible and offers an easy and convenient way to supply links adjacent to the data that is served. HAL will make your API explorable and its documentation easily discoverable from within the REST API itself. The easiest way to test these links is to use the Postman tool. You may want to explore the following links using Postman:

```
http://localhost:8080/profile
http://localhost:8080/profile/products
http://localhost:8080/profile/categories
```

Figure 7-4 shows what it looks like when you execute the GET on the link `http://localhost:8080/profile/products` in Postman.

Figure 7-4. *GET HTTP request using Postman*

Alternatively, you can now execute the Junit tests using Maven. The tests are provided in the folder named ch07-01\src\test\java\com\acme\ch07\ex01\product. The tests directly access the Mongo repository and do data operations. See Listing 7-8.

Listing 7-8. Junit Testing the Mongo Repository (ch07\ch07-01\src\test\java\com\acme\ch07\ex01\product\ProductRepositoryTest.java)

```
public class ProductRepositoryTest {

    @Autowired
    private ProductRepository productRepository;

    @Before
    public void setUp(){
        productRepository.deleteAll();
    }

    @Test
    public void testAddProduct(){

        productRepository.save(createProject());
        assertTrue("successfully saved",true);
    }

     @Test
     public void testFindAllProducts(){

        productRepository.save(createProject());
        List<Product> productList = productRepository.findAll();
        assertTrue(productList.size()>0);
     }

    @Test
    public void testProductByProductCategory(){
        Product product = createProject();
        productRepository.save(product);
        List<Product> productList =
                productRepository.findByProductCategoryName(
```

```
        product.getProductCategoryName());
        assertTrue(productList.size()>0);
    }
}
```

To execute the tests, assuming your Spring Boot application is already up, execute the following command:

```
cd ch07-01
D:\binil\gold\pack03\ch07\ch07-01>test
D:\binil\gold\pack03\ch07\ch07-01>mvn test
```

Developing Using the Spring HAL Browser, HATEOAS

A very convenient aspect of the hypermedia-driven REST interface is how you can discover all the RESTful endpoints using cURL (or whatever REST client you are using). There is no need to exchange a formal contract or interface document with your customers prior to the method invocation (query), if each response also provides information on what options are available next for the user to act on. The HAL format provides a consistent and easy way to hyperlink between resources in your API. HAL will make your REST API explorable, and its documentation is easily discoverable from within the API itself. This will make your API easier to work with in both manual and machine-readable mode and therefore more attractive to client developers. HATEOAS (Hypertext As The Engine Of Application State) is a REST pattern where the navigation links are provided as part of the response payload. The client can then determine the state and follow the transition URLs provided as part of that state.

Open source libraries available for most major programming languages are available in HAL, so APIs that adopt HAL can be easily served and consumed in multiple platforms and programming languages. It's so simple that you can just deal with it as you would with any other JSON.

The HAL Browser

The HAL Browser is a useful application based on the HAL specification for handling HAL+JSON data. It's a web app with HAL-powered JavaScript. You can point it to any HAL-compliant Spring Data REST API and use it to navigate the app and traverse through linked resources.

To enable your application with HAL Browser, all you have to do is include the "Rest Repositories HAL Browser" dependency in addition to your Spring Initializer along with the dependencies mentioned in Figure 7-1. So your pom.xml will have the additional dependency shown in Listing 7-9.

Listing 7-9. Maven Dependency for Spring REST HAL Browser (ch07\ch07-02\ pom.xml)

```
<dependencies>
    <dependency>
        <groupId>org.springframework.data</groupId>
        <artifactId>spring-data-rest-hal-browser</artifactId>
    </dependency>
</dependencies>
```

Note that the pom.xml has a few more configuration details, but all of those additional lines are for configuring Simple Logging Façade for Java (SL4J), which acts as a façade for commonly used logging frameworks, like Java Util Logging, Log4J, Log4J2, Logback, etc. When you write logging code against the SL4J API, you have the flexibility to plug in your desired logging framework at deployment time, which is made possible through an intermediate bridge/adapter layer. There is also an "Exclude" configuration to exclude the built-in Logback dependency since Spring Boot will pick and use Logback by default if present in the classpath.

Since the sample application kept in folder ch07\ch07-02 is similar to the code you saw in ch07\ch07-01, I won't explain it here. Make sure MongoDB is up and running. You may want to refer to Appendix A to get started with MongoDB.

You can build and run the application as follows:

```
cd ch07\ch07-02
D:\binil\gold\pack03\ch07\ch07-02>build
D:\binil\gold\pack03\ch07\ch07-02>mvn clean package -Dmaven.test.skip=true

cd ch07\ch07-02
D:\binil\gold\pack03\ch07\ch07-02>run
D:\binil\gold\pack03\ch07\ch07-02>mvn spring-boot:run
```

The spring-data-rest-hal-browser dependency autoconfigures the HAL Browser to be served up when you visit your application's root URI. You can point your browser to

```
http://localhost:8080
```

This will get redirected to the URL shown in Figure 7-5.

There are GET and Non-GET actions for the REST end points and you can either click the GET button and navigate and view one of the collections, or click the non-GET options to make changes to the collection. This is made possible automatically by enabling the HAL Browser to read the links from the response and display them on a list on the left side of the browser; on the right side of the browser are details from the response including headers and the body (a HAL document).

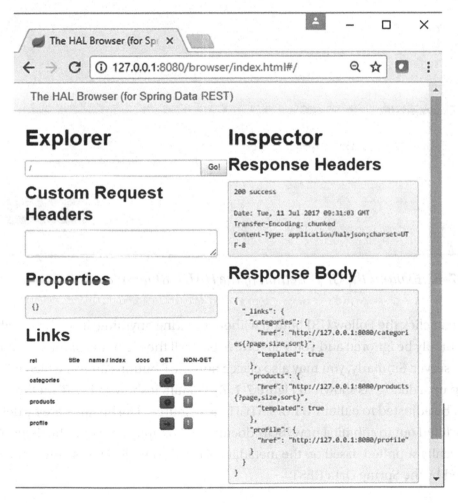

Figure 7-5. *Spring Data REST HAL Browser*

The HAL Browser speaks to the URI template. You may follow one of the GET methods next to Products or Categories via the question mark icon. An expansion dialog will pop up if you choose to navigate to it, as shown in Figure 7-6.

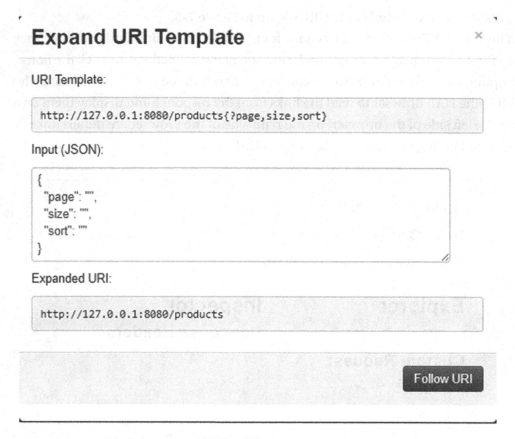

Figure 7-6. *Expand the GET method of the HAL URI template*

You can click the Follow URI button without entering anything; if so, the variables will essentially be ignored and you will receive back all the elements of the collection from the server. Similarly, you may also click a non-GET buttons above, which will then pop up a dialog, as shown in Figure 7-7. By default, it shows a POST method. This field can be adjusted to either PUT or PATCH the resource. The headers are by default properly filled out to submit a new JSON document. You may note that the fields are automatically supplied based on the metadata of the resources. This is automatically generated by the Spring Data REST.

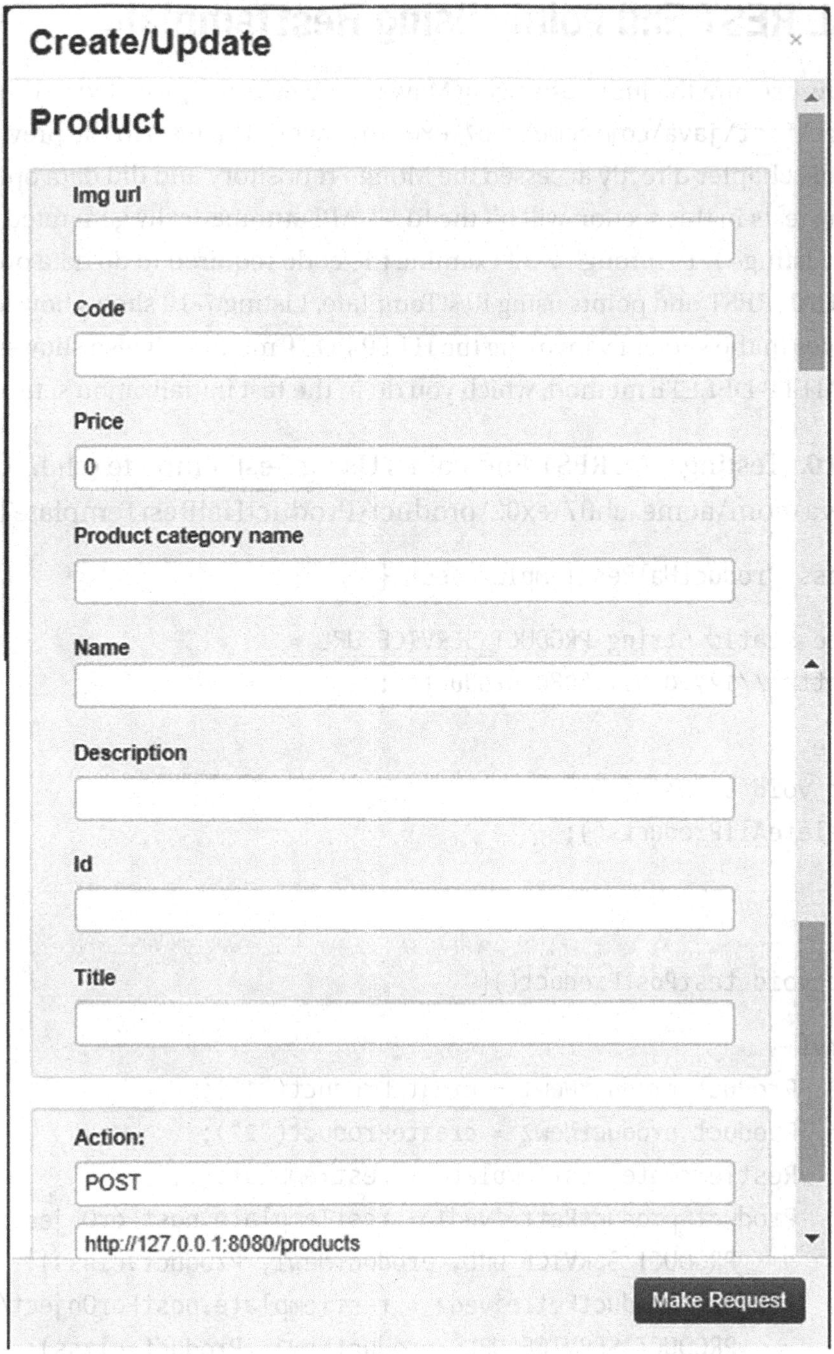

Figure 7-7. *Expand the non-GET method of the HAL URI template*

Test HAL REST End Points Using RestTemplate

You may now execute the Junit tests using Maven. The tests are provided in the folder ch07-02\src\test\java\com\acme\ch07\ex02\product. The tests in the previous section of this chapter directly accessed the Mongo repository and did data operations; however, the tests in this section will hit the REST API automatically generated by Spring Data REST. Listings 7-10 through 7-12 examine the code required to do data operations hitting the HAL REST end points using RestTemplate. Listing 7-10 shows how to create new resources in the server by invoking the HTTP POST method. It also shows how to invoke the HTTP DELETE method, which you do in the test initialization setup.

Listing 7-10. Testing HAL REST End Points Using RestTemplate (ch07\ch07-02\src\test\java\com\acme\ch07\ex02\product\ProductHalRestTemplateTest.java)

```java
public class ProductHalRestTemplateTest {

    private static String PRODUCT_SERVICE_URL =
        "http://127.0.0.1:8080/products";

    @Before
    public void setUp(){
        deleteAllProducts();
    }

    @Test
    public void testPostProduct(){

        try{
            Product productNew1 = createProduct("1");
            Product productNew2 = createProduct("2");
            RestTemplate restTemplate = restTemplate();
            Product productRetreived1 = restTemplate.postForObject(
                PRODUCT_SERVICE_URL, productNew1, Product.class);
            Product productRetreived2 = restTemplate.postForObject(
                PRODUCT_SERVICE_URL, productNew2, Product.class);
            assertTrue("successfully saved",true);
```

```
        }catch(Exception ex){
            assertTrue("successfully failed",true);
        }
    }

    public void deleteAllProducts(){

        RestTemplate restTemplate = restTemplate();
        List<Product> productList = getAllProducts();
        productList.forEach(item->restTemplate.delete(
            PRODUCT_SERVICE_URL + "/" + item.getId())
        );
    }

    private RestTemplate restTemplate() {
        ObjectMapper mapper = new ObjectMapper();
        mapper.configure(DeserializationFeature.FAIL_ON_UNKNOWN_PROPERTIES,
            false);
        mapper.registerModule(new Jackson2HalModule());
        MappingJackson2HttpMessageConverter converter =
            new MappingJackson2HttpMessageConverter();
        converter.setSupportedMediaTypes(
            MediaType.parseMediaTypes("application/hal+json"));
        converter.setObjectMapper(mapper);
        return new RestTemplate(Arrays.asList(converter));
    }
}
```

You can query the newly created resources using the HTTP GET method, as shown in Listing 7-11.

Listing 7-11. Testing HAL GET REST End Points Using RestTemplate

```
public class ProductHalRestTemplateTest {

    @Test
    public void testGetAllProducts(){
```

```
        testPostProduct();
        List<Product> productList = getAllProducts();
        assertTrue(productList.size() > 0);
    }

    public List<Product> getAllProducts(){

        RestTemplate restTemplate = restTemplate();
        ParameterizedTypeReference<PagedResources<Product>> responseTypeRef =
            new ParameterizedTypeReference<PagedResources<Product>>() {
            };
        ResponseEntity<PagedResources<Product>> responseEntity =
            restTemplate.exchange(PRODUCT_SERVICE_URL, HttpMethod.GET,
            (HttpEntity<Product>) null, responseTypeRef);
        PagedResources<Product> resources = responseEntity.getBody();
        Collection<Product> products = resources.getContent();
        List<Product> productList = new ArrayList<Product>(products);
        return productList;
    }

}
```

Listing 7-12 shows how to make changes to the resources in the server by invoking HTTP PUT using RestTemplate.

Listing 7-12. Testing HAL PUT End Points Using RestTemplate

```
public class ProductHalRestTemplateTest {

    @Test
    public void testPutProduct(){

        try{
            Product productNew3 = createProduct("3");
            RestTemplate restTemplate = restTemplate();
            Product productRetreived3 = restTemplate.postForObject(
                PRODUCT_SERVICE_URL, productNew3, Product.class);
            productRetreived3.setPrice(productRetreived3.getPrice() * 2);
```

```
        restTemplate.put( PRODUCT_SERVICE_URL + "/" +
            productRetreived3.getId(), productRetreived3, Product.class);
        Product productAgainRetrieved =
            restTemplate.getForObject(PRODUCT_SERVICE_URL + "/" +
            productRetreived3.getId(), Product.class);
        assertTrue("successfully saved",true);
    }catch(Exception ex){
        assertTrue("successfully failed",true);
    }
  }
}
```

To execute the tests, assuming your Spring Boot application is already up, execute the following command:

```
cd ch07-02
D:\binil\gold\pack03\ch07\ch07-02>test
D:\binil\gold\pack03\ch07\ch07-02>mvn test
```

Develop a RESTful Web Service

REST (Representational State Transfer) is an architectural style for designing distributed systems which was introduced by Roy Fielding in his doctoral dissertation in the year 2000. REST is a generic set of constraints applied to resources; however, it is commonly associated with HTTP. This section will introduce REST concepts and you will look at a complete implementation of a complete REST provider as well as a REST consumer using Spring Boot.

REST Basics

REST recommends a set of constraints, such as being stateless, having a client/server relationship, providing a uniform interface, request-response cycles being idempotent, and so on. REST is not strictly related to HTTP, but it is most commonly associated with it.

Summarized below are the principles of REST:

- Resources expose URIs, which are easily understood and directory-like structures, so that they are discoverable, linkable, and traversable.

- Representations transfer JSON or XML as wire-level formats to represent data objects and attributes.

- Operations or messages use HTTP methods explicitly (for example, GET, POST, PUT, and DELETE).

- Operations are stateless so that you store no client context on the server between requests. The client only holds session state so that when the number of clients increases, the server's scalability is not compromised by state data in big volumes.

There are other advantages if you use REST. One main advantage is that intermediaries like caches and proxies can provide cache hits so that the actual resource server is not stressed unless required. A cache server is a specialized proxy server that will help you improve web performance. Web performance can be improved either at the client end or at the server end or even between other intermediaries. Adhering to REST HTTP standards and gestures will help you leverage these optimizations, which you get freely since HTTP is a standard and many devices have provisions to configure for these optimizations.

HTTP Methods for CRUD Resources

The main methods in HTTP you can leverage for implementing REST are listed here:

- GET: GET is the simplest HTTP operation and its intention is to retrieve a resource from the server. 200 OK is the status code for a successful operation. All GET operations should be idempotent, which means regardless of how many times you repeat the operation with the same parameters, there should not be any change in state for the resource.

- POST[3]: HTTP POST provides an option for clients to send information to the server. POST is recommended for creating a new resource (even though it can also update an existing resource).

- PUT: HTTP PUT also provides an option for clients to send information to the server; however, the usage semantics of PUT are slightly different from that of POST as per HTTP. Using PUT, you can send a "new object" to the server to be put or placed at a location in the server represented by the URI, so the intent should be to replace the resource with a new one. A PUT request is idempotent as far as a single client is concerned. If only a subset of data elements is provided in a PUT request, the rest will be replaced with empty or null.

- DELETE: DELETE provides clients an option to remove a resource from the server. The URI identifies the resource to be deleted. The resource may not have to be removed immediately; instead it could be done by an asynchronous or long-running operation behind the scenes.

Develop a REST Controller in Spring Boot

You will use the same Product entity described in previous sections to build a fully functional REST service to do CRUD operations. Spring's approach in building RESTful web services is to use a controller to handle HTTP requests. Listings 7-13 through 7-16 show the complete code for building a HATEOS-based REST controller using Spring. Listing 7-13 shows how a product with a particular ID can be retrieved. The @RequestMapping annotation ensures that HTTP requests to /products/{id} are mapped to the getProduct() method.

---

[3]As per strict HTTP specifications, the difference between a POST and PUT is in how the server interprets the URI. In a POST, the URI normally identifies an object on the server that can process the included data. In a PUT, the URI identifies a resource in which the server should place the data. So a POST URI generally indicates a program or a script that can do processing; a PUT URI is usually the path and name for a resource.

Listing 7-13. HATEOAS-Enabled REST Controller with GET Operation
(ch07\ch07-03\src\main\java\com\acme\ch07\ex03\product\controller\
ProductRestController.java)

```java
@RestController
public class ProductRestController {

    @Autowired
    private ProductRepository productRepository;

    @RequestMapping(value = "/products/{id}", method = RequestMethod.GET,
        produces = MediaType.APPLICATION_JSON_VALUE)
    public ResponseEntity<Resource<Product>> getProduct(
        @PathVariable("id") String id) {

        Product product = productRepository.findOne(id);
        if (product == null) {
            return new ResponseEntity<Resource<Product>>
            (HttpStatus.NOT_FOUND);
        }
        Resource<Product> productRes = new Resource<Product>(product,
                linkTo(methodOn(ProductRestController.class).getProduct(
                product.getId())).withSelfRel());
        return new ResponseEntity<Resource<Product>>(productRes,
            HttpStatus.OK);
    }

    @RequestMapping(value = "/products", method = RequestMethod.GET,
            produces = {MediaType.APPLICATION_JSON_VALUE})
    public ResponseEntity<Resources<Resource<Product>>> getAllProducts() {

        List<Product> products = productRepository.findAll();
        Link links[] = {linkTo(methodOn(ProductRestController.class).
            getAllProducts()).withSelfRel(),linkTo(methodOn(
            ProductRestController.class).getAllProducts()).withRel(
            "getAllProducts")};
```

```
    if(products.isEmpty()){
        return new ResponseEntity<Resources<Resource<Product>>>(
            HttpStatus.NOT_FOUND);
    }
    List<Resource<Product>> list=new ArrayList<Resource<Product>> ();
    for(Product product:products){
        list.add(new Resource<Product>(product,
            linkTo(methodOn(ProductRestController.class).getProduct(
            product.getId()))).withSelfRel()));
    }
    Resources<Resource<Product>> productRes =
        new Resources<Resource<Product>>(list, links) ;
    return new ResponseEntity<Resources<Resource<Product>>>(
        productRes, HttpStatus.OK);
    }
}
```

The REST component is identified by the @RestController annotation, and the ProductRestController handles HTTP-based CRUD requests for the Product entity.

The implementation of the method body retrieves a product entity using the supplied id and returns a new Product object. This Product object data will be written directly to the HTTP response as JSON. Listing 7-13 also shows a bulk retrieval operation where you retrieve all Product resources.

A key difference between a traditional MVC controller and the RESTful web service controller above is the way that the HTTP response body is created. Rather than relying on a view technology to perform server-side rendering of the greeting data to HTML, this RESTful web service controller simply populates and returns a Greeting object. The object data will be written directly to the HTTP response as JSON.

This code uses Spring 4's @RestController annotation, which marks the class completely as a controller where every method returns a domain object instead of a view as compared to the a traditional MVC controller. It's shorthand for @Controller and @ResponseBody put together.

For converting the Product object to JSON, Spring uses the HTTP message converter support. You don't need to do this conversion manually since the Jackson 2 is on the classpath, so Spring's MappingJackson2HttpMessageConverter is automatically chosen to convert the Product instance to JSON.

Let's look at other operations. Listing 7-14 shows how to create new resources.

Listing 7-14. HATEOAS-Enabled REST Controller with a POST Operation

```
@RestController
public class ProductRestController {

    @RequestMapping(value = "/products", method = RequestMethod.POST)
    public ResponseEntity<Resource<Product>> postProduct(@RequestBody
    Product
        product,    UriComponentsBuilder ucBuilder) {
    List<Product> products =
        productRepository.findByCode(product.getCode());
    if (products.size() > 0) {
        LOGGER.debug("A Product with code {} already exist",
            product.getCode());
        return new ResponseEntity<Resource<Product>>
        (HttpStatus.CONFLICT);
    }
    Product newProduct = productRepository.save(product);

    HttpHeaders headers = new HttpHeaders();
    headers.setLocation(ucBuilder.path("/products/{id}").
    buildAndExpand(
        product.getId()).toUri());
    Resource<Product> productRes =new Resource<Product>(newProduct,
        linkTo(methodOn(ProductRestController.class).getProduct(
        newProduct.getId())).withSelfRel());
    return new ResponseEntity<Resource<Product>>(productRes,
        headers, HttpStatus.OK);
    }

}
```

You can make changes to the server side resources using the code snippet shown in Listing 7-15.

Listing 7-15. HATEOAS-Enabled REST Controller with a PUT Operation

```
@RestController
public class ProductRestController {

    @RequestMapping(value = "/products/{id}", method = RequestMethod.PUT)
    public ResponseEntity<Resource<Product>> updateProduct
    (@PathVariable("id")
            String id, @RequestBody Product product) {

        Product currentProduct = productRepository.findOne(id);
        if (currentProduct == null) {
            return new ResponseEntity<Resource<Product>>(HttpStatus.NOT_
            FOUND);
        }

        currentProduct.setName(product.getName());
        currentProduct.setCode(product.getCode());
        currentProduct.setTitle(product.getTitle());
        currentProduct.setDescription(product.getDescription());
        currentProduct.setImgUrl(product.getImgUrl());
        currentProduct.setPrice(product.getPrice());
        currentProduct.setProductCategoryName(
            product.getProductCategoryName());

        Product newProduct = productRepository.save(currentProduct);

        Resource<Product> productRes = new Resource<Product>(newProduct,
            linkTo(methodOn(ProductRestController.class).getProduct(
            newProduct.getId())).withSelfRel());
        return new ResponseEntity<Resource<Product>>(productRes,
            HttpStatus.OK);
    }
}
```

Finally, the DELETE method can delete a resource from the server. Listing 7-16 shows how to delete a product with a specific ID and how to delete all of the product resources.

Listing 7-16. HATEOAS-Enabled REST Controller with a DELETE Operation

```
@RestController
public class ProductRestController {

    @RequestMapping(value = "/products/{id}", method = RequestMethod.DELETE)
    public ResponseEntity<Product> deleteProduct(
            @PathVariable("id") String id) {

        Product product = productRepository.findOne(id);
        if (product == null) {
            return new ResponseEntity<Product>(HttpStatus.NOT_FOUND);
        }

        productRepository.delete(id);
        return new ResponseEntity<Product>(HttpStatus.NO_CONTENT);
    }

    @RequestMapping(value = "/products", method = RequestMethod.DELETE)
    public ResponseEntity<Product> deleteAllProducts() {

        productRepository.deleteAll();
        return new ResponseEntity<Product>(HttpStatus.NO_CONTENT);
    }
}
```

In the first section, you saw how to code a Spring Boot application. You will now build and package the application.

Since the sample application kept in folder ch07\ch07-02 is similar to the code you saw in ch07\ch07-01 and ch07\ch07-02, I won't explain it here. Make sure MongoDB is up and running. You may want to refer to Appendix A to get started with MongoDB.

You can build and run the application as follows:

```
cd ch07\ch07-03
D:\binil\gold\pack03\ch07\ch07-03>build
D:\binil\gold\pack03\ch07\ch07-03>mvn clean package -Dmaven.test.skip=true

cd ch07\ch07-02
D:\binil\gold\pack03\ch07\ch07-02>run
D:\binil\gold\pack03\ch07\ch07-02>mvn spring-boot:run
```

Test the REST Controller Using RestTemplate

Once the application is up, you can test it. You can use any REST client you wish. Listing 7-17 shows how to code a Java client using `RestTemplate` to consume the HATEOAS service. `RestTemplate` is Spring's central class for synchronous client-side HTTP invocations. `RestTemplate` simplifies communication with HTTP servers, and enforces REST principles. `RestTemplate` handles low-level HTTP connections, leaving application code to provide URLs (with possible template variables) and extract the responses back. `RestTemplate` by default relies on JDK facilities to establish HTTP connections; however, you may switch to use a different HTTP library such as Apache HttpComponents, Netty, or OkHttp.

Listing 7-17. Client Code Using RestTemplate to Consume a HATEOAS Service (ch07\ch07-03\src\test\java\com\acme\ch07\ex03\product\ProductControllerRestTemplateTest.java)

```java
public class ProductControllerRestTemplateTest {

    private static String PRODUCT_SERVICE_URL =
        "http://localhost:8080/products";

    @Test
    public void testPostProduct(){

        Product productNew1 = createProduct("1");
        RestTemplate restTemplate = restTemplate();
        Product productRetreived1 = restTemplate.postForObject(
            PRODUCT_SERVICE_URL,        productNew1, Product.class);
    }

    @Test
    public void testGetAProduct(){

        Product productNew2 = createProduct("2");
        RestTemplate restTemplate = restTemplate();
        Product productRetreived2 = restTemplate.postForObject(
            PRODUCT_SERVICE_URL, productNew2, Product.class);
```

```java
        String uri = PRODUCT_SERVICE_URL + "/" + productRetreived2.getId();
        Product productRetreivedAgain2 = restTemplate.getForObject(uri,
            Product.class);
    }

    @Test
    public void testPutProduct(){

        Product productNew3 = createProduct("3");
        RestTemplate restTemplate = restTemplate();
        Product productRetreived3 = restTemplate.postForObject(
            PRODUCT_SERVICE_URL, productNew3, Product.class);
        productRetreived3.setPrice(productRetreived3.getPrice() * 2);
        restTemplate.put( PRODUCT_SERVICE_URL + "/" +
            productRetreived3.getId(), productRetreived3, Product.class);
        Product productAgainRetreived3 =
            restTemplate.getForObject(PRODUCT_SERVICE_URL + "/" +
            productRetreived3.getId(), Product.class);
    }

    @Test
    public void testDeleteAProduct(){

        Product productNew4 = createProduct("4");
        RestTemplate restTemplate = restTemplate();
        Product productRetreived4 = restTemplate.postForObject(
            PRODUCT_SERVICE_URL, productNew4, Product.class);
        restTemplate.delete(PRODUCT_SERVICE_URL + "/" +
            productRetreived4.getId());
    }

    @Test
    public void testDeleteAllProducts(){

        RestTemplate restTemplate = restTemplate();
        Product productNew5 = createProduct("5");
        Product productRetreived5 = restTemplate.postForObject(
            PRODUCT_SERVICE_URL, productNew5, Product.class);
```

```
    Product productNew6 = createProduct("6");
    Product productRetreived6 = restTemplate.postForObject(
        PRODUCT_SERVICE_URL, productNew6, Product.class);
    restTemplate.delete(PRODUCT_SERVICE_URL);
}

private List<Product> getAllProducts(){

    RestTemplate restTemplate = restTemplate();
    ParameterizedTypeReference<PagedResources<Product>> responseTypeRef =
        new ParameterizedTypeReference<PagedResources<Product>>() {
        };
    ResponseEntity<PagedResources<Product>> responseEntity =
        restTemplate.exchange(PRODUCT_SERVICE_URL, HttpMethod.GET,
        (HttpEntity<Product>) null, responseTypeRef);
    PagedResources<Product> resources = responseEntity.getBody();
    Collection<Product> products = resources.getContent();
    List<Product> productList = new ArrayList<Product>(products);
    return productList;
}

private RestTemplate restTemplate() {

    ObjectMapper mapper = new ObjectMapper();
    mapper.configure(DeserializationFeature.FAIL_ON_UNKNOWN_PROPERTIES,
        false);
    mapper.registerModule(new Jackson2HalModule());
    MappingJackson2HttpMessageConverter converter =
        new MappingJackson2HttpMessageConverter();
    converter.setSupportedMediaTypes(MediaType.parseMediaTypes(
        "application/hal+json, application/json"));
    converter.setObjectMapper(mapper);
    return new RestTemplate(Arrays.asList(converter));
}
}
```

To execute the tests, assuming your Spring Boot application is already up, execute the following command:

```
cd ch07-03
D:\binil\gold\pack03\ch07\ch07-03>test
D:\binil\gold\pack03\ch07\ch07-03>mvn test
```

Summary

In this chapter, you learned about Spring Boot and how its opinionated view of the Spring platform and many other third-party Java libraries provides an easy and less scripted way of getting things done, leveraging code, and packaging by conventions. You then played with MongoDB, putting code to execute CRUD events over a custom entity or resource. You used both Postman and Curl to do simple testing. Code in later sections also introduced the concepts of HATEOAS and HAL. Next, you developed a complete REST controller sample so that you have a place on the server side where you can put complex business logic and custom rules and validations if required. In succeeding chapters, more code samples will be built over the samples present in this chapter. Further, most of the succeeding chapters leverage Spring Boot, so this chapter is a foundation for you to get the code working in the rest of the chapters. After Spring Boot, the next framework you want to look into is Spring Cloud, which provides implementations for common patterns in distributed microservices ecosystems. You will do so in the next chapter.

CHAPTER 8

Spring Cloud

In Chapter 7, you were introduced to the Spring Boot. You explored several examples built with Spring Boot so now you have the building blocks for an enterprise-level application, whether the application is medium scale or large scale. In this chapter, you will look into the next indispensable piece of Spring called Spring Cloud, which is built over Spring Boot itself. There are a bunch of common patterns in distributed, microservices ecosystems that can help you integrate the core services as a loosely coupled continuum, and Spring Cloud provides many powerful tools that enhance the behavior of Spring Boot applications to implement those patterns. You will learn only the major and critical blocks required to keep the discussion continuing in subsequent chapters, again with the help of concrete code samples. The samples in this chapter are incrementally built over the preceding samples, so please don't skip any section or you may not get the succeeding samples to run smoothly.

You will learn about the following in this chapter:

- The Feign client to make HTTP API calls

- Hystrix, the circuit breakers to gracefully degrade

- The Hystrix dashboard, showing a graphical overview of a circuit breaker in the system

- Ribbon, the client-side load balancer

- Eureka, a REST-based registry service

- Zuul, the API gateway, which is the front controller for your microservices

- The Config Server to externalize version control and manage configuration parameters for microservices

© Binildas Christudas 2019
B. Christudas, *Practical Microservices Architectural Patterns*, https://doi.org/10.1007/978-1-4842-4501-9_8

Spring Cloud for Microservices Architecture

The "The Architecture of Microservices" section in Chapter 4 talked about the major new concerns you need to deal with when you move from a traditional architecture to a microservices-based architecture. Due to the inversion effect in microservices architecture, many of the intra-application concerns now get moved to the inter (micro) services level, and when the number of microservices keeps growing, so does the inherent growth in associated outer architecture complexity.

Spring Cloud provides good out-of-the-box support for typical use cases and extensibility mechanisms required in the microservices ecosystem. A few of them are listed here:

- Distributed/versioned configuration

- Service registration and discovery

- Routing and load balancing

- Interservice calls

- Circuit breakers

- Distributed messaging

Similar to Spring Boot, Spring Cloud takes a very declarative approach, and often you get a lot of features with just an inclusion of a dependency in a classpath and/or an annotation. Let's look into a few of them now.

Feign Client Usage in Spring Cloud

The Feign client is a Java-to-HTTP client-side binder inspired by libraries like Retrofit, JAXRS-2.0, and WebSocket. Feign's intent is to reduce the complexity of invoking HTTP APIs by generalizing the binding denominator uniformly to HTTP APIs regardless of the maturity of the REST APIs (a.k.a. the restfulness of the APIs). Feign makes HTTP API calls simple by processing annotations into a templatized request. Just before sending the requests, arguments are applied to these templates in a straightforward fashion. However, Feign only supports text-based APIs. Nevertheless, Feign dramatically simplifies system aspects like replaying requests, unit testing, etc. You will look at invoking HTTP APIs in this section.

Design a Feign Client Scenario

Starting with this section and for all other examples in Spring Cloud in this chapter, you will use a simple yet representative real-world use case. You will look into the design of the use case first and then learn more. Figure 8-1 illustrates a simple scenario where there are two separate applications or, in our terms, two separate microservices: Product Web and Product Server.

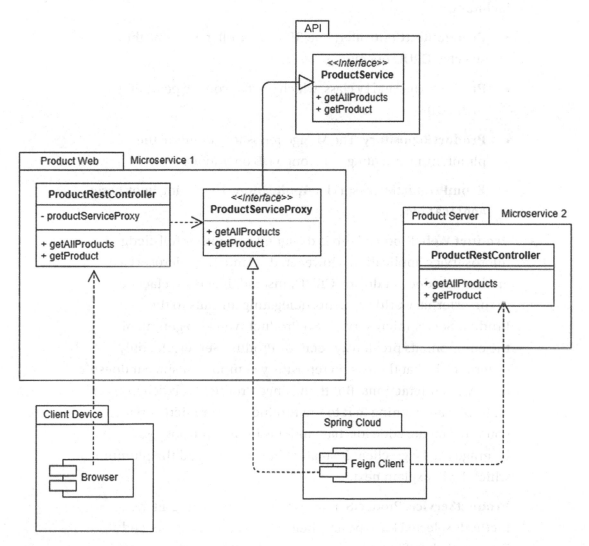

Figure 8-1. *A Feign client usage scenario*

Let's explore the components one by one:

- **Product Server**: Product Server is a full-fledged microservice application implementing a part of the CRUD operations. This microservice uses a Mongo DB to write to and read from the data pertaining to product entities. So the microservice encapsulates all the components required to do typical CRUD operations against a database and also to expose the functionality as REST-based services, including

  - **ProductRestController**: The REST controller exposing the selected CRUD operations

  - **Product**: The `Entity` class, which is what you are persisting to the DB

  - **ProductRepository**: The Mongo repository doing all the plumbing in executing the Mongo DB operations

  - **EcomProductMicroserviceApplication**: The Spring Boot-based `Application` class

- **Product Web**: Product Web is designed as another full-fledged microservice application. However, this time the microservice application doesn't do any CRUD; instead, it acts as a façade to the external world or clients delegating all calls to the Product Server microservice. So Product Web also gets all of the components previously seen for Product Server; the only difference is that there is no repository component since it doesn't do any DB interactions. But then, since Product Web delegates all REST calls coming to it to the Product Server microservice, you must create code for that, and it is for this purpose you will leverage the Feign client instead of hand-coding all the plumbing, which I will explain next.

- **ProductService**: ProductService is the interface listing all the methods selected for exposing, hence both Product Server and Product Web fulfill the contract specified in this interface.

186

- **ProductServiceProxy**: This component is another abstract interface that extends ProductService, so it gets all the methods expected out of both the Product Server and the Product Web interfaces. Moreover, ProductServiceProxy is the interface for annotating the Feign client's essential configuration. In every practical sense, this can be considered as the client-side proxy for the server-side functionality.

- **Spring Cloud Feign Client**: The Spring's Feign client is the actual implementation that Spring Cloud realizes on the fly. It is through this proxy implementation the calls from Product Web are delegated to Product Server.

The interactions described above are illustrated in Figure 8-2.

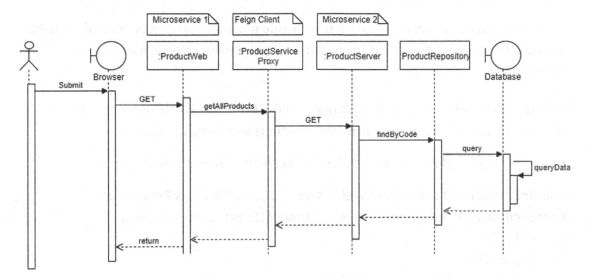

Figure 8-2. *Delegation of calls through the Feign client*

Here, requests from the browser will hit the Product Web microservice first. The Product Web microservice will in turn delegate the call to the Product Server microservice with the help of a ProductServiceProxy. The Product Server microservice will retrieve the data from the database and provide the response, which will be returned back through the call stack to the browser.

Code Using Feign Client

Since Feign is a declarative HTTP client, with one spring-cloud-starter-feign dependency mentioned in your Maven POM and with another single annotation of @EnableFeignClients, you have a fully functional HTTP client with a sensible, ready-to-go default configuration. Visit pom.xml to see the explicit mention of the Feign client dependency. See Listing 8-1.

Listing 8-1. Feign Client Dependency in Maven (ch08\ch08-01\ProductWeb\ pom.xml)

```
<dependency>
    <groupId>org.springframework.cloud</groupId>
    <artifactId>spring-cloud-starter-feign</artifactId>
</dependency>
```

With Feign added on the classpath, only one more annotation is needed to make everything work with the default configuration properties. This is mentioned in Listing 8-2.

Listing 8-2. Enable Feign Client (ch08\ch08-01\ProductWeb\src\main\java\ com\acme\ecom\product\controller\ProductRestController.java)

```
import org.springframework.cloud.netflix.feign.EnableFeignClients;

@EnableFeignClients(basePackageClasses = ProductServiceProxy.class)
@ComponentScan(basePackageClasses = ProductServiceProxy.class)
@CrossOrigin
@RestController
public class ProductRestController implements ProductService{

private ProductServiceProxy productServiceProxy;

    @Autowired
    public ProductRestController(ProductServiceProxy productServiceProxy){
        this.productServiceProxy = productServiceProxy;
    }
```

```
@RequestMapping(value = "/productsweb", method = RequestMethod.GET ,
    produces = {MediaType.APPLICATION_JSON_VALUE})
public ResponseEntity<Resources<Resource<Product>>> getAllProducts() {

    return productServiceProxy.getAllProducts();

}

@RequestMapping(value = "/productsweb/{productId}", method =
    RequestMethod.GET, produces = MediaType.APPLICATION_JSON_VALUE)
public ResponseEntity<Resource<Product>> getProduct(
    @PathVariable("productId") String productId) {

    return productServiceProxy.getProduct(productId);

}

}
```

ProductServiceProxy is injected into the code in Listing 8-2 in the Feign client proxy. Creating this REST proxy client is really easy, and most of the time all you need to do is create an interface and add some annotations. The Spring Cloud environment will create the implementation at runtime and make the call delegate work. Listing 8-3 shows the ProductServiceProxy in code.

Listing 8-3. Feign REST Client (ch08\ch08-01\ProductWeb\src\main\java\com\ acme\ecom\product\client\ProductServiceProxy.java)

```
import org.springframework.cloud.netflix.feign.FeignClient;

@FeignClient(name="product-proxy", url = "http://localhost:8080")
public interface ProductServiceProxy extends ProductService{

}
```

I will not explain the code for the Product Server microservice since it is very similar to the sample I already explained in the "Develop a RESTful Web Service" section in Chapter 7.

Build and Test the Feign Client

The complete code required to demonstrate the Feign client is in folder ch08-01. Make sure MongoDB is up and running. You may want to refer to Appendix A to get started with MongoDB.

You first build and package the executables for the Product Server microservice and bring up the server. There is a utility script provided which you can easily execute in folder ch08\ch08-01\ProductServer\make.bat:

```
cd ch08\ch08-01\ProductServer
D:\binil\gold\pack03\ch08\ch08-01\ProductServer>make
D:\binil\gold\pack03\ch08\ch08-01\ProductServer>mvn -Dmaven.test.skip=true
clean package
```

You can run the Spring Boot application in more than one way. The straightforward way is to execute the JAR file via the following commands:

```
D:\binil\gold\pack03\ch08\ch08-01\ProductServer>run
D:\binil\gold\pack03\ch08\ch08-01\ProductServer>java -jar -Dserver.
port=8080 ./target/Ecom-Product-Microservice-0.0.1-SNAPSHOT.jar
```

These commands will bring up the Product Server in port 8080. Note that an initialization component kept in the following place will pump a few Product instances into the MongoDB during startup, which will be handy for demonstrating your application later:

```
ch08\ch08-01\ProductServer\src\main\java\com\acme\ecom\
productInitializationComponent.java
```

Next, build and package the executables for the Product Web microservice and bring up the server:

```
cd ch08\ch08-01\ProductWeb
D:\binil\gold\pack03\ch08\ch08-01\ProductWeb>make
D:\binil\gold\pack03\ch08\ch08-01\ProductWeb>mvn -Dmaven.test.skip=true
clean package
D:\binil\gold\pack03\ch08\ch08-01\ProductWeb>run
D:\binil\gold\pack03\ch08\ch08-01\ProductWeb>java -jar -Dserver.port=8081
.\target\Ecom-Product-Microservice-0.0.1-SNAPSHOT.jar
```

Above command will bring up Product Web in port 8081

There is a quick utility provided in the following location to test the application:

ch08\ch08-01\ProductWeb\src\main\resources\product.html

Open this HTML utility preferably in the Chrome browser. Upon loading itself, the browser client will fire a request to the Product Web listening at port 8081, which will delegate the calls to the Product Server listening at 8080 by proxying through the Feign client.

If everything goes well, the browser widget will be filled with data from the back-end database (Figure 8-3). When you refresh the screen, the browser will hit the Product Web microservice first. The Product Web microservice will then call the Product Server microservice, which in turn will query the Mongo DB and return the results. The notable feature here is that in this demonstration you have created two different microservices and then one microservice made a call to the other microservice using Feign client. This is one of the ways by which microservices can communicate with each other using HTTP calls in a synchronous manner.

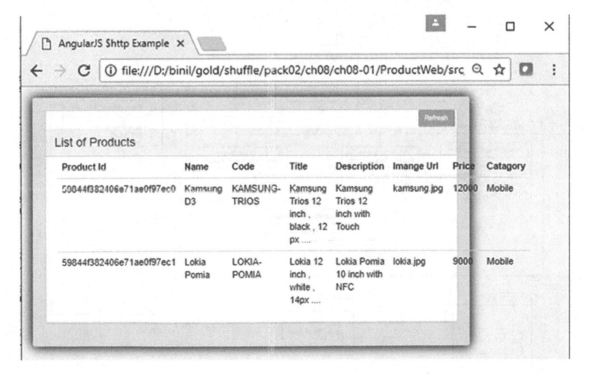

Figure 8-3. *Testing the Feign client*

Hystrix Fallback

There are times when a particular microservice is busy—or a particular database, or for that matter any resource—so it is not in a position to respond back within the expected SLA. In such scenarios, the caller service cannot wait on the dependent service endlessly, so there should be alternate strategies. You'll handle a scenario with the Hystrix circuit breaker falling back to an alternate strategy.

Circuit breakers can gracefully degrade functionality when a method call to a service or to a resource fails. Use of the circuit breaker pattern can allow a microservice to continue its operations when a dependent service fails. This will prevent the failure from cascading, thus giving the failing service enough time to recover.

Design a Hystrix Fallback Scenario

You are going to expand the sample from the previous section (illustrated in Figure 8-1). Figure 8-4 illustrates the simple scenario where there are three separate applications or, in our terms, three separate microservices: Product Web, Product Server 1, and Product Server 2.

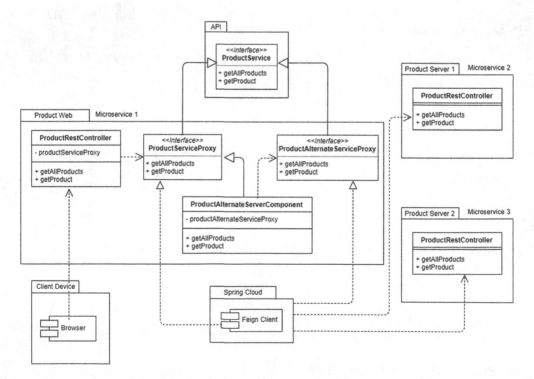

Figure 8-4. *A Hystrix fallback usage scenario*

The main components for the sample scenario are

- Product Server 1

- Product Server 2

- Product Web

- Product Service

- ProductServiceProxy

- ProductAlternateServiceComponent

- ProductAlternateServiceProxy

- Spring Cloud Feign Client

The explanation for many of the above components is the same as that provided in the "Feign Client" section earlier, so I won't duplicate it here. However, I will explain the new components.

- **ProductAlternateServiceComponent**: Product Web is designed to delegate all REST calls coming to it to the Product Server 1 microservice. However, if the Product Server 1 microservice is down or not responding for some reason, you can design a Hystrix callback to a fallback component named ProductAlternateServiceComponent. In real life, this can be a local cache from where you can respond to the client with alternate data. However, in your sample, you have already seen how a Feign client can be used to proxy calls to a remote service. So, you will have a ProductAlternateServiceProxy component to which calls can be proxied.

- **Product Server 2**: Product Server 2 is a full-fledged microservice application duplicating the CRUD operations implemented in Product Server 1. This microservice again uses a Mongo DB to write to and read from the data pertaining to product entities. This microservice acts as an alternate microservice implementation and can serve requests if Product Server 1 is not responding.

- **ProductAlternateServiceProxy**: The ProductAlternateServiceProxy component is another abstract interface that extends Product Service, so it gets all the methods expected out of both the Product Server and the Product Web interfaces. This is the interface you annotate with the Feign client essential configurations in such a way that all calls can be proxied to the Product Server 2 microservice.

You will split the component interaction into two, as shown in Figure 8-5 and Figure 8-6. In Figure 8-5, you can see that the query from the client-side browser hits Product Web, which is Microservice 1 in the sample. The Product Web microservice then proxies the query to Microservice 2, which is Product Server 1. If Product Server 1 is up and running, then the sample execution will end after responding back to the client with the response data, and so this sample will behave exactly like the previous sample from the "Feign Client" section. Instead, you can either not bring the Product Server 1 up or, if it's already up, you can bring it down. In that case, Hystrix will retry to the fallback service configured.

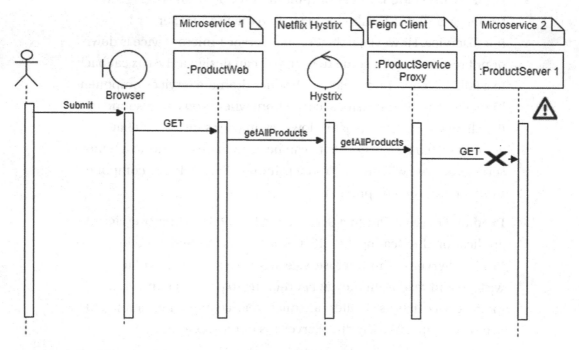

Figure 8-5. *Hystrix detects service non-availability*

Assuming the fallback microservice Product Server 2 is up, the query will be retried to hit this microservice and the execution will happen through the happy flow depicted in Figure 8-6.

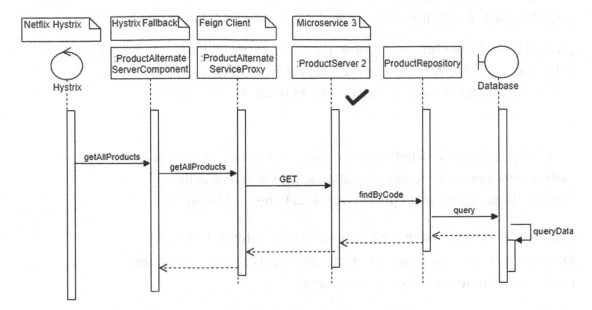

Figure 8-6. *Hystrix retries the alternate service*

Code the Hystrix Fallback Scenario

You have already seen how the Feign client is declared in your POM. Similarly, you can bring the Hystrix dependencies by declaring them again in the POM. All the code samples for this section are placed in folder ch08\ch08-02. Visit pom.xml to see the explicit mention of the Hystrix dependency. See Listing 8-4.

Listing 8-4. Spring Cloud Hystrix Dependency (ch08\ch08-02\ProductWeb\ pom.xml)

```
<dependency>
    <groupId>org.springframework.cloud</groupId>
    <artifactId>spring-cloud-starter-hystrix</artifactId>
</dependency>
```

Next, you need to mention the Hystrix fallback. This is mentioned in the ProductServiceProxy; see Listing 8-5.

Listing 8-5. Hystrix Fallback Declaration (ch08\ch08-02\ProductWeb\src\main\ java\com\acme\ecom\product\client\ProductServiceProxy.java)

```
@FeignClient(name="product-proxy", url = "http://localhost:8080",
fallback = ProductAlternateServerComponent.class)
public interface ProductServiceProxy extends ProductService{

}
```

Here you have instructed Hystrix to consider ProductAlternateServerComponent as the component to be retried as a fallback. Let's now look at the ProductAlternateServerComponent code mentioned in Listing 8-6.

Listing 8-6. Hystrix Fallback Implementation (ch08\ch08-02\ ProductWeb\src\main/java\com\acme\ecom\product\component\ ProductAlternateServerComponent.java)

```
@EnableFeignClients(basePackageClasses = ProductAlternateServiceProxy.class)
@ComponentScan(basePackageClasses = ProductAlternateServiceProxy.class)
@Component
public class ProductAlternateServerComponent implements
ProductServiceProxy{

private ProductAlternateServiceProxy productAlternateServiceProxy;

    @Autowired
    public ProductAlternateServerComponent(
            ProductAlternateServiceProxy productAlternateServiceProxy){

        this.productAlternateServiceProxy = productAlternateServiceProxy;
    }

    @Override
    public ResponseEntity<Resources<Resource<Product>>> getAllProducts() {
```

```
    return productAlternateServiceProxy.getAllProducts();
}

@Override
public ResponseEntity<Resource<Product>> getProduct(
        @PathVariable("productId") String productId) {

    return productAlternateServiceProxy.getProduct(productId);

}
}
```

One approach is to have ProductAlternateServerComponent respond with some kind of locally cached data as a fallback. However, since you have an alternate microservice designated as a fallback service, you can leverage it here. You have also leveraged the Feign client to delegate the call to the Product Server 2 microservice. For this Feign client, you will make use of ProductAlternateServiceProxy with the code from Listing 8-7.

Listing 8-7. Feign Client Proxy to Alternate Microservice (ch08\ch08-02\ProductWeb\src\main\java\com\acme\ecom\product\client\ProductAlternateServiceProxy.java)

```
@FeignClient(name="product-alternate-proxy", url = "http://localhost:8079")
public interface ProductAlternateServiceProxy extends ProductService{

}
```

Here you expect that the Product Server 2 microservice is available at http://localhost:8079, which will act as the fallback for the Product Server 1 microservice, which is expected to be available at http://localhost:8080.

You now need to enable Hystrix and configure its timeout interval, which you do in

ch08\ch08-02\ProductWeb\src\main\resources\application.properties:

```
feign.hystrix.enabled=true
hystrix.command.default.execution.isolation.thread.
timeoutInMilliseconds=2000
```

The rest of the code is similar to what you saw in the "Feign Client" section, so I won't repeat the explanation here. Instead, let's execute the code.

Build and Test the Hystrix Fallback Scenario

The complete code required to demonstrate the Hystrix fallback is kept inside folder ch08-02. Make sure MongoDB is up and running. You may want to refer to Appendix A to get started with MongoDB.

You first build and package the executables for the Product Server 1 microservice and bring up the server. A utility script that you can easily execute is in folder ch08\ch08-02\ProductServer\make.bat.

```
cd ch08\ch08-02\ProductServer
D:\binil\gold\pack03\ch08\ch08-02\ProductServer>make
D:\binil\gold\pack03\ch08\ch08-02\ProductServer>mvn -Dmaven.test.skip=true
clean package
```

You can run the Spring Boot application in more than one way. The straightforward way is to execute the JAR file via the following commands:

```
cd ch08\ch08-02\ProductServer
D:\binil\gold\pack03\ch08\ch08-02\ProductServer>run
D:\binil\gold\pack03\ch08\ch08-02\ProductServer>java -jar -Dserver.
port=8080 .\target\Ecom-Product-Microservice-0.0.1-SNAPSHOT.jar
```

These commands will bring up the Product Server in port 8080. You will now build and package the executables for the Product Server 2 microservice and bring up the server in a new command window:

```
cd ch08\ch08-02\ProductServerAlternate
D:\binil\gold\pack03\ch08\ch08-02\ProductServerAlternate>make
D:\binil\gold\pack03\ch08\ch08-02\ProductServerAlternate>mvn -Dmaven.test.
skip=true clean package
D:\binil\gold\pack03\ch08\ch08-02\ProductServerAlternate>run
D:\binil\gold\pack03\ch08\ch08-02\ProductServerAlternate>java -jar
-Dserver.port=8079 .\target\Ecom-Product-Microservice-0.0.1-SNAPSHOT.jar
```

Next, build and package the executables for the Product Web microservice and bring up the server:

```
cd ch08\ch08-02\ProductWeb
D:\binil\gold\pack03\ch08\ch08-02\ProductWeb>make
D:\binil\gold\pack03\ch08\ch08-02\ProductWeb>mvn -Dmaven.test.skip=true
clean package
D:\binil\gold\pack03\ch08\ch08-02\ProductWeb>run
D:\binil\gold\pack03\ch08\ch08-02\ProductWeb>java -jar -Dserver.port=8081
.\target\Ecom-Product-Microservice-0.0.1-SNAPSHOT.jar
```

These commands will bring up Product Web in port 8081. You may open this HTML utility preferably in the Chrome browser:

```
ch08\ch08-02\ProductWeb\src\main\resources\product.html
```

Upon loading itself, the browser client will fire a request to Product Web, which is listening on port 8081, and it will delegate the calls to Product Server 1 listening at 8080 by proxying through the Feign client.

Repeated browser refreshing will also point the hits to Product Server 1, which you can verify by looking at the log happening in its command window. To demonstrate Hystrix fallback, simply bring down Product Server 1 and refresh the browser. This time you will see the hits coming to Product Alternate Server. You can also see corresponding logs in the Product Web microservice console, as shown in Listing 8-8.

Listing 8-8. Hystric Fallback in Action

```
D:\binil\gold\pack03\ch08\ch08-02\ProductWeb>run
```

```
D:\binil\gold\pack03\ch08\ch08-02\ProductWeb>java -jar -Dserver.port=8081 .\
target\Ecom-Product-Microservice-0.0.1-SNAPSHOT.jar
```

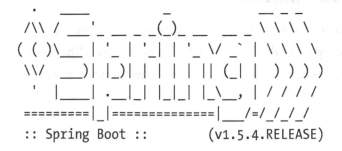

```
  .   ___          _            __ _ _
 /\\ / ___'_ __ _ _(_)_ __  __ _ \ \ \ \
( ( )\___ | '_ | '_| | '_ \/ _` | \ \ \ \
 \\/  ___)| |_)| | | | | || (_| |  ) ) ) )
  '  |____| .__|_| |_|_| |_\__, | / / / /
 =========|_|==============|___/=/_/_/_/
 :: Spring Boot ::        (v1.5.4.RELEASE)
```

```
2019-02-21 16:53:59 INFO  org.springframework.boot.SpringApplication.
logStartupProfileInfo:593 - No active profile set, falling back to default
profiles: default
2019-02-21 16:54:10 INFO  com.acme.ecom.product.InitializationComponent.
init:61- Start
2019-02-21 16:54:10 DEBUG com.acme.ecom.product.InitializationComponent.
init:63- Doing Nothing...
2019-02-21 16:54:10 INFO  com.acme.ecom.product.InitializationComponent.
init:65- End
2019-02-21 16:54:13 INFO  org.springframework.boot.StartupInfoLogger.
logStarted:57 - Started EcomProductMicroserviceApplication in 25.369 econds
(JVM running for 30.007)
2019-02-21 16:56:41 INFO  com.acme.ecom.product.controller.
ProductRestController.getAllProducts:84 - Delegating...
2019-02-21 16:56:57 INFO  com.acme.ecom.product.controller.
ProductRestController.getAllProducts:84 - Delegating...
2019-02-21 16:56:58 INFO  com.acme.ecom.product.component.ProductAlternateS
erverComponent.getAllProducts:78 - Delegating...
```

Hystrix Dashboard

A Hystrix dashboard can be used to provide a graphical overview of a circuit breaker in the system. In a typical microservices architecture, there will be more than one microservice processes and in such cases, you will need to monitor more than one circuit breaker in the application. For this, you can use Turbine, which is not explained here. In this section, you will see how to enable a Hystrix dashboard.

Redesign a Hystrix Fallback Method

You will now slightly modify the Feign and Hystrix design from the "Hystrix Fallback" section. The idea is to first demonstrate yet another way of defining a Hystrix fallback and afterwards demonstrate the Hystrix dashboard. The refactored design is shown in Figure 8-7.

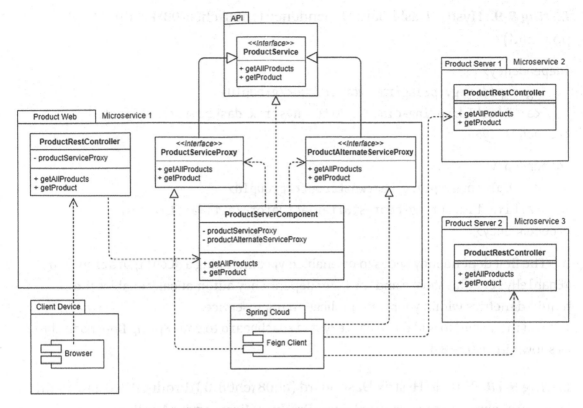

Figure 8-7. *Refactored design for the Hystrix fallback*

In the refactored design, all of the Feign client interactions have moved from the Controller to a Component class. So the Product Server Component now depends on the two proxies, which will get injected with Feign client proxies at runtime.

Code the New Design of Hystrix

All the code samples for this section are placed in folder ch08\ch08-03. The Hystrix dashboard application is yet another Spring Boot application. To enable it, you need to follow a few steps. Visit pom.xml to see the explicit mention of the Hystrix dashboard dependency in Listing 8-9.

Listing 8-9. Hystrix Dashboard Dependency (ch08\ch08-03\ProductWeb\
pom.xml)

```
<dependency>
    <groupId>org.springframework.cloud</groupId>
    <artifactId>spring-cloud-starter-hystrix-dashboard</artifactId>
</dependency>

<dependency>
    <groupId>org.springframework.boot</groupId>
    <artifactId>spring-boot-starter-actuator</artifactId>
</dependency>
```

The first dependency needs to be enabled via annotating a @Configuration with
@EnableHystrixDashboard and the latter dependency automatically enables the
required metrics within your web-application microservice.

You then need to add the @EnableHystrixDashboard to your Spring Boot main class,
as shown in Listing 8-10.

Listing 8-10. Enable Hystrix Dashboard (ch08\ch08-03\ProductWeb\src\main\
java\com\acme\ecom\product\EcomProductMicroserviceApplication.java)

```
@SpringBootApplication
@EnableCircuitBreaker
@EnableHystrixDashboard
@Configuration
public class EcomProductMicroserviceApplication {

    public static void main(String[] args) {

        SpringApplication.run(EcomProductMicroserviceApplication.class,
        args);
    }
}
```

The Rest Controller delegates all calls to ProductServerComponent, as shown in
Listing 8-11.

Listing 8-11. REST Controller (ch08\ch08-03\ProductWeb\src\main\java\com\
acme\ecom\product\controller\ProductRestController.java)

```
@RestController
public class ProductRestController implements ProductService{

    private ProductServerComponent productServerComponent;

    @Autowired
    public ProductRestController(ProductServerComponent
            productServerComponent){

        this.productServerComponent = productServerComponent;
    }

    @RequestMapping(value = "/productsweb", method = RequestMethod.GET ,
            produces = {MediaType.APPLICATION_JSON_VALUE})
    public ResponseEntity<Resources<Resource<Product>>> getAllProducts() {

        return productServerComponent.getAllProducts();
    }

    @RequestMapping(value = "/productsweb/{productId}",
        method = RequestMethod.GET,
        produces = MediaType.APPLICATION_JSON_VALUE)
    public ResponseEntity<Resource<Product>> getProduct(
            @PathVariable("productId") String productId) {

        return productServerComponent.getProduct(productTd);
    }
}
```

As you can see in Listing 8-11, ProductRestController simply delegates the call to
the ProductServerComponent. In ProductServerComponent, you mark the methods as
HystrixCommand, and for each HystrixCommand you also define fallback methods, as
shown in Listing 8-12.

Listing 8-12. Hystrix Commands (ch08\ch08-03\ProductWeb\src\main\java\ com\acme\ecom\product\component\ProductServerComponent.java)

```java
import com.netflix.hystrix.contrib.javanica.annotation.HystrixCommand;

@EnableFeignClients(basePackageClasses = {ProductServiceProxy.class,
    ProductAlternateServiceProxy.class})
@ComponentScan(basePackageClasses = {ProductServiceProxy.class,
        ProductAlternateServiceProxy.class})
public class ProductServerComponent implements ProductService{

    private ProductServiceProxy productServiceProxy;
    private ProductAlternateServiceProxy productAlternateServiceProxy;

@HystrixCommand(fallbackMethod = "getAllTheProducts")
    public ResponseEntity<Resources<Resource<Product>>> getAllProducts() {

        return productServiceProxy.getAllProducts();
    }

    @HystrixCommand(fallbackMethod = "getTheProduct")
    public ResponseEntity<Resource<Product>> getProduct(
            @PathVariable("productId") String productId) {

        return productServiceProxy.getProduct(productId);
    }

    public ResponseEntity<Resources<Resource<Product>>> getAllTheProducts() {

        return productAlternateServiceProxy.getAllProducts();
    }

    public ResponseEntity<Resource<Product>> getTheProduct(
            @PathVariable("productId") String productId) {

        return productAlternateServiceProxy.getProduct(productId);
    }
}
```

As you can see, if Product Server 1 is down, a call to productServiceProxy. getAllProducts() will fail, and since you have declared getAllTheProducts() as the fallback method, a retry will happen with a call to productAlternateServiceProxy. The fallback method is used by Hystrix in case of an error (the call to the productServiceProxy service fails or a timeout occurs) or to fast fail if the circuit is open.

Build and Test the Hystrix Fallback Scenario

The complete code required to demonstrate the Hystrix fallback is kept inside folder ch08-03. Make sure MongoDB is up and running. You can then build, pack, and run the three microservices in the following order:

```
cd ch08\ch08-03\ProductServer
D:\binil\gold\pack03\ch08\ch08-03\ProductServer>make
D:\binil\gold\pack03\ch08\ch08-03\ProductServer>mvn -Dmaven.test.skip=true
clean package
D:\binil\gold\pack03\ch08\ch08-03\ProductServer>run
D:\binil\gold\pack03\ch08\ch08-03\ProductServer>java -jar -Dserver.
port=8080 .\target\Ecom-Product-Microservice-0.0.1-SNAPSHOT.jar

cd ch08\ch08-03\ProductServerAlternate
D:\binil\gold\pack03\ch08\ch08-03\ProductServerAlternate>make
D:\binil\gold\pack03\ch08\ch08-03\ProductServerAlternate>mvn -Dmaven.test.
skip=true clean package
D:\binil\gold\pack03\ch08\ch08-03\ProductServerAlternate>run
D:\binil\gold\pack03\ch08\ch08-03\ProductServerAlternate>java -jar
-Dserver.port=8079 .\target\Ecom-Product-Microservice-0.0.1-SNAPSHOT.jar

cd ch08\ch08-03\ProductWeb
D:\binil\gold\pack03\ch08\ch08-03\ProductWeb>make
D:\binil\gold\pack03\ch08\ch08-03\ProductWeb>mvn -Dmaven.test.skip=true
clean package
D:\binil\gold\pack03\ch08\ch08-03\ProductWeb>run
D:\binil\gold\pack03\ch08\ch08-03\ProductWeb>java -jar -Dserver.port=8081
.\target\Ecom-Product-Microservice-0.0.1-SNAPSHOT.jar
```

The last command will bring up Product Web in port 8081. You may open this HTML utility preferably in the Chrome browser:

ch08\ch08-03\ProductWeb\src\main\resources\product.html

Upon loading itself, the browser client will fire a request to Product Web, listening in port 8081, which will delegate the calls to Product Server 1, listening at 8080, by proxying through the Feign client.

Repeated browser refreshing will also point the hits to Product Server 1, which you can verify by looking at the log happening in its command window. To demonstrate Hystrix fallback, simply bring down Product Server 1 and refresh the browser. This time you will see the hits coming to Product Server 2. You can also see corresponding logs in the Product Server microservice console.

Inspect Hystrix Dashboard

The Hystrix dashboard (Figure 8-8) is available at the following URL in your case:

http://localhost:8081/hystrix

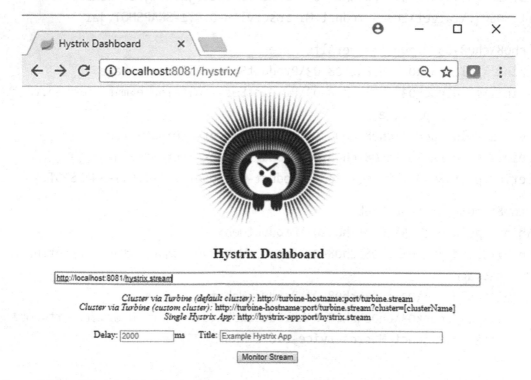

Figure 8-8. *Hystrix dashboard*

The Hystrix dashboard will ask for the URL of a Hystrix stream. Every Hystrix-enabled application produces a stream where the status of all circuits is constantly written. The URL is of the form `http://application-node:port/hystrix.stream`, and in your case the URL is `http://localhost:8081/hystrix.stream`. The stream can be monitored from the dashboard, as shown in Figure 8-9.

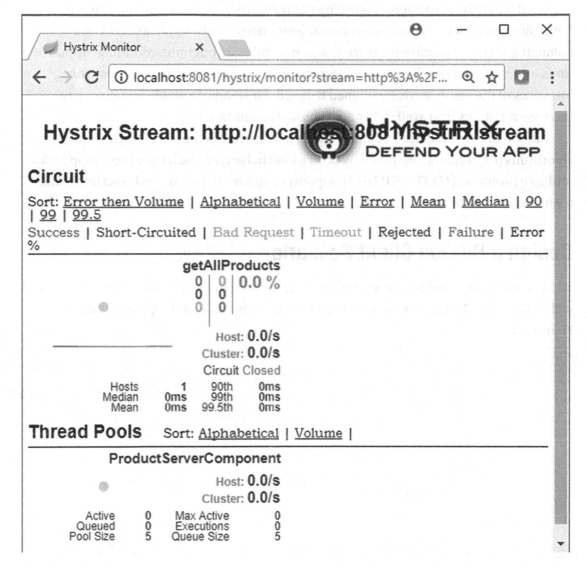

Figure 8-9. Stream monitoring in Hystrix dashboard

Ribbon, the Client-Side Load Balancer

Having looked at the Feign client and the Hystrix fallback, now is the right time to introduce the next important component in Spring Cloud: Ribbon. Ribbon is a client-side load balancer that gives you extra control over the behavior of HTTP and TCP clients. Feign already uses Ribbon, so understanding Ribbon is crucial.

Load balancing distributes incoming traffic between two or more microservices. It enables you to achieve fault tolerance in your microservice applications. Load balancing aims to optimize resource usage, maximize throughput, minimize response time, and avoid overloading any single microservice. Using multiple microservice instances of the same service with load balancing instead of a single instance may increase reliability and availability at the cost of redundancy.

Ribbon offers configuration options such as connection timeouts, retries, retry algorithms (exponential, bounded back off), load balancing, fault tolerance, support for multiple protocols (HTTP, TCP, UDP), support in an asynchronous and reactive model, caching, and batching.

Design a Ribbon Client Scenario

You will use the same design you used in the section for the Feign client. However, you will enhance the Feign client to internally leverage Ribbon. The design is shown in Figure 8-10.

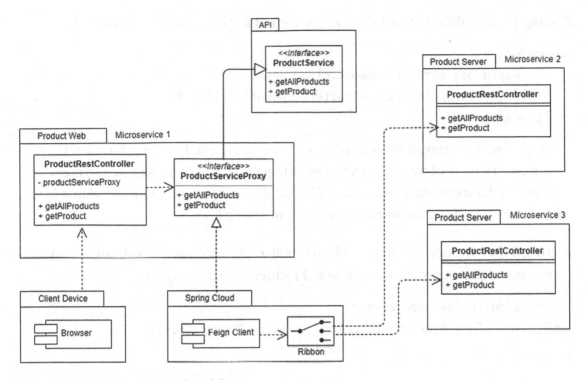

Figure 8-10. *Design with Ribbon*

You will use the same Product Server microservice module you used for previous sections in this chapter. In the previous sections, you also used the Product Server Alternate microservice module; however, in this section you will have only one module, the Product Server microservice module, but you will run two instances of it. This is important since I also want to demonstrate that a microservice can be instantiated to more than one in number (rather, replicated) to scale horizontally provided you have taken care of other design aspects like statelessness, idempotency, etc.

Code to Use Ribbon Client

All the code samples for this section are placed in folder ch08\ch08-04. Visit pom.xml to see the explicit mention of the Ribbon dependency. See Listing 8-13.

Listing 8-13. Ribbon Dependency (ch08\ch08-04\ProductWeb\pom.xml)

```
<dependency>
    <groupId>org.springframework.cloud</groupId>
    <artifactId>spring-cloud-starter-ribbon</artifactId>
</dependency>
```

The central concept of Ribbon is that of the named client. Each load balancer is part of an ensemble of components that work together to contact a remote server on demand, and the ensemble has a name that you give it as an application developer (e.g. using the @FeignClient annotation) as shown in Listing 8-14.

Listing 8-14. Named Client in Ribbon (ch08\ch08-04\ProductWeb\src\main\ java\com\acme\ecom\product\client\ProductServiceProxy.java)

```
@FeignClient(name="product-proxy")
public interface ProductServiceProxy extends ProductService{

}
```

You now need to provide configuration values to Ribbon, which you will do in ch08\ ch08-04\ProductWeb\src\main\resources\application.properties:

```
product-proxy.ribbon.listOfServers=localhost:8080,localhost:8081
```

This is it, and this will do all the required plumbing.

Build and Test the Ribbon Client

The complete code required to demonstrate Ribbon is kept inside folder ch08-04. Make sure MongoDB is up and running. You can then build, pack, and run the three microservices in the following order:

```
cd ch08\ch08-04\ProductServer
D:\binil\gold\pack03\ch08\ch08-04\ProductServer>make
D:\binil\gold\pack03\ch08\ch08-04\ProductServer>mvn -Dmaven.test.skip=true
clean package
```

```
D:\binil\gold\pack03\ch08\ch08-04\ProductServer>run1
D:\binil\gold\pack03\ch08\ch08-04\ProductServer>java -jar -Dserver.
port=8080 .\target\Ecom-Product-Microservice-0.0.1-SNAPSHOT.jar

cd ch08\ch08-04\ProductServer
D:\binil\gold\pack03\ch08\ch08-04\ProductServer>run2
D:\binil\gold\pack03\ch08\ch08-04\ProductServer>java -jar -Dserver.
port=8081 .\target\Ecom-Product-Microservice-0.0.1-SNAPSHOT.jar

cd ch08\ch08-03\ProductWeb
D:\binil\gold\pack03\ch08\ch08-04\ProductWeb>make
D:\binil\gold\pack03\ch08\ch08-04\ProductWeb>mvn -Dmaven.test.skip=true
clean package
D:\binil\gold\pack03\ch08\ch08-04\ProductWeb>run
D:\binil\gold\pack03\ch08\ch08-04\ProductWeb>java -jar -Dserver.port=8082
.\target\Ecom-Product-Microservice-0.0.1-SNAPSHOT.jar
```

The last command will bring up Product Web in port 8082. You should have noted that the two instances of the Product Server microservices are running in port 8080 and 8081. This explains why you used the following configuration:

```
product-proxy.ribbon.listOfServers=localhost:8080,localhost:8081
```

You may now open this HTML utility preferably in the Chrome browser:

```
ch08\ch08-04\ProductWeb\src\main\resources\product.html
```

Upon loading itself, the browser client will fire a request to the Product Web listening in port 8082, which will delegate the call to any one instance of the Product Server microservice by proxying through the Feign client.

Repeated browser refreshing will load balance the hits from the Product Web microservice to either of the Product Server microservice instances, which you can verify by looking at the log happening in the command window of the Product Server microservice. If you bring down one of the Product Server microservices and refresh the browser, you will see that the hits will always go to the other Product Server instance running. If you reinstate the Product Server microservice you brought down earlier, the Ribbon load balancing will again come into action, alternating calls from the Product Web microservice to both instances of the Product Server microservice.

Eureka, the Service Registry

Eureka is a REST-based registry service that is primarily used in public cloud-based deployments, especially in the AWS cloud. Using Eureka you can locate microservices for the purpose of load balancing and failover. Eureka is Spring Cloud's service registry, which acts as a phone book for your microservices. Each microservice self-registers with the service registry, telling the registry where it lives (host, node name, port, etc.) and perhaps other service-specific metadata. Eureka has two parts, the Eureka Server and a client component, the Eureka Client, which makes interactions with the registry service much easier. The client also has a built-in load balancer that does basic round-robin load balancing.

A service registry like Eureka has another feature that provides one or more levels of indirection for service consumers. This means service consumers can do a registry look-up using a logical service name, and this logical service name may be mapped to a different actual deployed service whose physical address entries are mapped against the above logical name. This insulates the service consumers from any changes happening to actual service details or whatever in the physical deployment environment. In the sample explained in the "Ribbon" section, you might have noticed hard-coded values for the service URL like:

```
localhost:8080,localhost:8081
```

This is not a good practice. A DNS (Domaine Name System) is used to resolve similar problems; however, a DNS is comparatively heavy when you consider hundreds of microservices within an enterprise application. Further, you do not want to expose the server details of your microservices outside your perimeter or DMZ (Demilitarized Zone). Typically the service consumers in a microservice-based enterprise application are other microservices. Hence these microservice have to ask questions like service topology ("Are there any 'product-services' available, and if so, where?") and service capabilities ("Can you handle A, B, and C?"). This is where service registries like Eureka and Consul come into play. Eureka does not impose any restrictions on the protocol or method of communication, so you can use Eureka to use protocols such as thrift, http(s) or any other RPC mechanisms.

You might still doubt the need for Eureka when there are already many software and hardware load balancers, including AWS Elastic Load Balancer and AWS Route 53. AWS Elastic Load Balancer is used to expose edge services, which typically connect to end-user web traffic whereas Eureka fills the need for mid-tier load balancing or, in our nomenclature, microservices registration and load balancing. Route 53 is analogous to a DNS service where you can host your DNS records even for non-AWS data centers, so it comes with the associated drawbacks of the traditional DNS-based load-balancing solutions where your traffic can still be routed to servers that may not be healthy or may not even exist, which is very typical in the case of public cloud-based deployments like AWS provisioned for auto scaling. Since you should prefer your microservices to be stateless (non-sticky), Eureka facilitates a much better scalability model since your microservices can be resilient to the outages of the load balancers (Eureka) because the information regarding the available servers is cached on the client. This does require a small amount of memory, but this increased resiliency doesn't penalize the overall resource concerns much.

Design a Eureka-Enabled Scenario

You will modify the design by introducing few new components, as shown in Figure 8-11. Here you replace ProductServiceProxy with RestTemplate. This means the Product Web microservice will now use RestTemplate to consume any of the instances of the Product Server microservice. RestTemplate simplifies communication with HTTP servers, and the "Develop a RESTful Web Service" section in Chapter 7 already explained how to use RestTemplate to communicate with RestController. You will extend that here. Another intention of using RestTemplate is that you can use Ribbon indirectly via an autoconfigured RestTemplate when RestTemplate is on the classpath and a LoadBalancerClient bean is defined so that you build over the previous sample of Ribbon itself.

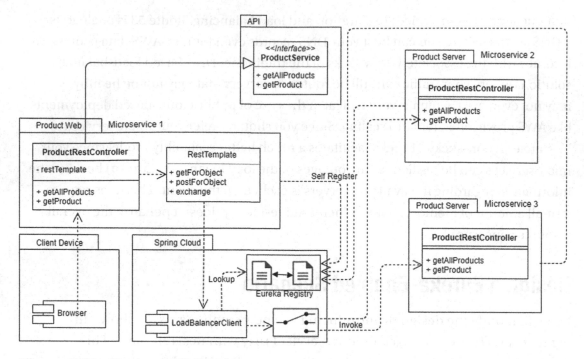

Figure 8-11. *Design with Eureka*

By enabling the Eureka registry, all microservices will self-register to the registry when brought up. Further, in a previous sample you saw how to bring redundancy by instantiating the same Product Server microservice more than once. You will follow the same pattern for Eureka so that there is redundancy at the service registry level too.

Code to Use Eureka

All the code samples for this section are placed in folder ch08\ch08-05. Visit pom.xml to see the explicit mention of the Eureka Server dependency. See Listing 8-15.

Listing 8-15. Eureka Dependency (ch08\ch08-05\Eureka\pom.xml)

```
<dependency>
    <groupId>org.springframework.cloud</groupId>
    <artifactId>spring-cloud-starter-eureka-server</artifactId>
</dependency>
```

Next, you need Spring Cloud's @EnableEurekaServer to stand up a registry that other microservices can talk to. This is done in your regular Spring Boot application main class with one annotation added to enable the service registry. See Listing 8-16.

Listing 8-16. Enable Eureka Server (ch08\ch08-05\Eureka\src\main\java\com\ acme\ecom\infra\EurekaRegistryApplication.java)

```
@EnableEurekaServer
@SpringBootApplication
public class EurekaRegistryApplication {

public static void main(String[] args) {

        SpringApplication.run(EurekaRegistryApplication.class, args);
    }
}
```

When Eureka comes up, it will attempt to register itself, so you need to disable that; see Listing 8-17.

Listing 8-17. Eureka Configuration (ch08\ch08-05\Eureka\src\main\resources\ application.properties)

```
spring.application.name=eureka-registry
server.port=8761
eureka.client.registerWithEureka=false
eureka.client.fetchRegistry=true
eureka.client.server.waitTimeInMsWhenSyncEmpty=0
eureka.client.serviceUrl.defaultZone=http://localhost:8761/eureka/,http://
localhost:8762/eureka/
eureka.server.enableSelfPreservation=false
```

If you want to bring multiple instances of Eureka registry with this single properties file, you need to override at least the first two parameters. You do so in the following two scripts:

```
ch08\ch08-05\Eureka\run1.bat
```

```
java -jar -Dserver.port=8761 -Dspring.application.name=eureka-registry1 .\
target\Ecom-Product-Microservice-0.0.1-SNAPSHOT.jar
```

```
ch08\ch08-05\Eureka\run2.bat
```

```
java -jar -Dserver.port=8762 -Dspring.application.name=eureka-registry2 .\
target\Ecom-Product-Microservice-0.0.1-SNAPSHOT.jar
```

Since you are dealing with HAL-based JSON data, you want to configure the REST template you want to use in the Product Web microservice to invoke calls in the Product Server microservice to deal with HAL-formatted data. See Listing 8-18.

Listing 8-18. Rest Template Configuration to Handle HAL JSON Format (ch08\ ch08-05\ProductWeb\src\main\java\com\acme\ecom\product\controller\ RestTemplateConfiguration.java)

```java
@Configuration
public class RestTemplateConfiguration{

@LoadBalanced
    @Bean
    public RestTemplate restTemplate() {

        return new RestTemplate(getRequiredMessageConvertors());
    }

    private List<HttpMessageConverter getRequiredMessageConvertors(){

        ObjectMapper mapper = new ObjectMapper();
        mapper.configure(DeserializationFeature.FAIL_ON_UNKNOWN_PROPERTIES,
            false);
        mapper.registerModule(new Jackson2HalModule());
        MappingJackson2HttpMessageConverter converter =
            new MappingJackson2HttpMessageConverter();
        converter.setSupportedMediaTypes(MediaType.parseMediaTypes(
            "application/hal+json, application/json"));
        converter.setObjectMapper(mapper);
        return Arrays.asList(converter);
    }
}
```

The Product Server microservice and the Product Web microservice must register themselves with the registry and use the Spring Cloud DiscoveryClient abstraction to interrogate the registry for their own host and port. You can use the @EnableEurekaClient to activate the Netflix Eureka DiscoveryClient implementation. EnableEurekaClient is a convenience annotation for clients to enable the Eureka discovery configuration (specifically). This annotation turns on discovery and lets the autoconfiguration find the Eureka classes if they are available. See Listing 8-19.

Listing 8-19. Enable Eureka Client (ch08\ch08-05\ProductServer\src\main\ java\com\acme\ecom\product\EcomProductMicroserviceApplication.java)

```
@SpringBootApplication
@EnableEurekaClient
public class EcomProductMicroserviceApplication {

public static void main(String[] args) {

        SpringApplication.run(EcomProductMicroserviceApplication.class,
        args);
    }
}
```

Visit pom.xml to see the explicit mention of the Eureka dependency. See Listing 8-20.

Listing 8-20. Eureka Dependency (ch08\ch08-05\ProductServer\pom.xml)

```
<dependency>
    <groupId>org.springframework.cloud</groupId>
    <artifactId>spring-cloud-starter-eureka</artifactId>
</dependency>
```

You saw the ProductController code in the "Develop a RESTful Web Service" section in Chapter 7 when retrieving the product data from the database using ProductRepository, so I will not explain the ProductController in the Product Server microservice again. However, you need to inspect the full code of the ProductController used by the Product Web microservice, since this code demonstrates how to disassemble a HATEOAS-based HTTP response completely and next assemble it back again to create a HATEOAS-based HTTP response to return back. Listing 8-21 shows the code for getAllProducts().

Listing 8-21. Dissemble and Assemble getAllProducts HAL JSON Data (ch08\
ch08-05\ ProductWeb\src\main\java\com\acme\ecom\product\controller\
ProductRestController.java)

```
@CrossOrigin
@RestController
public class ProductRestController implements ProductService{

    @Autowired
    RestTemplate restTemplate;

    private static String PRODUCT_SERVICE_URL =
        "http://product-service/products";

    @Autowired
    public ProductRestController(RestTemplate restTemplate){

        this.restTemplate = restTemplate;
    }

    @RequestMapping(value = "/productsweb",
        method = RequestMethod.GET,
        produces = {MediaType.APPLICATION_JSON_VALUE})
    public ResponseEntity<Resources<Resource<Product>>> getAllProducts() {

        ParameterizedTypeReference<PagedResources<Product>>
            responseTypeRef =
                new ParameterizedTypeReference<PagedResources<Product>>() {};
        ResponseEntity<PagedResources<Product>> responseEntity =
            restTemplate.exchange(PRODUCT_SERVICE_URL, HttpMethod.GET,
             (HttpEntity<Product>) null, responseTypeRef);
        PagedResources<Product> resources = responseEntity.getBody();
        Collection<Product> products = resources.getContent();
        List<Product> productList = new ArrayList<Product>(products);
```

```
Link links[] =
    {linkTo(methodOn(ProductRestController.class).getAllProducts()).
    withSelfRel(),linkTo(methodOn(ProductRestController.class).
    getAllProducts()).withRel("getAllProducts")};
if(products.isEmpty()){
    return new ResponseEntity<Resources<Resource<Product>>>(
        HttpStatus.NOT_FOUND);
}

List<Resource<Product>> list = new ArrayList<Resource<Product>> ();
for(Product product:products){
    list.add(new Resource<Product>(product,
        linkTo(methodOn(ProductRestController.class).
        getProduct(product.getId())).withSelfRel()));
}

Resources<Resource<Product>> productResponse =
    new Resources<Resource<Product>>(list, links) ;
return new ResponseEntity<Resources<Resource<Product>>>(
    productResponse, HttpStatus.OK);
    }
}
```

Listing 8-21 shows how to dissemble the Product entities you retrieved one by one, and further enrich them to be HAL-formatted data and assemble them to respond back to the client. Listing 8-22 shows similar code for a single product retrieval case.

Listing 8-22. Dissemble and Assemble getProduct HAL JSON Data

```
public class ProductRestController implements ProductService{

    @RequestMapping(value = "/productsweb/{id}", method =
        RequestMethod.GET, produces = MediaType.APPLICATION_JSON_VALUE)
    public ResponseEntity<Resource<Product>> getProduct(
        @PathVariable("id") String id) {
```

```
        Product product = restTemplate.getForObject(
            PRODUCT_SERVICE_URL + "/" + id, Product.class);
        if (product == null) {
            return new ResponseEntity<Resource<Product>>(
                HttpStatus.NOT_FOUND);
        }
        Resource<Product> productResponse = new Resource<Product>(
            product, linkTo(methodOn(ProductRestController.class).
            getProduct(product.getId())).withSelfRel());
        return new ResponseEntity<Resource<Product>>(
            productResponse, HttpStatus.OK);

    }
}
```

The rest of the code is more or less the same as you have seen in earlier samples, so it won't be explained.

Build and Test the Eureka Sample

The complete code required to demonstrate the Eureka registry is kept inside folder ch08-05. Make sure MongoDB is up and running. You can then build, pack, and run the different microservices in the following order:

You first bring up the Eureka registry microservices:

```
cd ch08\ch08-05\Eureka
D:\binil\gold\pack03\ch08\ch08-05\Eureka>make
D:\binil\gold\pack03\ch08\ch08-05\Eureka>mvn -Dmaven.test.skip=true clean
package
D:\binil\gold\pack03\ch08\ch08-05\Eureka>run1
D:\binil\gold\pack03\ch08\ch08-05\Eureka>java -jar -Dserver.port=8761
-Dspring.application.name=eureka-registry1 .\target\Ecom-Product-
Microservice-0.0.1-SNAPSHOT.jar
```

When the first Eureka starts up, it will complain with a stack trace in the console, since the registry cannot find a replica node to connect to. In a production environment, you will want more than one instance of the registry. For your sample purposes, you will bring up one more instance of Eureka.

```
D:\binil\gold\pack03\ch08\ch08-05\Eureka>run2
D:\binil\gold\pack03\ch08\ch08-05\Eureka>java -jar -Dserver.port=8762
-Dspring.application.name=eureka-registry2 .\target\Ecom-Product-
Microservice-0.0.1-SNAPSHOT.jar
```

Note in the Eureka console windows that both instances sync with each other. You may need to wait few seconds before you notice this synchronization. Also note that this kind of delay is characteristic at different stages of the demonstration of this sample, since registry registration, look-ups, and synchronizations all have little delays (which you can control by tweaking the configurations).

Since the registry is all set up now, you can bring up the application microservices next:

```
cd ch08\ch08-05\ProductServer
D:\binil\gold\pack03\ch08\ch08-05\ProductServer>make
D:\binil\gold\pack03\ch08\ch08-05/ProductServer>mvn -Dmaven.test.skip=true
clean package
```

```
D:/binil/gold/pack03/ch08/ch08-05/ProductServer>run1
D:/binil/gold/pack03/ch08/ch08-05/ProductServer>java -Dserver.port=8080
-Dspring.application.name=product-service -Deureka.client.serviceUrl.
defaultZone=http://localhost:8761/eureka/,http://localhost:8762/eureka/
-jar ./target/Ecom-Product-Microservice-0.0.1-SNAPSHOT.jar
```

Listing 8-23 provides a glimpse of what should happen in the Eureka console when you start the microservices.

Listing 8-23. Microservices Registering with Eureka

```
D:\binil\gold\pack03\ch08\ch08-05\Eureka>run1

D:\binil\gold\pack03\ch08\ch08-05\Eureka>java -jar -Dserver.port=8761
-Dspring.application.name=eureka-registry1 .\target\Ecom-Product-
Microservice-0.0.1-SNAPSHOT.jar
2019-02-21 19:09:38.836  INFO 16672 --- [        main] s.c.a.Annota
tionConfigApplicationContext : Refreshing org.springframework.context.
annotation.AnnotationConfigApplicationContext@28ba21f3: startup date [Thu
Feb 21 19:09:38 IST 2019]; root of context hierarchy
```

```
   .   ___          _            __ _ _
  /\\ / ___'_ __ _ _(_)_ __  __ _ \ \ \ \
 ( ( )\___ | '_ | '_| | '_ \/ _` | \ \ \ \
  \\/  ___)| |_)| | | | | || (_| |  ) ) ) )
   '  |____| .__|_| |_|_| |_\__, | / / / /
  =========|_|==============|___/=/_/_/_/
  :: Spring Boot ::        (v1.5.4.RELEASE)
```

2019-02-21 19:10:59.615 INFO 16672 --- [freshExecutor-0] com.netflix.
discovery.DiscoveryClient   : Getting all instance registry info from the
eureka server
2019-02-21 19:10:59.633 INFO 16672 --- [freshExecutor-0] com.netflix.
discovery.DiscoveryClient   : The response status is 200
2019-02-21 19:10:59.646 INFO 16672 --- [a-EvictionTimer] c.n.e.registry.
AbstractInstanceRegistry : Running the evict task with compensationTime 0ms
2019-02-21 19:11:08.318 INFO 16672 --- [nio-8761-exec-4] c.n.e.registry.
AbstractInstanceRegistry : Registered instance **PRODUCT-SERVICE/
tiger:product-service:8080** with status UP (replication=true)
2019-02-21 19:11:29.675 INFO 16672 --- [freshExecutor-0] com.netflix.
discovery.DiscoveryClient   : The response status is 200
2019-02-21 19:11:41.187 INFO 16672 --- [nio-8761-exec-8] c.n.e.registry.
AbstractInstanceRegistry : Registered instance **PRODUCT-SERVICE/
tiger:product-service:8081** with status UP (replication=true)
2019-02-21 19:11:59.647 INFO 16672 --- [a-EvictionTimer] c.n.e.registry.
AbstractInstanceRegistry : Running the evict task with compensationTime 0ms

cd ch08\ch08-05\ProductServer
D:\binil\gold\pack03\ch08\ch08-05\ProductServer>run2
D:\binil\gold\pack03\ch08\ch08-05\ProductServer>java -Dserver.port=8081
-Dspring.application.name=product-service -Deureka.client.serviceUrl.
defaultZone=http://localhost:8761/eureka/,http://localhost:8762/eureka/
-jar .\target\Ecom-Product-Microservice-0.0.1-SNAPSHOT.jar

Note that unlike in the case of Eureka instances, you have started all instances of the
Product Server microservice with the same application name. This is to make explicit
to the registry that both instances in fact point to the same microservice. This will help
Eureka to route to any one of these instances when a look-up comes to this microservice.

Next, bring up the Product Web microservice:

```
cd ch08\ch08-05\ProductWeb
D:\binil\gold\pack03\ch08\ch08-05\ProductWeb>make
D:\binil\gold\pack03\ch08\ch08-05\ProductWeb>mvn -Dmaven.test.skip=true
clean package
D:\binil\gold/pack03/ch08/ch08-05/ProductWeb>run
D:/binil/gold/pack03/ch08/ch08-05/ProductWeb>java -Dserver.port=8082
-Dspring.application.name=product-web -Deureka.client.serviceUrl.
defaultZone=http://localhost:8761/eureka/,http://localhost:8762/eureka/
-jar ./target/Ecom-Product-Microservice-0.0.1-SNAPSHOT.jar
```

The last command will bring up Product Web in port 8082.

You may inspect the Eureka console using a web browser by pointing to the following URLs where you have the registry services running:

```
http://localhost:8761/
http://localhost:8762/
```

See Figure 8-12.

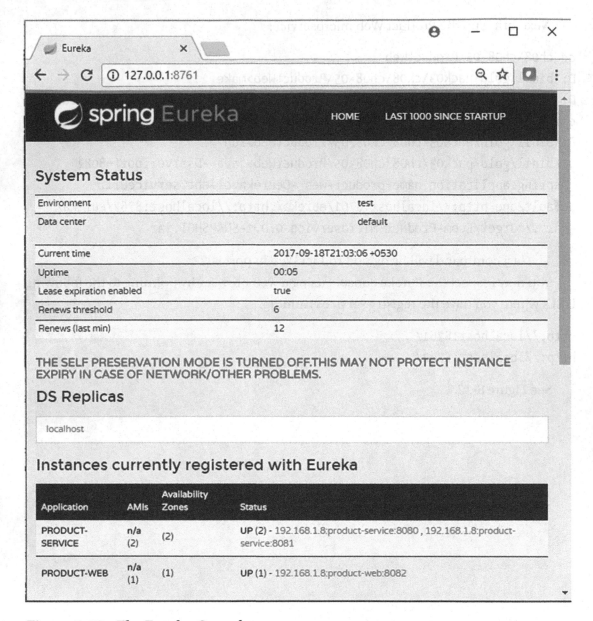

Figure 8-12. *The Eureka Console*

You may now open this HTML utility preferably in the Chrome browser: ch08\
ch08-05\ProductWeb\src\main\resources\product.html.

Upon loading itself, the browser client will fire a request to Product Web, listening
on port 8082, which will delegate the call to any one instance of the Product Server
microservice.

Repeated browser refreshing will load balance the hits from the Product Web microservice to the Product Server microservice instances, which you can verify by looking at the log happening in the command window of the Product Server microservices. If you bring down one of the Product Server microservices and refresh the browser, you will see that the hit will always go to the other Product Server instance running. This is because you use @LoadBalanced for the RestTemplate, which you use to hit the Product Server microservice from the Product Web microservice, as shown in Listing 8-18. If you can bring back the Product Server microservice you brought down earlier, the Ribbon load balancing will again come into action, alternating calls from the Product Web microservice to both instances of the Product Server microservice. Similarly, you may also want to test by bringing down one of the Eureka microservices. Eureka clients are built to handle the failure of one or more Eureka peers in the Eureka farm. Since Eureka clients have the registry information cached with them, they can operate reasonably well, even when all of the available Eureka peers goes down.

Bootstrap Your Bootstrap Server

You should understand by now that every service instance in a microservice-based enterprise application can be registered with the Eureka registry, and this is the case with Eureka registry instances. There is one exception to this, which is the API gateway, which you will look at the next section; until then, ignore this exception. I have said that the Eureka registry is the directory of services for any interested service consumer, so if the service consumer can somehow reach the registry with the name of the service it wants to consume, the registry will provide the information (host, port, etc.) on how to reach that service. Now the golden question is, how does any service consumer reach a registry to start with? In other words, the Eureka registry will help any microservice to bootstrap and advertise itself. But how can a Eureka registry ever advertise itself? How does the bootstrap server bootstrap itself?!

You need a standard set of well-identifiable addresses for Eureka servers. One mechanism is to have an internal DNS or similar service. However, such pinned (IP) addresses will only work in a traditional LAN environment. The moment we talk about deployment in a public cloud like AWS, the scenario changes. In a cloud like AWS, instances come and go. This means you cannot pin Eureka servers with a standard hostname or an IP address. Mechanisms like AWS EC2 Elastic IP addresses must be used here. An Elastic IP address is a static IPv4 address designed for dynamic cloud computing. With an Elastic IP address, you can mask the failure of a microservice by rapidly remapping the address to another instance in your account. You need one Elastic IP for every Eureka server in the cluster. Once you configure your Eureka Server with the list of Elastic IP addresses, the Eureka server deals with the hassle of finding the Elastic IP that is unused and binds it to itself during the start up.

Zuul, the API Gateway

Any service needs to be reached by using an address—more correctly, using a well-known address. Addresses like www.google.com or www.apple.com are examples. Similarly, when you host an enterprise application, it will need to have an address, specifically a home page URL. Such an URL when typed in a browser will lead your request to the landing resource in your web site. Typically, these names or well-known URLs are DNS resolved and directed to a physical IP or a combination of physical IPs. When you deploy applications in a cluster or farm for scalability reasons, you also need a load balancer, which will act as a reverse proxy where the request will land first and then will be load balanced to any one instance in the farm. Apache HTTP server and F5 are similar devices. AWS ELB (Elastic Load Balancer) is a load balancing solution for web services exposed to end-user traffic in an AWS cloud scenario. In all these cases, once you advertise the publicly exposed IP, from there onwards the internal details of the enterprise application, including the network and deployment details, are hidden from the outside world. This is a recommended pattern and you will follow the same in your microservice applications.

The Bootstrap URL

In the previous section, you saw that every microservice can self-register to the Eureka registry as and when they come up so that consumers can be directed to those services by the registry. In order to discover where the registry is, you will use well-known and fixed addresses for the registries. These registries only contain route mappings to internal microservices. Externally accessible resources and addresses are typically not indexed in the registry; instead, you need to expose them using other ways. DNS is one such mechanism. But you also know that subsequent queries or requests arising from those publicly accessible resources (like many AJAX calls from the home page and other pages) need to access those microservices. You require a mechanism to do this. This is where the API gateway will come into play. A set of microservices can be exposed to the clients from outside the perimeter using an API gateway whereas the rest of the microservices, which you don't want to expose, can still be kept unexposed. So your API gateway will become the bootstrap mechanism for those URLs by which the client accesses the publicly exposed microservices.

Figure 8-13 depicts how to set up an API gateway in an on-premises deployment. The "Mesh App and Services Architecture" section in Chapter 4 talked about the Mesh App and Services Architecture and I will extend the notion of MASA to accommodate the API gateway. There are many concerns to be addressed at the point of the API gateway in every enterprise application, and security is one such concern. This can all be addressed at the API gateway since the gateway will act as the single front door to your enterprise application landscape.

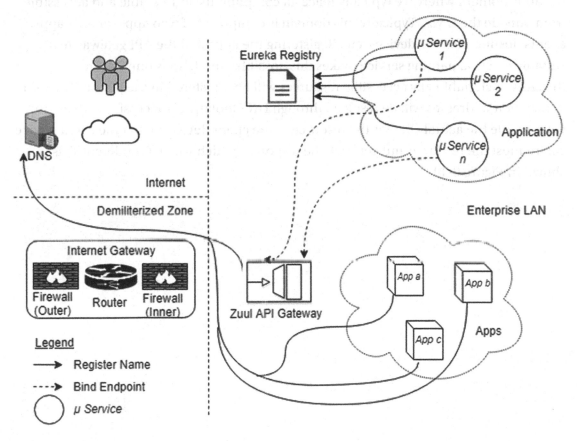

Figure 8-13. *Zuul, the API gateway on premises*

The following points are to be noted when you use an API gateway:

- Public services alone are bound to an API gateway. This means all microservice APIs that are to be addressable from outside the enterprise DMZ will be bound to the API gateway.

- For microservices that are not necessarily accessible from outside, there is no need to expose them at the API gateway.

In Figure 8-13, you can see that all microservices are registered at Eureka. Then, all microservices that are to be accessible from outside are bound to the API gateway too. However, microservices that are not necessarily accessible from outside, like Microservice 2, are not bound to the API gateway. The next notable aspect is that the API gateway itself should be addressable from outside. So is the case with all apps, since apps are to be accessible directly by client devices. In Figure 8-13, you can see the apps domain where we typically place all components addressable and accessible from outside the DMZ. Typically this domain is composed of web apps, mobile apps, agents destined for IoT devices, etc. Registering the apps and the API gateway to a suitable external naming service makes this possible, and DNS is one way of doing this. Any such publically accessible resources will be registered in the public DNS and hence their addresses will be resolved through DNS lookup. A successful DNS lookup will provide the actual URL for the resource to the client device so that the client device can request the resource and get back the response, which will get rendered. This is shown in Figure 8-14.

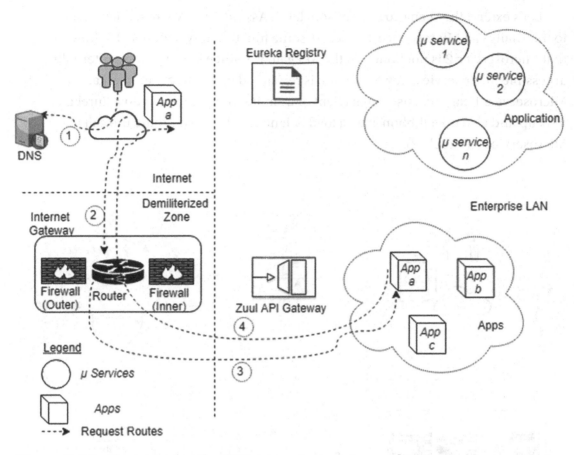

Figure 8-14. *Bootstraping the URL to a microservice application*

Once you receive the app content (the home page in a traditional web app context) and the same is rendered in the device, from then onwards all the rest of the hits from the client device to the server can be routed to one or more context root URLs. This means all subsequent requests from the app in the client device will hit the API gateway, as shown in Figure 8-15. This is marked with labels in the diagram. Since the API gateway is also publicly exposed, it makes sense to get its IP resolved through a naming service like DNS or alternatively the client app itself can remember the IP of the API gateway and hit (Label 7). The API gateway will first do a registry look up (Label 9) and subsequently route the request to the destination microservice (Label 10). Zuul by default uses Ribbon to locate an instance to forward the request to via discovery (e.g. Eureka in your case). So if your services are registered in Eureka, Zuul can also take care of instance lookup and carry the load balanced request forward.

Let's extend the scenario to one more level. Assume that Microservice 1 has to internally call Microservice 2 to access some functionality. Figure 8-13 shows that Microservice 2 is not bound to the API gateway since it is an always internally accessible microservice; however, it too is registered with a name in Eureka. Microservice 1 can then use Feign client or a similar mechanism to do a Eureka look up and also do a Ribbon-based load balance so that it can route the call to Microservice 2 (Label 12).

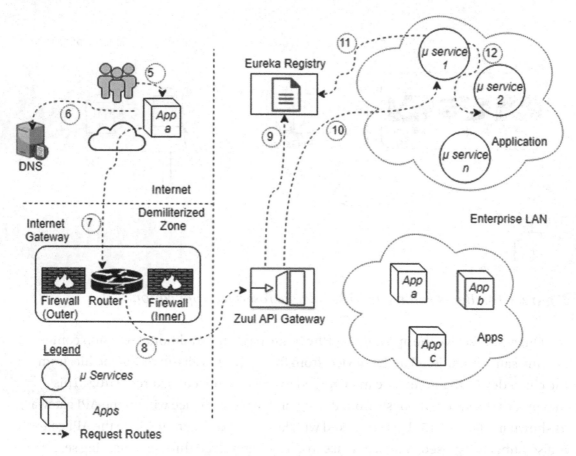

Figure 8-15. *Request from the client app to microservices*

You need to appreciate that the deployment architectures explained here are typical ones, and there can be multiple variations based on your enterprise requirements.

Design a Zuul-Enabled Scenario

You will modify your design in Figure 8-13 by introducing the Zuul API gateway; the modified design is shown in Figure 8-16. The flow is as explained in the previous section; however, I will not introduce all the complexities of DNS, etc. here. Let's look at the flow.

The client device, which is the browser in your case, will be used to render the product.html (Label 1). Once the product.html is loaded into the browser, it will fire a request to the Product Web microservice. You will not bind the Product Web microservice into the API gateway in this sample to keep it simple, so you will only bind the Product Server microservice to the API gateway. Hence the request from the client device to the Product Web microservice is a direct hit not through the API gateway (Label 3). The Product Web microservice now has to delegate the request to the Product Server microservice and in order to do so, it will route the request through the API gateway (Label 4). The API gateway will do a registry look up (Label 5) and return the server details where the Product Server microservices are hosted back to the Ribbon client in the Product Web microservice. The Product Web microservice takes this info and load balances the request to any one of the instances of the Product Server microservice (Label 6), since you will have two instances of Product Server microservices hosted.

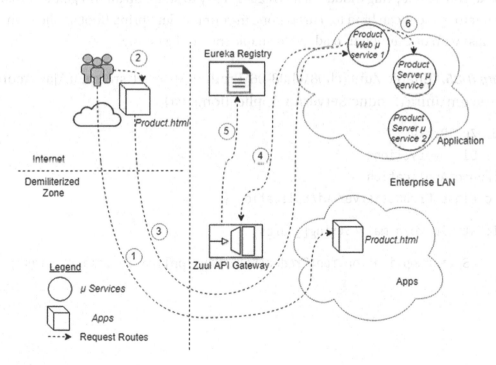

Figure 8-16. *Design with Zuul*

Code to Use Zuul

All the code samples for this section are in folder ch08\ch08-06.Visit pom.xml to see the explicit mention of the Zuul dependency. See Listing 8-24.

Listing 8-24. Zuul dependency (ch08\ch08-06\ProductApiZuul\pom.xml)

```
<dependency>
    <groupId>org.springframework.cloud</groupId>
    <artifactId>spring-cloud-starter-zuul</artifactId>
</dependency>
<dependency>
    <groupId>org.springframework.cloud</groupId>
    <artifactId>spring-cloud-starter-eureka</artifactId>
</dependency>
```

Note that Zuul by itself is a microservice, so it has to register itself to the registry just like any other normal microservice. Hence Zuul also needs a Eureka dependency, as shown in Listing 8-25.

Next, you need Spring Cloud's @EnableZuulProxy to stand up an API gateway that other microservices can bind to. This is done in your regular Spring Boot application main class with one annotation added to enable the Zuul gateway.

Listing 8-25. Enable Zuul (ch08\ch08-06\ProductApiZuul\src\main\java\com\ acme\ecom\infra\ProductServerApiApplication.java)

```
@EnableZuulProxy
@EnableDiscoveryClient
@SpringBootApplication
public class ProductServerApiApplication {

public static void main(String[] args) {

        SpringApplication.run(ProductServerApiApplication.class, args);
    }
}
```

You now need to define the routes at the API gateway, which you will do in application.yml. See Listing 8-26.

Listing 8-26. Define Routes in Zuul Gateway (ch08\ch08-06\ProductApiZuul\ src\main\resources\application.yml)

```
spring:
    application:
        name: product-service-api
server:
    port: 8082

zuul:
routes:
    product-api:
        path: /api/**
        service-id: product-service

eureka:
    client:
        serviceUrl:
            defaultZone: http://localhost:8761/eureka/

hystrix:
    command:
        default:
            execution:
                isolation:
                    thread:
                        timeoutInMilliseconds: 2000
```

Zuul will now get registered in Eureka in the name product-service-api. Further, any URLs of the pattern /api/** coming to Zuul will get routed to product-service.

The Product Server microservice code is similar to the code you saw in the "Code to Use Eureka" section except that you have removed the MongoDB dependency and instead use a simple in-memory representation of product data to make the sample simpler.

However, the Product Web microservice code needs explanation since it is in this place where you look up the Zuul API gateway to delegate requests to the Product Server microservice. See Listing 8-27.

Listing 8-27. Use API Gateway to Call Other Microservices (ch08\ch08-06\ ProductWeb\src\main\java\com\acme\ecom\product\controller\ ProductRestController.java)

```
@RestController
public class ProductRestController implements ProductService{

    @Autowired
    RestTemplate restTemplate;

    private static String PRODUCT_SERVICE_URL =
        "http://product-service-api/api/products";

    @Autowired
    public ProductRestController(RestTemplate restTemplate){

        this.restTemplate = restTemplate;
    }

    @RequestMapping(value = "/productsweb",
        method = RequestMethod.GET ,
        produces = {MediaType.APPLICATION_JSON_VALUE})
    public ResponseEntity<Resources<Resource<Product>>> getAllProducts() {

        ResponseEntity<PagedResources<Product>> responseEntity =
            restTemplate.exchange(PRODUCT_SERVICE_URL, HttpMethod.GET,
            (HttpEntity<Product>) null, responseTypeRef);
            // other code goes here…
    }
}
```

All of the other code remains similar to what you saw in the "Code to Use Eureka" section; however, the change is in the URL. The product-service-api portion of the URL http://product-service-api/api/products refers to the Zuul API gateway's address, so the call will first hit the gateway. In the API gateway you have configured that any URLs of the pattern /api/** coming to Zuul will get routed to product-service, hence the above full URL will get translated to the products end point in the Product Server microservice.

Build and Test the Zuul Sample

The complete code required to demonstrate the Eureka registry is in folder ch08-06. You don't require MongoDB for this sample. You can build, pack, and run the different microservices in the following order. You first bring up the Eureka registry microservices:

```
cd ch08\ch08-06\Eureka
D:\binil\gold\pack03\ch08\ch08-06\Eureka>make
D:\binil\gold\pack03\ch08\ch08-06\Eureka>mvn -Dmaven.test.skip=true clean
package
D:\binil\gold\pack03\ch08\ch08-06\Eureka>run
D:\binil\gold\pack03\ch08\ch08-06\Eureka>java -jar -Dserver.
port=8761 -Dspring.application.name=eureka-registry -Deureka.
client.registerWithEureka=false -Deureka.client.fetchRegistry=true
-Deureka.client.server.waitTimeInMsWhenSyncEmpty=0 -Deureka.client.
serviceUrl.defaultZone=http://localhost:8761/eureka/ -Deureka.server.
enableSelfPreservation=false .\target\Ecom-Product-Microservice-0.0.1-
SNAPSHOT.jar
```

You next bring up the Zuul API gateway:

```
D:\binil\gold\pack03\ch08\ch08-06\ProductApiZuul>make
D:\binil\gold\pack03\ch08\ch08-06\ProductApiZuul>mvn -Dmaven.test.skip=true
clean package
D:\binil\gold\pack03\ch08\ch08-06\ProductApiZuul>run
D:\binil\gold\pack03\ch08\ch08-06\ProductApiZuul>java -Dserver.port=8082
-Dspring.application.name=product-service-api -Deureka.client.serviceUrl.
defaultZone=http://localhost:8761/eureka/ -jar ./target/Ecom-Product-
Microservice-0.0.1-SNAPSHOT.jar
```

Since the registry and API gateway are all set up now, you can bring up the application microservices next:

```
cd ch08\ch08-06\ProductServer
D:\binil\gold\pack03\ch08\ch08-06\ProductServer>make
D:\binil\gold\pack03\ch08\ch08-06\ProductServer>mvn -Dmaven.test.skip=true
clean package
D:\binil\gold\pack03\ch08\ch08-06\ProductServer>run1
D:\binil\gold\pack03\ch08\ch08-06\ProductServer>java -Dserver.port=8080
-Dspring.application.name=product-service -Deureka.client.serviceUrl.
defaultZone=http://localhost:8761/eureka/ -jar .\target\Ecom-Product-
Microservice-0.0.1-SNAPSHOT.jar

cd ch08\ch08-06\ProductServer
D:\binil\gold\pack03\ch08\ch08-06\ProductServer>run2
D:\binil\gold\pack03\ch08\ch08-06\ProductServer>java -Dserver.port=8081
-Dspring.application.name=product-service -Deureka.client.serviceUrl.
defaultZone=http://localhost:8761/eureka/ -jar .\target\Ecom-Product-
Microservice-0.0.1-SNAPSHOT.jar
```

Next, bring up the Product Web microservice:

```
cd ch08\ch08-06\ProductWeb
D:\binil\gold\pack03\ch08\ch08-06\ProductWeb>make
D:\binil\gold\pack03\ch08\ch08-06\ProductWeb>mvn -Dmaven.test.skip=true
clean package
D:\binil\gold\pack03\ch08\ch08-06\ProductWeb>run
D:\binil\gold\pack03\ch08\ch08-06\ProductWeb>java -Dserver.port=8084
-Dspring.application.name=product-web -Deureka.client.serviceUrl.
defaultZone=http://localhost:8761/eureka/ -jar .\target\Ecom-Product-
Microservice-0.0.1-SNAPSHOT.jar
```

The last command brings up Product Web in port 8084.

You may inspect the Eureka console using a web browser by pointing to the following URL where you have the registry services running: http://localhost:8761/. See Figure 8-17.

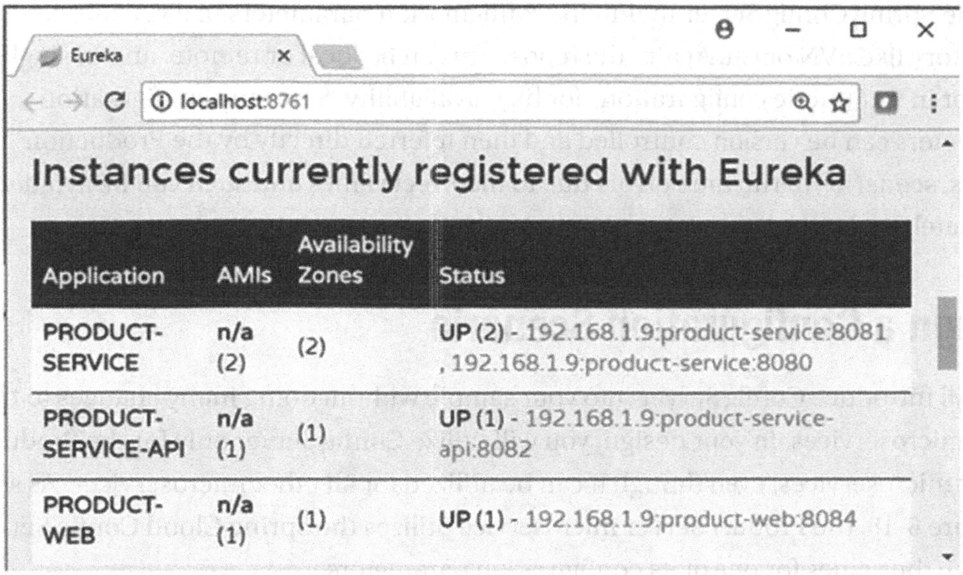

Figure 8-17. *Eureka Console*

You may now open this HTML utility, preferably in the Chrome browser: ch08\ch08-06\ProductWeb\src\main\resources\product.html.

Upon loading itself, the browser client will fire a request to Product Web, listening in port 8084, which will delegate the call to any instance of the Product Server microservice. The Product Web microservice now has to delegate the request to Product Server microservice and in order to do so, it will route the request through the API gateway. The API gateway will do a registry look up and return the server details where the Product Server microservices are hosted back to the Ribbon client in Product Web microservice. The Product Web microservice takes this info and load balances the request to any one of the instances of the Product Server microservices.

The Config Server

Externalizing configuration parameters is a critical characteristic that microservices exhibit. This is true for both application parameters and infrastructure parameters. When there are many microservices, maintaining the configuration parameters externally is a non-trivial task and Spring Cloud's Config Server comes to your rescue here.

The Spring Config Server maintains configuration parameters in a version-controlled repository like SVN or Git. Again, the repository can be local or remote, and in single node or in multinode configurations for high availability. Since the configuration parameters can be version controlled and then referred directly by the Production servers, scenarios of run time errors due to incorrect values and such can be avoided completely.

Design a Configuration Scenario

You will introduce Config Server into your sample without doing many changes to the other microservices. In your design, you will utilize Config Server only for the Product Server microservices, even though it can be utilized for all other microservices. As shown in Figure 8-18, the Product Server microservice utilizes the Spring Cloud Config Server to manage the values for one of its configuration parameters.

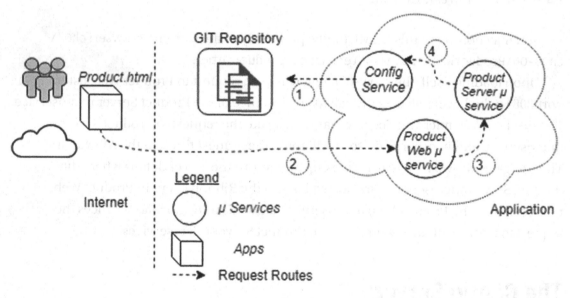

Figure 8-18. *Design for a Config Server scenario*

Code to Use Config Server

All the code samples for this section are in folder ch08/ch08-07. Visit pom.xml to see the explicit mention of the Config Server dependency. See Listing 8-28.

Listing 8-28. Config Server Dependency (ch08\ch08-07\ConfigServer\pom.xml)

```xml
<dependency>
    <groupId>org.springframework.cloud</groupId>
    <artifactId>spring-cloud-config-server</artifactId>
</dependency>
```

Next, you want to add @EnableConfigServer to the Application class, which is shown in Listing 8-29.

Listing 8-29. Enabling Config Server (ch08\ch08-07\ConfigServer\src\main\java\com\acme\ecom\product\EcomProductConfigApplication.java)

```java
@SpringBootApplication
@EnableConfigServer
public class EcomProductConfigApplication {

public static void main(String[] args) {

        SpringApplication.run(EcomProductConfigApplication.class, args);
    }
}
```

Next, configure the Config Server itself to point to the GIT URL. See Listing 8-30.

Listing 8-30. Spring Cloud Config Server Configurations (ch08\ch08-07\ConfigServer\src\main\resources\bootstrap.yml)

```yaml
server:
  port: 8888

spring:
  cloud:
    config:
      server:
        git:
          uri: file://D:/binil/gold/pack03/ch08/ch08-07/ConfigServer/
          config-repo
```

Here, since Port 8888 is the default port for the Config Server, even without explicit mention of server.port, the Config Server will bind to 8888. Next, you provide the GIT URL. It's in this repository where you need to place all your configuration files for the different microservices.

Next, you need to enable your microservice to access the Config Server. Visit the Maven dependency shown in Listing 8-31.

Listing 8-31. Config Server Client (ch08\ch08-07\ProductServer\pom.xml)

```xml
<dependency>
    <groupId>org.springframework.boot</groupId>
    <artifactId>spring-boot-starter-actuator</artifactId>
</dependency>

<dependency>
    <groupId>org.springframework.cloud</groupId>
    <artifactId>spring-cloud-starter-config</artifactId>
</dependency>
```

The Product Server microservice will act as the client for the Config Server. This is enabled by the spring-cloud-starter-config. You need to note the actuator dependency too, which is required for refreshing the configuration parameters when there is a change to the parameter in the Config Server. Next, inspect the microservice configuration file, shown in Listing 8-32.

Listing 8-32. Product Server Microservice Configurations (ch08\ch08-07\ ProductServer\src\main\resources\application.yml)

```yaml
server:
  port: 8081

spring:
  application:
    name: productservice
  cloud:
    config:
      server:
        uri: http://localhost:8888
```

```
management:
  security:
    enabled: false
```

The significant configuration parameters are

```
spring.application.name=productservice
spring.cloud.config.uri=http://localhost:8888
```

Here productservice is a logical name given to the Product Server microservice, which will also be treated as its service ID. The Config Server will look for productservice.yml in the repository to resolve any application configuration parameters. See Listing 8-33.

Listing 8-33. Product Server Configuration Parameters (ch08\ch08-07\ ConfigServer\config-repo\productservice.yml)

```
page:
  size: 3
```

You will see the relevance of the configuration parameter in Listing 8-33 in the next section. You may now move onto the Product Server microservice code shown in Listing 8-34.

Listing 8-34. Config Server Client (ch08\ch08-07\ProductServer\src\main\java\ com\acme\ecom\product\controller\ProductRestController.java)

```
@RestController
@RefreshScope
public class ProductRestController {

    @Value("${page.size}")
    private int size = 0;
    // other code goes here…
}
```

For demonstrating the centralized configuration of parameters and propagation of their changes, you have introduced an application-specific parameter named size, which is referred from the externalized configuration by the name page.size. In the application code, you use this parameter to control the number of rows of products returned when someone accesses them using the client.

Build and Test the Config Server

The complete code required to demonstrate the Config Server is in folder ch08-07. You don't require MongoDB for this sample too. You can build, pack, and run the different microservices in the following order.

You first bring up the Config Server microservices:

```
cd ch08\ch08-07\ConfigServer
D:\binil\gold\pack03\ch08\ch08-07\ConfigServer>make
D:\binil\gold\pack03\ch08\ch08-07\ConfigServer>mvn -Dmaven.test.skip=true
clean package
D:\binil\gold\pack03\ch08\ch08-07\ConfigServer>run
D:\binil\gold\pack03\ch08\ch08-07\ConfigServer>java -Dserver.port=8888
-Dspring.application.name=productservice -jar .\target\Ecom-Product-
Microservice-0.0.1-SNAPSHOT.jar
```

Once the Config Server is up, the configuration parameters in productservice. yml listed in Listing 8-33 can be inspected by typing http://localhost:8888/ productservice/default.

The first part in the URL is the microservice name. In your case, the microservice name is productservice. The microservice name is a logical name given to the application, using the spring.application.name property in application.yml of the Spring Boot (Product Server) application. Each application should have a unique name. The Config Server will use this name to resolve and pick up the appropriate .yml or .properties files from the Config Server repository. The application name is also referred to as a service ID. See Figure 8-19.

Figure 8-19. *Inspecting the Config Server*

Bring up the application microservices next:

```
cd ch08\ch08-07\ProductServer
D:\binil\gold\pack03\ch08\ch08-07\ProductServer>make
D:\binil\gold\pack03\ch08\ch08-07\ProductServer>mvn -Dmaven.test.skip=true
clean package
D:\binil\gold\pack03\ch08\ch08-07\ProductServer>run
D:\binil\gold\pack03\ch08\ch08-07\ProductServer>java -Dserver.port=8081
-Dspring.application.name=productservice -jar .\target\Ecom-Product-
Microservice-0.0.1-SNAPSHOT.jar
```

```
cd ch08\ch08-07\ProductWeb
D:\binil\gold\pack03\ch08\ch08-07\ProductWeb>make
D:\binil\gold\pack03\ch08\ch08-07\ProductWeb>mvn -Dmaven.test.skip=true
clean package
D:\binil\gold\pack03\ch08\ch08-07\ProductWeb>run
D:\binil\gold\pack03\ch08\ch08-07\ProductWeb>java -Dserver.port=8080
-Dspring.application.name=productweb -jar .\target\Ecom-Product-
Microservice-0.0.1-SNAPSHOT.jar
```

Open this HTML utility, preferably in the Chrome browser: ch08\ch08-07\
ProductWeb\src\main\resources\product.html.

Upon loading itself, the browser client will fire a request to Product Web, listening on
port 8080, which will delegate the call to the Product Server microservice. You can see as
many Product rows as configured in the productservice.yml listed in the client browser.

As a next step, change the value of `page.size productservice.yml` file (from 3 to 2 or 4) and save the file. You should be able to view this change in the Config Server by typing the Config server URL in a browser: `http://localhost:8888/productservice/default`.

You may now refresh the browser client. However, the change may not be reflected in the Product Server microservice. In order to force the Product Server microservice to reload the configuration parameters, call the `/refresh` endpoint of the Product Server microservice. This is the actuator's refresh endpoint. The following command will send an empty POST to the `/refresh` endpoint:

```
curl -d {} localhost:8081/refresh
```

Alternatively, you may also use Postman to send an empty POST request. If you refresh the browser client again, you will see that the change is reflected. The `/refresh` endpoint will refresh the locally cached configuration parameters of the Product Server microservice and reload[1] fresh values from the Config Server.

Summary

You explored the major building blocks of Spring Cloud in this chapter. Since Spring Cloud provides simple, easy-to-use, and Spring-friendly APIs and further since it's built on Spring's "convention over configuration" approach, Spring Cloud defaults all configurations and helps you to get off to a quick start. Many of the Spring Cloud features will be used to build your e-commerce sample application in later chapters, so the introductory level of knowledge provided in this chapter is essential for you to connect multiple microservices and visualize the complete picture. As you may have surmised, many of the Spring Cloud components are built from the ground up with the characteristics of fail safe and high availability in mind. This is of priority with increased outer architecture complexity for the microservices scenarios and you will do an end-to-end analysis of various essential high availability aspects and features in the next chapter.

---

[1]The Spring Cloud Bus provides an easy and automatic mechanism to refresh configurations across multiple instances without knowing how many instances there are or their locations, which is not covered here.

CHAPTER 9

High Availability and Microservices

High availability (HA) describes periods of time in which software services are available, as well as the time required by these systems to respond to a request made by a user. Eliminating single points of failure in your infrastructure that can cause a service interruption is key in designing HA systems. Duplicating or designing redundant components at every layer and at every stage is important to achieve HA, that too end to end. The "Outer Architecture Perspective" section in Chapter 4 talked about the outer architecture concerns of a microservices architecture. Various sections and samples in the last chapter provided you with concrete solutions to address a few of the concerns from that section in Chapter 4. You saw how to bring up more than one instance of a microservice. You also brought more than one instance of Eureka in the last chapter. In this chapter, you will explore further details of HA in general and HA of microservices in particular. You will also look at a comprehensive sample demonstrating end-to-end HA of a microservices architecture.

You will learn about the following in this chapter:

- Defining and measuring HA

- Decomposing HA at every layer, from the DNS lookup to storage backup

- Relooking at HA aspects in the context of microservices

- A code demonstration for HA using microservices and Spring Cloud

© Binildas Christudas 2019
B. Christudas, *Practical Microservices Architectural Patterns*, https://doi.org/10.1007/978-1-4842-4501-9_9

High Availability

High availability planning involves the identification of services that must be available for business continuity. Components that comprise each service should be identified, and list of possible points of failure for these systems should be made. A failure tolerance baseline should be established for each of them and failover strategies should be designed.

Measuring High Availability

Software availability is expressed as a percentage of yearly uptime. Using the nearly unachievable ideal of 100% availability as a baseline, the goal of the highest levels of service availability is considered to be "five nines," or 99.999% availability.

Downtime (usually expressed in outage minutes per year) is another way of expressing availability. Table 9-1 shows comparisons of different levels of availability.

Table 9-1. *Levels of Availability*

Availability	Unavailability	Five Nines	Downtime per Year
0.9	0.1	1	36 Days
0.99	0.01	2	87.7 Hours
0.999	0.001	3	8 Hours, 46 Minutes
0.9999	0.0001	4	52.5 Minutes
0.99999	0.00001	5	5 Minutes 16 Seconds
0.999999	0.000001	6	32 Seconds

I will not explain these levels or explore specific means to attain these levels of availability, since we have been describing and practicing them for decades and there are separate books[1] and references[2] to explain them. Our discussion will be just enough background for you to relate it to this microservices HA discussions.

---

[1] www.amazon.com/Blueprints-High-Availability-Evan-Marcus/dp/0471430269
[2] http://highscalability.com/

Baselining High Availability

High availability baselines can be defined based on two parameters:

- **Recovery Time Objective (RTO)**: The amount of time a business can function without the system's availability

- **Recovery Point Objective (RPO)**: How old the data will be once systems do recover

Based on the RTO and RPO baseline objectives and further based on the available budgets, accessible technologies, business criticality, and available technical expertise, software components are to be designed to attain the required level of availability.

Decomposing High Availability

If you have an infrastructure consisting of two identical, redundant web servers behind a load balancing router, traffic coming from client devices can be equally distributed between the web servers. However, if one of the servers goes down, the load balancer will redirect all subsequent traffic to the remaining online server. This is a simple mechanism which, if carefully extended, can be utilized to design HA for different elements. The Internet, internal networks, network devices, and software components are all elementary links of an end-to-end HA chain. You will look at the essential links required for our discussion so that the concepts and the sample demonstrated towards the end of the chapter will make sense to you. Also, I will explain aspects in the context of an on-premises or private data center in this chapter. In Chapter 16, when I describe advanced HA patterns, I will explain in the context of a public cloud so that you will have a broader view of how HA has to be looked at both in the context of a private and a public cloud.

DNS Redundancy

The "The Bootstrap URL" section in Chapter 8 introduced the Domain Name System (DNS) into the microservices architecture. Since the DNS serves as the phone book for the Internet by translating human-friendly computer hostnames into IP addresses, it serves as the bootstrap mechanism for most of the software-related operations through the Internet. It makes sense to understand availability starting from this point onwards. This means you need to understand mechanisms for DNS redundancy.

DNS outages may happen due to configuration errors, infrastructure failure, or a DDoS attack. DNS redundancy is a failsafe solution or a backup mechanism for such scenarios. If the DNS name servers are overloaded with more requests than they can serve, or they are down or responding sluggishly due to any of the above reasons, this creates latency in the DNS network, making the resolution process sluggish and eventually the DNS server will be rendered unavailable for most users. You can introduce DNS redundancy to the single-server architecture by expanding the number or choice of name servers that are available so that there are more name servers responding to the DNS queries. Figure 9-1 shows a typical redundant DNS setup where each DNS server has the capability to act as a primary server responding to DNS queries.

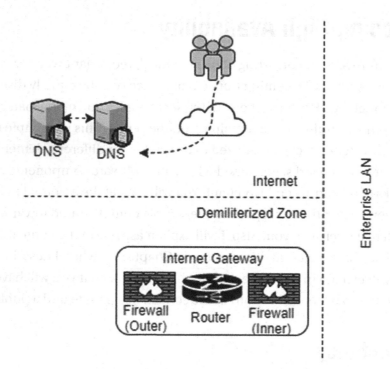

Figure 9-1. *DNS redundancy*

Let's look into more details of this now; see Figure 9-2. When setting up DNS redundancy, the servers can be set up as either primary, secondary or as primary, primary.[3] Maintaining multiple DNS providers and keeping them in sync is a complex process, but it ensures higher availability without compromising the advanced DNS functionalities supported by the DNS providers. When evaluating multiple DNS providers for your multi-DNS network, consider the global point of presence (PoP) of the providers and make sure these providers on separate networks can be seamlessly integrated using APIs.

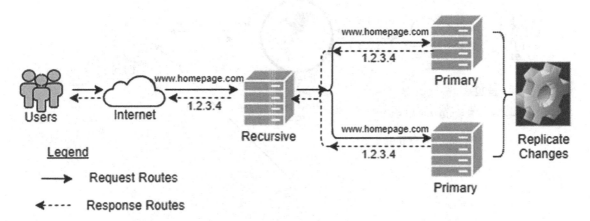

Figure 9-2. *How DNS redundancy works*

DNS Load Balancing

Once DNS redundancy is taken care, you need to think about DNS load balancing. A DNS load balancer reviews a list of servers and sends one connection to each server in turn. When a DNS change takes place, it has to be recorded on the ISP (Internet Service Provider) level. ISPs only refresh their DNS cache once every TTL (time to live) cycle. This implies that until the cache is updated, the ISPs are unaware of any changes that took place and continue to route traffic to the wrong server.

---

[3]A primary DNS server is the first point of contact for a browser, application, or device that needs to translate a human-readable hostname into an IP address. The primary DNS server contains a DNS record that has the correct IP address for the hostname. If the primary DNS server is unavailable, the device contacts a secondary DNS server, containing a recent copy of the same DNS records.

Instead of local load balancing, you can opt for global load balancing. Global DNS load balancing distributes traffic across multiple data centers to improve performance and availability; however, it again depends on your strategy for hosting across geographies. If your hosting is active-active across geographies, you can opt for global load balancing. There are solutions that can monitor connection quality between geographically dispersed sites at any given time, and also the actual requester geographical location and route traffic based on it. See Figure 9-3.

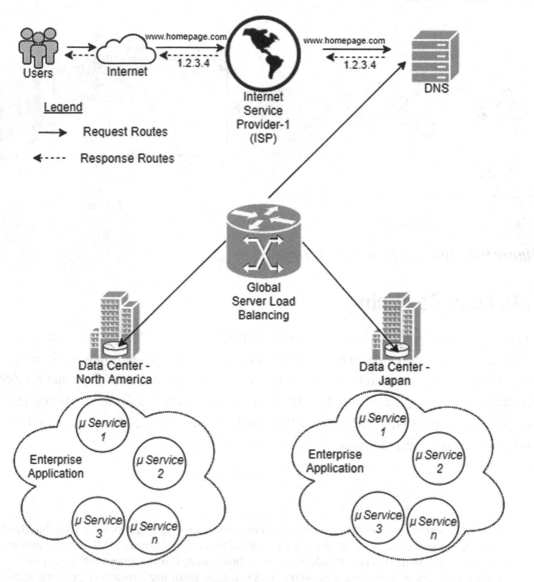

Figure 9-3. *Global server load balancing*

ISP Redundancy

ISPs provide you with pipes (or connections) from your enterprise to the Internet (Figure 9-4). If this pipe or path is down, it affects your network connectivity, which in turn affects your enterprise application availability. This is where ISP redundancy comes to your rescue.

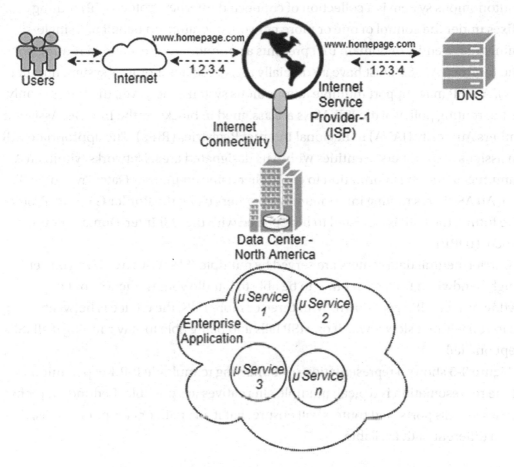

Figure 9-4. Enterprise connectivity to an ISP

Border Gateway Protocol (BGP) is one of the key protocols to use to achieve Internet connection redundancy. When you connect your network to more than one ISP, it is called multihoming. Multihoming[4] provides redundancy and network optimization. It selects the ISP that offers the best available path to a resource. Let's look into the details at a high level.

You need to start understanding from an autonomous system (AS) on the Internet. An autonomous system is a collection of connected Internet Protocol (IP) routing prefixes under the control of one or more network operators on behalf of a single administrative entity or domain that presents a common, clearly defined routing policy to the Internet. An ISP must have an officially registered autonomous system number (ASN). An ISP may support multiple autonomous systems; however, the Internet only sees the routing policy of the ISP. ASNs are assigned in blocks by the Internet Assigned Numbers Authority (IANA) to Regional Internet Registries (RIRs). The appropriate RIR then assigns AS numbers to entities within its designated area. Networks within an AS communicate routing information to each other using an Interior Gateway Protocol (IGP). An AS shares routing information with others using the Border Gateway Protocol. In the future, the BGP is expected to be replaced with the OSI Inter-Domain Routing Protocol (IDRP).

Carrier-neutral data centers are served by multiple ISPs. With two ISPs you get enough bandwidth from each other to be able to handle your traffic without any slowdowns if one ISP goes down. With three or more ISPs, the choice is between being able to run without slowdowns if one ISP fails and being able to stay running if all ISPs except one fail.

Figure 9-5 shows a representation of connecting to multiple ISP. Keep in mind that the representation is typical; multiple alternatives are possible. Redundant paths, switches, access ports, and routers will ensure that if any path or component fails, there is still a different path available.

---

[4]Multihoming is the practice of connecting a host or a computer network to more than one network. This can be done in order to increase reliability or performance.

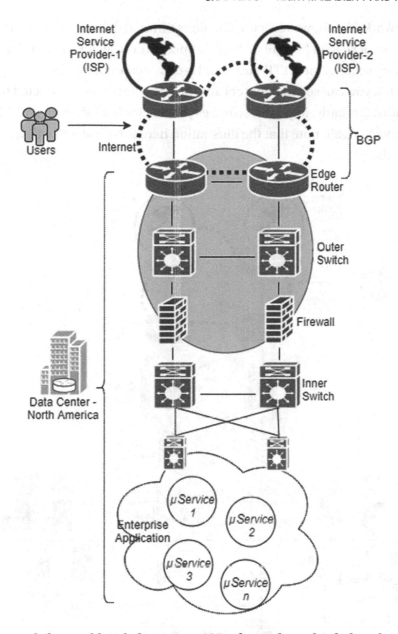

Figure 9-5. *Multihomed load sharing to ISPs through multiple local routers*

Application Architecture Redundancy

As illustrated in the previous section, the Internet-facing border routers peer directly to the ISPs. Intrusion prevention appliances that guard against worms, viruses, denial-of-service (DoS) traffic, and such, plus appliances like web security appliances (WSA) reside in this part of the network. The firewalls secure functions through the edge by implementation and enforcement of stateful firewall rules and application-level inspection. The DMZ provides primary security for HTTP-based and e-commerce applications.

In Figure 9-6, you can see that routers and switches are cross-connected to provide redundant paths. Similarly, app layer switches provide for load sharing and failover across web servers. Again note that the illustration here is typical and will vary based on enterprise needs.

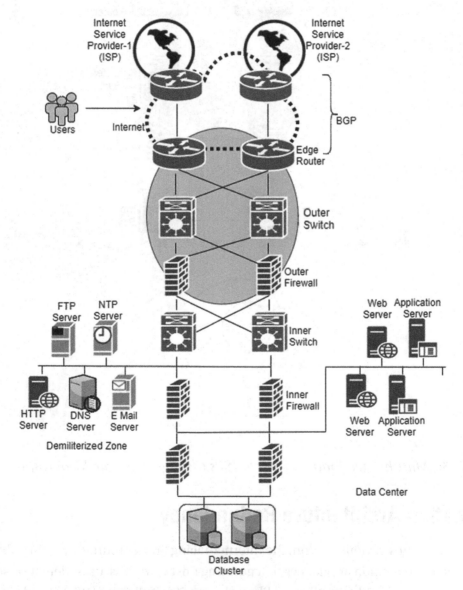

Figure 9-6. *Highly available application deployment architecture*

Public-facing services deployed in the DMZ are shown as single servers; however, they too can be deployed as redundant. The core servers in the data storage layer are again redundant.

Data and Storage Redundancy

Data is stored on either block-level storage arrays as in SANs (storage area networks), or file-based arrays (also known as NASs or network-attached storage arrays). They provide various levels of redundancy, so that if a single component in the array (whether a disk drive, controller, SAN or LAN access port, etc.) fails, it will not completely compromise the setup and data will still be accessible to the user. Server hardware based on x86 architecture is typically configured with redundant connections to SANs and Ethernet networks. Such connections to heterogeneous devices are done using dual port adapters or by using multiple (single port) adapters. The options of adapters depend on the space available in the servers (that is, the number of I/O expansion slots) as well as the level of hardware redundancy required. In short, the infrastructure is set up in such a way that it uses redundant paths, switches, and access ports for network and storage resources.

Figure 9-7 reveals that the paths are redundant and do not permit a single point of failure. If one of the Ethernet or SAN paths fails, there is still connectivity across a surviving path. In such a failure, failover will be triggered by some type of multipath or failover software.

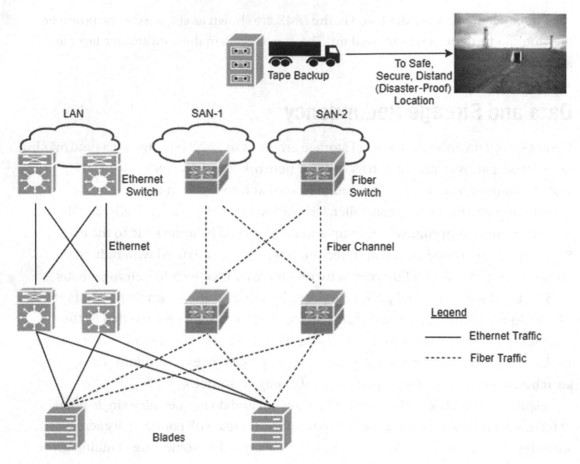

Figure 9-7. *Non-converged storage network*

Operating systems will have NIC (network interface card) drivers that will allow them to associate with more than one network card, thus enabling load balancing of network traffic across two paths. The same drivers also failover from failures if a physical network card, cable, or some other network component fails. Moreover, storage array vendors provide software that sits between the operating system and storage adapters, which can load balance traffic across available host bus adapters (HBAs) as shown Figure 9-7. When failure occurs in a HBA, path, or device, failover to redundant elements will happen.

From Figure 9-7 you can visualize so many network ports, storage ports, adapters, and cables to have redundancy. Large data centers with so many such components will increase the data center setup as well as operating cost. This is where converged networks come into play and where SAN and Ethernet traffic can be run over a single cable type. FCoE (Fiber Channel over Ethernet) is an example that uses FCoE-capable adapters, which can pass through both Ethernet and Fiber Channel traffic. Figure 9-8 shows this improvement.

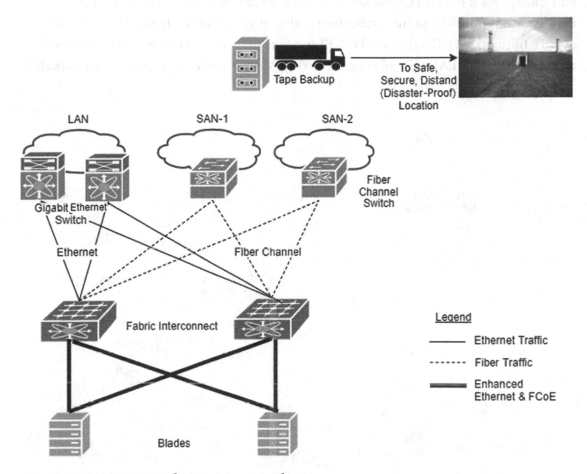

Figure 9-8. Converged storage network

Figure 9-8 makes it evident that you need fewer network ports, storage ports, adapters, and cables to have the same or better redundancy and failover as that required in Figure 9-7.

Figure 9-9 illustrates how you can replicate data centers across geography. SAN1 and SAN2 shown in Figure 9-9 can also be set up at distant geographies. One of the sites can then be regarded as a disaster recovery (DR) site. Vendor solutions can offer synchronous and asynchronous replication features, along with block-level incremental replication and granular snapshot features. Fiber Channel over IP (FCIP) that combines the features of the Fiber Channel and the IP is used to connect distributed SANs over large distances. FCIP encapsulates Fiber Channel and transports it over a TCP socket, hence it is a tunneling protocol, as it makes a transparent point-to-point connection between geographically separated SANs over IP networks. FCIP relies on TCP/IP services to establish connectivity between remote SANs over LANs (local area networks), MANs (metropolitan area networks), or WANs (wide area networks).

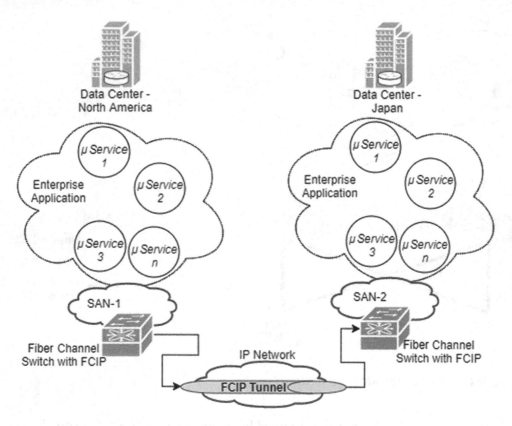

Figure 9-9. *SAN replication*

Last but not least, the stored bytes from the storage layer get archived into non-durable means and can be transported into secondary or DR sites, which again can be done by more than one service provider to improve reliability.

Highly Available Microservices

You can now extend the application deployment architecture explained in the "Application Architecture Redundancy" section earlier to accommodate the Mesh App and Service Architecture explained earlier. This is shown in Figure 9-10. Note that in the MASA style, apps are executed from the client device. They can be web apps, native mobile apps, IoT apps, etc. However, there is nothing wrong in representing them within the core data center behind the firewalls, which is the case in most of the web apps that also have server-side execution capability. If the apps are mobile apps, typically they are represented by an App Store (like Playstore, etc.). Further, if the apps don't have any server-side execution capability but get executed only in the client device, then they can also be hosted in the DMZ or closer to the perimeter for easy distribution to client devices. In such cases, the security concerns and other similar concerns will be further intercepted by the API layer, which you visited in the previous chapter.

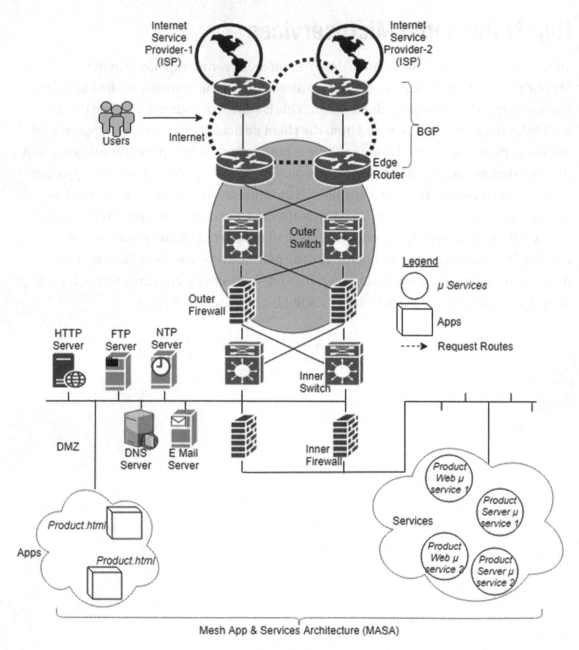

Figure 9-10. High availability for MASA-style deployment

The next thing to be noted in Figure 9-10 is that the apps and the services can be hosted with redundancy, especially when they are designed as microservices. If these concepts are difficult to digest, don't worry; all will be clarified in the working sample towards the end of this chapter.

A Highly Available Spring Cloud Microservice Demonstration

The previous section explained how the microservices architecture fits into the high availability reference architecture model from a deployment perspective. In this section, you will look at a real-world scenario where you will simulate many aspects of HA already discussed from a microservices perspective. You will simulate the HA building blocks essential for a microservices scenario alone; however, you will not attempt to demonstrate the rest of the general principles of infrastructure-level HA explained earlier in this chapter, since they are well proven and nothing is different even when applied to the microservices context.

Design a Highly Available Microservice Scenario

For the demonstration purpose of the microservices HA scenario, you will utilize the Eureka and Zuul components you used in Chapter 8. The scenario you will design is shown in Figure 9-11.

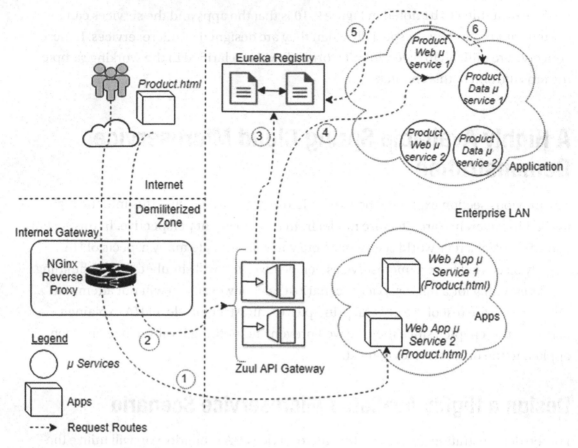

Figure 9-11. *Demonstrating high availability for microservices*

You have two instances each of Zuul and Eureka. Next, you divide the application components into three different microservices:

- **Web App μ Service**: This is the app component in the MASA style. In your sample, it hosts just an HTML page, so once this HTML is loaded by the browser from the server, then onwards all interactions from the HTML app to the server side will happen through the API gateway.

- **Product Web Server μ Service**: You have mocked this microservice as accepting all hits from outside the firewall from the clients, so this component will not do any major data operations. Instead, it will delegate the calls to the Product Data Server μ Service.

- **Product Data Server μ Service**: In this μ service, you will simulate CRUD operations. To keep the demo simple, you will not do actual CRUD operations against any database. Instead, you will simulate them from an in-memory data store.

All of the above microservices will also be instantiated twice so that at any point in time you will have redundancy.

You will next use an instance of Nginx server to simulate the reverse proxy. This reverse proxy will be configured in a load balanced mode so that it can load balance to the next layer of components.

You need to note two aspects with respect to the Nginx proxy configuration:

- **Web App μ Service**: The Web App μ Service is the app that must be downloaded into the client device first. Hence the bootstrap address for the application has to download and render this app into the client browser. In short, this component has to be directly addressable and accessible by client devices, so Nginx will reverse proxy requests from the client to this μ service directly.

- **Zuul API Gateway**: Once the Web App μ Service is rendered in the client device, from there onwards any subsequent hit from this app to the server will have to happen only through the API gateway. Hence the Zuul API gateway instances should also be configured in the Nginx reverse proxy.

I have removed the DNS, firewalls, and so on from the demonstration since their configuration is no different than from typical deployments, so your network architect will help you on this.

Code to Demonstrate Highly Available Microservices

All the code samples for this section are in folder ch09\ch09-01. Note that you are building over the examples in the previous chapter, especially the Eureka and Zuul examples in Chapter 8, so you should get an overview of those examples first before attempting to run this one. However, even if you skip those examples, you should still be able to run and understand this one. See Figure 9-12.

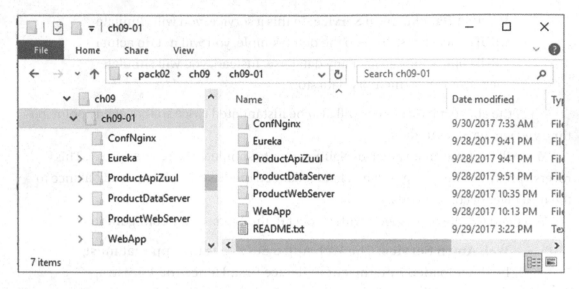

Figure 9-12. *Components to demonstrate a microservice's high availability*

Most of the components in this example were explained in Chapter 8, so I will avoid repetition. Instead, any incremental changes to the code in this section from that in Chapter 8 will be described here.

You will first look at the Nginx reverse proxy setup. The configurations are mentioned in the Nginx configuration file in Listing 9-1.

Listing 9-1. Nginx Configuration for Demonstrating High Availability (ch09\ch09-01\ConfNginx\nginx.conf)

```
http {
    upstream myapp1 {
        server localhost:8082;
        server localhost:8083;
    }
    upstream myapp2 {
        server localhost:9001;
        server localhost:9002;
    }
```

```
server {
    listen        8090;
    server_name   tiger;

    location / {
        proxy_pass http://myapp2;
    }
}

server {
    listen        8090;
    server_name   localhost;

    location / {
        proxy_pass http://myapp1;
    }
}
}
```

Note   You need to replace `tiger` in Listing 9-1 with the name of your host.

This file is usually found within the Nginx distribution. You need to edit the `nginx.conf` file to reflect the above changes within the Nginx distribution, which I found on my machine at the following location: `nginx-1.13.5\conf`.

You may also want to refer to Appendix C to get familiarized with Nginx.

The right way to use different names reflecting different sites is to use a local DNS server and then create some CNAMEs in DNS and refer them to the Nginx configuration. However, you will use a simple tweak here to get things running quickly. The hostname of my windows machine is `tiger`, and `localhost` also refers to this machine, so I can use these two different names to reference in my Nginx configuration to configure two different reverse proxy setups. So, `http://myapp1` and `http://myapp2` are the two reverse proxy setups, and `http://myapp1` refers to the API gateway whereas `http://myapp2` refers to the web app server farms where the default home page of the application can be fetched from.

You start Nginx only after you bring up the API gateway and the web app servers so that Nginx will start without any errors in its logs.

Since you have many more instances to be brought up, let's look at the design again, but with emphasis on the different ports and names of the microservices configured so that when I explain the relevant code sections it will be easy for you to understand. These details are marked in Figure 9-13.

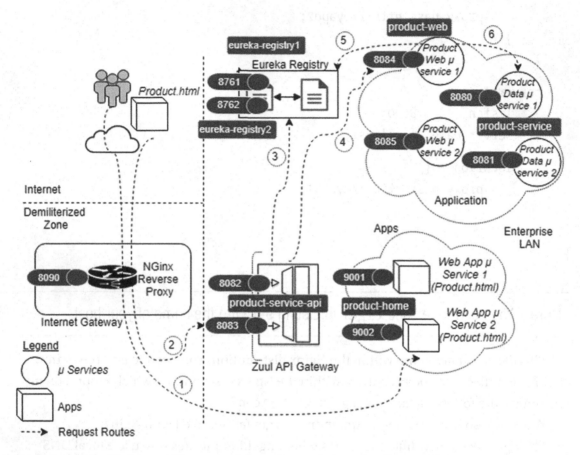

Figure 9-13. *Names and ports of the microservices for the HA demonstration*

There is no change in the Eureka configuration from what was explained in Chapter 8. In the Zuul API gateway, the only difference is the application configuration; see Listing 9-2.

Listing 9-2. Zuul API Gateway Route Configuration (ch09\ch09-01\ ProductApiZuul\src\main\resources\application.yml)

```
spring:
    application:
        name: product-service-api
```

```
zuul:
    routes:
        product-api:
            path: /myapp1/api/**
            service-id: product-service
        product-webapi:
            path: /myapp1/web/**
            service-id: product-web
```

The configuration is self-explanatory. It says that the application name of the API gateway is product-service-api. Further, any URLs of the pattern /myapp1/api/** will be routed to the product-service μ Service and any URLs of the pattern /myapp1/web/** will be routed to the product-web μ Service.

The Product Data Server μ Service is self-explanatory since it is similar to the Product Server microservice you visited in the "Code to Use Zuul" section in Chapter 8.

Likewise, the Product Web Server μ Service is similar to the ProductWeb microservice you visited in the "Code the New Design of Hystrix" section in Chapter 8, so it's not explained here.

However, the Web App μ Service requires a little explanation since you are using the constructs of such a microservice for the first time. The Web App μ Service is a first class μ Service; however, its purpose is to serve static content alone to the client device. In your sample, the contents are HTML files and JavaScript, which gets rendered in the client device. So as a first step you need to model the μ Service as a Spring MVC web application and you will use the spring-boot-starter-web dependency for that; see Listing 9-3.

Listing 9-3. Spring Boot Dependency for MVC (ch09\ch09-01\WebApp\pom.xml)

```
<dependency>
    <groupId>org.springframework.boot</groupId>
    <artifactId>spring-boot-starter-web</artifactId>
</dependency>
```

spring-boot-starter-web is the starter for building web, including RESTful, applications using Spring MVC and it uses Tomcat as the default embedded container. spring-boot-starter-web brings Tomcat with spring-boot-starter-tomcat, but spring-boot-starter-jetty and spring-boot-starter-undertow can be used instead by changing the configurations.

The Web App μ Service next gets only a single Java class, as shown in Listing 9-4.

Listing 9-4. Web App Microservice Application (ch09\ch09-01\WebApp\src\main\java\com\acme\ecom\product\EcomProductHomeMicroserviceApplication.java)

```
@SpringBootApplication
@EnableEurekaClient
public class EcomProductHomeMicroserviceApplication {

    public static void main(String[] args) {

        SpringApplication.run(EcomProductHomeMicroserviceApplication.class,
            args);

    }

}
```

The rest of the artifacts for the app are placed in folder ch09\ch09-01\WebApp\src\main\resources. They are the files required for an Angular JS-based web app. I will not go deep in exploring or explaining this app, since the scope of this book is not to deep dive into Angular or the web side of programming, but on the microservices aspects alone. So I will mention just two files here.

```
ch09\ch09-01\WebApp\src\main\resources\static\index.html
```

This is the welcome page that the client device will receive upon typing the bootstrap URL (http://tiger:8090) on the browser. This will get resolved by Nginx to myapp2, which will then get load balanced to any of following listener sockets shown in Listing 9-5.

Listing 9-5. Reverse Proxy Configurations

```
upstream myapp2 {
    server localhost:9001;
    server localhost:9002;
}
```

If you refer back to Figure 9-13 you can recollect that ports 9001 and 9002 host redundant instances of the Web App μ Service. You now need to appreciate that while the HTML is downloaded and rendered into the client device, the associated scripts too are downloaded into the device and hence the next file of interest is also downloaded into the device and will get executed from the device; see Listing 9-6.

Listing 9-6. Web App Contacting the API Gateway (ch09\ch09-01\WebApp\src\main\resources\static\js\service\product_service.js)

```
App.factory('ProductService', ['$http', '$q', function($http, $q){

    return {

        getApplication: function() {
            return $http.get('http://localhost:8090/myapp1/web/
            productsweb/')
                .then(
                    function(response){
                        return response.data._embedded.products;
                    },
                    function(errResponse){
                        console.error('Error while fetching application');
                        return $q.reject(errResponse);
                    }
                );
        }
    };
}]);
```

The main aspect to note here is the URL `http://localhost:8090/myapp1/web/productsweb/`, which will get resolved as

- `http://localhost:8090/myapp1/`: Nginx will resolve this to

```
upstream myapp1 {
        server localhost:8082;
        server localhost:8083;
}
```

Ports 8082 and 8083 host redundant instances of the API gateway.

- Next, /web/** will be resolved by the API gateway to the product-web
  μ Service:

```
zuul:
  routes:
    product-webapi:
      path: /myapp1/web/**
      service-id: product-web
```

- Finally, /productsweb/ is where the RestController of product-web μ
  Service method lies:

```
@RequestMapping(value = "/productsweb", method = RequestMethod.GET ,
    produces = {MediaType.APPLICATION_JSON_VALUE})
public ResponseEntity<Resources<Resource<Product>>>
getAllProducts() {

    return productServiceProxy.getAllProducts();
}
```

Finally, product-web μ Service has to delegate the request to the product-service
μ Service. This happens in the RestController of the product-web μ Service, shown in
Listing 9-7.

Listing 9-7. Product Web Microservice RestController (ch09\ch09-01\
ProductWebServer\src\main\java\com\acme\ecom\product\controller\
ProductRestController.java)

```
@EnableFeignClients(basePackageClasses = ProductServiceProxy.class)
@CrossOrigin
@RestController
public class ProductRestController implements ProductService{

    private ProductServiceProxy productServiceProxy;

    @Autowired
    public ProductRestController(ProductServiceProxy productServiceProxy){

        this.productServiceProxy = productServiceProxy;
    }
```

```
@RequestMapping(value = "/productsweb", method = RequestMethod.GET ,
    produces = {MediaType.APPLICATION_JSON_VALUE})
public ResponseEntity<Resources<Resource<Product>>> getAllProducts() {

    return productServiceProxy.getAllProducts();
}
}
```

The actual routing happens in the Feign client proxy shown in Listing 9-8.

Listing 9-8. Feign Client Proxy (ch09\ch09-01\ProductWebServer\src\main\
java\com\acme\ecom\product\client\ProductServiceProxy.java)

```
@FeignClient("product-service")
public interface ProductServiceProxy extends ProductService{

}
```

The product-service will be finally resolved by Eureka to the Product Data Service μ
Service, and that ends the full flow.

Build and Test the Microservices High Availability

The complete code required to demonstrate the Eureka registry is kept inside folder
ch09\ch09-01. You don't need MongoDB for this sample. You can build, pack, and run
the different microservices in the following order.

You first bring up the two instances of the Eureka microservices:

```
cd ch09\ch09-01\Eureka
D:\binil\gold\pack03\ch09\ch09-01\Eureka>make
D:\binil\gold\pack03\ch09\ch09-01\Eureka>mvn -Dmaven.test.skip=true clean
package
D:\binil\gold\pack03\ch09\ch09-01\Eureka>run1
D:\binil\gold\pack03\ch09\ch09-01\Eureka>java -jar -Dserver.
port=8761 -Dspring.application.name=eureka-registry1 -Deureka.client.
registerWithEureka=false -Deureka.client.fetchRegistry=true -Deureka.
client.server.waitTimeInMsWhenSyncEmpty=0-Deureka.client.serviceUrl.
```

```
defaultZone=http://localhost:8761/eureka/,http://localhost:8762/eureka/
-Deureka.server.enableSelfPreservation=false .\target\Ecom-Product-
Microservice-0.0.1-SNAPSHOT.jar
```

```
cd ch09\ch09-01\Eureka
D:\binil\gold\pack03\ch09\ch09-01\Eureka>run2
D:\binil\gold\pack03\ch09\ch09-01\Eureka>java -jar -Dserver.
port=8762 -Dspring.application.name=eureka-registry2 -Deureka.client.
registerWithEureka=false -Deureka.client.fetchRegistry=true -Deureka.
client.server.waitTimeInMsWhenSyncEmpty=0-Deureka.client.serviceUrl.
defaultZone=http://localhost:8761/eureka/,http://localhost:8762/eureka/
-Deureka.server.enableSelfPreservation=false .\target\Ecom-Product-
Microservice-0.0.1-SNAPSHOT.jar
```

You should note few aspects here:

- You explicitly disable Eureka registering to Eureka itself by configuring eureka.client.registerWithEureka=false.

- Each Eureka has the know-about of its peers looking at the values in eureka.client.serviceUrl.defaultZone.

- Unlike every other redundant instance of the same microservice, you have given each instance of Eureka different names.

You next bring up two instances of the Zuul API gateway:

```
cd ch09\ch09-01\ProductApiZuul
D:\binil\gold\pack03\ch09\ch09-01\ProductApiZuul>make
D:\binil\gold\pack03\ch09\ch09-01\ProductApiZuul>mvn -Dmaven.test.skip=true
clean package
D:\binil\gold\pack03\ch09\ch09-01\ProductApiZuul>run1
D:\binil\gold\pack03\ch09\ch09-01\ProductApiZuul>java -Dserver.port=8082
-Dspring.application.name=product-service-api -Deureka.client.serviceUrl.
defaultZone=http://localhost:8761/eureka/,http://localhost:8762/eureka/
-jar .\target\Ecom-Product-Microservice-0.0.1-SNAPSHOT.jar
```

```
cd ch09\ch09-01\ProductApiZuul
D:\binil\gold\pack03\ch09\ch09-01\ProductApiZuul>run2
```

```
D:\binil\gold\pack03\ch09\ch09-01\ProductApiZuul>java -Dserver.port=8083
-Dspring.application.name=product-service-api -Deureka.client.serviceUrl.
defaultZone=http://localhost:8761/eureka/,http://localhost:8762/eureka/
-jar .\target\Ecom-Product-Microservice-0.0.1-SNAPSHOT.jar
```

You will later see that the Zuul instances themselves will register to Eureka.

Since the Eureka registry and Zuul API gateway are all set up now, you can bring up the application microservices one by one.

First, you bring up two instances of the Product Data Server μ Service:

```
cd ch09\ch09-01\ProductDataServer
D:\binil\gold\pack03\ch09\ch09-01\ProductDataServer>make
D:\binil\gold\pack03\ch09\ch09-01\ProductDataServer>mvn -Dmaven.test.
skip=true clean package
D:\binil\gold\pack03\ch09\ch09-01\ProductDataServer>run1
D:\binil\gold\pack03\ch09\ch09-01\ProductDataServer>java -Dserver.port=8080
-Dspring.application.name=product-service -Deureka.client.serviceUrl.
defaultZone=http://localhost:8761/eureka/,http://localhost:8762/eureka/
-jar .\target\Ecom-Product-Microservice-0.0.1-SNAPSHOT.jar
```

```
cd ch09\ch09-01\ProductDataServer
D:\binil\gold\pack03\ch09\ch09-01\ProductDataServer>run2
D:\binil\gold\pack03\ch09\ch09-01\ProductDataServer>java -Dserver.port=8081
-Dspring.application.name=product-service -Deureka.client.serviceUrl.
defaultZone=http://localhost:8761/eureka/,http://localhost:8762/eureka/
-jar .\target\Ecom-Product-Microservice-0.0.1-SNAPSHOT.jar
```

Next, you bring up two instances of the Product Web μ Service:

```
cd ch09\ch09-01\ProductWebServer
D:\binil\gold\pack03\ch09\ch09-01\ProductWebServer>make
D:\binil\gold\pack03\ch09\ch09-01\ProductWebServer>mvn -Dmaven.test.
skip=true clean package
D:\binil\gold\pack03\ch09\ch09-01\ProductWebServer>run1
D:\binil\gold\pack03\ch09\ch09-01\ProductWebServer>java -Dserver.
port=8084 -Dspring.application.name=product-web -Deureka.client.serviceUrl.
defaultZone=http://localhost:8761/eureka/,http://localhost:8762/eureka/
-jar .\target\Ecom-Product-Microservice-0.0.1-SNAPSHOT.jar
```

```
cd ch09\ch09-01\ProductWebServer
D:\binil\gold\pack03\ch09\ch09-01\ProductWebServer>run2
D:\binil\gold\pack03\ch09\ch09-01\ProductWebServer>java -Dserver.
port=8085 -Dspring.application.name=product-web -Deureka.client.serviceUrl.
defaultZone=http://localhost:8761/eureka/,http://localhost:8762/eureka/
-jar .\target\Ecom-Product-Microservice-0.0.1-SNAPSHOT.jar
```

Finally, you bring up two instances of the Web App µ Service:

```
cd ch09\ch09-01\WebApp
D:\binil\gold\pack03\ch09\ch09-01\WebApp>make
D:\binil\gold\pack03\ch09\ch09-01\WebApp>mvn -Dmaven.test.skip=true clean
package
D:\binil\gold\pack03\ch09\ch09-01\WebApp>run1
D:\binil\gold\pack03\ch09\ch09-01\WebApp>java -Dserver.port=9001
-Dspring.application.name=product-home -Deureka.client.serviceUrl.
defaultZone=http://localhost:8761/eureka/,http://localhost:8762/eureka/
-jar .\target\Ecom-Product-Microservice-0.0.1-SNAPSHOT.jar
```

```
cd ch09\ch09-01\WebApp
D:\binil\gold\pack03\ch09\ch09-01\WebApp>run2
D:\binil\gold\pack03\ch09\ch09-01\WebApp>java -Dserver.port=9002
-Dspring.application.name=product-home -Deureka.client.serviceUrl.
defaultZone=http://localhost:8761/eureka/,http://localhost:8762/eureka/
-jar .\target\Ecom-Product-Microservice-0.0.1-SNAPSHOT.jar
```

By now, all of the microservices should be up. You can check them at the Eureka Console:

```
http://localhost:8761 or http://localhost:87612
```

See Figure 9-14.

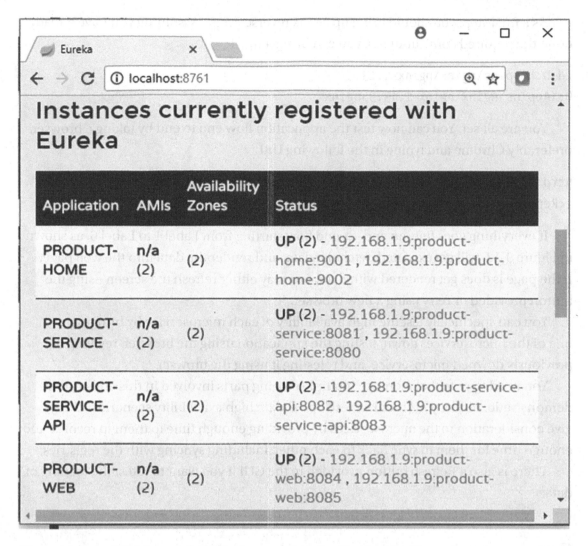

Figure 9-14. Highly available microservices in the Eureka Console

You can see that you have registered the externally available μ Service. In other words, the Web App μ Service (product-home) is registered in Eureka even though this is not required and you are not doing a look-up of it from the registry. Further, even the API gateway is seen registered in Eureka. This is also not mandatory. However, these variations can be made based on your specific requirements.

As a final step, you should bring up Nginx reverse proxy. Assuming you have already done the required configurations, you can bring it up at:

```
cd D:\Applns\nginx\nginx-1.13.5
D:\Applns\nginx\nginx-1.13.5>nginx
```

You are all set. You can now test the application flow end to end by taking a browser, preferably Chrome and typing in the following URL:

```
http://tiger:8090/
<<Replace "tiger" with your hostname>>
```

If everything goes fine, an end-to-end flow starting from Label 1 to Label 6, as shown in Figure 9-13, will get executed, fetch the data, and render the data into the web page. If the page is does get rendered with data, you may either refresh the screen using the button provided or retry using a new browser.

You can specifically test the high availability of each microservice by bringing one of the microservices down, testing the application using the browser, reviving the previously downed microservice, and retesting it using the browser.

You need to note that there are multiple moving parts involved in this end-to-end demonstration and if you "monkey test" to validate high availability scenarios, always give consideration to the microservices by providing enough time to them to recover and enough time for them to sync back to each other, including syncing with the registries.

There is also a Refresh button provided in the GUI if you want to retest the loading of data.

Summary

A chain is as strong as its weakest link, and the same saying holds true for many aspects of high availability. I have provided a ten-thousand-foot view of how HA and redundancy looks at every stage of an end-to-end deployment, starting from the client browser where data is originated and then to the web and application servers and further to the data management and data storage layer and finally to the archiving or the DR part. In Chapter 16, you will also look into advanced constructs and patterns in improving HA with an aim of making sure the sanity of every byte created by the user is preserved as per the intended data consistency rules in the end-to-end chain, regardless of whether you follow the traditional monolith-style architecture with strict ACID[5] compliance or a newer generation microservices-style architecture with relaxed ACID compliance. While provisioning HA and other related aspects need redundancy in processing nodes as well as network paths, there is a chance that the total number of network hops or thread-and-process-level context switches are increased in a microservices-based architecture compared to that of the monolith, so every effort should be taken to address the performance of individual microservices as well as that of the whole microservice application. You will do that in the next chapter.

---

[5]In computer science, ACID (Atomicity, Consistency, Isolation, Durability) is a set of properties of database transactions intended to guarantee validity even in the event of errors, power failures, etc. In the context of databases, a sequence of database operations that satisfies the ACID properties (and these can be perceived as a single logical operation on the data) is called a transaction.

CHAPTER 10

Microservice Performance

When you move from the traditional three-tier or n-tier architecture to the microservices architecture, one main observable characteristic is the increased number of interconnections between microservice processes. A computation that once took place completely within a single process now might get split into many microcomputations spanning across processes. This increases the number of interprocess communications, the number of context switches, the number of I/O operations involved, and so on. So it makes right sense to have a look at these aspects in more detail. In this chapter, you will explore a few performance aspects to be considered in microservices and you will look into the following:

- Synchronous vs. asynchronous HTTP
- The Servlet 3.0 spec for asynchronous HTTP
- Code to demonstrate asynchronous HTTP between browser and microservice
- Code to demonstrate asynchronous HTTP between microservices
- The Google Protocol Buffer
- Code to demonstrate using the Google Protocol Buffer between microservices

Communication Across the Outer Architecture

The "Outer Architecture Perspective" section in Chapter 4 introduced the outer architecture of microservices. There you saw how the internal complexities of a typical monolith architecture pop out to the "surface" when you move to a microservices-based architecture. One obvious change is the split of a single or a few computational processes into many more similar, but smaller computationally intensive processes. This change is better explained with the help of Figure 10-1.

279

© Binildas Christudas 2019
B. Christudas, *Practical Microservices Architectural Patterns*, https://doi.org/10.1007/978-1-4842-4501-9_10

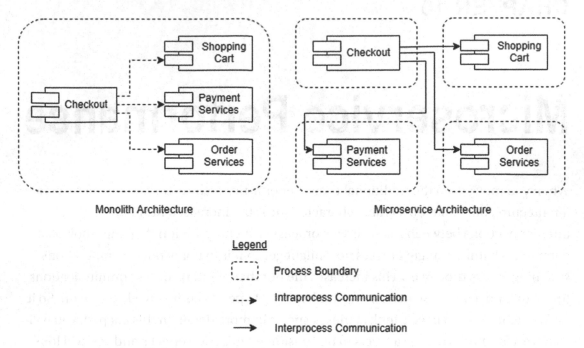

Figure 10-1. *Monolith vs. microservices boundaries*

In the traditional monolith, the multiple components that form the building blocks of a service realization get executed in a single container process. Method invocations or messaging between these components are "local" or "in process." This will allow processes, whether a container-managed process or a simple Java application process, to make a lot of assumptions and optimizations and complete the execution. However, when you rearchitect the same service from the monolith into the microservices architecture, the implementation gets split and deployed into more than one process. This is shown in Figure 10-1.

Interprocess communications are heavyweight compared to communications within a process. They involve more context switches, network wait and I/O operations, data marshalling and unmarshalling, etc. This increases the complexity involved in the outer architecture space of a microservices architecture.

Further, every microservice involves socket listeners listening to incoming traffic. So, compared to a traditional monolith, microservices architecture involves many more socket listeners, associated threads to process incoming traffic, and so on. A look into the details of a few of these handpicked concerns and analyzing the options to address them will give you a fair enough idea of the whole landscape.

Asynchronous HTTP

You briefly looked at distributed messaging in Chapter 6, where you also appreciated the differences between the synchronous and asynchronous style of communications between microservices. You saw that messaging is a first-class technology by which microservices can communicate asynchronously, and you saw via examples how you can correlate many asynchronous message transmissions so as to weave them together as pieces of a single, end-to-end request/response cycle. However, all of the samples in Chapter 8 used the HTTP protocol for intercommunications between microservices. You will look at the nature of these communications more closely in this section.

The Bad and the Ugly Part of HTTP

As stated, all of the samples in Chapter 8 use the HTTP protocol for intercommunications between microservices. If you examine these interactions again, you can observe that most of them are synchronous HTTP calls. Close observation of these communications reveals that an incoming request from a consumer microservice to your provider microservice server will capture one servlet connection and perform a blocking call to the remote service before it can send a response to the consumer microservice. It works, but it does not scale effectively if you have many such concurrent clients. Synchronous HTTP is a best fit for a user using a client application to get instant feedback or a response; however, that is not the case when it comes to server-side processing.

APIs for Asynchronous HTTP Processing

Typical containers in application servers like in Apache Tomcat normally use a server thread per client request. Under increased load conditions, this necessitates containers to have a large amount of threads to serve all the client requests. This limits scalability, which can arise due to running out of memory or exhausting the pool of container threads. Java EE has added asynchronous processing support for servlets and filters from the Servlet 3.0 spec onwards. A servlet or a filter, on reaching a potentially blocking operation when processing a request, can assign the operation to an asynchronous execution context and return the thread associated with the request immediately to the container without waiting to generate a response. The blocking operation can later complete in the asynchronous execution context in some different thread, which can

generate a response or dispatch the request to another servlet. The `javax.servlet.`
`AsyncContext` class is the API that provides the functionality that you need to perform
asynchronous processing inside service methods. The `startAsync()` method on the
`HttpServletRequest` object of your service method puts the request into asynchronous
mode and ensures that the response is not committed even after exiting the service
method. You have to generate the response in the asynchronous context after the
blocking operation completes or dispatch the request to another servlet.

The programming model is straightforward. Let's try to understand the difference by
first looking at the pseudo code for the traditional programming model of a `Controller`
class. See Listing 10-1.

Listing 10-1. Pseudo Code for a Sync Controller

```
@RestController
public class ProductRestController{

    @RequestMapping(value = "/products", method = RequestMethod.GET ,
        produces = {MediaType.APPLICATION_JSON_VALUE})
    public List<Product> getAllProducts() {
        //return "List of All Products";
    }
}
```

When you use Spring, the controller method can return a `java.util.concurrent.`
`Callable` to complete processing asynchronously. Spring MVC will then invoke the
`Callable` in a separate thread with the help of a TaskExecutor. A TaskExecutor is Spring's
abstraction for asynchronous execution and scheduling of tasks. The rewritten pseudo
code is shown in Listing 10-2.

Listing 10-2. Pseudo Code for an Async Controller Using Callable

```
@RestController
public class ProductRestController{

    @RequestMapping(value = "/products", method = RequestMethod.GET ,
        produces = {MediaType.APPLICATION_JSON_VALUE})
    public Callable<List<Product>> getAllProducts() {
```

```
    return new Callable<List<Product>>() {
        public Object call() throws Exception {
            // ...
            // return "List of All Products";
        }
    };
}
}
```

Spring 3.2 introduced `org.springframework.web.context.request.async.`
`DeferredResult`, which can again be returned by a `Controller` class. `DeferredResult`
provides an alternative to using a `Callable` for asynchronous request processing.
While a `Callable` is executed concurrently on behalf of the application, with a
`DeferredResult` the application can produce the result from a thread of its choice.
Here, the processing can happen in a thread not known to Spring MVC, similar to the
case when you need to get a response from a messaging channel, and so on. So, when
you use `DeferredResult`, even after you leave the controller handler method, the
request processing is not done. Instead, Spring MVC (using Servlet 3.0 capabilities)
will hold on with the response, keeping the idle HTTP connection. Even though the
HTTP Worker Thread is no longer used, the HTTP connection is still open. At a later
point in time, some other thread will resolve `DeferredResult` by assigning some value
to it. Spring MVC will immediately pick up this event and send a response to the client,
finishing the request processing.

The pseudo code for an async scenario using `DeferredResult` is shown in Listing 10-3.

Listing 10-3. Pseudo Code for an Async Controller Using DeferredResult

```
@RestController
public class ProductRestController{

    @RequestMapping(value = "/products", method = RequestMethod.GET ,
        produces = {MediaType.APPLICATION_JSON_VALUE})
    public DeferredResult<List<Product>> getAllProducts() {

        DeferredResult<List<Product>> deferredResult =
            new DeferredResult<List<Product>> ();
        // Add deferredResult to an internal memory holder
```

```
        // like a Queue or a Map...
        return deferredResult;
    }

    // In some other thread...
    deferredResult.setResult(data);
    // Remove deferredResult from the internal memory holder
}
```

Java 8 introduced `java.util.concurrent.CompletableFuture`, which can be used with Spring to create async endpoints that similarly free up request threads to perform other tasks. In this case, the `DeferredResult.setResult` may simply be replaced with `CompletableFuture.complete`. A `CompletableFuture` is a `java.util.concurrent.Future`. A `Future` represents the result of an asynchronous computation whereas a `CompletableFuture` is a `Future` that may be explicitly completed (setting its value and status) and may be used as a `CompletionStage`, supporting dependent functions and actions that trigger upon its completion. `CompletableFuture` makes handling complex asynchronous programming easier. It even lets you combine and cascade async calls, and also offers the static utility methods `runAsync` and `supplyAsync` to abstract away the manual creation of threads. See Listing 10-4.

Listing 10-4. Pseudo Code for an Async Controller using CompletableFuture

```
@RestController
public class ProductRestController{

    @RequestMapping(value = "/products", method = RequestMethod.GET,
        produces = {MediaType.APPLICATION_JSON_VALUE})
    public CompletableFuture<List<Product>> getAllProducts() {

        Future<List<Product>> future =
            new CompletableFuture<List<Product>>();
        return CompletableFuture.supplyAsync(() -> "in the background");
    }
}
```

Design a Scenario to Demo Async HTTP Between Microservices

You will use a trimmed down version of the same components used for previous examples. So your sample here will consist of three main components: an HTML-based client app and two microservices, as shown in Figure 10-2. I have removed all complexities of HATEOAS and any data repositories so that you can concentrate on async HTTP alone. Once you appreciate the design and the main components used to implement it, then you should be able to use a similar pattern for your other complex business scenarios.

In the design shown, the client app communicates with the Product Web microservice using the HTTP protocol; however, you want the client to do it using the async HTTP model. Similarly, the Product Web microservice communicates with the Product Server microservice, again using the HTTP protocol, and this intermicroservices communication is designed using the async HTTP model.

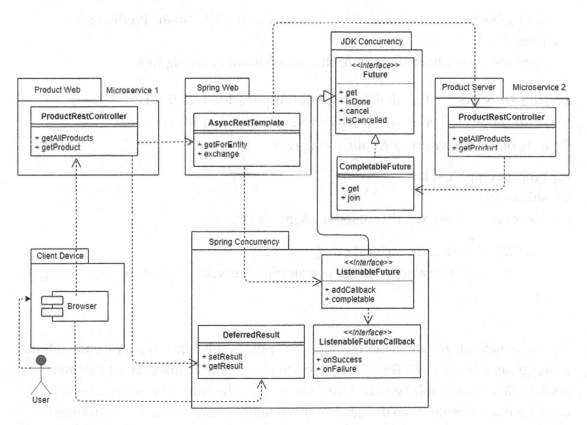

Figure 10-2. *Design an async HTTP scenario in Spring Boot*

Let's walk through the design in more detail by referring to the code snippets so that the concepts will be more clear.

Code to Use Async HTTP in Spring Boot

All the code samples for this section are in folder ch10\ch10-01. Visit pom.xml to see the explicit mention of the spring-boot-starter-web dependency for your Product Server microservice. See Listing 10-5.

Listing 10-5. Adding spring-boot-starter-web to Spring Boot (ch10\ch10-01\ ProductServer\pom.xml)

```
<dependency>
    <groupId>org.springframework.boot</groupId>
    <artifactId>spring-boot-starter-web</artifactId>
</dependency>
```

spring-boot-starter-web will add Tomcat and Spring MVC to the Product Server microservice.

Next, look at the Boot main application class shown in Listing 10-6.

Listing 10-6. Async Enabled Spring Boot Application (ch10\ch10-01\ProductServer\src\main\java\com\acme\ecom\product\ EcomProductMicroserviceApplication.java)

```
@SpringBootApplication
@EnableAsync
public class EcomProductMicroserviceApplication {

    public static void main(String[] args) {
        SpringApplication.run(EcomProductMicroserviceApplication.class, args);
    }
}
```

The @EnableAsync annotation switches on Spring's ability to run @Async methods in a background thread pool. This class also customizes the Executor backing the thread pool. By default, a SimpleAsyncTaskExecutor is used. The SimpleAsyncTaskExecutor does not reuse threads. Even though it supports limiting concurrent threads through the concurrencyLimit bean property, by default the number of concurrent threads is unlimited. In serious applications you should consider a thread-pooling TaskExecutor implementation instead.

Next, look at the Service component where you implement the async processing logic, shown in Listing 10-7.

Listing 10-7. Service Component Implementing Async Processing (ch10\
ch10-01\ProductServer\src\main\java\com\acme\ecom\product\service\
ProductService.java)

```
@Service
public class ProductService{

    @Async
    public CompletableFuture<List<Product>> getAllProducts()
            throws InterruptedException{

        List<Product> products = getAllTheProducts();
        if (products.size() == 0) {
            LOGGER.debug("No Products Retreived from the repository");
        }
        LOGGER.debug(Thread.currentThread().toString());
        Thread.sleep(2000L); // Delay to mock a long running task
        return CompletableFuture.completedFuture(products);
    }
}
```

The class is marked with the @Service annotation, making it a candidate for Spring's component scanning to detect it and add it to the application context. Next, the getAllProducts method is marked with Spring's @Async annotation, indicating it will run on a separate thread. The method's return type is CompletableFuture<List<Product>> instead of <List<Product>>, a requirement for any asynchronous service. This code uses the completedFuture method to return a CompletableFuture instance, which is already completed with the collection of results queried from the repository (a processing logic supposed to be taking considerable amount of time to complete).

Now, look at the Rest Controller of the Product Server microservice, shown in Listing 10-8.

Listing 10-8. Product Server Rest Controller Facilitating Async (ch10\ch10-01\ProductServer\src\main\java\com\acme\ecom\product\controller\ProductRestController.java)

```java
@RestController
public class ProductRestController {

    private final ProductService productService;

    @Autowired
    public ProductRestController(ProductService productService) {
        this.productService = productService;
    }

    @RequestMapping(value = "/products", method = RequestMethod.GET,
        produces = {MediaType.APPLICATION_JSON_VALUE})
    public CompletableFuture<List<Product>> getAllProducts()
            throws InterruptedException, ExecutionException{

        LOGGER.debug(Thread.currentThread().toString());

        return productService.getAllProducts()
            .thenApply(products -> {

                products.forEach(item->LOGGER.debug(item.toString()));
                LOGGER.debug(Thread.currentThread().toString());
                return products;
            });
    }
}
```

Note that the `CompletableFuture` response returned by `productService.getAllProducts()` allows you to manually control the moment when the future returns and also transform the output in the process. You then convert this simple `CompletableFuture` into the format you need with the help of `thenApply()`, which allows you to log some data about the current thread to make sure that the execution really happens asynchronously, that is, the thread that is finishing the work is not the thread that started the work. The Rest Controller too then returns the collection of the products once again as another CompletableFuture<List<Product>> so that Spring MVC will also act to execute the HTTP method in an async manner, making it a smartly implemented microservice! Keep in mind that this is an independent microservice; you will next look at a dependent microservice that depends on this independent microservice (as is shown in the design).

The dependent microservice is the Product Web microservice. The main code lies in the Controller class, shown in Listing 10-9.

Listing 10-9. Microservice Calling Async HTTP on Another Microservice (ch10\ ch10-01\ProductWeb\src\main\java\com\acme\ecom\product\controller\ ProductRestController.java)

```java
@RestController
public class ProductRestController{

    private final AsyncRestTemplate asyncRestTemplate =
        new AsyncRestTemplate();
    private static String PRODUCT_SERVICE_URL =
        "http://localhost:8080/products/";

    @RequestMapping(value = "/productsweb", method = RequestMethod.GET,
        produces = {MediaType.APPLICATION_JSON_VALUE})
    public DeferredResult<List<Product>> getAllProducts() {

        LOGGER.debug(Thread.currentThread().toString());
        DeferredResult<List<Product>> deferredResult = new DeferredResult<>();

        ParameterizedTypeReference<List<Product>> responseTypeRef =
            new ParameterizedTypeReference<List<Product>>() {};
        ListenableFuture<ResponseEntity<List<Product>>> entity =
            asyncRestTemplate.exchange(PRODUCT_SERVICE_URL,
            HttpMethod.GET, (HttpEntity<Product>) null, responseTypeRef);

        entity.addCallback(new
            ListenableFutureCallback<ResponseEntity<List<Product>>>() {

                @Override
                public void onFailure(Throwable ex) {
```

```
                    LOGGER.debug(Thread.currentThread().toString());
                    LOGGER.error(ex.getMessage());
                }

                @Override
                public void onSuccess(ResponseEntity<List<Product>> result) {

                    List<Product> products = result.getBody();
                    products.forEach(item->LOGGER.debug(item.toString()));
                        LOGGER.debug(Thread.currentThread().toString());
                        deferredResult.setResult(products);
                }
        });

        LOGGER.debug(Thread.currentThread().toString());
        return deferredResult;
    }
}
```

The PRODUCT_SERVICE_URL here refers to the independent microservice. The Product Web microservice has to invoke the Product Server microservice. You have already made the Product Server microservice methods asynchronous. Let's now make the Product Web microservice method asynchronous too so that all the containers hosting these microservices can better utilize container resources by implementing asynchronous characteristics to the runtime model. You are not done; you want to invoke the Product Server microservice too in an asynchronous mode so that both the microservice implementations as well as the intermicroservices communications are in smart, asynchronous mode!

org.springframework.web.client.AsyncRestTemplate is Spring's central class for asynchronous client-side HTTP access. It exposes methods similar to those of RestTemplate; however, it returns ListenableFuture wrappers as opposed to concrete results. By default, AsyncRestTemplate relies on standard JDK facilities to establish HTTP connections. Here again you can switch to a different HTTP library such as Apache HttpComponents, Netty, or OkHttp by using a constructor accepting an AsyncClientHttpRequestFactory. The AsyncRestTemplate gives you a ListenableFuture, so the container thread will not wait for the response to be received back; instead it will continue with the next steps of processing since you are using AsyncRestTemplate. ListenableFuture has the capability to accept completion callbacks, so you add callbacks on failure and success scenarios. If success, you set the result to the body of the DeferredResult. Since the Spring MVC is holding on to the response through the idle HTTP connection, as soon as you set the result to the DeferredResult, the client will receive it.

product_service.js has the code that the Angular JS client will use to invoke the Product Web microservice; see Listing 10-10.

Listing 10-10. Web Client Invoking Async HTTP (ch10\ch10-01\ProductWeb\src\main\resources\static\js\service\product_service.js)

```
App.factory('ProductService', ['$http', '$q', function($http, $q){

    return {

        getApplication: function() {
            return $http.get('http://localhost:8081/productsweb/')
                .then(
                    function(response){
                        return response.data;
                    },
                    function(errResponse){
                        console.error('Error while fetching application');
                        return $q.reject(errResponse);
                    }
                );
        }
    };

}]);
```

Build and Test Asynchronous HTTP Between Microservices

The complete code required to demonstrate asynchronous HTTP between microservices is in folder ch10\ch10-01. You don't require MongoDB for this sample. You can build, pack, and run the different microservices in the following order.

Bring up the Product Server microservice first:

```
cd ch10\ch10-01\ProductServer
D:\binil\gold\pack03\ch10\ch10-01\ProductServer>make
D:\binil\gold\pack03\ch10\ch10-01\ProductServer>mvn -Dmaven.test.skip=true
clean package
D:\binil\gold\pack03\ch10\ch10-01\ProductServer>run
D:\binil\gold\pack03\ch10\ch10-01\ProductServer>java -jar -Dserver.
port=8080 .\target\Ecom-Product-Microservice-0.0.1-SNAPSHOT.jar
```

Refer to Appendix D to get an overview of cURL and Postman. You can use any of these tools to test the above microservice by pointing to http://localhost:8080/products/.

Next, bring up the Product Web microservice:

```
cd ch10\ch10-01\ProductWeb
D:\binil\gold\pack03\ch10\ch10-01\ProductWeb>make
D:\binil\gold\pack03\ch10\ch10-01\ProductWeb>mvn -Dmaven.test.skip=true
clean package
D:\binil\gold\pack03\ch10\ch10-01\ProductWeb>run
D:\binil\gold\pack03\ch10\ch10-01\ProductWeb>java -jar -Dserver.port=8081
.\target\Ecom-Product-Microservice-0.0.1-SNAPSHOT.jar
```

You can again use cURL or Postman to test the Product Web microservice pointing to http://localhost:8081/productsweb/.

Alternatively, you may open this HTML utility preferably in the Chrome browser:

```
ch10\ch10-01\ProductWeb\src\main\resources\product.html.
```

Upon loading itself, the browser client will fire a request to Product Web, listening on port 8081, which will delegate the request to the Product Server microservice listening on port 8080. All is good until now, as far as the request routes are concerned. In fact, the HTTP conduit between the client and the Product Web microservice as well as the one between the Product Web microservice and the Product Server microservice are kept open and idle, and the container threads in both the microservices will return to be available for context switching. So, your Postman client or the HTML utility client will keep waiting over the idle HTTP connection. On the server side, processing happens in different threads and as soon as the results are available, they are written back to the open HTTP connection.

The thread dynamics can be understood by carefully observing the logs of the microservices consoles. Listing 10-11 shows the console output for the called (ProductServer) microservice.

Listing 10-11. Console Log of ProductServer (Called) Microservice

```
D:\binil\gold\pack03\ch10\ch10-01\ProductServer>run

D:\binil\gold\pack03\ch10\ch10-01\ProductServer>java -jar -Dserver.
port=8080 .\target\Ecom-Product-Microservice-0.0.1-SNAPSHOT.jar


  .   ___           _            __ _ _
 /\\ / ___'_ __ _ _(_)_ __  __ _ \ \ \ \
( ( )\___ | '_ | '_| | '_ \/ _` | \ \ \ \
 \\/  ___)| |_)| | | | | || (_| |  ) ) ) )
  '  |____| .__|_| |_|_| |_\__, | / / / /
 =========|_|==============|___/=/_/_/_/
 :: Spring Boot ::        (v1.5.4.RELEASE)


2019-02-23 10:11:33 INFO  StartupInfoLogger.logStarting:48 - Starting
2019-02-23 10:11:40 INFO  StartupInfoLogger.logStarted:57 - Started
EcomProductMicroserviceApplication in 8.231 seconds (JVM running for 9.827)
2019-02-23 10:13:34 INFO  ProductRestController.getAllProducts:94 - Start
2019-02-23 10:13:34 DEBUG ProductRestController.getAllProducts:95 -
Thread[http-nio-8080-exec-10,5,main]
2019-02-23 10:13:34 INFO  ProductService.getAllProducts:78 - Start
2019-02-23 10:13:34 DEBUG ProductService.getAllProducts:79 - Fetching all
the products from the repository
2019-02-23 10:13:34 INFO  ProductService.getAllTheProducts:109 - Start
2019-02-23 10:13:34 INFO  ProductService.getAllTheProducts:136 - Ending...
2019-02-23 10:13:34 DEBUG ProductService.getAllProducts:86 -
Thread[SimpleAsyncTaskExecutor-1,5,main]
2019-02-23 10:13:34 INFO  ProductService.getAllProducts:87 - Ending
2019-02-23 10:13:36 DEBUG ProductRestController.lambda$null$1:100 - Product
[productId=1, ...]
```

```
2019-02-23 10:13:36 DEBUG ProductRestController.lambda$null$1:100 - Product
[productId=2, ...]
2019-02-23 10:13:36 DEBUG ProductRestController.lambda$getAllProducts$2:101 -
Thread[SimpleAsyncTaskExecutor-1,5,main]
```

Listing 10-11 shows that `ProductRestController` gets executed in the context of `Thread[http-nio-8080-exec-10,5,main]` and so is the case with `ProductService`. In `ProductService`, just after the `ProductService.getAllTheProducts:136 - Ending...` log has happened, the following two lines of code release the executing thread:

```
Thread.sleep(2000L); // Delay to mock a long running task
return CompletableFuture.completedFuture(products);
```

You need to differentiate between the above two lines of code, and I will explain them:

1. The first line just makes a delay so that the caller (line of code from `ProductRestController` of the ProductWeb microservice reproduced below) will feel a perceived delay from the called microservice:

    ```
    ListenableFuture<ResponseEntity<List<Product>>> entity =
        asyncRestTemplate.exchange(PRODUCT_SERVICE_URL, HttpMethod.GET,
        (HttpEntity<Product>) null, responseTypeRef);
    ```

2. The second line of code actually returns the executing thread, so `Thread[http-nio-8080-exec-10,5,main]` will be returned back to the embedded web container's HTTP pool.

Later when `CompletableFuture.completedFuture(products)` resumes, it will get executed in some other thread context (`Thread[SimpleAsyncTaskExecutor-1,5,main]` in your case, as shown in Listing 10-11).

Similarly, Listing 10-12 shows the console output for the called (ProductServer) microservice.

Listing 10-12. Console Log of ProductWeb (Caller) Microservice

```
D:\binil\gold\pack03\ch10\ch10-01\ProductWeb>run

D:\binil\gold\pack03\ch10\ch10-01\ProductWeb>java -jar -Dserver.port=8081
.\target\Ecom-Product-Microservice-0.0.1-SNAPSHOT.jar

  .   ___          _            __ _ _
 /\\ / ___'_ __ _ _(_)_ __  __ _ \ \ \ \
( ( )\___ | '_ | '_| | '_ \/ _` | \ \ \ \
 \\/  ___)| |_)| | | | | || (_| |  ) ) ) )
  '  |____| .__|_| |_|_| |_\__, | / / / /
 =========|_|==============|___/=/_/_/_/
 :: Spring Boot ::        (v1.5.4.RELEASE)

2019-02-23 10:12:33 DEBUG StartupInfoLogger.logStarting:51 - Running with
Spring Boot v1.5.4.RELEASE, Spring v4.3.9.RELEASE
2019-02-23 10:12:38 INFO  StartupInfoLogger.logStarted:57 - Started
EcomProductMicroserviceApplication in 6.804 seconds (JVM running for 8.494)
2019-02-23 10:13:34 INFO  ProductRestController.getAllProducts:87 - Start
2019-02-23 10:13:34 DEBUG ProductRestController.getAllProducts:88 -
Thread[http-nio-8081-exec-7,5,main]
2019-02-23 10:13:34 DEBUG ProductRestController.getAllProducts:113 -
Thread[http-nio-8081-exec-7,5,main]
2019-02-23 10:13:37 DEBUG ProductRestController$2.lambda$onSuccess$0:107 -
Product [productId=1, ...]
2019-02-23 10:13:37 DEBUG ProductRestController$2.lambda$onSuccess$0:107 -
Product [productId=2, ...]
2019-02-23 10:13:37 DEBUG ProductRestController$2.onSuccess:108 -
Thread[SimpleAsyncTaskExecutor-1,5,main]
```

Listings 10-11 and 10-12 assert that the background processing happens in threads from SimpleAsyncTaskExecutor whereas the container threads of the format http-nio-*.* have already completed the request part of the transaction and were given back to the pool. This is a powerful way of bridging the synchronous, blocking paradigm of a RESTful interface with the asynchronous, non-blocking processing performed on the server side.

Google Protocol Buffer Between Spring Boot Microservices

The previous section talked about effectively utilizing the microservices' server resources like HTTP connections and threads. Equally important are the other possible optimizations in intercommunications between microservices. Since microservices are spread across process boundaries, the amount of data sent across microservices matter. This boils down to the marshalling and unmarshalling of data structures across microservices. You will look into this with examples in this section.

Protocol Buffer

Protocol buffers are Google's platform-neutral and language-neutral mechanism for marshalling and unmarshalling structured data. You need to define how you want your data to be structured to use Protocol Buffer, and then you can use generated source code in multiple platforms and languages to easily write and read your structured data to and from a variety of data streams. One benefit of using Protocol Buffer is that you can even update your data structure without breaking already deployed application code that is compiled against the "old" format. This is especially important in architecting applications capable of adapting or evolving to future requirement changes.

You will now look into the dynamics of using Protocol Buffer. You first need to specify how you want the information you're serializing to be structured in `.proto` files. In doing so, you use the Protocol Buffer message types. Each Protocol Buffer message is a logical grouping of information, containing a series of name-value pairs. Listing 10-13 is a sample of a `.proto` file that defines a message containing information about a `Product`, which you used in all of your previous samples.

Listing 10-13. Sample .proto File

```
message Product {

    string productId = 1;
    string name = 2;
    string code = 3;
    string title = 4;
    string description = 5;
```

```
    string imgUrl = 6;
    double price = 7;
    string productCategoryName = 8;
}
```

Each message (message `Product` in your sample) type has one or more uniquely numbered fields, and each field has a name and a value type, where value types can be numbers (integer or floating-point), bools, strings, or raw bytes. Your Protocol Buffer message can also be other protocol buffer message types, as shown in the container message defined in Listing 10-14 to hold a collection of `Product` instances.

Listing 10-14. .proto File for a Collection of Other .proto Types

```
message Products {
    repeated Product product = 1;
}
```

You can specify fields as optional, required, and/or repeated, as shown in the `Products` message.

Once you define your messages, you can run the Protocol Buffer compiler for the application's programming language of your choice on your .proto file to generate entity classes. These entity classes provide you with simple accessors for each field (like `code()` and `set_code()`) as well as methods to serialize/parse the whole structure to/from raw bytes. In your scenario, if your chosen language is Java, running the compiler on the above sample will generate a class called `Product`. You can use this entity class in your application to marshal and unmarshal `Product` protocol buffer messages. Your code will look like that in Listing 10-15.

Listing 10-15. Marshalling and Unmarshalling .proto Types

```
Product product =
    Product.newBuilder().setProductId(id)
        .setName("Kamsung D3")
        .setCode("KAMSUNG-TRIOS")
        .setTitle("Kamsung Trios 12 inch , black , 12 px ....")
        .setDescription("Kamsung Trios 12 inch with Touch")
```

```
        .setImgUrl("kamsung.jpg")
        .setPrice(12000.00)
        .setProductCategoryName("Mobile").build();
```

```
// write
FileOutputStream output = new FileOutputStream("D:/Product.ser");
product.writeTo(output);
output.close();
```

```
// read
Product productFromFile = Product.parseFrom(new FileInputStream("D:/
Product.ser"));
```

You can now add new fields to your message formats without breaking backwards-compatibility; any old program binaries will ignore any new fields when parsing. So by using protocol buffers as the data format, you can extend your message protocol without having to worry about breaking existing code.

Google's documentation on Protocol Buffer lists the advantages of using Protocol Buffer as follows:

- Simpler

- 3 to 10 times smaller

- 20 to 100 times faster

- Less ambiguous

- Generate data access classes that are easier to use programmatically

The second and third bullet points are of great significance especially when you want to design numerous chit-chat kinds of interactions between microservices, which are again too many in number in any serious enterprise-grade application.

Let's now look at a complete example to explain the usage of Protocol Buffer between microservices.

A Scenario to Demonstrate Protocol Buffer Between Microservices

You will modify the same example you used in your earlier demonstrations to leverage Protocol Buffer. You will use a trimmed down version of the same components used in Chapter 8. So your example here will consist of three main components: an HTML-based client app and two microservices, as shown in Figure 10-3. Here again I have removed all complexities of HATEOAS and data repositories so that you can concentrate on the usage of Protocol Buffer alone.

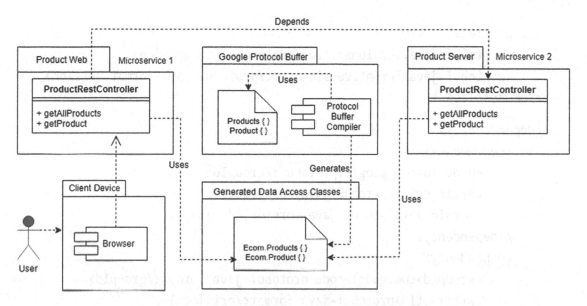

Figure 10-3. *Use Protocol Buffer between microservices*

In your example design, you use a .proto file where you spec out the entities you want to use. The next step is to run the Protocol Buffer compiler for the application's programming language (Java, in your case) on your .proto file to generate similar classes. Now both the dependent and the independent microservices can be programmed against the generated entity classes, thus making intermicroservices communication using protocol buffer a straightforward step.

Code to Use Protocol Buffer in Spring Boot

All the code samples for this section are in folder ch08\ch10-02. You will look at the code for the independent microservice first, the Product Server microservice. Visit pom.xml to see the explicit mention of the protobuf-java and the protobuf-java-format dependency for your Product Server microservice. See Listing 10-16.

Listing 10-16. Adding a Protocol Buffer Compiler and Runtime to the Maven Build (ch10\ch10-02\ProductServer\pom.xml)

```
<project>

    <properties>
        <protobuf-java.version>3.1.0</protobuf-java.version>
        <protobuf-java-format.version>1.4</protobuf-java-format.version>
    </properties>

    <dependencies>
        <dependency>
            <groupId>com.google.protobuf</groupId>
            <artifactId>protobuf-java</artifactId>
            <version>${protobuf-java.version}</version>
        </dependency>
        <dependency>
            <groupId>com.googlecode.protobuf-java-format</groupId>
            <artifactId>protobuf-java-format</artifactId>
            <version>${protobuf-java-format.version}</version>
        </dependency>
        <dependency>
            <groupId>org.springframework.boot</groupId>
            <artifactId>spring-boot-starter-web</artifactId>
        </dependency>
    </dependencies>
```

```
<build>
    <plugins>
        <plugin>
            <groupId>org.springframework.boot</groupId>
            <artifactId>spring-boot-maven-plugin</artifactId>
        </plugin>
        <plugin>
            <groupId>com.github.os72</groupId>
            <artifactId>protoc-jar-maven-plugin</artifactId>
            <version>3.1.0</version>
            <executions>
                <execution>
                    <phase>generate-sources</phase>
                    <goals>
                        <goal>run</goal>
                    </goals>
                    <configuration>
                        <protocVersion>3.1.0</protocVersion>
                        <includeStdTypes>true</includeStdTypes>
                        <includeDirectories>
                            <include>
                                src/main/resources
                            </include>
                        </includeDirectories>
                        <inputDirectories>
                            <include>
                                src/main/protobuf
                            </include>
                        </inputDirectories>
                    </configuration>
                </execution>
            </executions>
        </plugin>
    </plugins>
</build>

</project>
```

protoc-jar-maven-plugin performs protobuf code generation using the multi-platform executable protoc-jar. At build time, this Maven plugin detects the platform and executes the corresponding protoc binary so that it can compile .proto files using protoc-jar embedded protoc compiler, providing some portability across the major platforms (Linux, Mac/OSX, and Windows). In the pom.xml above, the compiler compiles .proto files in the main cycle and places the generated files into target/generated-sources, including google.protobuf standard types, and includes any additional imports required.

The protobuf-java Maven artifact provides the Java APIs required to serialize the generated message objects in Java. So it acts as the runtime for Protocol Buffer.

Note that the compiler version should be same as the Java API version. In your sample, you use the 3.1.0 version.

The protobuf-java-format Maven artifact provides serialization and deserialization of different formats based on Google's protobuf Message. It enables overriding the default (byte array) output to text based formats such as XML, JSON, and HTML.

Now, look at the Protocol Buffer type declaration shown in Listing 10-17.

Listing 10-17. Type Declaration in product.proto (ch10\ch10-02\ProductServer\ src\main\resources\product.proto)

```
syntax = "proto3";

package binildas;

option java_package = "com.acme.ecom.product.model";
option java_outer_classname = "ECom";

message Products {

    repeated Product product = 1;
}
message Product {

    string productId = 1;
    string name = 2;
    string code = 3;
    string title = 4;
    string description = 5;
```

```
    string imgUrl = 6;
    double price = 7;
    string productCategoryName = 8;
}
```

Since you use version 3 of both the protocol buffer compiler and the protocol buffer language runtime, the .proto file must start with the syntax = "proto3" declaration. If a compiler version 2 is used instead, this declaration would be omitted.

The .proto file should next have a package declaration, which helps prevent naming conflicts between different type declarations across different projects. In Java, this package name is also used as the Java package unless you have explicitly specified a java_package, as you have here.

Next are two Java-specific options: the java_package and java_outer_classname. The java_package option specifies in what Java package your generated classes should live. If you don't specify this explicitly, it matches the package name given by the package declaration. The java_outer_classname option defines the container class name, which should contain all of the classes generated in the type definition file.

Next, you add a message for each data structure you want to serialize and then specify a name and a type for each field in the message. A message is an aggregate containing a set of typed fields. Many standard simple data types are available as field types, including bool, int32, float, double, and string. You can also add other message types as field types; in your example, the Products message contains Product messages. The = 1, = 2, = 3, etc. are markers on each element to identify the unique "tag" that the field uses in the binary encoding.

Fields can be annotated with one of the following modifiers:

- **required**: Indicates that a value for the field must be provided; otherwise the message will be considered "uninitialized."

- **optional**: Indicates that the field may or may not be set. If an optional field value isn't set, a default value is used, like zero for numeric types, the empty string for strings, false for Booleans, etc.

- **repeated**: Indicates that the field may be repeated any number of times (including zero). The order of the repeated values will be preserved in the protocol buffer.

Next, look at the Product Server Controller in Listing 10-18.

Listing 10-18. Product Rest Controller to Emit Protocol Buffer (ch10\ch10-02\ProductServer\src\main\java\com\acme\ecom\product\controller\ProductRestController.java)

```
package com.acme.ecom.product.controller;

import com.acme.ecom.product.model.ECom.Product;
import com.acme.ecom.product.model.ECom.Products;

@RestController
public class ProductRestController {

    @RequestMapping(value = "/products", method = RequestMethod.GET)
    public  Products getAllProducts() {

        List<Product> products = getAllTheProducts();
        if(products.isEmpty()){
            LOGGER.debug("No products retreived from repository");
        }
        products.forEach(item->LOGGER.debug(item.toString()));
        Products productsParent =
            Products.newBuilder().addAllProduct(products).build();
        return productsParent;
    }
}
```

There is no major noticeable difference in the Rest Controller except the fact that you need to import Products and Product Java types defined within the outer container class, ECom.

You now need to instrument the microservice runtime with the required libraries to serialize and deserialize to the Protocol Buffer format. Spring's ProtobufHttpMessageConverter comes handy to internally leverage Google's libraries. This converter supports by default application/x-protobuf and text/plain with the official com.google.protobuf:protobuf-java library. It is to be noted that other formats can also be supported with the correct additional libraries on the classpath. You will instantiate this bean in a configuration class; see Listing 10-19.

Listing 10-19. Configuring Protocol Buffer Message Converter (ch10\ch10-02\ProductServer\src\main\java\com\acme\ecom\product\controller\ProductRestControllerConfiguration.java)

```
import org.springframework.http.converter.protobuf.
ProtobufHttpMessageConverter;

@Configuration
public class ProductRestControllerConfiguration{

    @Bean
    ProtobufHttpMessageConverter protobufHttpMessageConverter() {
        return new ProtobufHttpMessageConverter();
    }
}
```

That's all for the Product Server microservice. Now you will look at the code for the Product Web microservices. All of the code snippets you have seen and the explanations I have made for the Product Server microservice are still valid, so I will not repeat them here for brevity; instead, I will explain any additional requirements.

The Product Web microservice must delegate requests to the Product Server microservice. To make this delegation work, you need a bean of the RestTemplate type to be registered in a configuration class. This RestTemplate is injected with another bean of the ProtobufHttpMessageConverter type, which will help to automatically transform the received protocol buffer messages. This is shown in Listing 10-20.

Listing 10-20. Rest Template to Invoke Protocol Buffer (ch10\ch10-02\ProductWeb\src\main\java\com\acme\ecom\product\controller\ProductRestControllerConfiguration.java)

```
@Configuration
public class ProductRestControllerConfiguration{

    @Bean
    RestTemplate restTemplate(ProtobufHttpMessageConverter hmc) {
        return new RestTemplate(Arrays.asList(hmc));
    }
```

```
@Bean
ProtobufHttpMessageConverter protobufHttpMessageConverter() {
    return new ProtobufHttpMessageConverter();
}
}
```

Next, the Rest Controller for the Product Web microservice will leverage the above RestTemplate to delegate calls to the Product Server microservice, as shown in Listing 10-21.

Listing 10-21. Rest Controller Delegating Calls to Microservice Spitting Protocol Buffer (ch10\ch10-02\ProductWeb\src\main\java\com\acme\ecom\product\controller\ProductRestController.java)

```
@RestController
public class ProductRestController{

    @Autowired
    RestTemplate restTemplate;

    private static String PRODUCT_SERVICE_URL =
        "http://localhost:8081/products/";

    @Autowired
    public ProductRestController(RestTemplate restTemplate){
        this.restTemplate = restTemplate;
    }

    @RequestMapping(value = "/productsweb", method = RequestMethod.GET,
        produces = {MediaType.APPLICATION_JSON_VALUE})
    public  Products getAllProducts() {

        Products products = restTemplate.getForObject(PRODUCT_SERVICE_URL,
            Products.class);
        List<Product> productsList = products.getProductList();
        Products productsParent =
        Products.newBuilder().addAllProduct(productsList).build();
        return productsParent;
    }
}
```

Build and Test the Protocol Buffer Between Microservices

Once your message structure is defined in a .proto file, you need a protoc compiler to convert this language-neutral content to Java code. Follow the instructions in the Protocol Buffer's repository (https://github.com/google/protobuf) in order to get an appropriate compiler version. Alternatively, you can download a prebuilt binary compiler from the Maven central repository by searching for the com.google.protobuf:protoc artifact and then picking an appropriate version for your platform.

Next, you need to run the compiler, specifying the path to search for the .proto files, the destination directory where you want the generated code to go, and the absolute path to your .proto. In your case, it will look like:

```
D:\Applns\Google\ProtocolBuffer\protoc-3.4.0-win32\bin\protoc --proto_path
.\src\main\resources --java_out .\src\main\java .\src\main\resources\
product.proto
```

Because you want Java classes, you use the --java_out option; however, similar options are provided for other supported languages.

The above steps are handy, but they are not straightforward to weave into the Maven build. That's why you used the protoc-jar-maven-plugin in the pom.xml in Listing 10-16; it performs protobuf code generation using the multiplatform executable protoc-jar. Hence no manual steps are needed to build and run the samples. Let's get started.

The complete code required to demonstrate intermicroservices communication using Protocol Buffer is kept inside folder ch10\ch10-02. You don't need MongoDB for this sample. You can build, pack, and run the different microservices in the following order.

Bring up the Product Server microservice first:

```
cd ch10\ch10-02\ProductServer
D:\binil\gold\pack03\ch10\ch10-02\ProductServer>make
D:\binil\gold\pack03\ch10\ch10-02\ProductServer>rem D:\Applns\Google\
ProtocolBuffer\protoc-3.4.0-win32\bin\protoc --proto_path .\src\main\
resources --java_out .\src\main\java .\src\main\resources\product.proto
D:\binil\gold\pack03\ch10\ch10-02\ProductServer>mvn -Dmaven.test.skip=true
clean package
D:\binil\gold\pack03\ch10\ch10-02\ProductServer>run
D:\binil\gold\pack03\ch10\ch10-02\ProductServer>java -jar -Dserver.
port=8080 .\target\Ecom-Product-Microservice-0.0.1-SNAPSHOT.jar
```

The above command will bring up the Product Server microservice in port 8080. You also want to inspect the format of the messages flowing through the wire, so you use Apache TCPMon as a proxy. See Appendix E to start TCPMon as a proxy.

```
cd D:\Applns\apache\TCPMon\tcpmon-1.0-bin\build
D:\Applns\apache\TCPMon\tcpmon-1.0-bin\build>tcpmon 8081 127.0.0.1 8080
```

This will bring up TCPMon so that all requests hitting port 8081 in the host where the TCPMon is running (localhost, in your case) will be proxied to port 8080 in host 127.0.0.1 in the above case. See Figure 10-4.

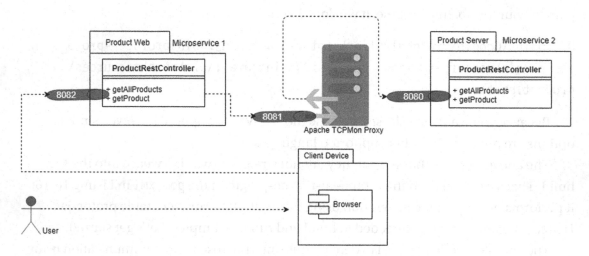

Figure 10-4. *TCPMon Proxy set to monitor requests and responses*

Next, bring up the Product Web microservice:

```
cd ch10\ch10-02\ProductWeb
D:\binil\gold\pack03\ch10\ch10-02\ProductWeb>make

D:\binil\gold\pack03\ch10\ch10-02\ProductWeb>mvn -Dmaven.test.skip=true
clean package
D:\binil\gold\pack03\ch10\ch10-02\ProductWeb>run
D:\binil\gold\pack03\ch10\ch10-02\ProductWeb>java -Dserver.port=8082 -jar
.\target\Ecom-Product-Microservice-0.0.1-SNAPSHOT.jar
```

You can now test the application by pointing to the URL to retrieve the HTML-based client app, preferably using the Chrome browser:

`http://localhost:8082/`

Upon loading itself, the browser client will fire a request to Product Web, listening on port 8082, which will delegate the request to the Apache TCPMon Proxy listening on port 8081. This request hitting port 8081 in the host where the TCPMon is running (localhost, in your case) will be proxied to port 8080 in localhost, again where the Product Server microservice is listening. If everything goes as planned, you should be able to see the products listed on the web page. If you inspect the TCPMon Proxy console, you should be able to validate that the communication between the two microservices uses Protocol Buffer as the wire-level protocol in handshaking the HTTP-based REST invocation.

The Impact of Using Protocol Buffer

Let's inspect the response content length while using Protocol Buffer for intermicroservices communications. For this comparison, you will look at three scenarios.

Protocol Buffer Encoding

The sample demonstration in the previous section explained how to use Protocol Buffer for intermicroservices communications. You can observe the TCPMon Proxy console where you should be able to validate that the communication between the two microservices uses Protocol Buffer. It will also say that the response content length is 265 (which is representative). See Figure 10-5.

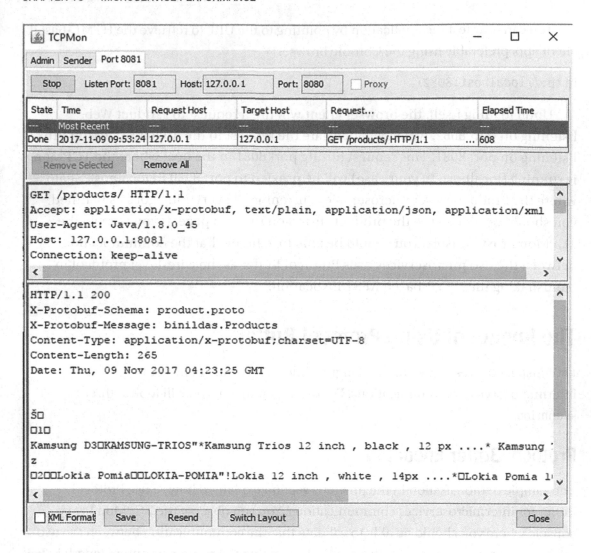

Figure 10-5. *Inspect the Protocol Buffer encoding using TCPMon*

XML Encoding

You can use Chrome and hit the TCPMon Proxy directly so that the client doesn't explicitly ask for Protocol Buffer during content negotiation using the URL http://localhost:8081/products/. This will show the response in XML format; see Figure 10-6.

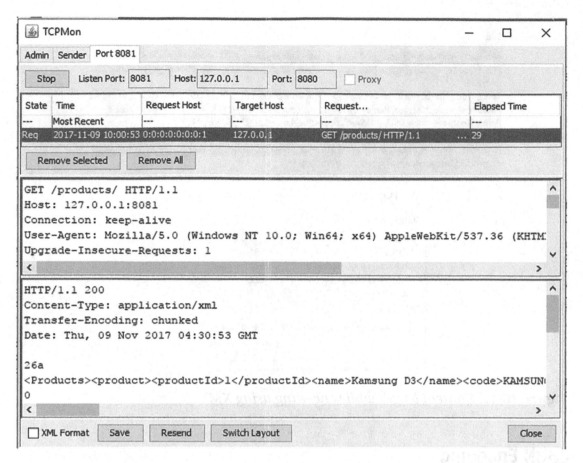

Figure 10-6.   *Inspect the XML encoding using TCPMon*

You can examine the content size using any tool (I use Microsoft Word in Figure 10-7).

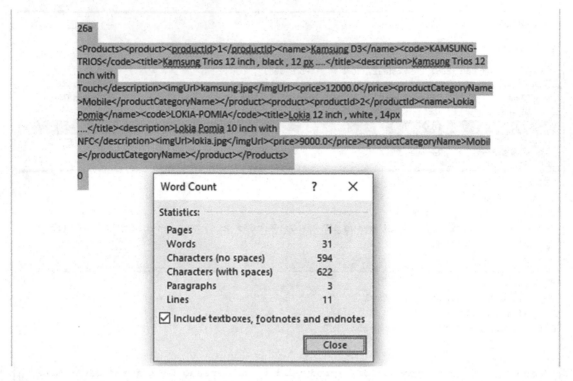

Figure 10-7. *Content length while encoding using XML*

JSON Encoding

One easy method to force JSON encoding between the microservices call is to slightly change the application code in the Product Server microservice. See Listing 10-22.

Listing 10-22. Enforce JSON Encoding (ch10\ch10-02\ProductServer\src\main\java\com\acme\ecom\product\controller\ProductRestController.java)

```
@RequestMapping(value = "/products", method = RequestMethod.GET,
    produces = {MediaType.APPLICATION_JSON_VALUE})
//@RequestMapping(value = "/products", method = RequestMethod.GET)
public  Products getAllProducts() {
```

```
    List<Product> products = getAllTheProducts();
    Products productsParent =        Products.newBuilder().
                                     addAllProduct(products).build();

    return productsParent;
}
```

You can now rebuild and restart the Product Server microservice and rerun the client application by going to `http://localhost:8082/`.

If you inspect the TCPMon Proxy console, you should be able to see that JSON encoding is opted in this case, as shown in Figure 10-8.

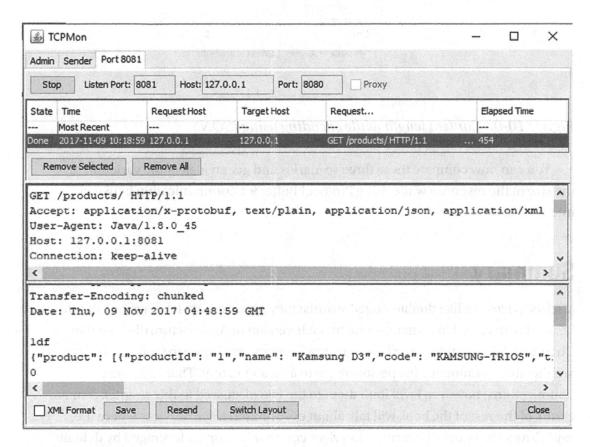

Figure 10-8. *Inspect JSON encoding using TCPMon*

You can again examine the content size using any tool (see Figure 10-9).

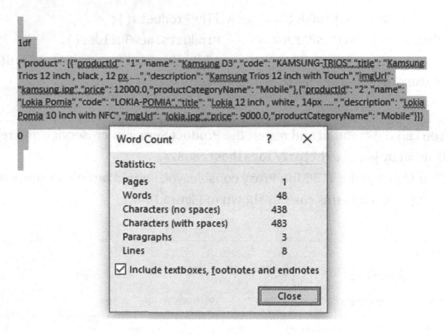

Figure 10-9. *Content length while encoding using JSON*

You can now compare these three scenarios and get an idea of the variation in the size of the response while using Protocol Buffer for communication between microservices.

Summary

Microservices are like double-edged swords: they provide extra leverage but should be used with care. This is mainly due to the Inversion of Architecture discussed in Chapter 4. You learned two refactoring processes you can bring to your microservices architecture to influence the performance to a greater extent. There are more optimizations; however, I will limit them to the two discussed in this chapter. A major chunk of the rest of the book will talk about event-based microservices where the asynchronous nature of intermicroservices communications is leveraged by default using messaging instead of HTTP. You'll start getting into those aspects in the next chapter.

CHAPTER 11

Events, Eventuality, and Consistency

A handshake with one of your colleagues provides you back the same feeling of the handshake, instantaneously. Similar is the case of a hug or a kiss with your partner—you also receive the same back, instantaneously (assuming your partner's mood doesn't invite a slap as response!). What if your partner in any of the above described contexts is not near you but you still want to pass similar greetings to him or her? You can send an email or a message through any kind of digital media available today. Your partner will (sooner or later) receive your message and will be able to respond to you. The end effect is that, even though your partner is not nearby or even listening to you at the exact time you initiate your gesture, you will sooner or later get the response gesture back. These scenarios and gestures are typical of a microservices application too. Once you have split your application into microservices based on domain boundaries, which can be deployed, brought up, and operated on their own, independent of other microservices, it also means that those microservices should have the capability to continue providing functionality irrespective of their counterpart microservices. This is where the importance of event-driven architecture (EDA) must be discussed. You will look into EDA in general plus a selected few concerns in this chapter. At the end, you will be in a position to appreciate events and EDA, and you'll be better equipped to decide whether you want asynchronous events or synchronous request/response-style interactions between microservices.

You will learn the following in this chapter:

- Introduction to EDA

- Different styles of EDA

- Relevance of EDA in the evolution of a microservices architecture

© Binildas Christudas 2019

B. Christudas, *Practical Microservices Architectural Patterns*, https://doi.org/10.1007/978-1-4842-4501-9_11

- The role of EDA in making different microservices eventually consistent

- The Scale Cube and the need for partitioning computational activity

- The CAP Theorem and the CAP Pyramid

- BASE transactions

Event-Driven Architecture

Event-driven architecture is a software architecture pattern promoting the production, detection, consumption, and reaction to events. An event-driven system typically consists of event emitters (or agents), event consumers (or sinks), and event channels through which the events propagate. Let's look into these components in detail.

Events

An event is an occurrence or a happening within a particular system or domain; it is something that has occurred or is contemplated as having occurred in that domain.

An event can be defined as a change in state. For example, when an order is shipped, the order's state changes from "pending" to "shipped." An e-commerce microservices architecture may treat this state change as an event whose occurrence can be made known to other microservices within the architecture or for that matter even to other components outside the microservices boundary. From a formal perspective, what is produced, published, propagated, detected, or consumed is a (typically asynchronous) message called the event notification, and not the event itself. If so, the event is the state change that triggered the message emission. Events do not travel; they just occur. However, the terms "event" and "event notifications" are often used interchangeably to denote the notification message itself.

EDA Components

An EDA-based application typically consists of event emitters (source or agents), event consumers (sinks), and event channels. Event emitters have the responsibility to generate, detect, gather, and transfer events. When an event emitter does so, it doesn't know the consumers of the event, it doesn't even know if any consumer exists, and if it exists, it doesn't know how or when or where the event is used for further processing. Event sinks have the responsibility of reacting as soon as an interested event is sensed. The reaction provided by the sink may be complete or partial. If the reaction is partial, it is possible that the same event is also interesting to other sinks and they may add to the reaction.

Event channels are conduits through which events are transmitted from an event source to an event sink. The information required for the correct distribution of events to the right sink is exclusively present within the event channel. However, such event channels with distribution knowledge are rather rigid in terms of addressing, and in physical terms they are often represented by message queues.

In other words, the physical implementation of such event channels can be based on traditional components such as message-oriented middleware using point-to-point communication, typically represented by message queues.

Figure 11-1 represents the point-to-point kind of event processing typically leveraging message queues. When you use a queue, the event source and sink are tightly coupled and this is shown in Figure 11-1. A better approach is to have topics representing those conduits. Here, the event channels have little information as to where to distribute the events; rather, it's up to the event sinks to attach themselves to the interested event channels and get notified whenever an interesting event is available.

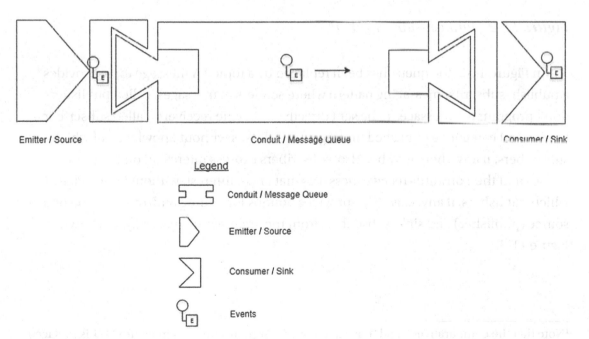

Figure 11-1. Point-to-point EDA

The latter approach is more flexible in terms of the expandability of a microservices application, and you will see the details soon. Figure 11-2 shows that the relationship of the event source and sink with respect to the message conduit (Message Topic, in this case) is relatively flexible.

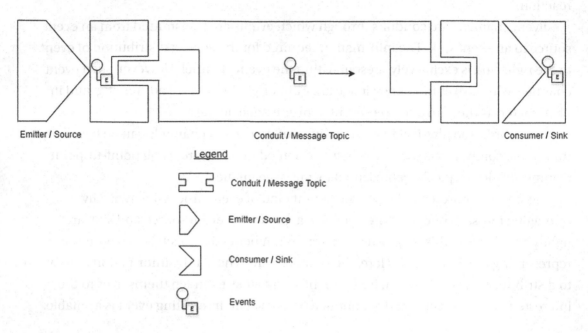

Figure 11-2. *Publish-subscribe EDA*

In Figure 11-2, the queue has been replaced by a topic.[1] A message topic provides a publish–subscribe messaging pattern where senders of messages, called publishers, don't program the messages to be sent directly to specific receivers, called subscribers, but instead categorize published messages into classes without knowledge of which subscribers, if any, there may be. Also, subscribers express interest in one or more classes and then onwards receive messages that are of interest, without knowledge of which publishers, if any, exist. This provides options for adding and/or removing both source (publisher) and sink (subscriber) from the architecture on the fly, as shown in Figure 11-3.

---

[1]Note that the comparatively rigid "dove tail" connector representation in Figure 11-1 is replaced with a flexible, "slide in and slide out" connector in Figure 11-2

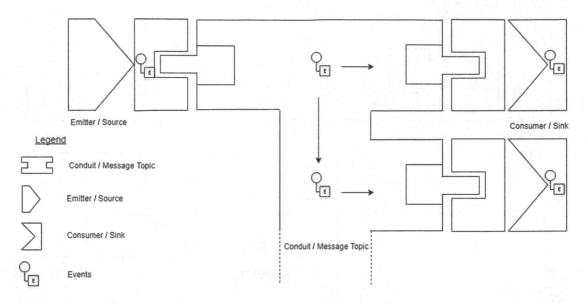

Figure 11-3. *Flexible publish-subscribe EDA*

As depicted in Figure 11-3, while following the publish-subscribe pattern, the conduit itself is open and continuous in the sense that it can accommodate more sink in future, on the fly.

Microservices and Event-Driven Architecture

Having talked about the point-to-point and publish-subscribe patterns of EDA, let's now look into some concerns you will face when designing microservices in the flexible, publish-subscribe pattern.

Evolution of Microservices

Most of the software applications are built with a set of requirements in mind to start with, and then have a natural evolution over a period of a few years. Incorporating change requests and new requirements will happen over the years until the application is finally retired. Traditional or monolith applications are changed at the source code level to accommodate these changes and then the entire application has to be regression tested, performance validated, and redeployed. There will be inevitable downtime, also.

Figure 11-4 shows an e-commerce application that uses the publish-subscribe microservices pattern.

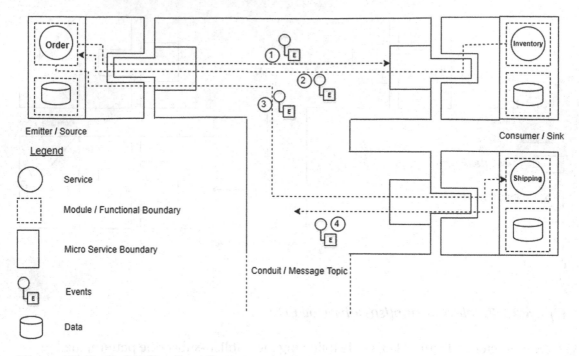

Figure 11-4. Publish-subscribe microservices

With reference to Figure 11-4, the microservices interact as follows:

1. The Order Service creates an Order in a pending state and publishes an OrderCreated event.

2. The Inventory Service receives the event and attempts to update the inventory for items based on that Order. It then publishes either an InventoryUpdated event or a NotEnoughInventory event.

3. If an InventoryUpdated event occurs, then the Order status must change from pending to confirmed, which will again fire an OrderConfirmed event.

4. The Shipping Service receives the OrderConfirmed event and arranges for shipping the product. Once arrangements have completed and the item has shipped, it fires an OrderShipped event.

So far, so good, but say the e-commerce company wants to boost customer experience, and as a part of that, the IT department wants to enhance the application to include prompt notifications to customers through e-mail and other channels.

The solution is to introduce another microservice called Notification Service. Since you have designed the application based on a publish-subscribe pattern, you should be able to introduce the new microservice without any downtime to the application. In other words, you should develop, test, benchmark the performance, baseline the Notification microservice, and deploy "hot" to the existing application infrastructure. Once deployed, from then onwards the Notification microservice will start consuming the OrderConfirmed event to promptly notify the customer that his order has been confirmed. Similarly, it may also start consuming the OrderShipped event to promptly notify the customer that his order has been shipped. This is depicted in Figure 11-5.

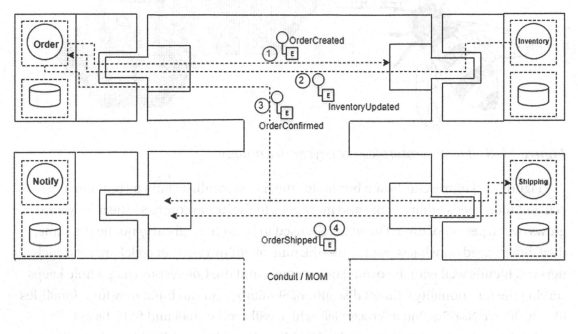

Figure 11-5.   *The evolution of the microservices application*

What you have seen is seamless evolution. You don't touch or disrupt any of the existing microservices; however, you can hook or attach more and more microservices to significantly alter application behavior or functionality! You should now better understand the honeycomb analogy mentioned in the "Extensible Microservices" section in Chapter 3, which is duplicated in Figure 11-6.

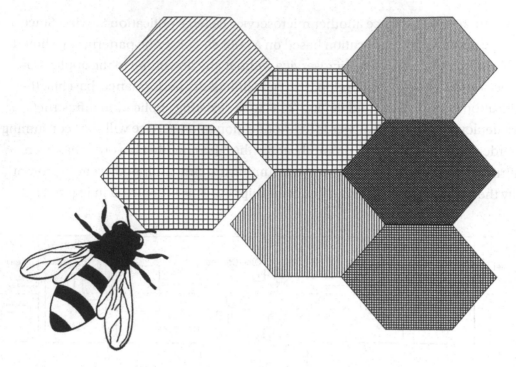

Figure 11-6. *The microservices honeycomb analogy*

Figure 11-6 represents how a bee builds the honeycomb. It starts by building the first cell and then keeps adding more and more cells to the honeycomb. So the honeycomb grows over a period of time. The materials used to build the cells may not be the same; they differ based on what is available at the time of building of that cell. However, each new cell blends well with the overall honeycomb, and the honeycomb as a whole keeps serving the functionality without disruption. Similarly, you can build new functionalities like the above Notification microservice, which will send e-mail and SMS-based notifications of order statuses, seamlessly adding this enhanced functionality to the application without any downtime for existing (microservices of the) application.[2]

---

[2]Refer back to Figure 2-5 in Chapter 2 to refresh your notion of "application" and "microservices" and the relationship between the two.

Eventual Consistency and Microservices

Let's now explore the interesting intricacies of microservices. Monolithic applications typically use a single relational database. A key benefit of using a relational database is that your application can leverage ACID transactions. Figure 11-7 depicts a typical monolithic application.

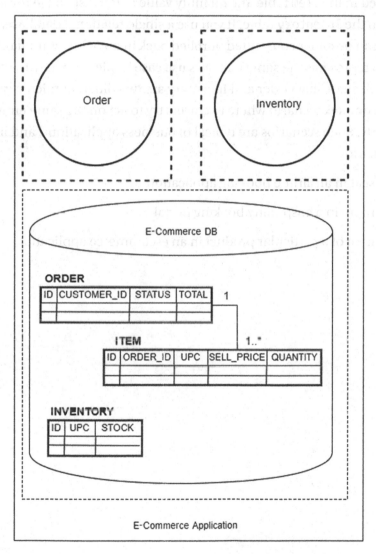

Figure 11-7. An e-commerce monolith application

Multiple entities in your domain can be represented by separate tables in a schema in your single relational database. In the current example, Order, Item, and Inventory are such entities. A customer will add multiple product items to his shopping cart and finally check out via a single button click. When that happens, a new row gets created in the Order table representing a new order. With this Order ID as a foreign key, as many rows are created in the Items table as there are items in the shopping cart. Further, for each row created in the Item table, the quantity value in the respective rows must be decremented in the Inventory table. If you use a single relational database, all of the above actions can be either committed or rolled back in an ACID-compliant manner.

Figure 11-8 represents the same business use case implemented with the help of microservices. Assume that Order and Inventory are two different microservices. Now, let's analyze a complex scenario where two users try to act on the same entity, more or less concurrently. Such scenarios are typical of business applications, and listed here are a few such scenarios:

- Last seat in an airline booking application

- Last room in a hospitality booking portal

- Last item of a particular product in an e-commerce application

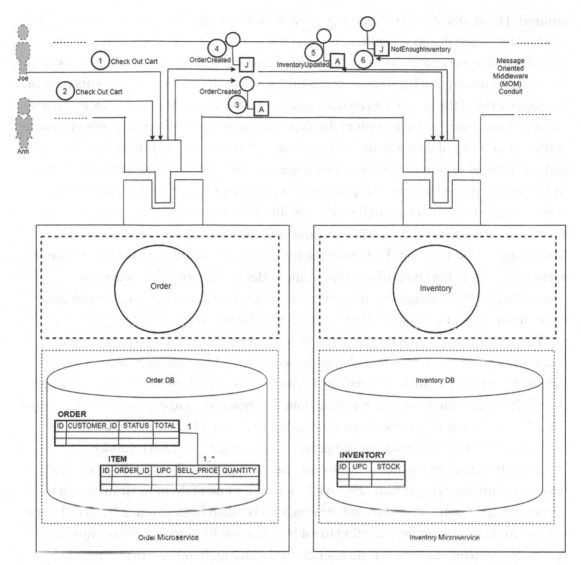

Figure 11-8. *Microservices race condition*

Assume that Joe and Ann, sitting at two different parts of the globe, are both interested in an older version of Mac Book Pro, which is offered at a good discount on the e-commerce site. Also assume that there is just one of this item left for sale on the e-commerce site. Both Joe and Ann have searched, reviewed, and finally added this item to their shopping cart. Now assume that both of them click the Confirm purchase button (Labels 1 and 2 in Figure 11-8) more or less at the same time. An EDA-based microservice architecture (shown in Figure 11-8) will allow the creation of an Order by the Order microservice on behalf of both Joe and Ann, and OrderCreated event will be

325

emitted. The status of both Orders is now "New." You can further assume that there are two OrderCreated events submitted, more or less concurrently (Labels 3 and 4). The Inventory microservice instances will consume the OrderCreated events; again, assume this event consumption happens concurrently. Since both OrderCreated events refer to the single item of the product, even if the microservices try to process the OrderCreated events concurrently, at the inventory database management level, one inventory update on behalf of either of these OrderCreated events will be allowed to progress, so the stock will get reduced to zero and an InventoryUpdated event will be emitted (Label 5). The Inventory microservice, processing on behalf of the other OrderCreated event, cannot succeed since there is not enough stock available, so it will emit a NotEnoughInventory event. The Order microservice will consume both the OrderCreated event and the NotEnoughInventory event. The Order microservice, on consuming the OrderCreated event, will change the status of corresponding Order to Confirmed; however, on consuming the NotEnoughInventory event, it will change the status of corresponding Order from "New" to "Cancelled" or "Cannot be Fulfilled" or whatever.

The scenario explained here is perfectly normal and acceptable, so what is the problem? Careful inspection reveals that for some period of time both Orders created on behalf of Joe and Ann are in a "New" or "Created" state. At this moment, both users get the feedback that their orders are getting honored; however, one of them is disappointed later. The system gives an "illusionary" snapshot to the user in place of "factual" snapshot. (However, whoever doesn't get the product does get a full refund.)

If you turn back to the architecture described in Figure 11-7, you will realize that if Joe and Ann are trying to purchase that last item, for one of them the transaction is successful and for the other the entire transaction is rolled back atomically, all (all steps leading to success or all steps leading to rollback) as one unit, so that at any moment system is consistent and there is no later disappointment. In other words, there is either instantaneous disappointment or instantaneous happiness; no chance for an eventual disappointment or eventual happiness. Now the golden question: When your architecture is changed from that shown in Figure 11-7 to that shown in Figure 11-8, is this eventuality acceptable for the business?

Microservices and the CAP Theorem

This discussion leads to another interesting constraint in distributed computing postulated as the CAP Theorem, which you will look in the context of microservices in this section.

The Scale Cube

Highly transactional systems have to serve millions of requests per unit of time and the transactions per second (TPS) in such systems is high. This is particularly true when we talk about web scale architectures. By increasing the compute power of nodes serving the requests, we can increase throughput; this is called vertical scaling. However, there is a limit beyond which an increase in compute will not yield proportionately in the same node, and this is shown in Figure 11-9.

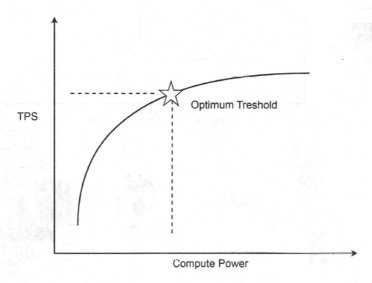

Figure 11-9. *Vertical scaling*

Further increase in throughput can be attained by horizontal scaling techniques. Here, operating software at web scale requires distributing many copies of the software runtime. This also means there are many copies of the data sets distributed across many nodes.

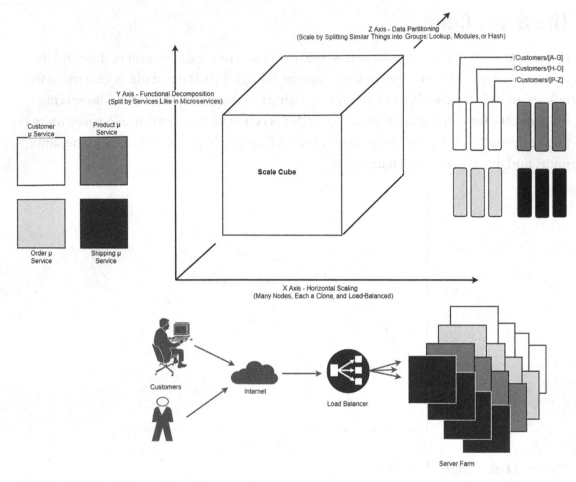

Figure 11-10.   *The scale cube*

Let's talk about the Scale Cube, which concerns three-axis scaling. Figure 11-10 depicts the three-axis scaling where each axis represents scaling your application at different levels:

- **X axis (horizontal scaling)**: Here you replicate many instances of the same microservice and use load balancers to distribute traffic.

- **Y axis (functional decomposition)**: Microservices are one approach of Y axis scaling where you split the application components based on functionality.

- **Z axis (data partitioning)**: Here, each microservices or functionality can be further split based on some criterion. A web scale application can distribute traffic and so all first names starting from A to G go to server farm X, H to O go to server farm Y, and P to Z go to server farm Z. This technique is called name sharding.

Each of these scaling methods must address data consistency issues. You have master data, or look-up data, and transactional data in enterprise applications. While master data is more or less static, transactional data keeps changing state with transactions. X-, Y-, and Z-axis scaling depends on the network for distributed services to share data.

So, you can distribute data and services on each axis to increase scalability, or have more than one node hosting services to increase availability. The moment you have more than one node, you require a network for interconnectivity, so the network provides partition tolerance. Also, if you have more than one copy of either data or code (service runtime), you need to address data consistency. I will describe this more in the next section.

The CAP Theorem

The CAP Theorem describes the three architectural properties that are linked together with mutual dependencies as

- Consistency

- Availability

- Partition tolerance

The theorem states that you can guarantee any two of the three properties. If you add or increase one of these properties, you do it by taking away from one (or both) of the others. In other words, you can have a highly available, consistent system but its partitionability will be low, or you can have a highly available and partitionable system but you would likely need to give up on consistency.

Figure 11-11 depicts the CAP Theorem pictorially. It says, you can pick any two from the list of C, A, and P, but you can't achieve all three at the same time. Let's understand better what that means. First, let's look at the definition of C, A, and P in the CAP Theorem.

- **Consistency:** All microservice nodes have the same view of the data.

- **Availability:** Every microservice can read or write to any other microservice, all the time.

- **Partition tolerance:** The microservices application as a whole works well despite physical network partitions between the microservices.

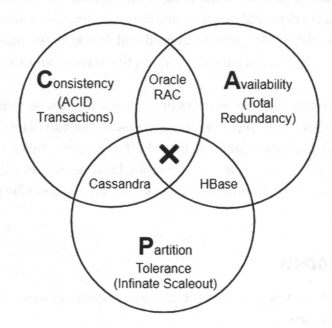

Figure 11-11. *The CAP Theorem*

Relational databases like Oracle are great at providing consistency because they focus on ACID properties and provide consistency by also providing fine control over transaction isolation so that in the earlier e-commerce example when Customer Joe confirms the purchase of the last item of a particular product in stock and simultaneously decreases the inventory in stock by one, any intermediate states are isolated from Customer Ann, who must wait a few milli- or microseconds for the RDBMS table or row locks to be released while the data store is made consistent.

Availability means the service is available to operate fully as far as the transaction is concerned. Cluster-aware proxies or client stubs are used in enterprise applications to fall back to redundant instances, if a particular instance of a service is down. The Oracle Real Application Cluster (RAC) is noteworthy here due to its firm promise to provide consistency of data on disk and availability of the DBMS service in runtime process at the same time. Once you are able to transport your data bits up to the disk level by using the techniques mentioned in the "Data or Storage Redundancy" section in Chapter 9, you can be sure that your bits are made durable enough. However, the techniques mentioned in that section will increase the probability of partitions forming!

When you use a SQL client and issue "Select for Update"[3] or similar commands from the same node where you run your Oracle database, your node acts as a kind of atomic processor in that it either works or it doesn't (i.e. if it has crashed, it's not available, but it won't cause data inconsistency either). When you start to separate and spread processing logic from data around different nodes either for scalability or availability, there's a risk of partitions forming. A partition happens when, for example, a network switch malfunctions, a network cable gets unplugged, or a power failure makes your other node unavailable.

Architecture trade-offs must be made when designing microservices to address the limitations imposed by the CAP Theorem. You may design systems without partitions if you have to stop them from network failures. In order to do this, you need to put everything related to that transaction on one machine, or in one atomically-failing unit like a single rack. Ah, does it sound familiar? Are we talking about "a microservice here?" You have seen that a microservice by definition is an independently deployable, self-contained unit that owns and governs its own data! Here comes the next caveat: even a rack can have partial failures. Further, a microservice itself has to scale, which means you need to think about redundancy. Moreover, if horizontal layers of a single microservice have to be deployed best to address SLAs, then the need to partition comes back. Yes, you are going round in circles in your design thinking, and the characteristics of your application, the context of your business, and many other technical and even cultural factors must be taken into account to decide where the sweet spot for your microservices architecture is in the above circular continuum.

---

[3]The SELECT FOR UPDATE statement allows you to lock the records in the cursor result set. You are not required to make changes to the records in order to use this statement. The record locks are released when the next commit or rollback statement is issued.

BASE (Basically Available, Soft State, Eventually Consistent) Systems

Having touched upon the CAP Theorem and assuming that you are well versed with the familiar and perfectly consistent ACID transactions, let's look at the BASE alternative to ACID. BASE is the acronym for Basically Available, Soft state, Eventually consistent, which is diametrically opposed to the ACID principles. While ACID is based on pessimistic assumptions and forces consistency at the end of every operation, BASE is based on optimistic assumptions and accepts that the database consistency will be in a state of flux to a level acceptable to the business transaction in consideration. BASE design encourages designing systems in such a way that

- If a portion of the application is down or not functioning properly, a few other functionalities of the application should still work, or

- If a few nodes' failure of the customer database impacts only the 30 percent of the customers on that particular host, the rest of the customers should still be able to use the system.

- Etc.

All or most of the above characteristics can be realistically met if you define a set of properties for coordination of systems or services as follows:

- A system is basically available when supporting partial failures, which may be appreciated than total system failure.

- The state of the system is "soft" in that it can change over time even in cases where no further updates are made, because some of the past changes are yet to be applied since they are "still on the fly", originated from other partitions.

- The system will eventually become consistent if no more new updates are made to the system.

CAP Pyramid

The CAP Pyramid is an inverted tetrahedron[4] pivoted on its vertex with the opposite face (base) kept parallel to the pivoted plane (ground), as shown in Figure 11-12.

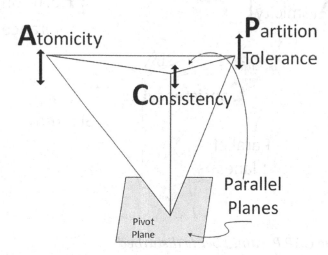

Figure 11-12. *The CAP Pyramid in unstable equillibrium*

If we assume the height from the pivot plane of each corner of the top face of the CAP Pyramid representing consistency, availability, and partition tolerance, you will always have a balance between these three characteristics in the equilibrium state, which is a BASE state. At the BASE state, all of the three characteristics are not too low or not too high; instead, they are at a nominal level to keep the CAP Pyramid in an unstable equilibrium.[5]

The CAP Theorem says you can pick any two from the list of consistency, availability, and partition tolerance, but you can't achieve all three at the same time.

---

[4]A tetrahedron is a four-sided pyramid (base plus three sides). The tetrahedron has the extra interesting property of having all four triangular sides congruent. The base is a triangle (any of the four faces can be considered the base), so a tetrahedron is also known as a "triangular pyramid." An Egyptian pyramid has a square base and four triangular sides.

[5]Unstable equilibrium is a state of equilibrium of a body (as a pendulum standing directly upward from its point of support) such that when the body is slightly displaced, it departs further from the original position.

In Figure 11-13, the pyramid is tilted to bring the corners near the tilted point to come nearer to the pivot plane so that the corners opposite the tilted point are raised further from the pivot plane.

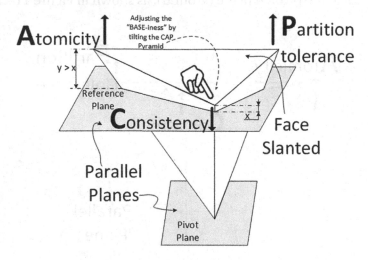

Figure 11-13. *The CAP Pyramid being disturbed*

As shown in Figure 11-13, without changing the pivot point, you can tend to increase any two at the max at a time. Here I attempt to increase (Label "y > x") atomicity and partition tolerance at the cost of reduced consistency (Label x).

When you disturb the unstable equilibrium of the BASE state, any two of the below characteristics can be improved to your desire:

- A system can be changed from basically available to available at five-nines.

- The state of the system is "not soft" in that it will not change over time since all updates are applied atomically, and no more updates are expected that are "still on the fly."

- The system is always consistent, since no new updates are expected.

You should now be able to relate this to the core design principles of a microservices architecture. For example, even if your Order microservice is not functioning properly, customers should still be able to search and browse through product listing and product details pages. Thus when BASE allows for (partial) availability by leveraging multiple partitioned microservices, opportunities to relax consistency have to be identified.

It is true that this relaxation of consistency cannot be completely hidden from a user experience point of view. To make it more clear, when your Order microservice and your Inventory microservice are partitioned, it is possible that even after the last item in stock has been order confirmed for Joe for purchase, Ann may still add the same item to her shopping cart and confirm check out. She will only eventually come to know that this particular item is no longer in stock. From a microservices design point of view, these are temporal inconsistencies, which be eventually be consistent and hence the temporal unhappiness of Ann will also eventually be converted to happiness since she will either be informed by the system before payment that the item is no longer available or, in the worst case where the payment has already been made for a non-available item, a refund will be initiated.

There are more intricacies when you do actual system design and implementation, but let's park them until Chapter 13 on transactions.

Summary

Architecture is all about trade-offs, and judicious trade-offs are of increased importance in microservices architecture. You saw the Inversion of Architecture in the context of microservices in Chapter 4, which has increased the outer architecture complexities to an exponential level. This has made networks inevitable, so techniques to attain partition tolerance must be built into the architecture by design, not as an afterthought. The amount of partition tolerance will influence the application's availability and consistency, and deciding the balance between these three characteristics is key in architecting microservices applications. In Chapter 5, you separated out the Command and Query parts of the application in the CQRS pattern, and this is a fine example of introducing partitions in the architecture. It's now time to look at some code in action to explain many of these concepts so turn to Chapter 12.

CHAPTER 12

Axon for CQRS Architecture

In Chapter 11, you learned about events and event-driven architecture, and you also looked into the theorems and constraints within which any EDA-based application can operate. Microservices architecture inherently bring partitions, hence concrete mechanisms to attain partition tolerance are of great importance. You will do that in this chapter with the help of Axon. Axon is a lightweight framework that will help you develop applications following the CQRS pattern. The Axon framework is licensed under the Apache 2 license so you can use the framework in any application for free. However, if you need professional services around Axon, they are provided by AxonIQ B.V., which is based in Amsterdam.

Axon is not mandatory to build CQRS-based systems, nor is a CQRS pattern mandatory to build systems using Axon. However, any new framework is an additional layer of debt in your application stack, so one of the primary reasons for you to use Axon in your application would be your urge to follow the CQRS pattern in building applications. Again, CQRS is not a mandatory prerequisite for you to architect microservices; however, CQRS provides leverage to address distributed enterprise software system concerns about scalability, so Axon and microservices go hand in hand.

You went into enough depth on Spring Boot and Spring Cloud in Chapter 7 and Chapter 8, and you will be leveraging both extensively while using Axon in this chapter. This marriage of CQRS with Spring Cloud will arm you with the combination of the most powerful tools from both worlds.

You will do the following in this chapter:

- Meet Axon, the Java CQRS framework

- Understand the building blocks of Axon

- Build and run an introductory CQRS example

- Build and run a fully distributed CQRS microservices example

© Binildas Christudas 2019
B. Christudas, *Practical Microservices Architectural Patterns*, https://doi.org/10.1007/978-1-4842-4501-9_12

Introducing Axon, the CQRS Framework

There are quite a few frameworks that allow you to architect CQRS-based solutions in the open source community and in the commercial world, both in Java and the .NET platforms. I picked Axon due to its free nature of the open source license and its integration options with other mainstream languages and platforms, including Java and Spring.

In this chapter, you will look at working examples using both Axon and Spring Boot. As I introduce the examples, I will also cover the essential concepts and APIs. You are advised to refer to the Axon documentation for detailed coverage on the usage of the framework since I will not attempt to duplicate the Axon documentation here. Instead, I will walk you through the core concepts with examples so that you are geared up to speed quickly.

You will be using two different versions of Axon for these examples. You will first use Axon 2.4.1. Here, you require explicit wiring of components, either through annotations or using XML configurations. Moreover, the Axon 2.4.1 example will leverage the 1.3.5.RELEASE version of Spring Boot. Later in the book, you will also look at examples in Axon 3.0.5 where you use the Spring Boot 1.5.3.RELEASE version. In Axon 3.0.5, a lot of explicit wiring can be avoided since Axon uses the Spring Application Context to locate specific implementations of building blocks and provides a default for those that are not there. Even though this will make life easier for the developer, if you are not an experienced Axon developer, you may not be able to appreciate what is happening under the hood. In Axon 2.4.1, much of this wiring is explicit and thus visible in code as annotations or in configurations as XML, so you can get a better understanding what is happening in the underlying layers. For that reason, you will use the previous (2.4.1) version[1] of Axon for the examples to start with. However, I will give you an easy roadmap for later Axon versions[2] by providing the same examples in those versions too.

What Is Axon?

The Axon framework helps developers apply the CQRS architectural pattern and build modular, SOA-based solutions. Traditional SOA architecture addresses some mainstream concerns in software architectures; however, Axon fills the gap that has been found in the experience while using SOA over the last two decades.

---

[1]Axon framework 2.4 Reference guide: www.axonframework.org/docs/2.4/
[2]Axon framework 2.4 API Documentation: https://axoniq.io/apidocs/2.4/

Axon provides implementations of the most important building blocks, such as aggregates, repositories, and event buses (the dispatching mechanism for events). Aggregates take care of grouping entities in a parent-child hierarchy and prescribe clear responsibility to aggregate roots to manage the lifecycle of the entity tree in terms of data consistency and synchronization. Event buses help you to do away with all the nitty-gritty details of creating, maintaining, and tracking correlation ids between different parts of your application. Axon guarantees the delivery of events to the right event listeners and processing them in parallel as well as in the intended sequence. Next, Axon uses Java annotation support, which means you can build aggregates and event listeners without tying your code to Axon-specific logic.

Where Can You Use Axon?

Axon is free and open source, and has the tag line of *The Jargon CQRS* (which many of your peers are still searching the Internet to understand what it means), which is quite enough to maintain the attention of executive management for a long time, so why not use it in every new application you build? Unfortunately, CQRS is not simple and straightforward compared to traditional one-to-one and synchronous architecture styles. Conceiving future complexities to an extent at the start of architecture design is required; further your design has to accommodate and evolve more combinations of scenarios, states, and flows compared to traditional SOA or for that matter even compared to microservices without CQRS. However, if you understand this and if you attempt it, the effort will be paid back in more than one way. Here are some scenarios where CQRS makes more sense:

- **Extensible architectures**: Typical applications are built with a span of life in mind, say 10, 20, or even 50 years (if you still program in assembly or mainframe); however, during this span many of these applications are likely to be extended with more functionality. It's the same story for applications built today, getting deployed to clouds and containers. However, business continuity is paramount, and extensions both in terms of functionality and quality of system (QoS) have to be effected with zero disruption to running systems. Can you do this? Is this expectation realistic or still a myth? Well, the answer depends not on the technologies and frameworks available alone. You need to combine them with your architectural thoughts too, put aside all other advancements in DevOps, etc.

- **High read-to-write ratio**: Recollect the discussion about the look-to-book ratio in Chapter 5. A system will have to accommodate hundreds or thousands of read transactions before it gets converted into a single write transaction. Building the operational QoS into your read transactions similar to write transactions would be disastrous in today's enterprise software paradigm, especially in the cloud native scenarios, where every CPU cycle or every bit stored or transported adds to your cost. Your read transactions are your LEAD transactions, and your write transactions are your LAG transactions. The first one converts "intent" to "decision" of purchase whereas the second one converts your "inventory" to "realized margin." Both are important; however, the criticality is different. An unsuccessful write transaction due to functional or system issues is priceless, whereas an unsuccessful read transaction will have less of an impact since it can be either retried or ignored; its value lost is considerably low compared to that of an unsuccessful write transaction. Data sources for queries are to be tuned differently than those used for command execution, and they should be optimized for fast querying with relaxed locks in resources; however, for write transactions, your data sources should ensure strict ACID compliancy so that once a traveler successfully purchases the last seat on your airplane, you will have all the means to respect that purchase so that you don't need to later send a regret e-mail to that traveler telling him that the seat is not available for so-and-so reason and hence he will be provided with a refund!

- **Single source of truth, many views**: "Resources" were first defined on the World Wide Web as documents or files identified by their URLs. However, today they have a much more generic and abstract definition that encompasses every thing or every entity that can be identified, named, addressed, or handled, in any way whatsoever, on the Web. In a RESTful web service, requests made to a resource's URI will elicit a response that may be in CSV, XML, HTML, JSON, or some other format. The same data in your application may be represented in many ways, some optimized for quick searching, others in a cached state for maximum responsiveness, and others in the form of canned reports like an Excel or PDF file. This is the application-level reality of the single source of truth of resource existing in many views. CQRS addresses this requirement explicitly and also helps you keep the different views in sync with the single source of truth whenever a change occurs in the form of raising events.

- **Application with varied interactions**: Some applications will have a user base at varied levels of interaction with the system. For example, an e-commerce application has end users or customers doing retail purchases as one set of the user base, and that number will be huge; also, these customers expect a split-second response time. The next set is the back office storekeepers who manage the inventories, whose numbers are limited and who suffer if the software is slow or sluggish at times. A third set is the B2B interfaces connecting with the supply chain, whose number is even smaller, in the form of a few known IP addresses, and who also suffer if the interfaces are down for a few minutes because then they have to retry at a later time. Depending upon the type of interacting parties and the overall value and criticality of the transactions on behalf of these parties, software services within the same application may have to exhibit different levels of access, security, performance, and so on. Microservices architectures will help you here, and adopting CQRS will provide you the extra leverage to address these heterogeneous kinds of interactions.

- **Applications with autonomous interfaces**: The IoT and the WoT are current software paradigms that pose a new set of challenges to software architects. The strict definition of an application's API using commands and events makes it easier to integrate with such interfaces of things and devices. Any interface can send commands or listen to events generated by the host interface.

The above list provides only a general list of problem characteristics where CQRS will value add; it's in no way exhaustive.

What You Need to Run Axon

The Axon framework has been built and tested against Java 6, making that more or less the only requirement. You can use Gradle or Maven for the build and also use any IDE of your choice. Since Axon doesn't create any connections or threads by itself, it is safe to run on an application server. Axon abstracts all asynchronous behavior by using executors, which decouple task submission from the mechanics of how each task will be run. So you can even easily pass a container-managed thread pool, for example. If you don't use an application server (e.g. Tomcat, Jetty, or a stand-alone app), you can use the Executors class or the Spring Framework to create and configure thread pools.

You will now look at some concrete examples and see Axon code in action.

Command and Event Handling in the Same JVM

Simple things first, so let's keep the first example in Axon simple. However, I can't make it simpler. To introduce Axon, you must first understand a simple scenario in the Axon way and then look at the details of what each of the steps mean in Axon.

The Sample Scenario

The first Axon example is a single microservice from an e-commerce application. There are two entities in the domain, order and product. Users can buy a product, which will create a new order. When a new order is created, the product stock will get depreciated. Just that. Figure 12-1 depicts the architecture with the complete flow labelled.

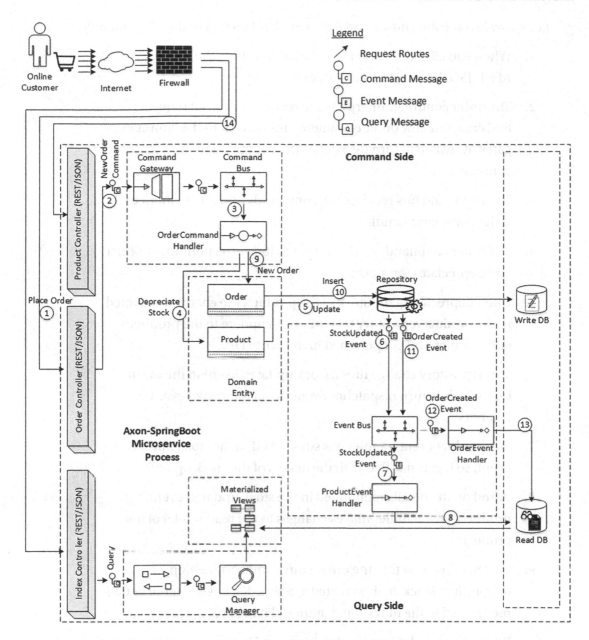

Figure 12-1. *Axon command and event handling in the same JVM*

The "A Meta Model for Event-Based CQRS Design" section in Chapter 5 shows a meta model for a CQRS-based architecture. Figure 12-1 is a concrete incarnation of that abstract meta model represented in Figure 5-5 in Chapter 5.

Let's now explore the end-to-end flow, which is labelled in the diagram as follows:

1. When you click the "Order One Now!" button in the browser, a REST/JSON request hits the order controller.

2. The order controller interprets the request as a write request and creates a new order command and sends it to the command gateway, which in turn dispatches the command to the command bus.

3. The command bus receives the commands and routes them to the order command handler.

4. The order command handler retrieves the corresponding product and depreciates the stock.

5. Upon depreciating the stock of the product, the change is effected in the product repository by sending an update to the product entity, which will get persisted in the Write DB.

6. This repository change fires a stock updated event to the event bus, which in turn dispatches events to all interested event listeners.

7. The product event handler has subscribed to the stock updated event, so it gets notified with the details of the stock update.

8. Based on the details mentioned in the stock updated event, the product event handler makes changes to the read model of the product.

9. In step 4, you saw that the order command handler depreciated the product stock. It also created a new order, based on the details mentioned in the new order command it received.

10. When a new order is created, it is effected in the order repository by sending an insert of a new order entity, which will subsequently get persisted in the Write DB.

11. This repository insert fires an order created event to the event bus, which in turn dispatches events to all interested event listeners.

12. The order event handler has subscribed to the order created event, so it gets notified with the details of the new order created.

13. Based on the details mentioned in the order created event, the order event handler makes changes to the read model of the order.

14. The browser can refresh itself to keep the view updated from querying the read model of the entities.

Code the Sample Scenario

All the code examples for this section are in folder ch12\ch12-01. Visit pom.xml to see the explicit mention of the Axon dependency. See Listing 12-1.

Listing 12-1. Axon Maven Dependency (ch12\ch12-01\Ax2-Commands-Events-Same-JVM\pom.xml)

```
<dependency>
    <groupId>org.axonframework</groupId>
    <artifactId>axon-core</artifactId>
    <version>2.4.1</version>
</dependency>
```

This first Axon example is a first class Spring Boot citizen, hence there is nothing special in the main application class; still you can look at the code in Listing 12-2.

Listing 12-2. Spring Boot Application Class (ch12\ch12-01\Ax2-Commands-Events-Same-JVM\src\main\java\com\acme\ecom\EcomApplication.java)

```
@SpringBootApplication
public class EcomApplication {

    public static void main(String[] args) {

        SpringApplication.run(EcomApplication.class, args);
    }
}
```

Next is the most important class of this example where you do the setup of all Axon components; see Listing 12-3.

Listing 12-3. Spring Axon Configurations (ch12\ch12-01\Ax2-Commands-Events-Same-JVM\src\main\java\com\acme\ecom\EcomAppConfiguration.java)

```java
@Configuration
public class EcomAppConfiguration {

    @PersistenceContext
    private EntityManager entityManager;

    @Bean
    public SimpleCommandBus commandBus() {

        return new SimpleCommandBus();
    }

    @Bean
    public SimpleEventBus eventBus() {

        return new SimpleEventBus();
    }

    @Bean
    AnnotationCommandHandlerBeanPostProcessor
            annotationCommandHandlerBeanPostProcessor() {

        AnnotationCommandHandlerBeanPostProcessor handler =
            new AnnotationCommandHandlerBeanPostProcessor();
        handler.setCommandBus(commandBus());
        return handler;
    }

    @Bean
    AnnotationEventListenerBeanPostProcessor
            annotationEventListenerBeanPostProcessor() {

        AnnotationEventListenerBeanPostProcessor listener =
            new AnnotationEventListenerBeanPostProcessor();
        listener.setEventBus(eventBus());
        return listener;
    }
```

```
@Bean
public DefaultCommandGateway commandGateway() {

    return new DefaultCommandGateway(commandBus());
}

@Bean
@Qualifier("productRepository")
public GenericJpaRepository<Product> productJpaRepository() {

    SimpleEntityManagerProvider entityManagerProvider =
        new SimpleEntityManagerProvider(entityManager);
    GenericJpaRepository<Product> genericJpaRepository =
        new GenericJpaRepository(entityManagerProvider, Product.class);
    genericJpaRepository.setEventBus(eventBus());
    return genericJpaRepository;
}

@Bean
@Qualifier("orderRepository")
public GenericJpaRepository<Order> orderJpaRepository() {

    SimpleEntityManagerProvider entityManagerProvider =
        new SimpleEntityManagerProvider(entityManager);
    GenericJpaRepository<Order> genericJpaRepository =
        new GenericJpaRepository(entityManagerProvider, Order.class);
    genericJpaRepository.setEventBus(eventBus());
    return genericJpaRepository;
}
}
```

I will explain the Axon-specific components now. The SimpleCommandBus does straightforward processing of commands in the same thread that dispatches them. After a command is processed, the modified aggregate(s) are saved and any generated events are published in that same thread.

An aggregate is an entity or group of entities that are always kept in a consistent state. An aggregate root is the object on top of the aggregate tree that is responsible for maintaining this consistent state. For example, an order aggregate could contain entities like line items and a delivery address. In order to keep the full aggregate in a consistent state, changing the address of this order should be done via the order aggregate, not by directly accessing the address entity.

The SimpleCommandBus maintains the notion of a unit of work (UoW) for each command published. Since all command processing is done in the same thread, this implementation is limited to a single JVM's boundaries.

A unit of work is a set of modifications to be made to aggregates. Execution of a command typically happens within the scope of a unit of work. When a command handler finishes execution, the UoW is committed and all actions are finalized. This means that any repositories are notified of state changes in their aggregates and events scheduled for publication are sent to the event bus. This is a convenient grouping that will help to prevent individual events from being published before a number of aggregates have been processed. In the back, it allows repositories to manage resources, such as locks, over an entire transaction. Locks, for example, will only be released when the unit of work is either committed or rolled back.

A unit of work is not a replacement for traditional ACID-style transactions. It is merely a buffer where changes are grouped and staged. When a unit of work is committed, all staged changes are only committed; however, this commit is not atomic. That means if a commit fails, a few changes might have already been persisted, while others not. So Axon best practices dictate that a command should always containing one action. If you have more actions in your unit of work, then you should consider attaching a transaction to the unit of work's commit, for which you can refer to the Axon documentation.

The SimpleEventBus, as the name suggests, is a very basic implementation of the EventBus interface and is a mechanism used to dispatch events to the subscribed event listeners. It is good when the event dispatching is done synchronously and locally (i.e. in a single JVM). It manages subscribed EventListeners and forwards all incoming events to all subscribed listeners. EventListeners must be explicitly registered with the event bus in order for them to receive events. The registration process is thread safe and listeners may register and unregister for events at any time. If an EventListener throws an exception, the event dispatching stops and the exception is propagated to the component publishing the event.

AnnotationCommandHandlerBeanPostProcessor will automatically register classes containing command handler methods (i.e. methods annotated with the @ CommandHandler annotation) with a command bus.

- This bean post processor will scan the application context for all beans with an @CommandHandler annotated method.

- All such command handlers will be automatically recognized and subscribed to the command bus.

AnnotationEventListenerBeanPostProcessor will automatically register classes containing event handler methods (i.e. methods annotated with the @EventHandler annotation) in your application context and automatically connect them to the event bus.

- This bean post processor will scan the application context for all the beans with an @EventHandler annotated method.

- All such event listener will be automatically recognized and subscribed to the event bus.

The command gateway is a convenient interface for the command dispatching mechanism. Usage of a gateway to dispatch commands is optional; however, it is generally the easiest option to do so. CommandGateway is the interface and DefaultCommandGateway is the default implementation provided by Axon. The gateway provides a number of methods that allow you to send a command and wait for a result either synchronously, with a timeout, or asynchronously.

The GenericJpaRepository is a repository implementation that can store aggregates that are JPA compatible. It is configured with an EntityManager that manages the actual persistence and classes specifying the actual type of aggregate stored in the repository, Product and Order in your case. All the JPA-annotated aggregates must implement the AggregateRoot and have the proper JPA annotations. The repository may be configured with a locking scheme. The repository will always force optimistic locking in the backing persistent store. An optional lock can be configured for the repository, in which case it will be in addition to this optimistic lock. Locks on one repository instance will not be shared with other repository instances. When this repository is requested to persist changes to an aggregate, it will also flush the EntityManager, during which it will enforce checking of database constraints and optimistic locks. Let's look at your AggregateRoot entities now; see Listing 12-4.

Listing 12-4. Order Aggregate Entity (ch12\ch12-01\Ax2-Commands-Events-Same-JVM\src\main\java\com\acme\ecom\order\model\Order.java)

```java
import org.axonframework.domain.AbstractAggregateRoot;

@Entity
@Table(name="ECOM_ORDER")
@Data
@EqualsAndHashCode(exclude = { "id" })
public class Order extends AbstractAggregateRoot<Integer> {

    @Id
    private Integer id;

    @Column(name="PRICE")
    private Double price;

    @Column(name="NUMBER")
    private Integer number;

    @Column(name="ORDER_STATUS")
    @Enumerated(EnumType.STRING)
    private OrderStatusEnum orderStatus; ;

    @ManyToOne(fetch=FetchType.LAZY)
    @JoinColumn(name="PRODUCT_ID")
    private Product product;

    @Override
    public Integer getIdentifier() {
        return id;
    }

    public Order(Integer id, Double price, Integer number,
            OrderStatusEnum orderStatus, Product product) {

        super();
        this.id = id;
        this.price = price;
        this.number = number;
```

```
        this.orderStatus = orderStatus;
        this.product = product;
        registerEvent(new OrderCreatedEvent(id, price, number,
            product.getDescription(), orderStatus.toString()));
    }
}
```

Order extends AbstractAggregateRoot, a very basic implementation of the AggregateRoot interface. It provides the mechanism to keep track of all uncommitted events and also maintains a version number based on the number of events generated, which can be used for validation during committing. Further, the Order entity also registers events to be published when the aggregate is saved using the registerEvent method. Next, you will look at the Product aggregate in Listing 12-5.

Listing 12-5. Product Aggregate Entity (ch12\ch12-01\Ax2-Commands-Events-Same-JVM\src\main\java\com\acme\ecom\product\model\Product.java)

```
@Entity
@Table(name="ECOM_PRODUCT")
@Data
@EqualsAndHashCode(exclude = { "id" })
public class Product extends AbstractAggregateRoot<Integer> {

    @Id
    private Integer id;

    @Column(name="PRICE")
    private Double price;

    @Column(name="STOCK")
    private Integer stock;

    @Column(name="DESCRIPTION")
    private String description;

    @Override
    public Integer getIdentifier() {
        return id;
    }
```

```java
    public void depreciateStock(int count) {

        if(this.stock >= count){
            this.stock = this.stock - count;
            registerEvent(new StockUpdatedEvent(id, stock));
        }else{
            throw new RuntimeException("Out of stock");
        }
    }
}
```

The Product aggregate is similar in structure and functionality to that of the Order aggregate, hence the explanation won't be repeated here.

Next, you will look at commands. They are straight DTO-like classes, as shown in Listing 12-6.

Listing 12-6. New Order Command (ch12\ch12-01\Ax2-Commands-Events-Same-JVM\src\main\java\com\acme\ecom\order\api\command\NewOrderCommand.java)

```java
import lombok.Data;

@Data
public class NewOrderCommand {

    private final Double price;
    private final Integer number;
    private final Integer productId;
}
```

It's good practice for a command to express its intent by its name. So you can use the Java class name to figure out what needs to be done, and the fields of the command object should provide the information required to act based on the command.

Now you will see the creation of the above command. When you click the "Order One Now!" button in the browser, a REST/JSON request hits the order controller, as shown in Listing 12-7.

Listing 12-7. Order REST Controller (ch12\ch12-01\Ax2-Commands-Events-Same-JVM\src\main\java\com\acme\ecom\web\controller\OrderController.java)

```
@RestController
public class OrderController {

    @Autowired
    private DataSource dataSource;

    @Autowired
    private CommandGateway commandGateway;

    @RequestMapping(value = "/orders", method = RequestMethod.POST)
    @Transactional
    public ResponseEntity<Void> addNewOrder(@RequestBody OrderDTO orderDTO)
{

        commandGateway.sendAndWait(new NewOrderCommand(orderDTO.getPrice(),
            orderDTO.getNumber(), orderDTO.getProductId()));
        return new ResponseEntity<>( HttpStatus.OK);
    }
}
```

The `Controller` method will create a new command and send it to the command bus and wait for it to execute. The result of the execution is returned when available. This `sendAndWait` method will block indefinitely, until a result is available or until the current thread is interrupted. If the thread is interrupted, this method returns null. If an exception occurs during processing, it is wrapped in a CommandExecutionException.

Listing 12-8 shows the CommandHandler.

Listing 12-8. Axon Order Command Handler (ch12\ch12-01\Ax2-Commands-Events-Same-JVM\ src\main\java\com\acme\ecom\order\commandhandler\OrderCommandHandler.java)

```
@Component
public class OrderCommandHandler {

    @Autowired
    @Qualifier("orderRepository")
```

353

```
    private Repository<Order> orderRepository;

    @Autowired
    @Qualifier("productRepository")
    private Repository<Product> productRepository;

    @CommandHandler
    public void handle(NewOrderCommand newOrderCommand){

        Product product =
            productRepository.load(newOrderCommand.getProductId());
        product.depreciateStock(newOrderCommand.getNumber());
        Order order = new Order(new Random().nextInt(),
            newOrderCommand.getPrice(),
            newOrderCommand.getNumber(), OrderStatusEnum.NEW, product);
        orderRepository.add(order);
    }
}
```

The CommandHandler marker annotation will mark the handle method on the OrderCommandHandler as being a CommandHandler. The annotated method's first parameter is the command handled by that method. Optionally, the command handler may specify a second parameter of type UnitOfWork. The active unit of work will be passed if that parameter is supplied. A type of command can be handled by only one type of command handler. So an order command handler instance will handle a new order command, and when such a command arrives, it will retrieve the corresponding domain object, Product (aggregates) in your case, from a repository, and execute methods on it to change the state (depreciate the stock and also create a new order in your case). These aggregates typically contain the actual business logic and are therefore responsible for guarding their own invariants. The state changes of aggregates result in the generation of domain events. In the above code, the product stock depreciation and the creation of the new order generate events. Both the domain events and the aggregates form the domain model.

You will now look at the code for the events generated. Events are simple data-encapsulated POJO classes. See Listing 12-9 and Listing 12-10.

Listing 12-9. Order Created Event (ch12\ch12-01\Ax2-Commands-Events-Same-JVM\ src\main\java\com\acme\ecom\order\api\event\OrderCreatedEvent.java)

```java
public class OrderCreatedEvent {

    private final Integer id;
    private final Double price;
    private final Integer number;
    private final String productDescription;
    private final String orderStatus;
}
```

Listing 12-10. Stock Updated Event (ch12\ch12-01\Ax2-Commands-Events-Same-JVM\ src\main\java\com\acme\ecom\product\api\event\StockUpdatedEvent.java)

```java
public class StockUpdatedEvent {

    private final Integer id;
    private final Integer stock;
}
```

Now look at the event handlers capable of handling these events. If you recollect, for command handling, a type of command can be handled by only one type of command handler. However, for event handling, a type of event may be handled by zero or more types of event handlers. This is synonymous to the publish-subscribe pattern using a message topic where a message may be consumed by more than one subscriber. More on this later; let's now look at the code for the event handlers in Listing 12-11.

Listing 12-11. Event Handler for Order (ch12\ch12-01\Ax2-Commands-Events-Same-JVM\ src\main\java\com\acme\ecom\order\eventhandler\OrderEventHandler.java)

```java
@Component
public class OrderEventHandler {

    @Autowired
    DataSource dataSource;
```

355

```
@EventHandler
public void handleOrderCreatedEvent(OrderCreatedEvent event) {

    JdbcTemplate jdbcTemplate = new JdbcTemplate(dataSource);
    jdbcTemplate.update("INSERT INTO ecom_order_view VALUES(?,?,?,?,?)",
        new Object[]{event.getId(),
    event.getPrice(), event.getNumber(), event.getProductDescription(),
        event.getOrderStatus()});
}
}
```

The order event handler receives the order created event after a new order has been created. Hence the only task left is to update the Order Read DB, which is done by the above code. The other event handler left is product event handler, shown in Listing 12-12.

Listing 12-12. Event Handler for Product (ch12\ch12-01\Ax2-Commands-Events-Same-JVM\src\main\java\com\acme\ecom\product\eventhandler\ProductEventHandler.java)

```
@Component
public class ProductEventHandler {

    @Autowired
    DataSource dataSource;

    @EventHandler
    public void handleProductStockUpdatedEvent(StockUpdatedEvent event) {

        JdbcTemplate jdbcTemplate = new JdbcTemplate(dataSource);
        jdbcTemplate.update("UPDATE ecom_product_view SET stock=? WHERE ID=?",
            new Object[]{event.getStock(), event.getId()});
    }
}
```

The product event handler will update the change in stock level of the product to the Product Read DB. In this way, every new order creation changes the Order and Product Write DBs, and all these changes are eventually propagated to the Read DB too.

Build and Test the Example Scenario

The complete code required to demonstrate this simple Axon example is in folder ch12\ ch12-01. First, update the configuration files to suit to your environment:

```
ch12\ch12-01\Ax2-Commands-Events-Same-JVM\src\main\resources\application.
properties
spring.datasource.url=jdbc:mysql://localhost/ecom01
spring.datasource.username=root
spring.datasource.password=rootpassword
```

Make sure MySQL is up and running. You may want to refer to Appendix H to get started with MySQL.

```
First Bring Up MySQL Server.
D:\Applns\MySQL\mysql-8.0.14-winx64\bin>mysqld --console

Now Open MySQL prompt
D:\Applns\MySQL\mysql-8.0.14-winx64\bin>mysql -u root -p

mysql> use ecom01;
Database changed
mysql>
```

To start with clean tables, delete any tables with the names you want for your examples:

```
mysql> drop table ecom_order;
mysql> drop table ecom_product;
mysql> drop table ecom_order_view;
mysql> drop table ecom_product_view;
```

Now, the ecom_order and ecom_product tables will be created when the microservice starts up. However, you need to explicitly create the Read DB tables:

```
mysql> create table ecom_product_view(id INT , price DOUBLE, stock INT
,description VARCHAR(255));
mysql> create table ecom_order_view(id INT , price DOUBLE, number INT
,description VARCHAR(225),status VARCHAR(50));
```

You will now build and package the executables for the Axon microservice and bring up the server. Since you used the `mysql-8.0.14-winx64.zip` archive while installing the MySQL server (see Appendix H), you need to use version 8.0.14 of the `mysql-connector-java` Maven artifact in the Maven build script `pom.xml`. There is a utility script provided in folder `ch12\ch12-01\Ax2-Commands-Events-Same-JVM\make.bat`:

```
cd D:\binil\gold\pack03\ch12\ch12-01\Ax2-Commands-Events-Same-JVM
D:\binil\gold\pack03\ch12\ch12-01\Ax2-Commands-Events-Same-JVM>make
D:\binil\gold\pack03\ch12\ch12-01\Ax2-Commands-Events-Same-JVM>mvn clean install
```

You can now run the Axon Spring Boot application in more than one way. The straightforward way is to execute the JAR file via the following commands:

```
D:\binil\gold\pack03\ch12\ch12-01\Ax2-Commands-Events-Same-JVM>run
D:\binil\gold\pack03\ch12\ch12-01\Ax2-Commands-Events-Same-JVM>mvn spring-boot:run
```

This will bring up the Axon Spring Boot Server in port 8080. The `ecom_order` and `ecom_product` tables would have been created by now. You need to prepopulate the `ecom_product` and `ecom_product_view` tables with some initial data:

```
mysql> insert into ecom_product(id,description,price,stock,version)
values(1,'Shirts',100,5,0);
mysql> insert into ecom_product(id,description,price,stock,version)
values(2,'Pants',100,5,0);
mysql> insert into ecom_product(id,description,price,stock,version)
values(3,'T-Shirt',100,5,0);
mysql> insert into ecom_product(id,description,price,stock,version)
values(4,'Shoes',100,5,0);

mysql> insert into ecom_product_view(id,description,price,stock)
values(1,'Shirts',100,5);
mysql> insert into ecom_product_view(id,description,price,stock)
values(2,'Pants',100,5);
mysql> insert into ecom_product_view(id,description,price,stock)
values(3,'T-Shirt',100,5);
mysql> insert into ecom_product_view(id,description,price,stock)
values(4,'Shoes',100,5);
```

You can use a browser (preferably Chrome) and point to `http://localhost:8080/`. You can now test the example by clicking any one of the buttons in Figure 12-2.

Figure 12-2. *Testing the Axon command and event handling in the same JVM*

When you click, a new order is created in the Order Write DB. Eventually, the Order Read DB will be updated with this new order. Also, the corresponding product stock will be reduced by one in the Product Write DB. This change will also be eventually updated in the Product Read DB. The change is reflected in Figure 12-3.

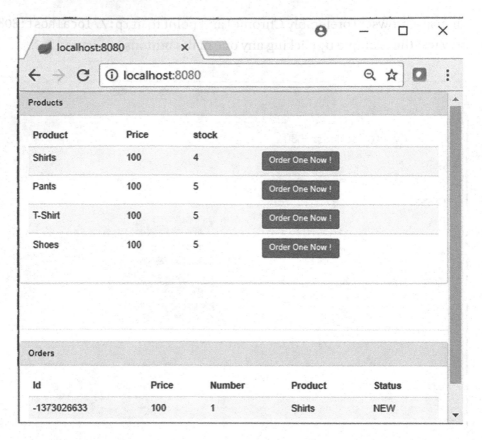

Figure 12-3. *Product view synched with product write data*

Distributed Command and Event Handling

Enterprise-grade applications distribute processing into multiple compute nodes and multiple processes to leverage the full power of multicore processors as well as to attain maximum parallelism so as to improve overall performance. The microservices architecture is no exception, and in this example you are going to completely distribute the different Axon components across JVMs. Since the example is distributed across processes, you can practically distribute them across nodes too; however, you will execute the examples with each main Axon components in a single node (my personal laptop, in my case) for simplicity.

The Example Scenario

You are using the same scenario as in the previous section. While the previous example was implemented as a single microservice, you will split the same functionality into four different microservices in this example and you will additionally introduce another microservice too. This new, fifth microservice is the Event Handler Audit microservice. The Event Handler Audit microservice has an event handler, AuditEventHandler, which too is subscribed to the order created event. So, you now have two microservices (the Event Handler Audit microservice and the Event Handle Core microservice) with two event handler types, both interested in the same order created event! Figure 12-4 shows the design.

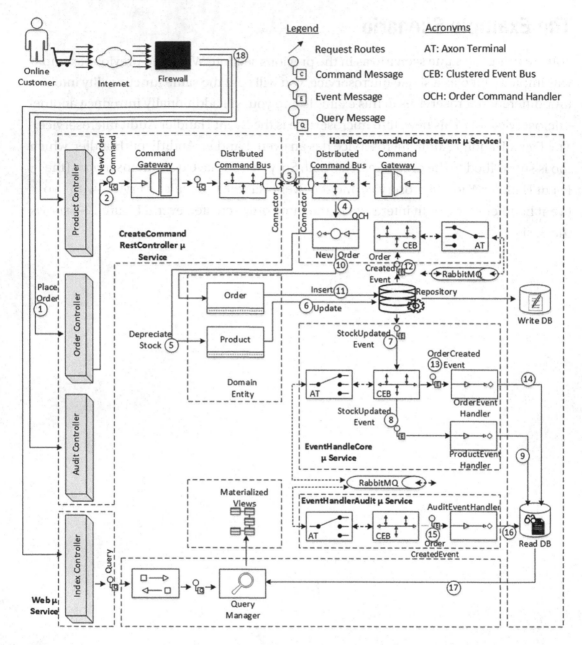

Figure 12-4. *The design of the distributed command and event handling in Axon*

The "Command Query Segregation Using Events" section in Chapter 5 represented the meta model for an event-based CQRS architecture. Figure 12-4 is a concrete incarnation of that abstract meta model represented in Figure 5-6 in Chapter 5.

The command and event flow in the architecture is also similar to the previous example; however, there are subtle differences. Let's relook at the end-to-end flow, which is labelled in the diagram as follows:

1. When you click the "Order One Now!" button in the browser, a REST/JSON request hits the order controller.

2. The order controller in the Create Command Rest Controller microservice interprets the request as a write request and creates a new order command and sends it to the command gateway, which in turn dispatches the command to the distributed command bus.

3. The distributed command bus forms a bridge between the command bus implementations across JVMs. The distributed command bus on each JVM is called a segment.

4. The command bus receives commands and routes them to the order command handler, both of them being present in the Handle Command and Create Event microservices.

5. The order command handler retrieves the corresponding product and depreciates the stock.

6. Upon depreciating the stock of the product, the change is effected in the product repository by sending an update to the product entity, which will get persisted in the Write DB.

7. This repository change fires a stock updated event to the event bus, which in turn dispatches events to all interested event listeners.

8. The product event handler in the Event Handle Core microservice has subscribed to the stock updated event, so it gets notified with the details of the stock update.

9. Based on the details mentioned in the stock updated event, the product event handler makes changes to the read model of the product.

10. In step 5, the order command handler depreciated the product stock. Along with that, it also created a new order, based on the details mentioned in the new order command it received.

11. When a new order is created, it is effected in the order repository by sending an insert of a new order entity, which subsequently gets persisted in the Write DB.

12. This repository insert fires an order created event to the event bus, which in turn dispatches events to all interested event listeners. There are two interested event listeners, both of them in foreign (different process or nodes) microservices, the Event Handle Core microservice and the Event Handler Audit microservice.

13. The order event handler in the Event Handle Core microservice has subscribed to the order created event, so it gets notified with the details of the new order created.

14. Based on the details mentioned in the order created event, the order event handler makes changes to the read model of the order, inserting a new row in this case.

15. The audit event handler in the Event Handler Audit microservice has also subscribed to the order created event, so it gets notified with the details of the new order created.

16. Based on the details mentioned in the order created event, the audit event handler makes changes to the read model of the audit.

17. The browser can refresh itself to keep the view updated from querying the read model of the entities.

18. The user can view changes using the browser.

Code the Example Scenario

The complete code required to demonstrate the simple Axon example is in folder ch12\ch12-02. There are five microservices to be coded, and you will look into them one by one.

Microservice 1: 01-Ecom-web

This microservice is a typical Spring Boot web application without any Axon components, so I will not discuss it.

Microservice 2: 02-Ecom-CreateCommandRestController

Visit pom.xml to see the axon-distributed-commandbus dependency; see Listing 12-13.

Listing 12-13. Axon Distributed Command Bus Maven Dependency (ch12\
ch12-02\Ax2-Commands-Multi-Event-Handler-Distributed\02-Ecom-
CreateCommandRestController\pom.xml)

```
<dependency>
    <groupId>org.axonframework</groupId>
    <artifactId>axon-distributed-commandbus</artifactId>
    <version>2.4.1</version>
</dependency>
```

A major part of the code for this example is similar to the previous example, so I will not repeat it here; instead, I will explain all new code as well as any changes to the code from the previous example. The most important class of this example is where you do the setup of all the distributed Axon components, shown in Listing 12-14.

Listing 12-14. Distributed Command Bus Configuration (ch12\
ch12-02\Ax2-Commands-Multi-Event-Handler-Distributed\02-Ecom-
CreateCommandRestController\src\main\java\com\acme\ecom\
EcomAppConfiguration.java)

```
@Configuration
public class EcomAppConfiguration {

    @Bean
    public XStreamSerializer xstreamSerializer() {
        return new XStreamSerializer();
    }

    @Bean
    @Qualifier("distributedCommandGateway")
    public CommandGatewayFactoryBean<CommandGateway>
            commandGatewayFactoryBean() {
        CommandGatewayFactoryBean<CommandGateway> factory =
            new CommandGatewayFactoryBean<>();
```

```
        factory.setCommandBus(distributedCommandBus());
        return factory;
    }

    @Bean
    public JGroupsConnector getJGroupConnector() {

        JGroupsConnector connector = new JGroupsConnector(
            new JChannel("udp_config.xml"), "myCluster",
            localSegment(), xstreamSerializer());
        connector.connect(100);
        return connector;
        return null;
    }

    @Bean
    @Qualifier("distributedCommandBus")
    public DistributedCommandBus distributedCommandBus() {

        DistributedCommandBus distributedCommandBus =
            new DistributedCommandBus(getJGroupConnector());
        return distributedCommandBus;
    }

    @Bean
    @Qualifier("localCommandBus")
    public SimpleCommandBus localSegment() {

        SimpleCommandBus simpleCommandBus = new SimpleCommandBus();
        simpleCommandBus.setDispatchInterceptors(Arrays.asList(
            new BeanValidationInterceptor()));
        return simpleCommandBus;
    }
}
```

The DistributedCommandBus forms a bridge between command bus implementations across JVMs. In your case, you want to bridge between the 02-Ecom-CreateCommandRestController microservice and the 03-Ecom-HandleCommandAndCreateEvent microservice, since the former microservice generates commands that are to be handled by the later microservice. So the DistributedCommandBus instances on each JVM are called segments and are qualified with the name localCommandBus in code, as shown in Figure 12-5.

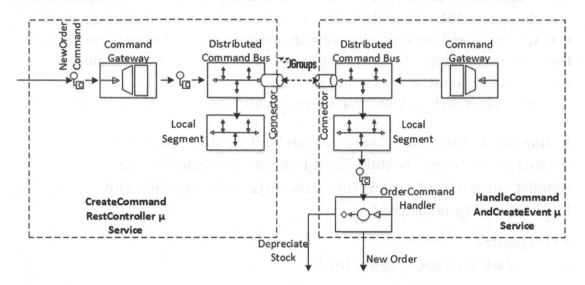

Figure 12-5. *Distributed command and event handling in Axon*

The DistributedCommandBus relies on the CommandBusConnector, which implements the communication protocol between the JVMs. In your case, you use a JGroupsConnector, which uses JGroups to discover and connect to other JGroupsConnectors in the network. Depending on the configuration of the channel that was provided, this implementation allows for dynamic discovery and addition of new members. When members disconnect, their portion of the processing is divided over the remaining members. This dynamic addition and retraction of nodes or JVM or microservices is very important for the required extensibility of your software, which was discussed in the first section in this chapter.

There are no changes other than this configuration as far as the code for the Ecom-CreateCommandRestController microservice is concerned, but you may visit the corresponding section in the previous example for an explanation of the rest of the code in this microservice.

Microservice 3: 03-Ecom-HandleCommandAndCreateEvent

This microservice has to handle any commands created by the 02-Ecom-Create CommandRestController microservice and reaching through the DistributedCommandBus from the remote JVM. Further, this microservice also creates events that are supposed to be consumed by distributed event handlers in remote JVMs or foreign microservices. Hence the configuration of this microservice is going to be little complex in order to accommodate all those connectors and routings.

Visit EcomAppConfiguration.java to see the main configuration, shown in Listing 12-15.

Listing 12-15. Distributed Command Bus Configuration (Visit ch12\ ch12-02\Ax2-Commands-Multi-Event-Handler-Distributed\03-Ecom-HandleCommandAndCreateEvent\src\main\java\com\acme\ecom\ EcomAppConfiguration.java)

```
@Configuration
public class EcomAppConfiguration {

    @PersistenceContext
    private EntityManager entityManager;

    @Qualifier("transactionManager")
    @Autowired
    protected PlatformTransactionManager txManager;

    @Bean
    @Qualifier("distributedCommandGateway")
    public CommandGatewayFactoryBean<CommandGateway>
            commandGatewayFactoryBean() {

        CommandGatewayFactoryBean<CommandGateway> factory =
            new CommandGatewayFactoryBean<>();
        factory.setCommandBus(distributedCommandBus());
        return factory;
    }

    @Bean
    @Qualifier("localCommandGateway")
    public CommandGatewayFactoryBean<CommandGateway>
```

```java
        localCommandGatewayFactoryBean() {

    CommandGatewayFactoryBean<CommandGateway> factory =
        new CommandGatewayFactoryBean<>();
    factory.setCommandBus(localSegment());
    return factory;
}

@Bean
public JGroupsConnector getJGroupConnector() {

    JGroupsConnector connector = new JGroupsConnector(
        new JChannel("udp_config.xml"), "myCluster",
        localSegment(), xstreamSerializer());
    connector.connect(100);
    return connector;
}

@Bean
@Qualifier("distributedCommandBus")
public DistributedCommandBus distributedCommandBus() {

    DistributedCommandBus distributedCommandBus =
        new DistributedCommandBus(getJGroupConnector());
    return distributedCommandBus;
}

@Bean
@Qualifier("localCommandBus")
public SimpleCommandBus localSegment() {

    SimpleCommandBus simpleCommandBus = new SimpleCommandBus();
    SpringTransactionManager transcationMgr =
        new SpringTransactionManager(txManager);
    simpleCommandBus.setTransactionManager(transcationMgr);
    simpleCommandBus.setDispatchInterceptors(Arrays.asList
        new BeanValidationInterceptor()));
    return simpleCommandBus;
}
```

```
@Bean
public AnnotationCommandHandlerBeanPostProcessor
        annotationCommandHandlerBeanPostProcessor() {

    AnnotationCommandHandlerBeanPostProcessor processor =
        new AnnotationCommandHandlerBeanPostProcessor();
    processor.setCommandBus(distributedCommandBus());
    return processor;
}

}
```

You already saw the explanation for the distributed command bus configuration of Listing 12-14, so I will now explain the distributed command processing infrastructure in Listing 12-15. Let's move on to the event infrastructure; see Listing 12-16.

Listing 12-16. Clustered Event Bus Configuration

```
@Configuration
public class EcomAppConfiguration {

    @PersistenceContext
    private EntityManager entityManager;

    @Qualifier("transactionManager")
    @Autowired
    protected PlatformTransactionManager txManager;

    @Bean
    public ConnectionFactory connectionFactory() {

        CachingConnectionFactory connectionFactory =
            new CachingConnectionFactory();
        connectionFactory.setAddresses(rabbitMQAddress);
        connectionFactory.setUsername(rabbitMQUser);
        connectionFactory.setPassword(rabbitMQPassword);
        connectionFactory.setVirtualHost(rabbitMQVhost);
        connectionFactory.setConnectionTimeout(500000);
        connectionFactory.setRequestedHeartBeat(20);
```

```java
    return connectionFactory;
}

@Bean
public FanoutExchange eventBusExchange() {

    return new FanoutExchange(rabbitMQExchange, true, false);
}
@Bean
public Queue eventBusQueue() {

    return new Queue(rabbitMQQueue, true, false, false);
}

@Bean
public Binding binding() {

    return BindingBuilder.bind(eventBusQueue()).to(eventBusExchange());
}

@Bean
public EventBus eventBus() {

    ClusteringEventBus clusteringEventBus = new ClusteringEventBus(
        new DefaultClusterSelector(simpleCluster()), terminal());
    return clusteringEventBus;
}

@Bean
public DefaultAMQPMessageConverter defaultAMQPMessageConverter() {

    return new DefaultAMQPMessageConverter(xstreamSerializer());
}

@Bean
ListenerContainerLifecycleManager listenerContainerLifecycleManager() {

    ListenerContainerLifecycleManager listenerContainerLifecycleManager =
        new ListenerContainerLifecycleManager();
    listenerContainerLifecycleManager.setConnectionFactory(
        connectionFactory());
```

```
            return listenerContainerLifecycleManager;
    }

    @Bean
    public AnnotationEventListenerBeanPostProcessor
            annotationEventListenerBeanPostProcessor() {

        AnnotationEventListenerBeanPostProcessor processor =
            new AnnotationEventListenerBeanPostProcessor();
        processor.setEventBus(eventBus());
        return processor;
    }

    @Bean
    public EventBusTerminal terminal() {

        SpringAMQPTerminal terminal = new SpringAMQPTerminal();
        terminal.setConnectionFactory(connectionFactory());
        terminal.setSerializer(xstreamSerializer());
        terminal.setExchangeName(rabbitMQExchange);
        terminal.setListenerContainerLifecycleManager(
        listenerContainerLifecycleManager());
        terminal.setDurable(true);
        terminal.setTransactional(true);
        return terminal;
    }

    SimpleCluster simpleCluster() {

        SimpleCluster simpleCluster = new SimpleCluster(rabbitMQQueue);
        return simpleCluster;
    }
}
```

The ClusteringEventBus dispatches events to event handlers across different machines. A ClusteringEventBus has to be configured with a ClusterSelector, which selects a Cluster instance for each of the registered EventListeners, and an EventBusTerminal, which is responsible for dispatching events to each of the relevant clusters. In the code above, you use DefaultClusterSelector as the ClusterSelector, which always selects the same cluster. This implementation can serve as a delegate for other cluster selectors for event listeners that do not belong to a specific cluster. The DefaultClusterSelector in turn uses a simple Cluster implementation that invokes each of the members of a cluster when an event is published. The next important component is the EventBusTerminal, which is a mechanism that connects event bus clusters. The terminal is responsible for delivering published events with all of the clusters available in the event bus (either locally or remotely). Terminals are typically bound to a single event bus instance, but may be aware that multiple instances exist in order to form a bridge between these event buses. You use a SpringAMQPTerminal, which is an implementation of EventBusTerminal that uses an AMQP 0.9-compatible message broker to dispatch event messages. This is because you are using Rabbit MQ, which is AMQP-compatible, as the message queue provider that provides the backbone for the distributed event channel. All outgoing messages are sent to a configured exchange. This terminal does not dispatch events internally, as it relies on each cluster to listen to its own AMQP queue. Again, as shown in the code, the terminal is configured with the ConnectionFactory providing the connections and channels to send messages. Although they are a little too complex to understand, the good thing is that Axon abstracts much of these complexities and you can visualize the whole set up as shown in Figure 12-6.

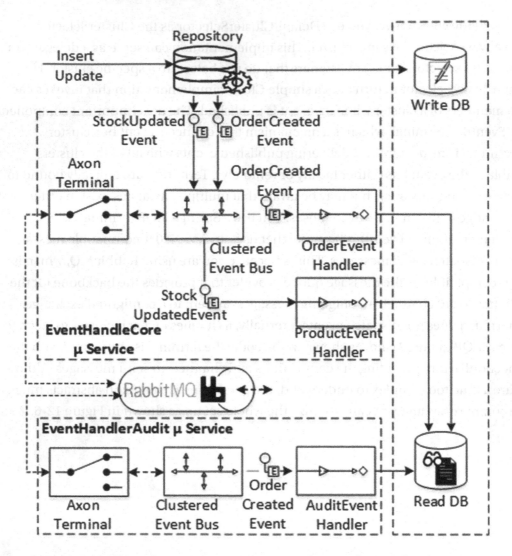

Figure 12-6. *Distributed event processing in a clustered event bus*

If you understand the previous example, there is absolutely nothing new in this microservice.

Microservice 4: 04-Ecom-EventHandleCore

Again, if you have followed the previous example, there is nothing new in this microservice, so I will not do a code walkthrough. As the name of the microservice hints, it contains the two main event handlers, OrderEventHandler and ProductEventHandler, and the functionality and code snippets are similar to those in the previous example.

Microservice 5: 05-Ecom-EventHandlerAudit

This is a new microservice. The intention is to demonstrate the extensibility of the Axon-based CQRS architecture where, in the future if you have a new functionality that wants to subscribe to existing events and add to the existing overall functionality of the application, you should be able to do that without any downtime of the existing running application.

Listing 12-17 shows the code for the newly added event handler, which is expecting to be notified of the previously handled event itself.

Listing 12-17. Event Handler for the newly introduced Microservice (ch12\ch12-02\ Ax2-Commands-Multi-Event-Handler-Distributed\05-Ecom-EventHandlerAudit\ src\main\java\com\acme\ecom\order\eventhandler\AuditEventHandler.java)

```
@Component
public class AuditEventHandler {

    @Autowired
    DataSource dataSource;

    @EventHandler
    public void handleOrderCreatedEvent(OrderCreatedEvent event) {

        JdbcTemplate jdbcTemplate = new JdbcTemplate(dataSource);
        jdbcTemplate.update("INSERT INTO ecom_order_audit VALUES(?,?,?)",
            new Object[]{event.getId(),
        event.getOrderStatus(), new Date()});
    }
}
```

Build and Test the Example Scenario

As the first step, you need to bring up the RabbitMQ server. You may want to refer to Appendix B to get started with RabbitMQ server.

```
D:\Applns\RabbitMQ\rabbitmq_server-3.6.3\sbin>D:\Applns\RabbitMQ\rabbitmq_
server-3.6.3\sbin\rabbitmq-server.bat
```

Make sure MySQL is up and running. You may want to refer to Appendix H to get started with MySQL.

To start with clean tables, delete any tables with the names you want for this example:

```
mysql> drop table ecom_order;
mysql> drop table ecom_product;
mysql> drop table ecom_order_view;
mysql> drop table ecom_product_view;
mysql> drop table ecom_order_audit;
```

Newly create the required tables. Now the ecom_order table and the ecom_product table will be created when the microservice starts up. However, you need to explicitly create the Read DB tables and the table for Audit:

```
mysql>create table ecom_product_view(id INT , price DOUBLE, stock INT
,description VARCHAR(255));
mysql>create table ecom_order_view(id INT , price DOUBLE, number INT
,description VARCHAR(225),status VARCHAR(50));
mysql>create table ecom_order_audit(id INT ,status VARCHAR(50),date
TIMESTAMP);
```

The example has a Maven module that contains the common classes used by all other microservices. Hence this has to be built first:

```
cd D:\binil\gold\pack03\ch12\ch12-02\Ax2-Commands-Multi-Event-Handler-
Distributed\06-Ecom-common
D:\binil\gold\pack03\ch12\ch12-02\Ax2-Commands-Multi-Event-Handler-
Distributed\06-Ecom-common>make
D:\binil\gold\pack03\ch12\ch12-02\Ax2-Commands-Multi-Event-Handler-
Distributed\06-Ecom-common>mvn clean install
```

Next, there are five microservices to build and get running. You will do one at a time.

Microservice 1: 01-Ecom-web

First, update the configuration files to suit to your environment:

```
ch12\ch12-02\Ax2-Commands-Multi-Event-Handler-Distributed\01-Ecom-web\src\
main\resources\application.properties
server.port=8080
```

I advise you not to make any changes here.

Now, build and package the executables for the Ecom-web microservice and bring up the server. There is a utility script at ch12\ch12-02\Ax2-Commands-Multi-Event-Handler-Distributed\01-Ecom-web\make.bat:

```
cd D:\binil\gold\pack03\ch12\ch12-02\Ax2-Commands-Multi-Event-Handler-
Distributed\01-Ecom-web
D:\binil\gold\pack03\ch12\ch12-02\Ax2-Commands-Multi-Event-Handler-
Distributed\01-Ecom-web>make
D:\binil\gold\pack03\ch12\ch12-02\Ax2-Commands-Multi-Event-Handler-
Distributed\01-Ecom-web>mvn clean install
```

You can run the Spring Boot application in more than one way. The straightforward way is to execute the JAR file via the following commands:

```
D:\binil\gold\pack03\ch12\ch12-02\Ax2-Commands-Multi-Event-Handler-
Distributed\01-Ecom-web>run
D:\binil\gold\pack03\ch12\ch12-02\Ax2-Commands-Multi-Event-Handler-
Distributed\01-Ecom-web>java -jar .\target\01-Ecom-web-0.0.1-SNAPSHOT.jar
```

This will bring up the 01-Ecom-web Spring Boot Server in port 8080.

Microservice 2: 02-Ecom-CreateCommandRestController

The JGroups configuration is provided at ch12\ch12-02\Ax2-Commands-Multi-Event-Handler-Distributed\02-Ecom-CreateCommandRestController\src\main\resources\udp_config.xml.

However, don't worry about the contents of this file too much for now.

Update the configuration files to suit to your environment:

```
ch12\ch12-02\Ax2-Commands-Multi-Event-Handler-Distributed\02-Ecom-
CreateCommandRestController\src\main\resources\application.properties
server.port=8081
spring.datasource.url=jdbc:mysql://localhost/ecom01
spring.datasource.username=root
spring.datasource.password=rootpassword
```

Now, build the microservice:

```
cd D:\binil\gold\pack03\ch12\ch12-02\Ax2-Commands-Multi-Event-Handler-
Distributed\02-Ecom-CreateCommandRestController
D:\binil\gold\pack03\ch12\ch12-02\Ax2-Commands-Multi-Event-Handler-
Distributed\02-Ecom-CreateCommandRestController>make
D:\binil\gold\pack03\ch12\ch12-02\Ax2-Commands-Multi-Event-Handler-
Distributed\02-Ecom-CreateCommandRestController>mvn clean install
```

You can run the 02-Ecom-CreateCommandRestController Axon Spring Boot application in more than one way. The straightforward way is to execute the JAR file via the following commands:

```
D:\binil\gold\pack03\ch12\ch12-02\Ax2-Commands-Multi-Event-Handler-
Distributed\02-Ecom-CreateCommandRestController>run
D:\binil\gold\pack03\ch12\ch12-02\Ax2-Commands-Multi-Event-Handler-
Distributed\02-Ecom-CreateCommandRestController>java -jar .\target\02-Ecom-
CreateCommandRestController-0.0.1-SNAPSHOT.jar
```

This will bring up the 02-Ecom-CreateCommandRestController Axon Spring Boot Server in port 8081.

Microservice 3: 03-Ecom-HandleCommandAndCreateEvent

Update the configuration files to suit to your environment:

```
ch12\ch12-02\Ax2-Commands-Multi-Event-Handler-Distributed\03-Ecom-
HandleCommandAndCreateEvent\src\main\resources\application.properties
server.port=8082
spring.datasource.url=jdbc:mysql://localhost/ecom01
spring.datasource.username=root
spring.datasource.password=rootpassword

ecom.amqp.rabbit.address= 127.0.0.1:5672
ecom.amqp.rabbit.username= guest
ecom.amqp.rabbit.password= guest
ecom.amqp.rabbit.vhost=/
ecom.amqp.rabbit.exchange=Ecom-02
ecom.amqp.rabbit.queue=Ecom-createcommand
```

```
cd D:\binil\gold\pack03\ch12\ch12-02\Ax2-Commands-Multi-Event-Handler-
Distributed\03-Ecom-HandleCommandAndCreateEvent
D:\binil\gold\pack03\ch12\ch12-02\Ax2-Commands-Multi-Event-Handler-
Distributed\03-Ecom-HandleCommandAndCreateEvent>make
D:\binil\gold\pack03\ch12\ch12-02\Ax2-Commands-Multi-Event-Handler-
Distributed\03-Ecom-HandleCommandAndCreateEvent>mvn clean install
```

You can run the 03-Ecom-HandleCommandAndCreateEvent Axon Spring Boot
application in more than one way. The straightforward way is to execute the JAR file via
the following commands:

```
D:\binil\gold\pack03\ch12\ch12-02\Ax2-Commands-Multi-Event-Handler-
Distributed\03-Ecom-HandleCommandAndCreateEvent>run
D:\binil\gold\pack03\ch12\ch12-02\Ax2-Commands-Multi-Event-Handler-
Distributed\03-Ecom-HandleCommandAndCreateEvent>java -jar .\target\03-Ecom-
HandleCommandAndCreateEvent-0.0.1-SNAPSHOT.jar
```

This will bring up the 02-Ecom-CreateCommandRestController Axon Spring Boot
Server in port 8082.

Microservice 4: 04-Ecom-EventHandleCore

Update the configuration files to suit to your environment:

```
ch12\ch12-02\Ax2-Commands-Multi-Event-Handler-Distributed\04-Ecom-
EventHandleCore\src\main\resources\application.properties
server.port=8083
spring.datasource.url=jdbc:mysql://localhost/ecom01
spring.datasource.username=root
spring.datasource.password=rootpassword

ecom.amqp.rabbit.address= 127.0.0.1:5672
ecom.amqp.rabbit.username= guest
ecom.amqp.rabbit.password= guest
ecom.amqp.rabbit.vhost=/
ecom.amqp.rabbit.exchange=Ecom-02
ecom.amqp.rabbit.queue=Ecom-event-core
```

```
cd D:\binil\gold\pack03\ch12\ch12-02\Ax2-Commands-Multi-Event-Handler-
Distributed\04-Ecom-EventHandleCore
D:\binil\gold\pack03\ch12\ch12-02\Ax2-Commands-Multi-Event-Handler-
Distributed\04-Ecom-EventHandleCore>make
D:\binil\gold\pack03\ch12\ch12-02\Ax2-Commands-Multi-Event-Handler-
Distributed\04-Ecom-EventHandleCore>mvn clean install
```

You can run the 04-Ecom-EventHandleCore Axon Spring Boot application in more than one way. The straightforward way is to execute the JAR file via the following commands:

```
D:\binil\gold\pack03\ch12\ch12-02\Ax2-Commands-Multi-Event-Handler-
Distributed\04-Ecom-EventHandleCore>run
D:\binil\gold\pack03\ch12\ch12-02\Ax2-Commands-Multi-Event-Handler-
Distributed\04-Ecom-EventHandleCore>java -jar .\target\04-Ecom-
EventHandleCore-0.0.1-SNAPSHOT.jar
```

This will bring up the 04-Ecom-EventHandleCore Axon Spring Boot Server in port 8083.

Microservice 5: 05-Ecom-EventHandlerAudit

This is the last microservice you want to bring up in this example. Update the configuration files to suit to your environment:

```
ch12\ch12-02\Ax2-Commands-Multi-Event-Handler-Distributed\05-Ecom-
EventHandlerAudit\src\main\resources\application.properties
server.port=8084
spring.datasource.url=jdbc:mysql://localhost/ecom01
spring.datasource.username=root
spring.datasource.password=rootpassword

ecom.amqp.rabbit.address= 127.0.0.1:5672
ecom.amqp.rabbit.username= guest
ecom.amqp.rabbit.password= guest
ecom.amqp.rabbit.vhost=/
ecom.amqp.rabbit.exchange=Ecom-02
ecom.amqp.rabbit.queue=Ecom-event-history
```

```
cd D:\binil\gold\pack03\ch12\ch12-02\Ax2-Commands-Multi-Event-Handler-
Distributed\05-Ecom-EventHandlerAudit
D:\binil\gold\pack03\ch12\ch12-02\Ax2-Commands-Multi-Event-Handler-
Distributed\05-Ecom-EventHandlerAudit>make
D:\binil\gold\pack03\ch12\ch12-02\Ax2-Commands-Multi-Event-Handler-
Distributed\05-Ecom-EventHandlerAudit>mvn clean install
```

You can run the 05-Ecom-EventHandlerAudit Axon Spring Boot application again in more than one way. The straightforward way is to execute the JAR file via the following commands:

```
D:\binil\gold\pack03\ch12\ch12-02\Ax2-Commands-Multi-Event-Handler-
Distributed\05-Ecom-EventHandlerAudit>run
D:\binil\gold\pack03\ch12\ch12-02\Ax2-Commands-Multi-Event-Handler-
Distributed\05-Ecom-EventHandlerAudit>java -Dserver.port=8084 -Dspring.
application.name=product-audit-01 -jar .\target\05-Ecom-EventHandlerAudit-
0.0.1-SNAPSHOT.jar
```

This will bring up the 05-Ecom-EventHandlerAudit Axon Spring Boot Server in port 8084.

You want to prepopulate the ecom_product and ecom_product_view tables with some initial data:

```
mysql> insert into ecom_product(id,description,price,stock,version)
values(1,'Shirts',100,5,0);
mysql> insert into ecom_product(id,description,price,stock,version)
values(2,'Pants',100,5,0);
mysql> insert into ecom_product(id,description,price,stock,version)
values(3,'T-Shirt',100,5,0);
mysql> insert into ecom_product(id,description,price,stock,version)
values(4,'Shoes',100,5,0);

mysql> insert into ecom_product_view(id,description,price,stock)
values(1,'Shirts',100,5);
mysql> insert into ecom_product_view(id,description,price,stock)
values(2,'Pants',100,5);
mysql> insert into ecom_product_view(id,description,price,stock)
values(3,'T-Shirt',100,5);
```

```
mysql> insert into ecom_product_view(id,description,price,stock)
values(4,'Shoes',100,5);
```

You can use a browser (preferably Chrome) and point to http://localhost:8080/.

You can now test the example by clicking any one of the buttons in Figure 12-7. When you click, a new order is created in the Order Write DB. Eventually, the Order Read DB will be updated with this new order. Also, the corresponding product stock will be reduced by one in the Product Write DB. This change will also be eventually updated in the Product Read DB.

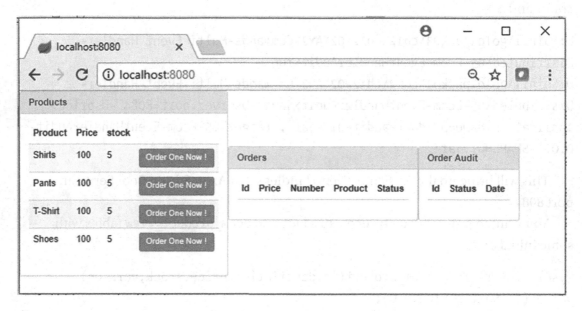

Figure 12-7. *Testing the distributed command and event processing example*

There is another aspect to be noted here. The new microservice you added in this example is responsible for the audit log entries, so the Audit Read DB is updated with records. When you refresh the screen, the change is as reflected in Figure 12-8. (If the change is not reflected, you may close the browser session and make a new browser instance and try the above URL. Again, there may be little gotchas in the GUIs provided with the examples in the book since this book's concentration is on microservices, not on the perfectness of their UIs.)

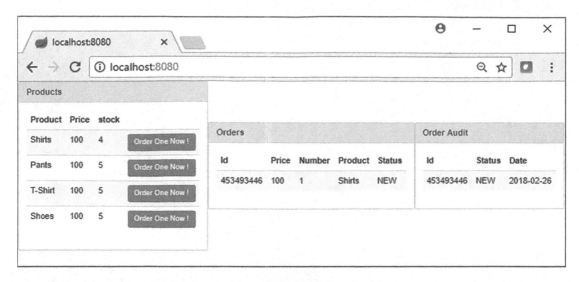

Figure 12-8. *Product view synced with product write data*

What is different from the example in the previous section is that in the current example, the same event OrderCreatedEvent is consumed by two event handlers. This demonstrates the extensibility of the architecture. To make it clear, you may create a sixth microservice with a new event handler for the same event, and if you can bring it up without disturbing the already existing five microservices, then from next command onwards the event will be consumed by the newly attached sixth microservice too!

Summary

You have reached a major milestone in this book by executing the examples in this chapter, since they are live code in action and they explain many of the concepts discussed in this book so far. You saw what a CQRS application will look like in the familiar Spring Boot framework, and you also saw how to distribute one into multiple microservices, also communicating with other using events over a messaging middleware. So far, so good; however, you have now invited "Satan"[3] into your architecture: the partition. By bringing the capability to partition your single JVM CQRS application in the first example into multiple microservices in the second example, you now need to address the consistency aspects you explored via the CAP theorem in Chapter 11. To discuss that in detail further, you should first know the foundations of consistency in the context of microservices, so move on to Chapter 13.

---

[3]Satan is the name used by Christians and Jews for the Devil (= a powerful evil force and the enemy of God).

CHAPTER 13

Distributed Transactions

You looked at using the Axon framework to implement different scenarios of the CQRS pattern in the previous chapter. In this chapter, you will be revisiting Axon for more scenarios in the microservices context, including executing long-running computational processing. To do that effectively, let's start the discussion with a few basics, including transactions. A transaction in its simple form is a change or exchange of values between entities. The parties involved can be a single entity or more than one entity. When the party involved is a single entity, typically the transaction is a local transaction. If more than one party is involved, the transaction can be classified as either a local transaction or a distributed transaction, depending on the nature and location of the entities involved.

A transaction may involve a single step or multiple steps. Whether a single step or multiple steps, a transaction is a single unit of work that embodies these individual steps. For the successful completion of a transaction, each of the involved individual steps should succeed. If any of the individual steps fail, the transaction should undo any of the effects of the other steps it has already done within that transaction.

With this preface, you will look into the details of transactions, especially distributed transactions. I will only touch base on the essentials of transactions; I'll spend more time on the practical implication aspects, especially in the context of microservices. Detailing out transactions to any more depth would require its own complete book, so this coverage will be limited to discussions around microservices and few practical tools you can use to build reliable microservices.

In this chapter you will learn about

- The indeterministic characteristics of computer networks

- Transaction aspects in general

- Distributed transactions vs. local transactions

© Binildas Christudas 2019

B. Christudas, *Practical Microservices Architectural Patterns*, https://doi.org/10.1007/978-1-4842-4501-9_13

- ACID vs. BASE transactions

- A complete example demonstrating distributed transactions using multiple resource managers

The Two Generals Paradox

In computer networking (particularly with regard to the Transmission Control Protocol), literature shows that TCP can't guarantee (complete) state consistency between endpoints. This is illustrated by the Two Generals Paradox (also known as the Two Generals Problem or the Two Armies Problem or the Coordinated Attack Problem), which is a thought experiment illustrating the pitfalls and connected design challenges while attempting to coordinate an action by communicating over an unreliable link.

The Two Generals Paradox is unsolvable in the face of arbitrary communication failures; however, the same problem provides a base for realistic expectations for any distributed consistency protocols. So to understand the problem, you need to understand the associated indeterminism involved, which will provide a perfect analogy to learn more about transactions.

Illustrating the Two Generals Paradox

This section will illustrate the Two Generals Paradox with the classical example scenario. Figure 13-1 shows two armies, each led by a different general who are jointly preparing to attack a fortified city, shown in the center. Both armies are encamped near the city, but in their own valleys. A third valley separates the two hills of the valleys occupied by the two generals, and the only way for the two generals to communicate is by sending messengers across the third valley. The third valley is occupied by the city's defenders, so there's a chance that any messenger sent through the valley may be captured.

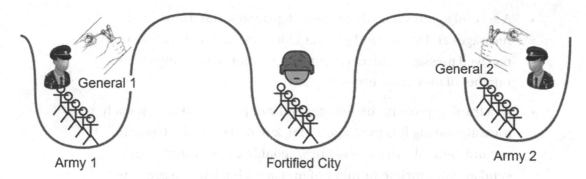

Figure 13-1. *Illustrating the Two Generals Paradox*

The two generals have agreed that they will attack; however, they have yet to agree upon a time for attack. The attack will only succeed if both armies attack the city at the same time; the lone attacker army will die trying. So the generals must communicate with each other to decide on a time to attack and agree to jointly attack at that time; each general must also know that the other general knows that they have jointly agreed to the attack plan. An acknowledgement of message receipt can be lost as easily as the original message itself, thus a potentially infinite series of messages are required to come to (near) consensus. Both generals will always be left wondering whether their last messenger got through.

Solution Approaches

Computer networks are the spine of distributed systems; however, the reliability of any network has to be examined. Distributed systems are required to address scalability and flexibility of software systems, so a network is a necessary evil. Schemes should accept the uncertainty of the networks and not attempt to eliminate it; rather, they should mitigate it to an acceptable degree.

In the Two Generals Paradox, you can think of many acceptable mechanisms, such as

- The first general can send 50 messengers, anticipating that the probability of all 50 being captured is low. This general will have fixed the time of attack to include enough time for all or a few or many of those 50 messengers to reach the other general. He will then attack at the communicated time no matter what, and the second general will also attack if any of the messages are received.

- A second approach is where the first general sends a stream of messages and the second general sends acknowledgments to each received message, with each general's comfort increasing with the number of messages received.

- In a third approach, the first general can put a marking on each message saying it is message 1 of n, 2 of n, 3 of n, etc. Here the second general can estimate how reliable the channel is and send an appropriate number of messages back to ensure a high probability of at least one message being received. If the network is highly reliable, then one message will suffice and additional messages won't help; if not, the last message is as likely to get lost as the first one.

Microservices as Generals

When you have split the state of a monolith that has been "living happily thereafter, together" to the state of "living happily ever after, separated," you have split the army from one general into multiple generals. Each microservice has their own general or is a general by itself, and more than one general may be required to coordinate any useful functionality. By adopting polyglot, each microservice will have its own resource, whether it's a database or file storage. The network is the only way these microservices can coordinate and communicate. The effect of changes made to resources cross-microservices has to be made consistent. This consistency depends on which schema or protocol you choose to coordinate and communicate the commands to make changes and the acknowledgements, which act as the agreement to effect that change between microservices.

TCP/IP, the Valley Between the Generals

The Internet Protocol (IP) is not reliable. It may be delayed or dropped or duplicate data can come or data can come in order not as per the original intention. The Transmission Control Protocol adds a more reliable layer over IP. TCP can retransmit missing packets, eliminate duplicates, and assemble packets in the order in which the sender intended to transmit. However, while TCP can hide packet loss, duplication, or reordering, it may not be able to remove delays in the network, since they are packet switched. Traditional fixed-line telephone networks are extremely reliable, and delayed audio frames and dropped calls are very rare. This is because a fixed, guaranteed amount of bandwidth is allocated for your call in the network, along the entire route between the two callers; this is referred to as circuit switched. However, data center networks and the Internet are not circuit switched. Their backbone, the Ethernet and IP, are packet switched protocols, which suffer from queueing, which can cause unbounded delays in the network.

Each microservice has its own memory space for computation and resources for persistence and storage, and one microservice cannot access another microservice's memory or resource (except by making requests to the other microservice over the network, through an exposed API). The Internet and most internal networks in data centers (often Ethernet) have the characteristics explained above, and these networks become the only way microservices can coordinate and communicate. In this kind of network, one microservice can send a message to another microservice, but the network gives no guarantees as to when it will arrive or whether it will arrive at all. If you send a request and expect a response, many things could go wrong in between.

The sending microservice can't even tell whether the request or message was delivered. The next best option is for the recipient microservice to send a response message, which may also in turn be lost or delayed. These issues are indistinguishable in an asynchronous network. When one microservice sends a request to another microservice and doesn't receive a response, it is impossible to tell why. The typical way of handling such issues is by using timeouts: after some time you give up waiting and assume that the response is never going to arrive. However, if and when a timeout occurs, you still don't know whether the remote microservice got your request or not, and if the request is still queued somewhere, there is a chance that it may still be delivered to the recipient microservice, even if the sender microservice has given up on the previous request and might have resent the request, in which case a duplicate request will get fired. Advanced solutions to this problem are addressed in the reference.[1]

---

[1]Atomikos Microservices Transaction Patterns online course: `https://atomikos.teachable.com/p/microservice-transaction-patterns`

Transactions

Transactions help you control how access is given to the same data set, whether it is for read or write purposes. Data in a changing state might be inconsistent, hence other reads and writes should have to wait while the state transitions from "changing" to either "committed" or "rolled back." You will look at the details related to transactions now.

Hardware Instruction Sets at the Core of Transactions

For transactions at a single database node, atomicity is implemented at the storage level. When a transaction commits, the database makes the transaction's writes durable (typically in a write-ahead log[2]) and subsequently appends a commit record to the log on disk. So, the controller of the disk drive handling that write takes a crucial role in asserting that the write has happened.

A transaction once committed cannot be undone. You cannot change your mind and retroactively undo a transaction after it has been committed. This is because, once data has been committed, it may become visible to other transactions and thus other transactions may have already started relying on that data.

The ACID in the Transaction

For a transaction to comply with the specification, it should exhibit the ACID (Atomicity, Consistency, Isolation, and Durability) properties. Let's look into them one by one.

- **Atomicity:** The outcome of a transaction, if it's a commit, is that all of the transaction's writes are made durable as a single unit of work. If it's an abort, then all of the transaction's writes are rolled back (i.e., undone or discarded) as a single unit of work. If you go back to the previous section where I described that it's the single controller of one particular disk drive that sits in the core and takes the commit or rollback decision, you need to appreciate that whether it's the write

---

[2]Write-ahead logging (WAL) is a family of techniques for providing atomicity and durability (two of the ACID properties) in database systems. The changes are first recorded in the log, which must be written to stable storage, before the changes are written to the database.

of a single word[3] or multiple words (depending on 32-bit or 64-bit), it's the support available from the hardware level that helps you club them together as the write of a single unit of work.

- **Consistency:** This property guarantees that a transaction will leave the data in a consistent state, irrespective of whether the transaction is committed or rolled back. To understand what this "consistent state" means, it refers to the adherence of the constraints or rules of the database. It is common to model business rule constraints in terms of database integrity constraints. So, maintaining consistency is a dual effort by both a resource manager and the application. While the application ensures consistency in terms of keys, referential integrity, and so on, the transaction manager ensures that the transaction is atomic, isolated, and durable. For example, if your transaction is to assign the last seat on the flight to one of two travelers who are concurrently booking for that same flight, the transaction will be consistent if one seat is removed from the inventory of free seats and assigned to one and only one of the travelers and at the same time show that the same seat is not assigned or assignable any more to the other traveler trying booking concurrently.

- **Isolation:** The isolation property guarantees that the changes ongoing in a transaction will not affect the data accessed by another transaction. This isolation can be controlled to finer levels, and "Transaction Isolation Mechanisms" section describes them.

- **Durability:** This property requires that when a transaction is committed, any changes the transaction makes to the data must be recorded permanently. When a transaction commits, the database makes the transaction's writes durable (typically in a write-ahead log) and subsequently appends a commit record to the log on disk.

---

[3]64-bit computing is the use of processors that have datapath widths, integer size, and memory address widths of 64 bits (eight octets). Also, 64-bit computer architectures for central processing units (CPUs) and arithmetic logic units (ALUs) are based on processor registers, address buses, or data buses of that size.

If the database crashes in the middle of this process, the transaction can be recovered from the log when the database restarts. In cases where the commit record is already written to disk before the crash, the transaction is considered committed. If not, any writes from that transaction are rolled back. So the moment at which the disk finishes writing the commit record is the single deciding point to commit; before that moment, it is still possible to abort (due to a crash), but after that moment, the transaction is committed (even if the database crashes just afterwards). So, it is the controller of the disk drive handling the write that makes the commit atomic. Having said that, if an error or crash happens during the process, the above logs can be used to rebuild or recreate the data changes.

Transaction Models

Transaction models refer to how the coordination of individual transactions under the context of an enclosing transaction are structured. You will look at the major transaction models here:

- **Flat transactions:** In a flat transaction, when one of the steps fails, the entire transaction is rolled back. In a flat transaction, the transaction completes each of its steps before going on to the next one. Each step accesses corresponding resources sequentially. When the transaction uses locks, it can only wait for one object at a time.

- **Nested transactions:** In a nested transaction, atomic transactions are embedded in other transactions. The top-level transaction can open subtransactions, and each subtransaction can open further subtransactions, and this nesting can continue. The effect of an individual embedded transaction will not affect the parent transaction. When a parent aborts, all of its subtransactions are aborted. However, when a subtransaction aborts, the parent can decide whether to abort or not. In a nested transaction, a subtransaction can be another nested transaction or a flat transaction.

- **Chained transactions:** In a chained transaction, each transaction relies on the result and resources of the previous transaction. A chained transaction is also called a serial transaction. Here the distinguishing feature is that when a transaction commits, its resources, like cursors, are retained and are available for the next transaction in the chain. So, transactions inside the chain can see the result of the previous commit within the chain; however, transactions outside of the chain cannot see or alter the data being affected by transactions within the chain. If one of the transactions should fail, only that one will be rolled back and the previously committed transactions will not.

- **Saga:** Sagas are similar to nested transactions; however, each of the transactions has a corresponding compensating transaction. If any of the transactions in a saga fail, the compensating transactions for each transaction that was successfully run previously will be invoked.

Transaction Attributes in EJB vs. Spring

Both Spring and EJB give the user the freedom to choose from programmatic and declarative transaction management. For programmatic transaction management, you need to code against the JDBC and JTA APIs. With the declarative approach, you externalize transaction control to configuration files. Also, you need to choose from the available transaction attributes to get the required behavior. The EJB specification defines six basic transaction attributes. Subsequently, Spring has counterparts for all six transaction attributes. In fact, Spring has more:

- **PROPAGATION_REQUIRED (REQUIRED in EJB):** Supports a current transaction; creates a new one if none exist.

- **PROPAGATION_REQUIRES_NEW (REQUIRES_NEW in EJB):** Creates a new transaction; suspends the current transaction if one exists.

- **PROPAGATION_NOT_SUPPORTED (NOT_SUPPORTED in EJB):** Executes non-transactionally; suspends the current transaction if one exists.

- **PROPAGATION_SUPPORTS (SUPPORTS in EJB):** Supports a current transaction; executes non-transactionally if none exist.

- **PROPAGATION_MANDATORY (MANDATORY in EJB):** Supports a current transaction; throws an exception if none exist.

- **PROPAGATION_NEVER (NEVER in EJB):** Executes non-transactionally; throws an exception if a transaction exists.

- **PROPAGATION_NESTED (No equivalent in EJB):** Executes within a nested transaction if a current transaction exists, or else behave like PROPAGATION_REQUIRED. There is no analogous feature in EJB. Actual creation of a nested transaction will only work on specific transaction managers. Out of the box, this only applies to the JDBC DataSourceTransactionManager when working on a JDBC 3.0 driver. Some JTA providers might support nested transactions as well.

Transaction Isolation Mechanisms

Transaction isolation refers to the protection of one transaction from the effects of the other, when multiple concurrent transactions happen, often on the same data set. Transaction managers rely on two mechanisms to achieve transaction isolation:

- **Locking:** Locking controls access to a transaction to a particular data set. Read locks are non-exclusive and allow multiple transactions to read data concurrently. However, write locks are exclusive locks and only a single transaction is allowed to update data.

- **Serialization:** When multiple transactions happen concurrently, serialization is a mechanism to guarantee that the effects are as if they are executing sequentially, not concurrently. Locking is a means of enforcing serialization.

Transaction Isolation Levels

The types of serialization and locks used as well as the extent to which they are affected determine the level of isolation that a transaction will execute under. Java Enterprise Edition specifies the following types of isolation levels, as defined in the java.sql. Connection interface:

- **TRANSACTION_NONE:** Indicates that transactions are not supported.

- **TRANSACTION_READ_COMMITTED:** Indicates that dirty reads are prevented; non-repeatable reads and phantom[4] reads can occur.

- **TRANSACTION_READ_UNCOMMITTED:** Indicates that dirty reads, non-repeatable reads, and phantom reads can occur. This level allows a row changed by one transaction to be read by another transaction before any changes in that row have been committed (a dirty read). If any of the changes are rolled back, the second transaction will have retrieved an invalid row.

- **TRANSACTION_REPEATABLE_READ:** Indicates that dirty reads and non-repeatable reads are prevented; phantom reads can occur.

- **TRANSACTION_SERIALIZABLE:** Indicates that dirty reads, non-repeatable reads, and phantom reads are prevented. This level prohibits the situation where one transaction reads all rows that satisfy a WHERE condition, a second transaction inserts a row that satisfies that WHERE condition, and the first transaction rereads for the same condition, retrieving the additional phantom row in the second read.

The level of relaxation or the strictness of enforcement of the serialization and locks are determined by the type of concurrency the application is willing to tolerate with respect to staleness of data. The next section will explain this concept.

Transaction Concurrency

When multiple concurrent transactions happen, often on the same data set, the effect of one transaction from the effects of the other can be controlled via the level of concurrency the application is willing to tolerate. The levels are the following:

- **Dirty read:** Dirty reads happen when a transaction reads data that has been written by another transaction but has not yet been committed by the other transaction.

---

[4]A phantom read occurs when, in the course of a transaction, new rows are added or removed by another transaction to the records being read.

- **Non-repeatable read:** If a transaction reads data, and if it gets a different result if it rereads the same data within the same transaction, it is a non-repeatable read.

- **Phantom read:** When a single transaction reads against the same data set more than once, a phantom read happens when another transaction slips in and inserts additional data.

Transaction Isolation Control Methods

Strict levels of transaction isolation may cause negative performance scenarios, and in such cases there are two general approaches to locking:

- **Optimistic locking:** Optimistic locking takes a pragmatic approach and encourages clients to be "optimistic" that data will not change while they are using it and allows them to access same data concurrently. If for any reason the transaction on behalf of any particular client wants to update, the update is committed if and only if the data that was originally provided to the client is the same as the current data in the database. This approach is less ideal for hot-spot data because the comparison will fail often.

- **Pessimistic locking:** Pessimistic locking may use semaphore[5] or any of the transaction mechanisms previously discussed. For every read, you need a read lock, and for every write, you need a write lock. Read locks are not exclusive whereas write locks are. A typical read lock may be obtained when you query similar to

```
SELECT * FROM QUOTES_TABLE WHERE QUOTES_ID=5 FOR UPDATE;
```

---

[5]A semaphore is a variable or abstract data type used to control access to a common resource by multiple processes in a concurrent system such as a multitasking operating system. A trivial semaphore is a plain variable that is changed (for example, incremented, decremented, or toggled) depending on programmer-defined conditions.

Both locks will be released only when the usage of data is completed. A read lock can be given to a transaction on request, provided no other transaction holds the write lock. For a transaction to update, it requires a write lock, and during the duration that transaction holds the write lock, other transactions are allowed to read the data if and only if they don't require a read lock. Moreover, if a transaction holds a write, it will not allow another transaction to read its changing data until those changes have been committed.

Enterprise Transaction Categories

Transactions have different connotations depending on the context in which we use them. It can be in the context of multiple operations within a monolith system, or in the context of multiple monoliths or multiple microservices, or in the context of multiple enterprises with common (or conflicting) interests. You will briefly look at the different transaction categories in this context.

ACID Transactions

ACID transactions are related to atomic transactions where multiple steps or operations are executed with the intent that either all of them succeed together or all of them return back to the previous state due to the failure of one or more of the steps. A major portion of the discussion in previous sections of this chapter concerned ACID transactions, so enough explanation has already been done. You will now look at the architecture of an ACID transaction processing (TP) system. Figure 13-2 depicts a typical architecture consisting of multiple resource managers.

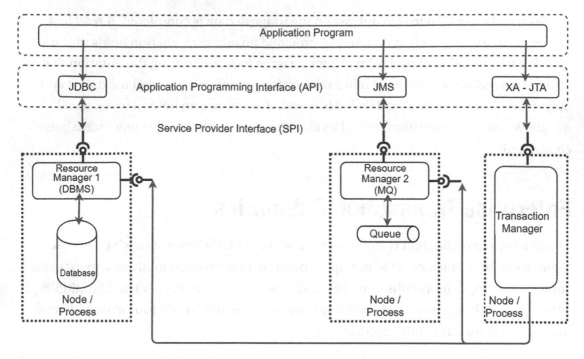

Figure 13-2. Distributed ACID transactions with multiple resources

BASE = ACID in Slices

ACID is the only style that can guarantee data consistency. However, if a distributed system uses ACID transactions, everything has to happen in lockstep mode, everywhere. This requires all components to be available and it also increases the lock times on the data. BASE is an architectural style that relaxes these requirements, simply by cutting the (overall, ideal) ACID transaction into smaller pieces, each of them still ACID in themselves.

Messaging is used to make changes ripple through the system, where each change is ideally processed by an ACID transaction. The messages are asynchronous rather than synchronous, meaning that there is a delay between the first and last ACID transaction in a BASE system.

This is why this style exhibits "eventual consistency:" one has to wait for all messages to ripple through the system and be applied where appropriate. The "Eventual Consistency of Microservices" section in Chapter 11 discussed this in detail.

I'll now introduce BASE in various incremental steps, by cutting more and more into the ACID transaction scope.

BASE Transactions

Figure 13-3 shows a BASE architecture with four different microservices. Each microservice still has ACID properties (independent of the other microservices of the system).

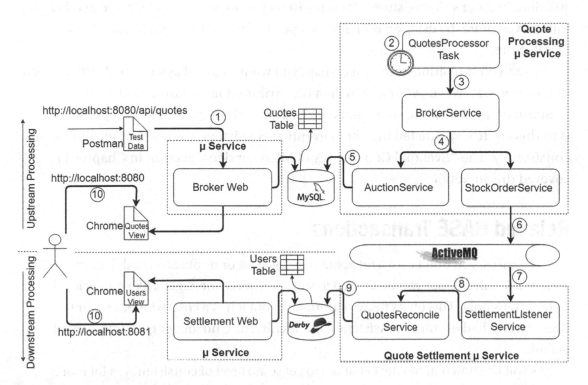

Figure 13-3. *BASE architecture where each microservice still has ACID guarantees by means of XA transactions*

This is the architecture of a microservice ecosystem in BASE style that sends or receives messages in ACID style. You will look at the functionality of each microservice in a later section (the "Design the Example Scenario" subsection under the "Distributed Transaction Example" section); however, pay attention to the technical components depicted here for the time being. It is BASE because via ActiveMQ you don't know or care where the messages go to or come from; all that the quote processing and quote settlement see between them is the queues (whereas a classical ACID architecture would create one big ACID transaction for quote settlement and quote processing). You use JTA/XA to ensure that messages are processed exactly once, since you don't want to lose messages (or get duplicates). Messages that are received from the queue are guaranteed to make it to the database, even with intermediate crashes. Messages that are sent are guaranteed to have their domain object status updated in the database, even with intermediate crashes.

For systems that require strong guarantees on data consistency, this is a good solution. In other systems, strong data consistency is not that vital and you can relax things even more–by using an even finer scope of ACID transactions in your BASE architecture.

When you transition to microservices, you want to avoid system-wide distributed transactions. However, your actual data is distributed more compared to the scenario of the monolith, so the need for distributed transactions is very real. And it is in this context we are talking about eventual consistency in place of instantaneous consistency. The "Eventual Consistency of Microservices" section in Chapter 11 covered this in detail.

Relaxed BASE Transactions

In some cases, you don't care a lot about message loss or duplicates, and the scope of your ACID transactions can be limited to single resource managers, like purely local transactions only. This offers more performance but it has a cost: whereas so far the BASE system had eventual consistency, this architecture no longer guarantees that by default.

As will be shown in the next chapter, to get some level of consistency, a lot more work has to be done by the application developers; in some cases, eventual consistency may even be impossible, notably in the case of message loss.

Figure 13-4 shows a typical architecture consisting of multiple resource managers in a relaxed BASE transaction.

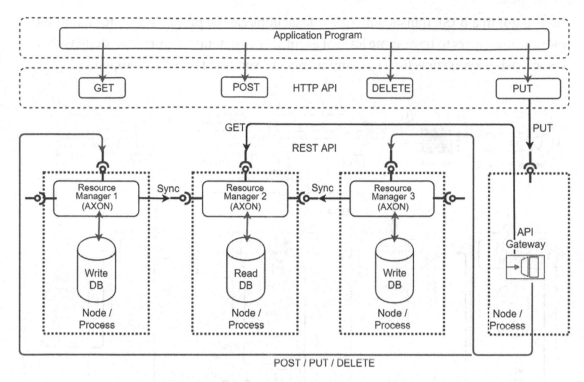

Figure 13-4. *Distributed, relaxed BASE transactions with multiple resources*

Microservice resources are distributed across nodes. You want to avoid distributed transactions since locking of resources across nodes will impede system scalability. Further, you are OK for eventual consistency but you don't mind if you can't achieve it perfectly. If so, Figure 13-4 illustrates how to follow the relaxed BASE model. Applications interact either directly with one or more of the involved resource managers, or, more typically, through some load balancer or gateway that distributes incoming requests to a pool of resource managers with symmetrical responsibilities and capabilities. Requests are served by one or more resource managers, and changes are propagated to one or more other resource managers subsequently. The number of resource managers involved depends on the sharding model (covered in Chapter 11's "The Scale Cube" section) and the system configuration chosen, ranging from a single node (single replica) to a quorum of nodes to, theoretically, all replicas of a given data record.

Axon provides many features with which you can span BASE transactions across resource managers without using a distributed transaction manager or transaction coordinator. To rephrase, there is no distributed transaction manager or transaction coordinator in a BASE transaction; still, transactions can be propagated across multiple resource managers to have some level of eventual consistency. Figure 13-5 depicts this scenario where you show the key components in Axon that make this happen.

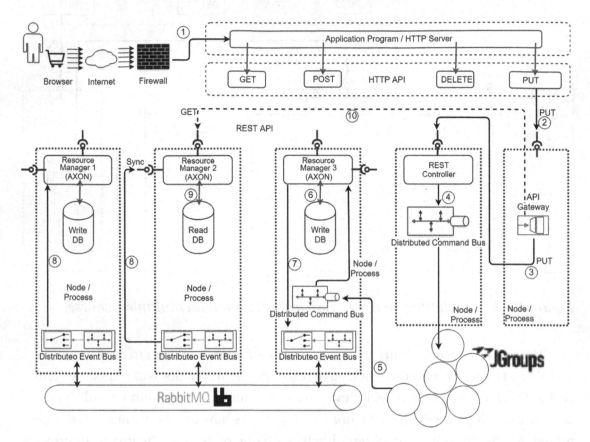

Figure 13-5. *Axon components to support BASE transactions*

You will look at typical relaxed BASE transactional steps, referring to Figure 13-5. A write request from a browser will come as a HTTP PUT at the HTTP server or the load balancer.

1. The request is routed to the API gateway.

2. The API gateway routes this request to the first point of contact of the request to the Axon application, which is the (front) REST Controller.

3. The REST Controller, after unpacking the request, interprets it as a request for an entity change and creates a command, following the CQRS pattern. This command is send to the distributed command bus, starting a local transaction.

4. The distributed command bus transports this command to the node containing the respective command handler (Resource Manager 3).

5. The command handler effects the write to the entity with the help of the repository in the Write DB.

6. The above repository change also triggers an event (the "Design the Example Scenario" section under the "Command and Event Handling in Same JVM" section in Chapter 12 provides detailed narration) and this event is sent to the clustered event bus.

7. In Figure 13-5, you can see that the two different event handlers (Resource Manager 1 and Resource Manager 2) are interested in the previous event, and they may also do whatever state changes they dictate.

8. You can see that Resource Manager 2 is in effect synchronizing itself (the Read DB) of any interesting changes in the system.

9. Any subsequent query (HTTP GET) also sees these changes. Eventually, everyone see the changes.

ACID vs. BASE

Such a comparison is like comparing apples and oranges: they are not intended to replace each other, and both are equally good (or bad) at serving their own purpose. This is an easily said statement; however, no CTO-level discussion can end with that straight explanation. Having said that, understanding this distinction is key in "mastering microservices." If you understand this difference, the main intention of this book is met!

BASE transactions are the base for microservices architecture where we want to stay away from ACID transactions. However, they serve different purposes. There is not much point in debating one over the other, since both solve orthogonal concerns–the reason why the CAP theorem is significant. But then, do you want to completely put aside ACID transactions? It's like asking whether you as the captain of your fighter jet should have direct control of the seat ejection button or are you comfortable even if you don't have direct reach to it but you are (almost) sure that your co-pilot will activate it for you at your command? In the former case, you are very sure that you can escape instantaneously, at your own will, when a sudden need arises. In the latter case, you are almost sure that you will still be able to escape; however, there is a percentage of skepticism as to whether the escape will be instantaneous or delayed either due to your co-pilot taking time to execute your command or in the unfortunate event that your co-pilot is not in a position to move his own muscles to act! To restate, the former is synonymous to an ACID transaction, which is relatively more deterministic, whereas the latter is synonymous to a BASE transaction, which (may) eventually happen.

We still need ACID, if not all the time.

Let's now come to BASE. If you still use ACID at the right level (as in Figure 13-3), then things are easy. On the other hand, an even more relaxed BASE approach is not going to ease your life; in fact, relaxed BASE is going to give you far more complexities than ACID.

Having said that, one way to understand and appreciate the complexities involved in BASE transactions is to understand ACID transactions themselves, so you will do that in the following sections.

Distributed Transactions Revisited

Before you look into concrete examples, you need to understand a few concepts that will set the context for the examples you will explore.

Local Transactions

If you take a typical resource manager, typically that single resource will be confined to a single host or node (even though that may not be the case mandatorily). Operations confined to such a single resource are local transactions and they affect only one transactional resource. Within a single node, there are less (or for practical considerations, nil) nondeterministic operations, hence a command sent to a single node must be considered deterministic, and in case of any catastrophes, there are local recovery mechanisms. These resources have their own transactional APIs, and the notion of a transaction is often exhibited as the concept of a session, which can encapsulate a unit of work with demarcating APIs to tell the resource when the buffered work should be committed to the underlying resource. Thus, from a developer perspective, you do not manage with transactions in a local transaction, but with just "connections."

The java.sql.Connection interface is a transactional resource that can wrap a database. By default, a Connection object is in auto-commit mode, which means that it automatically commits changes after executing each statement. If auto-commit mode is disabled, the method commit must be called explicitly in order to commit changes; otherwise, database changes will not be saved. It is preferable to collect several related statements into a batch and then commit all, or none, when you have more than one statement. You do this by first setting the Connection's setAutoCommit() method to false and later explicitly calling Connection.commit() or Connection.rollback() at the end of the batch. See Listing 13-1.

Listing 13-1. A Local Transaction Sample

```
try{
    connection.setAutoCommit(false);
    Statement statement = conn.createStatement();

    String insertString = "insert into " +  dbName + ".SHIPPING VALUES ("
        + orderId + ", 'NEW')";
    statement.executeUpdate(insertString);

    String updateString = "update " + dbName + ".ORDERS set STATUS =
        'PROCESSED' where ORDER_ID = " + orderId;
    statement.executeUpdate(updateString);

    connection.commit();
}catch(SQLException se){
    connection.rollback();
}
```

In Listing 13-1, both the statements will be committed together or rolled back together. However, it is a local transaction, not a distributed transaction.

Distributed Transactions

Typically for the scenario of a distributed transaction to exist, it must span at least two resource managers. Databases, message queues, transaction processing (TP) monitors like IBM's CICS, BEA's Tuxedo, SAP Java Connector, and Siebel Systems are common transactional resources, and often, if the transactions has to be distributed, it has to span a couple of such resources. A distributed transaction can be seen as an atomic operation that must be synchronized (or provide ACID properties) among multiple participating resources that are distributed among different physical locations.

Java EE application servers like Oracle Weblogic and IBM Websphere support JTA out of the box, and there are third-party, standalone implementations of JTA like

- **JOTM:** JOTM is an open source transaction manager implemented in Java. It supports several transaction models and specifications providing transaction support for clients using a wide range of middleware platforms (J2EE, CORBA, Web Services, OSGi).

- **Narayana:** Narayana, formerly known as JBossTS and Arjuna Transaction Service, comes with a very robust implementation that supports both the JTA and JTS APIs. It supports three extended transaction models: nested top-level transactions, nested transactions, and a compensation-based model based on sagas. Further, it also supports web service and RESTful transactions. There is a need for manual integration with the Spring framework, but it provides out-of-the-box integration with Spring Boot.

- **Atomikos TransactionsEssentials:** Atomikos TransactionsEssentials is a production quality implementation that also supports recovery and some exotic features beyond the JTA API. It provides out-of-the-box Spring integration and support for pooled connections for both database and JMS resources.

- **Bitronix JTA:** Bitronix claims to support transaction recovery as well as or even better than some of the commercial products. Bitronix also provides connection pooling and session pooling out of the box.

Distributed Transactions in Java

Coordination of transactions spanning multiple resources are specified by the X/Open standards by opengroup. Java supports X/Open standards by providing two interfaces: JTA (Java Transaction API) and JTS (Java Transaction Service). As shown in Figure 13-2, JTA is used by application developers to communicate to transaction managers. Since resources can be provided by multiple vendors following different platforms and programming languages, if all of these resources must be coordinated, they have to agree again to the X/Open standards. Here, JTS, which follows CORBA OTS (Object Transaction Service), provides the required interoperability between different transaction managers sitting with distributed resources.

I have discussed the "distributed nature" in distributed transactions. The two-phase commit protocol is used for coordination of transactions across multiple resource managers.

Distributed Transaction Example Using MySQL, ActiveMQ, Derby, and Atomikos

The easiest way to do away with many data consistency problems, especially when multiple resource managers are involved, is to use XA or distributed transactions even in BASE, as in Figure 13-3. However, if you want to transition to even more relaxed BASE microservices, the design mechanisms have to be more fault tolerant since your XA transaction managers are absent, and they would have done all the hard work. You will walk through the major consistency concern scenarios with the help of an example. Again, I could have demonstrated the concern scenarios straight without using distributed transactions in the example; however, I will take the reverse route and use XA transactions to illustrate the perfect scenario and simulate the various fault conditions by cutting down the ACID scope even more since it is rather easy for you, the reader, to comprehend aspects in this manner. XA transactions allow us to do that by "abusing" the transaction attributes to make the transaction scope smaller than it would normally be. This means that I can reuse the same code to illustrate the anomalies of relaxed BASE incrementally.

The Example Scenario

The example is not trivial, as shown in Figure 13-3, so the scenario requires a little explanation. The example scenario is a simple stock trade processing system. Here are the building blocks:

1. New quotes for stock transactions can be pushed to the Broker Web microservice. New quotes get inserted into a Quotes table, which is in a MySQL DB, with a status of "New."

2. The Quotes processor task is a quartz scheduled task and it polls the Quotes table in the MySQL DB for any new quotes with a status of "New."

3. When a new quote with a status of "New" is found, it invokes the processNewQuote method of the broker service, always with a transaction, passing the unique identifier for the new quote into the Quotes table.

4. The broker service makes use of the other transactional services, the auction service and the stock order service, and the execution of both has to be atomic.

5. The auction service confirms the quote received by changing the status of the quote to "Confirmed" within a transaction.

6. The stock order service creates a JMS message out of the information contained in the new quote and is sent to an ActiveMQ queue for settlement of the quote, again within the above (5) transaction.

7. The settlement listener service is listening on the ActiveMQ queue for any new confirmed quote. All confirmed quotes on reaching the ActiveMQ queue are picked up by onMessage of the settlement listener service, within a transaction.

8. The settlement listener service invokes the quotes reconcile service for reconciliation of the quote, again within the above (7) transaction.

9.   The quotes reconcile service needs to reconcile the value of the stock traded to the respective user account of the seller and the buyer, within the above (7) transaction.

10. The Broker Web microservice and the Settlement Web microservice are just utilities that provide a dashboard view of the operational data on both the Quotes table as well as the User table to provide live views.

Having seen the high-level business of the example scenario, let's now pay attention to other infrastructural aspects in the architecture. The Quote Processing microservice has to do atomic operations across two resources, MySQL and ActiveMQ. You need a distributed transaction manager here. Similarly, the Quote Settlement microservice must also do atomic operations across two resources, Derby and ActiveMQ. You need a distributed transaction manager here also.

Code the Example Scenario

The complete code required to demonstrate the distributed transaction example is in folder ch13\ch13-01. There are four microservices to be coded. You will look into them one by one.

Microservice 1: Quote Processing (Broker-MySQL-ActiveMQ)

Visit pom.xml to see the Atomikos distributed transaction manager dependency. See Listing 13-2.

Listing 13-2. Maven Dependencies for the Distributed Transactions Example Using MySQL and ActiveMQ (ch13\ch13-01\XA-TX-Distributed\Broker-MySQL-ActiveMQ\pom.xml)

```
<dependencies>

    <dependency>
        <groupId>javax.transaction</groupId>
        <artifactId>jta</artifactId>
        <version>1.1</version>
    </dependency>
```

```
<dependency>
    <groupId>com.atomikos</groupId>
    <artifactId>transactions</artifactId>
    <version>3.9.3</version>
</dependency>

<dependency>
    <groupId>com.atomikos</groupId>
    <artifactId>transactions-hibernate3</artifactId>
    <version>3.9.3</version>
</dependency>

<dependency>
    <groupId>com.atomikos</groupId>
    <artifactId>transactions-api</artifactId>
    <version>3.9.3</version>
</dependency>

<dependency>
    <groupId>com.atomikos</groupId>
    <artifactId>transactions-jms</artifactId>
    <version>3.9.3</version>
</dependency>

<dependency>
    <groupId>com.atomikos</groupId>
    <artifactId>transactions-jdbc</artifactId>
    <version>3.9.3</version>
</dependency>

<dependency>
    <groupId>com.atomikos</groupId>
    <artifactId>transactions-jta</artifactId>
    <version>3.9.3</version>
</dependency>
```

```xml
<dependency>
    <groupId>org.apache.activemq</groupId>
    <artifactId>activemq-core</artifactId>
    <version>5.7.0</version>
</dependency>

<dependency>
    <groupId>mysql</groupId>
    <artifactId>mysql-connector-java</artifactId>
    <version>8.0.14</version>
</dependency>

</dependencies>
```

These library dependencies will be clearer when you look at the configuration in detail. Before you do that, let's inspect the main components in the architecture.

You will first look at the Quotes Processor Task, which is a Quartz scheduler that will timeout at configured intervals so the processNewQuotes() will get triggered at definite intervals. See Listing 13-3.

Listing 13-3. Scheduled Task for Processing New Quotes (ch13\ch13-01\XA-TX-Distributed\Broker-MySQL-ActiveMQ\src\main\java\com\acme\ecom\schedule\QuotesProcessorTask.java)

```java
public class QuotesProcessorTask {

@Autowired
@Qualifier("brokerServiceRequired_TX")
BrokerService brokerServiceRequired_TX;

    public void processNewQuotes() {

        List<QuoteDTO> newQuotes = brokerServiceRequired_TX.findNewQuotes();
        newQuotes.forEach(item->{
```

```
            if(((QuoteDTO) item).getStatus().equals(Quote.NEW)){
                brokerServiceRequired_TX.processNewQuote(
                    ((QuoteDTO) item).getId());
            }
        });
    }
}
```

If "New" quotes are found, the scheduler invokes the processNewQuote() method of the broker service, once for each new quote, passing the ID of the new quote found. Note that this method invocation happens within a transaction, the configuration of which you will see soon. You will look at the broker service next in Listing 13-4.

Listing 13-4. Broker Service Coordinating New Quote Processing (ch13\ch13-01\ XA-TX-Distributed\Broker-MySQL-ActiveMQ\src\main\java\com\acme\ecom\ service\BrokerServiceImpl.java)

```
public class BrokerServiceImpl implements BrokerService{

private static volatile boolean flipFlop = false;

    @Autowired
    @Qualifier("auctionServiceRequired_TX")
    AuctionService auctionServiceRequired_TX;

    @Autowired
    @Qualifier("stockOrderServiceRequired_TX")
    StockOrderService stockOrderServiceRequired_TX;

    @Autowired
    @Qualifier("auctionServiceRequiresNew_TX")
    AuctionService auctionServiceRequiresNew_TX;

    @Autowired
    @Qualifier("stockOrderServiceRequiresNew_TX")
    StockOrderService stockOrderServiceRequiresNew_TX;

    private static synchronized void flipFlop() throws QuotesBaseException{
```

```
        if(flipFlop){
            flipFlop = false;
        }
        else{
            flipFlop = true;
        }
        if(flipFlop){
            throw new QuotesBaseException("Explicitly thrown by Broker
                Application to Roll Back!");
        }
    }

    @Override
    public List<QuoteDTO> findNewQuotes(){

        List<QuoteDTO> newQuotes = auctionServiceRequired_
TX.findNewQuotes();
        return newQuotes;
    }

    @Override
    public void processNewQuote(Long id)throws QuotesBaseException{

        Optional<QuoteDTO> quoteQueried =
            auctionServiceRequired_TX.findQuoteById(id);
        QuoteDTO quoteDTO = (QuoteDTO) quoteQueried.get();
        Integer testCase = quoteDTO.getTest();

        If((testCase == 1)  || (testCase == 5) || (testCase == 6)
                || (testCase == 7)){
            auctionServiceRequired_TX.confirmQuote(quoteDTO);
            stockOrderServiceRequired_TX.sendOrderMessage(quoteDTO);
        }
        else if(testCase == 2){
            auctionServiceRequired_TX.confirmQuote(quoteDTO);
            stockOrderServiceRequired_TX.sendOrderMessage(quoteDTO);
            flipFlop();
        }
```

413

```
        else if(testCase == 3){
            auctionServiceRequired_TX.confirmQuote(quoteDTO);
            try{
                stockOrderServiceRequiresNew_TX.sendOrderMessage(quoteDTO);
            }
            catch(QuotesMessageRollbackException
                    quotesMessageRollbackException){
                LOGGER.error(quotesMessageRollbackException.getMessage());
            }
        }
        else if(testCase == 4){
            try{
                auctionServiceRequiresNew_TX.confirmQuote(quoteDTO);
            }
            catch(QuotesConfirmRollbackException
                    quotesConfirmRollbackException){
                LOGGER.error(quotesConfirmRollbackException.getMessage());
            }
            stockOrderServiceRequired_TX.sendOrderMessage(quoteDTO);
        }
        else if(testCase == 8){
            try{
                auctionServiceRequiresNew_TX.confirmQuote(quoteDTO);
                // PROPAGATION_REQUIRES_NEW Because, during next time out
                // of QuotesProcessorTask we shouldn't fetch this quote
            }
            catch(QuotesConfirmRollbackException
                    quotesConfirmRollbackException){
                LOGGER.error(quotesConfirmRollbackException.getMessage());
            }
            stockOrderServiceRequired_TX.sendOrderMessage(quoteDTO);
        }
        else{
            LOGGER.debug("Undefined Test Case");
        }
    }
}
```

You auto-configure the references to the auction service and the stock order service within the broker service. You have two references of each of these services; this is just a hack to arrange the fixtures for the various test scenarios you are going to validate. To make it clear, you have two references of auction service with the names auctionServiceRequired_TX and auctionServiceRequiresNew_TX. As the name implies, the write methods in auctionServiceRequired_TX get executed in a PROPAGATION_REQUIRED context whereas those in auctionServiceRequiresNew_TX get executed in a PROPAGATION_REQUIRES_NEW context. The rest of the code checks the incoming parameter where you have piggy-backed an indicator (an integer value) to identify which test scenario (test case) you are executing. The general strategy is to use PROPAGATION_REQUIRED if you want to propagate transactions between parent and child services and to use PROPAGATION_REQUIRES_NEW wherever you explicitly generate error conditions so that the error is confined to the context of that respective service method alone, that too in a controlled manner (by using try-catch) and the rest of the execution flow can happen; again, this is to facilitate the fixture for the demonstration purposes.

You need to be aware that, in a real production scenario, you do not want the arrangement of the test scenarios; so if you want atomic operations across services, you just configure everything using PROPAGATION_REQUIRED, the (testCase == 1) scenario alone.

There is another utility method called flipFlop()[6] defined in the broker service. This method flip-flops the simulation of error creation during an operation between two consecutive executions, so if you have simulated an error in one execution of the method, the next execution of the same method will not simulate the error. In this way, if you have executed a test case to validate for an error scenario in one pass, you will also be able to see how the invariants will be if the same flow is executed without that error scenario. This is useful if you want to see if the message consumptions fails between the first pass so that when an attempt to reconsume happens, it will happen without failure in the next pass; in that manner, it is easy for you to test and visualize the results. Leave this here for the time being; it will be clearer when you execute the tests.

Next, look at the auction service shown in Listing 13-5.

---

[6]A flip-flop is an electronic circuit with two stable states that can be used to store binary data.

Listing 13-5. Auction Service Confirming New Quotes into MySQL DB (ch13\
ch13-01\XA-TX-Distributed\Broker-MySQL-ActiveMQ\src\main\java\com\
acme\ecom\service\AuctionServiceImpl.java)

```java
@Service
public class AuctionServiceImpl implements AuctionService{

    @Autowired
    private QuoteRepository quoteRepository;

    @Override
    public QuoteDTO confirmQuote(QuoteDTO quoteDTO)
            throws QuotesConfirmRollbackException{

        Integer testCase = quoteDTO.getTest();
        Optional quoteQueried = quoteRepository.findById(quoteDTO.getId());
        Quote quote = null;
        Quote quoteSaved = null;
        if(quoteQueried.isPresent()){
            quote = (Quote) quoteQueried.get();
            quote.setStatus(Quote.CONFIRMED);
            quote.setUpdatedAt(new Date());
            quoteSaved = quoteRepository.save(quote);
        }

        if(testCase == 4){
            flipFlop();
        }
        return getQuoteDTOFromQuote((Quote) quoteQueriedAgain.get());
    }
}
```

The auction service changes the status of a new quote to "Confirmed."

The broker service, after invoking the auction service, will call the stock order service. The stock order service is a JMS message sender and is shown in Listing 13-6.

Listing 13-6. Stock Order Service Sending Messages to ActiveMQ Against
Confirmed Quotes (ch13\ch13-01\XA-TX-Distributed\Broker-MySQL-ActiveMQ\
src\main\java\com\acme\ecom\messaging\StockOrderServiceImpl.java)

```java
public class StockOrderServiceImpl implements StockOrderService{

    private JmsTemplate jmsTemplate;

    public void setJmsTemplate(JmsTemplate jmsTemplate) {
        this.jmsTemplate = jmsTemplate;
    }

    public void sendOrderMessage(final QuoteDTO quoteDTO)
            throws QuotesMessageRollbackException{

        Integer testCase = quoteDTO.getTest();

        jmsTemplate.send(new MessageCreator() {

            public Message createMessage(Session session) throws
            JMSException {

                return session.createObjectMessage(quoteDTO);
            }
        });

        if(testCase == 3){
            throw new QuotesMessageRollbackException(
                "Explicitly thrown by Message Sender to Roll Back!");
        }
    }
}
```

For the sake of completeness of the code, Listing 13-7 shows the Quote model class.

Listing 13-7. A Quote Entity (ch13\ch13-01\XA-TX-Distributed\Broker-MySQL-ActiveMQ\src\main\java\com\acme\ecom\model\quote\Quote.java)

```java
@Entity
@Table(name = "quote")
@Data
@EqualsAndHashCode(exclude = { "id" })
public class Quote{

    public static final String NEW = "New";
    public static final String CONFIRMED = "Confirmed";

    @Id
    @GeneratedValue(strategy = GenerationType.AUTO)
    private Long id;

    @NotBlank
    @Column(name = "symbol", nullable = false, updatable = false)
    private String symbol;

    @Column(name = "sellerid", nullable = false, updatable = false)
    private Long sellerId;

    @Column(name = "buyerid", nullable = false, updatable = false)
    private Long buyerId;

    @Column(name = "amount", nullable = false, updatable = false)
    private Float amount;

    @Column(name = "status", nullable = false, updatable = true)
    private String status;

    @Column(name = "test", nullable = true, updatable = true)
    private Integer test;

    @Column(name = "delay", nullable = true, updatable = true)
    private Integer delay = 0;

    @Column(name = "createdat", nullable = true, updatable = false)
    @Temporal(TemporalType.TIMESTAMP)
    private Date createdAt;
```

```
@Column(name = "updatedat", nullable = true, updatable = true)
@Temporal(TemporalType.TIMESTAMP)
private Date updatedAt;
}
```

That's all of the main Java files for the example. The main configuration of wiring the above classes with the Atomikos XA transaction manager is done in the file spring-sender-mysql.xml, shown in Listing 13-8.

Listing 13-8. Spring Wiring for Distributed Transactions Example Using MySQL, ActiveMQ, and Atomikos (ch13\ch13-01\XA-TX-Distributed\Broker-MySQL-ActiveMQ\src\main\resources\spring-sender-mysql.xml)

```
<beans>

    <bean id="stockOrderTarget"
            class="com.acme.ecom.messaging.StockOrderServiceImpl">
        <property name="jmsTemplate" ref="jmsTemplate"/>
    </bean>

    <bean id="stockOrderServiceRequired_TX"class="org.springframework.
            transaction.interceptor.TransactionProxyFactoryBean">
        <property name="transactionManager">
            <ref bean="transactionManager" />
        </property>
        <property name="target"><ref bean="stockOrderTarget"  /></property>
        <property name="transactionAttributes">
            <props>
                <prop key="sendOrderMessage*">
                    PROPAGATION_REQUIRED,
                    -QuotesMessageRollbackException,
                    +QuotesNoRollbackException
                </prop>
            </props>
        </property>
    </bean>
```

```
<bean id="stockOrderServiceRequiresNew_TX" class="org.springframework.
        transaction.interceptor.TransactionProxyFactoryBean">
    <property name="transactionManager">
        <ref bean="transactionManager" />
    </property>
    <property name="target"><ref bean="stockOrderTarget"  /></property>
    <property name="transactionAttributes">
        <props>
            <prop key="sendOrderMessage*">
                PROPAGATION_REQUIRES_NEW,
                -QuotesMessageRollbackException, +QuotesNoRollbackException
            </prop>
        </props>
    </property>
</bean>

<bean id="auctionTarget" class= "com.acme.ecom.service.AuctionServiceImpl">
</bean>

<bean id="auctionServiceRequired_TX" class="org.springframework.
        transaction.interceptor.TransactionProxyFactoryBean">
    <property name="transactionManager">
        <ref bean="transactionManager" />
    </property>
    <property name="target"><ref bean="auctionTarget"  /></property>
    <property name="transactionAttributes">
        <props>
            <prop key="confirm*">
                PROPAGATION_REQUIRED,
                -QuotesConfirmRollbackException, +QuotesNoRollbackException
            </prop>
            <prop key="find*">PROPAGATION_SUPPORTS, readOnly</prop>
        </props>
    </property>
</bean>
```

```
<bean id="auctionServiceRequiresNew_TX" class="org.springframework.
    transaction.interceptor.TransactionProxyFactoryBean">
  <property name="transactionManager"><ref bean="transactionManager" />
  </property>
  <property name="target"><ref bean="auctionTarget"  /></property>
  <property name="transactionAttributes">
      <props>
          <prop key="confirm*">
              PROPAGATION_REQUIRES_NEW,
              -QuotesConfirmRollbackException,
              +QuotesNoRollbackException</prop>
          <prop key="find*">PROPAGATION_SUPPORTS, readOnly</prop>
      </props>
  </property>
</bean>

<bean id="brokerTarget" class= "com.acme.ecom.service.BrokerServiceImpl">
</bean>

<bean id="brokerServiceRequired_TX" class="org.springframework.
    transaction.interceptor.TransactionProxyFactoryBean">
  <property name="transactionManager">
      <ref bean="transactionManager" />
  </property>
  <property name="target"><ref bean="brokerTarget"  /></property>
  <property name="transactionAttributes">
      <props>
          <prop key="process*">
              PROPAGATION_REQUIRED,
              -QuotesBaseException, +QuotesNoRollbackException
          </prop>
          <prop key="find*">PROPAGATION_SUPPORTS, readOnly</prop>
      </props>
  </property>
</bean>

</beans>
```

You touched on local transactions in the "Distributed Transactions Revisited" section earlier and Spring's PlatformTransactionManager supports local transactions in JDBC, JMS, AMQP, Hibernate, JPA, JDO, and many others usage scenarios. When you want to use XA transactions, `org.springframework.transaction.jta.JtaTransactionManager` can be used. JtaTransactionManager is a PlatformTransactionManager implementation for JTA, delegating to a back-end JTA provider. This is typically used to delegate to a Java EE server's transaction coordinator like Oracle WebLogicJtaTransactionManager or IBM WebSphereUowTransactionManager, but may also be configured with a local JTA provider that is embedded within the application like Atomikos. Embedded transaction managers give you the freedom of not using a full-fledged app server; you still get much of the XA transaction support similar to what you get from an app server in your standalone JVM applications.

In the current example, there are operations in two resource managers, which are to be transactional:

- `AuctionService.confirmQuote()`

- `StockOrderService.sendOrderMessage()`

The first one uses a JPA repository to merge an entity's changed state to the underlying repository and subsequently to the backing persistent store. The second one uses JMS to send messages to an ActiveMQ queue. You want to make both above operations atomic, so either both of them should succeed or both of them should roll back. To ease the control, you enclose both above transactional methods within a third method:

- `BrokerService.processNewQuote()`

You now leverage `org.springframework.transaction.interceptor.TransactionProxyFactoryBean`, designed to cover the typical use case of declarative transaction demarcation, by wrapping a singleton target object with a transactional proxy, proxying all the interfaces that the target implements. This is done in the XML configuration. You then also configure the transaction type required for all three methods:

- `AuctionService.confirmQuote()`

  - `<prop key="confirm*">PROPAGATION_REQUIRED</prop>`

- `StockOrderService.sendOrderMessage()`

- <prop key="sendOrderMessage*">PROPAGATION_REQUIRED</prop>

- BrokerService.processNewQuote()

  - <prop key="process*">PROPAGATION_REQUIRED</prop>

Further, the recommended way to indicate to the Spring Framework's transaction infrastructure that a transaction's work is to be rolled back is to throw an exception from code that is currently executing in the context of a transaction. The Spring Framework's transaction infrastructure code will catch any unhandled exception as it bubbles up the call stack and will mark the transaction for rollback.

That's all you want to do to wire the business components. Now, if there is an error within any of the above three methods, it will roll back the state changes affected by all three business methods in the underlying resource managers taking part in the XA transaction.

You can now concentrate on the infrastructure plumbing. There are two resources you need to configure, the JMS resource and the JDBC resource. See Listing 13-9 for the XA JMS resource.

Listing 13-9. Spring Wiring for XA JMS Resources for the Distributed Transactions Example ActiveMQ Atomikos (ch13\ch13-01\XA-TX-Distributed\Broker-MySQL-ActiveMQ\src\main\resources\spring-sender-mysql.xml)

```
<beans>

    <bean id="XaFactory"
          class="org.apache.activemq.ActiveMQXAConnectionFactory">
        <property name="brokerURL" value="tcp://127.0.0.1:61616"/>
    </bean>

    <bean id="connectionFactory"
          class="com.atomikos.jms.AtomikosConnectionFactoryBean">
        <property name="uniqueResourceName" value="JMS-Producer"/>
        <property name="xaConnectionFactory" ref="XaFactory"/>
        <property name="localTransactionMode" value="false"/>
    </bean>
```

```
<bean id="jmsTemplate"
        class="org.springframework.jms.core.JmsTemplate">
    <property name="connectionFactory" ref="connectionFactory"/>
    <property name="defaultDestinationName"
        value="notification.queue"/>
    <property name="deliveryPersistent" value="true"/>
    <property name="sessionTransacted" value="true"/>
    <property name="sessionAcknowledgeMode" value="0"/>
</bean>

</beans>
```

The JmsTemplate used by StockOrderService uses `com.atomikos.jms.AtomikosConnectionFactoryBean`, which is the Atomikos's JMS 1.1 connection factory for JTA-enabled JMS operations. You can use an instance of this class to make JMS participate in JTA transactions without having to issue the low-level XA calls yourself. You set whether local transactions are desired by using the `localTransactionMode` property, which defaults to false. With local transactions, no XA enlist will be done; rather, the application should perform session-level JMS commits or rollbacks instead. Note that this feature also requires support from your JMS provider, ActiveMQ in your case. The `xaConnectionFactory` property is the basic connection factory that encapsulates the plumbing for connecting to the ActiveMQ broker. In your case, the bean is an instance of `ActiveMQXAConnectionFactory` type, which is a special connection factory class that you must use when you want to connect to the ActiveMQ broker with support for XA transactions.

See Listing 13-10 for the XA JDBC resource.

Listing 13-10. Spring Wiring for XA JDBC Resources for the Distributed Transactions Example Using MySQL and Atomikos (ch13\ch13-01\XA-TX-Distributed\Broker-MySQL-ActiveMQ\src\main\resources\spring-sender-mysql.xml)

```
<beans>

    <bean id="datasourceAtomikos-01"
            class="com.atomikos.jdbc.AtomikosDataSourceBean">
        <property name="uniqueResourceName"><value>JDBC-1</value></property>
        <property name="xaDataSource">
```

```
            <ref bean="xaDataSourceMySQL-01"  />
        </property>
        <property name="xaProperties">
            <props>
                <prop key="maxPoolSize">4</prop>
                <prop key="uniqueResourceName">xads1</prop>
            </props>
        </property>
        <property name="poolSize"><value>4</value></property>
    </bean>

    <bean id="xaDataSourceMySQL-01"
            class="com.mysql.cj.jdbc.MysqlXADataSource">
        <property name="url">
            <value>jdbc:mysql://localhost:3306/ecom01</value>
        </property>
        <property name="pinGlobalTxToPhysicalConnection">
            <value>true</value>
        </property>
        <property name="user"><value>root</value></property>
        <property name="password"><value>rootpassword</value></property>
    </bean>

    <bean id="atomikosTransactionManager"
            class="com.atomikos.icatch.jta.UserTransactionManager">
        <property name="forceShutdown"><value>true</value></property>
    </bean>

    <bean id="atomikosUserTransaction"
            class="com.atomikos.icatch.jta.UserTransactionImp">
        <property name="transactionTimeout"><value>300</value></property>
    </bean>
```

```xml
<bean id="transactionManager"
        class="org.springframework.transaction.jta.JtaTransactionManager">
    <property name="transactionManager">
        <ref bean="atomikosTransactionManager"  />
    </property>
    <property name="userTransaction">
        <ref bean="atomikosUserTransaction"  />
    </property>
</bean>

<bean id="springJtaPlatformAdapter"
        class="com.acme.ecom.AtomikosJtaPlatform">
    <property name="jtaTransactionManager" ref="transactionManager" />
</bean>

<bean id="hibernateJpaVendorAdapter" class=
        "org.springframework.orm.jpa.vendor.HibernateJpaVendor
        Adapter"/>

<bean id="quoteEntityManager"class="org.springframework.
        orm.jpa.LocalContainerEntityManagerFactoryBean">

    <property name="dataSource" ref="datasourceAtomikos-01"/>
    <property name="jpaVendorAdapter" ref="hibernateJpaVendorAdapter"/>
    <property name="jpaProperties">
        <props>
            <prop key="hibernate.transaction.jta.platform">
                com.acme.ecom.AtomikosJtaPlatform
            </prop>
            <prop key="javax.persistence.transactionType">JTA</prop>
        </props>
    </property>
    <property name="packagesToScan" value="com.acme.ecom.model.quote"/>
    <property name="persistenceUnitName" value="quotePersistenceUnit" />
</bean>
```

```
<jpa:repositories base-package="com.acme.ecom.repository.quote"
    entity-manager-factory-ref="quoteEntityManager"/>

</beans>
```

You can use an instance of the com.atomikos.jdbc.AtomikosDataSourceBean class if you want to use Atomikos JTA-enabled connection pooling. You need to construct an instance and set the required properties, and the resulting bean will automatically register with the transaction service and take part in active transactions. All SQL done over connections received from this class will participate in JTA transactions. Starting with Connector/J 5.0.0, the javax.sql.XADataSource interface is implemented using the com.mysql.jdbc.jdbc2.optional.MysqlXADataSource class, which supports XA distributed transactions when used in combination with MySQL server version 5.0 and later. You set an instance of MysqlXADataSource as the xaDataSource property for the AtomikosDataSourceBean class.

Next, the LocalContainerEntityManagerFactoryBean is Spring's FactoryBean that creates a JPA EntityManagerFactory, which can then be passed to JPA-based DAOs via dependency injection. Starting with Spring 3.1, the persistence.xml is no longer necessary and LocalContainerEntityManagerFactoryBean supports a packagesToScan property where the packages to scan for @Entity classes can be specified.

To teach Hibernate how to participate in the Atomikos transaction, earlier you must set a property, the hibernate.transaction.manager_lookup_class. However, Hibernate 4.3 removed the long-deprecated TransactionManagerLookup. Hibernate4 doesn't know to work with Atomikos out of the box. The JTA provider must implement org.hibernate.engine.transaction.jta.platform.spi. JtaPlatform to resolve the JTA UserTransaction and TransactionManager from the Spring-configured JtaTransactionManager implementation. An abstract implementation of JTA Platform is already available within Hibernate, namely org.hibernate.engine.transaction.jta.platform.internal.AbstractJtaPlatform. Using it makes writing a JTA Platform for Atomikos a breeze. You need to implement this class and set the hibernate.transaction.jta.platform property explicitly. See Listing 13-11.

Listing 13-11.   Resolving JTA UserTransaction and TransactionManager (ch13\
ch13-01\XA-TX-Distributed\Broker-MySQL-ActiveMQ\src\main\java\com\
acme\ecom\AtomikosJtaPlatform.java)

```java
import javax.transaction.TransactionManager;
import javax.transaction.UserTransaction;

import org.hibernate.engine.transaction.jta.platform.internal.
AbstractJtaPlatform;
import org.springframework.transaction.jta.JtaTransactionManager;

@SuppressWarnings("serial")
public class AtomikosJtaPlatform extends AbstractJtaPlatform {

    static TransactionManager transactionManager;
    static UserTransaction userTransaction;

    @Override
    protected TransactionManager locateTransactionManager() {

        Assert.notNull(transactionManager,
            "TransactionManager has not been setted");
        return transactionManager;
    }

    @Override
    protected UserTransaction locateUserTransaction() {

        Assert.notNull(userTransaction, "UserTransaction has not been setted");
        return userTransaction;
    }

    public void setJtaTransactionManager(JtaTransactionManager
            jtaTransactionManager) {

        transactionManager = jtaTransactionManager.getTransactionManager();
        userTransaction = jtaTransactionManager.getUserTransaction();
    }
```

```
public void setTransactionManager(TransactionManager transactionManager) {

    this.transactionManager = transactionManager;
}

public void setUserTransaction(UserTransaction userTransaction) {

    this.userTransaction = userTransaction;
}
}
```

Having looked at the overall configurations, let's also look into more details of the infrastructure configurations with reference to Listing 13-9 and Listing 13-10.

You need to set the `dataSource` property of LocalContainerEntityManager FactoryBean to a JDBC DataSource that the JPA persistence provider is supposed to use for accessing the database. The DataSource passed in here will be used as a nonJtaDataSource on the PersistenceUnitInfo passed to the PersistenceProvider. Note that this variant typically works for JTA transaction management as well; if it does not, consider using the explicit property `jtaDataSource` instead. You use the AtomikosDataSourceBean explained previously to set this property.

Next, you need a service provider interface implementation that allows you to plug in vendor-specific behavior into Spring's EntityManagerFactory creators. HibernateJpaVendorAdapter is an implementation for Hibernate EntityManager. It supports the detection of annotated packages along with other things. The JPA module of Spring Data contains a custom namespace, <jpa:repositories, that allows the defining of repository beans. It also contains certain features and element attributes that are special to JPA. Generally, the JPA repositories can be set up using the repositories element. In this example, Spring is instructed to scan `com.acme.ecom.repository.quote` and all its subpackages for interfaces extending `Repository` or one of its subinterfaces. For each interface found, the infrastructure registers the persistence technology-specific FactoryBean to create the appropriate proxies to handle invocations of the query methods. Each bean is registered under a bean name that is derived from the interface name, so your interface of QuoteRepository would be registered under quoteRepository. The entity-manager-factory-ref will help to explicitly wire the EntityManagerFactory to be used with the repositories being detected by the repositories element. This property is usually used if multiple EntityManagerFactory beans are used within the

application. If not explicitly configured, Spring will automatically look up the single EntityManagerFactory configured in the ApplicationContext.

This completes the configuration of both XA resources. Next, you must configure the XA transaction manager.

You need `org.springframework.transaction.jta.JtaTransactionManager`, which is an implementation of PlatformTransactionManager. You need to provide implementations of `javax.transaction.TransactionManager` and `javax.transaction.UserTransaction` to create a `JtaTransactionManager`.

The `javax.transaction.UserTransaction` interface provides the application the ability to control transaction boundaries programmatically. This interface may be used by Java client programs or Enterprise Java Beans. The `UserTransaction.begin()` method starts a global transaction and associates the transaction with the calling thread. The transaction-to-thread association is managed transparently by the transaction manager. Thus the `UserTransaction` is the user-facing API.

`com.atomikos.icatch.jta.UserTransactionManager` is a straightforward, zero-setup implementation of `javax.transaction.TransactionManager`. Standalone Java applications can use an instance of this class to get a handle to the transaction manager and automatically start up or recover the transaction service on first use. `com.atomikos.icatch.jta.UserTransactionImp` is the `javax.transaction.UserTransaction` implementation from Atomikos which you can use for standalone Java applications. This class again automatically starts up and recovers the transaction service on first use.

`org.springframework.transaction.jta.JtaTransactionManager` is a PlatformTransactionManager implementation for JTA, delegating to back-end JTA providers. It is typically used to delegate to a Java EE server's transaction coordinator, but in your case, you have configured with Atomikos JTA provider, which is embedded within the application.

Microservice 2: Broker-Web

This microservice is straightforward, with REST controllers. You can invoke the test cases by sending HTTP requests to this microservice. You can also keep watching the dashboard, which will provide you with view for the Quotes table so that you can visualize the effect of your test. Figure 13-6 shows how various interactions can be done with the Broker Web microservice.

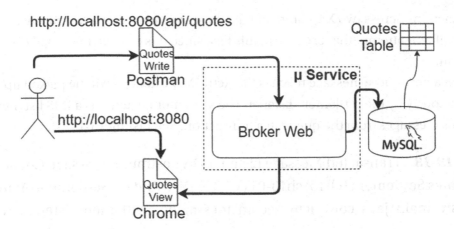

Figure 13-6. *The Broker Web console*

Microservice 3: Quote Settlement (Settlement-ActiveMQ-Derby)

Visit pom.xml to see the Atomikos distributed transaction manager dependency. You have all of the dependencies described already in Microservice 2, the Broker-MySQL-ActiveMQ microservice. However, as depicted in the architecture diagram, you are using a Derby database in place of MySQL for the downstream settlement of quotes. I will not repeat the dependencies you have already seen; Listing 13-12 shows the dependency for the Derby client alone.

Listing 13-12. Maven Dependency for the Derby Client (ch13\ch13-01\XA-TX-Distributed\Settlement-ActiveMQ-Derby\pom.xml)

```
<dependencies>
    <dependency>
        <groupId>org.apache.derby</groupId>
        <artifactId>derbyclient</artifactId>
        <version>10.14.1.0</version>
    </dependency>
</dependencies>
```

My intention with using a Derby database in place of MySQL is just to make you, the reader, comfortable using XA transactions with an additional XA-compliant resource, a Derby database, so that as a subsequent exercise you have all the tools to try for yourself

XA transactions across two XA-compliant databases within a single XA transactions. But you will not attempt that exercise in this text, since it is outside the scope of our discussion.

When a new quote message reaches the ActiveMQ queue, it will be picked up instantaneously by the settlement listener. The settlement listener is a JMS listener and it consumes messages from the queue in a transaction. See Listing 13-13.

Listing 13-13. Transacted Message Listener Orchestrating Message Consumtion and Quotes Settlement (ch13\ch13-01\XA-TX-Distributed\Settlement-ActiveMQ-Derby\src\main\java\com\acme\ecom\messaging\SettlementListener.java)

```java
public class SettlementListener implements MessageListener {

    @Autowired
    @Qualifier("quotesReconcileServiceRequired_TX")
    QuotesReconcileService quotesReconcileServiceRequired_TX;

    @Autowired
    @Qualifier("quotesReconcileServiceRequiresNew_TX")
    QuotesReconcileService quotesReconcileServiceRequiresNew_TX;

    public void onMessage(Message message) {

        try {
            reconcile((QuoteDTO) objectMessage.getObject());
        }
        catch (JMSException e) {
            throw new RuntimeException(e);
        }
        catch (QuotesBaseException e) {
            throw new RuntimeException(e);
        }
    }

    private void reconcile(QuoteDTO quoteDTO)throws QuotesBaseException{
```

```java
Integer testCase = quoteDTO.getTest();

if(testCase.equals(1) || testCase.equals(2) || testCase.equals(4) ||
        testCase.equals(8)){

    quotesReconcileServiceRequired_TX.reconcile(quoteDTO);
}
else if(testCase.equals(5)){

    try{
        quotesReconcileServiceRequiresNew_TX.reconcile(quoteDTO);
    }
    catch(QuotesBaseException quotesBaseException){
        LOGGER.error(quotesBaseException.getMessage());
    }
        flipFlop();
}
else if(testCase.equals(6)){

    try{
        quotesReconcileServiceRequiresNew_TX.reconcile(quoteDTO);
    }
    catch(QuotesBaseException quotesBaseException){
        LOGGER.error(quotesBaseException.getMessage());
    }

}
else if(testCase.equals(7)){

    try{
        quotesReconcileServiceRequired_TX.reconcile(quoteDTO);
    }
    catch(QuotesBaseException quotesBaseException){
        LOGGER.error(quotesBaseException.getMessage());
    }
    flipFlop();
}
```

```
    else{
        LOGGER.debug("Undefined Test Case");
    }
  }
}
```

On consuming the message, the settlement listener will invoke the QuotesReconcileService.reconcile(QuoteDTO) method to reconcile and settle the quote, again in a transaction. See Listing 13-14.

Listing 13-14. Quotes Reconcile Service Doing Settlement Reconciliation (ch13\ ch13-01\XA-TX-Distributed\Settlement-ActiveMQ-Derby\src\main\java\com\ acme\ecom\service\QuotesReconcileServiceImpl.java)

```
public class QuotesReconcileServiceImpl implements QuotesReconcileService{

    @Autowired
    private UserRepository userRepository;

    @Override
    public void reconcile(QuoteDTO quoteDTO)throws QuotesBaseException{

        Integer testCase = quoteDTO.getTest();

        Optional sellerQueried =
            userRepository.findById(quoteDTO.getSellerId());
        Optional buyerQueried  =
            userRepository.findById(quoteDTO.getBuyerId());
        User seller = null;
        User buyer = null;
        User sellerSaved = null;
        User buyerSaved = null;
        Date updatedDate = null;

        seller = (User) sellerQueried.get();
        buyer  = (User) buyerQueried.get();
        updatedDate = new Date();
```

```
        seller.setAmountSold(seller.getAmountSold() + quoteDTO.getAmount());
        seller.setUpdatedAt(updatedDate);
        seller.setLastQuoteAt(quoteDTO.getCreatedAt());
        sellerSaved = userRepository.save(seller);

        buyer.setAmountBought(buyer.getAmountBought() + quoteDTO.getAmount());
        buyer.setUpdatedAt(updatedDate);
        buyer.setLastQuoteAt(quoteDTO.getCreatedAt());
        buyerSaved = userRepository.save(buyer);

        if(testCase.equals(6)){
            throw new QuotesReconcileRollbackException(
                "Explicitly thrown by Reconcile Application to Roll Back!");
        }
        if(testCase.equals(7)){
            flipFlop();
        }
    }
}
```

During reconciliation, you update the amountSold and the amountBought attributes of the Seller and the Buyer respectively, thus these two attributes represent the running totals as shown in code Listing 13-14. For the completeness of the discussion, Listing 13-15 shows the User entity.

Listing 13-15. User Entity (ch13\ch13-01\XA-TX-Distributed\Settlement-ActiveMQ-Derby\src\main\java\com\acme\ecom\model\user\User.java)

```
@Entity
@Table(name = "stockuser")
@Data
@EqualsAndHashCode(exclude = { "id" })
public class User {

    @Id
    @Column(name = "id", nullable = false, updatable = false)
    private Long id;
```

435

```
@Column(name = "name", nullable = false, updatable = false)
private String name;

@Column(name = "amountsold", nullable = true, updatable = true)
private Double amountSold;

@Column(name = "amountbought", nullable = true, updatable = true)
private Double amountBought;

@Column(name = "lastquoteat", nullable = true, updatable = true)
@Temporal(TemporalType.TIMESTAMP)
private Date lastQuoteAt;

@Column(name = "createdat", nullable = false, updatable = false)
@Temporal(TemporalType.TIMESTAMP)
private Date createdAt;

@Column(name = "updatedat", nullable = false, updatable = true)
@Temporal(TemporalType.TIMESTAMP)
private Date updatedAt;
}
```

That's all the main Java files for the microservice. The main configuration of wiring the above classes with the Atomikos XA transaction manager is done in the file spring-listener-derby1.xml, shown in Listing 13-16.

Listing 13-16. Spring Wiring for the Distributed Transactions Example Using Derby, ActiveMQ, and Atomikos (ch13\ch13-01\XA-TX-Distributed\Settlement-ActiveMQ-Derby\src\main\resources\spring-listener-derby1.xml)

```
<beans>
    <bean id="datasourceAtomikos-02"
            class="com.atomikos.jdbc.AtomikosDataSourceBean>
        <property name="uniqueResourceName"><value>JDBC-2</value>
        </property>
        <property name="xaDataSourceClassName"
            value="org.apache.derby.jdbc.ClientXADataSource" />
        <property name="xaProperties">
```

```
      <props>
          <prop key="databaseName">
              D:/Applns/apache/Derby/derbydb/exampledb
          </prop>
          <prop key="serverName">localhost</prop>
          <prop key="portNumber">1527</prop>
      </props>
      </property>
</bean>

<bean id="atomikosTransactionManager"
        class="com.atomikos.icatch.jta.UserTransactionManager">
    <property name="forceShutdown"><value>true</value></property>
</bean>

<bean id="atomikosUserTransaction"
        class="com.atomikos.icatch.jta.UserTransactionImp">
    <property name="transactionTimeout"><value>300</value></property>
</bean>

<bean id="transactionManager"
        class="org.springframework.transaction.jta.
        JtaTransactionManager">

    <property name="transactionManager">
        <ref bean="atomikosTransactionManager"  />
    </property>
    <property name="userTransaction">
        <ref bean="atomikosUserTransaction"  />
    </property>
</bean>

<bean id="springJtaPlatformAdapter"
        class="com.acme.ecom.AtomikosJtaPlatform">
    <property name="jtaTransactionManager" ref="transactionManager" />
</bean>
```

```xml
<bean id="hibernateJpaVendorAdapter" class="org.springframework.
        orm.jpa.vendor.HibernateJpaVendorAdapter"/>

<bean id="userEntityManager" class="org.springframework.
        orm.jpa.LocalContainerEntityManagerFactoryBean">
    <property name="dataSource" ref="datasourceAtomikos-02"/>
    <property name="jpaVendorAdapter" ref="hibernateJpaVendorAdapter"/>
    <property name="jpaProperties">
        <props>
            <prop key="hibernate.transaction.jta.platform">
                com.acme.ecom.AtomikosJtaPlatform
            </prop>
            <prop key="javax.persistence.transactionType">JTA</prop>
        </props>
    </property>
    <property name="packagesToScan" value="com.acme.ecom.model.user"/>
    <property name="persistenceUnitName" value="userPersistenceUnit" />
</bean>

<jpa:repositories base-package="com.acme.ecom.repository.user"
    entity-manager-factory-ref="userEntityManager"/>

<bean id="XaFactory"
        class="org.apache.activemq.ActiveMQXAConnectionFactory">
    <property name="brokerURL"
        value="failover:(tcp://127.0.0.1:61616)?timeout=10000"/>
</bean>

<bean id="connectionFactory"
        class="com.atomikos.jms.AtomikosConnectionFactoryBean">
    <property name="uniqueResourceName" value="JMS-Consumer"/>
    <property name="xaConnectionFactory" ref="XaFactory"/>
    <property name="localTransactionMode" value="false"/>
</bean>

<bean id="notificationListenerContainer" class="org.springframework.
        jms.listener.DefaultMessageListenerContainer">
```

```xml
    <property name="messageListener" ref="notificationListener"/>
    <property name="receiveTimeout" value="10000"/>
    <property name="connectionFactory" ref="connectionFactory"/>
    <property name="destinationName" value="notification.queue"/>
    <property name="transactionManager" ref="transactionManager"/>
    <property name="sessionTransacted" value="true"/>
    <property name="sessionAcknowledgeMode" value="0"/>
</bean>

<bean id="notificationListener"
        class="com.acme.ecom.messaging.SettlementListener">
    <property name="quotesReconcileServiceRequired_TX">
        <ref bean="quotesReconcileServiceRequired_TX"  />
    </property>
    <property name="quotesReconcileServiceRequiresNew_TX">
        <ref bean="quotesReconcileServiceRequiresNew_TX"  />
    </property>
</bean>

<bean id="quotesReconcileServiceTarget"
    class="com.acme.ecom.service.QuotesReconcileServiceImpl">
</bean>

<bean id="quotesReconcileServiceRequired_TX" class="org.springframework.
        transaction.interceptor.TransactionProxyFactoryBean">
    <property name="transactionManager">
        <ref bean="transactionManager" />
    </property>
    <property name="target">
        <ref bean="quotesReconcileServiceTarget"  />
    </property>
    <property name="transactionAttributes">
    <props>
        <prop key="reconcile*">
            PROPAGATION_REQUIRED,
            -QuotesReconcileRollbackException,+QuotesNoRollbackException
        </prop>
```

```xml
                <prop key="find*">PROPAGATION_SUPPORTS, readOnly</prop>
        </props>
        </property>
    </bean>

    <bean id="quotesReconcileServiceRequiresNew_TX" class="org.
    springframework.
            transaction.interceptor.TransactionProxyFactoryBean">
        <property name="transactionManager">
            <ref bean="transactionManager" />
        </property>
        <property name="target">
            <ref bean="quotesReconcileServiceTarget"  />
        </property>
        <property name="transactionAttributes">
            <props>
                <prop key="reconcile*">
                    PROPAGATION_REQUIRES_NEW,
                    -QuotesReconcileRollbackException,
                    +QuotesNoRollbackException
                </prop>
                <prop key="find*">PROPAGATION_SUPPORTS, readOnly</prop>
            </props>
        </property>
    </bean>
</beans>
```

I have already explained all of the configurations above except that of DefaultMessage ListenerContainer. DefaultMessageListenerContainer is a message listener container variant that uses plain JMS client APIs, specifically a loop of MessageConsumer.receive() calls that also allow for transactional reception of messages when registered with an XA transaction manager. This is designed to work in a native JMS environment as well as in a Java EE environment. You first set your standard JMS message listener, which is the settlement listener, so that messages can be picked up by the SettlementListener. onMessage().

Microservice 4: Settlement-Web

This microservice is again straightforward, with REST controllers. You can also keep watching the dashboard, which will provide you with view for the User table so that you can visualize the effect of your test. You will also use this microservice to create a few initial users in the system for test purposes. Figure 13-7 shows how various interactions can be done with the Settlement Web microservice.

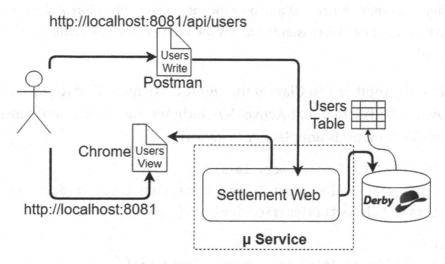

Figure 13-7. *The Settlement Web console*

There is a junit Test class that simply loads the bean definitions into spring-sender-mysql.xml and puts the main test application in sleep mode so that the scheduler can time out to check for any new quotes received at predefined intervals. See Listing 13-17.

Listing 13-17. Main Test Class at the Quote Processor End (ch13\ch13-01\
XA-TX-Distributed\Broker-MySQL-ActiveMQ\src\test\java\com\acme\ecom\
test\BrokerServiceTest.java)

```
@RunWith(SpringJUnit4ClassRunner.class)
@ContextConfiguration(locations="classpath:spring-sender-mysql.xml")
public class BrokerServiceTest {

    @Autowired
    @Qualifier("brokerServiceRequired_TX")
    BrokerService brokerService;
```

```
@Test
public void testSubmitQuote() throws Exception{

    Thread.sleep(1000 * 60 * 60);
  }
}
```

Similarly, there is another junit Test class that simply loads the bean definitions into spring-listener-derby.xml and puts the main test application in sleep mode so that the JMS listener can keep listening to any incoming messages in the ActiveMQ. See Listing 13-18.

Listing 13-18. Another Test Class at the Quote Settlement End (ch13\ch13-01\ XA-TX-Distributed\Settlement-ActiveMQ-Derby\src\test\java\com\acme\ ecom\test\SettlementListenerServiceTest.java)

```
@RunWith(SpringJUnit4ClassRunner.class)
@ContextConfiguration(locations="classpath:spring-listener-derby.xml")
public class SettlementListenerServiceTest {

    @Test
    public void testSettleQuote() throws Exception{
        Thread.sleep(1000 * 60 * 60);
    }
}
```

Build and Test the Example's Happy Flow

As the first step, you need to bring up the ActiveMQ server. You may want to refer to Appendix F to get started with ActiveMQ.

You configure a queue that will act as the bridge between the upstream and downstream processing. Listing 13-19 gives the configuration of a queue that can be done in activemq.xml.

Listing 13-19. The ActiveMQ Queue Configuration (D:\Applns\apache\ActiveMQ\apache-activemq-5.13.3\conf\activemq.xml)

```
<beans>
    <broker>
        <destinations>
            <queue physicalName="notification.queue" />
        </destinations>
    </broker>
</beans>
```

You may now bring up the ActiveMQ Server:

```
cd D:\Applns\apache\ActiveMQ\apache-activemq-5.13.3\bin
D:\Applns\apache\ActiveMQ\apache-activemq-5.13.3\bin>activemq start
```

Next, make sure MySQL is up and running. You may want to refer to Appendix H to get started with MySQL.

```
D:\Applns\MySQL\mysql-5.7.14-winx64\bin>mysqld --console
```

Now open a MySQL prompt:

```
D:\Applns\MySQL\mysql-5.7.14-winx64\bin>mysql -u root -p
```

```
mysql> use ecom01;
Database changed
mysql>
```

To start with clean tables, delete any tables with the names you want for your examples:

```
mysql> drop table quote;
```

Next, create the table with the schema required for this example:

```
mysql> create table quote (id BIGINT PRIMARY KEY AUTO_INCREMENT, symbol
VARCHAR(4), sellerid BIGINT, buyerid BIGINT, amount FLOAT, status VARCHAR(9),
test INTEGER, delay INTEGER, createdat DATETIME, updatedat DATETIME);
```

Next, make sure the Derby database is up and running in network mode. You may want to refer to Appendix G to get started with Derby.

```
D:\Applns\apache\Derby\db-derby-10.14.1.0-bin\bin>startNetworkServer
```

You can also use the Derby ij tool to create the database exampledb and open a connection to an already created database using the embedded driver using the following command:

```
D:\Applns\apache\Derby\derbydb>ij
ij> connect 'jdbc:derby://localhost:1527/D:/Applns/apache/Derby/derbydb/
exampledb;create=false';
```

Note   You are using the ij tool from a base location different from your Derby installation, assuming that your database is in a location different from that of the Derby installation, which is a best practice. For further details on how to create a new database, refer to Appendix G.

Here again you will start with clean tables. Delete any tables with the names you want for your examples:

```
ij> drop table stockuser;
```

Next, create the table with the schema required for this example:

```
ij> create table stockuser (id bigint not null, amountbought double,
amountsold double, createdat timestamp not null, lastquoteat timestamp,
name varchar(10) not null, updatedat timestamp not null, primary key (id));
ij> CREATE SEQUENCE hibernate_sequence START WITH 1 INCREMENT BY 1;
```

This completes the infrastructure required to build and run the example.

Next, there are four microservices to build and get running. You will do this one by one.

Microservice 1: Quote Processing Microservice

See Listing 13-9 to tweak the ActiveMQ-specific configuration in

```
ch13\ch13-01\XA-TX-Distributed\Broker-MySQL-ActiveMQ\src\main\resources\
spring-sender-mysql.xml
```

```
<property name="brokerURL" value="tcp://127.0.0.1:61616"/>
```

Also, you need to tweak the MySQL-specific configuration:

```
<bean id="xaDataSourceMySQL-01" class="com.mysql.cj.jdbc.
MysqlXADataSource">
    <property name="url">
        <value>jdbc:mysql://localhost:3306/ecom01</value>
    </property>
    <property name="user"><value>root</value></property>
    <property name="password"><value>rootpassword</value></property>
</bean>
```

Now build and package the executables for the Quote Processing microservice and bring up the scheduled processor. There is a utility script provided that you can easily execute in folder ch13\ch13-01\XA-TX-Distributed\Broker-MySQL-ActiveMQ\make.bat:

```
cd D:\binil\gold\pack03\ch13\ch13-01\XA-TX-Distributed\Broker-MySQL-ActiveMQ
D:\binil\gold\pack03\ch13\ch13-01\XA-TX-Distributed\Broker-MySQL-ActiveMQ>make
D:\binil\gold\pack03\ch13\ch13-01\XA-TX-Distributed\Broker-MySQL-
ActiveMQ>mvn -Dmaven.test.skip=true clean install
```

Now, the junit test can be run by using the script provided:

```
D:\binil\gold\pack03\ch13\ch13-01\XA-TX-Distributed\Broker-MySQL-ActiveMQ>run
D:\binil\gold\pack03\ch13\ch13-01\XA-TX-Distributed\Broker-MySQL-
ActiveMQ>mvn -Dtest=BrokerServiceTest#testSubmitQuote test
```

Microservice 2: Broker Web Microservice

First, you want to update the configuration files to suit to your environment:

ch13\ch13-01\XA-TX-Distributed\Broker-Web\src\main\resources\application.
properties

```
server.port=8080
spring.datasource.url = jdbc:mysql://localhost:3306/ecom01?autoReconnect=true&
useUnicode=true&characterEncoding=UTF-8&allowMultiQueries=true&useSSL=false
spring.datasource.username = root
spring.datasource.password = rootpassword
spring.jpa.properties.hibernate.dialect = org.hibernate.dialect.
MySQL5Dialect
spring.jpa.hibernate.ddl-auto = update
spring.freemarker.cache=false
```

You can now build and package the executables for the Broker Web microservice and bring up the server. There is a utility script provided in folder ch13\ch13-01\XA-TX-Distributed\Broker-Web\make.bat:

```
cd D:\binil\gold\pack03\ch13\ch13-01\XA-TX-Distributed\Broker-Web
D:\binil\gold\pack03\ch13\ch13-01\XA-TX-Distributed\Broker-Web>make
D:\binil\gold\pack03\ch13\ch13-01\XA-TX-Distributed\Broker-Web>mvn -Dmaven.
test.skip=true clean package
```

You can run the Spring Boot application, again in more than one way. The straightforward way is to execute the JAR file via the following commands:

```
D:\binil\gold\pack03\ch13\ch13-01\XA-TX-Distributed\Broker-Web>run
D:\binil\gold\pack03\ch13\ch13-01\XA-TX-Distributed\Broker-Web>java -jar
-Dserver.port=8080 .\target\quotes-web-1.0.0.jar
```

This will bring up the Broker Web Spring Boot Server in port 8080.

You can use a browser (preferably Chrome) and point to the following URL to keep monitoring the processing of all new incoming quotes: http://localhost:8080/.

Microservice 3: Quote Settlement Microservice

See Listing 13-16 to tweak the ActiveMQ-specific configuration in

```
ch13\ch13-01\XA-TX-Distributed\Settlement-ActiveMQ-Derby\src\main\
resources\spring-listener-derby.xml
```

```
<property name="brokerURL" value="failover:(tcp://127.0.0.1:61616)?
timeout=10000"/>
```

Also, you need to tweak the Derby-specific configuration:

```
<property name="xaProperties">
<props>
    <prop key="databaseName">D:/Applns/apache/Derby/derbydb/exampledb</prop>
    <prop key="serverName">localhost</prop>
    <prop key="portNumber">1527</prop>
    </props>
</property>
```

Now build and package the executables for the Quote Settlement microservice and bring up the message listener. There is a utility script provided in folder ch13\ch13-01\ XA-TX-Distributed\Settlement-ActiveMQ-Derby\make.bat:

```
cd D:\binil\gold\pack03\ch13\ch13-01\XA-TX-Distributed\Settlement-ActiveMQ-
Derby
D:\binil\gold\pack03\ch13\ch13-01\XA-TX-Distributed\Settlement-ActiveMQ-
Derby>make
D:\binil\gold\pack03\ch13\ch13-01\XA-TX-Distributed\Settlement-ActiveMQ-
Derby>mvn -Dmaven.test.skip=true clean install
```

Now, the junit test can be run by using the script provided:

```
D:\binil\gold\pack03\ch13\ch13-01\XA-TX-Distributed\Settlement-ActiveMQ-
Derby>run
D:\binil\gold\pack03\ch13\ch13-01\XA-TX-Distributed\Settlement-ActiveMQ-
Derby>mvn -Dtest=SettlementListenerServiceTest#testSettleQuote test
```

Microservice 4: Settlement Web Microservice

First, you want to update the configuration files to suit to your environment:

ch13\ch13-01\XA-TX-Distributed\Settlement-Web\src\main\resources\
application.properties

```
server.port=8081
spring.datasource.url=jdbc:derby://localhost:1527/D:/Applns/apache/Derby/
derbydb/exampledb;create=false
spring.datasource.initialize=false
spring.datasource.driver-class-name=org.apache.derby.jdbc.ClientDriver
spring.jpa.properties.hibernate.dialect=org.hibernate.dialect.
DerbyTenSevenDialect
spring.freemarker.cache=false
```

Now build and package the executables for the Settlement Web microservice and bring up the server. There is a utility script provided in folder ch13\ch13-01\XA-TX-Distributed\Settlement-Web\make.bat:

```
cd D:\binil\gold\pack03\ch13\ch13-01\XA-TX-Distributed\Settlement-Web
D:\binil\gold\pack03\ch13\ch13-01\XA-TX-Distributed\Settlement-Web>make
D:\binil\gold\pack03\ch13\ch13-01\XA-TX-Distributed\Settlement-Web>mvn
-Dmaven.test.skip=true clean package
```

You can run the Spring Boot application in more than one way. The straightforward way is to execute the JAR file via the following commands:

```
D:\binil\gold\pack03\ch13\ch13-01\XA-TX-Distributed\Settlement-Web>run
D:\binil\gold\pack03\ch13\ch13-01\XA-TX-Distributed\Settlement-Web>java
-jar -Dserver.port=8081 .\target\user-web-1.0.0.jar
```

This will bring up the Settlement Web Spring Boot Server in port 8080.

You can use a browser (preferably Chrome) and point to the following URL to keep monitoring the running account status of the users and how the account balance changes as each new incoming quote is settled: http://localhost:8081/.

There are altogether eight test cases that you will execute one by one to validate the example. See Figure 13-8.

Test Case	Broker	Auction (DB Update)	Delay (s)	Stock Order (Send Message)	Settlement Listener (Receive Message)	Record User Transaction (DB Update)	Comments
1	No Error	No Error	2	No Error	No Error	No Error	Happy Flow - All Good
2	Error No Error	No Error No Error	2	No Error No Error	No Error	No Error	New Quote gets Processed only in the second run
3	No Error	No Error	2	Error			Message Lost. Quote Never Settled
4	No Error No Error	Error No Error	2 2	No Error No Error	No Error No Error	No Error No Error	Duplicate Message send, 2nd time only Quote marked processed; Hence. Quote Settled twice
5	No Error	No Error	2	No Error	Error No Error	No Error No Error	Duplicate settlement caused by message consumed more than once. Quote Settled twice
6	No Error	No Error	2	No Error	No Error	Error	Quote Processed, however Quote Never Settled
7	No Error	No Error	2	No Error	Error No Error	Error No Error	Message ReDelivery comes to rescue - Quote Settled second chance
8	No Error No Error	No Error No Error	1st: 120 2nd: 2	No Error No Error	No Error No Error	No Error No Error	Message Received out of order!

Figure 13-8. *Test cases*

In the truest sense, there are only three test cases that validate the example and they are the first, second, and the seventh test cases. All other test cases invalidate the example either by simulating various failure conditions or by adjusting the transaction semantics applied to service methods. I do that to make you understand possible error scenarios that can occur in a distributed transactions environment.

In this section, you will look at the first test case, which demonstrates strict ACID compliant transaction in the end-to-end flow. This means either all of the state changes in the resources will be approved or all of them will be rolled back. The rest of the test cases will be executed in the subsequent sections one by one.

As a first step, you will create two test users in the system. Take Postman and create two test users as shown (see Figure 13-9):

```
http://localhost:8081/api/users
METHOD: POST; BODY: Raw JSON

{ "id" : 11, "name" : "Sam", "amountSold" : 1000.0, "amountBought" : 1000.0 }
{ "id" : 21, "name" : "Joe", "amountSold" : 5000.0, "amountBought" : 5000.0 }
```

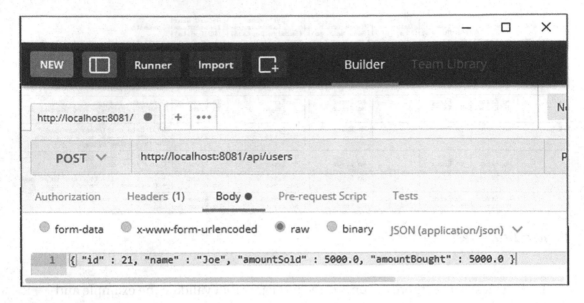

Figure 13-9. *Create test users*

The moment the test users are created, they will be visible in the settlement console, as shown in Figure 13-10.

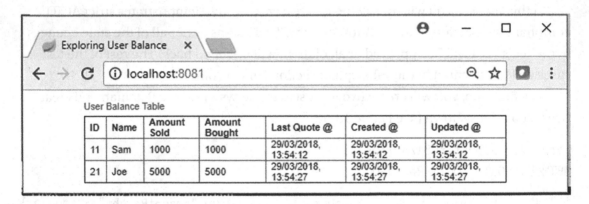

Figure 13-10. *Test user console*

To start the first test case, take Postman and create a new quote, as shown in Figure 13-11:

```
http://localhost:8080/api/quotes
METHOD: POST; BODY: Raw JSON

{ "symbol" : "AAPL", "sellerId" : 11, "buyerId" : 21, "amount" : 100,
"test" : 1, "delay" : 2 }
```

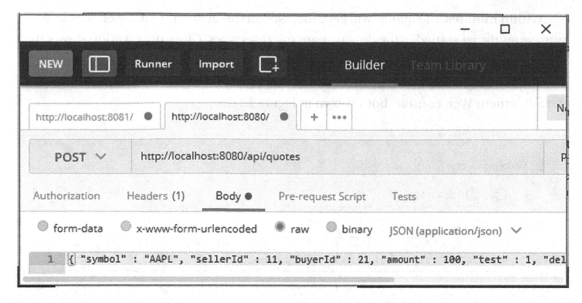

Figure 13-11. *Create a new quote*

Keep watching the consoles of the broker web service and the settlement web service together. When a new quote is created, as shown in Figure 13-11, it instantaneously gets reflected in the broker web console, as shown in Figure 13-12.

Exploring Quotes   ✕

← → C   ⓘ localhost:8080   🔍 ☆ ▣ ⋮

Quotes Table

ID	Symbol	SellerId	BuyerId	Amount	Status	Test	Delay	Created @	Updated @
1	AAPL	11	21	100	New	1	2	29/03/2018, 13:58:22	29/03/2018, 13:58:22

Exploring User Balance   ✕

← → C   ⓘ localhost:8081   🔍 ☆ ▣ ⋮

User Balance Table

ID	Name	Amount Sold	Amount Bought	Last Quote @	Created @	Updated @
11	Sam	1000	1000	29/03/2018, 13:54:12	29/03/2018, 13:54:12	29/03/2018, 13:54:12
21	Joe	5000	5000	29/03/2018, 13:54:27	29/03/2018, 13:54:27	29/03/2018, 13:54:27

Figure 13-12. *A new quote arrived for Test Case 1*

Within minutes, the quotes will get processed in the upstream microservices and will subsequently get settled in the downstream microservices. Close observation shows that the status of the quote changes from "New" to "Confirmed" in the broker web console and the running balances of the users will get changed by the amount of quotes also in the Settlement Web console, both shown in Figure 13-13.

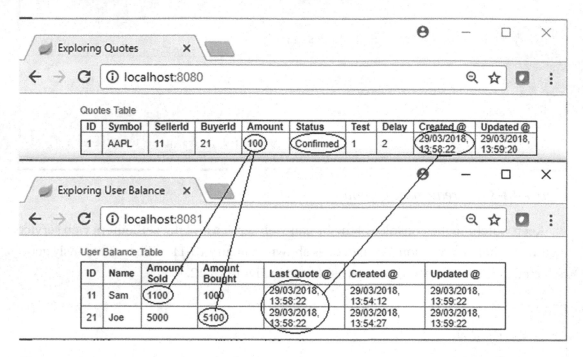

Figure 13-13. *Test Case 1 console*

You should also note another aspect in Figure 13-13, which will be relevant in Test Case 8, in the "Test the Message Received Out of Order Scenario" section later. The latest quote creation time in the upstream system gets updated as the Last Quote Time for users whenever the respective user account gets updated.

Since you already looked at every detail of the code in the earlier sections, you will not look at what is happening under the hood again in detail. Instead, you will now concentrate on the transaction semantics.

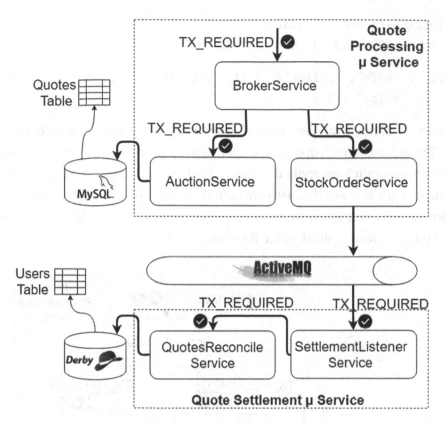

Figure 13-14. *Test Case 1 transaction semantics*

As shown in Figure 13-14, you applied TX_REQUIRED transaction semantics to all service methods. This means either all of the state changes in the resources will be made or all of them will be rolled back. In the current test case, you have not simulated any errors or failure conditions, hence all of the transactions succeeded.

In subsequent test cases you are going to simulate error conditions to better understand possible failure conditions in enterprise scenarios. A thorough understanding of all of these possible failure conditions will arm you with better insight, which is very much required when you design for "true microservices," where you want to stay away from distributed transactions!

Test the Transaction Rollback Scenario

To test the Transaction Rollback test case, take Postman again and create another new quote, as shown in Figure 13-11:

```
http://localhost:8080/api/quotes
METHOD: POST; BODY: Raw JSON
```

```
{ "symbol" : "AMZN", "sellerId" : 11, "buyerId" : 21, "amount" : 200,
"test" : 2, "delay" : 2 }
```

In Figure 13-3, the upstream processing and the downstream processing are separate. There is no strict "super transaction coordinator" across these two domains. If transaction semantics are applied to Figure 13-3, you get Figure 13-15. So within a domain (upstream alone or downstream alone) you may decide to have coordinated transactions across multiple resources, and when it comes to coordination across those domains you may need to think of the BASE approach.

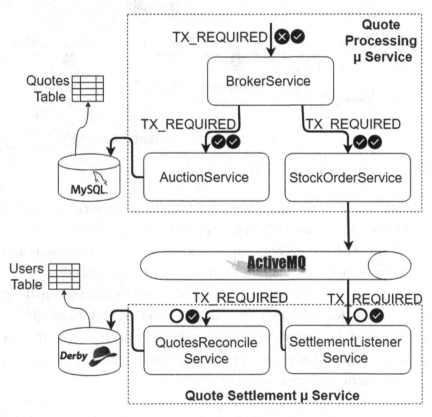

Figure 13-15. *Test Case 2 transaction semantics*

As shown in Figure 13-15, TX_REQUIRED transaction semantics have been applied to all service methods. This means either all of the state changes in the resources will be made or all of them will be rolled back.

454

In the first pass of execution when the Quotes Processor Task picks up the new quote for processing, you simulate an error within the broker service. This is marked by an X sign in Figure 13-15. So, even though the corresponding transactions in the auction service and stock order service were ready to commit, as shown by the ✓ sign, they will be rolled back since both of them were called within the context of the parent transaction of the broker service where you simulate the error. This is shown in the Quote Processing microservice's console in Figure 13-16.

Moreover, since in the first pass the transactions were rolled out, the New Quote message delivery to ActiveMQ is not committed, so no action takes place in the Quote Settlement microservice (see Figure 13-16). This is depicted by a blank circle in the first pass in Figure 13-15 for brevity.

```
2018-03-28 10:53:52 DEBUG c.a.e.s.QuotesProcessorTask.lambda$processNewQuotes$0:
35 - New
2018-03-28 10:53:52 INFO  c.a.e.s.BrokerServiceImpl.processNewQuote:67 - Start
2018-03-28 10:53:52 INFO  c.a.e.s.AuctionServiceImpl.findQuoteById:93 - Start
2018-03-28 10:53:52 DEBUG c.a.e.s.AuctionServiceImpl.findQuoteById:98 - Quote Qu
eried : 3
2018-03-28 10:53:52 INFO  c.a.e.s.AuctionServiceImpl.findQuoteById:106 - return
2018-03-28 10:53:52 DEBUG c.a.e.s.BrokerServiceImpl.processNewQuote:78 - Quote Q
ueried : 3
2018-03-28 10:53:52 DEBUG c.a.e.s.BrokerServiceImpl.processNewQuote:86 - Test Ca
se : 2
2018-03-28 10:53:52 INFO  c.a.e.s.AuctionServiceImpl.confirmQuote:45 - Start
2018-03-28 10:53:52 DEBUG c.a.e.s.AuctionServiceImpl.confirmQuote:54 - Quote Que
ried : Quote(id=3, symbol=AMZN, sellerId=11, buyerId=21, amount=200.0, status=Ne
w, test=2, delay=2, createdAt=2018-03-28 10:52:57.0, updatedAt=2018-03-28 10:52:
57.0)
2018-03-28 10:53:52 DEBUG c.a.e.s.AuctionServiceImpl.confirmQuote:61 - Quote Que
ried Again : Quote(id=3, symbol=AMZN, sellerId=11, buyerId=21, amount=200.0, sta
tus=Confirmed, test=2, delay=2, createdAt=2018-03-28 10:52:57.0, updatedAt=Wed M
ar 28 10:53:52 IST 2018)
2018-03-28 10:53:52 INFO  c.a.e.s.AuctionServiceImpl.confirmQuote:69 - return
2018-03-28 10:53:52 INFO  c.a.e.m.StockOrderService.sendOrderMessage:29 - Start
2018-03-28 10:53:52 DEBUG c.a.e.m.StockOrderService.sendOrderMessage:34 - Sleepi
ng for : 2 seconds
2018-03-28 10:53:54 DEBUG c.a.e.m.StockOrderService.sendOrderMessage:41 - Waking
 up after : 2 seconds
2018-03-28 10:53:54 INFO  c.a.e.m.StockOrderService.createMessage:48 - Inside cr
eateMessage
2018-03-28 10:53:54 INFO  c.a.e.m.StockOrderService.sendOrderMessage:57 - End
2018-03-28 10:53:54 INFO  c.a.e.s.AuctionServiceImpl.findQuoteById:93 - Start
2018-03-28 10:53:54 DEBUG c.a.e.s.AuctionServiceImpl.findQuoteById:98 - Quote Qu
eried : 3
2018-03-28 10:53:54 INFO  c.a.e.s.AuctionServiceImpl.findQuoteById:106 - return
2018-03-28 10:53:54 DEBUG c.a.e.s.BrokerServiceImpl.processNewQuote:93 - Quote Q
ueried again : QuoteDTO(id=3, symbol=AMZN, sellerId=11, buyerId=21, amount=200.0
, status=Confirmed, test=2, delay=2, createdAt=2018-03-28 10:52:57.0, updatedAt=
Wed Mar 28 10:53:52 IST 2018)
2018-03-28 10:53:54 WARN  c.a.j.AbstractConnectionProxy.logWarning:12 - Forcing
close of pending statement: com.mysql.jdbc.jdbc2.optional.JDBC42PreparedStatemen
tWrapper@5afb26e1
2018-03-28 10:53:54 ERROR c.a.e.s.QuotesProcessorTask.lambda$processNewQuotes$0:
40 - Explicitly thrown by Broker Application to Roll Back!
```

Figure 13-16. Test Case 2 processing first pass

Wait until the Quotes Processor Task picks up the previous quote again (since the status is still New) in the next scheduled trigger, which is shown in Figure 13-17.

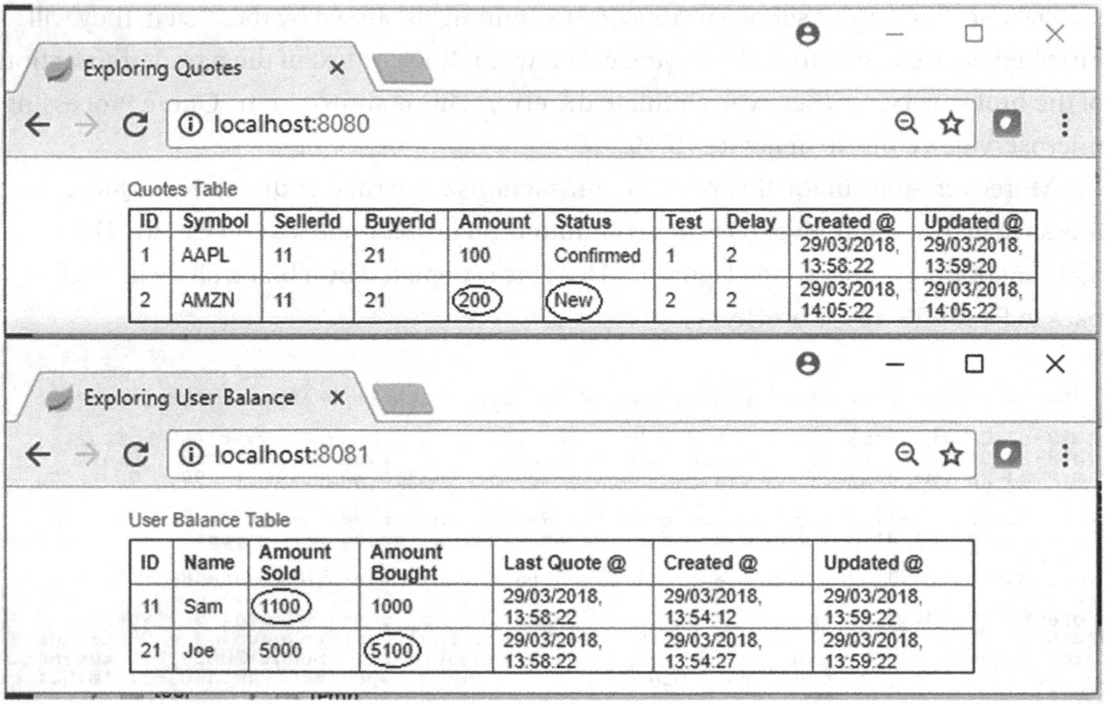

Figure 13-17. *New quote arrived for Test Case 2*

In the second pass of executing the Quotes Processor Task, it again picks up the new quote corresponding to Test Case 2 for processing. In the second pass, you do not simulate any error conditions, as shown by the ✓ sign in Figure 13-15. So, the transactions in the auction service and stock order service that are ready to commit as shown by the ✓ sign are committed, since both of them were called within the context of the parent transaction of the broker service, which is also committed. Since the new quote message delivery to ActiveMQ is committed, the Quote Settlement microservice will receive the quote message for settlement. As shown in Figure 13-15 by the ✓ sign in this second pass for the settlement listener service and the record user transaction service, the complete transactions within the Quote Settlement microservice will be committed. This is reflected in the console in Figure 13-18.

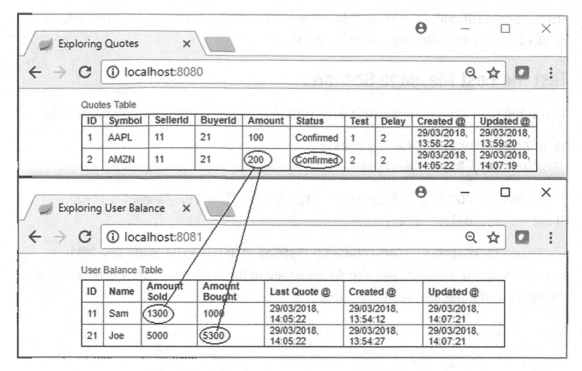

Figure 13-18.   *Test Case 2 console*

Caution   As a reader, if you follow the execution of tests mentioned in this chapter exactly, it is easy for you to visualize the effects and understand based on the explanation and screenshots provided here. So you are strongly advised to follow exactly as directed. Further, this setup automatically makes the first pass fail and the second pass succeed for few of the test cases. This mechanism is designed in that manner to make intervention from the reader at a minimum during the test execution. However, the test fixtures will work only if you execute tests cases with a single test client (Postman Browser client). So do not (monkey) test the example with concurrent test clients. Later, when you are comfortable executing the tests as described and can follow the explanations provided, then you may start tweaking the code and test fixtures to test further scenarios of your own.

Simulating Relaxed Base Anomalies

So far you implemented a BASE system with a reasonable degree of ACID transactions so you are sure that eventual consistency is preserved. Now, let's abuse the transaction attributes to artificially "cut down" the scope of ACID transactions even more, which brings you into the following relaxed BASE situations.

Test the Lost Message Scenario

To test the Lost Message test case, take Postman again and create another new quote:

```
http://localhost:8080/api/quotes
METHOD: POST; BODY: Raw JSON
```

```
{ "symbol" : "GOOG", "sellerId" : 11, "buyerId" : 21, "amount" : 300,
"test" : 3, "delay" : 2 }
```

Figure 13-19 shows the new quote for Test Case 3. It has a status of "New." When settled, the quote amount, 300, should get added to the respective running balances of the buyer and seller shown in the figure.

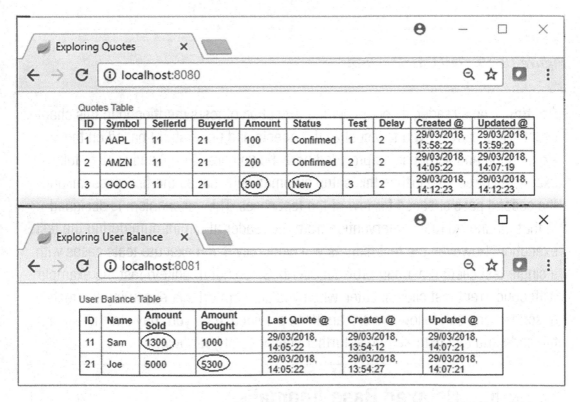

Figure 13-19. *Test Case 3 console at first*

Let's now look at the transaction semantics. See Figure 13-20.

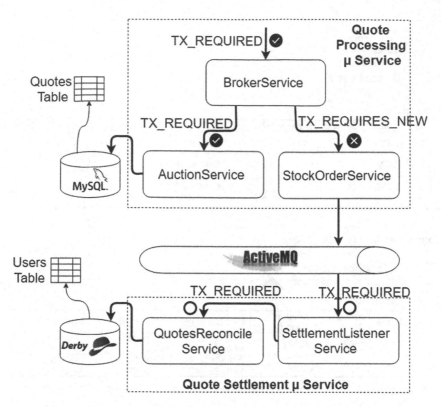

Figure 13-20. *Test Case 3 transaction semantics*

Here, the Quotes Processor Task picks up the new quote for processing. You simulate an error within the stock order service. This is marked by an X sign in Figure 13-19. The peer transaction in the auction service has to succeed, so it's marked with the ✓ sign. The parent transaction in the broker service also needs to succeed. This means the error in the stock order service shouldn't affect the parent transaction in the broker service or the peer transaction in auction service, so you put TX_REQUIRES_NEW semantics for the stock order service. The net effect is that the quote will be marked as "Confirmed;" however, the new quote message to ActiveMQ will fail. Since the quote is already marked as "Confirmed," the Quotes Processor Task will not pick up this quote for processing again in the next scheduled trigger. The net effect is this quote will never get settled in the downstream Quote Settlement microservice, which is shown in Figure 13-21! The message is lost.

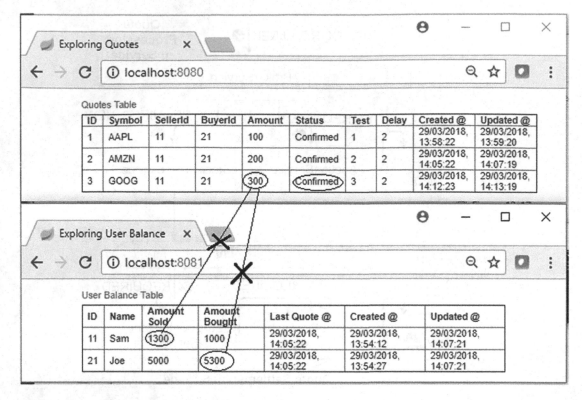

Figure 13-21. *Test Case 3 console at completion*

Test the Duplicate Message Sent Scenario

To validate the Duplicate Message Sent test case, take Postman again and create another new quote:

```
http://localhost:8080/api/quotes
METHOD: POST; BODY: Raw JSON
```

```
{ "symbol" : "NFLX", "sellerId" : 11, "buyerId" : 21, "amount" : 400,
"test" : 4, "delay" : 2 }
```

Figure 13-22 shows the new quote for Test Case 4. It has a status of "New." When settled, the quote amount, 400, should get added to the respective running balances of the buyer and seller, as shown in the figure.

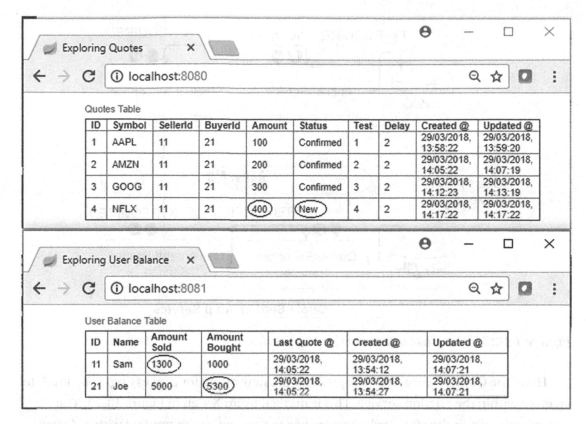

***Figure 13-22.** Test Case 4 console, initially*

Let's now look at the transaction semantics in Figure 13-23.

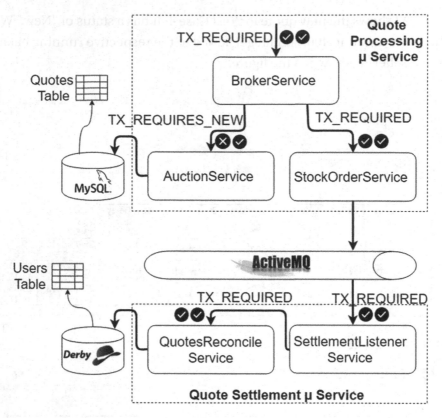

Figure 13-23. *Test Case 4 transaction semantics*

Here, the Quotes Processor Task picks up the new quote for processing. You simulate an error within the auction service. This is marked by an X sign in Figure 13-23. The peer transaction in the stock order service has to succeed, so it's marked with a ✓ sign. The parent transaction in the broker service also needs to succeed. This means the error in the auction service shouldn't affect the parent transaction in the broker service or the peer transaction in the stock order service, so you put TX_REQUIRES_NEW semantics for the auction service. The net effect is that the status of the quote marked as "Confirmed" will be rolled back; however, the new quote message to ActiveMQ will succeed.

Since the new quote message delivery to ActiveMQ is committed, the Quote Settlement microservice will receive the quote message for settlement. As shown in Figure 13-23 by the ✓ sign in the first pass for the settlement listener service and the record user transaction service, the complete transactions within the Quote Settlement microservice will be committed. This is reflected in the console in Figure 13-24.

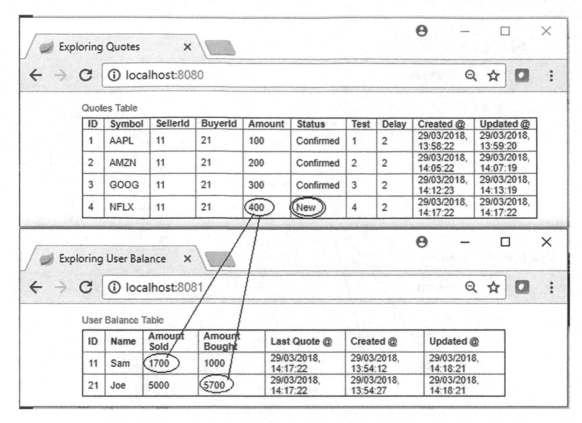

Figure 13-24. *Test Case 4 console, intermediate view*

Alarmingly enough, you can see that the quote settlement happened and the quote amount of 400 gets added to the respective running balances of the buyer and seller, as shown in Figure 13-24; however, in the upstream systems, the quote is yet not marked as "Confirmed." This is because the auction service, which marked the quote as "Confirmed," got rolled back!

The effect is the next time out the Quotes Processor Task picks up the new quote for processing a second time. In your test execution, you won't simulate the error within the auction service this time. Thus, for a second time, the end-to-end processing of this quote is repeated and Figure 13-25 reflects the result!

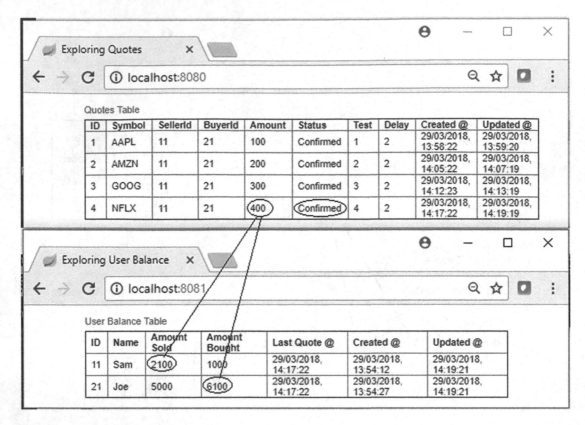

Figure 13-25. *Test Case 4 console at completion*

This is not intended. The duplicate message caused the duplicate settlement of the quote!

Test the Duplicate Message Consumption Scenario

To test the Duplicate Message Consumption test case, take Postman again and create another new quote:

```
http://localhost:8080/api/quotes
METHOD: POST; BODY: Raw JSON
```

```
{ "symbol" : "TSLA", "sellerId" : 11, "buyerId" : 21, "amount" : 500,
"test" : 5, "delay" : 2 }
```

Figure 13-26 shows the new quote for Test Case 5. It has a status of "New." When settled, the quote amount, 500, should get added to the respective running balances of the buyer and seller, shown in the figure.

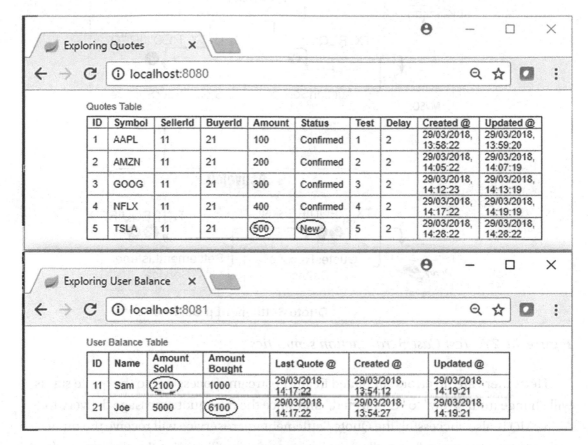

Figure 13-26. *Test Case 5 console, initially*

Let's now look at the transaction semantics in Figure 13-27.

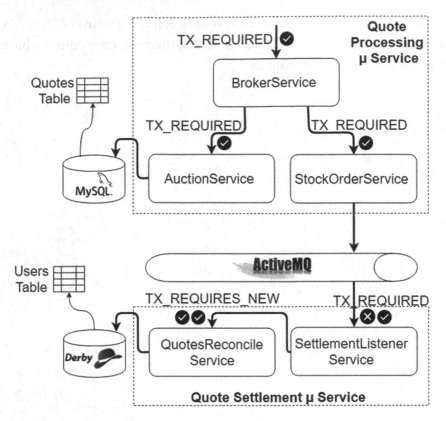

Figure 13-27. *Test Case 5 transaction semantics*

Here, there are no errors simulated in any upstream processing, so the quote status will change from "New" to "Confirmed," and since the new quote message delivery to ActiveMQ is also successful, the Quote Settlement microservice will receive the quote message for settlement. The settlement listener service will receive the message and subsequently invoke the quote reconcile service for settlement. Settlement happens during which the running balances of the buyer and seller are updated. However, once the control comes back from the quote reconcile service, an error is simulated, as shown in Figure 13-27 by the X sign in the first pass for the settlement listener service.

A few things to be noted here:

- The settlement done by the quote reconcile service is done within a TX_REQUIRES_NEW transaction context, so the error happens at the enclosing or the parent transaction (the transaction of the settlement listener service) will not have any effect on the transaction of the quote reconcile service, so the effect of the settlement is committed.

- Even though the settlement listener service has read the message from ActiveMQ, the message listener method, which is in a TX_ REQUIRED transaction context, will not commit the message read from ActiveMQ. Hence for ActiveMQ, the message delivery didn't succeed, so it will try to deliver the message again.

During retry of message delivery (i.e., during the second pass of the message listener processing), you do not simulate any error, and this is indicated by the sign (✓) in both services in Figure 13-27. Hence the transactions by the settlement listener service and the quote reconcile service will both be successful and committed. However, there is a bigger problem: the quote will get settled once again, which will cause double addition and double deduction in the buyer's and seller's accounts, respectively. See Figure 13-28.

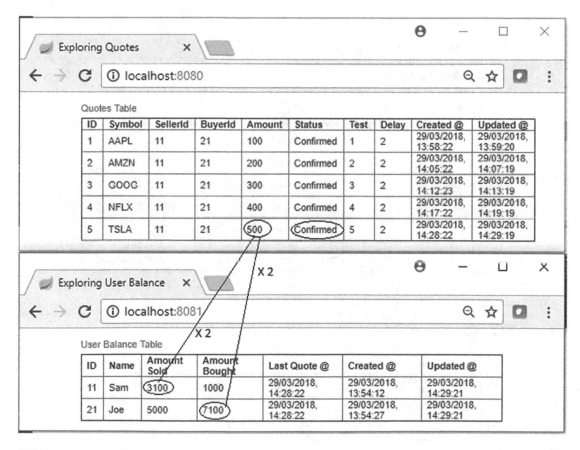

Figure 13-28. *Test Case 5 transaction semantics*

Test the Message Consumed, Processing Failure Scenario

To test the Message Consumed, Processing Failure test case, take Postman again and create another new quote:

```
http://localhost:8080/api/quotes
METHOD: POST; BODY: Raw JSON
```

```
{ "symbol" : "MSFT", "sellerId" : 11, "buyerId" : 21, "amount" : 600,
"test" : 6, "delay" : 2 }
```

Figure 13-29 shows the new quote for Test Case 6. It has a status of "New." When settled, the quote amount, 600, should get added to the respective running balances of the buyer and seller, as shown in the figure.

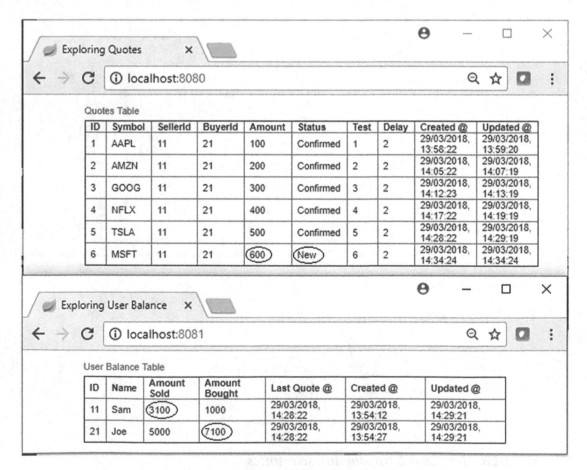

Figure 13-29. *Test Case 6 console, initially*

Let's now look at the transaction semantics shown in Figure 13-30.

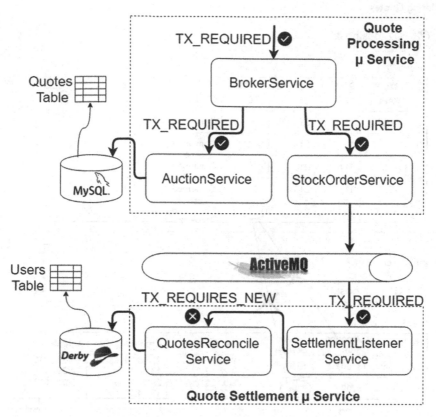

Figure 13-30. *Test Case 6 transaction semantics*

Here again there are no errors simulated in any upstream processing, so the quote status will change from "New" to "Confirmed," and since the new quote message delivery to ActiveMQ is also successful, the Quote Settlement microservice will receive the quote message for settlement. The settlement listener service will receive the message and subsequently invoke the quote reconcile service for settlement. Settlement happens during which it attempts to update the running balances of the buyer and seller. However, an error is simulated within the quote reconcile service transaction, as shown in Figure 13-30 by the X sign. Since the quote reconcile service transaction is configured with TX_REQUIRES_NEW semantics, the settlement will be rolled back. Since the message consumption succeeded, the net effect is that the quote remains unsettled forever in the downstream system! See Figure 13-31.

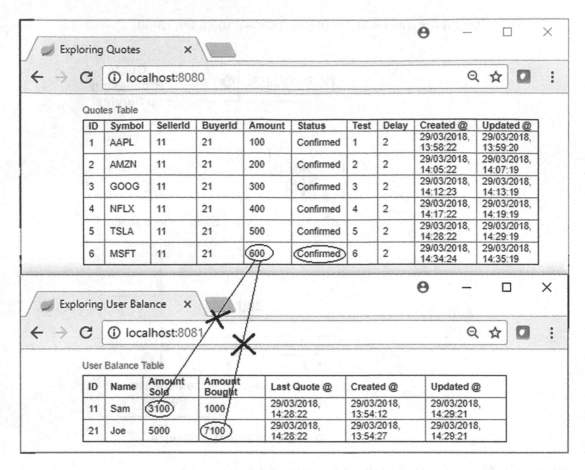

Figure 13-31. *Test Case 6 console, complete*

Test the Message Redelivery Scenario

JMS offers no ordering guarantees regarding message delivery, so messages sent first can arrive after messages sent at a later time. This holds regardless of whether you use XA transactions or not.

To test the Message Redelivery test case, take Postman again and create another new quote:

```
http://localhost:8080/api/quotes
METHOD: POST; BODY: Raw JSON
```

```
{ "symbol" : "ORCL", "sellerId" : 11, "buyerId" : 21, "amount" : 700,
"test" : 7, "delay" : 2 }
```

Figure 13-32 shows the new quote for Test Case 7. It has a status of "New." When settled, the quote amount, 700, should get added to the respective running balances of the buyer and seller, as shown in the figure.

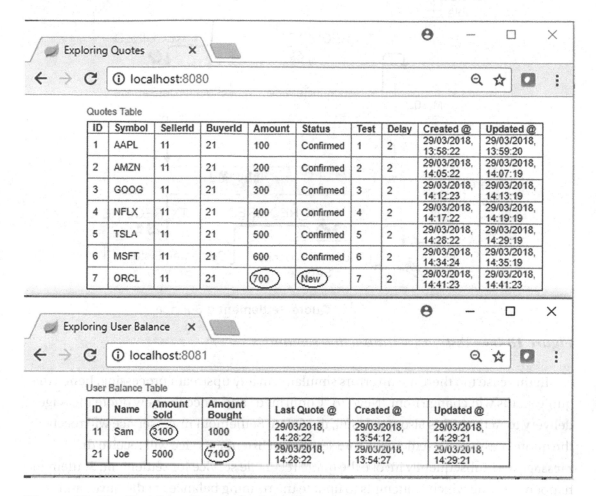

Figure 13-32. *Test Case 7 console, initially*

Let's now look at the transaction semantics shown in Figure 13-33.

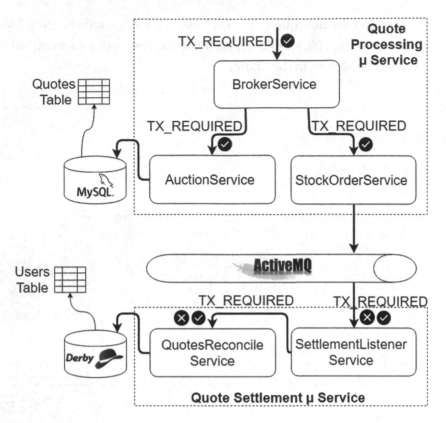

Figure 13-33. *Test Case 7 transaction semantics*

In this case too there are no errors simulated in any upstream processing, hence the quote status will change from "New" to "Confirmed" and since the new quote message delivery to ActiveMQ is also successful, the Quote Settlement microservice will receive the quote message for settlement. The settlement listener service will receive the message and subsequently invoke the quote reconcile service for settlement. Settlement happens, during which it attempts to update the running balances of the buyer and seller. However, during the first pass, an error is simulated within the quote reconcile service transaction, as shown in Figure 13-33 by the X sign. Further, once the control comes back from the quote reconcile service, another error is simulated within the settlement listener service, as shown in Figure 13-33 by the X sign in the first pass by the settlement listener service.

Even though the settlement listener service has read the message from ActiveMQ, the message listener method, which is in a TX_REQUIRED transaction context, will not commit the message read from ActiveMQ. Hence for ActiveMQ, the message delivery didn't succeed, so it will try to deliver the message again. During the retry (i.e., during the second pass of the message listener processing), you do not simulate any error, and this is indicated by the ✓ sign in both the services. Hence the transactions by the settlement listener service and the quote reconcile service will both be successful and committed. And the effect is that the quote will get settled correctly in the second pass. See Figure 13-34.

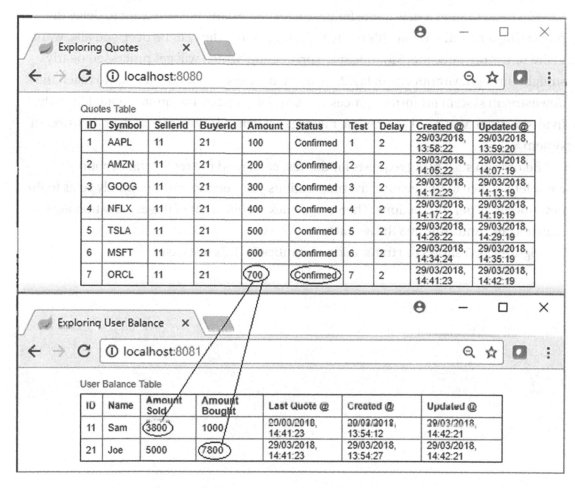

Figure 13-34. *Test Case 7 console, complete*

Common Messaging Pitfalls

In this section, I will demonstrate few common messaging pitfalls which can occur in distributed scenarios if you have not designed the system carefully.

Test the Message Received Out of Order Scenario

Testing for this scenario is slightly tricky since you need to coordinate the timing of each action as per the test fixtures. I will explain based on the configuration for my test fixtures, and they should work for you too if you have not done any changes to the example configurations.

You need to send a new quote for upstream processing but you want to delay the processing for a little. While this quote is waiting for the delay to be over, you also want to fire one more new quote for upstream processing, which will get processed nearly straight through without any delay. As a result, the quote created later has to reach the downstream system for further processing first, followed by the quote created initially. In this manner, you need to simulate messages arriving out of order at the downstream system.

Before you start firing requests for this test case, read the rest of this section completely once to understand the preparations you need to make mentally so as to fire new quotes as per instructions. Then come back to this point of the explanation again, read it again, and continue the actual test.

Figure 13-35 shows the transaction semantics for this test case.

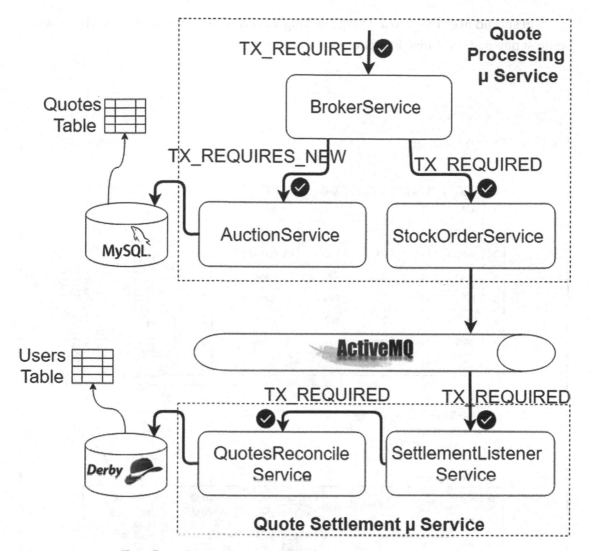

Figure 13-35. *Test Case 8 transaction semantics*

As shown in Figure 13-35, you don't simulate any error scenarios; instead, you simulate only messages reaching out of order.

To test this test case, take Postman again and fire a new quote:

```
http://localhost:8080/api/quotes
METHOD: POST; BODY: Raw JSON

{ "symbol" : "QCOM", "sellerId" : 11, "buyerId" : 21, "amount" : 800,
"test" : 8, "delay" : 90}
```

You should note that you are piggybacking a delay of 90 seconds along with the test request payload, as shown in Figure 13-36.

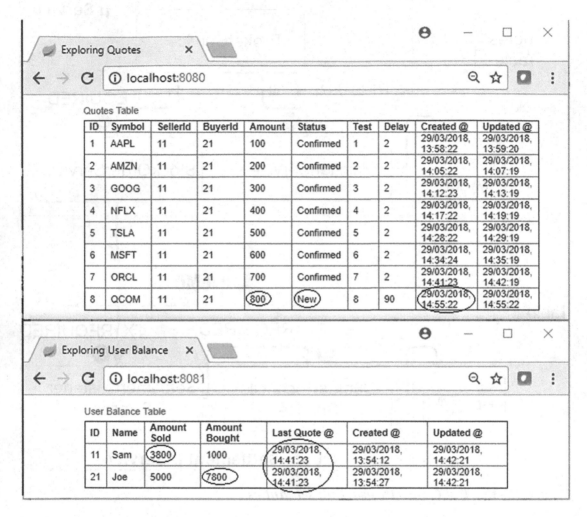

Figure 13-36. *Test Case 8 console, creating the first quote*

Keep watching upstream microservice console (command screen). When the Quote Processor Task times out, it will fetch this new quote, changing the status from "New" to "Confirmed," but before completing the end-to-end transaction, it will sleep for the 90 seconds delay you have provided; this is shown in Figure 13-37.

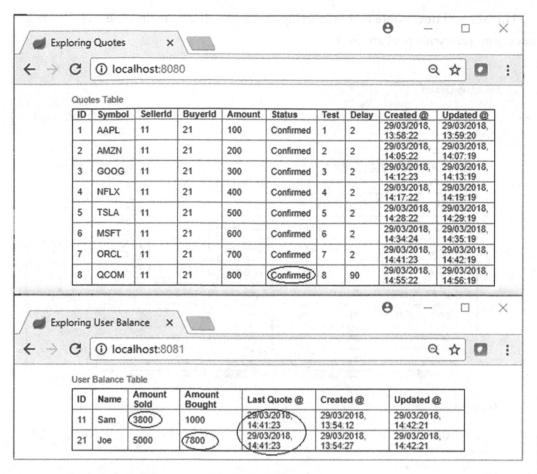

Figure 13-37. *Test Case 8 console, showing the delay*

This 90 seconds has a significance because the next time-out of the Quote Processor Task will happen in the next 60 seconds, and during that time-out it shouldn't fetch this quote because it is already in a processing state (the quote status is not "New").

Here comes the trick. As soon as (within 10 to 20 seconds) the Quote Processor Task picks up the quote for processing and further goes to sleep for the delay of 90 seconds provided, you need to fire another new quote (ideally, you have another Postman session with the data ready), like so:

```
http://localhost:8080/api/quotes
METHOD: POST; BODY: Raw JSON
```

```
{ "symbol" : "GILD", "sellerId" : 11, "buyerId" : 21, "amount" : 900,
"test" : 8, "delay" : 2 }
```

This second new quote is shown in Figure 13-38. That's all, and the steps for test execution from your part are over.

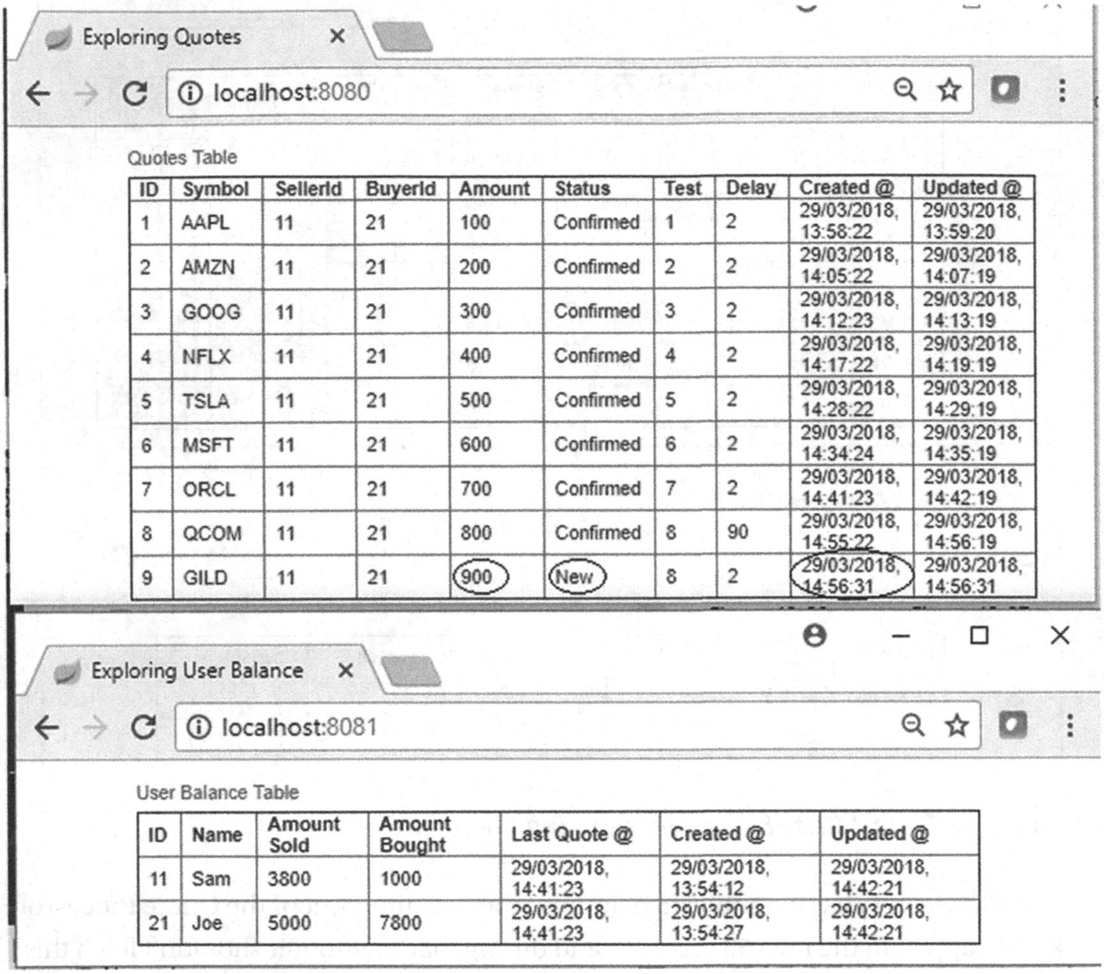

ID	Symbol	SellerId	BuyerId	Amount	Status	Test	Delay	Created @	Updated @
1	AAPL	11	21	100	Confirmed	1	2	29/03/2018, 13:58:22	29/03/2018, 13:59:20
2	AMZN	11	21	200	Confirmed	2	2	29/03/2018, 14:05:22	29/03/2018, 14:07:19
3	GOOG	11	21	300	Confirmed	3	2	29/03/2018, 14:12:23	29/03/2018, 14:13:19
4	NFLX	11	21	400	Confirmed	4	2	29/03/2018, 14:17:22	29/03/2018, 14:19:19
5	TSLA	11	21	500	Confirmed	5	2	29/03/2018, 14:28:22	29/03/2018, 14:29:19
6	MSFT	11	21	600	Confirmed	6	2	29/03/2018, 14:34:24	29/03/2018, 14:35:19
7	ORCL	11	21	700	Confirmed	7	2	29/03/2018, 14:41:23	29/03/2018, 14:42:19
8	QCOM	11	21	800	Confirmed	8	90	29/03/2018, 14:55:22	29/03/2018, 14:56:19
9	GILD	11	21	900	New	8	2	29/03/2018, 14:56:31	29/03/2018, 14:56:31

ID	Name	Amount Sold	Amount Bought	Last Quote @	Created @	Updated @
11	Sam	3800	1000	29/03/2018, 14:41:23	29/03/2018, 13:54:12	29/03/2018, 14:42:21
21	Joe	5000	7800	29/03/2018, 14:41:23	29/03/2018, 13:54:27	29/03/2018, 14:42:21

Figure 13-38. *Test Case 8 console, creating a second quote*

When the Quote Processor Task times out next, it will fetch this second new quote alone. This is because even though the first quote is still under process in the upstream system, the status of the quote has already been updated to "Confirmed," as shown in Figure 13-38. This is shown by marking the transaction of the Auction Service as TX_REQUIRES_NEW, as is evident in Figure 13-35 (another hack for demonstration purposes).

For the second new quote, there is negligible process delay and it comes out of upstream processing, gets through ActiveMQ, and reaches downstream for further processing. You expect the first quote to still be at the process stage in the upstream system. This way, the message is out of order in the downstream system. This will be settled as shown in Figure 13-39.

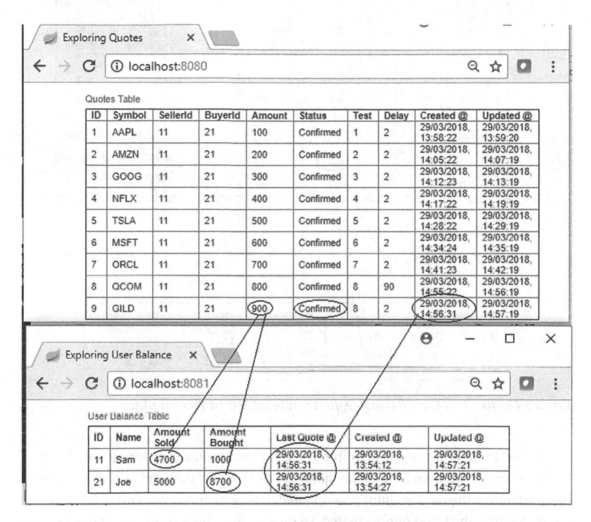

Figure 13-39. *Test Case 8 console, second quote settled first*

Keep watching the browser consoles. Quite soon, you will see the running balances of users in the downstream system change. This is the effect of the first quote, whose upstream processing has been delayed, so it reaches the downstream system out of order and finally gets settled, as shown in Figure 13-40.

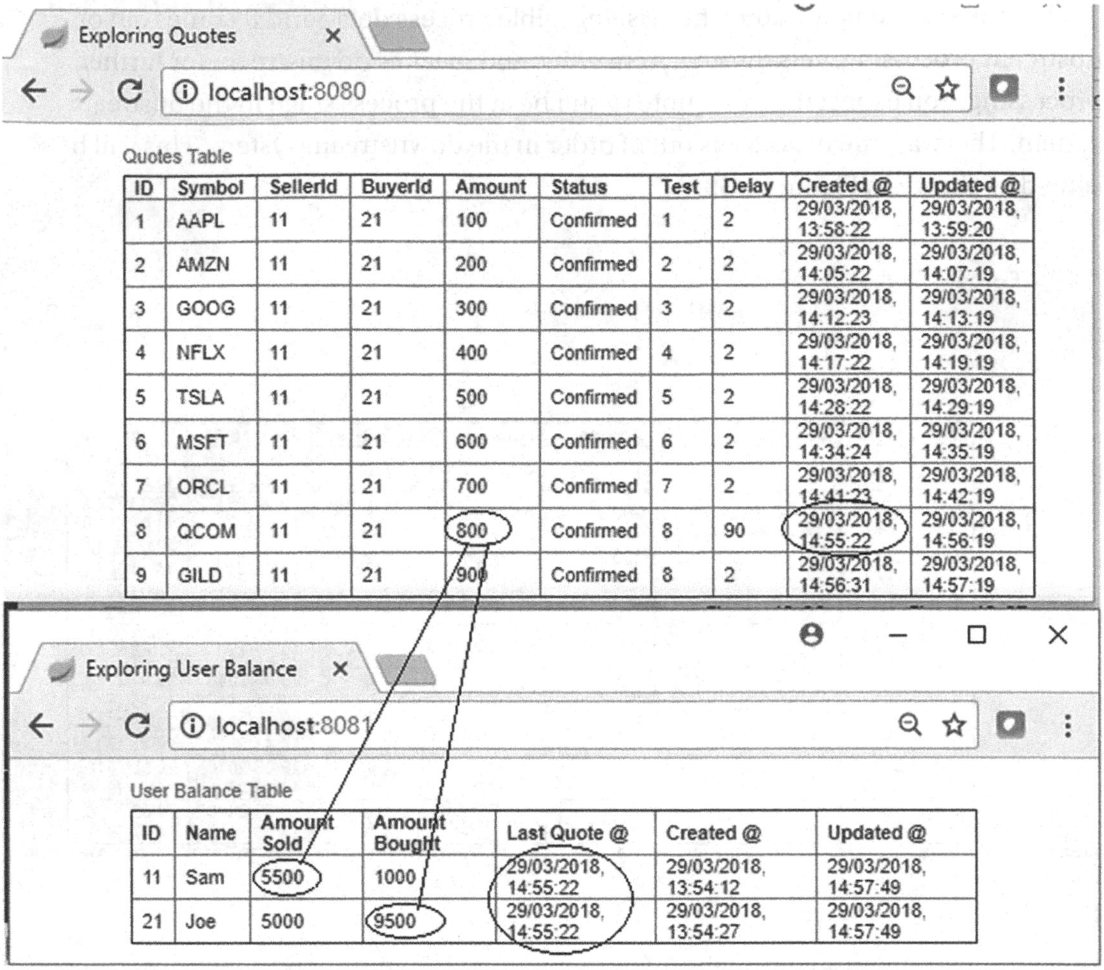

Figure 13-40. *Test Case 8 console, first quote settled in second place*

In the "Build and Test the Example's Happy Flow" section earlier, you read that the latest quote creation time in the upstream system gets updated as the last quote time whenever the user account gets updated. Going by this logic, Quote ID 9 in Figure 13-40 is the latest quote created, so the creation timestamp of that quote should be the last quote time for the users. However, since Quote ID 8 and Quote ID 9 reached the downstream systems out of order, this sanity of data attribute rule went wrong!

Summary

Transactions are the bread and butter for the dynamics of any enterprise-class application. Local transactions are good; however, distributed transactions across partitioned domains are not among the good guys. When you shift from a monolith-based architecture to a microservices-based architecture, you still need transactions; however, you are better off with BASE transactions in place of ACID transactions for domains across partitions and keep ACID or XA compliant transactions within partitions or domains. In this chapter, you saw many error scenarios possible in distributed enterprise systems, and you also saw how such error scenarios could be avoided had you been using ACID transactions. When you shift from monolith- to microservices-based architecture, there is no reduction in the above error scenarios; instead, there is a magnitude of increase in such error scenarios since the degree of distribution of microservices-based architectures are increased manyfold. In the next chapter, you will see techniques you can use in architecting distributed systems to safeguard against such error scenarios, so continue happy reading!

CHAPTER 14

Transactions and Microservices

Chapter 13 covered distributed transactions extensively. You now understand distributed transactions clearly so you use them judiciously. To make it clear, you want to avoid distributed transactions as much as possible in the microservices world across partitions and domains. I do not say that distributed transactions should be deprecated completely in microservices architecture because there are areas where you want to use them by trading loose coupling for reliability; however, the essence is that you can do most of the design without actually using distributed transactions when cross-partitions and cross-domains are involved. You will look at how to do this in detail[1] in this chapter. The examples in this chapter are a continuation of the examples from Chapter 13, so you may want to read and understand Chapter 13 before you attempt to run the examples in this chapter.

You will look into these aspects in this chapter:

- The effect of distributing data across microservices

- Distinguishing between global and local transactions

- Enhancing the example in Chapter 13 to make it fault tolerant

- Exploring further design refactorings that you can use in your actual microservices work

---

[1]For more details, visit the online course at https://atomikos.teachable.com/p/
microservice-transaction-patterns

© Binildas Christudas 2019

B. Christudas, *Practical Microservices Architectural Patterns*, https://doi.org/10.1007/978-1-4842-4501-9_14

Partitioning and Microservices

The best method to maximize consistency is to avoid partitions. No partitions means you have a single software process handling all of your processing. Time has revealed that software processes have limitations, and vertical scaling cannot be increased linearly if not exponentially after a certain limit; this was discussed in Chapter 11's "The Scale Cube" section. It is in this context that people use horizontal scaling methodologies to improve scalability. The moment you split processing into more than one software process, you have introduced probability for partitions, and the more partitions you have, the less consistency you can achieve. Microservices are no exception. When you split a monolith application into a microservices-based architecture, you have increased the number of nodes or software processes across which you have split your processing logic, and the coordination of this processing has to be done using a network. Network or process boundaries bring all the associated complexities and uncertainties, and you can no longer be certain on how and when end-to-end software processing will complete. It is in this context that you have been leveraging two-phase commit protocols to decrease uncertainty.

Software processes that execute requests as part of a two-phase commit protocol need to be able to communicate with one another to coordinate their actions when the transaction commits. In the first phase of the two-phase commit protocol, the coordinator, which is typically the process originating the transaction, will ask all the participants if they are prepared to commit; in the second phase, the coordinator instructs them to commit (or abort) the transaction. If a participant resource manager can commit its part of a transaction, it will agree as soon as it has recorded the changes it has made (to the resources) and its status in permanent storage, and is therefore prepared to commit. Thus the two-phase commit protocol consists of a voting phase and a completion phase. All of these additional steps add to the main processing instructions and in this manner two-phase commit protocols are comparatively expensive since they take more time to complete compared to local transactions.

Even two-phase commit protocols are not completely error free. There are cases where towards the end of the two-phase commit protocol, after all of the participants have agreed to commit, some resources can go out of order where the commit will not get completed. However, the protocol by design can tolerate such failures (server crashes, network failures, or lost messages) and is guaranteed to complete eventually, with or without manual intervention, although it is not possible to specify a time limit within which it will be completed.

Microservices and Distributed Data

Typical monolith applications have all or most data collocated in a single database, and this offers simplicity and many control options for the application in terms of consistency. For example, look at the two data tables introduced in Chapter 13, shown here as Figure 14-1.

User Balance Table

ID	Name	Amount Sold	Amount Bought	Last Quote @	Created @	Updated @
11	Sam	1000	1000	29/03/2018, 13:54:12	29/03/2018, 13:54:12	29/03/2018, 13:54:12
21	Joe	5000	5000	29/03/2018, 13:54:27	29/03/2018, 13:54:27	29/03/2018, 13:54:27

Figure 14-1. *The User Balance table*

Figure 14-1 shows the User Balance table, which is an aggregated view of the running balance for the users. Figure 14-2 shows the Quotes table, which maintains the transaction history.

Quotes Table

ID	Symbol	SellerId	BuyerId	Amount	Status	Test	Delay	Created @	Updated @
1	AAPL	11	21	100	Confirmed	1	2	29/03/2018, 13:58:22	29/03/2018, 13:59:20
2	AMZN	11	21	200	Confirmed	2	2	29/03/2018, 14:05:22	29/03/2018, 14:07:19
3	GOOG	11	21	300	Confirmed	3	2	29/03/2018, 14:12:23	29/03/2018, 14:13:19

Figure 14-2. *The Quotes table*

You know that when a new quote is created, its status is "New." When a quote is processed and settled, its status gets updated to "Confirmed" and simultaneously the value of the quote gets added to the running balances of both the buyer and the seller in the User Balance table. These two actions must be atomic, and if it's a monolith system, you can make the operations atomic within the span of a local transaction. See Listing 14-1.

Listing 14-1. Transactions in a Monolith application

```
Start Local Transaction
    Update Quote Status
    Increment or Decrement User Balance
End Local Transaction
```

When you split the processing into more than one microservice, as per the principle of microservices design, each microservice will manage its own data. This means, the Quote Processing microservice will own and manage the Quotes table, whereas the Quote Settlement microservice will own and manage the User Balance table. If you use two-phase commit global transactions, the actions will be as shown in Listing 14-2.

Listing 14-2. Global Transactions in Microservices

```
Start Global Transaction
    Update Quote Status
    Increment or Decrement User Balance
End Global Transaction
```

If you do not use two-phase commit transaction for the operations described in Listing 14-2, then the two actions will have to be done separate by the two microservices and this means the atomicity between these two actions has to be relaxed. See Listing 14-3.

Listing 14-3. Local Transactions in Microservices

```
Start Local Transaction
    Update Quote Status
End Local Transaction
Start Local Transaction
    Increment or Decrement User Balance
End Local Transaction
```

There is a possibility that when the quote status is changed from "New" to "Confirmed" something will go wrong just after this change in such a manner that the addition-deduction of the value of the quote to the buyer and the seller in the User Balance table won't happen, so the quote settlement is missed! See Listing 14-4.

Listing 14-4. Local Transactions in Microservice Error Scenario

```
Start Local Transaction
    Update Quote Status
End Local Transaction
Start Local Transaction
    Increment or Decrement User Balance
End Local Transaction !ERROR
```

Whether this state is admissible to the application depends upon the impact if the above action in the User Balance table is missed. Even though the update of data in the User Balance table is missed, the same is already tracked in a different form in the Quotes table. In this example, the data in the User Balance table is to be looked at as a summary view, which is a kind of cache of the aggregated total for each user. This is present for faster lookup of the trading balance of each user in the system. If the application assumes that these balances for users are estimates alone, whose correct value can always be verified for accuracy using data from the Quotes table, then the error described earlier, missing the addition of the value of the quote to the buyer and the seller in the User Balance table, is acceptable. In such a scenario, the data present in the User Balance table is not expected to be 100% accurate.

The "Test the Lost Message Scenario" section in Chapter 13 simulated an error scenario like this where the quote status change from "New" to "Confirmed" was successful; however, the downstream settlement was missed because the message sent from the upstream to the downstream microservice failed to reach through. It introduced the messaging middleware between the two microservices as a bridge so that the microservices were loosely coupled. Alas, when you decoupled the microservices like this, you introduced another headache: managing consistency across one microservice and the messaging middleware. Such scenarios are common when you have many microservices in your application. You will look into the complexities involved when you get to the messaging middleware later in the "Global vs. Local Resources" section; however, let's keep aside the queue for the time being.

Idempotent Operations and Microservices

One easy way to handle the error scenario in Listing 14-4 is to simply reverse the order of transactions. See Listing 14-5.

Note   This reversal of order of transaction works in this specific scenario; for your case, it may require a different approach.

Listing 14-5. Local Transactions in Microservice Scenario Reversed

```
Start Local Transaction
    Increment or Decrement User Balance
End Local Transaction
Start Local Transaction
    Update Quote Status
End Local Transaction
```

By reversing the order of transactions as listed above, you can always make sure that you will attempt to change the quote status if and only if you are sure that the user balance update is successful. In this manner, you can be sure that if the quote processing is completed by changing the quote status from "New" to "Confirmed," the quote is already settled for sure by making corresponding changes in the User Balance table.

There arises a new scenario then. What if the quote processing fails after the quote is settled in the User Balance table? Here, the user balance is updated; however, the quote remains in the status of "New," as shown in Listing 14-6.

Listing 14-6. Local Transactions in Microservice Scenario Reversed Error

```
Start Local Transaction
    Increment or Decrement User Balance
End Local Transaction
Start Local Transaction
    Update Quote Status
End Local Transaction !ERROR
```

If so, when the Quotes Processor Task, which is a scheduled timer, times out the next time, it will attempt to process the same quote again since the quote status is still "New." This will cause duplicate transactions in the user balance. The "Test the Duplicate Message Being Sent Scenario" and "Test the Duplicate Message Consumption Scenario" sections in Chapter 13 simulated error scenarios like this. In the first case, the quote status change from "New" to "Confirmed" was not successful in the first pass, so duplicate messages were sent to the downstream settlement microservice. In the second case, the duplicate message consumption scenario was simulated, which caused duplicate transactions in the user balance.

The effect of duplicate transactions can be nullified provided the transaction is idempotent. Idempotent operations are those that can be repeatedly applied without any side effects. Additions and deductions are not idempotent, as is evident from the nature of the actions itself. Update operations that simply set a value in a single-threaded environment are idempotent; however, in a multi-threaded environment where you have concurrency, even such update operations are not idempotent. This is because the context that was assumed to be the precondition for such update operations could have been changed by another concurrent thread. Or the application of such updates can happen out of order from what is desired. You need to have mechanisms to handle these cases, and you will look into them in the enhanced example section later in this chapter. In general, idempotent consumer implementations can be tricky, as illustrated in the reference.[2]

Global vs. Local Resources

Chapter 13 discussed ACID transactions, and Figure 13-2 showed a typical scenario of two separate resources, one a database resource and another a message middleware resource. Queues of message middleware resources are first class citizens for storing the state of entities in motion, temporarily in a node, or in a process. When you split the monolith Quote application into two microservices, the Quote Processing microservice and the Quote Settlement microservice, you need a communication mechanism between them. If you prefer reactive or event-based approaches for this communication over synchronous-style REST calls, message middleware resources are good choices, and that is what is represented in Figure 13-2. However, this figure depicts a completely

---

[2]www.atomikos.com/Blog/IdempotentJmsConsumerPitfalls

distributed architecture where all the resource managers and even the transaction managers are distributed globally in the network, hence full global transactions are required if you must apply ACID-style, two-phase commit operations.

If the queues should have fault tolerance, they are to be persistent. A queue to be persistent should be backed up with a suitable persistent mechanism, usually by a database itself. So if we redraw Figure 13-2 to represent a persistent queue participating in the global transaction, it will look like Figure 14-3.

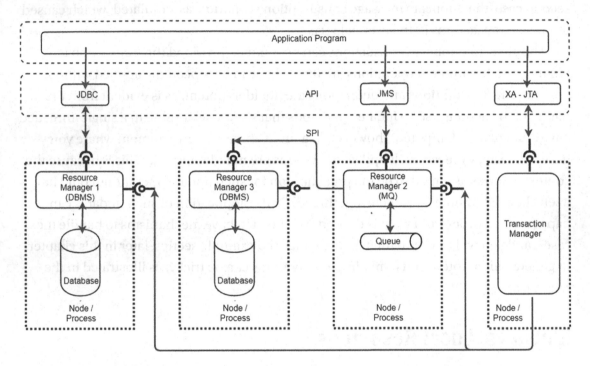

Figure 14-3. *Distributed ACID transactions with distributed resources*

Figure 14-3 retains the Resource Manager 1 and Resource Manager 2 from Figure 13-2 however, it shows a backing store for the JMS resource (Resource Manager 2) represented by Resource Manager 3. You then can represent your microservices architecture similar to that shown in Figure 14-4.

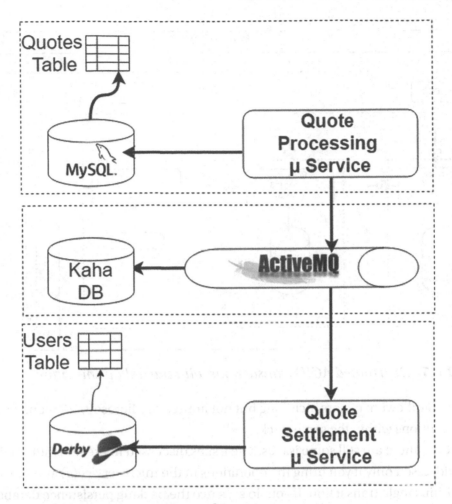

Figure 14-4. *Quotes microservices architecture*

It's again typical that middleware vendors provide database solutions and message middleware solutions together. If so, you can do one optimization to the architecture shown in Figure 14-3, and it is shown in Figure 14-5.

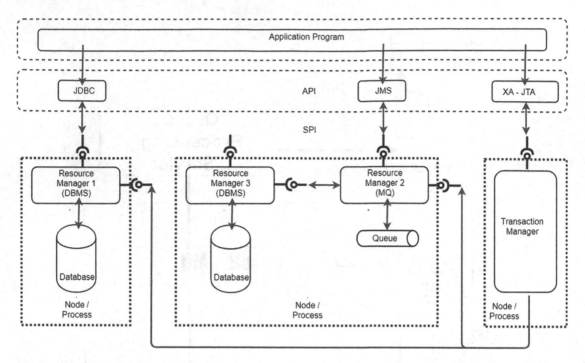

Figure 14-5. *Distributed ACID transactions with partial optimization*

Many middleware majors including but not limited to Microsoft, IBM, and Oracle provide solutions within the same stack.

However, there are still some issues. The issues discussed in previous subsections can be addressed only if you bring the operations in the microservice(s) and the message queue within single transaction. If you do so, since the backing persistence database of the queue and the database used by the microservices are different resources, global two-phase transactions are required.

You will optimize the architecture in Figure 14-5 further to address the above issue; see Figure 14-6.

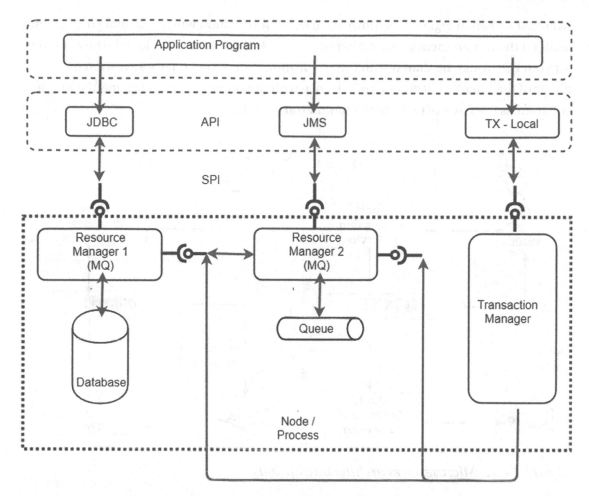

Figure 14-6. *Distributed transactions optimized into local transactions*

The technique is to ensure that the backing persistence is on the same resource as the database, as shown in Figure 14-6. Note that the label of the transaction in Figure 14-6 has changed from XA-JTA to TX-Local. Moreover, when partitioning is avoided, you can minimize or even avoid communications happening at the network level. This too is shown in Figure 14-6. Compared to Figure 14-3 or Figure 14-5, the transaction managers, resource managers, and backing resources all reside in the same partition or node. If they are all from the same vendor, then there are options for optimizations using tight integration choices, like bypassing published APIs and making optimized calls through published or even non-published SPIs (service provider interfaces).

Let's now look at the microservices architectures possible with such a resource sharing setup. The architecture options shown in Figure 14-7 are surely improvisations over that shown in Figure 14-4; however, careful observation will reveal that you have not avoided the requirement to use global two-phase transactions completely. The resource for your queue can be shared with the application transaction database resource of either of the microservices, not both. Hence with the other microservice and the queue, still there is the issue of two-phase commit transactions.

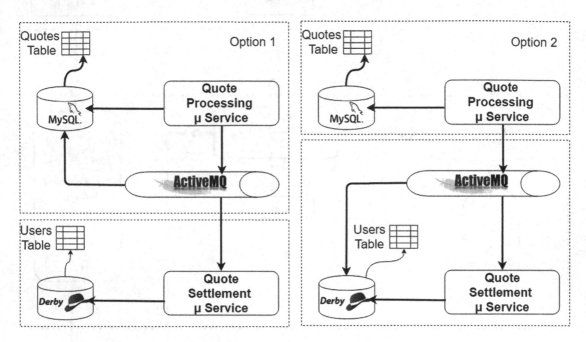

Figure 14-7. *Microservices architecture options*

Here you need to do an architecture trade-off depending upon the business involved. Perhaps Option 1 is better since you want to process any number of new quotes throttled to the Quote Processing microservice. By queueing a persistent message within the same transaction as the update to the new quote by changing the status of the quote from "New" to "Confirmed," the information needed to update the running balances on the User Balance table in the foreign microservice has been safely captured. The transaction is contained on a single database instance and therefore maximum throughput can be achieved by limiting transactions locally. This is also desirable if you assume that there are humans interacting with the Quote Processing microservice where, once the transactions has completed, a response has to be provided to their device or browser (even though the example in Chapter 13 doesn't have humans waiting; instead, it uses scheduled jobs to process quotes).

If you chose Option 1 for the architecture, then when you dequeue messages from the queue for settlement by the Quotes Settlement microservice, you still have the two-phase transaction problem. If you consider quote settlement as a pure back-office process, one justification for you to still continue with the two-phase commit transactions there is that you maximized the throughput and hence the availability of your customer-facing microservices while trading off with comparatively lower responsiveness for your back-office microservices. Similar is the case where you want to deal with "expensive" or "high consequence" transactions like those involved in the financial domain where you would still want to continue with two-phase commit transactions where the benefits outweigh the costs involved.

Again, as is shown in Figure 14-7, in Option 2 the design is restructured. However, it only reveals that you haven't completely avoided the need for two-phase commit transactions; instead, it shifted the necessity from downstream to upstream!

Distributed Transactions Example: Refactoring Towards Less ACID

In the "Idempotent Operations and Microservices" section, you saw the problem arising due to partial failures in enterprise systems. When you relax ACID constraints, there should be mechanisms to take care of scenarios including but not limited to

- Partial failures

- Lost messages

- Duplicate messages

- Retry attempts

- Message redelivery

- Message received out of order

As you know, all of the above scenarios were covered in Chapter 13. The end goal is to choose between distributed transactions and local transactions based on the nature and context of the use case involved. But Figure 14-7 illustrates that you can live with local transactions alone if your application is a monolith. The moment you split your monolith into microservices, you introduce partitions in the architecture and there you need to trade off. Option 1 in Figure 14-7 is the preferred option where you avoid distributed transactions from microservices that require high responsiveness like those that interact with human users, and retain some form of distributed transactions in other microservices where you justify using distributed transactions to pieces of your microservices architecture where you require comparatively lower responsiveness, since they are your back-office microservices.

So far, so good. What if distributed transactions or two-phase transactions are simply never acceptable in your microservices? Can this problem be ever solved? Let's relook at an example from Chapter 13.

Towards Relaxed BASE: Redesign For Dealing with Duplicates and Out-Of-Order Messages

The aim here is not to deprecate distributed transactions straight away. Instead, you will bring relaxations to the design from Chapter 13, simulate failure scenarios, and see if you are able to overcome the shortcomings seen in Chapter 13. Once you understand this enhanced design, you will have a good grip of the underlying basics in designing distributed systems that are more resilient and fault tolerant. Once you have these basics in your toolset, then it's a matter of architectural creativity in designing fault tolerant microservices.

The main design change I introduce here is to have a new table with the name QuotesTX in the downstream system, as shown in Figure 14-8.

Transactions Table

ID	Quote ID	Symbol	Seller	Buyer	Amount	Status	Quote Created @	Test
123	1	AAPL	11	21	100	Settled	10/04/2018, 16:22:13	1
124	2	AMZN	11	21	200	Settled	10/04/2018, 16:23:27	2

Figure 14-8. *Quotes Transactions table*

You need a way to track which quotes received through the messaging middleware have been settled and which are still outstanding. The transactions to the QuotesTX table have been handled by a new entity in the system called StockTransaction, and all actions on this entity are owned by a new transactional component service, QuotesTransactionService. The enhanced architecture is shown in Figure 14-9.

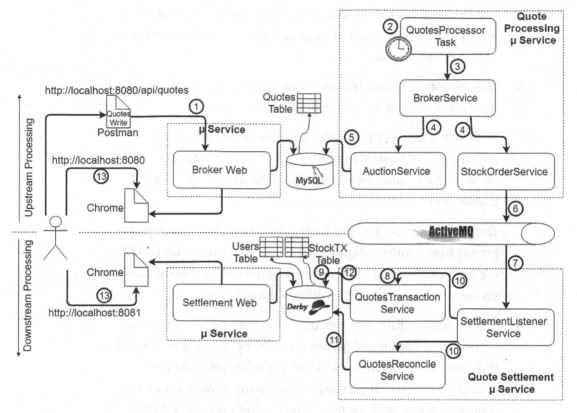

Figure 14-9. *The architecture for the relaxed XA transaction example*

The business flow for the relaxed design explaining the new building blocks for your example is as follows:

1. New quotes for stock transactions can be pushed to the Broker Web microservice. New quotes will get inserted into a Quotes table, which is in a MySQL DB, with a status of "New."

2. The Quotes Processor Task is a Quartz scheduled task, and it polls the Quotes table in the MySQL DB for any quotes with a status of "New."

3. When a quote with a status of "NEW" is found, it invokes the processNewQuote method of the broker service, always with a transaction, passing the unique identifier for the new quote in the Quotes table.

4. The broker service makes use of two other transactional services, the auction service and the stock order service. The execution of both must be atomic.

5. The auction service confirms the quote received by changing the status of the quote to "Confirmed," in a transaction.

6. The stock order service creates a JMS message out of the information contained in the new quote and it is sent to an ActiveMQ queue for settlement of the quote, again in a transaction.

7. The settlement listener service listens on the ActiveMQ queue for any new confirmed quote. All confirmed quotes on reaching the ActiveMQ queue are picked up by the onMessage of the settlement listener service, within a transaction.

8. The settlement listener service invokes the quotes transaction service for recording all quotes received by the system. To make this record happen irrespective of any other processing in peer transactions within the enclosed parent transaction, the transaction semantic for this recording action is REQUIRES_NEW. This record action will not raise any errors on finding duplicate entries received.

9. The quotes transaction service attempts to safely record all quote transactions the downstream microservice receives through the messaging bridge.

10. The settlement listener service makes use of two other transactional services, the quotes reconcile service and the quotes transaction service (again), the execution of both of which must be atomic.

11. The quotes reconcile service needs to reconcile the value of the stock traded to the respective user account of the seller and the buyer, in a transaction.

12. At the same time, the quotes transaction service marks the quotes transaction entry as settled in the QuotesTX table by changing its status from "New" to "Settled."

13. The Broker Web microservice and the Settlement Web microservice are just utilities that provide a dashboard view of the operational data on the Quotes table, the User table, and the QuotesTX table to provide you with live views.

A little more discussion is required about the new design. In the new design, the StockTransaction entity is nothing but a copy of the message the microservices receive as such. In a messaging and distributed system, it is a best practice to record what is coming in and going out of (sub) systems so that if you need to later track what happened during transactions, it is possible to correlate entity states with respect to temporal actions. The downside in doing this is that you eat up more storage space in terms of duplicating data. However, you need to go back to another basic principle of microservices: a microservice should have all of what is required for the service to serve without any external dependency.

In that way, duplicating the required data and caching it in the microservices has to be done in certain scenarios. This is also one of the after-effects of the CQRS architecture introduced in Chapter 12 where, while one microservices will own the "write" governance for an entity, there can be many other microservices that are interested in the "read" models, and here too you will have read data duplicated and attached along with the interested microservices so that these microservices can function on their own with no external dependency.

The next aspect is that the StockTX table is also a mechanism for the downstream microservice to identify duplicate messages coming through the messaging middleware. This is done using the transaction ID pattern. Here, the StockTX table will also record a transaction ID send by the sender microservices along with the message payload. The sender and receiver microservices have to agree on a common schema where these transaction IDs are unique in the way that any two different messages will not have the same transaction ID. If so, the receiver microservice can record this transaction ID along with the message. In this manner, whenever the receiver microservice receives a message, it can check if it's a duplicate message, and if so, it can be silently ignored.

Boundary level actions of microservices are to be done in isolation from internal processing and also with more fault tolerant design patterns. This is because microservices boundaries have a dependency of system resources like networks, I/O, and so on, which are more error-prone. Hence, when the downstream microservice receives a message from the message network, your aim should be to make the "record new message" action independent and isolated from further internal microservice processing, since internal microservice processing is in the control of that microservice alone (no external resources, like previously mentioned) and can be retried in case of errors. This is achieved in the new design by making the transaction semantic for the new message recording action as REQUIRES_NEW so that it will succeed irrespective of the outcome of the peer transactions or the parent transaction.

Code the Relaxed Example Scenario

The complete code required to demonstrate the distributed transaction example with enhanced resiliency for relaxed BASE anomalies is in folder ch14\ch14-01. There are no major changes in the code of the upstream microservices from what you saw in Chapter 13, so I will not duplicate the code here. I have introduced new code as well as updates to existing code in the downstream microservices, so I will explain it all here. The main changes are in the Quote Settlement downstream microservice.

Microservice 3: Quote Settlement (Settlement-ActiveMQ-Derby)

When a new quote message reaches the ActiveMQ queue, it will be picked up instantaneously by the settlement listener. The settlement listener code has changed from what you saw in Chapter 13, so look at Listing 14-7.

Listing 14-7. Settlement Listener Orchestrator (ch14\ch14-01\XA-TX-Resilient\ Settlement-ActiveMQ-Derby\src\main\java\com\acme\ecom\messaging\ SettlementListener.java)

```
public class SettlementListener implements MessageListener {

    @Autowired
    @Qualifier("quotesTransactionServiceRequired_TX")
    QuotesTransactionService quotesTransactionServiceRequired_TX;

    @Autowired
    @Qualifier("quotesTransactionServiceRequiresNew_TX")
    QuotesTransactionService quotesTransactionServiceRequiresNew_TX;
```

```
@Autowired
@Qualifier("quotesReconcileServiceRequired_TX")
QuotesReconcileService quotesReconcileServiceRequired_TX;

@Autowired
@Qualifier("quotesReconcileServiceRequiresNew_TX")
QuotesReconcileService quotesReconcileServiceRequiresNew_TX;

public void onMessage(Message message) {

    QuoteDTO quoteDTO = null;
    try {
        quoteDTO = (QuoteDTO) ((ObjectMessage) message). getObject();
    }
    catch (JMSException e) {
        throw new RuntimeException(e);
    }

    quotesTransactionServiceRequiresNew_TX.insertUniqueNoErrorOnDuplicate(
            quoteDTO);

    try {
        reconcile(quoteDTO);
    }
    catch (QuotesBaseException e) {
        throw new RuntimeException(e);
    }
  }
}
```

As shown in Listing 14-7, on consuming the message, the settlement listener will at the very next instance attempt to record the incoming quote message backed up by a persistent resource. To make this record happen irrespective of the outcome (success or failure) of any other processing in peer transactions within the enclosed parent transaction, the transaction semantic for this recording action is REQUIRES_NEW. This record action will not raise any errors on finding duplicate entries received. Next, the listener will do a check to see if a quote similar to the one received has already been settled. This happens in cases of duplicate messages. See Listing 14-8.

Listing 14-8. Settlement Listener Reconciliation (ch14\ch14-01\XA-TX-Resilient\Settlement-ActiveMQ-Derby\src\main\java\com\acme\ecom\messaging\SettlementListener.java)

```java
public class SettlementListener implements MessageListener {

    private void reconcile(QuoteDTO quoteDTO)throws QuotesBaseException{

        User seller = null;
        User buyer = null;
        StockTransaction stockTransaction = null;
        Integer testCase = quoteDTO.getTest();

        if(!quotesTransactionServiceRequired_TX.isNotSettled(
                quoteDTO.getId()))){
            LOGGER.debug("Quote will not be attempted to be settled again");
            return;
        }

        if(testCase.equals(1) || testCase.equals(2) ||
                testCase.equals(4) || testCase.equals(8)){
            try{
                quotesReconcileServiceRequired_TX.reconcile(quoteDTO);
                quotesTransactionServiceRequired_TX.markSettled(
                quoteDTO.getId());
            }
            catch(QuotesBaseException quotesBaseException){
                LOGGER.error(quotesBaseException.getMessage());
            }
        }
        else if(testCase.equals(5)){
            try{
                quotesReconcileServiceRequiresNew_TX.reconcile(quoteDTO);
                quotesTransactionServiceRequiresNew_TX.markSettled(
                    quoteDTO.getId());
            }
```

```
                catch(QuotesBaseException quotesBaseException){
                    LOGGER.error(quotesBaseException.getMessage());
                }
                flipFlop();
            }
            else if(testCase.equals(6)){
                try{
                    quotesReconcileServiceRequiresNew_TX.reconcile(quoteDTO);
                    quotesTransactionServiceRequired_TX.markSettled(
                    quoteDTO.getId());
                }
                catch(QuotesBaseException quotesBaseException){
                    LOGGER.error(quotesBaseException.getMessage());
                }
            }
            else if(testCase.equals(7)){
                try{
                    quotesReconcileServiceRequired_TX.reconcile(quoteDTO);
                    quotesTransactionServiceRequired_TX.markSettled(
                    quoteDTO.getId());
                }
                catch(QuotesBaseException quotesBaseException){
                    LOGGER.error(quotesBaseException.getMessage());
                }
                flipFlop();
            }
            else{
                LOGGER.debug("Undefined Test Case");
            }
        }
    }
}
```

If the quote is not a duplicate, reconciliation will be attempted, as shown in Listing 14-8. As a last step, the listener will mark the stock transaction in the StockTX table as "Settled" so that, if further duplicate messages arrive for the same quote, the listener will not settle it again. Listing 14-9 shows the stock transaction.

Listing 14-9. Stock Transaction Entity (ch14\ch14-01\XA-TX-Resilient\
Settlement-ActiveMQ-Derby\src\main\java\com\acme\ecom\model\trade\
StockTransaction.java)

```java
@Entity
@Table(name = "stocktx")
@Data
@EqualsAndHashCode(exclude = { "id" })
public class StockTransaction {

    public static final String NEW = "New";
    public static final String SETTLED = "Settled";

    @Id
    @GeneratedValue(strategy = GenerationType.AUTO)
    private Long id;

    @Column(name = "stocksymbol", nullable = false, updatable = false)
    private String stockSymbol;

    @Column(name = "sellerid", nullable = false, updatable = false)
    private Long sellerId;

    @Column(name = "buyerid", nullable = false, updatable = false)
    private Long buyerId;

    @Column(name = "amount", nullable = false, updatable = false)
    private Float amount;

    @Column(name = "quoteid", nullable = false, updatable = false, unique=true)
    private Long quoteId;

    @Column(name = "status", nullable = false, updatable = true)
    private String status;

    @Column(name = "quotecreated", nullable = false, updatable = false)
    @Temporal(TemporalType.TIMESTAMP)
    private Date quoteCreated;
```

```
@Column(name = "test", nullable = true, updatable = true)
private Integer test;

@Column(name = "createdat", nullable = false, updatable = false)
@Temporal(TemporalType.TIMESTAMP)
private Date createdAt;

@Column(name = "updatedat", nullable = true, updatable = true)
@Temporal(TemporalType.TIMESTAMP)
private Date updatedAt;
}
```

The fields for the StockTransaction entity in Listing 14-9 are chosen to demonstrate the required test cases in later sections. You will now look at the QuotesTransactionService, which is responsible for managing the stock transaction entity life cycle, in Listing 14-10.

Listing 14-10. Quotes Transaction Service (ch14\ch14-01\XA-TX-Resilient\ Settlement-ActiveMQ-Derby\src\main\java\com\acme\ecom\service\ QuotesTransactionServiceImpl.java)

```
public class QuotesTransactionServiceImpl implements
QuotesTransactionService{

    @Autowired
    private StockTransactionRepository stockTransactionRepository;

    @Override
    public boolean insertUniqueNoErrorOnDuplicate(QuoteDTO quoteDTO){

        StockTransaction stockTransaction = null;
        StockTransaction stockTransactionSaved = null;
        boolean inserted = false;
        Optional stockTransactionQueried =
            stockTransactionRepository.findOptionalByQuoteId(quoteDTO.getId());
        if(!stockTransactionQueried.isPresent()){

            stockTransaction = convertQuoteToStockTransaction(quoteDTO);
            stockTransaction.setStatus(StockTransaction.NEW);
```

```
            Date now = new Date();
            stockTransaction.setCreatedAt(now);
            stockTransaction.setUpdatedAt(now);
            stockTransactionSaved =
                stockTransactionRepository.save(stockTransaction);
            inserted = true;
        }
        else{
            LOGGER.debug("Stock Transaction with quoteId : {} exist;
            Cannot insert duplicate", quoteDTO.getId());
            // Do Nothing - we know this is a duplicate message
        }
        return inserted;
    }
}
```

The notable aspect in Listing 14-10 is the silent manner in which you are ignoring duplicate messages. Further, the isNotSettled and markSettled utility methods are also shown in Listing 14-11.

Listing 14-11. Quotes Transaction Service (ch14\ch14-01\XA-TX-Resilient\
Settlement-ActiveMQ-Derby\src\main\java\com\acme\ecom\service\
QuotesTransactionServiceImpl.java)

```
public class QuotesTransactionServiceImpl implements
QuotesTransactionService{

    @Autowired
    private StockTransactionRepository stockTransactionRepository;

    @Override
    public void markSettled(Long quoteId){

        StockTransaction stockTransaction = null;
        StockTransaction stockTransactionSaved = null;
        Optional stockTransactionQueried =
            stockTransactionRepository.findOptionalByQuoteId(quoteId);
```

```
        if(stockTransactionQueried.isPresent()){
            stockTransaction =
                (StockTransaction) stockTransactionQueried.get();
            stockTransaction.setStatus(StockTransaction.SETTLED);
            stockTransaction.setUpdatedAt(new Date());
            stockTransactionSaved =
                stockTransactionRepository.save(stockTransaction);
        }
        else{
            LOGGER.debug("Stock Transaction cannot be tracked");
        }
    }

    @Override
    public boolean isNotSettled(Long quoteId){

        boolean isNotSettled = true;
        StockTransaction stockTransaction = null;
        Optional stockTransactionQueried =
            stockTransactionRepository.findOptionalByQuoteId(quoteId);
        if(stockTransactionQueried.isPresent()){
            stockTransaction =
                (StockTransaction) stockTransactionQueried.get();
            if(stockTransaction.getStatus().equals(StockTransaction.
            SETTLED)){
                isNotSettled = false;
            }
        }
        return isNotSettled;
    }

    public Optional<StockTransaction> findOptionalByQuoteId(Long quoteId){
        return stockTransactionRepository.findOptionalByQuoteId(quoteId);
    }
}
```

The quotes reconcile service has also been updated from what you saw in Chapter 13 to take care of the messages coming out of order. Look at the code in Listing 14-12 to understand the method of handling messages coming out of order.

Listing 14-12. Enhanced Quotes Reconcile Service Code (ch14\ch14-01\XA-TX-Resilient\Settlement-ActiveMQ-Derby\src\main\java\com\acme\ecom\service\QuotesReconcileServiceImpl.java)

```java
public class QuotesReconcileServiceImpl implements QuotesReconcileService{

    @Autowired
    private UserRepository userRepository;

    @Override
    public void reconcile(QuoteDTO quoteDTO)throws QuotesBaseException{
        Integer testCase = quoteDTO.getTest();
        Optional sellerQueried =
            userRepository.findById(quoteDTO.getSellerId());
        Optional buyerQueried  =
            userRepository.findById(quoteDTO.getBuyerId());
        User seller = null;
        User buyer = null;
        User sellerSaved = null;
        User buyerSaved = null;
        Date updatedDate = null;

        if(sellerQueried.isPresent() && buyerQueried.isPresent()){
            seller = (User) sellerQueried.get();
            buyer  = (User) buyerQueried.get();
            updatedDate = new Date();
            seller.setAmountSold(seller.getAmountSold() +
                quoteDTO.getAmount());
            seller.setUpdatedAt(updatedDate);
            if(quoteDTO.getCreatedAt().after(seller.getLastQuoteAt())){
                seller.setLastQuoteAt(quoteDTO.getCreatedAt());
            }
```

```
            sellerSaved = userRepository.save(seller);
            buyer.setAmountBought(buyer.getAmountBought() +
                quoteDTO.getAmount());
            buyer.setUpdatedAt(updatedDate);
            if(quoteDTO.getCreatedAt().after(buyer.getLastQuoteAt())){
                buyer.setLastQuoteAt(quoteDTO.getCreatedAt());
            }
            buyerSaved = userRepository.save(buyer);
            if(testCase.equals(6)){
                throw new QuotesReconcileRollbackException("Explicitly thrown
                    by Reconcile Application to Roll Back!");
            }
            if(testCase.equals(7)){
                flipFlop();
            }
        }
        else{
            LOGGER.debug("Reconciliation Not Done");
        }
    }
}
```

The quotes reconcile service has a helper method to retrieve user details, shown in Listing 14-13.

Listing 14-13. Enhanced Quotes Reconcile Service Helper Method

```
public class QuotesReconcileServiceImpl implements QuotesReconcileService{

    @Autowired
    private UserRepository userRepository;

    @Override
    public Optional findUserById(Long id){
        return userRepository.findById(id);
    }
}
```

The way you take care of quote messages arriving out of order is by using the check in Listing 14-14.

Listing 14-14. Handling Messages Arriving Out of Order

```
if(quoteDTO.getCreatedAt().after(seller.getLastQuoteAt())){
    seller.setLastQuoteAt(quoteDTO.getCreatedAt());
}

if(quoteDTO.getCreatedAt().after(buyer.getLastQuoteAt())){
    buyer.setLastQuoteAt(quoteDTO.getCreatedAt());
}
```

These checks will update the timestamp of last quote for a buyer or a seller if and only if the corresponding creation timestamp of the original quote message recorded by the upstream microservice is later than the current timestamp of last quote for the respective buyer or the seller.

Build and Test the Duplicate Message Being Sent Scenario

Since this example is a continuation of the example in Chapter 13, I won't explain the scenario in detail. Instead, your aim is to understand how to manage the duplicate messages and the messages coming out of order so that you know how to better design for them in a microservices architecture. Hence you will look into three test cases in detail, shown in Figure 14-10.

Test Case	Broker	Auction (DB Update)	Delay (s)	Stock Order (Send Message)	Settlement Listener (Receive Message)	Record User Transaction (DB Update)	Comments
1	No Error	No Error	2	No Error	No Error	No Error	Happy Flow - All Good
2	Error / No Error	No Error / No Error	2	No Error / No Error	No Error	No Error	New Quote gets Processed only in the second run
3	No Error	No Error	2	Error			Message Lost, Quote Never Settled
4	No Error / No Error	Error / No Error	2 / 2	No Error / No Error	No Error / No Error	No Error / No Error	Duplicate Message send, 2nd time only Quote marked processed; However, Quote NOT Settled twice
5	No Error	No Error	2	No Error	Error / No Error	No Error / No Error	Duplicate settlement caused by message consumed more than once. However, Quote NOT Settled twice
6	No Error	No Error	2	No Error	No Error	Error	Quote Processed, however Quote Never Settled
7	No Error	No Error	2	No Error	Error / No Error	Error / No Error	Message ReDelivery comes to rescue - Quote Settled second chance
8	No Error / No Error	No Error / No Error	1st: 90 / 2nd: 2	No Error / No Error	No Error / No Error	No Error / No Error	Message Received out of order! However, Original order taken care

Figure 14-10. *XA transaction resiliency test cases*

The test cases of interest for you are

- Test Case 4 : Duplicate messages sent

- Test Case 5 : Duplicate consumption of messages

- Test Case 8 : Messages reached out of order

You will look at Test Case 4 in this section and the other two test cases in the subsequent two sections.

You need to do steps similar to those explained in Chapter 13; however, there are a few extra steps. Hence the complete steps to run the examples will be explained again here. Further, as a prerequisite of running these test cases, I'll assume that you have experience in running the test scenarios explained in Chapter 13.

As the first step, you need to bring up the ActiveMQ server. You may want to refer to Appendix F to get started with the ActiveMQ server.

You will configure a queue that will act as the bridge between the upstream and downstream processing. Listing 14-15 gives the configuration of a queue, which can be done in `activemq.xml`.

Listing 14-15. The ActiveMQ Queue configuration (D:\Applns\apache\ ActiveMQ\apache-activemq-5.13.3\conf\activemq.xml)

```
<beans>
    <broker>
        <destinations>
            <queue physicalName="notification.queue" />
        </destinations>
    </broker>
</beans>
```

You may now bring up the ActiveMQ server:

```
cd D:\Applns\apache\ActiveMQ\apache-activemq-5.13.3\bin
D:\Applns\apache\ActiveMQ\apache-activemq-5.13.3\bin>activemq start
```

Next, make sure MySQL is up and running. You may want to refer to Appendix H to get started with MySQL.

```
First Bring Up MySQL Server
D:\Applns\MySQL\mysql-5.7.14-winx64\bin>mysqld --console
```

```
Now Open MySQL prompt
D:\Applns\MySQL\mysql-5.7.14-winx64\bin>mysql -u root -p
```

```
mysql> use ecom01;
Database changed
mysql>
```

To start with clean tables, delete any tables with the names you want for your examples:

```
mysql> drop table quote;
```

Next, create the table with the schema required for this example:

```
mysql> create table quote (id BIGINT PRIMARY KEY AUTO_INCREMENT, symbol
VARCHAR(4), sellerid BIGINT, buyerid BIGINT, amount FLOAT, status
VARCHAR(9), test INTEGER, delay INTEGER, createdat DATETIME, updatedat
DATETIME);
```

Next, make sure the Derby database is up and running in network mode. You may want to refer to Appendix G to get started with Derby.

```
D:\Applns\apache\Derby\db-derby-10.14.1.0-bin\bin>startNetworkServer
```

You can also use the Derby ij tool to create the database named exampledb and open a connection to an already created database using the embedded driver via the following command:

```
D:\Applns\apache\Derby\derbydb>ij
ij> connect 'jdbc:derby://localhost:1527/D:/Applns/apache/Derby/derbydb/
exampledb;create=false';
```

Note   You are using the ij tool from a base location different from your Derby installation, assuming that your database is in a location different from that of the Derby installation, which is a best practice. For further details on how to create a new database, refer to Appendix G.

Here again you will start with clean tables. Delete any tables with the names you want for your examples:

```
ij> drop table stockuser;
ij> drop table stocktx;
```

Next, create the table with the schema required for this example:

```
ij> create table stockuser (id bigint not null, amountbought double,
amountsold double, createdat timestamp not null, lastquoteat timestamp, name
varchar(255) not null, updatedat timestamp not null, primary key (id));
ij> create table stocktx (id bigint generated by default as identity,
amount float not null, buyerid bigint not null, createdat timestamp not
null, quotecreated timestamp not null, quoteid bigint not null, sellerid
bigint not null, status varchar(255) not null, stocksymbol varchar(255) not
null, test integer, updatedat timestamp, primary key (id));
ij> alter table stocktx add constraint stocktx_001 unique (quoteid);
ij> CREATE SEQUENCE hibernate_sequence START WITH 1 INCREMENT BY 1;
```

This completes the infrastructure required to build and run the example.

For this example, there are four microservices to build and get running. You will do so one by one.

Microservice 1: Quote Processing Microservice

Tweak the ActiveMQ-specific configuration in `spring-sender-mysql.xml`:

```
ch14\ch14-01\XA-TX-Resilient\Broker-MySQL-ActiveMQ\src\main\resources\
spring-sender-mysql.xml
```

```
<property name="brokerURL" value="tcp://127.0.0.1:61616"/>
```

Also, tweak the MySQL-specific configuration:

```
<bean id="xaDataSourceMySQL-01" class="com.mysql.cj.jdbc.
MysqlXADataSource">
    <property name="url">
        <value>jdbc:mysql://localhost:3306/ecom01</value>
    </property>
```

```
<property name="pinGlobalTxToPhysicalConnection">
    <value>true</value>
</property>
<property name="user"><value>root</value></property>
<property name="password"><value>rootpassword</value></property>
</bean>
```

You will now build and package the executables for the Quote Processing microservice and bring up the scheduled processor. There is a utility script in folder ch14\ch14-01\XA-TX-Resilient\Broker-MySQL-ActiveMQ\make.bat:

```
cd D:\binil\gold\pack03\ch14\ch14-01\XA-TX-Resilient\Broker-MySQL-ActiveMQ
D:\binil\gold\pack03\ch14\ch14-01\XA-TX-Resilient\Broker-MySQL-
ActiveMQ>make
D:\binil\gold\pack03\ch14\ch14-01\XA-TX-Resilient\Broker-MySQL-ActiveMQ>mvn
-Dmaven.test.skip=true clean install
```

Now, the junit test can be run by using the script provided:

```
D:\binil\gold\pack03\ch14\ch14-01\XA-TX-Resilient\Broker-MySQL-ActiveMQ>run
D:\binil\gold\pack03\ch14\ch14-01\XA-TX-Resilient\Broker-MySQL-ActiveMQ>mvn
-Dtest=BrokerServiceTest#testSubmitQuote test
```

Microservice 2: Broker Web Microservice

First, update the configuration files to suit to your environment:

ch14\ch14-01\XA-TX-Resilient\Broker-Web\src\main\resources\application.
properties

```
server.port=8080
spring.datasource.url = jdbc:mysql://localhost:3306/oauth2?autoReconnect=true
&useUnicode=true&characterEncoding=UTF-8&allowMultiQueries=true&useSSL=false
spring.datasource.username = root
spring.datasource.password = rootpassword
spring.jpa.properties.hibernate.dialect = org.hibernate.dialect.
MySQL5Dialect
spring.jpa.hibernate.ddl-auto = update
spring.freemarker.cache=false
```

I advise you not to make any changes here.

Now build and package the executables for the Broker Web microservice and bring up the server. There is a utility script in folder ch14\ch14-01\XA-TX-Resilient\Broker-Web\make.bat:

```
cd D:\binil\gold\pack03\ch14\ch14-01\XA-TX-Resilient\Broker-Web
D:\binil\gold\pack03\ch14\ch14-01\XA-TX-Resilient\Broker-Web>make
D:\binil\gold\pack03\ch14\ch14-01\XA-TX-Resilient\Broker-Web>mvn -Dmaven.
test.skip=true clean package
```

You can run the Spring Boot application in more than one way. The straightforward way is to execute the JAR file via the following commands:

```
D:\binil\gold\pack03\ch14\ch14-01\XA-TX-Resilient\Broker-Web>run
D:\binil\gold\pack03\ch14\ch14-01\XA-TX-Resilient\Broker-Web>java -jar
-Dserver.port=8080 .\target\quotes-web-1.0.0.jar
```

This will bring up the Broker Web Spring Boot Server in port 8080.

You can use a browser (preferably Chrome) and point to this URL to keep monitoring the processing of all new incoming quotes: http://localhost:8080/.

Microservice 3: Quote Settlement Microservice

Tweak the ActiveMQ-specific configuration in

```
ch13\ch13-01\XA-TX-Distributed\Settlement-ActiveMQ-Derby\src\main\
resources\spring-listener-derby.xml
```

```
<property name="brokerURL"
    value="failover:(tcp://127.0.0.1:61616)?timeout=10000"/>
```

Also, you need to tweak the Derby-specific configuration:

```
<property name="xaProperties">
    <props>
    <prop key="databaseName">D:/Applns/apache/Derby/derbydb/exampledb</prop>
    <prop key="serverName">localhost</prop>
    <prop key="portNumber">1527</prop>
    </props>
</property>
```

Now build and package the executables for the Quote Settlement microservice and bring up the message listener. There is a utility script provided the folder ch14\ch14-01\ XA-TX-Resilient\Settlement-ActiveMQ-Derby\make.bat:

```
cd D:\binil\gold\pack03\ch14\ch14-01\XA-TX-Resilient\Settlement-ActiveMQ-
Derby
D:\binil\gold\pack03\ch14\ch14-01\XA-TX-Resilient\Settlement-ActiveMQ-
Derby>make
D:\binil\gold\pack03\ch14\ch14-01\XA-TX-Resilient\Settlement-ActiveMQ-
Derby>mvn -Dmaven.test.skip=true clean install
```

Now, the junit test can be run by using the script provided:

```
D:\binil\gold\pack03\ch14\ch14-01\XA-TX-Resilient\Settlement-ActiveMQ-
Derby>run
D:\binil\gold\pack03\ch14\ch14-01\XA-TX-Resilient\Settlement-ActiveMQ-
Derby>mvn -Dtest=SettlementListenerServiceTest#testSettleQuote test
```

Microservice 4: Settlement Web Microservice

First, update the configuration files to suit to your environment:

```
ch14\ch14-01\XA-TX-Resilient\Settlement-Web\src\main\resources\application.
properties
```

```
server.port=8081
spring.datasource.url=jdbc:derby://localhost:1527/D:/Applns/apache/Derby/
derbydb/exampledb;create=false
spring.datasource.initialize=false
spring.datasource.driver-class-name=org.apache.derby.jdbc.ClientDriver
spring.jpa.properties.hibernate.dialect=org.hibernate.dialect.
DerbyTenSevenDialect
spring.freemarker.cache=false
```

I advise you not to make any changes here.

Now build and package the executables for the Settlement Web microservice and bring up the server. There is a utility script provided in folder ch13\ch13-01\XA-TX-Distributed\Settlement-Web\make.bat:

```
cd D:\binil\gold\pack03\ch14\ch14-01\XA-TX-Resilient\Settlement-Web
D:\binil\gold\pack03\ch14\ch14-01\XA-TX-Resilient\Settlement-Web>make
D:\binil\gold\pack03\ch14\ch14-01\XA-TX-Resilient\Settlement-Web>mvn
-Dmaven.test.skip=true clean package
```

You can run the Spring Boot application in more than one way. The straightforward way is to execute the JAR file via the following commands:

```
D:\binil\gold\pack03\ch14\ch14-01\XA-TX-Resilient\Settlement-Web>run
D:\binil\gold\pack03\ch14\ch14-01\XA-TX-Resilient\Settlement-Web>java -jar
-Dserver.port=8081 .\target\user-web-1.0.0.jar
```

This will bring up the Settlement Web Spring Boot Server in port 8081.

You can use a browser (preferably Chrome) and point to this URL to keep monitoring the running account status of the users and how the account balance changes as each new incoming quote is settled: `http://localhost:8081/`.

Observe that this same console will also show the new table introduced, the Transactions table.

Before you start executing any test case, you want to create two test users in the system. Take Postman and create the two test users shown:

```
http://localhost:8081/api/users
METHOD: POST; BODY: Raw JSON
```

```
{ "id" : 11, "name" : "Sam", "amountSold" : 1000.0, "amountBought" : 1000.0 }
{ "id" : 21, "name" : "Joe", "amountSold" : 5000.0, "amountBought" : 5000.0 }
```

As mentioned, the intention is to execute Test Case 4; however, to relate easily to the execution of the test cases in Chapter 13, you will execute all test cases starting from Test Case 1.

To test the first test case, take Postman and create a new quote, as shown:

```
http://localhost:8080/api/quotes
METHOD: POST; BODY: Raw JSON
```

```
{ "symbol" : "AAPL", "sellerId" : 11, "buyerId" : 21, "amount" : 100,
"test" : 1, "delay" : 2 }
```

Keep watching all three consoles. Once you make sure Test Case 1 is completed, execute the second test case by again taking Postman and creating another new quote, as shown:

```
{ "symbol" : "AMZN", "sellerId" : 11, "buyerId" : 21, "amount" : 200,
"test" : 2, "delay" : 2 }
```

Once Test Case 2 has completed fully processed, execute the third test case:

```
{ "symbol" : "GOOG", "sellerId" : 11, "buyerId" : 21, "amount" : 300,
"test" : 3, "delay" : 2 }
```

If you have followed along exactly, at the completion of Test Case 3, your consoles will look like Figure 14-11 and Figure 14-12.

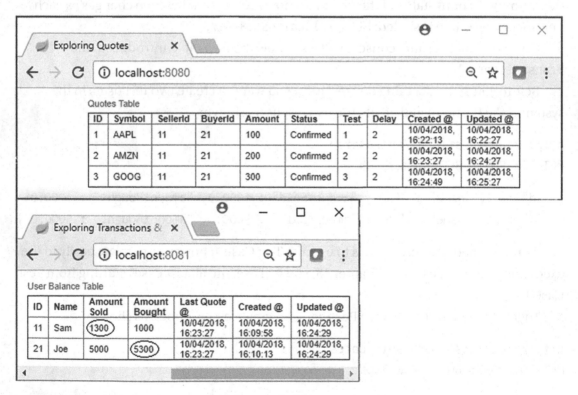

Figure 14-11. Quotes and User tables, pre-Test Case 4

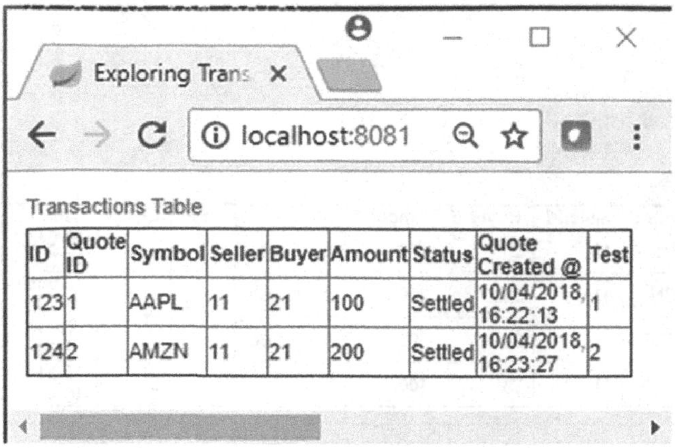

ID	Quote ID	Symbol	Seller	Buyer	Amount	Status	Quote Created @	Test
123	1	AAPL	11	21	100	Settled	10/04/2018, 16:22:13	1
124	2	AMZN	11	21	200	Settled	10/04/2018, 16:23:27	2

Figure 14-12. *Stock Transaction table, pre-Test Case 4*

You may want to note in Figure 14-12 that, even though three new quotes were processed in the upstream microservice, there are only two transactions recorded in the `Stock Transaction` table. This is because the quote message of Test Case 3 was lost upstream and never reached the downstream microservice. For the same reason, the quote amount of 300 in Test Case 3 was also not added to the buyer and seller, as shown in Figure 14-11.

Now let's execute the test case you intend to do and validate the effect of the design for resiliency. To test the Duplicate Message Being Sent test case, take Postman again and create another new quote, as shown:

```
http://localhost:8080/api/quotes
METHOD: POST; BODY: Raw JSON
```

```
{ "symbol" : "NFLX", "sellerId" : 11, "buyerId" : 21, "amount" : 400,
"test" : 4, "delay" : 2 }
```

Figure 14-13 shows the new quote for Test Case 4. It has a status of "New." When settled, the quote amount, 400, should get added to the respective running balances of the buyer and seller, as shown in Figure 14-11.

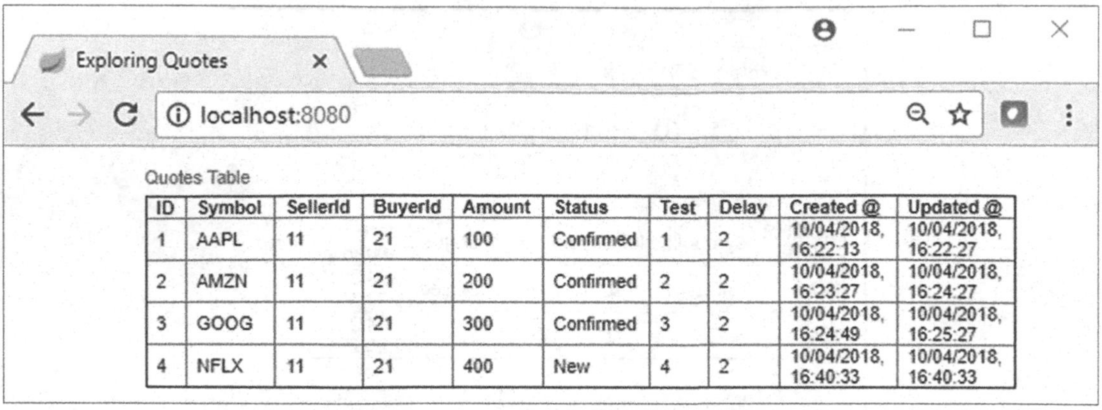

ID	Symbol	SellerId	BuyerId	Amount	Status	Test	Delay	Created @	Updated @
1	AAPL	11	21	100	Confirmed	1	2	10/04/2018, 16:22:13	10/04/2018, 16:22:27
2	AMZN	11	21	200	Confirmed	2	2	10/04/2018, 16:23:27	10/04/2018, 16:24:27
3	GOOG	11	21	300	Confirmed	3	2	10/04/2018, 16:24:49	10/04/2018, 16:25:27
4	NFLX	11	21	400	New	4	2	10/04/2018, 16:40:33	10/04/2018, 16:40:33

Figure 14-13. *Test Case 4 console, initially*

The "Test the Duplicate Message Being Sent Scenario" section in Chapter 13 may be referenced for a detailed explanation of the test scenario you are executing. Here you simulate duplicate quote messages being sent by the upstream microservice. In that section, you saw that the quote was settled twice, which is undesirable.

In the test case you execute in this section, you simulate duplicate quote messages being send by the upstream microservice. The simulation is effected by successfully sending the message and making the status update of the quote change from "New" to "Confirmed" fail. This is shown in Figure 14-14. Here, the quote amount is already added during quote settlement by the downstream microservice.

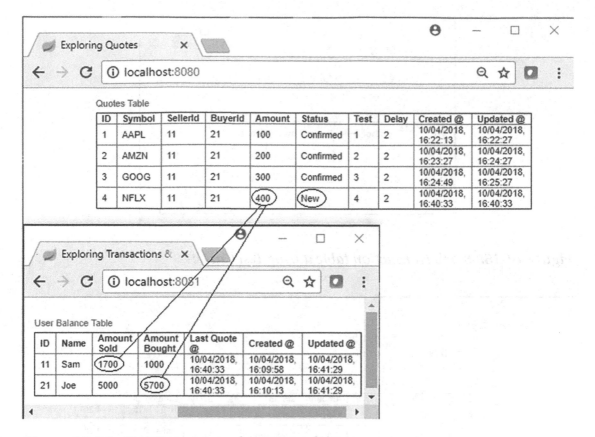

Figure 14-14. *Test Case 4 console, intermediate*

You may also view the Stock Transaction console in Figure 14-15 and see that the settlement of the quote for Test Case 4 has been recorded.

In the next pass of the Quote Processor Task of the upstream microservice, it will pick up the same quote of Test Case 4 a second time for processing. This time you also send a quote message to the downstream microservice; however, you do not simulate the error while you update the status of the quote from "New" to "Confirmed." When this quote message reaches the downstream microservice as a duplicate, due to the enhanced design of the solution, the downstream microservice is now smart enough to understand by looking in the Stock Transaction table (Figure 14-15) that this quote message is a duplicate and so it will not settle. All of this is shown in Figure 14-16.

ID	Quote ID	Symbol	Seller	Buyer	Amount	Status	Quote Created @	Test
123	1	AAPL	11	21	100	Settled	10/04/2018, 16:22:13	1
124	2	AMZN	11	21	200	Settled	10/04/2018, 16:23:27	2
125	4	NFLX	11	21	400	Settled	10/04/2018, 16:40:33	4

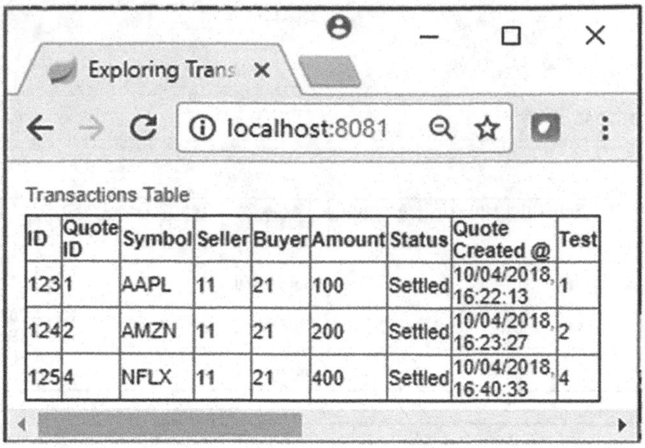

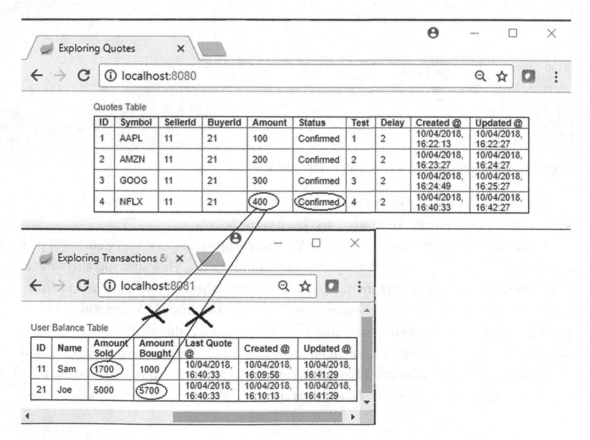

***Figure 14-15.** Stock Transaction table during Test Case 4*

ID	Symbol	SellerId	BuyerId	Amount	Status	Test	Delay	Created @	Updated @
1	AAPL	11	21	100	Confirmed	1	2	10/04/2018, 16:22:13	10/04/2018, 16:22:27
2	AMZN	11	21	200	Confirmed	2	2	10/04/2018, 16:23:27	10/04/2018, 16:24:27
3	GOOG	11	21	300	Confirmed	3	2	10/04/2018, 16:24:49	10/04/2018, 16:25:27
4	NFLX	11	21	400	Confirmed	4	2	10/04/2018, 16:40:33	10/04/2018, 16:42:27

ID	Name	Amount Sold	Amount Bought	Last Quote @	Created @	Updated @
11	Sam	1700	1000	10/04/2018, 16:40:33	10/04/2018, 16:09:58	10/04/2018, 16:41:29
21	Joe	5000	5700	10/04/2018, 16:40:33	10/04/2018, 16:10:13	10/04/2018, 16:41:29

***Figure 14-16.** Test Case 4 console at completion*

Test the Duplicate Message Consumption Scenario

To test the Duplicate Message Consumption test case, take Postman again and create another new quote, as shown (see Figure 14-17):

```
http://localhost:8080/api/quotes
METHOD: POST; BODY: Raw JSON

{ "symbol" : "TSLA", "sellerId" : 11, "buyerId" : 21, "amount" : 500,
"test" : 5, "delay" : 2 }
```

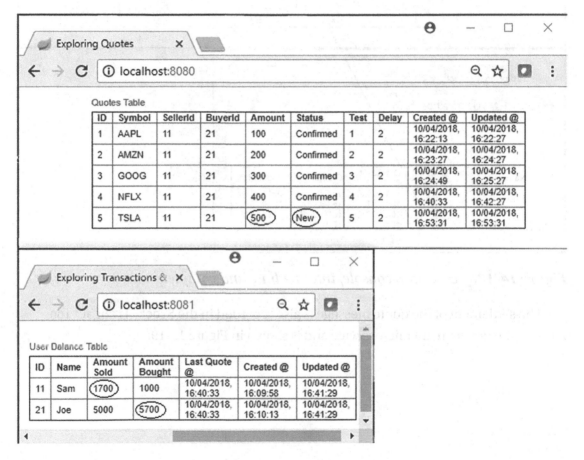

Figure 14-17. *Test Case 5 console, initially*

In this test case, all works fine in the upstream microservices. You settle the quote message at the downstream microservice and then you simulate an error in the reading of message by the downstream microservice's message listener. The state at this point is shown in Figure 14-18.

523

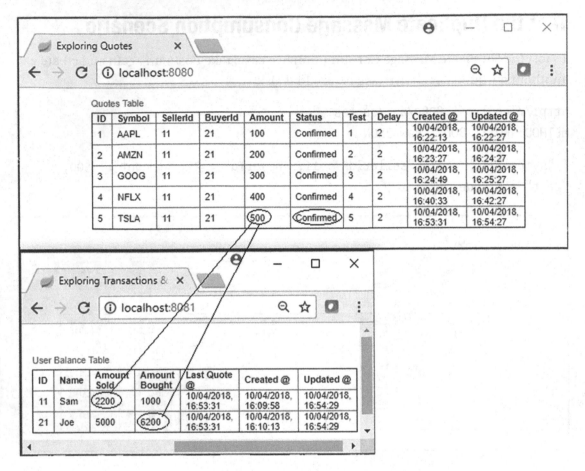

Figure 14-18. *Test Case 5 console, intermediate and complete*

The settlement of the quote message is also recorded in the Stock Transaction table by the downstream microservice and is shown in Figure 14-19.

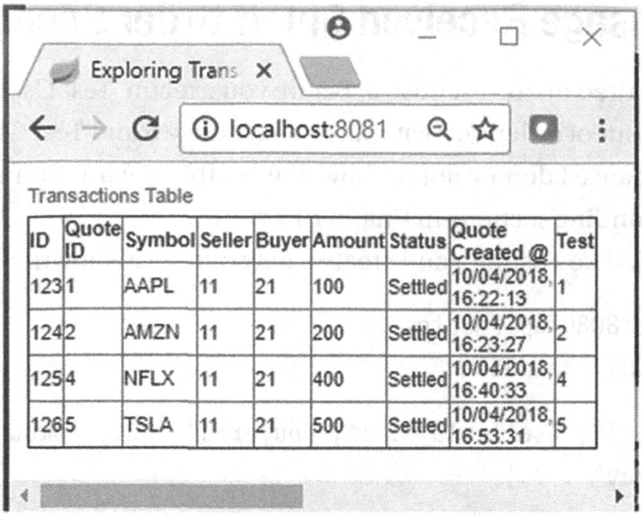

ID	Quote ID	Symbol	Seller	Buyer	Amount	Status	Quote Created @	Test
123	1	AAPL	11	21	100	Settled	10/04/2018, 16:22:13	1
124	2	AMZN	11	21	200	Settled	10/04/2018, 16:23:27	2
125	4	NFLX	11	21	400	Settled	10/04/2018, 16:40:33	4
126	5	TSLA	11	21	500	Settled	10/04/2018, 16:53:31	5

***Figure 14-19.** Stock Transaction table during Test Case 5*

Because you simulated an error in the reading of message by the downstream microservice's message listener, the message broker will redeliver the message to the downstream microservice. But when this quote message reaches the downstream microservice as a duplicate, due to the enhanced design of the solution, the downstream microservice is now smart enough to understand by looking in the `Stock Transaction` table (in Figure 14-19) that this quote message is a duplicate and will not settle again; the final state of the user balances remains as shown in Figure 14-18.

> *"If the consumer uses messages to simply write (and never overwrite) a value in a database, then receiving a message more than once is no different than receiving it exactly once".*[3]

This is true for some applications, but not for all. At the very least, it requires the application to interpret incoming messages accordingly. There are many other aspects on messaging to the above statement with respect to microservices; however, we will park them for another textbook on this, because the linked aspects are manyfold.

[3]O'Reilly, *New Designs for Streaming Architecture*

Test the Message Received Out of Order Scenario

You have now executed up to Test Case 5. Before you execute Test Case 8 to simulate a message reaching out of order, you will execute Test Case 6 and Test Case 7, but I won't explain further because I don't want to showcase anything extra from what you already saw in the corresponding sections in Chapter 13.

For Test Case 6, take Postman and create a new quote, as shown:

```
http://localhost:8080/api/quotes
METHOD: POST; BODY: Raw JSON

{ "symbol" : "MSFT", "sellerId" : 11, "buyerId" : 21, "amount" : 600,
"test" : 6, "delay" : 2 }
```

Keep watching all three consoles. Once you make sure Test Case 6 is completed, execute Test Case 7 by again taking Postman and creating another new quote, as shown:

```
{ "symbol" : "ORCL", "sellerId" : 11, "buyerId" : 21, "amount" : 700,
"test" : 7, "delay" : 2 }
```

If you have followed along exactly as directed, at the completion of Test Case 7, your consoles will look like Figure 14-20 and Figure 14-21.

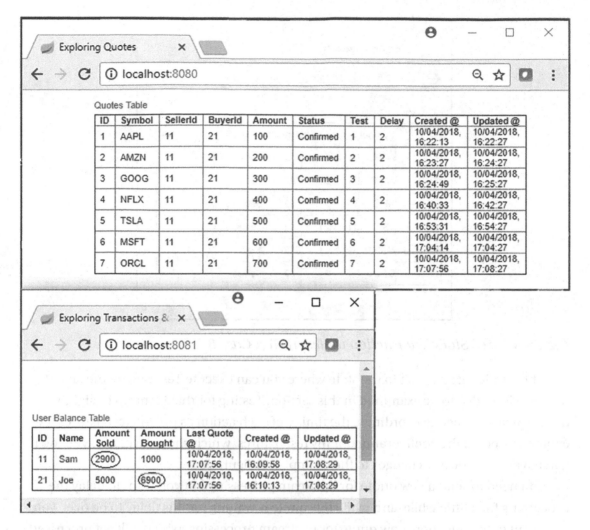

Figure 14-20. *Quotes and User table, pre-Test Case 8*

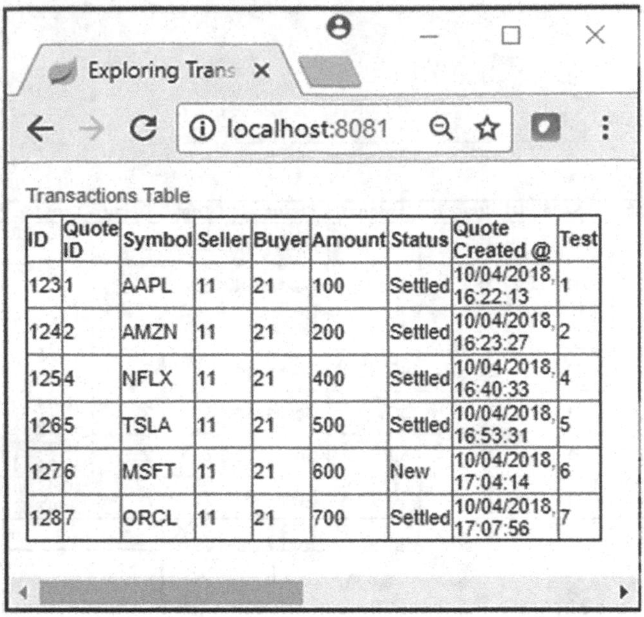

ID	Quote ID	Symbol	Seller	Buyer	Amount	Status	Quote Created @	Test
123	1	AAPL	11	21	100	Settled	10/04/2018, 16:22:13	1
124	2	AMZN	11	21	200	Settled	10/04/2018, 16:23:27	2
125	4	NFLX	11	21	400	Settled	10/04/2018, 16:40:33	4
126	5	TSLA	11	21	500	Settled	10/04/2018, 16:53:31	5
127	6	MSFT	11	21	600	New	10/04/2018, 17:04:14	6
128	7	ORCL	11	21	700	Settled	10/04/2018, 17:07:56	7

Figure 14-21. *Stock Transaction table, pre-Test Case 8*

The entities are now set to the state where you can execute Test Case 8, the actual test case intended to be examined in this section. Testing for this scenario is slightly tricky since you need to coordinate the timing of each action as per the test fixtures. I will explain based on the configuration for my test fixtures, which should work for you too if you have not made any changes to the example configurations.

You need to send a new quote for upstream processing but you want to delay the processing for a little while, and while this quote is waiting for this delay to be over, you also want to fire one more new quote for upstream processing, which will get processed nearly straight through without any delay. In this manner, the quote created later will reach the downstream system for further processing first, followed by the quote created initially. In this manner, you will simulate messages reaching out of order at the downstream system.

Before you start firing requests for this test case, read this section completely once to understand the preparations you need to make mentally so as to fire the new quotes as per instructions. Then come back to this point of explanation and continue the actual test.

Take Postman again and fire a new quote, as shown:

```
http://localhost:8080/api/quotes
METHOD: POST; BODY: Raw JSON
```

Note that you are piggybacking a delay of 90 seconds along with the test request payload, as shown in Figure 14-22.

```
{ "symbol" : "QCOM", "sellerId" : 11, "buyerId" : 21, "amount" : 800,
"test" : 8, "delay" : 90}
```

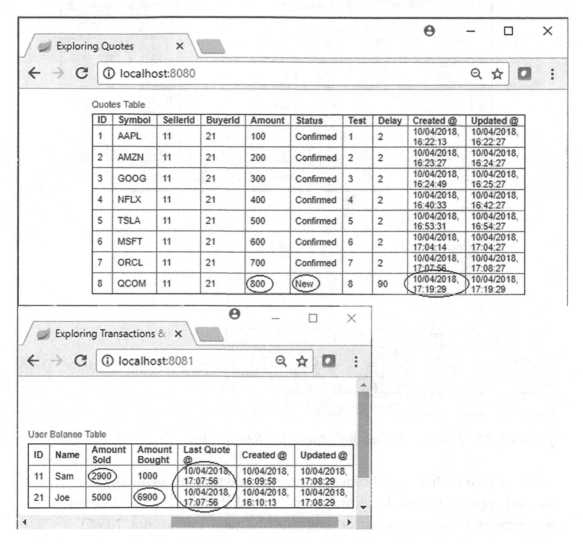

Figure 14-22. *Test Case 8 console, creating the first quote*

Keep watching the upstream microservice console (command prompt console) and when the Quote Processor Task times out, it will fetch this new quote and change the status from "New" to "Confirmed," but before completing the end-to-end transaction, it will sleep for the 90 seconds delay you have provided. See Figure 14-23.

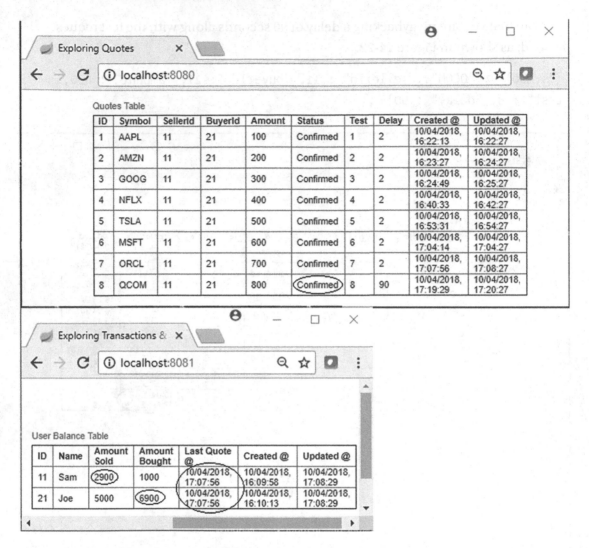

Figure 14-23. *Test Case 8 console, processing first quote*

This 90 seconds has a significance because the next time-out of the Quote Processor Task will happen in the next 60 seconds, and during that time-out it shouldn't fetch this quote because it is already in a processing state (the quote status is not "New").

Here comes the trick: as soon as (within 10 to 20 seconds) the Quote Processor Task picks up the quote for processing and further goes to sleep for the delay of 90 seconds provided, you need to fire another new quote (ideally, you have another Postman session with the data ready), like so:

```
http://localhost:8080/api/quotes
METHOD: POST; BODY: Raw JSON
```

```
{ "symbol" : "GILD", "sellerId" : 11, "buyerId" : 21, "amount" : 900,
"test" : 8, "delay" : 2 }
```

This second new quote is shown in Figure 14-24. That's all, and the steps for test execution are over.

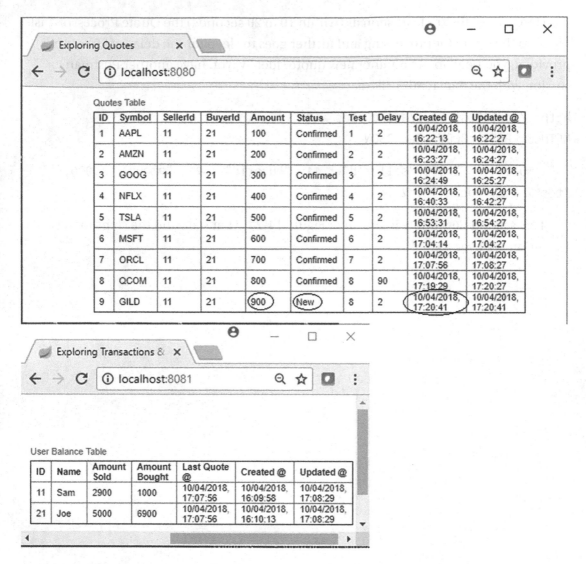

Figure 14-24. *Test Case 8 console, creating a second quote*

When the Quote Processor Task times out next, it will fetch this second new quote alone. This is because even though the first quote is still under process in the upstream system, the status of the quote has already been updated to "Confirmed," as shown in Figure 14-24. This is effected by marking the transaction of Auction Service in the upstream microservice as TX_REQUIRES_NEW.

For the second new quote, there is a negligible process delay and it comes out of the upstream processing, gets through ActiveMQ, and reaches downstream for further processing. You expect that the first quote is still in the process stage in the upstream system. This way, the message is out of order in the downstream system. This will be settled as shown in Figure 14-25.

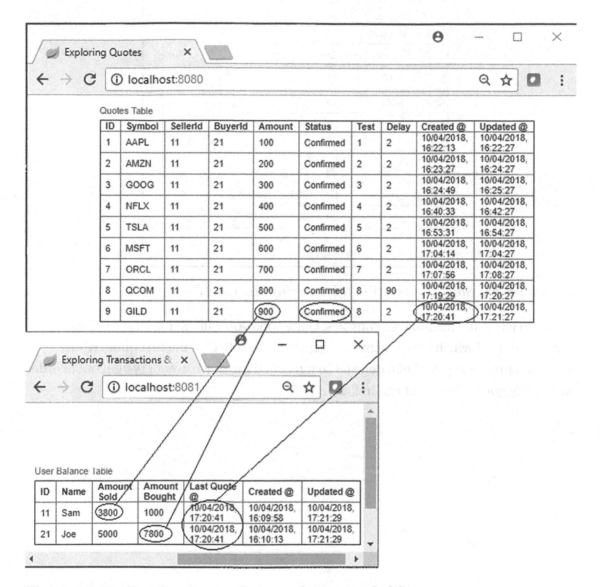

Figure 14-25. *Test Case 8 console, second quote settled first*

Figure 14-26 also asserts that the quote created second during Test Case 8 is in fact recorded in the Stock Transaction table and that the quote is in a settled state.

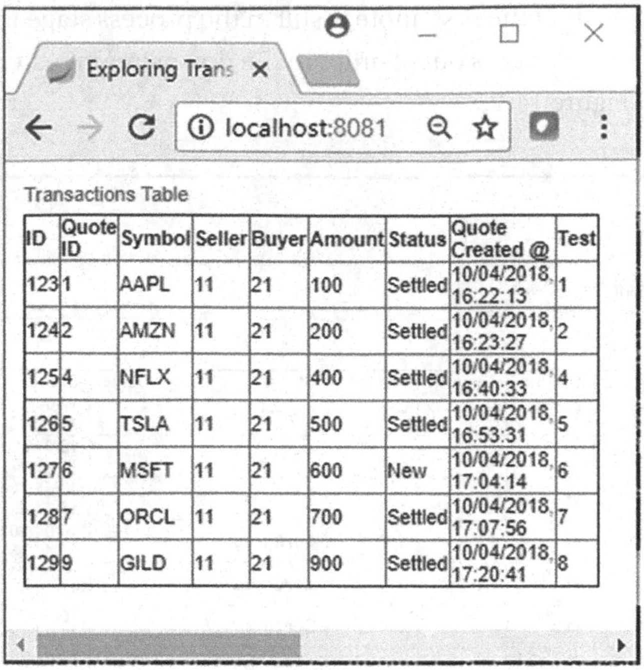

Transactions Table

ID	Quote ID	Symbol	Seller	Buyer	Amount	Status	Quote Created @	Test
123	1	AAPL	11	21	100	Settled	10/04/2018, 16:22:13	1
124	2	AMZN	11	21	200	Settled	10/04/2018, 16:23:27	2
125	4	NFLX	11	21	400	Settled	10/04/2018, 16:40:33	4
126	5	TSLA	11	21	500	Settled	10/04/2018, 16:53:31	5
127	6	MSFT	11	21	600	New	10/04/2018, 17:04:14	6
128	7	ORCL	11	21	700	Settled	10/04/2018, 17:07:56	7
129	9	GILD	11	21	900	Settled	10/04/2018, 17:20:41	8

Figure 14-26. *Stock Transaction table during Test Case 8*

Keep watching the browser consoles. Quite soon you will see the running balances of users in the downstream system change. This is the effect of the first quote whose upstream processing has been delayed so it reached the downstream system out of order and finally got settled, as shown in Figure 14-27.

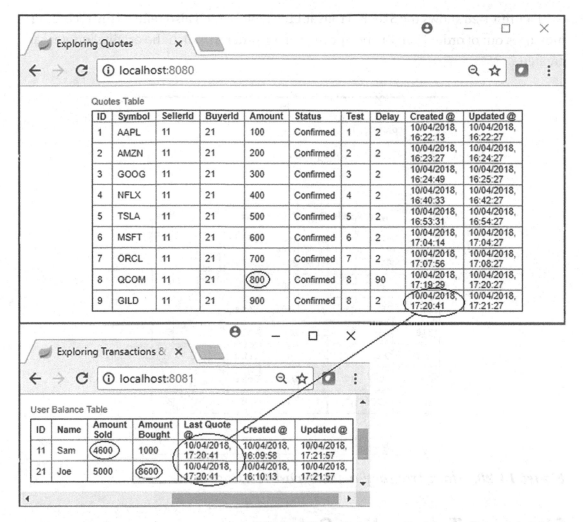

Figure 14-27. *Test Case 8 console, first quote settled as second*

In the "Build and Test the Example's Happy Flow" section in Chapter 13, you read
that the latest quote creation time in the upstream system was updated as the last quote
time whenever the user account was updated. In the demonstration here, the last quote
time of the user accounts were not changed as per the first quote created, which came
last. This is correct, but you were not able to achieve in this in Chapter 13. Due to the
enhanced design of the solution, the downstream microservice is now smart enough
to understand by looking in detail at the arrived quote messages that for messages
arriving out of order too the requirement is met. In general, regardless what transaction
paradigm you use (relaxed BASE or not) you should always add code and design to
address out-of-order messages when message ordering is important.

Figure 14-28 shows the `Stock Transaction` table, which also reflects the recording of messages out of order from the perspective of the order in which the original quote was created.

ID	Quote ID	Symbol	Seller	Buyer	Amount	Status	Quote Created @	Test
123	1	AAPL	11	21	100	Settled	10/04/2018, 16:22:13	1
124	2	AMZN	11	21	200	Settled	10/04/2018, 16:23:27	2
125	4	NFLX	11	21	400	Settled	10/04/2018, 16:40:33	4
126	5	TSLA	11	21	500	Settled	10/04/2018, 16:53:31	5
127	6	MSFT	11	21	600	New	10/04/2018, 17:04:14	6
128	7	ORCL	11	21	700	Settled	10/04/2018, 17:07:56	7
129	9	GILD	11	21	900	Settled	10/04/2018, 17:20:41	8
130	8	QCOM	11	21	800	Settled	10/04/2018, 17:19:29	8

Figure 14-28. *Stock Transaction table, post-Test Case 8*

Choosing Transaction Options

You concluded the "Global vs. Local Resource" section by justifying that if you chose Option 1 for the architecture, then when you dequeue messages from the queue for settlement by the Quotes Settlement microservice, you still have the two-phase transaction problem. If you consider quote settlement as a pure back-office process, one justification for you to still continue with the two-phase transactions is that you maximized the throughput and hence the availability of your customer-facing microservices while trading off comparatively lower responsiveness for your back-office microservices.

But what if a two-phase commit transaction is never acceptable in some parts of your microservice architecture? There are a bunch of implications associated with a two-phase commit transaction even if you justify using them for specific use cases, as discussed earlier. Here are a few of them:

- Two-phase commit transaction coordinators are single points of failure. You would require distributed and replicated logs to keep state and keep the coordinator stateless to address this.[4]

- Two-phase commit transactions are chatty in the order of two times the number of roundtrips to the resource compared to local transactions.

- Resource locks last a bit longer, which can impede scalability in some cases.

- Last but not least, two-phase commit transaction can't solve every problem. You may still need manual intervention when something goes wrong, like when you want to bring back a database from a crash. To avoid this, a form of hot failover architecture is preferred.

You need to judiciously select between two-phase and local transactions on a case-by-case basis, and this will be the case for many of the microservice architectures you develop in future. To make the scenario more specific, assume that Architecture Option 1 shown in Figure 14-7 is more acceptable than Option 2. If so, if there is a need, how can you further avoid two-phase transactions between the Quote Settlement microservice and the ActiveMQ message broker and still take care of integrity of data? Let's open this Pandora's box in the next section.

Message Queues, Peek, and Client Acknowledge

Suppose that you want to adopt the Architecture Option 1 shown in Figure 14-7 and still want to avoid two-phase commit transactions between the Quote Settlement microservice and the ActiveMQ message broker. When you avoid two-phase commit transactions, if the database operations and the message queue operations are backed up by partitioned resources, they can't be effected atomically. If they cannot be effected atomically, you don't want to encapsulate the read and read-acknowledgement of messages from the queue to happen automatically; rather, the client program or the client code should control that. The JMS specification supports two types of message

---

[4]www.atomikos.com/Documentation/LogCloud shows a new generation of coordinator.

delivery: persistent and non-persistent. Persistent messages should be used if you want messages to always be available to a message consumer after they've been delivered to the broker, even if that consumer isn't running when the message was sent. When a message is consumed and acknowledged by a message consumer, it's typically deleted from the broker's message store.

Javax.jms.Session may be specified as transacted. When transacted, session supports a single series of transactions. Each transaction groups a set of message sends and a set of message receives into an atomic unit of work. In effect, transactions organize a session's input message stream and output message stream into series of atomic units. When a transaction commits, its atomic unit of input is acknowledged and its associated atomic unit of output is sent. If a transaction rollback is done, the transaction's sent messages are destroyed and the session's input is automatically recovered.

Note   Unlike XA transactions, JMS transactions concern only on the JMS messages of a single connection. A rollback or commit does not extend beyond a single connection.

In the examples in the current chapter and in Chapter 13, you use the following configuration:

```
<bean id="jmsTemplate" class="org.springframework.jms.core.JmsTemplate">
    <property name="sessionTransacted" value="true"/>
</bean>
```

Alternatively, the SESSION_TRANSACTED value may be passed as the argument to the method `createSession(int sessionMode)` on the `Connection` object to specify that the session should use a local transaction. When used, it rolls up acknowledgments with `Session.commit()`.

```
Session session = connection.createSession(true, Session.SESSION_TRANSACTED);
```

By specifying false and AUTO_ACKNOWLEDGE, you can create a nontransacted session and the session automatically acknowledges messages. A message is automatically acknowledged when it successfully returns from the `receive()` method or the `onMessage()` method. If a failure occurs while executing the `receive()` method or the `onMessage()` method, the message is automatically redelivered. The JMS provider manages message redelivery and guarantees once-only delivery semantics. However, messages can still be lost if the application crashes right after `receive()` returns and before the message can be processed.

```
Session session = connection.createSession(false, Session.AUTO_ACKNOWLEDGE);
```

If you create the receiver's session and specify false as `createSession()`'s first argument and Session.CLIENT_ACKNOWLEDGE as its second argument, you create the Session in the client acknowledgement mode. This creates a nontransacted session and invoking the `Message` class's `acknowledge()` method explicitly is required to acknowledge the messages. By invoking `acknowledge()` on a consumed message, a client acknowledges all messages consumed by the session that the message was delivered to. A client may individually acknowledge each message as it is consumed, or it may choose to acknowledge messages as an application-defined group (which is done by calling `acknowledge()` on the last received message of the group, thereby acknowledging all messages consumed by the session). And messages that have been received but not acknowledged may be redelivered, and this is that double-edged sword: it's a blessing as well as a curse. A blessing in the sense that, if not acknowledged, you can be sure that messages will be redelivered at some later time. At the same time, it's a curse because if your application design doesn't have the mechanisms to deal with duplicate messages, it will cause duplicate processing, which will have adverse effects.

Let's look more into this aspect. See Listing 14-16.

Listing 14-16. ActiveMQ and Derby Within Two-Phase Tx

```
Start 2-Phase Transaction
    Start ActiveMQ Transaction-01
        Read Message from ActiveMQ
        Start Derby Transaction-01
            Record Quote Received in Derby
        End Derby Transaction-01
        Start Derby Transaction-02
            Reconcile User Balances in Derby
            Change Quote Status
        End Derby Transaction-02
    End ActiveMQ Transaction-01
End 2-Phase Transaction
```

The message consumption from the ActiveMQ queue and the database operations in the Derby database you saw in the downstream processing in the previous example in this chapter can be pseudo coded as shown in Listing 14-16. If you remove the two-phase transactions, the same can be rewritten as Listing 14-17.

Listing 14-17. ActiveMQ and Derby Without Two-Phase Tx

```
Read Message from ActiveMQ
Start Derby Transaction-01
    Record Quote Received in Derby
End Derby Transaction-01
Start Derby Transaction-02
    Reconcile User Balances in Derby
    Change Quote Status
End Derby Transaction-02
Acknowledge Message Read from ActiveMQ
```

This is equivalent to Listing 14-18.

Listing 14-18. ActiveMQ and Derby with Local Tx

```
Peek Message from ActiveMQ
Start Derby Transaction-01
    Record Quote Received in Derby
End Derby Transaction-01
Start Derby Transaction-02
    Reconcile User Balances in Derby
    Change Quote Status
End Derby Transaction-02
Remove Message from ActiveMQ
```

The pseudocode in Listing 14-18 depends upon the capability of peeking at a message in the queue without removing it and removing the messages from the queue once successfully processed. This can be done with two or more independent transactions if necessary, as shown in the pseudocode: one on the message queue, another one on the user database to record the quote message, and a third one to reconcile the user balances and change the quote status. User balance reconciliation and quote status change are committed atomically; however, no two-phase transactions are required since both operations happen in the same local resource. Queue operations are not committed unless database operations successfully commit. A partial failure during the database operations will keep the queue operation uncommitted so that the message is redelivered sooner or later and processing starts over again. The algorithm now supports partial failures and still provides transactional guarantees. This algorithm or method is one attempt to implement eventual consistency between distributed microservices without the use of distributed and two-phase commit transactions. The example code provided here can be enhanced to implement multiple variants of the above methodology; this is left as an exercise for you to get your hands wet with the code. Note that this requires an implementation of the "idempotent consumer pattern," which is hard to do correctly.[5] Additional testing is required, beyond the basic exploratory test cases in this chapter, so that every possible failure mode is taken into account

Summary

Just like many of my colleagues, I too loved transactions. I have been using declarative transaction management since 1999 where we were thrilled to be among the first few to download the *Sun's Reference Implementation of J2EE Server with EJB[6] (Enterprise Java Beans) Containers* in the process of implementing an expert system for optimizing operations of an airline passenger reservation system for a European airline. It's been 20 years since then, and we still love transactions, both local and distributed. However, the point is that the choice between distributed and local transactions has to be done on a case-by-case basis based on the context, functionality, and criticality of the microservice involved. Designing systems leveraging distributed transaction managers in cases where you don't mandatorily need them will be costly since it may increase the operations cost as well as slightly affect the performance. You saw a few techniques in this chapter that you can use to design fault-tolerant microservices that must be eventually consistent, although I did not address all possible anomalies. In the next chapter, you will extend this learning to look at few other scenarios including but not limited to long-running transactions.

---

[5]`www.atomikos.com/Blog/IdempotentJmsConsumerPitfalls`

[6]The EJB specification was originally developed in 1997 by IBM and later adopted by Sun Microsystems (EJB 1.0 and 1.1) in 1999 and enhanced under the Java Community Process as JSR 19 (EJB 2.0), JSR 153 (EJB 2.1), JSR 220 (EJB 3.0), JSR 318 (EJB 3.1) and JSR 345 (EJB 3.2).

CHAPTER 15

Transactions Optimized for Microservices

While Chapter 13 covered distributed transactions with working code, you relooked at those examples with an enhanced design in Chapter 14 with an aim to understand the nitty-gritty details and concerns while architecting solutions for BASE transactional support. So far, so good, but the question is whether there is a way to abstract the details you saw in those two chapters and still attain the required level of data consistency in a microservices architecture. You will look at this in detail in this chapter. The examples in this chapter are not a continuation of the examples you covered in Chapters 13 and 14, so you can skip those two chapters if you are in a hurry to understand the examples in this chapter. However, you are going to leverage Axon framework again in this chapter, so you are strongly advised to go through Chapter 12 first to get an introduction to Axon so that you know the programming paradigm during this discussion.

You will be looking into the following in this chapter:

- An introduction to saga

- Distributed saga and microservices

- A complete saga example using Axon 2

Saga for Microservices Transactions

The section titled "Transaction Models" in Chapter 13 introduced the concept of saga, and in this section you will look at saga in detail.

© Binildas Christudas 2019
B. Christudas, *Practical Microservices Architectural Patterns*, https://doi.org/10.1007/978-1-4842-4501-9_15

Saga Explained

The concept of saga was first introduced in a paper in 1987, and the concept gained traction in the context of microservices. Sagas are similar to nested transactions. In a nested transaction, atomic transactions are embedded in other transactions. In sagas, each of these transactions has a corresponding compensating transaction. If any of the transactions in a saga fails, the compensating transactions for each transaction that was successfully run previously will be invoked so as to nullify the effect of previously successful transactions.

Sagas are typically used for modelling long-lived transactions like those involved in workflows. It is not advisable to use two-phase transactions to control long-lived transactions since the locking of resources for prolonged durations is not at all advisable. In the context of microservices, sagas become relevant even when long-lived transactions are not involved due to the reason why you want to say NO to two-phase commit transactions. When two-phase commit transactions can't be used and when you still want to exercise control at each stage of a multi-step transaction, sagas will help you.

Even before the evolution of microservices, the concept of saga was very popular, and in the truest sense many real-world problems have been addressed using sagas. Maintaining consistency across location and/or trust boundaries can't easily be handled using the classic ACID model and many real-world scenarios involve these complexities. A transfer of money from an account in one bank to another account in another bank is a classic example where there is no reason to assume that the software systems of these banks are near or together. And you can relate to this from your daily experience when you do such fund transfers. Even if a money transfer happens near real time so that it appears to be instantaneous in every aspect, most probably the involved transactions were not carried out in a two-phase commit transaction, but instead in some kind of saga. This means, when you do a fund transfer, the associated debit and credit in most cases will happen as two correlated steps, coordinated by some means other than a two-phase transaction coordinator so that all the involved steps will either happen or all the involved steps will be rolled back eventually.

Another classical example is when you book a flight, hotel, and rental cab. It's very unlikely that a single enterprise owns inventory for all these resources, but it's highly likely that end user wants to book one or more of these resources in a single transaction, because a confirmed hotel booking with a non-confirmed flight booking is not very useful for him. Another aspect here is that, if you look at the resource managers or the resource owners in such cases, they may fall outside trust boundaries, and in many cases they might be competing enterprises. My current firm is involved in building software systems for the travel and hospitality industry, and I can relate to many instances in our software design where similar transactions can and will only be designed to be eventually consistent.

Figure 15-1 illustrates a state diagram representing how individual transactions will progress, stage by stage, within a saga.

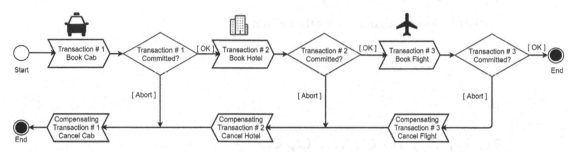

Figure 15-1. *State diagram illustrating saga*

As shown in Figure 15-1, in saga, if one of the transactions fails, the compensating transactions for each of the transactions that successfully ran will be executed. This is coordinated by the saga transaction coordinator.

Distributed Saga

The concept of saga as described in the previous section is rather trivial to build, since many of the workflow and Business Process Model and Notation (BPMN) frameworks are built using the same analogy where you want to orchestrate long-running transactions. If you want to coordinate the same in a microservices environment, this involves coordinating multiple decentralized nodes and processes, which is non-trivial.

You will first look at the various components needed for a distributed saga at the conceptual level. See Figure 15-2.

- Transactions and compensation transactions:

    A saga transaction in a microservices context is better called a request (HTTP) or an event (commands and events); however, for the simplicity of our discussion, we will retain the term transactions.

A distributed saga is a collection of transactions:

T1, T2, ..., Tn

Each transaction has a compensating transaction:

C1, C2, ..., Cn

A compensating transaction (Cn) will semantically undo a previously completed corresponding transaction (Tn).

A distributed saga guarantees that either

T1, T2, ..., Tn

or

T1, T2, ..., Ti, Ci, ..., C2, C1

happens so that, as shown in Figure 15-1, if one of the transactions fails, the compensating transactions for each of the transactions that successfully ran will be executed.

- The saga log:

  The saga log is a distributed log that's used to persist the state of every transaction/operation during the execution of a given saga. The saga log contains various state-changing operations, such as begin saga, end saga, abort saga, begin Ti, end Ti, begin Ci, and end Ci. The saga log is often implemented using a distributed log, and systems such as Kafka are commonly used for the implementation.

- The saga execution coordinator (SEC):

  The SEC orchestrates the entire logic and is responsible for the execution of the saga. All of the steps in a given saga are recorded in the saga log and the SEC writes to and reads from and interprets the records of the saga log. A SEC has the following subcomponents:

  - Control bus: A control bus effectively administers a messaging system that is distributed across multiple nodes and processes.

  - Process manager: A process manager maintains the state of the sequence and determine the next processing step based on intermediate results.

  - Message correlation: The sender correlates the response it received to the request it sent originally. The MessageID and CorrelationID properties of the message are used to correlate the request and response messages. Thus a correlation identifier is a unique identifier that indicates which request message this reply is for.

  - Message sequence: This is required to retain the order of the messages send as per original intention.

  - Guaranteed delivery: With guaranteed delivery, the system uses built-in data stores to persist messages. Each node the messaging system is installed on has its own data store so that the messages can be stored locally. When the sender sends a message, the send operation does not complete successfully until the message is safely stored in the sender's data store. Subsequently, the message is not deleted from one data store until it is successfully forwarded to and stored in the next data store. In this way, once the sender successfully sends the message, it is always stored on disk on at least one computer until it is successfully delivered to and acknowledged by the receiver.

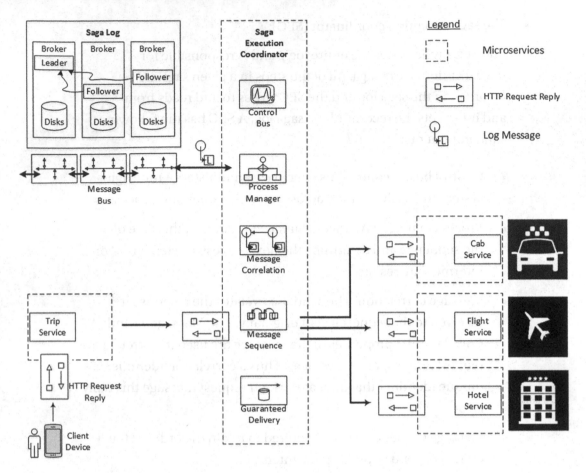

Figure 15-2. *Distributed saga, illustrated*

The SEC is not a special process that has central control of the entire execution. It operates as a centralized runtime, but the runtime is dumb and the execution logic is kept out of the SEC in the distributed saga log. So when an SEC crashes, another SEC instance could be brought live and continue by looking at the saga log. It is required to make sure that SEC is up and running all the time. In the event of an SEC failure, a new SEC process should be started based on the same distributed saga log. The distributed saga log is also distributed and replicated so that there is no single point of data loss.

Having looked at the various components needed for a distributed saga, you will now look at how a distributed saga executes. See Figure 15-3.

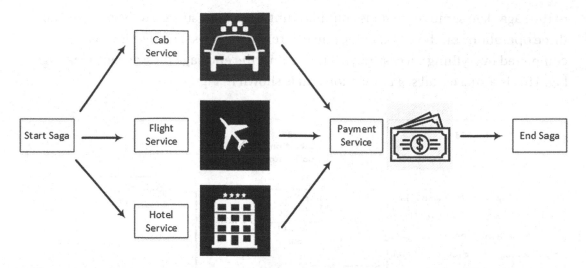

Figure 15-3. Distributed saga as a directed acyclic graph

A distributed saga is a directed acyclic graph (DAG) and the SEC's task is to execute that DAG. A directed acyclic graph is a finite directed graph[1] with no directed cycles. That is, it consists of finitely many vertices and edges (also called arcs), with each edge directed from one vertex to another, such that there is no way to start at any vertex (v) and follow a consistently-directed sequence of edges that eventually loop back to v again. Equivalently, a DAG is a directed graph that has a topological ordering, a sequence of the vertices such that every edge is directed from earlier to later in the sequence.

Referring to Figure 15-2, once the trip service gets a booking request, SEC initiates a saga by writing to the saga log with a start saga instruction along with any other metadata required to process the saga. Once the record is durably committed into the log, SEC can move to executing the next instruction. Then, based on the DAG of the saga in Figure 15-3, SEC can pick one of the flight, hotel, or cab rental transactions (given that all three can work in parallel). Suppose that the flight transaction is executed first. In that case, the SEC logs a start flight transaction message to the saga log. Then, the SEC executes the book flight operation. Once the SEC receives the response from the flight service, it commits the end flight transaction message along with the response from the flight service, which you may need during the latter part

---

[1]A directed graph (or digraph) is a graph that is made up of a set of vertices connected by edges, where the edges have a direction associated with them.

of the saga. The same set of steps continues until you have successfully executed all three operations on the flight, hotel, and cab rental services. Finally, since you have completed everything successfully, SEC commits the end saga message into the saga log. This is a successful saga execution and is shown in Figure 15-4.

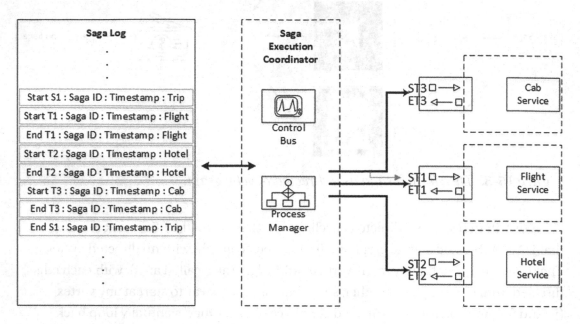

Legend

ST: Start Transaction   ET: End Transaction

Figure 15-4. *Execution steps of a successful distributed saga*

Figure 15-5 shows a saga failure case.

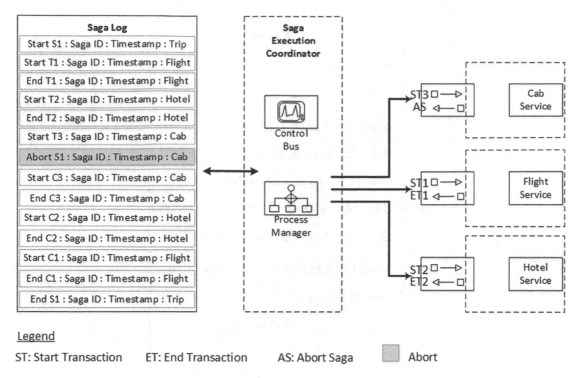

Legend

ST: Start Transaction   ET: End Transaction   AS: Abort Saga   ▨ Abort

Figure 15-5. *Execution steps of a failed distributed saga*

It's the same set of steps as discussed earlier, but in this case, the cab rental process fails (there are no cabs available on the specified dates, for example). Since you have detected a failure of a particular subtransaction (i.e., the cab booking), you need to roll back all the other subtransaction you made so far. So, in the saga log you can find the start cab rental log (Start T3) but now the cab booking has failed. Now you have to walk through the inverted DAG of saga that you executed so far and end the saga as unsuccessful.

You will now look at some interesting aspects of a distributed saga. We discussed earlier that SEC can pick one of the flight, hotel, or cab rental transactions (given that all three can work in parallel). This means saga transactions may be executed in parallel, and saga logs might be interleaved, as shown in Figure 15-6.

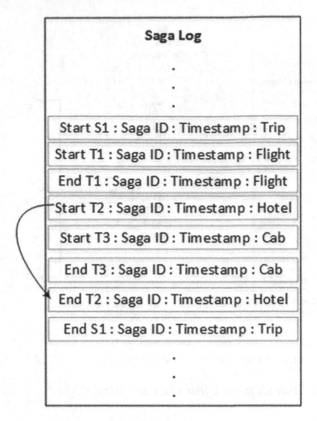

Figure 15-6. *Distributed saga executing transactions in parallel*

This means the SEC shouldn't depend on the order of individual log entries in the saga log. You should relook at the discussion in the "Test the Message Received Out of Order Scenario" section in Chapter 14 where you saw the technique to deal with such scenarios.

Next, for every transaction in a distributed saga the messaging semantics should be as follows:

- Transactions: At most once

- Compensating transactions: At least once

You should now revisit the sections titled "Build and Test the Duplicate Message Being Sent Scenario" and "Test the Duplicate Message Consumption Scenario" in Chapter 14. By suitably combining the techniques described in those two sections, you can conceptualize how the "at most once" and "at least once" semantics can be tailored into the overall solution. Using the same techniques, you should also take care of the extra characteristics required for the transactions of a distributed saga as listed in Table 15-1.

Table 15-1. *Distributed Saga Transaction Characteristics*

Characteristics	Transaction (T)	Compensating Transaction (C)
Idempotent	a	a
Can Abort	a	×
Commutative	NA	a

A little discussion needs to take place about the commutative characteristic required for compensating transactions described in Table 15-1. Refer to Figure 15-7.

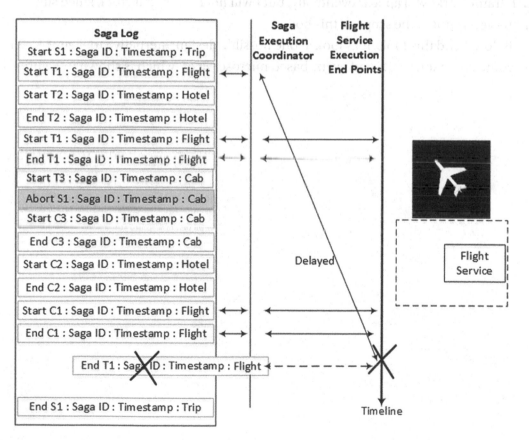

Figure 15-7. *Message delays in distributed saga*

There are two Start T1 transactions. This is because the SEC can replay Start T1 if it didn't receive it and End T1 within a defined timeout. Such a delayed Start T1 might reach the service to be executed after a compensating transaction (Start C1, End C1) was successfully effected, in which case the Start T1, which reached later, shouldn't be attempted to be executed. So semantically

```
T1 -> C1
```

or

```
C1 -> T1
```

Both should have the same effect.

There are more such complexities, but you should have the hang of it by now. Ideally a framework should abstract all these complexities for you. Even though as of this writing I couldn't find a complete framework to execute our earlier discussion, I hope such frameworks will appear eventually, but I will not discuss it further, since such a discussion is not in the scope of this book.

Before I end this topic, let's look at one possible design alternative to Figure 15-2 in the context of Axon CQRS and event-based microservices, which is shown in Figure 15-8.

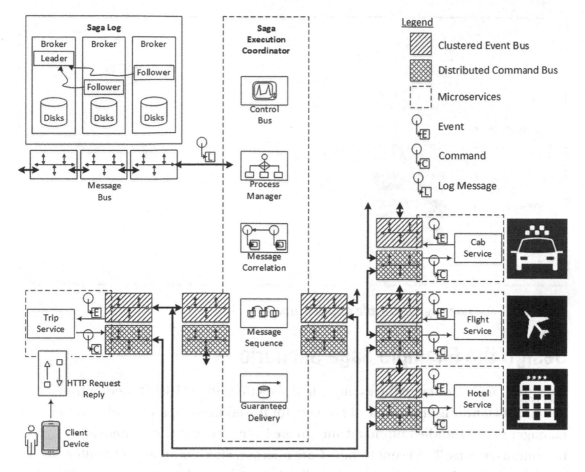

***Figure 15-8.** Distributed saga in an event-driven CQRS context, illustrated*

Be informed that the design shown in Figure 15-8 is just for illustrative purposes, and you will see in the next section that Axon CQRS has a comparable saga implementation, not necessarily the exact as per the design shown.

Saga Example Code Using Axon

You are going to extend the example code from in Chapter 12, which is a portion of an e-commerce application. There are two entities in your domain, the order and the product. Users can buy a product, which will create a new order. When a new order is created, the status of the order will be in a "New" state and the product stock will get depreciated. Creating a new order will also make an entry to the Audit table. The example application is shown in Figure 15-9.

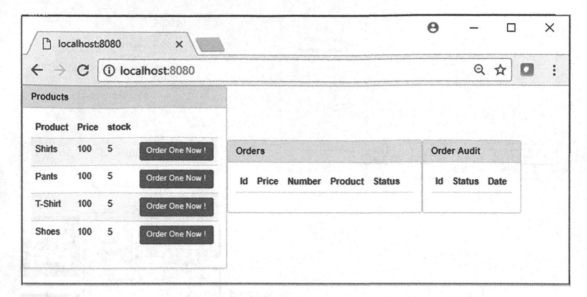

Figure 15-9.   *The saga example application*

Design the Example Saga Scenario

This example is similar to the example in the section titled "Distributed Command and Event Handling" in Chapter 12, except for the addition of a saga transaction manager in the Handle Command and Create Event microservice. There are five microservices. The Event Handle Core microservice has an event handler, OrderEventHandler, and the Event Handler Audit microservice has an event handler, AuditEventHandler. Both are subscribed to the order created event. So, you have two microservices (the Event Handler Audit microservice and the Event Handle Core microservice) with two event handler types, both interested in the same order created event. Also, the Handle Command and Create Event microservice has a saga, OrderProcessSaga, which is also interested in the order created event. Figure 15-10 shows the design.

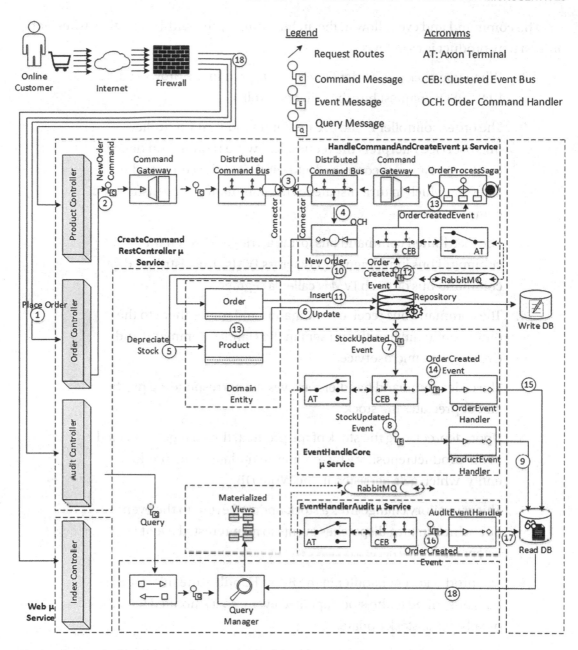

Figure 15-10. *Start saga for a new order*

The command and event flow in the architecture for the end-to-end flow when you order a new product is as follows:

1. When you click the "Order One Now!" button in the browser, a REST/JSON request hits the order controller.

2. The order controller in the Create Command Rest Controller microservice interprets the request as a write request and hence creates a new order command and sends it to the command gateway, which in turn dispatches the command to the distributed command bus.

3. The distributed command bus forms a bridge between the command bus implementations across JVMs. The distributed command bus on each JVM is called a segment.

4. The command bus receives commands and routes them to the order command handler present in the Handle Command and Create Event microservice.

5. The order command handler retrieves the corresponding product and depreciates the stock.

6. Upon depreciating the stock of the product, the change is effected in the product repository by sending an update to the product entity, which gets persisted in the Write DB.

7. This repository change fires a stock updated event to the event bus, which in turn dispatches events to all interested event listeners.

8. The product event handler in the Event Handle Core microservice has subscribed to the stock updated event, so it's notified with the details of the stock update.

9. Based on the details mentioned in the stock updated event, the product event handler makes changes to the read model of the product.

10. In step 5, the order command handler depreciates the product stock. It also creates a new order, based on the details mentioned in the new order command it received.

11. When a new order is created, it is effected in the order repository by sending an insert of a new order entity, which subsequently gets persisted in the Write DB, with the status of the new order as "New," as shown in Figure 15-11.

12. This repository insert fires an order created event to the event bus, which in turn dispatches events to all interested event listeners. There are two interested event listeners in two foreign microservices, the Event Handle Core microservice and the Event Handler Audit microservice. Further, the order process saga is also interested in the order created event.

13. The order process saga on receiving the order created event starts a new saga.

14. The order event handler in the Event Handle Core microservice has subscribed to the order created event so it's notified with the details of the new order created.

15. Based on the details mentioned in the order created event, the order event handler makes changes to the read model of the order, inserting a new row in this case.

16. The audit event handler in the Event Handler Audit microservice has also subscribed to the order created event, so it's notified with the details of the new order created.

17. Based on the details mentioned in the order created event, the audit event handler makes a new entry to the read model of the audit.

18. The browser can refresh itself to keep the view updated from querying the read model of the entities.

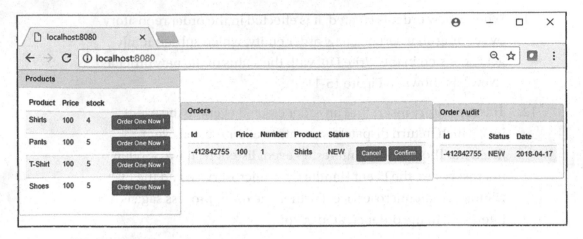

Figure 15-11. *New order created*

Event handling in a saga event handler is similar to that of a regular event listener, as you saw in Listing 12-11 in Chapter 12. The same rules for method and parameter resolution apply here too; however, there is one difference. While there is a single instance of an event listener that deals with all incoming events, multiple instances of a saga may exist, each interested in events targeted to a saga of different entity instances. To make it clear, a saga that manages a transaction around an order with an ID of x will not be interested in events targeted to an order with an ID of y, and vice versa.

The new saga started earlier will exist in memory backed up with persistence. As shown in Figure 15-11, the order workflow can progress from "New" to either "Cancelled" or "Confirmed." You will look into them separately.

First, you will look at the saga transitioning from status "New" to "End" as a result of confirming the order. See Figure 15-12.

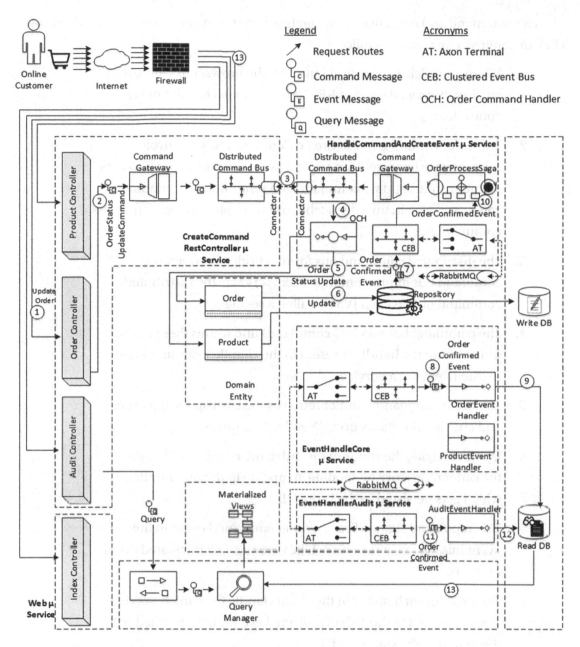

Figure 15-12. *End saga after order confirmation*

The command and event flow in the architecture for the end-to-end flow when you click to confirm a new order as follows:

1. When you click the Confirm button in the browser to confirm an already created order, a REST/JSON request hits the order controller.

2. The order controller in the Create Command Rest Controller microservice interprets the request as a write request and creates an order status update command and sends it to the command gateway, which in turn dispatches the command to the distributed command bus.

3. The distributed command bus forms a bridge between the command bus implementations across JVMs. The distributed command bus on each JVM is called a segment.

4. The command bus receives commands and routes them to the order command handler present in the Handle Command and Create Event microservice.

5. The order command handler retrieves the corresponding order and changes the status from "New" to "Confirmed."

6. Upon changing the status of the order, the change is effected in the order repository by sending an update to the order entity, which gets persisted in the Write DB.

7. This repository change fires an order confirmed event to the event bus, which in turn dispatches events to all interested event listeners.

8. The order event handler in the Event Handle Core microservice has subscribed to the order confirmed event, so it's notified with the details of the status update.

9. Based on the details mentioned in the order confirmed event, the order event handler makes changes to the read model of the order.

10.   As mentioned, the saga is also interested in the order confirmed event. On receiving the order confirmed event, the saga is transitioned to the "End Saga" state.

11.   The audit event handler in the Event Handler Audit microservice has also subscribed to the order confirmed event, so it's also notified with the details of the new order created.

12.   Based on the details mentioned in the order confirmed event, the audit event handler will make a new entry to the read model of the audit.

13.   The browser can refresh itself to keep the view updated from querying the read model of the entities

Lastly, you will look at the saga transitioning from status "New" to "End" as a result of cancelling an already created order. See Figure 15-13.

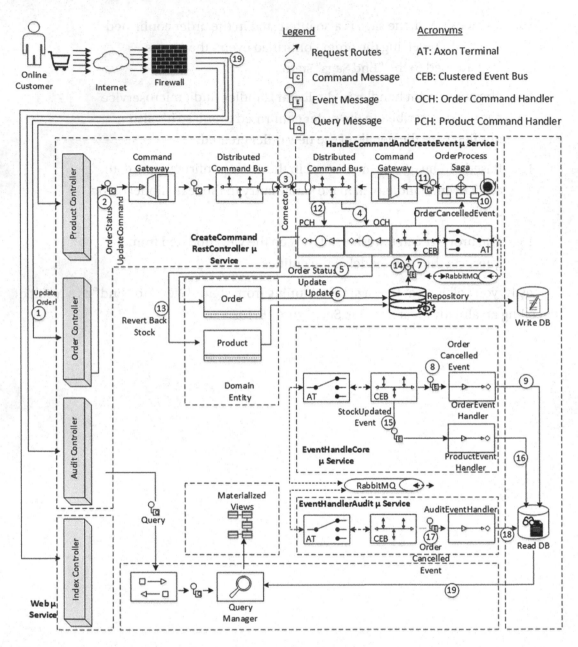

Figure 15-13. *End saga after order cancellation*

The command and event flow in the architecture for the end-to-end flow when you click to cancel an already created order is as follows:

1. When you click the Cancel button in the browser to cancel an already created order, a REST/JSON request hits the order controller.

2. The order controller in the Create Command Rest Controller microservice interprets the request as a write request and creates an order status update command and sends it to the command gateway, which in turn dispatches the command to the distributed command bus.

3. The distributed command bus forms a bridge between the command bus implementations across JVMs. The distributed command bus on each JVM is called a segment.

4. The command bus receives commands and routes them to the order command handler present in the Handle Command and Create Event microservice.

5. The order command handler retrieves the corresponding order and changes the status of the order from "New" to "Cancelled."

6. Upon changing the status of the order, the change is effected in the order repository by sending an update to the order entity, which gets persisted in the Write DB.

7. This repository change will fire an order cancelled event to the event bus, which in turn dispatches events to all interested event listeners.

8. The order event handler in the Event Handle Core microservice has subscribed to order cancelled event, so it's notified with the details of the status update.

9. Based on the details mentioned in the order cancelled event, the order event handler will make changes to the read model of the order.

10.   As mentioned earlier, the saga is also interested in the order cancelled event. On receiving the order cancelled event, the saga is transitioned to the "End Saga" state.

11.   The saga while transitioning to the end state as a result of cancelling an order will also spit out a new product stock revert command to the distributed command bus.

12.   The product command handler in Handle Command and Create Event microservice retrieves the corresponding product and reverts the stock count by the number of items ordered in the cancelled order.

13.   Upon reverting back the stock of the product, the change is effected in the product repository by sending an update to the product entity, which gets persisted in the Write DB.

14.   This repository change will fire a stock updated event to the event bus, which in turn dispatches events to all interested event listeners.

15.   The product event handler in the Event Handle Core microservice has subscribed to the stock updated event, so it's notified with the details of the stock update.

16.   Based on the details mentioned in the stock updated event, the product event handler will make changes to the read model of the product.

17.   The audit event handler in the Event Handler Audit microservice has also subscribed to the order cancelled event, so its's notified with the details of the order cancelled.

18.   Based on the details mentioned in the order cancelled event, the audit event handler will make a new entry to the read model of the audit.

19.   The browser can refresh itself to keep the view updated from querying the read model of the entities.

Code the Example Saga Scenario

The complete code required to demonstrate the simple Axon example is in ch15\
ch15-01. Since this example is an extension of the example in the "Distributed
Command and Event Handling" section in Chapter 12, I will explain only the newly
added or changed code, so refer back to that section to get the explanation of the rest
of the code. There are five microservices to be coded, and you will look into them one
by one.

Microservice 1: 01-Ecom-web

This microservice is a typical Spring Boot web application without any Axon
components, so I will not discuss it further.

Microservice 2: 02-Ecom-CreateCommandRestController

You will start with the order controller, which handles the HTTP requests to create a new
order and to confirm or cancel the order. See Listing 15-1.

Listing 15-1. Order Controller (ch15\ch15-01\Ax2-Saga\02-Ecom-Create
CommandRestController\src\main\java\com\acme\ecom\web\controller\
OrderController.java)

```
@RestController
public class OrderController {

    @Autowired
    private DataSource dataSource;

    @Autowired
    @Qualifier("distributedCommandGateway")
    private CommandGateway commandGateway;

    @RequestMapping(value = "/orders", method = RequestMethod.GET,
            produces = { MediaType.APPLICATION_JSON_VALUE })
    public ResponseEntity<List<OrderDTO>> getAllOrders() {
```

```
    JdbcTemplate jdbcTemplate = new JdbcTemplate(dataSource);
    List<OrderDTO> queryResult = jdbcTemplate.query(
        "SELECT * from ecom_order_view order by id", (rs, rowNum) ->
        {return new OrderDTO(rs.getInt("id"), rs.getDouble("price"),
        rs.getInt("number"), rs.getString("description"),
        rs.getString("status"));
    });
    return new ResponseEntity<>(queryResult, HttpStatus.OK);
}

@RequestMapping(value = "/orders", method = RequestMethod.POST)
@Transactional
public ResponseEntity<Void> addNewOrder(@RequestBody OrderDTO orderDTO)
{
    commandGateway.sendAndWait(new NewOrderCommand(orderDTO.getPrice(),
    orderDTO.getNumber(), orderDTO.getProductId()));
    return new ResponseEntity<>( HttpStatus.OK);
}

@RequestMapping(value = "/orders", method = RequestMethod.PUT)
@Transactional
public ResponseEntity<Void> updateOrder(@RequestBody
OrderStatusUpdateDTO
        orderStatusUpdateDTO) {

    commandGateway.sendAndWait(
        new OrderStatusUpdateCommand(orderStatusUpdateDTO.getOrderId(),
        orderStatusUpdateDTO.getOrderStatus()));
    return new ResponseEntity<>( HttpStatus.OK);
}
}
```

The main methods of interest are

- addNewOrder: This is a HTTP POST method that creates a new order.
  As a result, it also sends a new order command to the distributed
  command bus.

- updateOrder: This HTTP PUT method handles both confirmation and cancellation of orders. An order status update command is triggered to handle updates to the order status.

The other main classes are `ProductController` and `OrderAuditController`; both are simple REST controllers providing a view for the respective view models.

Microservice 3: 03-Ecom-HandleCommandAndCreateEvent

This microservice has to handle any commands created by the 02-Ecom-CreateCommandRestController microservice and reaching through the distributed command bus from the remote JVM. Further, this microservice also creates events, which are supposed to be consumed by distributed event handlers in remote JVMs or foreign microservices. Listing 15-2 shows the order command handler first.

Listing 15-2. Order Command Handler (ch15\ch15-01\Ax2-Saga\03-Ecom-HandleCommandAndCreateEvent\src\main\java\com\acme\ecom\order\commandhandler\OrderCommandHandler.java)

```
@Component
public class OrderCommandHandler {

    @Autowired
    @Qualifier("orderRepository")
    private Repository<Order> orderRepository;

    @Autowired
    @Qualifier("productRepository")
    private Repository<Product> productRepository;

    @CommandHandler
    public void handleNewOrder(NewOrderCommand newOrderCommand){

        Product product =
            productRepository.load(newOrderCommand.getProductId());
        product.depreciateStock(newOrderCommand.getNumber());
        Integer id = new Random().nextInt();
```

```
        Order order = new Order(id, newOrderCommand.getPrice(),
            newOrderCommand.getNumber(), OrderStatusEnum.NEW, product);
        orderRepository.add(order);
        newOrderCommand.getNumber(), product.getId()});
    }

    @CommandHandler
    public void handleUpdateOrder(
            OrderStatusUpdateCommand orderStatusUpdateCommand){

        Order order =
            orderRepository.load(orderStatusUpdateCommand.getOrderId());
        order.updateOrderStatus(orderStatusUpdateCommand.getOrderStatus());
        orderStatusUpdateCommand.getOrderStatus()});
    }
}
```

Next, Listing 15-3 shows the product command handler.

Listing 15-3. Product Command Handler (ch15\ch15-01\Ax2-Saga\03-Ecom-HandleCommandAndCreateEvent\ src\main\java\com\acme\ecom\product\commandhandler\ProductCommandHandler.java)

```
@Component
public class ProductCommandHandler {

    @Autowired
    @Qualifier("productRepository")
    private Repository<Product> productRepository;

    @CommandHandler
    public void handleNewOrder(ProductStockRevertCommand
            productStockRevertCommand){

        Product product =
            productRepository.load(productStockRevertCommand.getProductId());
        product.revertStock(productStockRevertCommand.getCount());
    }
}
```

The order command handler and the product command handler are self-explanatory. Hence you will look at the next and most important code in this example, the saga, shown in Listing 15-4.

Listing 15-4. Order Process Saga (ch15\ch15-01\Ax2-Saga\03-Ecom-HandleCommandAndCreateEvent\src\main\java\com\acme\ecom\saga\ OrderProcessSaga.java)

```java
public class OrderProcessSaga extends AbstractAnnotatedSaga {

    private static final long serialVersionUID = -7209131793034337691L;

    private Integer orderId;
    private Integer productId;
    private Integer count;

    @Autowired
    @Qualifier("distributedCommandGateway")
    private transient CommandGateway commandGateway;

    @StartSaga
    @SagaEventHandler(associationProperty = "orderId")
    public void handleOrderCreationEvent(OrderCreatedEvent orderCreated
    Event) {

        orderId = orderCreatedEvent.getOrderId();
        productId = orderCreatedEvent.getProductId();
        count - orderCreatedEvent.getNumber();
    }

    @SagaEventHandler(associationProperty = "orderId")
    @EndSaga
    public void handleOrderCanceledEvent(
            OrderCancelledEvent orderCancelledEvent) {

        // This is the compensating command
        commandGateway.send(new ProductStockRevertCommand(productId, count));
    }
```

```java
@SagaEventHandler(associationProperty = "orderId")
@EndSaga
public void handleOrderConfirmationEvent(
        OrderConfirmedEvent orderConfirmedEvent) {
    // Nothing to do
}

public CommandGateway getCommandGateway() {
    return commandGateway;
}
public void setCommandGateway(CommandGateway commandGateway) {
    this.commandGateway = commandGateway;
}

public Integer getProductId() {
    return productId;
}
public void setProductId(Integer productId) {
    this.productId = productId;
}

public Integer getCount() {
    return count;
}
public void setCount(Integer count) {
    this.count = count;
}

public Integer getOrderId() {
    return orderId;
}
public void setOrderId(Integer orderId) {
    this.orderId = orderId;
}
}
```

A single saga instance is responsible for managing a single saga transaction. Hence, if there are two orders, you will have two instances of the above saga. So a new saga is only started if no suitable existing saga (of the same type) can be found in the system.

You should indicate the start and end of a saga's life cycle. The abstract annotated saga allows you to annotate event handlers with the annotation @SagaEventHandler. If the handler method signifies the start of a transaction, you add another annotation to that same method: @StartSaga. This annotation creates a new saga and invokes its event handler method when a matching event is published, the order created event in your case. In your case, there are two cases that can bring the saga to an end state: when an order confirmed event is intercepted or when an order cancelled event is intercepted. If a certain event always indicates the end of a saga's life cycle, annotate that event's handler on the saga with @EndSaga, in your case the handle order canceled event and the handle order confirmation event handlers. The saga's life cycle will be ended after the invocation of the handler.

The saga event handler annotation indicates that the annotated method is an event handler method for the saga instance. For each event, only a single annotated method will be invoked. This method is resolved in the following order of preference:

- First, the event handler methods of the actual class (at runtime) are searched.

- If a method is found with a parameter that the domain event can be assigned to, it is marked as eligible.

- After a class has been evaluated (but before any super class), the most specific event handler method is called. That means that if an event handler for class X and one for class Y are eligible, and Y is a subclass of X, then the method with a parameter of type Y will be chosen.

- If no method is found in the actual class, its super class is evaluated.

- If still no method is found, the event listener ignores the event.

Instead of publishing all events to all saga instances in the system, Axon will only publish events containing properties that the saga has been associated with. This is done using association values. An association value consists of a key and a value. The key represents the type of identifier used, for example orderId in the code above. The value represents the corresponding value of the order ID. The @SagaEventHandler annotation has two attributes, of which associationProperty is the most important one. This is the name of the property on the incoming event that should be used to find associated sagas. The key of the association value is the name of the property. The value is the value returned by property's getter method.

Microservice 4: 04-Ecom-EventHandleCore

As the name of the microservice hints, it contains the two main event handlers, OrderEventHandler and ProductEventHandler, and their functionality is to update the views of Order and Product respectively, in response to the following events:

- OrderCreatedEvent

- OrderConfirmedEvent

- OrderCancelledEvent

- StockUpdatedEvent

Listing 15-5 shows the order event handler code, which updates the order view.

Listing 15-5. Order Event Handler (ch15\ch15-01\Ax2-Saga\04-Ecom-EventHandleCore\src\main\java\com\acme\ecom\order\eventhandler\OrderEventHandler.java)

```
@Component
public class OrderEventHandler {

    @Autowired
    DataSource dataSource;

    @EventHandler
    public void handleOrderCreatedEvent(OrderCreatedEvent event) {

        JdbcTemplate jdbcTemplate = new JdbcTemplate(dataSource);
        jdbcTemplate.update("INSERT INTO ecom_order_view VALUES(?,?,?,?,?)",
            new Object[]{event.getOrderId(), event.getPrice(),
            event.getNumber(), event.getProductDescription(), NEW});
    }
```

```
@EventHandler
public void handleOrderConfirmedEvent(OrderConfirmedEvent event) {

    JdbcTemplate jdbcTemplate = new JdbcTemplate(dataSource);
    jdbcTemplate.update("UPDATE ecom_order_view SET status=?
        WHERE id =?", new Object[]{CONFIRMED, event.getOrderId()});
}

@EventHandler
public void handleOrderCancelledEvent(OrderCancelledEvent event) {

    JdbcTemplate jdbcTemplate = new JdbcTemplate(dataSource);
    jdbcTemplate.update("UPDATE ecom_order_view SET status=?
        WHERE id =?", new Object[]{CANCELLED, event.getOrderId()});
}
}
```

Listing 15-6 shows the product event handler code, which updates the product view.

Listing 15-6. Product Event Handler (ch15\ch15-01\Ax2-Saga\04-Ecom-EventHandleCore\src\main\java\com\acme\ecom\product\eventhandler\ProductEventHandler.java)

```
@Component
public class ProductEventHandler {

    @Autowired
    DataSource dataSource;

    @EventHandler
    public void handleProductStockUpdatedEvent(StockUpdatedEvent event) {

        JdbcTemplate jdbcTemplate = new JdbcTemplate(dataSource);
        jdbcTemplate.update("UPDATE ecom_product_view SET stock=?
            WHERE ID=?", new Object[]{event.getStock(), event.getId()});
    }
}
```

Microservice 5: 05-Ecom-EventHandlerAudit

This microservice makes audit entries to all major events happening against the domain entities. Listing 15-7 shows the audit event handler.

Listing 15-7. Audit Event Handler (ch15\ch15-01\Ax2-Saga\05-Ecom-EventHandlerAudit\src\main\java\com\acme\ecom\order\eventhandler\AuditEventHandler.java)

```
@Component
public class AuditEventHandler {

    @Autowired
    DataSource dataSource;

    @EventHandler
    public void handleOrderCreatedEvent(OrderCreatedEvent event) {

        JdbcTemplate jdbcTemplate = new JdbcTemplate(dataSource);
        jdbcTemplate.update("INSERT INTO ecom_order_audit VALUES(?,?,?)",
            new Object[]{event.getOrderId(), event.getOrderStatus(),
                new Date()});
    }

    @EventHandler
    public void handleOrderConfirmedEvent(OrderConfirmedEvent event) {

        JdbcTemplate jdbcTemplate = new JdbcTemplate(dataSource);
        jdbcTemplate.update("INSERT INTO ecom_order_audit VALUES(?,?,?)",
            new Object[]{event.getOrderId(), CONFIRMED, new Date()});
    }

    @EventHandler
    public void handleOrderCancelledEvent(OrderCancelledEvent event) {

        JdbcTemplate jdbcTemplate = new JdbcTemplate(dataSource);
        jdbcTemplate.update("INSERT INTO ecom_order_audit VALUES(?,?,?)",
            new Object[]{event.getOrderId(), CANCELLED, new Date()});
    }
}
```

The audit event handler creates audit rows and updates them as the status of order changes.

That's all of the main classes. There are few other classes like the `Command`, `Event`, and `Data Transfer` classes, which are simple and straightforward so I won't explain them here.

Build and Test the Saga Example

As the first step, you need to bring up MongoDB. You may want to refer to Appendix A to get started with MongoDB.

```
D:\Applns\MongoDB\Server\3.2.6\bin>mongod.exe --dbpath D:\Applns\MongoDB\
Server\3.2.6\data
```

Next, you need to bring up the RabbitMQ server. You may want to refer to Appendix B to get started with the RabbitMQ server.

```
D:\Applns\RabbitMQ\rabbitmq_server-3.6.3\sbin>D:\Applns\RabbitMQ\rabbitmq_
server-3.6.3\sbin\rabbitmq-server.bat
```

Make sure MySQL is up and running. You may want to refer to Appendix H to get started with MySQL.

```
Bring Up MySQL Server
cd D:\Applns\MySQL\mysql-8.0.14-winx64\bin
D:\Applns\MySQL\mysql-8.0.14-winx64\bin>mysqld --console
```

```
Now Open MySQL prompt
D:\Applns\MySQL\mysql-8.0.14-winx64\bin>mysql -u root -p
```

```
mysql> use ecom01;
Database changed
mysql>
```

To start with clean tables, delete any tables with the names you want for your examples:

```
mysql> drop table ecom_order;
mysql> drop table ecom_product;
mysql> drop table ecom_order_view;
```

```
mysql> drop table ecom_product_view;
mysql> drop table ecom_order_audit;
```

Newly create the required tables:

```
mysql>create table ecom_order (id integer not null, last_event_sequence_
number bigint, version bigint, number integer, order_status varchar(255),
price double precision, product_id integer, primary key (id)) ENGINE=InnoDB
mysql>create table ecom_product (id integer not null, last_event_sequence_
number bigint, version bigint, description varchar(255), price double
precision, stock integer, primary key (id)) ENGINE=InnoDB
mysql>alter table ecom_order add constraint FK_f3rnd79i90twafllfhpo1sihi
foreign key (product_id) references ecom_product (id)
mysql>create table ecom_product_view(id INT , price DOUBLE, stock INT
,description VARCHAR(255));
mysql>create table ecom_order_view(id INT , price DOUBLE, number INT
,description VARCHAR(225),status VARCHAR(50));
mysql>create table ecom_order_audit(id INT ,status VARCHAR(50),date
TIMESTAMP);
```

The example has a Maven module that contains common classes used by all other microservices. Hence it must be built first:

```
cd D:\binil\gold\pack03\ch15\ch15-01\Ax2-Saga\06-Ecom-common
D:\binil\gold\pack03\ch15\ch15-01\Ax2-Saga\06-Ecom-common>make
D:\binil\gold\pack03\ch15\ch15-01\Ax2-Saga\06-Ecom-common>mvn clean install
```

Next, there are five microservices to build and get running. You will do so one by one.

Microservice 1: 01-Ecom-web

First, update the configuration files to suit to your environment:

```
ch15\ch15-01\Ax2-Saga\01-Ecom-web\src\main\resources\application.properties
server.port=8080
```

Note   I advise you not to make any changes here.

Now build and package the executables for the Ecom-web microservice and bring up the server. There is a utility script in folder ch15\ch15-01\Ax2-Saga\01-Ecom-web\make. bat.

```
cd D:\binil\gold\pack03\ch15\ch15-01\Ax2-Saga\01-Ecom-web
D:\binil\gold\pack03\ch15\ch15-01\Ax2-Saga\01-Ecom-web>make
D:\binil\gold\pack03\ch15\ch15-01\Ax2-Saga\01-Ecom-web>mvn clean install
```

Now run the Spring Boot application. The straightforward way is to execute the JAR file via the following commands:

```
D:\binil\gold\pack03\ch15\ch15-01\Ax2-Saga\01-Ecom-web>run
D:\binil\gold\pack03\ch15\ch15-01\Ax2-Saga\01-Ecom-web>java -jar .\
target\01-Ecom-web-0.0.1-SNAPSHOT.jar
```

This will bring up the 01-Ecom-web Spring Boot Server in port 8080.

Microservice 2: 02-Ecom-CreateCommandRestController

The JGroups configuration is provided in the following file:

```
ch15\ch15-01\Ax2-Saga\02-Ecom-CreateCommandRestController\src\main\
resources\udp_config.xml
```

However, let's not worry about the contents of this file too much for now.

Update the next configuration file to suit to your environment:

```
ch15\ch15-01\Ax2-Saga\02-Ecom-CreateCommandRestController\src\main\
resources\application.properties
server.port=8081
spring.datasource.url=jdbc:mysql://localhost/ecom01
spring.datasource.username=root
spring.datasource.password=rootpassword
```

```
cd D:\binil\gold\pack03\ch15\ch15-01\Ax2-Saga\02-Ecom-CreateCommandRest
Controller
D:\binil\gold\pack03\ch15\ch15-01\Ax2-Saga\02-Ecom-CreateCommandRest
Controller>make
D:\binil\gold\pack03\ch15\ch15-01\Ax2-Saga\02-Ecom-CreateCommandRest
Controller>mvn clean install
```

You can now run the 02-Ecom-CreateCommandRestController Axon Spring Boot application, again in more than one way. The straightforward way is to execute the JAR file via the following commands:

```
D:\binil\gold\pack03\ch15\ch15-01\Ax2-Saga\02-Ecom-CreateCommandRestControl
ler>run
D:\binil\gold\pack03\ch15\ch15-01\Ax2-Saga\02-Ecom-CreateCommandRest
Controller>java -Dserver.port=8081 -Dlog4j.configurationFile=log4j2-spring.
xml -jar .\target\02-Ecom-CreateCommandRestController-0.0.1-SNAPSHOT.jar
```

This will bring up the 02-Ecom-CreateCommandRestController Axon Spring Boot Server in port 8081.

Microservice 3: 03-Ecom-HandleCommandAndCreateEvent

Update the configuration files to suit to your environment and see Listing 15-8:

```
ch12\ch12-02\Ax2-Commands-Multi-Event-Handler-Distributed\03-Ecom-Handle
CommandAndCreateEvent\src\main\resources\application.properties
```

Listing 15-8. Microservice 3 Configuration Parameters

```
spring.data.mongodb.uri=mongodb://localhost:27017/test

server.port=8082
spring.datasource.url=jdbc:mysql://localhost/ecom01
spring.datasource.username=root
spring.datasource.password=rootpassword

ecom.amqp.rabbit.address= 127.0.0.1:5672
ecom.amqp.rabbit.username= guest
ecom.amqp.rabbit.password= guest
ecom.amqp.rabbit.vhost=/
ecom.amqp.rabbit.exchange=Ecom-02
ecom.amqp.rabbit.queue=Ecom-createcommand_01
```

Note   The MongoDB URL is used by the microservice to persist the saga. Even though you provide the full path to the `test` database, the microservice will create any saga-related collections only in a different database called `axonframework`.

```
cd D:\binil\gold\pack03\ch15\ch15-01\Ax2-Saga\03-Ecom-HandleCommandAnd
CreateEvent
D:\binil\gold\pack03\ch15\ch15-01\Ax2-Saga\03-Ecom-HandleCommandAndCreate
Event>make
D:\binil\gold\pack03\ch15\ch15-01\Ax2-Saga\03-Ecom-HandleCommandAndCreate
Event>mvn clean install
```

You can run the 03-Ecom-HandleCommandAndCreateEvent Axon Spring Boot application, again in more than one way. The straightforward way is to execute the JAR file via the following commands:

```
D:\binil\gold\pack03\ch15\ch15-01\Ax2-Saga\03-Ecom-HandleCommandAndCreate
Event>run
D:\binil\gold\pack03\ch15\ch15-01\Ax2-Saga\03-Ecom-HandleCommandAnd
CreateEvent>java -Dserver.port=8082 -Dlog4j.configurationFile=log4j2-
spring.xml -jar .\target\03-Ecom-HandleCommandAndSaga-0.0.1-SNAPSHOT.jar
```

This will bring up the 02-Ecom-CreateCommandRestController Axon Spring Boot Server in port 8082.

Microservice 4: 04-Ecom-EventHandleCore

Update the configuration files to suit to your environment and see Listing 15-9:

```
ch15\ch15-01\Ax2-Saga\04-Ecom-EventHandleCore\src\main\resources\
application.properties
```

Listing 15-9. Microservice 4 Configuration Parameters

```
server.port=8083
spring.datasource.url=jdbc:mysql://localhost/ecom01
spring.datasource.username=root
spring.datasource.password=rootpassword
```

```
ecom.amqp.rabbit.address= 127.0.0.1:5672
ecom.amqp.rabbit.username= guest
ecom.amqp.rabbit.password= guest
ecom.amqp.rabbit.vhost=/
ecom.amqp.rabbit.exchange=Ecom-02
ecom.amqp.rabbit.queue=Ecom-event-core_01
```

```
cd D:\binil\gold\pack03\ch15\ch15-01\Ax2-Saga\04-Ecom-EventHandleCore
D:\binil\gold\pack03\ch15\ch15-01\Ax2-Saga\04-Ecom-EventHandleCore>make
D:\binil\gold\pack03\ch15\ch15-01\Ax2-Saga\04-Ecom-EventHandleCore>mvn
clean install
```

You can now run the 04-Ecom-EventHandleCore Axon Spring Boot application. The straightforward way is to execute the JAR file via the following commands:

```
D:\binil\gold\pack03\ch15\ch15-01\Ax2-Saga\04-Ecom-EventHandleCore>run
D:\binil\gold\pack03\ch15\ch15-01\Ax2-Saga\04-Ecom-EventHandleCore>java
-Dserver.port=8083 -jar .\target\04-Ecom-EventHandlerCore-0.0.1-SNAPSHOT.jar
```

This will bring up the 04-Ecom-EventHandleCore Axon Spring Boot Server in port 8083.

Microservice 5: 05-Ecom-EventHandlerAudit

This is the last microservice you want to bring up in this example. Update the configuration files to suit to your environment and see Listing 15-10:

```
ch15\ch15-01\Ax2-Saga\05-Ecom-EventHandlerAudit\src\main\resources\
application.properties
```

Listing 15-10. Microservice 5 Configuration Parameters

```
server.port=8084
spring.datasource.url=jdbc:mysql://localhost/ecom01
spring.datasource.username=root
spring.datasource.password=rootpassword

ecom.amqp.rabbit.address= 127.0.0.1:5672
ecom.amqp.rabbit.username= guest
ecom.amqp.rabbit.password= guest
```

```
ecom.amqp.rabbit.vhost=/
ecom.amqp.rabbit.exchange=Ecom-02
ecom.amqp.rabbit.queue=Ecom-event-history_01
```

```
cd D:\binil\gold\pack03\ch15\ch15-01\Ax2-Saga\05-Ecom-EventHandlerAudit
D:\binil\gold\pack03\ch15\ch15-01\Ax2-Saga\05-Ecom-EventHandlerAudit>make
D:\binil\gold\pack03\ch15\ch15-01\Ax2-Saga\05-Ecom-EventHandlerAudit>mvn
clean install
```

You can now run the 05-Ecom-EventHandlerAudit Axon Spring Boot application, again in more than one way. The straightforward way is to execute the JAR file via the following commands:

```
D:\binil\gold\pack03\ch15\ch15-01\Ax2-Saga\05-Ecom-EventHandlerAudit>run
D:\binil\gold\pack03\ch15\ch15-01\Ax2-Saga\05-Ecom-EventHandlerAudit>java
-Dserver.port=8084 -Dspring.application.name=product-audit-01 -jar .\
target\05-Ecom-EventHandlerHistory-0.0.1-SNAPSHOT.jar
```

This will bring up the 05-Ecom-EventHandlerAudit Axon Spring Boot Server in port 8084.

Prepopulate the ecom_product and ecom_product_view tables with some initial data:

```
mysql> insert into ecom_product(id,description,price,stock,version) values
(1,'Shirts',100,5,0);
mysql> insert into ecom_product(id,description,price,stock,version) values
(2,'Pants',100,5,0);
mysql> insert into ecom_product(id,description,price,stock,version) values
(3,'T-Shirt',100,5,0);
mysql> insert into ecom_product(id,description,price,stock,version) values
(4,'Shoes',100,5,0);

mysql> insert into ecom_product_view(id,description,price,stock) values
(1,'Shirts',100,5);
mysql> insert into ecom_product_view(id,description,price,stock) values
(2,'Pants',100,5);
mysql> insert into ecom_product_view(id,description,price,stock) values
(3,'T-Shirt',100,5);
```

```
mysql> insert into ecom_product_view(id,description,price,stock)
values(4,'Shoes',100,5);
```

You can use a browser (preferably Chrome) and point to `http://localhost:8080/`. This will bring up the screen shown in Figure 15-9. You can test the example by clicking the "Order One Now" button against any one of the products in Figure 15-9. When you click, a new order is created in the Order Write DB. Eventually, the Order Read DB will be updated with this new order. Also, the corresponding product stock will be reduced by one in the Product Write DB. This change will also be eventually updated in the Product Read DB. The Audit Read DB too is updated with records. When you refresh the screen, the change is as shown in Figure 15-11.

The moment you create the first order, a saga will be started. To verify this, you may use a console to check the collections in the MongoDB, as shown in Listing 15-11.

Listing 15-11. Saga Persisted in MongoDB Collection

```
D:\Applns\MongoDB\Server\3.2.6\bin>D:\Applns\MongoDB\Server\3.2.6\bin\mongo
MongoDB shell version: 3.2.6
connecting to: test
> show dbs
ecom    0.000GB
local   0.000GB
test    0.000GB
> show dbs
axonframework   0.000GB
ecom            0.000GB
local           0.000GB
test            0.000GB
> use axonframework
switched to db axonframework
> show collections
sagas
> db.sagas.find()
{ "_id" : ObjectId("5c7f689a75c90e3adeb78318"), "sagaType" : "com.acme.
ecom.saga.OrderProcessSaga", "sagaIdentifier" : "3aeffc45-4ddd-419b-ab00-
d2e32914c9ce", "serializedSaga" : BinData(0,"rO0ABXNyACNjb20uYWNtZS5lY
```

29tLnNhZ2EuT3JkZXJQcm9jZXNzU2FnYZvoBNRxNqJlAgADTAAFY291bnRoABNMamF2YS9
sYW5nL0ludGVnZXI7TAAHb3JkZXJJZHEAfgABTAAJcHJvZHVjdElkcQB+AAF4cgA3b3JnLmF
4b25mcmFtZXdvcmsuc2FnYS5hbm5vdGF0aW9uLkFic3RyYWNOQW5ub3RhdGVkU2FnYSEZT
tg8hhaCAgADWgAIaXNBY3RpdmVMABFhc3NvY2lhdGlvblZhbHVlc3QAKkxvcmcvYXhvbmZyYW
1ld29yay9zYWdhL0Fzc29jaWF0aW9uVmFsdWVzOOwACmlkZW50aWZpZXJOABJMamF2YS9sYW5
nL1NOcmluZzt4cAFzcgA3b3JnLmF4b25mcmFtZXdvcmsuc2FnYS5hbm5vdGF0aW9uLkFzc29
jaWF0aW9uVmFsdWVzSW1wbHLSJtX04PrCAgABTAAGdmFsdWVzdAAPTGphdmEvdXRpbC9TZXQ
7eHBzcgAoamF2YS51dGlsLmNvbN 1cnJlbnQuQ29weU9uV3JpdGVBcnJheVNldEu90JKQFWn
XAgABTAACYWx0ACtMamF2YS91dGlsL2NvbNN1cnJlbnQvQ29weU9uV3JpdGVBcnJheUxpc3Q7
eHBzcgApamF2YS51dGlsLmNvbNN1cnJlbnQuQ29weU9uV3JpdGVBcnJheUxpc3R4XZ/VRquQww
MAAHhwdwQAAAACc3IAJ29yZy5heG9uZnJhbWV3b3JrLnNhZ2EuQXNzb2NpYXRpb25WYWx1
ZTGYTDwHQAy9AgACTAALcHJvcGVydHlLZXlxAH4ABEwADXByb3BlcnR5VmFsdWVxAH4ABHhwd
AAOc2FnYU1kZW50aWZpZXJOACQzYWVmZmONSOOZGRkLTQxOWItYWIwMC1kMmUzMjkxNGM5Y2V
zcQB+AA5OAAdvcmRlcklkdAAJNTEwMzcOMTg1eHEAfgARc3IAEWphdmEuBGFuZy5JbnRlZ2
VyEuKgpPeBhzgCAAFJAAV2YWx1ZXhyABBqYXZhLmxhbmcuTnVtYmyhqyVHQuU4IsCAAB4
cAAAAAFzcQB+ABUea7Epc3EAfgAVAAAAAQ=="), "associations" : [{ "key":
"sagaIdentifier", "value" : "3aeffc45-4ddd-419b-ab00-d2e32914c9ce" }, {
"key": "orderId", "value" : "510374185" }] }

Note   If the microservices are not responding as per the intended manner, you
may want to flush the RabbitMQ queues. This can be done easily by bringing down
RabbitMQ, deleting the data folders, and then bringing back RabbitMQ. Refer to
Appendix B for related details.

(If the change is not reflected, close the browser session and take a new browser
instance and try the above URL.)

Create two more orders so that you can execute all test cases. On refreshing the
screen, you will see all new orders as well as the audit logs for the orders, as shown in
Figure 15-14.

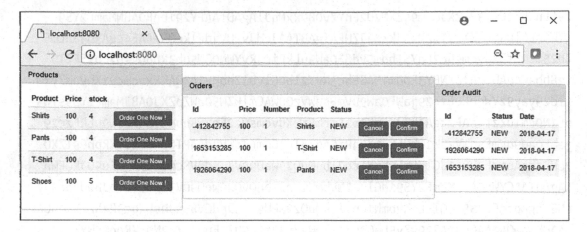

Figure 15-14. *Three new orders created*

If you click Cancel button against one of the orders, it will cancel that order and end the saga. Not only that, since the order is cancelled, the product number is added back to the stock of corresponding product. The cancel action will create its own audit log. Refresh the screen again and you will see the changes shown in Figure 15-15.

Figure 15-15. *Order cancelled*

If you click the Confirm button against one of the order, it will confirm that order and again end the saga. Since the order is confirmed, the product stock, which got reduced while you ordered, will remain the same. The confirm action will create its own audit log. Refresh the screen again and you will see the changes shown in Figure 15-16.

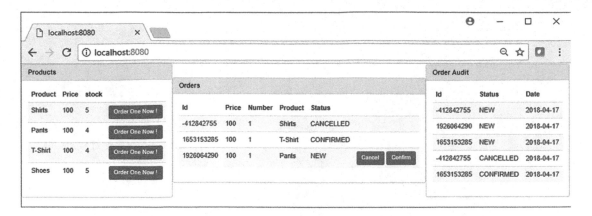

Figure 15-16. *Order confirmed*

Lastly, take a note of the order, which remains in the "New" status. If you do nothing further with this order, it will remain in that status, and this is due to the persistent nature of the saga, which will also remain in that status. This demonstrates a long-running workflow, in your case a saga.

Summary

While Chapters 13 and 14 covered transactions in detail, this chapter covered transactions specifically in the context of microservices. You learned about saga and how distributed sagas can be utilized by grouping a given transaction into a sequence of subtransactions and corresponding compensating transactions. All transactions in a saga either complete successfully or, in the event of a failure, the compensating transactions are rolled back. You also saw the complete working code of how to implement saga using the Axon 2 framework. Having looked at transactions, next you will relook at high availability and scalability with an emphasis on CQRS design in Chapter 16.

CHAPTER 16

Advanced High Availability and Scalability

In Chapter 9, you looked at various elements contributing to high availability (HA) for a software architecture, most of which are relevant for both a microservices architecture and a monolith architecture. There you looked at the various components of a private cloud or an on-premises deployment infrastructure and glanced through the HA aspects. In this chapter, you will look into details of selected concerns that have significant impact in designing CQRS-based systems. To make things simple and relatable to concepts you already know or have been using, I will examine these concerns in the context of a database familiar to most of us, Oracle. Once you understand the concepts, then it's straightforward to extend that learning to any other vendor's solution or to other free and open source solutions. Interestingly, you will look at many of these concepts in the context of Oracle just to make sure you leverage such solutions only when it's absolutely required, which again leads to the core point that in many situations there are alternate and possibly cheaper solutions.

You will be exploring the following in this chapter:

- Architecture templates to address an increasing amount of scalability

- Code samples demonstrating HA and scalability design using Axon 2 CQRS

- Read scalability vs. write scalability

- Techniques to allow concurrent modification of entities

- Code samples demonstrating concurrent modification of entities using Axon 2 CQRS

© Binildas Christudas 2019
B. Christudas, *Practical Microservices Architectural Patterns*, https://doi.org/10.1007/978-1-4842-4501-9_16

High Availability and Scalability Templates Using an Oracle DB as a Reference

As mentioned, you will use an Oracle database as a solution to explain various HA templates. While doing so, you will also use the public cloud, Amazon Web Services (AWS) in your case, as the deployment environment. This is because, as you will shortly see, there are some caveats to the templates, which I will explain when it comes to the public cloud.

You will consider the application architecture as a life cycle, each stage of the cycle representing the various stages of growth, from inception until the level when the architecture reaches maturity and operates at economies and efficiencies of scale, and further beyond where you need to web scale at an exponential or infinite level.

The Simple, Inception Architecture

This is the simplest form of any distributed or microservices architecture and will suit only for serving application services for personal use or for the use of small start-ups. In its basic form, it consists of a middle tier providing application services, and this middle tier connects to a single, simple database instance for persistence services. Figure 16-1 depicts how this looks when deployed in a public cloud, Amazon Web Services.

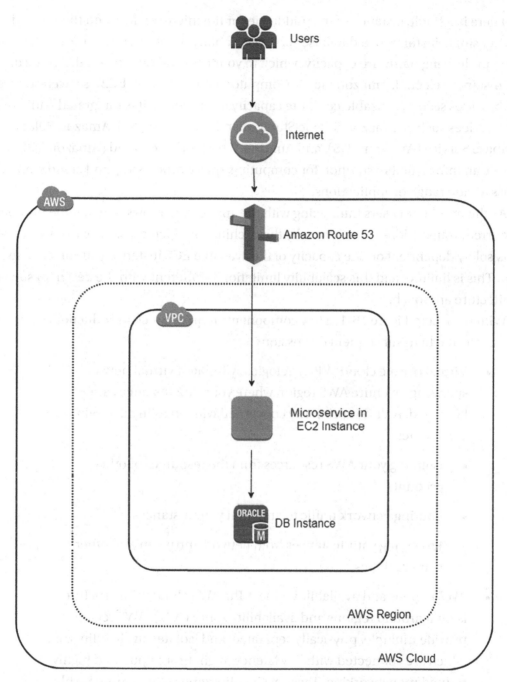

Figure 16-1. *The simple inception architecture*

There is a single instance of the middle tier or the microservices and then there is another single instance of a database server. Scalability of this architecture is determined by the underlying hardware capacity, which in your case will depend on the grade of EC2 instance selected. Amazon Elastic Compute Cloud (Amazon EC2) is a web service that provides secure, resizable compute capacity in the cloud. It is integrated with most AWS services such as Amazon Simple Storage Service (Amazon S3), Amazon Relational Database Service (Amazon RDS), and Amazon Virtual Private Cloud (Amazon VPC) to provide an infrastructure solution for computing, query processing, and cloud storage across a wide range of applications.

As the number of users interfacing with the application grows or when the number of concurrent transactions to be served by this architecture increases, the capacity to scale out is solely dependent on the capacity of the available EC2 instance you can choose from. This is limited, and this scalability limitation is inherent with the design of such an architecture approach.

With respect to Figure 16-1, a few components require quick introduction, since they will be referred to in subsequent discussions:

- Virtual private cloud (VPC): A logically isolated virtual network spanning an entire AWS region where your EC2 instances are launched. A VPC is primarily concerned with enabling the following capabilities:

  - Isolating your AWS resources from the resources of other accounts

  - Routing network traffic to and from your instances

  - Protecting your instances from network intrusion and other vulnerabilities

- AWS regions and availability zones: The AWS cloud infrastructure is built around regions and availability zones (AZs). AWS regions provide multiple, physically separated, and isolated availability zones which are connected with low latency, high throughput, and highly redundant networking. These availability zones offer a more highly available, fault tolerant, and scalable infrastructure than traditional single datacenter infrastructures or multi-datacenter infrastructures. AWS regions are completely isolated from other AWS regions.

The AWS cloud currently spans 54 availability zones within 18 geographic regions and one local region around the world. An AWS region is depicted in Figure 16-1 whereas an availability zone will be shown in next section where it's relevant.

The Simple, Scaled Out Architecture

The simple inception architecture described in the previous section is a bare minimum, and is the one with less hassles. If circumstances permit, you may want to live with that minimalist architecture, since it will give you peace of mind. However, if your business is successful with that architecture, that in a sense implies that you are going to need an enhanced architecture for scalability, since a growing business can in no way be served by the above minimalist architecture. The simple, scaled out architecture is shown in Figure 16-2.

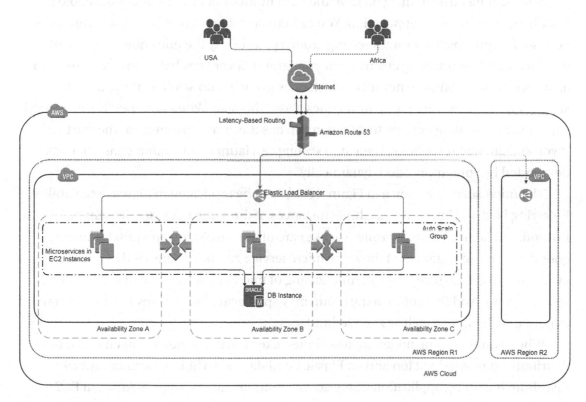

Figure 16-2. *The simple, scaled out architecture*

The simple, scaled out architecture is not that simple, but it's simpler compared to the architectures you are going to visit next, hence the name. The simple, scaled out architecture leverages regions, availability zones, and auto scale groups. Each region is a separate geographic area in the AWS cloud. Each region has multiple, isolated locations known as availability zones. Amazon EC2 provides the ability to place resources, such as instances, and data in multiple locations. If you host all your instances in a single location, none of your instances will be available if that location is badly affected. AWS regions and availability zones will help you here. Each region is completely independent. Each availability zone is also isolated, but the availability zones within a region are connected through low-latency links. When you launch an EC2 instance, you can select an availability zone or let AWS choose one for you. If you distribute your EC2 instances across multiple availability zones and if one of the instances fails and if you have designed your application appropriately, an instance in another availability zone can still handle requests.

Auto scaling ensures that you have the right number of EC2 instances available to handle the load for your application. You can create collections of EC2 instances, called auto scaling groups. To the auto scaling groups you specify the minimum number of instances, and auto scaling ensures that your group never goes below this size. You can also specify the maximum number of instances in each auto scaling group, and auto scaling ensures that your group never goes above this size. When you specify the desired capacity, auto scaling ensures that your group has this many instances at the start. If you specify scaling policies, then auto scaling can launch or terminate instances as demanded by your application dynamically.

The microservice instance in Figure 16-1 has to be replicated to increase scalability. Referring back to Figure 16-2, multiple instances of the same microservice can be instantiated in an availability zone. To take care of the case when an availability zone goes down, more instances of the same microservice can be instantiated in another availability zone. To take care dynamic scaling of microservices, you can design an auto scaling group. And this auto scaling group may span availability zones so that you have dynamic scalability as well as zone redundancy.

When your compute nodes are distributed like above, you need a mechanism to distribute your workload too and an Elastic Load Balancer (ELB) can automatically distribute incoming application traffic across multiple targets, such as Amazon EC2 instances, containers, and IP addresses. An ELB can handle the varying load of your application traffic in a single availability zone or across multiple availability zones. ELBs are of three types:

- Application Load Balancer: An ALB is best suited for load balancing of HTTP and HTTPS traffic, operating at the individual request level at OSI Layer 7.

- Network Load Balancer: A NLB load balances TCP traffic where extreme performance is required, operating at the connection level at OSI Layer 4.

- Classic Load Balancer: A CLB is intended for applications that were built within the EC2-Classic network. It provides basic load balancing across multiple Amazon EC2 instances and operates at both the request level and connection level.

Another aspect to discuss is the need to distribute data globally. This can be due to multiple reasons. One reason can be that the user base is distributed globally and hence users should be directed to microservice instances located near to that geography for low latency. Another reason might be to comply with data privacy requirements like GDPR[1] (General Data Protection Regulation). AWS regions can be leveraged here where you want to leverage microservice instances located across regions. This is also depicted in Figure 16-2 in a non-expanded form. Regional traffic routing or latency-based traffic routing can be done using AWS Route 53. Amazon Route 53 is a highly available and scalable cloud Domain Name System (DNS) web service. Route 53 makes it easy for you to manage traffic globally through a variety of routing types, including latency-based routing, Geo DNS, geoproximity, and weighted round robin—all of which can be combined with DNS failover too.

The simple, scaled out architecture in Figure 16-2 is an improvement over the simple inception architecture in Figure 16-1; however, careful observation of Figure 16-2 reveals other concerns and limitations. The first one is that the data across regions is disparate; it's not in sync automatically. Maybe that is justified by the very reason that compelled you to distribute applications across regions, like privacy. But then, concentrate within a

---

[1]The General Data Protection Regulation is a regulation in EU law on data protection and privacy for all individuals within the European Union (EU) and the European Economic Area (EEA). It also addresses the export of personal data outside the EU and EEA areas.

region. Even though you can design microservices to have many instances, your backing data store is still a single instance, which is your single source of truth. This single database instance will still have the scalability issues discussed. You need to improvise further, which you will look at next.

Architecture to Address the Database Bottleneck

The improvement you want to bring to the simple, scaled out architecture is required to address the scalability of the database instance too. Oracle Real Application Cluster (RAC) is a cluster database with a shared cache architecture that overcomes the limitations of traditional shared-nothing and shared-disk approaches to provide high scalability and availability to database. In a RAC environment, the database itself is shared across a pool of servers, which means that if any server in the server pool fails, the database continues to run on surviving servers, thus avoiding any single point of failure. Since there are a pool of servers, the combined memory capacity and processing power of the clustered database servers provide high scalability too. RAC is an active-active distributed architecture with shared database storage. The shared storage plays a central role in enabling automatic failover, no data loss, 100% data consistency, and in preventing application downtime.

There is a catch when it comes to a public cloud like AWS. As of this writing, Amazon Web Services does not currently enable Oracle RAC natively on Amazon EC2 or Amazon RDS. Oracle RAC has the following infrastructure requirements that are not directly available in AWS:

- Shared high-performance storage accessible from all nodes in the cluster

- Multicast-enabled network between all nodes in the cluster

- Separate networks for different types of traffic: client, cluster interconnect, and storage

But the happy news is that there are solutions by third-party providers that allow you to run Oracle RAC on AWS using AWS-native components, such as Amazon EC2, Amazon Elastic Block Store (Amazon EBS), and Amazon VPC. Figure 16-3 depicts a possible architecture approach leveraging Oracle RAC to improve on the simple, scaled out architecture.

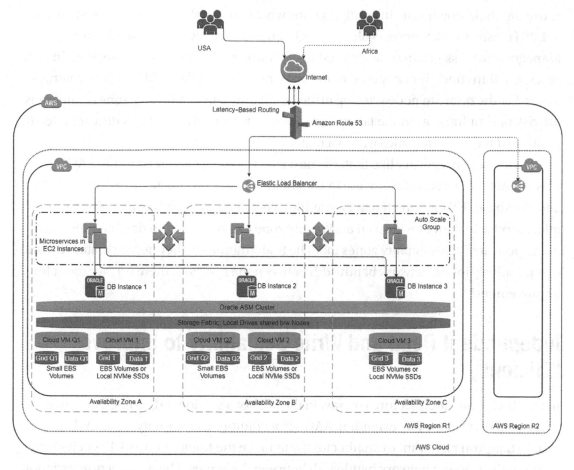

Figure 16-3. *Architecture to address a database bottleneck*

Referring to the architecture shown in Figure 16-3, two or three node clusters are recommended for enhanced reliability. Clusters with four or more nodes can also be used for extra HA or performance. Grid infrastructure clusters with four or more nodes containing several two-node or three-node database clusters are possible. Nodes of a cluster can be in one availability zone or can be spread across availability zones.

Most of the AWS regions are limited to three availability zones. Figure 16-3 shows three RAC nodes. Placing the quorum nodes in the same availability zones as the RAC nodes still allows achieving most of the expected HA capabilities. Such a three-node cluster can tolerate the loss of any two nodes or the loss of any one availability zone without database downtime. However, simultaneous loss of two availability zones will cause database downtime. In configurations where local NVMe SSDs[2] are used instead of EBS (Elastic Block Storage) volumes, high redundancy ASM[3] (Automatic Storage Management) disk groups may be used to provide extra layer of data protection. In such cases, the third node is configured as a storage node with NVMe SSDs or EBS volumes instead of the quorum node. Placing instances in different availability zones eliminates the risk of simultaneous node failures, except for the unlikely event of a disaster affecting multiple data center facilities within a region.

Having set up a cluster like that, the next step is to distribute load to the RAC cluster. The architecture leverages HA capabilities built into Oracle Clusterware, ASM, and Database. This is depicted in Figure 16-3 where database calls originating from microservice instances within an availability zone can be routed to database instances in the pool across availability zones too. The trade-offs are higher network latencies and comparatively lower network bandwidth between the nodes. Is there further room for improvement?

Independent Read and Write Scalability to Improve Efficiency

In the RAC-based architecture you saw in the previous section, I discussed how to bring additional redundancy by extending RAC across multiple availability zones. When you do that, you also want to architecturally manage the higher network latencies and comparatively lower network bandwidth between the nodes. The architecture variation depicted in Figure 16-4 shows one such option.

---

[2]NVMe (non-volatile memory express) is a host controller interface and storage protocol created to accelerate the transfer of data between enterprise and client systems and solid-state drives (SSDs) over a computer's high-speed Peripheral Component Interconnect Express (PCIe) bus.

[3]Automatic Storage Management (ASM) is a feature provided by Oracle within the Oracle Database from release Oracle 10g (revision 1) onwards. ASM aims to simplify the management of database datafiles, control files, and log files. To do so, it provides tools to manage file systems and volumes directly inside the database, allowing database administrators (DBAs) to control volumes and disks with familiar SQL statements in standard Oracle environments. Thus DBAs do not need extra skills in specific file systems or volume managers (which usually operate at the level of the operating system).

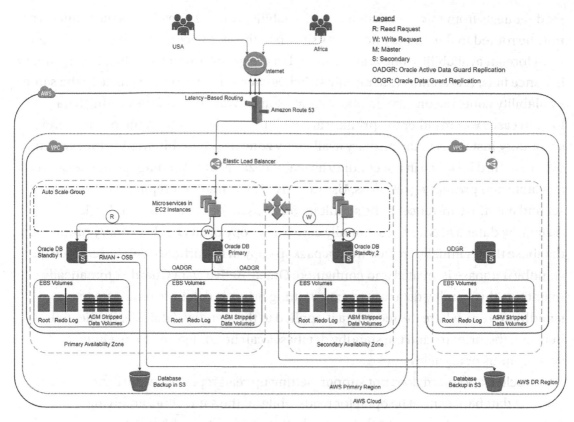

Figure 16-4. *Data architecture to improve read scalability*

There are many scenarios where the number of read requests or queries far exceeds the total number of write requests an application has to handle. You explored the aspect of the look to book ratio in Chapter 12. The architecture option in Figure 16-4 uses the notion of primary and secondary (standby) database nodes. It uses Oracle Data Guard Replication[4] (ODGR) and Oracle Active Data Guard Replication (OADGR) to implement the concept of primary and standby. Distribution of the load across multiple availability zones is done by using Oracle Active Data Guard. Replicating with Active Data Guard allows you to use the replicated standby instances for read-only loads, allowing load distribution. This is evident in Figure 16-4 where all read requests are routed to standby nodes in respective availability zones. By doing so, the primary node is not loaded with

---

[4]The software that Oracle markets as Oracle Data Guard forms an extension to the Oracle RDBMS. It aids in establishing and maintaining secondary standby databases as alternative/supplementary repositories to production primary databases. Data Guard supports both physical standby and logical standby sites.

read requests from microservices across availability zones. Instead, all write requests can now be routed to the primary nodes. As shown in the architecture, write requests even from foreign availability zones can be routed to the primary node. Further, if the primary instance fails, this architecture rapidly switches over to the second instance in the same availability zone, making the database continuously available and preventing data loss. In cases where either the primary availability zone fails or both the primary and secondary instances in the primary availability zone fail, then this architecture switches over to a third instance in a secondary availability zone, thus keeping the database still available and preventing data loss. Use of Active Data Guard for replication allows the second and third instances to be simultaneously used for read-only workloads.

A standby database is a transactionally consistent copy of an Oracle primary production database that is initially created from a backup copy of the primary database. Once the standby database is created and configured, Oracle Active Data Guard automatically maintains the standby database by transmitting primary database redo data to the standby system, where the redo data is applied to the standby database. Replication between the primary and the standby databases can be configured to be either synchronous or asynchronous.

Oracle Data Guard does not support setting up read replicas because the physical standby database cannot be open for reads while, at the same time, archiving transactions from the primary database, since it can function either in managed-recovery mode or in read-only mode, but not in both modes at the same time. Oracle Active Data Guard built upon Oracle Data Guard is an option that allows for the setup of read replicas. In addition to the functionality described previously, Oracle Active Data Guard enables read-only access to the standby databases while at the same time being kept up to date by archiving transactions from the primary database. This allows you to run read queries and reports on the standby instances, and to perform your backups from a standby instance. It is typical to perform data backup in such architectures either by using EBS snapshots to Amazon S3 or using Oracle Recovery Manager[5] (RMAN) and Oracle Secure Backup Cloud Module (OSB).

---

[5]RMAN (Recovery Manager) is a backup and recovery manager supplied for Oracle databases. It provides database backup, restore, and recovery capabilities addressing high availability and disaster recovery concerns.

Sharding for Web Scale Architecture

Having managed to separate the management of write scalability from that of read scalability, it's yet not time for you to rest and relax. Sooner or later you will start to feel that your separated read nodes or if your business is too successful (like many businesses today), even your write nodes by themselves are putting limitations, many times due to the sheer volume of transactions it has to handle or due to the volume of data it has to manage. This is especially true when enterprises operate globally and open up their applications for global customer use. Many social network applications and messaging applications fall in this category, which are to be web scale. "Divide and rule" is the mantra, and sharding is one such approach. Sharding can be applied to a services layer or a data layer. The architecture in Figure 16-5 shows one such concept.

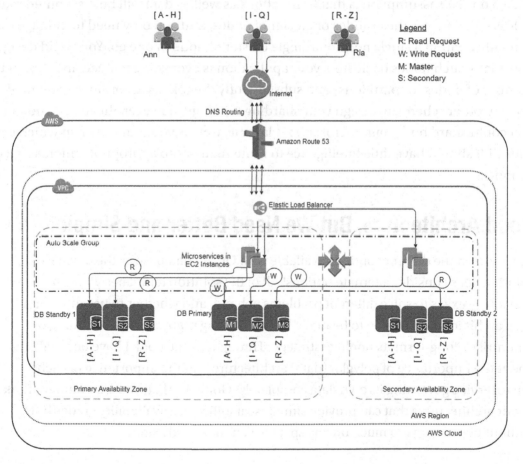

Figure 16-5. *Data architecture to improve read scalability*

The concept of a sharding architecture is that you will have many nodes so that all or few of the nodes will also have redundant data and then each node will have unique tokens and you use those tokens to divide upon the entire data to write and read to and from the database.

Refer to Figure 16-5, and I will use an analogy. Suppose your application is similar to the popular social networking application we use today. You know there are too many users in the system and there are too many user actions that you want to manage in your application. If both of my daughters, Ann and Ria, are users in the application along with many other millions of users, one easy way to design the token is to go with the alphabet and divide the users into nodes based on the first initial of their name. There are nodes or cluster of nodes dedicated to handle requests and data for users whose names start with letters A-H and similarly another set of nodes or cluster of nodes dedicated to handle requests and data for users whose names start with I-Q, and so on. The assumption is that transactions as well as data will be distributed more or less equal across these nodes or cluster of nodes, and you only need to manage the scalability within a single node or a single cluster of node in one go. You could design how many such nodes or clusters your application is ever going to need and design the number of nodes (or partitions) and subsequently the tokens accordingly. You may use any other schema to design your sharding topology; however, the idea is the same. You could shard both your microservices layer as well as your data layer, in which case your ELB should have little intelligence to route requests to appropriate microservice instance.

Good Architecture, But We Need Better and Simpler

Having seen the different options available with Oracle database as the database solution, let's consider alternate options! All of the solution templates you saw previously exists to solve different problems at hand, and whether to use them or not is an architectural decision to be made by considering many aspects including the enterprise's long-term technology strategy. Throughout the book I have been talking about the importance of polyglot (data) architecture and the importance of each microservice governing its own data completely. Going by that, you also want to think about architectures that can provide similar scalability and availability grades but without depending too much on any specific vendor's costly stack.

Microservices architecture by themselves are a way of functionally decomposing systems into many separate pieces so that you can better manage the availability and scalability of each piece independently. Then you have sharding to further manage volumes. With or without shards, you can also look at separating read from writes, and the CQRS introduced in Chapter 12 is apt for that. The combination of the right principles will help you to web scale.

Highly Available and Scalable CQRS Example in Axon

Leaving behind the various vendor offerings from the previous section in defining HA templates, you will return to Axon CQRS, which was introduced in Chapter 12. There you looked at a working code where you completely distribute the different Axon components across JVMs. Since that example was distributed across processes, you can practically distribute them across nodes too; however, you demonstrated the examples with each Axon processor in a single node for simplicity. In the current example, you are going to distribute them into multiple instances of Axon components to validate how to bring redundancy and subsequently HA and scalability to an Axon-based CQRS architecture.

Design the Sample Scenario

You are going to follow the same design as in the "Distributed Command and Event Handling" section in Chapter 12, so I won't repeat all the explanations. There are two entities in your domain, the order and the product. Users can buy a product, which will create a new order. When a new order is created, the product stock will get depreciated. Just that. Revisit that section to get a detailed overview of the architecture of the business scenario you are going to execute in the example here.

You will extend the deployment architecture of the example in Chapter 12 to bring redundancy. You may want to refer to the section titled "Design a Microservice HA Scenario" in Chapter 9 where you already demonstrated the high availability concepts in Spring Cloud. You will follow a similar deployment topology in the current example; however, to make the overall complexity of the example within a certain limit and to concentrate on the point of discussion, HA and scalability in Axon CQRS components alone, you will omit the Spring Cloud components from current example, and the deployment architecture will be as shown in Figure 16-6.

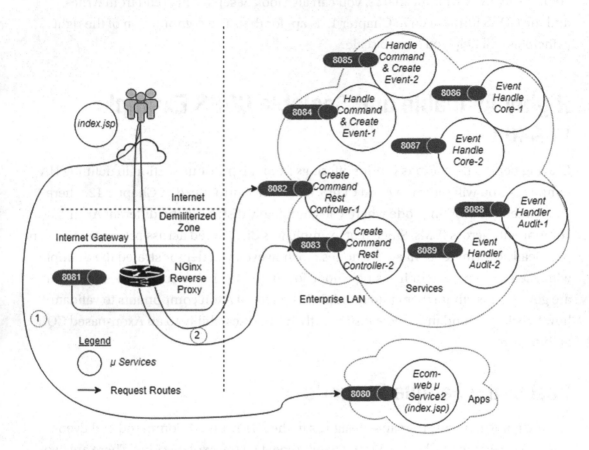

Figure 16-6. *Demo of high availability for Axon CQRS*

The major change in current deployment architecture from that of the sample in the corresponding section in Chapter 12 is that the microservices hosting the command creators, command handlers, event creators, and event handlers are instantiated more than once. Hence the deployment ecosystem has the following characteristics:

- There is more than one type of event handlers interested in the same kind of event.

- There is more than one instance of the same kind of command handler as well as event handler.

In Figure 16-6, you are not routing the request to the web app through Nginx since there is only one instance of the web app, but nothing will prevent you from instantiating more and reverse proxy requests through Nginx. The aim is to validate HA of Axon components alone, hence you're purposefully not replicating the web app, again to keep the complexity of the demonstration in control. However, the REST Controller microservice responsible for creating commands as a result of intercepting HTTP requests is instantiated twice and the requests are routed through the Nginx reverse proxy. This will help to route requests from the web browser to be alternated across these two instances of the REST Controller microservice. In doing so, you make both instances participate in creating commands and spit them to the distributed command bus, which will be further propagated to the application through the JGroups connector. Even though all of the other microservices shown in Figure 16-6 are also listening to HTTP traffic through the embedded HTTP connector, their communication with the other components of the application happens through either JGroups or through the RabbitMQ channel in terms of creating and consuming commands as well as events.

Code the Sample Scenario

The complete code required to demonstrate the simple Axon sample is in folder ch16\ch16-01. There is no major difference in the code from that of Chapter 12, so I won't reproduce it.

Build and Test the High Availability Scenario

As the first step, bring up the RabbitMQ server. You may want to refer to Appendix B to get started with RabbitMQ server.

```
D:\Applns\RabbitMQ\rabbitmq_server-3.6.3\sbin>D:\Applns\RabbitMQ\rabbitmq_
server-3.6.3\sbin\rabbitmq-server.bat
```

Make sure MySQL is up and running. You may want to refer to Appendix H to get started with MySQL.

```
First Bring Up MySQL Server
D:\Applns\MySQL\mysql-8.0.14-winx64\bin>mysqld --console
```

```
Now Open MySQL prompt
D:\Applns\MySQL\mysql-8.0.14-winx64\bin>mysql -u root -p

mysql> use ecom01;
Database changed
mysql>
```

To start with clean tables, delete any tables with the names you want for your samples:

```
mysql> drop table ecom_order;
mysql> drop table ecom_product;
mysql> drop table ecom_order_view;
mysql> drop table ecom_product_view;
mysql> drop table ecom_order_audit;
```

Now the ecom_order and ecom_product tables will be created when the microservice starts up, if they don't exist already. However, you need to explicitly create the Read DB tables and the table for Audit. In your case, you will create all the required tables.

```
mysql> create table ecom_order (id integer not null, last_event_
sequence_number bigint, version bigint, number integer, order_status
varchar(255), price double precision, product_id integer, primary key (id))
ENGINE=InnoDB;
mysql> create table ecom_product (id integer not null, last_event_sequence_
number bigint, version bigint, description varchar(255), price double
precision, stock integer, primary key (id)) ENGINE=InnoDB;
mysql> alter table ecom_order add constraint FK_f3rnd79i90twafllfhpo1sihi
foreign key (product_id) references ecom_product (id);
mysql> create table ecom_product_view(id INT , price DOUBLE, stock INT ,
description VARCHAR(255));
mysql> create table ecom_order_view(id INT , price DOUBLE, number INT ,
description VARCHAR(225),status VARCHAR(50));
mysql> create table ecom_order_audit(id INT ,status VARCHAR(50),
date TIMESTAMP);
```

The sample has a Maven module that contains common classes used by all other microservices. Hence it must be built first:

```
cd D:\binil\gold\pack03\ch16\ch16-01\Ax2-Multi-Command-Multi-Event-Handler-
Instance\06-Ecom-common
D:\binil\gold\pack03\ch16\ch16-01\Ax2-Multi-Command-Multi-Event-Handler-
Instance\06-Ecom-common>make
D:\binil\gold\pack03\ch16\ch16-01\Ax2-Multi-Command-Multi-Event-Handler-
Instance\06-Ecom-common>mvn clean install
```

Next, there are five microservices to build and get running, so you will do so one by one.

Microservice 1: 01-Ecom-web

First, update the configuration files to suit to your environment:

```
ch16\ch16-01\Ax2-Multi-Command-Multi-Event-Handler-Instance\01-Ecom-web\
src\main\resources\application.properties
server.port=8080
```

Note   Don't make any changes here.

Now build and package the executables for the Ecom-web microservice and bring up the server. There is a utility script provided at ch16\ch16-01\Ax2-Multi-Command-Multi-Event-Handler-Instance\01-Ecom-web\make.bat.

```
cd D:\binil\gold\pack03\ch16\ch16-01\Ax2-Multi-Command-Multi-Event-Handler-
Instance\01-Ecom-web
D:\binil\gold\pack03\ch16\ch16-01\Ax2-Multi-Command-Multi-Event-Handler-
Instance\01-Ecom-web>make
D:\binil\gold\pack03\ch16\ch16-01\Ax2-Multi-Command-Multi-Event-Handler-
Instance\01-Ecom-web>mvn clean install
```

You can run the Spring Boot application in more than one way. The straightforward way is to execute the JAR file via the following commands:

```
D:\binil\gold\pack03\ch16\ch16-01\Ax2-Multi-Command-Multi-Event-Handler-
Instance\01-Ecom-web>run
D:\binil\gold\pack03\ch16\ch16-01\Ax2-Multi-Command-Multi-Event-Handler-
Instance\01-Ecom-web>java -Dserver.port=8080 -jar .\target\01-Ecom-
web-0.0.1-SNAPSHOT.jar
```

This will bring up the 01-Ecom-web Spring Boot Server in port 8080.

Microservice 2: 02-Ecom-CreateCommandRestController

The JGroups configuration is provided in the following file:

```
ch16\ch16-01\Ax2-Multi-Command-Multi-Event-Handler-Instance\02-Ecom-
CreateCommandRestController\src\main\resources\udp_config.xml
```

However, let's not worry about the contents of this file too much for now.
Update the configuration files to suit to your environment:

```
ch16\ch16-01\Ax2-Multi-Command-Multi-Event-Handler-Instance\02-Ecom-
CreateCommandRestController\src\main\resources\application.properties
server.port=8082
spring.datasource.url=jdbc:mysql://localhost/ecom01
spring.datasource.username=root
spring.datasource.password=rootpassword
```

```
cd D:\binil\gold\pack03\ch16\ch16-01\Ax2-Multi-Command-Multi-Event-Handler-
Instance\02-Ecom-CreateCommandRestController
D:\binil\gold\pack03\ch16\ch16-01\Ax2-Multi-Command-Multi-Event-Handler-
Instance\02-Ecom-CreateCommandRestController>make
D:\binil\gold\pack03\ch16\ch16-01\Ax2-Multi-Command-Multi-Event-Handler-
Instance\02-Ecom-CreateCommandRestController>mvn clean install
```

You can run the 02-Ecom-CreateCommandRestController Axon Spring Boot application in more than one way. The straightforward way is to execute the JAR file via the following commands:

```
D:\binil\gold\pack03\ch16\ch16-01\Ax2-Multi-Command-Multi-Event-Handler-
Instance\02-Ecom-CreateCommandRestController>run1
D:\binil\gold\pack03\ch16\ch16-01\Ax2-Multi-Command-Multi-Event-Handler-
Instance\02-Ecom-CreateCommandRestController>java -Dserver.port=8082 -jar
.\target\02-Ecom-CreateCommandRestController-0.0.1-SNAPSHOT.jar
```

This will bring up the 02-Ecom-CreateCommandRestController Axon Spring Boot
Server in port 8082.

Bring up another instance clone for the same microservice:

```
cd D:\binil\gold\pack03\ch16\ch16-01\Ax2-Multi-Command-Multi-Event-Handler-
Instance\02-Ecom-CreateCommandRestController
D:\binil\gold\pack03\ch16\ch16-01\Ax2-Multi-Command-Multi-Event-Handler-
Instance\02-Ecom-CreateCommandRestController>run2
D:\binil\gold\pack03\ch16\ch16-01\Ax2-Multi-Command-Multi-Event-Handler-
Instance\02-Ecom-CreateCommandRestController>java -Dserver.port=8083 -jar
.\target\02-Ecom-CreateCommandRestController-0.0.1-SNAPSHOT.jar
```

This will bring up the one more instance of 02-Ecom-CreateCommandRestController
Axon Spring Boot Server in port 8083.

Microservice 3: 03-Ecom-HandleCommandAndCreateEvent

Update the configuration files to suit to your environment; see Listing 16-1.

Listing 16-1. Microservice 3 Configuration (ch16\ch16-01\Ax2-Multi-Command-
Multi-Event-Handler-Instance\03-Ecom-HandleCommandAndCreateEvent\src\
main\resources\application.properties)

```
server.port=8084
spring.datasource.url=jdbc:mysql://localhost/ecom01
spring.datasource.username=root
spring.datasource.password=rootpassword

ecom.amqp.rabbit.address= 127.0.0.1:5672
ecom.amqp.rabbit.username= guest
ecom.amqp.rabbit.password= guest
ecom.amqp.rabbit.vhost=/
```

```
ecom.amqp.rabbit.exchange=Ecom-02
ecom.amqp.rabbit.queue=Ecom-createcommand_03
```

```
cd D:\binil\gold\pack03\ch16\ch16-01\Ax2-Multi-Command-Multi-Event-Handler-
Instance\03-Ecom-HandleCommandAndCreateEvent
D:\binil\gold\pack03\ch16\ch16-01\Ax2-Multi-Command-Multi-Event-Handler-
Instance\03-Ecom-HandleCommandAndCreateEvent>make
D:\binil\gold\pack03\ch16\ch16-01\Ax2-Multi-Command-Multi-Event-Handler-
Instance\03-Ecom-HandleCommandAndCreateEvent>mvn clean install
```

You can run two instances of the 03-Ecom-HandleCommandAndCreateEvent Axon Spring Boot application in more than one way. The straightforward way is to execute the JAR file via the following commands:

```
D:\binil\gold\pack03\ch16\ch16-01\Ax2-Multi-Command-Multi-Event-Handler-
Instance\03-Ecom-HandleCommandAndCreateEvent>run1
D:\binil\gold\pack03\ch16\ch16-01\Ax2-Multi-Command-Multi-Event-Handler-
Instance\03-Ecom-HandleCommandAndCreateEvent>java -Dserver.port=8084 -jar .\
target\03-Ecom-HandleCommandAndCreateEvent-0.0.1-SNAPSHOT.jar
```

This will bring up the 02-Ecom-CreateCommandRestController Axon Spring Boot Server in port 8084.

```
cd D:\binil\gold\pack03\ch16\ch16-01\Ax2-Multi-Command-Multi-Event-Handler-
Instance\03-Ecom-HandleCommandAndCreateEvent
D:\binil\gold\pack03\ch16\ch16-01\Ax2-Multi-Command-Multi-Event-Handler-
Instance\03-Ecom-HandleCommandAndCreateEvent>run2
D:\binil\gold\pack03\ch16\ch16-01\Ax2-Multi-Command-Multi-Event-Handler-
Instance\03-Ecom-HandleCommandAndCreateEvent>java -Dserver.port=8085
-jar .\target\03-Ecom-HandleCommandAndCreateEvent-0.0.1-SNAPSHOT.jar
```

And this will bring up the 02-Ecom-CreateCommandRestController Axon Spring Boot Server in port 8085.

Microservice 4: 04-Ecom-EventHandleCore

Update the configuration files to suit to your environment, as shown in Listing 16-2.

Listing 16-2. Microservice 4 Configuration (ch16\ch16-01\Ax2-Multi-Command-Multi-Event-Handler-Instance\04-Ecom-EventHandleCore\src\main\resources\application.properties)

```
server.port=8086
spring.datasource.url=jdbc:mysql://localhost/ecom01
spring.datasource.username=root
spring.datasource.password=rootpassword

ecom.amqp.rabbit.address= 127.0.0.1:5672
ecom.amqp.rabbit.username= guest
ecom.amqp.rabbit.password= guest
ecom.amqp.rabbit.vhost=/
ecom.amqp.rabbit.exchange=Ecom-02
ecom.amqp.rabbit.queue=Ecom-event-core_03

cd D:\binil\gold\pack03\ch16\ch16-01\Ax2-Multi-Command-Multi-Event-Handler-
Instance\04-Ecom-EventHandleCore
D:\binil\gold\pack03\ch16\ch16-01\Ax2-Multi-Command-Multi-Event-Handler-
Instance\04-Ecom-EventHandleCore>make
D:\binil\gold\pack03\ch16\ch16-01\Ax2-Multi-Command-Multi-Event-Handler-
Instance\04-Ecom-EventHandleCore>mvn clean install
```

You can run two instances of the 04-Ecom-EventHandleCore Axon Spring Boot application again in more than one way. The straightforward way is to execute the JAR file via the following commands:

```
D:\binil\gold\pack03\ch16\ch16-01\Ax2-Multi-Command-Multi-Event-Handler-
Instance\04-Ecom-EventHandleCore>run1
D:\binil\gold\pack03\ch16\ch16-01\Ax2-Multi-Command-Multi-Event-Handler-
Instance\04-Ecom-EventHandleCore>java -Dserver.port=8086 -jar .\target\04-
Ecom-EventHandleCore-0.0.1-SNAPSHOT.jar
```

This will bring up the 04-Ecom-EventHandleCore Axon Spring Boot Server in port 8086.

```
cd D:\binil\gold\pack03\ch16\ch16-01\Ax2-Multi-Command-Multi-Event-Handler-
Instance\04-Ecom-EventHandleCore
```

```
D:\binil\gold\pack03\ch16\ch16-01\Ax2-Multi-Command-Multi-Event-Handler-
Instance\04-Ecom-EventHandleCore>run2
D:\binil\gold\pack03\ch16\ch16-01\Ax2-Multi-Command-Multi-Event-Handler-
Instance\04-Ecom-EventHandleCore>java -Dserver.port=8087 -jar .\target\04-
Ecom-EventHandleCore-0.0.1-SNAPSHOT.jar
```

And this will bring up the 04-Ecom-EventHandleCore Axon Spring Boot Server in port 8087.

Microservice 5: 05-Ecom-EventHandlerAudit

This is the last microservice you want to bring up in this sample. Update the configuration files to suit to your environment, as shown in Listing 16-3.

Listing 16-3. Microservice 5 Configuration Parameters (ch16\ch16-01\Ax2-Multi-Command-Multi-Event-Handler-Instance\05-Ecom-EventHandlerAudit\src\main\resources\application.properties)

```
server.port=8088
spring.datasource.url=jdbc:mysql://localhost/ecom01
spring.datasource.username=root
spring.datasource.password=rootpassword

ecom.amqp.rabbit.address= 127.0.0.1:5672
ecom.amqp.rabbit.username= guest
ecom.amqp.rabbit.password= guest
ecom.amqp.rabbit.vhost=/
ecom.amqp.rabbit.exchange=Ecom-02
ecom.amqp.rabbit.queue=Ecom-event-history_03

cd D:\binil\gold\pack03\ch16\ch16-01\Ax2-Multi-Command-Multi-Event-Handler-
Instance\05-Ecom-EventHandlerAudit
D:\binil\gold\pack03\ch16\ch16-01\Ax2-Multi-Command-Multi-Event-Handler-
Instance\05-Ecom-EventHandlerAudit>make
D:\binil\gold\pack03\ch16\ch16-01\Ax2-Multi-Command-Multi-Event-Handler-
Instance\05-Ecom-EventHandlerAudit>mvn clean install
```

You can run two instances of 05-Ecom-EventHandlerAudit Axon Spring Boot application in more than one way. The straightforward way is to execute the JAR file via the following commands:

```
D:\binil\gold\pack03\ch16\ch16-01\Ax2-Multi-Command-Multi-Event-Handler-
Instance\05-Ecom-EventHandlerAudit>run1
D:\binil\gold\pack03\ch16\ch16-01\Ax2-Multi-Command-Multi-Event-Handler-
Instance\05-Ecom-EventHandlerAudit>java -Dserver.port=8088 -Dspring.
application.name=product-audit-01 -jar .\target\05-Ecom-EventHandlerAudit-
0.0.1-SNAPSHOT.jar
```

This will bring up the 05-Ecom-EventHandlerAudit Axon Spring Boot Server in port 8088.

```
cd D:\binil\gold\pack03\ch16\ch16-01\Ax2-Multi-Command-Multi-Event-Handler-
Instance\05-Ecom-EventHandlerAudit
D:\binil\gold\pack03\ch16\ch16-01\Ax2-Multi-Command-Multi-Event-Handler-
Instance\05-Ecom-EventHandlerAudit>run2
D:\binil\gold\pack03\ch16\ch16-01\Ax2-Multi-Command-Multi-Event-Handler-
Instance\05-Ecom-EventHandlerAudit>java -Dserver.port=8089 -Dspring.
application.name=product-audit-02 -jar .\target\05-Ecom-EventHandlerAudit-
0.0.1-SNAPSHOT.jar
```

And this will bring up the 05-Ecom-EventHandlerAudit Axon Spring Boot Server in port 8089.

This finishes the starting of all microservices.

Now, prepopulate the ecom_product and ecom_product_view tables with some initial data:

```
mysql> insert into ecom_product(id,description,price,stock,version)
values(1,'Shirts',100,5,0);
mysql> insert into ecom_product(id,description,price,stock,version)
values(2,'Pants',100,5,0);
mysql> insert into ecom_product(id,description,price,stock,version)
values(3,'T-Shirt',100,5,0);
mysql> insert into ecom_product(id,description,price,stock,version)
values(4,'Shoes',100,5,0);
```

```
mysql> insert into ecom_product_view(id,description,price,stock)
values(1,'Shirts',100,5);
mysql> insert into ecom_product_view(id,description,price,stock)
values(2,'Pants',100,5);
mysql> insert into ecom_product_view(id,description,price,stock)
values(3,'T-Shirt',100,5);
mysql> insert into ecom_product_view(id,description,price,stock)
values(4,'Shoes',100,5);
```

Next, you need to configure Nginx as a reverse proxy. Apply the relevant parts of ch16\ch16-01\Ax2-Multi-Command-Multi-Event-Handler-Instance\ConfNginx\ nginx.conf to your Nginx configuration; see Listing 16-4.

Listing 16-4. Nginx Configuration Parameters (D:\Applns\nginx\nginx-1.13.5\ conf\nginx.conf)

```
http {

    upstream myapp1 {
        server localhost:8082;
        server localhost:8083;
    }

    server {
        listen        8081;
        server_name  localhost;

        location / {
            proxy_pass http://myapp1;
            root    html;
            index   index.html index.htm;
        }
    }
}
```

You may want to refer to Appendix C to get started with Nginx.

After making above said configuration changes, bring up Nginx:

```
cd D:\Applns\nginx\nginx-1.13.5
D:\Applns\nginx\nginx-1.13.5>nginx
```

You can use a browser (preferably chrome) and point to `http://localhost:8080/`. If the change is not reflected, you may close the browser session and take a new browser instance and try the above URL.

You may test the sample by following the steps described previously in the subsection titled "Build and Test the Sample Scenario" under the section "Distributed Command and Event Handling" in Chapter 12. While you test the sample, if you keep watching the console windows of the microservice instances, you can verify that the HTTP requests will alternate hitting both instances of the CreateCommandRestController microservice since Nginx will reverse proxy the requests to both these instances. Similarly, the command handling and event handling will alternate between both instances of the respective microservices. You may also want to bring down any one instance of the microservice for a while, during which, if you keep testing by pumping requests, you can see that the corresponding processing happens in the other live instance of the microservice always. Later, if you bring back the previously down instance, you can see that the processing gets evenly distributed again across both the instances.

Scaling Aggregate Root Entities in Write Nodes for AXON CQRS

The previous section demonstrated how to scale the CQRS architecture in Axon by adding more nodes to handle commands and events. Let's explore the caveats involved in scaling the write node or the command handling node.

Concurrently Modify Requests to Clone of Same Entity

In the section titled "Independent Read and Write Scalability to improve Efficiency" you saw the architecture template based on Oracle where there is a single write node or primary database where you route all writes and multiple read nodes or a secondary database to manage queries. You know the reason to favor this kind of architecture:

to manage the high look to book ratio or similar characteristics of most business applications where the number of read transactions is much higher compared to that of write transactions.

When you add the CQRS layer on top of data persistence, you have partitioned the command and query handling into nodes or processes separate from that of the data persistence. Further, when you replicate the microservices handling the command and query handling into multiple instances, a typical architecture is as shown in Figure 16-7.

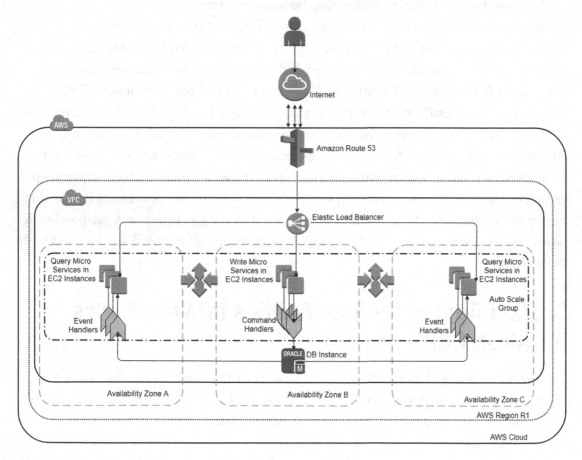

Figure 16-7. *Scaled out CQRS architecture*

Referring to Figure 16-7, scaling out event handlers is straightforward, since all of the event handlers will be notified and all of them can take whatever actions, refreshing the materialized views or cache with them in most cases. If you look at the scaling out scenario of command handlers, there can be more complexities. Figure 16-8 depicts a scenario where you have many instances of microservices hosting the command handlers.

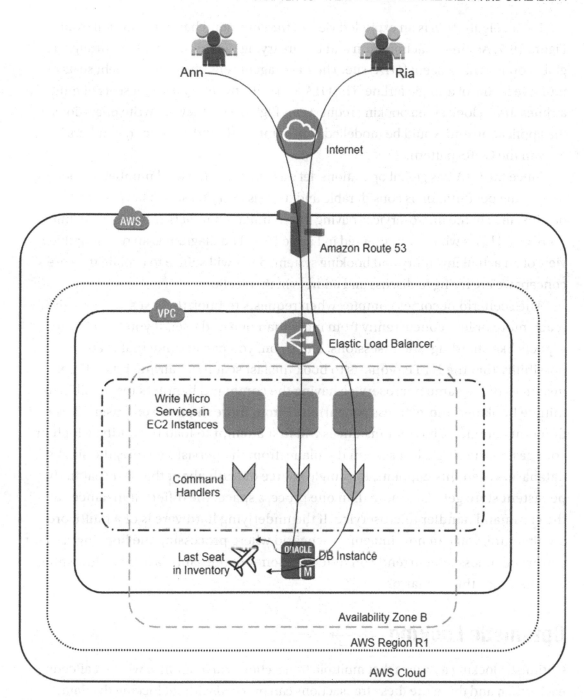

Figure 16-8. Scaled out command handlers

In fact Figure 16-8 is an exploded view of the command handling portion from Figure 16-7. Assume that both Ann and Ria are trying to book a flight seat through a global online travel agent (OTA) site. The travel agent sells inventory of flight seats of multiple flights of a single airline. The OTA also sells inventory of flight seats of multiple airlines. If you look at the booking requests for flight seats, they are write operations to the application and would be modelled with commands and command handlers if you go with the CQRS pattern.

Since the OTA has global operations, let's assume that the total number of bookings happening per duration is considerable and there is every reason to have more than one instance of the microservices having the command handlers responsible to initiate bookings. This is what is represented in Figure 16-8. The diagram is an oversimplified view of an actual inventory and booking system, but it will suffice to explain the core concept we are trying to discuss and address in this section.

The scenario becomes complex when requests to book the last seat in an airline reach more or less concurrently from more than one end user. If you forget other aspects like sharding, sticky sessions, and so on, you can assume that there is a possibility that the HTTP requests to book the last seat in an airline hits different instances of the same microservice having the command handlers responsible to initiate bookings, more or less concurrently from more than one end user. These different command handler instances will first attempt to load the entity, which in your case is the single last seat on the plane, from the persistent store, the single database. When this happens, the single source of truth about that last seat in the persistent store gets into more than one process space, the different instances of the command handler microservice. If the underlying hardware is of a multicore architecture, you can now imagine a scenario where processing the booking request gets more or less concurrently on different clones of the same last seat. How should you deal with this scenario?

Optimistic Locking

Optimistic locking assumes that multiple transactions can complete without affecting each other, and therefore these transactions can proceed without locking the data resources that they affect. However, before committing, each transaction verifies that no other transaction has modified its data. If the validation conflicts, the committing transaction rolls back.

Optimistic locking is typically used for long transactions or conversations that span several database transactions. But the same strategy can also be used for short transactions. You can store versioning information in the entity so that if the same entity is updated by more than one conversation, the subsequent commit attempts are informed of the conflict and do not override the previous conversation's work. This approach guarantees some isolation, but scales well and works particularly well in read-often, write-sometimes situations. Hibernate provides two different mechanisms for storing versioning information, a dedicated version number or a timestamp.

For this examples, you are using Hibernate as the persistence service provider. So, in cases where there is more than one transactions getting progressed in the same entity, Hibernate will allow one of them to commit (typically the one that gets completed first) and the other transaction will get a `org.hibernate.StaleObjectStateException,` and this exception will carry information about the particular entity instance that was the source of the failure. A sample is provided here:

```
Caused by: org.hibernate.StaleObjectStateException: Row was updated or
deleted by another transaction (or unsaved-value mapping was incorrect) :
[com.axon.concurrency.user.model.User#1]
```

Upon receiving such an exception, the persistence provider will interpret that an optimistic locking conflict occurred and throw a `javax.persistence.OptimisticLockException.` This exception may be thrown as part of an API call, a flush, or at commit time. When doing so, the current transaction, if one is active, will be marked for rollback.

Conflict Detection and Resolution in Axon

One of the major advantages of being explicit about the meaning of changes is that you can detect conflicting changes with more precision. Typically, these conflicting changes occur when two users are acting on the same data more or less concurrently. Referring to Figure 16-8, if Ann and Ria, both looking at a specific version of the data, believe that the status of the last seat they both looked is "Available for Booking," then they both can decide to make a change to that data. They will both send a command like "on version X of this aggregate, do that," where X is the expected version of the aggregate on which the changes are to be applied; at least, this is what both Ann and Ria expect. In this case, one of them will have the changes actually applied to the expected version. By the time the system is about to apply the changes on behalf of the other user, the expected version on which the changes are to be applied would have changed, hence the changes on behalf of that particular user will not be applied.

`org.axonframework.domain.AggregateRoot<I>` is the interface defining a contract for entities that represent the aggregate root where I represents the type of the identifier of this aggregate. AggregateRoot provides a method called `Long getVersion()`.

`AggregateRoot.getVersion()` returns the current version number of the aggregate or null if the aggregate is a newly created one. This version must reflect the version number of the aggregate on which the changes are applied. Each time the aggregate is modified and stored in a repository, the version number must be increased by at least 1. This version number can be used by optimistic locking strategies and detection of conflicting concurrent modification.

Typically the sequence number of the last committed event on this aggregate is used as a version number.

As a convenience measure, Axon also provides `org.axonframework.domain.AbstractAggregateRoot<I>`, which is a very basic implementation of the AggregateRoot interface. It provides the mechanism to keep track of uncommitted events and maintains a version number based on the number of events generated. For most of the cases, it is enough that you extend your Aggregate Root entities from this abstract class.

Example Demonstrating Optimistic Locking in Axon CQRS

In this section, you will look at a working example demonstrating the optimistic locking strategy of Axon. You will set up an environment similar to that shown in Figure 16-8; however, you will not deploy in the cloud. Instead you will run in your own PC and also you will have only two instances of the microservices, since if the working can be demonstrated for two microservices it can be assumed to work in scenarios involving more than two instances of the microservice.

Design the Sample Scenario

You will simulate two users attempting to modify the same entity concurrently. For that, you will have a simple Axon microservice consisting of a REST Controller and a command handler. The REST Controller can accept POST and PUT requests to create and modify records of the User entity. See Figure 16-9.

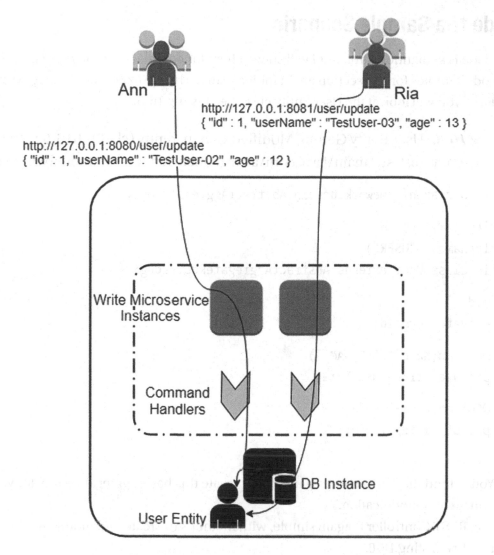

Figure 16-9. *Design for sample scenario to test optimistic locking*

You need to tweak the processing of the "modify" operation in such a manner as to simulate the concurrent modification scenario. For that, you will introduce a delay by using the Thread.sleep() method so that while the first modification operation is in the sleep state you have enough time to also start a second modification request.

Code the Sample Scenario

The code is straightforward., but I will show it here for completeness of the example. All the code samples for this section are in folder ch16\ch16-02\Ax2-Cuncurrency-Test.

First, you will look at the User Entity class. See Listing 16-5.

Listing 16-5. User Entity Getting Modified Concurrently (ch16\ch16-02\Ax2-Cuncurrency-Test\src\main\java\com\axon\concurrency\user\model\User.java)

```
import org.axonframework.domain.AbstractAggregateRoot;

@Entity
@Table(name = "USER")
public class User extends AbstractAggregateRoot<Long> {

    @Id
    private Long id;

    @Column(name="USER_NAME")
    private String userName;

    @Column(name="AGE")
    private Integer age;
}
```

You extend the AbstractAggregateRoot to create this basic aggregate entity for you to test concurrent modification.

The REST Controller is again simple, with methods to create and modify the User entities. See Listing 16-6.

Listing 16-6. REST Controller creating Commands (ch16\ch16-02\Ax2-Cuncurrency-Test\src\main\java\com\axon\concurrency\user\web\UserController.java)

```
@RestController
public class UserController {

    @Autowired
    private CommandGateway commandGateway;
```

```
@RequestMapping(method = RequestMethod.POST,path="/user/create")
public void createNewUser(@RequestBody UserDTO userDTO){

    UserCreationCommand command = new UserCreationCommand(userDTO.getId(),
            userDTO.getUserName(), userDTO.getAge());
    try{
        commandGateway.sendAndWait(command);
    }
    catch(RuntimeException runtimeException){
        LOGGER.error(runtimeException.getMessage());
    }
}

@RequestMapping(method = RequestMethod.PUT,path="/user/update")
public void updateUser(@RequestBody UserDTO userDTO){

    UserModificationCommand command = new UserModificationCommand(
            userDTO.getId(), userDTO.getUserName(), userDTO.getAge());
    try{
        commandGateway.sendAndWait(command);
    }
    catch(RuntimeException runtimeException){
        LOGGER.error(runtimeException.getMessage());
    }
}
}
```

You create and send a UserCreationCommand for new user creation. You also create and send a UserModificationCommand for a user modification request. Both the UserCreationCommand and the UserModificationCommand are handled by the UserCommandHandler. See Listing 16-7.

Listing 16-7. Axon Command Handler (ch16\ch16-02\Ax2-Cuncurrency-Test\src\main\java\com\axon\concurrency\user\command\handler\UserCommandHandler.java)

```java
@Component
public class UserCommandHandler {

    @Autowired
    @Qualifier(value = "userRepository")
    private Repository<User> userRepository;

    @CommandHandler
    public void handleUserCreationCommand(UserCreationCommand
            userCreationCommand) {

        User user = new User(userCreationCommand.getId(),
            userCreationCommand.getUserName(), userCreationCommand.getAge());
        userRepository.add(user);
    }

    @CommandHandler
    public void handleUserModifyCommand(UserModificationCommand
            userModificationCommand) {

        User user = userRepository.load(userModificationCommand.getId());
        user.setAge(userModificationCommand.getAge());
        user.setUserName(userModificationCommand.getUserName());

        Long seconds = 60L;
        LOGGER.debug("Thread Sleeping for {} seconds", seconds);
        try{
            Thread.sleep(1000 * seconds);
        }catch(Exception exception){
            LOGGER.error(exception.getMessage());
        }
    }
}
```

That completes the main code.

Build and Test the Sample Scenario

As the first step, you need to bring up MySQL Server. You may want to refer to Appendix H to get started with MySQL Server.

```
D:\Applns\MySQL\mysql-8.0.14-winx64\bin>mysqld --console
```

Now open a MySQL prompt:

```
D:\Applns\MySQL\mysql-8.0.14-winx64\bin>mysql -u root -p
```

```
mysql> use ecom01;
Database changed
mysql>
```

To start with clean tables, delete any tables with the names you want for your samples:

```
mysql> drop table user;
```

Update the configuration files to suit to your environment; see Listing 16-8.

Listing 16-8. MySQL Configuration (ch16\ch16-02\Ax2-Cuncurrency-Test\src\ main\resources\application.properties)

```
server.port: 8080
spring.datasource.url=jdbc:mysql://localhost/ecom01
spring.datasource.username=root
spring.datasource.password=rootpassword
```

Note   Don't make any changes here.

You will now build and package the executables for the Concurrency Test microservice and bring up two instances of the server. There is a utility script in folder ch16\ch16-02\Ax2-Cuncurrency-Test\make.bat.

```
cd D:\binil\gold\pack03\ch16\ch16-02\Ax2-Cuncurrency-Test
D:\binil\gold\pack03\ch16\ch16-02\Ax2-Cuncurrency-Test>make
D:\binil\gold\pack03\ch16\ch16-02\Ax2-Cuncurrency-Test>mvn clean install
```

You can run the Spring Boot application in more than one way. The straightforward way is to execute the JAR file via the following commands:

```
D:\binil\gold\pack03\ch16\ch16-02\Ax2-Cuncurrency-Test>run1
D:\binil\gold\pack03\ch16\ch16-02\Ax2-Cuncurrency-Test>java -Dserver.
port=8080 -jar .\target\Axon-Concurrency-test-0.0.1-SNAPSHOT.jar
```

This will bring up your first instance of the command handler in port 8080. This will also create the required User table in the database for this example. You may want to note the additional fields, last_event_sequence_number and version, that Axon has created to manage the AggregateRoot entity in Listing 16-9.

Listing 16-9. User Table for the AggregateRoot Entity

```
mysql> desc user;
+----------------------------+--------------+------+-----+---------+-------+
| Field                      | Type         | Null | Key | Default | Extra |
+----------------------------+--------------+------+-----+---------+-------+
| id                         | bigint(20)   | NO   | PRI | NULL    |       |
| last_event_sequence_number | bigint(20)   | YES  |     | NULL    |       |
| version                    | bigint(20)   | YES  |     | NULL    |       |
| age                        | int(11)      | YES  |     | NULL    |       |
| user_name                  | varchar(255) | YES  |     | NULL    |       |
+----------------------------+--------------+------+-----+---------+-------+
5 rows in set (0.04 sec)
mysql>
```

You need at least one more instance of the same microservice to simulate concurrent modification requests on different clones of the same Axon Aggregate. You will do this in another window.

```
cd D:\binil\gold\pack03\ch16\ch16-02\Ax2-Cuncurrency-Test
D:\binil\gold\pack03\ch16\ch16-02\Ax2-Cuncurrency-Test>run2
D:\binil\gold\pack03\ch16\ch16-02\Ax2-Cuncurrency-Test>java -Dserver.
port=8081 -jar .\target\Axon-Concurrency-test-0.0.1-SNAPSHOT.jar
```

This will bring up your second instance of the command handler in port 8081.

You need to create a User entity in your domain. Take Postman and send a HTTP POST request sending the User data in the JSON format to create a new user, as shown in Figure 16-10. You may want to refer to Appendix D to know more about Postman.

```
HTTP POST: http://127.0.0.1:8080/user/create
Body: JSON(application/json)
{ "id" : 1, "userName" : "TestUser-01", "age" : 11 }
```

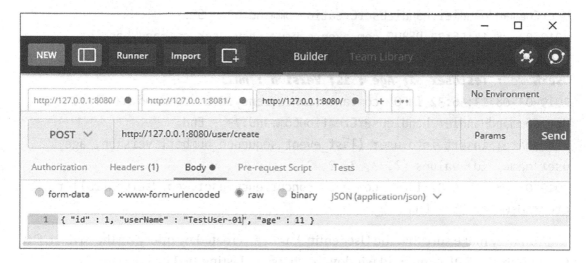

Figure 16-10. *Create a new user*

Listing 16-10 shows the microservice console showing the logs for the user creation.

Listing 16-10. Microservice Console Showing User Creation

```
D:\binil\gold\pack03\ch16\ch16-02\Ax2-Cuncurrency-Test>run1

D:\binil\gold\pack03\ch16\ch16-02\Ax2-Cuncurrency-Test>java -Dserver.
port=8080 -jar .\target\Axon-Concurrency-test-0.0.1-SNAPSHOT.jar


  .   ___          _            __ _ _
 /\\ / ___'_ __ _ _(_)_ __  __ _ \ \ \ \
( ( )\___ | '_ | '_| | '_ \/ _` | \ \ \ \
 \\/  ___)| |_)| | | | | || (_| |  ) ) ) )
  '  |____| .__|_| |_|_| |_\__, | / / / /
 =========|_|==============|___/=/_/_/_/
 :: Spring Boot ::        (v1.3.5.RELEASE)
```

```
...
2019-03-08 13:53:39 INFO  org.springframework.boot.StartupInfoLogger.
logStarted:57 - Started AxonApplication in 36.376 seconds (JVM running for 39.958)
...
2019-03-08 13:56:32 INFO  com.axon.concurrency.user.web.UserController.
createNewUser:67 - Start
2019-03-08 13:56:32 INFO  com.axon.concurrency.user.command.handler.
UserCommandHandler.handleUserCreationCommand:69 - Start
2019-03-08 13:56:32 DEBUG com.axon.concurrency.user.command.handler.
UserCommandHandler.handleUserCreationCommand:72 - New User Created : ID : 1;
UserName : TestUser-01; Age : 11; Version : null
2019-03-08 13:56:32 INFO  com.axon.concurrency.user.command.handler.
UserCommandHandler.handleUserCreationCommand:73 - End
Hibernate: insert into user (last_event_sequence_number, version, age,
user_name, id) values (?, ?, ?, ?, ?)
2019-03-08 13:56:32 INFO  com.axon.concurrency.user.web.UserController.
createNewUser:76 - End
```

You may make sure that the User entity has been created by querying the MySQL DB through the MySQL command window, as shown in Listing 16-11.

Listing 16-11. Inspecting the Newly Created User

```
mysql> select * from user;
+----+----------------------------+---------+------+-------------+
| id | last_event_sequence_number | version | age  | user_name   |
+----+----------------------------+---------+------+-------------+
|  1 |                       NULL |       0 |   11 | TestUser-01 |
+----+----------------------------+---------+------+-------------+
1 row in set (0.00 sec)

mysql>
```

You should now target to modify the above created User from more than one client, more or less concurrently. The User modification processing is now configured with a delay of 60 seconds. That means after you fire the first modification request, you should also fire another modification request within the next 60 seconds (within the next 60 – delta seconds, to be on the safer side).

Take Postman and send a HTTP PUT request sending the User data in JSON format to update the previously created user, as shown in Figure 16-11.

```
HTTP PUT http://127.0.0.1:8080/user/update
BODY Raw JSON(application/json)
{ "id" : 1, "userName" : "TestUser-02", "age" : 12 }
```

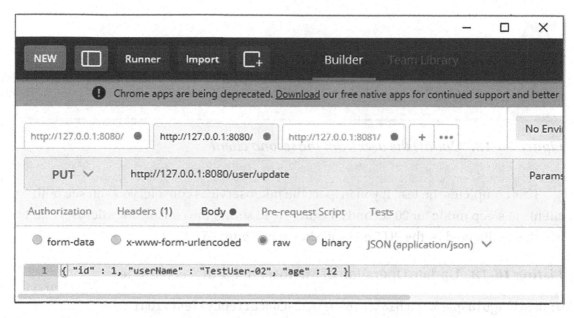

Figure 16-11. *Update the user from the first client*

Without losing much time, fire one more HTTP PUT request sending the User data in JSON format to update the previously created user with slightly different data so that you will be able to distinguish between updates effected by above two actions, as shown in Figure 16-12.

```
HTTP PUT http://127.0.0.1:8081/user/update
BODY Raw JSON(application/json)
{ "id" : 1, "userName" : "TestUser-03", "age" : 13 }
```

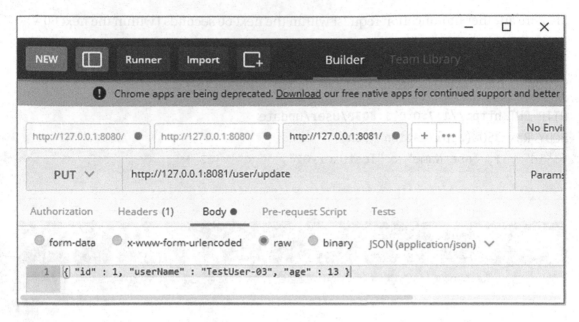

Figure 16-12. *Update the user from the second client*

This completes the test. If you inspect the microservices console, you can see both clients in sleep mode for 20 seconds. Listing 16-12 shows the console for Microservice 1, which was affected by the PUT method shown in Figure 16-11.

Listing 16-12. Update Operation of Microservice 1 in Sleep Mode

```
D:\binil\gold\pack03\ch16\ch16-02\Ax2-Cuncurrency-Test>run1

D:\binil\gold\pack03\ch16\ch16-02\Ax2-Cuncurrency-Test>java -Dserver.
port=8080 -jar .\target\Axon-Concurrency-test-0.0.1-SNAPSHOT.jar


  .   ____          _            __ _ _
 /\\ / ___'_ __ _ _(_)_ __  __ _ \ \ \ \
( ( )\___ | '_ | '_| | '_ \/ _` | \ \ \ \
 \\/  ___)| |_)| | | | | || (_| |  ) ) ) )
  '  |____| .__|_| |_|_| |_\__, | / / / /
 =========|_|==============|___/=/_/_/_/
 :: Spring Boot ::        (v1.3.5.RELEASE)
```

630

...
2019-03-08 13:53:39 INFO org.springframework.boot.StartupInfoLogger.
logStarted:57 - Started AxonApplication in 36.376 seconds (JVM running for 39.958)
...
2019-03-08 13:56:32 INFO com.axon.concurrency.user.web.UserController.
createNewUser:67 - Start
2019-03-08 13:56:32 INFO com.axon.concurrency.user.command.handler.
UserCommandHandler.handleUserCreationCommand:69 - Start
2019-03-08 13:56:32 DEBUG com.axon.concurrency.user.command.handler.
UserCommandHandler.handleUserCreationCommand:72 - **New User Created : ID :
1; UserName : TestUser-01; Age : 11; Version : null**
2019-03-08 13:56:32 INFO com.axon.concurrency.user.command.handler.
UserCommandHandler.handleUserCreationCommand:73 - End
Hibernate: insert into user (last_event_sequence_number, version, age,
user_name, id) values (?, ?, ?, ?, ?)
2019-03-08 13:56:32 INFO com.axon.concurrency.user.web.UserController.
createNewUser:76 - End
2019-03-08 14:00:56 INFO com.axon.concurrency.user.web.UserController.
updateUser:82 - Start
2019-03-08 14:00:56 INFO com.axon.concurrency.user.command.handler.
UserCommandHandler.handleUserModifyCommand:79 - Start
Hibernate: select user0_.id as id1_0_0_, user0_.last_event_sequence_
number as last_eve2_0_0_, user0_.version as version3_0_0_, user0_.age
as age4_0_0_, user0_.user_name as user_nam5_0_0_ from user user0_ where
user0_.id=?
2019-03-08 14:00:56 DEBUG com.axon.concurrency.user.command.handler.
UserCommandHandler.handleUserModifyCommand:82 - **User Found : ID : 1;
UserName : TestUser-01; Age : 11; Version : 0; versionInitial : 0**
2019-03-08 14:00:56 DEBUG com.axon.concurrency.user.command.handler.
UserCommandHandler.handleUserModifyCommand:85 - **User Modified to : ID : 1;
UserName : TestUser-02; Age : 12; Version : 0**
2019-03-08 14:00:56 DEBUG com.axon.concurrency.user.command.handler.
UserCommandHandler.handleUserModifyCommand:88 - **User Queried : ID : 1;
UserName : TestUser-02; Age : 12; Version : 0; versionQueried : 0.**

```
2019-03-08 14:00:56 DEBUG com.axon.concurrency.user.command.handler.
UserCommandHandler.handleUserModifyCommand:90 - Thread Sleeping for
60 seconds
```

Listing 16-13 shows the console for Microservice 2, which was affected by the PUT method shown in Figure 16-12.

Listing 16-13. Update Operation of Microservice 2 in Sleep Mode

```
D:\binil\gold\pack03\ch16\ch16-02\Ax2-Cuncurrency-Test>run2

D:\binil\gold\pack03\ch16\ch16-02\Ax2-Cuncurrency-Test>java -Dserver.
port=8081 -jar .\target\Axon-Concurrency-test-0.0.1-SNAPSHOT.jar


  .   ____          _            __ _ _
 /\\ / ___'_ __ _ _(_)_ __  __ _ \ \ \ \
( ( )\___ | '_ | '_| | '_ \/ _` | \ \ \ \
 \\/  ___)| |_)| | | | | || (_| |  ) ) ) )
  '  |____| .__|_| |_|_| |_\__, | / / / /
 =========|_|==============|___/=/_/_/_/
 :: Spring Boot ::        (v1.3.5.RELEASE)

...
2019-03-08 13:53:39 INFO  org.springframework.boot.StartupInfoLogger.
logStarted:57 - Started AxonApplication in 29.656 seconds
(JVM running for 31.918)

...
2019-03-08 14:01:01 INFO  com.axon.concurrency.user.web.UserController.
updateUser:82 - Start
2019-03-08 14:01:01 INFO  com.axon.concurrency.user.command.handler.
UserCommandHandler.handleUserModifyCommand:79 - Start
Hibernate: select user0_.id as id1_0_0_, user0_.last_event_sequence_
number as last_eve2_0_0_, user0_.version as version3_0_0_, user0_.age
as age4_0_0_, user0_.user_name as user_nam5_0_0_ from user user0_ where
user0_.id=?
```

```
2019-03-08 14:01:01 DEBUG com.axon.concurrency.user.command.handler.
UserCommandHandler.handleUserModifyCommand:82 - User Found : ID : 1;
UserName : TestUser-01; Age : 11; Version : 0; versionInitial : 0
2019-03-08 14:01:01 DEBUG com.axon.concurrency.user.command.handler.
UserCommandHandler.handleUserModifyCommand:85 - User Modified to : ID : 1;
UserName : TestUser-03; Age : 13; Version : 0
2019-03-08 14:01:01 DEBUG com.axon.concurrency.user.command.handler.
UserCommandHandler.handleUserModifyCommand:88 - User Queried : ID : 1;
UserName : TestUser-03; Age : 13; Version : 0; versionQueried : 0
2019-03-08 14:01:01 DEBUG com.axon.concurrency.user.command.handler.User
CommandHandler.handleUserModifyCommand:90 - Thread Sleeping for 60 seconds
```

Look closely at Listing 16-12 and Listing 16-13 and appreciate that both clients have attempted to effect the updates using different values.

Now refer back to the section titled "Transaction Isolation Control Methods" in Chapter 13 where I defined optimistic locking, which takes a pragmatic approach and encourages clients to be "optimistic" that data will not change while they are using it and so allows them to access same data concurrently. Wait until both of the corresponding updates processing, which are in the sleep mode, wake up and finish the update and attempt to commit the transaction. You will see that one of the clients has succeeded in updating.

Listing 16-14 shows the console of Microservice 1, which woke up first (since it started sleeping first) is successful in commiting the update.

Listing 16-14. Update Operation of Microservice 1 Committed

```
D:\binil\gold\pack03\ch16\ch16-02\Ax2-Cuncurrency-Test>run1

D:\binil\gold\pack03\ch16\ch16-02\Ax2-Cuncurrency-Test>java -Dserver.
port=8080 -jar .\target\Axon-Concurrency-test-0.0.1-SNAPSHOT.jar

  .   ____          _            __ _ _
 /\\ / ___'_ __ _ _(_)_ __  __ _ \ \ \ \
( ( )\___ | '_ | '_| | '_ \/ _` | \ \ \ \
 \\/  ___)| |_)| | | | | || (_| |  ) ) ) )
  '  |____| .__|_| |_|_| |_\__, | / / / /
 =========|_|==============|___/=/_/_/_/
 :: Spring Boot ::        (v1.3.5.RELEASE)
```

```
...
2019-03-08 13:53:39 INFO  org.springframework.boot.StartupInfoLogger.
logStarted:57 - Started AxonApplication in 36.376 seconds (JVM running for
39.958)
...
2019-03-08 14:00:56 DEBUG com.axon.concurrency.user.command.handler.
UserCommandHandler.handleUserModifyCommand:90 - Thread Sleeping for
60 seconds
2019-03-08 14:01:57 DEBUG com.axon.concurrency.user.command.handler.
UserCommandHandler.handleUserModifyCommand:98 - User Queried Again : ID : 1;
UserName : TestUser-02; Age : 12; Version : 0; versionQueriedAgain : 0
2019-03-08 14:01:57 INFO  com.axon.concurrency.user.command.handler.
UserCommandHandler.handleUserModifyCommand:99 - End
Hibernate: update user set last_event_sequence_number=?, version=?, age=?,
user_name=? where id=? and version=?
2019-03-08 14:01:57 INFO  com.axon.concurrency.user.web.UserController.
updateUser:91 - End
```

Listing 16-15 shows the console of the Microservice 2, which woke up second
(since it started sleeping second) is not successful in commiting the update. It gets an
exception, as shown in Listing 16-15. This is because on optimistic concurrent access,
if for any reason the transaction on behalf of any particular client wants to update, the
update is committed if and only if the data that was originally provided to the client is the
same as the current data in the database.

Listing 16-15. Update Operation of Microservice 2 Rolled Back

```
D:\binil\gold\pack03\ch16\ch16-02\Ax2-Cuncurrency-Test>run2

D:\binil\gold\pack03\ch16\ch16-02\Ax2-Cuncurrency-Test>java -Dserver.
port=8081 -jar .\target\Axon-Concurrency-test-0.0.1-SNAPSHOT.jar
```

```
  .   ___          _           __ _ _
 /\\ / ___'_ __ _ _(_)_ __  __ _ \ \ \ \
( ( )\___ | '_ | '_| | '_ \/ _` | \ \ \ \
 \\/  ___)| |_)| | | | | || (_| |  ) ) ) )
  '  |____| .__|_| |_|_| |_\__, | / / / /
 =========|_|==============|___/=/_/_/_/
 :: Spring Boot ::        (v1.3.5.RELEASE)
```

...

2019-03-08 14:01:01 DEBUG com.axon.concurrency.user.command.handler.
UserCommandHandler.handleUserModifyCommand:90 - Thread Sleeping for
60 seconds
2019-03-08 14:02:01 DEBUG com.axon.concurrency.user.command.handler.
UserCommandHandler.handleUserModifyCommand:98 - **User Queried Again : ID : 1;
UserName : TestUser-03; Age : 13; Version : 0; versionQueriedAgain : 0**
2019-03-08 14:02:01 INFO com.axon.concurrency.user.command.handler.
UserCommandHandler.handleUserModifyCommand:99 - End
Hibernate: update user set last_event_sequence_number=?, version=?, age=?,
user_name=? where id=? and version=?
2019-03-08 14:02:01 ERROR com.axon.concurrency.user.web.UserController.
updateUser:88 - Command execution resulted in a checked exception that was
not declared on the gateway
org.axonframework.commandhandling.**CommandExecutionException**: Command
execution resulted in a checked exception that was not declared on the
gateway
        at org.axonframework.commandhandling.gateway.GatewayProxyFactory$Wrap
        NonDeclaredCheckedExceptions.invoke(GatewayProxyFactory.java:524)
...
        at java.lang.Thread.run(Unknown Source)
Caused by: **javax.persistence.OptimisticLockException: Row was updated or
deleted by another transaction (or unsaved-value mapping was incorrect) :
[com.axon.concurrency.user.model.User#1]**
...

```
        at org.axonframework.repository.GenericJpaRepository.doSaveWithLock
        (GenericJpaRepository.java:78)
        at org.axonframework.repository.LockingRepository.
        doSave(LockingRepository.java:128)
        at org.axonframework.repository.AbstractRepository$SimpleSave
        AggregateCallback.save(AbstractRepository.java:183)
        at org.axonframework.unitofwork.DefaultUnitOfWork$AggregateEntry.
        saveAggregate(DefaultUnitOfWork.java:322) .
...
Caused by: org.hibernate.StaleObjectStateException: Row was updated or
deleted by another transaction (or unsaved-value mapping was incorrect) :
[com.axon.concurrency.user.model.User#1]
...
        at org.hibernate.internal.SessionImpl.flush(SessionImpl.java:1258)
        at org.hibernate.jpa.spi.AbstractEntityManagerImpl.
        flush(AbstractEntityManagerImpl.java:1335)
        ... 84 more
2019-03-08 14:02:01 INFO  com.axon.concurrency.user.web.UserController.
updateUser:91 - End
```

If you query the database, you can validate that the update attempted by the client who succeeded alone is effected as shown in Listing 16-16.

Listing 16-16. Update from Only One Client Successful

```
mysql> select * from user;
+----+---------------------------+---------+------+-------------+
| id | last_event_sequence_number | version | age  | user_name   |
+----+---------------------------+---------+------+-------------+
| 1  |                      NULL |       1 |   12 | TestUser-02 |
+----+---------------------------+---------+------+-------------+
1 row in set (0.00 sec)

mysql>.
```

Summary

Provisioning for HA and scalability is an art as well as an engineering activity. There can be more than one design suitable for a specific scenario, and choosing the right one with future requirements in mind is a challenging task. This chapter covered a few techniques, starting from the simple to more advanced to complex scenarios of HA design. In doing so, you also relooked at the CQRS pattern and dissected core aspects of scaling read and write nodes independently. While scaling read nodes is rather straightforward, the same is not the case when scaling write nodes, since you need to deal with concurrency issues while changing entity states. However, nothing is impossible, and you saw code in action on how to scale write nodes too, utilizing the basic principles of transaction control you learned in Chapter 14. With this, you have reached yet another milestone in your journey in this book. Accumulating all the knowledge gained thus far, it's time now to look into more serious code, and you will do so in the next chapter when you look at complete end-to-end enterprise-grade microservices application. Take a break. When you're ready, start the next chapter.

CHAPTER 17

Axon CQRS Microservices E-Commerce

By now, you have covered selected and basic minimum technical details from multiple frameworks, including but not limited to Spring Boot, Spring Cloud, and Axon CQRS. Now let's see how they fit together so that you can architect and build real-world applications. For this purpose, you will design and build a basic e-commerce web site.

As you can appreciate by now, microservices architecture is not simple or straightforward compared to traditional or monolith architecture, so even the little e-commerce web site you are going to build in this chapter is non-trivial and requires dedication in terms of time and effort on your part so that all the critical aspects are understood by you. To help you in this objective, I will not repeat any aspect you have already seen and felt in previous chapters like high availability, high scalability, etc. This means you will play around with only a single instance of the microservice. However, nothing limits you from playing with the example in your own way by instantiating more instances of the same microservice.

Secondly, since this chapter will be long, I will cover only a few critical and basic flows. I have omitted other aspects like payment integration and so on. Even though nothing limits you from extending the code to add more features to make it production ready (which by itself is one of the aims of microservices), the current scope of the example in this chapter is minimalistic and I advise you to test the example as is prescribed in this chapter in the first pass so that you have a fairly good understanding of what is happening under the hood. You may monkey test it to fail in a subsequent pass of the test.

You are going to explore the following in this chapter:

- A traditional monolithic style architecture for an e-commerce application

© Binildas Christudas 2019

B. Christudas, *Practical Microservices Architectural Patterns*, https://doi.org/10.1007/978-1-4842-4501-9_17

- What the same e-commerce application will look like when architected using microservices

- A detailed design for selected major use cases for the microservices e-commerce application using CQRS

- Complete code for the microservices e-commerce application

- How to configure and run all microservices for the e-commerce application

- How to execute the above said selected use cases

Note   This chapter uses Axon 2 for building the example. In Chapter 19, we will refactor the same application using a later version of Axon.

Revisiting a Traditional E-Commerce Application

Let's start the discussion from the basic requirements for an online e-commerce web site. Once you cover the requirements, you will look at how a typical logical architecture of the basic building blocks will look if you architect it using the traditional or the monolith approach. In the next section, you will look at what changes are required if you rearchitect the design using a microservices-based approach.

The E-Commerce Business Summarized

The sample e-commerce enterprise is named ACME Shop. ACME has an online presence, and customers or end users can do online shopping at the web site. The ACME back office employees also interact with the same web site to fulfill customer orders.

ACME Shop specializes in selling fashion accessories, and it has classified its product portfolio under different categories called product categories. Under each product category, ACME Shop lists a set of products for sale. When an (anonymous) user accesses the ACME home page, all of the product categories are listed and by default, the products under one of the categories are expanded and listed further. The user can click one of the products to view the product details. The product details also show the available stock or inventory. A user can further specify how many of the selected product to purchase and add them to the shopping cart. Once added to the shopping cart, it will be displayed in the user's cart icon on the web site. The user can select his cart and opt to check out. In the next step, the user can confirm the purchase.

To confirm a purchase, the user has to log in. If the user has previously created a user profile, he or she can log in using those credentials. A new user can click the New User link to newly create a user profile. After creating a profile, the user can select the cart again to check out. He can log in this time and confirm the purchase.

Upon successful purchase, an order will be created. Once an order is created, it will be available for viewing in the "Your Orders" link under the appropriate submenu.

A user can cancel an order until it gets fulfilled.

The ACME back office employees log in using super credentials to interact with the same web site to fulfill customer orders. Once an order is created by a user, the next action is for the back office employee to ship that order. Once an order is shipped, the order can't be cancelled by the user. Instead, the user can view the "Shipped State" under the "In Progress" submenu of his "Orders."

The next stage in the order fulfilment process is the order delivery. The ACME back office employees must go to the "To Deliver" submenu and act on it. There are two actions, "Delivered" or "Delivery Failed," based on which whether you want to simulate a successful order delivery or a failure case.

E-Commerce Architecture Revisited

A typical monolith architecture for the above described business application is depicted in Figure 17-1.

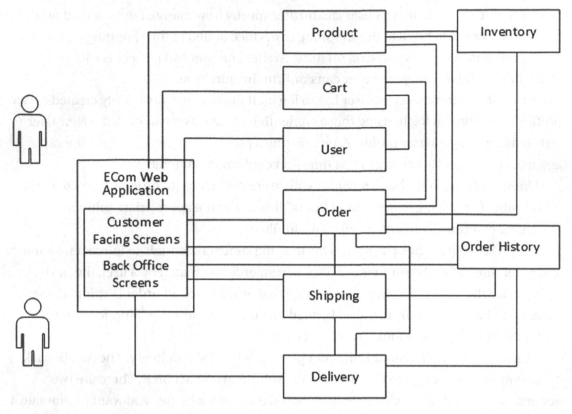

Figure 17-1. *Monolith e-commerce logical architecture*

The web application is typically a single web archive (.war) file. Components from the web application send requests to the services available in the middle tier. The logical architecture of the middle tier depicts multiple modules, and these modules interact with the web as well as with each other usually using request-response style synchronous communications.

Figure 17-2 attempts to depict the interdependency between components in the monolith architecture. Note that Figures 17-1 and 17-2 are representative, not exhaustive, intended just to illustrate the chit-chattiness between components.

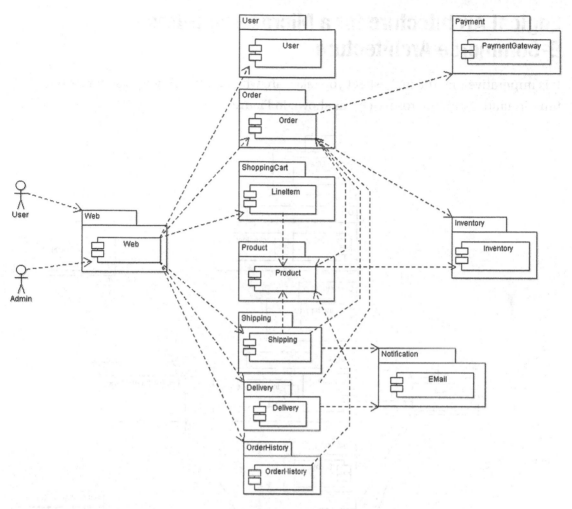

Figure 17-2. *Monolith e-commerce component dependency*

The E-Commerce Microservice Application

In previous chapters, I described the need for microservices-based architecture, so I won't repeat that information. Instead, let's relook at the architecture represented in the previous section to see what is to be changed.

It is clear that you need similar or enhanced features, functional as well as non-functional, in the new architecture. At the same time, you want to reduce the ill effects of the architecture depicted in the previous section, so let's do that.

Logical Architecture for a Microservice-Based E-Commerce Architecture

It is imperative that the first aspect you take care when refactoring is to separate out functionalities into microservices, as shown in Figure 17-3.

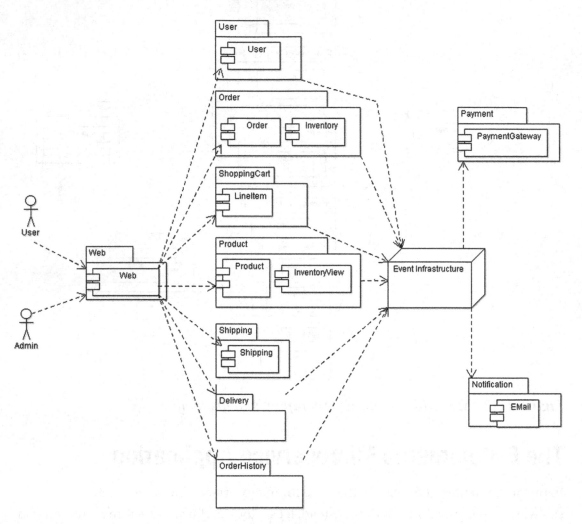

Figure 17-3. *E-commerce microservices dependency*

There is little or zero direct dependency between microservices; instead, microservices communicate with each other through the event-based infrastructure. All of these microservices will be deployed in separate processes, and may or may not be in separate physical nodes too.

The ACID Within the BASE

Compare the architectures in Figures 17-2 and 17-3 one more time. Careful observation will reveal two notable aspects:

- **Replicated read models**: You can see that inventory data is replicated and kept at more than one microservice level. This is to take care of query requirements of data not owned by the host microservice, which is what you saw in detail in the CQRS pattern in Chapter 12. To make it clear, when product details are displayed, the available stock information too need to be displayed on the screen and this can be done from the inventory materialized view maintained at the Product microservice level.

- **Domain affinity for enhanced consistency**: Figure 17-2 depicts Order and Inventory as two separate domains. However, in the redesign in Figure 17-3 you can see that both of these domain entities are brought together and maintained in same space (process or node). The reason is that you want to have stronger data consistency across the Order and Inventory domain entities.

While you want ACID-similar consistency across these two entities, you want to avoid distributed transactions across nodes. But there is a caveat here: for whatever reason you are attempting to split the monolith into microservices, the same forces are now putting constraints to join them back together at the cost of consistency! While you don't want to join everything back to attain strongest consistency with zero partitions, let's keep Order and Inventory for the time being and live with the "ACID within the BASE" scenario.

Worry not; you are going to look into a further refactored design where you have true BASE transaction characteristics in Chapter 19 when you look at Axon 3.

The Design of the E-Commerce Microservices

The Business Domain Object Model (BDOM) or the Common Information Model (CIM) for the e-commerce application is shown in Figure 17-4.

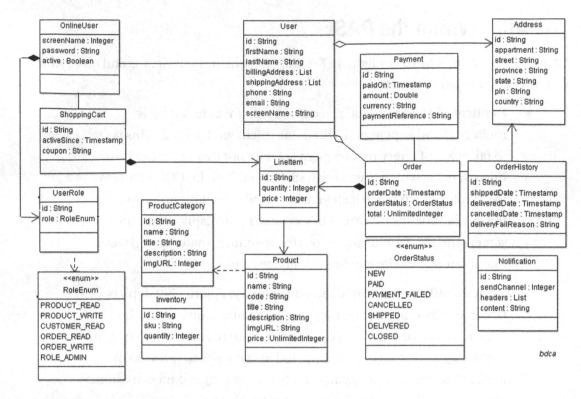

Figure 17-4. *E-commerce domain object model*

Even though you have to design the e-commerce application based on a microservices architecture, the BDOM is following the traditional UML class diagram style. Hence the dependency shown in the e-commerce class diagram above may not map one-to-one when you decide the microservices boundaries. Instead, when you decide the microservices boundaries based on domain-driven design, some of the dependencies shown here will get split across microservices boundaries, in which case some microservices must maintain materialized views of data owned by foreign microservices.

Technical Architecture for the Microservice-Based E-Commerce Architecture

Having looked at the rationale behind the approach to be taken in architecting the microservices-based e-commerce application, you can arrive at the initial view of the technical architecture, shown in Figure 17-5.

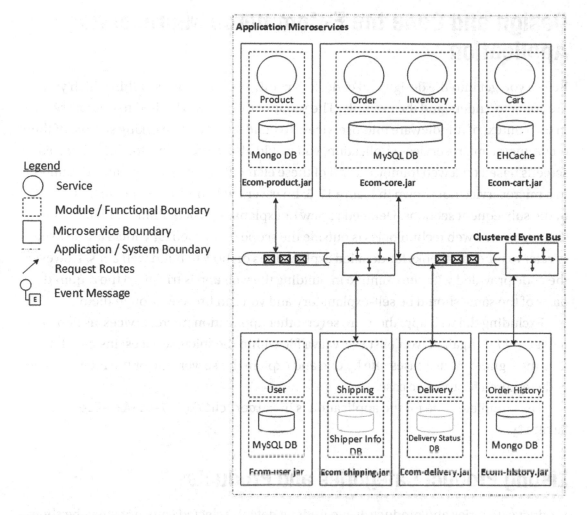

Figure 17-5. E-commerce microservices technical architecture

You are attempting to remove all direct intermicroservices dependencies and direct all intermicroservices communications through an event-driven architecture . You use Axon's clustered event bus for the same. You leverage polyglot persistence for storing data so that multiple data storage technologies can be chosen based upon the way data is being used by individual microservices. For the Shipping microservice and the Delivery microservice, you are not using any persistence to make the application simpler, so they are blurred out in Figure 17-5.

Design and Code the E-Commerce Microservice Application

Before you get into the design and code, let's clarify the boundaries within which you are going to understand the example. The scope of this book is limited to microservices in the context of middleware microservices. To build a complete working sample of the e-commerce microservices application, you would also want to develop HTML-based screens based on a web framework. All of these elements of the web app are contained in a microservice not shown in Figure 17-5; however I will introduce that microservice in the subsequent sections. Detailed review or explanations of building HTML screens and associated web technologies is outside the scope of this book. Readers are advised to refer to other textbooks for detailed explanations on how to build web apps. However, the code provided with the example in building the web app is trivial, so the required parts of the same should be self-explanatory and you can browse through them.

Excluding the web app, there are seven other application microservices, as depicted in Figure 17-5. Again, I won't list every Java file within the microservices; instead, I'll take the significant use cases one by one and explain the server side or the microservices code required for that use case.

The complete code for the application is in folder `ch17\ch17-01\Ax2-Ecom-No-Security`.

Listing Product Categories and Products

Product categories and products listed under a default selected category are to be shown on the ACME Shop home page. Listing 17-1 shows this portion of the code.

Listing 17-1. ProductCategoryRepository (ch17\ch17-01\Ax2-Ecom-No-Security\Ecom-product\src\main\java\com\acme\ecom\product\repository\ProductCategoryRepository.java)

```
@RepositoryRestResource(collectionResourceRel = "categories", path =
"categories")
public interface ProductCategoryRepository extends MongoRepository
<ProductCategory, String>  {

}
```

This repository is an interface and it allows you to perform various operations involving ProductCategory objects. It gets these operations by extending the Mongo Repository, which is a Mongo-specific Repository interface, which in turn extends the PagingAndSortingRepository interface defined in Spring Data Commons. At runtime, Spring Data REST will create an implementation of this interface automatically. Then it will use the @RepositoryRestResource annotation to direct Spring MVC to create RESTful endpoints at /categories:

product_service.js retrieves all product categories as follows:

```
http.get(sessionStorage.getItem('apiUrl')+'/product/categories/')
```

Note   All of the code for the web application is in the folder ch17\ch17-01\ Ax2-Ecom-No-Security\Ecom-web\src\main\resources\static.

Next, you should be able to retrieve all of the products under a product category with the code in Listing 17-2.

Listing 17-2.   productsByCategory (ch17\ch17-01\Ax2-Ecom-No-Security\ Ecom-product\src\main\java\com\acme\ecom\product\controller\ ProductRestController.java)

```
@RestController
public class ProductRestController {

    @RequestMapping(value = "/productsByCategory", method = RequestMethod.GET,
            produces = { MediaType.APPLICATION_JSON_VALUE })
    public ResponseEntity<Resources<Resource<Product>>>getAllProductsByCategory
            (@RequestParam("category") String category) {

        List<Product> products =
            productRepository.findByProductCategoryName(category);
        Link links[] = { };
        if (products.isEmpty()) {
            return new ResponseEntity<Resources<Resource<Product>>>(
                HttpStatus.NOT_FOUND);
        }
```

```
        List<Resource<Product>> list = new ArrayList<Resource<Product>>();
        addLinksToProduct(products, list);
        Resources<Resource<Product>> productRes =
            new Resources<Resource<Product>>(list, links);
        return new ResponseEntity<Resources<Resource<Product>>>(
            productRes, HttpStatus.OK);
    }
}
```

product_service.js retrieves all products listed under a product category as follows:

```
http.get(sessionStorage.getItem('apiUrl')+'/product/productsByCategory?
category='+category)
```

Listing Product Details Mashed Up with Inventory Data

The next main use case is to retrieve information when a user clicks on a specific product to list the product details. The product details can be retrieved using the code in Listing 17-3.

Listing 17-3. Get Product Details (ch17\ch17-01\Ax2-Ecom-No-Security\ Ecom-product\src\main\java\com\acme\ecom\product\controller\ ProductRestController.java)

```
@RestController
public class ProductRestController {

    @RequestMapping(value = "/products/{id}", method = RequestMethod.GET,
            produces = MediaType.APPLICATION_JSON_VALUE)
    public ResponseEntity<Resource<Product>> getProduct(
            @PathVariable("id") String id) {

        Product product = productRepository.findOne(id);
        if (product == null) {
            return new ResponseEntity<Resource<Product>>(HttpStatus.NOT_
            FOUND);
        }
```

```
Resource<Product> productRes = new Resource<Product>(
    product,new Link[]{linkTo(methodOn(ProductRestController.class).
    getProduct(product.getId())).withSelfRel(), linkTo(
    ProductRestController.class).slash("productImg").slash(
    product.getImgUrl()).withRel("imgUrl")});
    return new ResponseEntity<Resource<Product>>(productRes,
        HttpStatus.OK);
    }
}
```

`product_service.js` retrieves all products listed under a product category as follows:

```
http.get(sessionStorage.getItem('apiUrl')+'/product/products/'+id)
```

The product details should be mashed up with stock information so the user can tell if he can add any number of that product to the shopping cart. The architecture in Figure 17-5 shows that the inventory information is available only in the "core" microservice, which is outside the Product microservice.

You could make an architectural decision by allowing the browser to retrieve product details by requesting the Product microservice and then requesting the core microservice to retrieve the stock information for that particular product, thus performing a data mashup at the client tier.

But the principles of microservices say that microservices are to be self-sufficient and independent. This means, if you consider the Product and core microservices, each one should be able to independently live and serve irrespective of whether the other is up and running or not. If the core microservice is down, the ACME online shop should still function with a reduced functionality by allowing users to reach the home page and browse through the product categories, list products under a product category, view details of a selected product (with stock information too, perhaps!), select and add items to cart, etc. Maybe the create order functionality will work only after the core microservice is up and running again. So you are going to follow a different architectural approach, by allowing the Product microservice to maintain a materialized view of the inventory, which is a read replica.

To retrieve the inventory details of a product from this read replica, you have the inventory repository, shown in Listing 17-4.

Listing 17-4. Inventory Read Repository (ch17\ch17-01\Ax2-Ecom-No-Security\ Ecom-product\src\main\java\com\acme\ecom\product\inventory\repository\ InventoryRepository.java)

```
@RepositoryRestResource(collectionResourceRel = "inventory",
    path = "inventory")
public interface InventoryRepository extends
        MongoRepository<Inventory, String>  {

    public Inventory findByInventoryId(
        @Param("inventoryId") Long  inventoryId);
    public Inventory findBySku(@Param("sku") String  sku);
}
```

product_service.js retrieves all Products listed under a Product Category as below:

http.get(sessionStorage.getItem('apiUrl')+'/product/inventory/search/ findBySku?sku='+productCode)

Now it's trivial to mashup data from above two API sources and the client tier.

Add a Product to the Cart

This is a straightforward implementation of adding items selected to order into an org. springframework.cache.CacheManager and retrieving it back, so the code snippets are not shown here. The code is placed in folder ch17\ch17-01\Ax2-Ecom-No-Security\ Ecom-cart.

Create a New Order

The use cases you are going to explore from now on are non-trivial since there are multiple directions for the control flow across the microservices. As explained, you are not using any synchronous style intermicroservices communication; instead, you leverage the Axon CQRS event-driven infrastructure to facilitate end-to-end control flow. You will use a representation similar to that shown in Figure 17-6 so that it will be easy to understand the control flow and state changes during the execution of the use cases.

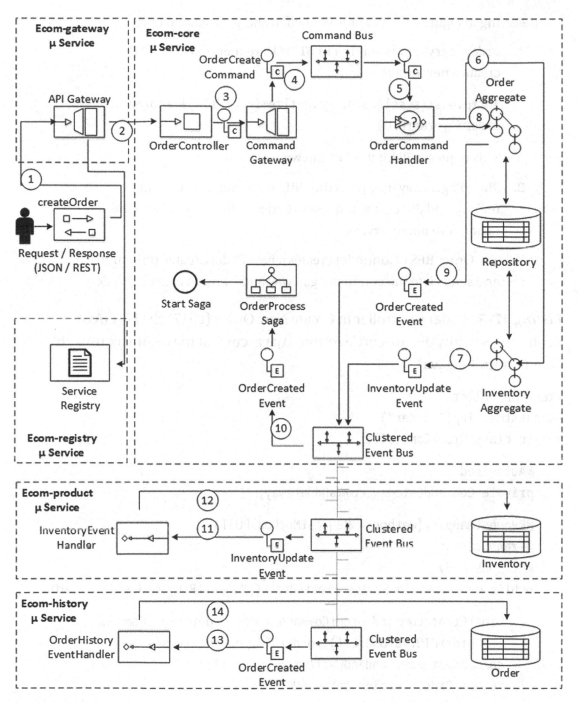

Figure 17-6. *Create a new order*

Referring to Figure 17-6, the flow is labelled and is explained here.

1. order_service.js sends a REST JSON request over HTTP to create a new order:

    $http.post(sessionStorage.getItem('apiUrl')+'/core/order/',orderDTO)

    This request will hit the API gateway.

2. The API gateway interprets the URL by looking at the service registry and directs the request to Order REST Controller in the Ecom-core microservice.

3. The Order REST Controller creates a new OrderCreateCommand and sends it to the command gateway and waits. See Listing 17-5.

Listing 17-5. Order Controller to Create New Order (ch17\ch17-01\Ax2-Ecom-No-Security\Ecom-core\src\main\java\com\acme\ecom\core\web\OrderController.java)

```
@RestController
@RequestMapping("/order")
public class OrderController {

    @Autowired
    private CommandGateway commandGateway;

    @RequestMapping(method = RequestMethod.POST)
    @Transactional
    @ResponseBody
    public OrderCreationStatus createOrder(@RequestBody OrderDTO orderDTO) {

        OrderCreateCommand orderCommand = new OrderCreateCommand(
            orderDTO.getUserId(), orderDTO.getLineItems());
        commandGateway.sendAndWait(orderCommand);
        return OrderCreationStatus.SUCCESS;
    }
}
```

4. The command gateway delivers the OrderCreateCommand to the command bus.

5. The OrderCommandHandler consumes the OrderCreateCommand from the command bus. See Listing 17-6.

Listing 17-6. OrderCommandHandler handleNewOrder (ch17\ch17-01\ Ax2-Ecom-No-Security\Ecom-core\src\main\java\com\acme\ecom\core\ order\command\handler\OrderCommandHandler.java)

```java
@Component
public class OrderCommandHandler {

    @Autowired
    @Qualifier(value = "orderRepository")
    private Repository<Order> orderRepository;

    @CommandHandler
    public void handleNewOrder(OrderCreateCommand orderCreatedCommand) {
        Order order = new Order(Long.valueOf(new Random().nextInt()));
        order.setOrderDate(new Date());
        order.setOrderStatus(OrderStatus.PAID);
        order.setUserId(orderCreatedCommand.getUserId());
        double total = 0;
        if (orderCreatedCommand.getLineItems() != null) {
            for (LineItemDTO lineItemDto :
                    orderCreatedCommand.getLineItems()) {
                if (lineItemDto.getInventoryId() != null) {
                    LineItem lineItem = new LineItem(new Random().nextLong(),
                        lineItemDto.getProductId(), lineItemDto.getQuantity(),
                        lineItemDto.getPrice(), lineItemDto.getInventoryId());
                    total = total + lineItemDto.getPrice();
                    order.addLineItem(lineItem);
                    Inventory inventory = inventoryRepository.load
                    (lineItemDto.getInventoryId());
                    inventory.updateProductStock(lineItemDto.getQuantity(),
                        ProductStockOperation.DEPRECIATE);
```

```
                    }
                }
            }
        order.setTotal(total);
        order.notifyOrderCreation();
        orderRepository.add(order);
    }
}
```

Command handling processes are atomic, so it should either be processed entirely or not at all. The Axon framework uses the Unit of Work (UoW) to track actions performed by the command handlers. After the command handler completes, Axon tries to commit the actions registered with the UoW. This involves storing modified aggregates in their respective repository and publishing events on the event bus. However, the UoW is not a replacement for a transaction. The UoW only ensures that changes made to aggregates are stored upon successful execution of a command handler. If an error occurs while storing an aggregate, any aggregates already stored are not rolled back. You can bind a transaction to a UoW. CommandBus implementations like the SimpleCommandBus and DisruptorCommandBus allow you to configure a transaction manager. This transaction manager is used to create the transactions to bind to the UoW that is used to manage the process of a command. This is shown in Listing 17-7.

Listing 17-7. Bind Transactions to Unit of Work (ch17\ch17-01\Ax2-Ecom-No-Security\Ecom-core\src\main\java\com\acme\ecom\core\EcomCoreAppConfiguration.java)

```
@Configuration
@RefreshScope
public class EcomCoreAppConfiguration {

    @Bean
    public SimpleCommandBus commandBus() {
```

```
    SimpleCommandBus simpleCommandBus = new SimpleCommandBus();
    simpleCommandBus.setDispatchInterceptors(
        Arrays.asList(new BeanValidationInterceptor()));
    SpringTransactionManager transcationMgr =
        new SpringTransactionManager(txManager);
    simpleCommandBus.setTransactionManager(transcationMgr);
    return simpleCommandBus;
    }
}
```

Here, SpringTransactionManager is a TransactionManager implementation that uses a PlatformTransactionManager as the underlying transaction manager.

Note that you use two aggregate entities (inventory and order) in a single transaction, but there are no distributed transactions involved since both the aggregate entities are managed by the same resource manager in a single node.

6. The OrderCommandHandler first depreciates the available inventory in the inventory AXON aggregate. See Listing 17-8.

Listing 17-8. Inventory Aggregate updateProductStock (ch17\ch17-01\Ax2-Ecom-No-Security\Ecom-core\src\main\java\com\acme\ecom\core\inventory\model\Inventory.java)

```
@Entity
@Table(name = "INVENTORY")
public class Inventory extends AbstractAggregateRoot<Long> {

    public void updateProductStock(Integer count,
            ProductStockOperation stockoperation) {

        if (stockoperation.equals(ProductStockOperation.DEPRECIATE)) {
            if (this.quantity - count >= 0) {
                this.quantity = this.quantity - count;
            } else {
                throw new OutOfStockException(this.id);
            }
```

657

```
        } else {
            this.quantity = this.quantity + count;
        }
        registerEvent(new InventoryUpdateEvent(id, sku, quantity));
    }
}
```

When you view the product listing page or the product details page, the stock you see there is coming from the cached data in the materialized view of inventory in the Ecom-product microservice. However, when you create an order, the required inventory is validated with the available stock, which happens against the inventory aggregate entity, which is the write model of the inventory. Scenarios like this are common in many business processes, like selling hotel rooms and flight seats. When you start shopping for hotel rooms or flight seats, the initial availability of rooms or seats are "nearly accurate" approximations, perhaps coming from caches or from intermediary demand-supply gateways. When the actual booking is done, there is always an instantaneous or eventual validation of the number of seats or rooms requested against the actual availability in the single source of truth, which is the write model.

7. While depreciating the stock, the inventory aggregate registers an InventoryUpdateEvent into the clustered event bus.

8. The OrderCommandHandler, on consuming the OrderCreateCommand in Step 5, also creates a new order on successfully depreciating the inventory. See Listing 17-9.

Listing 17-9. Order notifyOrderCreation (ch17\ch17-01\Ax2-Ecom-No-Security\ Ecom-core\src\main\java\com\acme\ecom\core\order\model\Order.java)

```
@Entity(name="order")
@Table(name = "CUSTOMER_ORDER")
public class Order extends AbstractAggregateRoot<Long> {
```

```java
@OneToMany(cascade = CascadeType.ALL, mappedBy="order",
orphanRemoval=true)
private Set<LineItem> lineItems;

public void addLineItem(LineItem lineItem){

    if(this.lineItems==null){
        this.lineItems=new HashSet<LineItem>();
    }
    lineItem.setOrder(this);
    this.lineItems.add(lineItem);
}

public void notifyOrderCreation() {

    List<LineItemDTO> lineItemDTOs = new ArrayList<LineItemDTO>();
    for (LineItem lineItem : lineItems) {
        lineItemDTOs.add(new LineItemDTO(lineItem.getProduct(),
        lineItem.getPrice(), lineItem.getQuantity(),
        lineItem.getInventoryId()));
    }
    registerEvent(new OrderCreatedEvent(id, userId, orderStatus.name(),
        total, orderDate, lineItemDTOs));

}
}
```

9. Once the order aggregate is notified of a new order creation, it registers a OrderCreatedEvent into the clustered event bus.

10. For every new OrderCreatedEvent, a new order process saga instance is instantiated, as shown in Listing 17-10.

Listing 17-10. Start Saga on New Order Creation (ch17\ch17-01\Ax2-Ecom-No-Security\Ecom-core\src\main\java\com\acme\ecom\core\order\saga\handler\OrderProcessSaga.java)

```
public class OrderProcessSaga extends AbstractAnnotatedSaga {

    private Long orderId;

    @StartSaga
    @SagaEventHandler(associationProperty = "orderId")
    public void handleOrderCreationEvent(OrderCreatedEvent orderCreatedEvent) {
        this.orderId = orderCreatedEvent.getOrderId();
    }
}
```

11. When depreciating the stock in Step 7, the inventory aggregate registers an InventoryUpdateEvent into the clustered event bus. This InventoryUpdateEvent is consumed by the inventory event handler in the Ecom-product microservice.

12. The InventoryEventHandler in the Ecom-product microservice refreshes its own materialized view of the inventory read model, as shown in Listing 17-11.

Listing 17-11. Product handleInventoryUpdates (ch17\ch17-01\Ax2-Ecom-No-Security\Ecom-product\src\main\java\com\acme\ecom\product\inventory\event\handler\InventoryEventHandler.java)

```
@Component
public class InventoryEventHandler {

    @Autowired
    private InventoryRepository inventoryRepository;

    @EventHandler
    public void handleInventoryUpdates(InventoryUpdateEvent event,
            Message eventMessage, @Timestamp DateTime moment) {
```

```
        Inventory inventory =
            inventoryRepository.findByInventoryId(event.getId());
        if(inventory == null){
            inventory=new Inventory();
            inventory.setInventoryId(event.getId());
            inventory.setSku(event.getSku());
        }else{
            logger.debug("Inventory  existing - updating...............");
        }
        inventory.setQuantity(event.getQuantity());
        inventoryRepository.save(inventory);
    }
}
```

13. In Step 9, when the order aggregate is notified of a new order creation, it will register an OrderCreatedEvent into the clustered event bus. This OrderCreatedEvent is consumed by the order history event handler in the Ecom-history microservice

14. The order history event handler in the Ecom-history microservice creates a new record in the Order History table. See Listing 17-12.

Listing 17-12. handleOrderCreationEvent (ch17\ch17-01\Ax2-Ecom-No-Security\Ecom-history\src\main\java\com\acme\ecom\order\history\event\handler\OrderHistoryEventHandler.java)

```
@Component
public class OrderHistoryEventHandler {

    @Autowired
    private OrderHistoryRepository orderHistoryRepository;

    @EventHandler
    public void handleOrderCreationEvent(OrderCreatedEvent event,
            Message eventMessage, @Timestamp DateTime moment) {
```

```
        Order order =new Order();
        order.setOrderId(event.getOrderId());
        order.setUserId(event.getUserId());
        order.setCreationDate(new Date());
        order.setOrderStatus(event.getOrderStatus());
        List<LineItem> lineItems=new ArrayList<LineItem>();
        if(event.getLineItems()!=null){
            for(LineItemDTO lineItemDTO:event.getLineItems()){
                LineItem lineItem=new LineItem();
                lineItem.setProductId(lineItemDTO.getProductId());
                lineItem.setPrice(lineItemDTO.getPrice());
                lineItem.setQuantity(lineItemDTO.getQuantity());
                lineItems.add(lineItem);
            }
        }
        order.setLineItems(lineItems);
        orderHistoryRepository.save(order);
    }
}
```

Later you will also see that whenever the status of the order aggregate in the Ecom-core microservice changes, the same is also updated in this history table. If a need arises, BI or analytics can be executed over these records, since they are in a microservice separate from the order aggregate in the Ecom-core microservice, so it will not affect the performance of the order aggregate.

This completes the "create new order" flow. Later you will look at the execution of the actual use case in the subsection titled "Create New Order" under the section titled "Test E-Commerce Microservice Use Cases."

Cancel an Order

A newly created order, if it's not being processed in the fulfilment cycle, can be cancelled by the user. Figure 17-7 depicts the various states different entities undergo once the Cancel command is initiated.

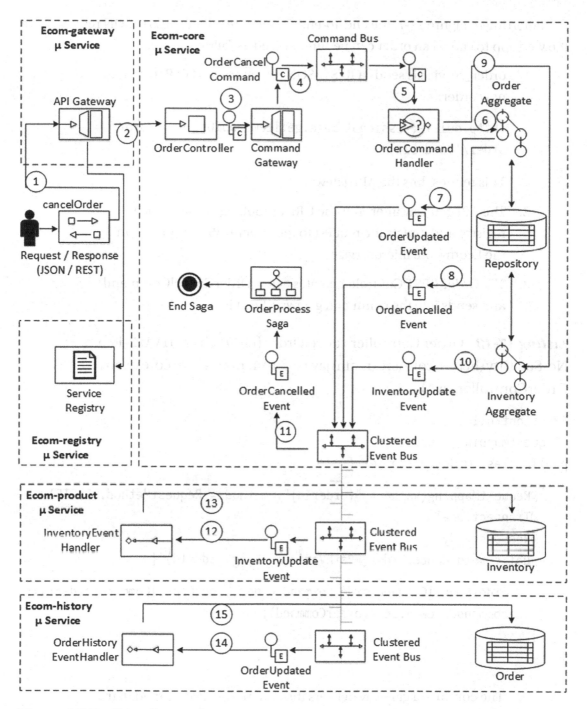

Figure 17-7. Cancel an order

Referring to Figure 17-7, the end-to-end flow as a result of a REST JSON request from the web app to cancel an order can be summarized as follows:

1. order_service.js sends a REST JSON request over HTTP to create a new order:

   ```
   $http.delete(sessionStorage.getItem('apiUrl')+'/core/
   order/'+orderId)
   ```

   This request hits the API gateway.

2. The API gateway interprets the URL by looking at the service registry and directs the request to the Order REST Controller in the Ecom-core microservice.

3. The Order REST Controller creates a new OrderCancelCommand and sends it to the command gateway. See Listing 17-13.

Listing 17-13. Order Controller cancelOrder (ch17\ch17-01\Ax2-Ecom-No-Security\Ecom-core\src\main\java\com\acme\ecom\core\web\OrderController.java)

```
@RestController
@RequestMapping("/order")
public class OrderController {

    @RequestMapping(value = "{orderId}", method = RequestMethod.DELETE)
    @Transactional
    @ResponseBody
    public void cancelOrder(@PathVariable Long orderId) {

        OrderCancelCommand orderCommand = new OrderCancelCommand(orderId);
        commandGateway.send(orderCommand);
    }
}
```

4. The command gateway delivers the OrderCancelCommand to the command bus.

5. The OrderCommandHandler consumes the OrderCreateCommand from the command bus. See Listing 17-14.

Listing 17-14. OrderCommandHandler handleOrderCancel (ch17\ch17-01\Ax2-Ecom-No-Security\Ecom-core\src\main\java\com\acme\ecom\core\order\command\handler\OrderCommandHandler.java)

```java
@Component
public class OrderCommandHandler {

    @CommandHandler
    public void handleOrderCancel(OrderCancelCommand orderCancelCommand) {

        Order order = orderRepository.load(orderCancelCommand.getOrderId());
        order.cancelOrder();
        rollbackInventory(order);
    }

    private void rollbackInventory(Order order){

        for(LineItem lineItem:order.getLineItems()){
            Inventory inventory =
                inventoryRepository.load(lineItem.getInventoryId());
            inventory.updateProductStock(lineItem.getQuantity(),
                ProductStockOperation.ADD);
        }
    }

}
```

6. The OrderCommandHandler retrieves the respective order from the repository and invokes cancelOrder. The selected order aggregate changes its status to OrderStatus.CANCELLED. See Listing 17-15.

Listing 17-15. Order Aggregate cancelOrder (ch17\ch17-01\Ax2-Ecom-No-Security\Ecom-core\src\main\java\com\acme\ecom\core\order\model\Order.java)

```java
@Entity(name="order")
@Table(name = "CUSTOMER_ORDER")
public class Order extends AbstractAggregateRoot<Long> {
```

```
public void cancelOrder(){

    this.orderStatus=OrderStatus.CANCELLED;
    registerEvent(new OrderUpdatedEvent(this.id, orderStatus.name(),
        new Date(),null));
    registerEvent(new OrderCancelledEvent(this.id));
}
}
```

7. The order aggregate sends the OrderUpdatedEvent to the clustered event bus.

8. The order aggregate will also send the OrderCancelledEvent to the clustered event bus.

9. As a result of Step 5, the OrderCommandHander also retrieves the inventory items of all the products associated with the order and invokes updateProductStock. The objective is to revert the stock to account for the effect of cancelling the order so that those inventories can be made available for sales again. The rollbackInventory in Listing 17-14 depicts this.

    See Listing 17-8 to go through the updateProductStock code in the inventory aggregate entity.

10. While reinstating the stock, each inventory aggregate registers an InventoryUpdateEvent into the clustered event bus.

11. The OrderCancelledEvent registered during Step 8 is consumed by the order process saga. See Listing 17-16.

Listing 17-16. OrderProcessSaga handleOrderCanceledEvent (ch17\ch17-01\ Ax2-Ecom-No-Security\Ecom-core\src\main\java\com\acme\ecom\core\ order\saga\handler\OrderProcessSaga.java)

```
public class OrderProcessSaga extends AbstractAnnotatedSaga {

    private Long orderId;

    @EndSaga
    @SagaEventHandler(associationProperty = "orderId")
```

```
public void handleOrderCanceledEvent(
    OrderCancelledEvent orderCancelledEvent) {

        // Do Nothing
}
}
```

The saga's life cycle ends after the invocation of the handleOrderCanceledEvent handler since you annotated that event's handler on the saga with @EndSaga.

It is easy to make a saga take action when an event happens, like the OrderCancelledEvent event in your case. But what if you want your saga to do something when nothing happens even after so long? Deadlines are used in such scenarios. While the confirmation of a credit card payment should occur within a few seconds, in the case of an online order like the one in your case, it can be few hours or days. You can use an EventScheduler to schedule an event for publication to honor deadlines. Axon provides two EventScheduler implementations: SimpleEventScheduler, a pure Java one and QuartzEventScheduler using Quartz 2 as a backing scheduling mechanism. I have not used them in this example; that's left as an exercise for you, the reader.

12. While reinstating the stock in Step 10, the inventory aggregate registers an InventoryUpdateEvent into the clustered event bus. This InventoryUpdateEvent is consumed by the InventoryEventHandler in the Ecom-product microservice.

13. The InventoryEventHandler in the Ecom-product microservice refreshes its own materialized view of the inventory read model. Listing 17-11 shows the code of handleInventoryUpdates doing this.

14. In Step 7 when the order aggregate is notified of an order cancellation, it registers an OrderUpdatedEvent into the clustered event bus. This OrderUpdatedEvent is consumed by the Order History Event Handler in the Ecom-history microservice.

15. The Order History Event Handler in the Ecom-history microservice updates the corresponding record of Order in the Order History table. See Listing 17-17.

Listing 17-17. OrderHistoryEventHandler handleOrderUpdatedEvent (ch17\ch17-01\Ax2-Ecom-No-Security\Ecom-history\src\main\java\com\acme\ecom\order\history\event\handler\OrderHistoryEventHandler.java)

```
@Component
public class OrderHistoryEventHandler {

    @EventHandler
    public void handleOrderUpdatedEvent(OrderUpdatedEvent event,
            Message eventMessage, @Timestamp DateTime moment) {

        Order order =orderHistoryRepository.findByOrderId(event.getOrderId());
        order.setOrderStatus(event.getOrderStatus());
        if(event.getOrderStatus().equals("SHIPPED")){
            order.setShippedDate(event.getDate());
        }else if(event.getOrderStatus().equals("DELIVERED")){
            order.setDeliveredDate(event.getDate());
        }else if(event.getOrderStatus().equals("CANCELLED")){
            order.setCancelledDate(event.getDate());
        }else if(event.getOrderStatus().equals("DELIVERY_FAILED")){
            order.setDeliveryFailReason(event.getDescription());
        }
        orderHistoryRepository.save(order);
    }
}
```

This completes the "cancel an order" flow, and you will look at the execution of the actual use case in subsequent section.

Ship an Order Received

In the "Create a New Order" subsection you the flow of creating a new order. All new orders created will be available for the back office admin to take and trigger the fulfilment processing. The first step in order fulfilment is to trigger a shipping command. Figure 17-8 illustrates the state changes of various entities during the shipping step.

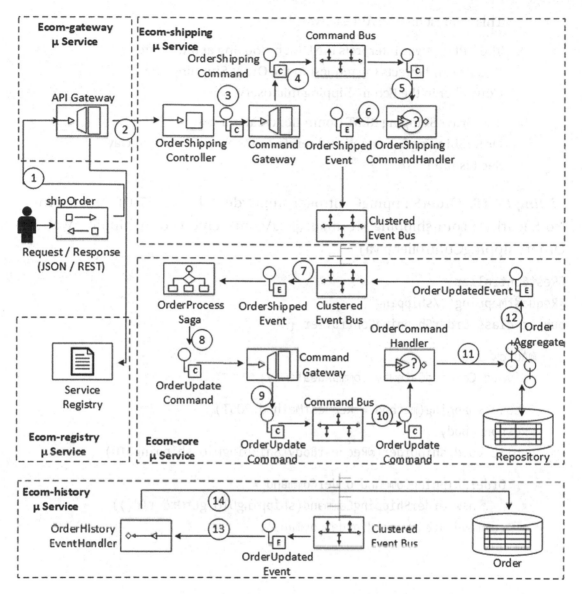

Figure 17-8. *Ship an Order*

Referring to Figure 17-8, the end-to-end flow as a result of a REST JSON request using the web app from the back office admin to ship an order can be summarized as follows:

1. order_service.js sends a REST JSON request over HTTP to ship a newly created order:

    $http.post(sessionStorage.getItem('apiUrl')+'/shipping/
    shipping',shippingDTO)

This request hits the API gateway.

2. The API gateway interprets the URL by looking at the Service Registry and directs the request to the Order Shipping REST Controller in the Ecom-shipping microservice.

3. The Order Shipping REST Controller creates a new OrderShippingCommand and sends it to the command gateway. See Listing 17-18.

Listing 17-18. OrderShippingController shipOrder (ch17\ch17-01\Ax2-Ecom-No-Security\Ecom-shipping\src\main\java\com\acme\ecom\shipping\web\OrderShippingController.java)

```
@RestController
@RequestMapping("/shipping")
public class OrderShippingController {

    @Autowired
    private CommandGateway commandGateway;

    @RequestMapping(method = RequestMethod.POST)
    @ResponseBody
    public void shipOrder(@RequestBody ShippingDTO shippingDTO) {

        OrderShippingCommand orderCommand =
            new OrderShippingCommand(shippingDTO.getOrderId());
        commandGateway.send(orderCommand);
    }
}
```

4. The command gateway delivers the OrderShippingCommand to the command bus.

5. The OrderShippingCommandHandler consumes the OrderShippingCommand from the command bus. See Listing 17-19.

Listing 17-19. OrderShippingCommandHandler handleOrderShipping (ch17\
ch17-01\Ax2-Ecom-No-Security\Ecom-shipping\src\main\java\com\acme\
ecom\shipping\command\handler\ OrderShippingCommandHandler.java)

```
@Component
public class OrderShippingCommandHandler {

    @Autowired
    private EventBus eventBus;

    @CommandHandler
    public void handleOrderShipping(
            OrderShippingCommand orderShippingCommand) {
        eventBus.publish(asEventMessage(new OrderShippedEvent(
            orderShippingCommand.getOrderId(), new Date())));
    }
}
```

6. The OrderShippingCommandHandler creates a new
    OrderShippedEvent and sends it to the clustered event bus.

7. When an OrderShippedEvent appears in the clustered event
    bus, the handleOrderShippedEvent SagaEventHandler of
    OrderProcessSaga picks it up.

8. The handleOrderShippedEvent in OrderProcessSaga is similar to
    a normal event handler in Axon. It doesn't start or end the existing
    saga; instead, it needs to do a certain action alone, sending a new
    OrderUpdateCommand to the command gateway in your case.
    See Listing 17-20.

Listing 17-20. OrderProcessSaga handleOrderShippedEvent (ch17\ch17-01\
Ax2-Ecom-No-Security\Ecom-core\src\main\java\com\acme\ecom\core\
order\saga\handler\OrderProcessSaga.java)

```
public class OrderProcessSaga extends AbstractAnnotatedSaga {

    private Long orderId;

    @SagaEventHandler(associationProperty = "orderId")
    public void handleOrderShippedEvent(OrderShippedEvent orderShippedEvent) {
```

```
        commandGateway.send(new OrderUpdateCommand(
            orderShippedEvent.getOrderId(),OrderStatus.SHIPPED));
    }
}
```

9. The command gateway delivers the OrderUpdateCommand to the command bus.

10. The OrderCommandHandler is interested in the OrderUpdateCommand. See Listing 17-21.

Listing 17-21. OrderCommandHandler handleOrderUpdate (ch17\ch17-01\ Ax2-Ecom-No-Security\Ecom-core\src\main\java\com\acme\ecom\core\ order\command\handler\OrderCommandHandler.java)

```
@Component
public class OrderCommandHandler {

    @Autowired
    @Qualifier(value = "orderRepository")
    private Repository<Order> orderRepository;

    @CommandHandler
    public void handleOrderUpdate(OrderUpdateCommand orderUpdateCommand) {

        Order order = orderRepository.load(orderUpdateCommand.getOrderId());
        order.updateOrderStatus(orderUpdateCommand.getOrderStatus());
    }
}
```

11. The handleOrderUpdate first retrieves the corresponding order and calls updateOrderStatus, as shown in Listing 17-22.

Listing 17-22. updateOrderStatus (ch17\ch17-01\Ax2-Ecom-No-Security\Ecom-core\src\main\java\com\acme\ecom\core\order\model\Order.java)

```
@Entity(name="order")
@Table(name = "CUSTOMER_ORDER")
public class Order extends AbstractAggregateRoot<Long> {
```

```
@Id
private Long id;

@Enumerated(EnumType.STRING)
@Column(name="ORDER_STATUS")
private OrderStatus orderStatus;

public void updateOrderStatus(OrderStatus orderStatus){

    this.orderStatus=orderStatus;
    registerEvent(new OrderUpdatedEvent(this.id, orderStatus.name(),
        new Date(), null));
    }
}
```

12. The order aggregate sends an OrderUpdatedEvent to the clustered
     event bus.

13. The OrderUpdatedEvent is consumed by the Order History Event
     Handler in the Ecom-history microservice.

14. The Order History Event Handler in the Ecom-history
     microservice updates the corresponding record of order in the
     Order History table.

Listing 17-17 shows the code of the Order History Event Handler handling order
updates.

This completes the "ship an order" flow, and you will later look at the execution of
the actual use case.

Deliver a Shipped Order

You just saw the flow of shipping a new order. All shipped orders will be available further
for the back office admin to pick and trigger the last step in the fulfilment cycle, the order
delivery. Figure 17-9 illustrates the state changes of various entities during the delivery
step.

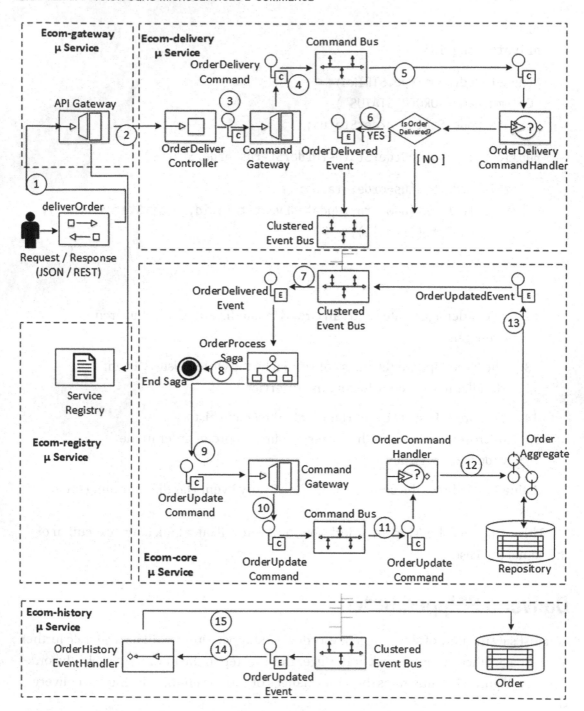

Figure 17-9. *Order delivery success*

Referring to Figure 17-9, the end-to-end flow as a result of a REST JSON request using the web app from the back-office admin to ship an order can be summarized as follows:

1. order_service.js sends a REST JSON request over HTTP to deliver an already shipped order:

   ```
   $http.post(sessionStorage.getItem('apiUrl')+'/delivery/
   delivery',deliveryDTO)
   ```

   This request hits the API gateway.

2. The API gateway interprets the URL by looking at the service registry and directs the request to the Order Deliver REST Controller in the Ecom-delivery microservice.

3. The Order Deliver REST Controller creates a new OrderDeliveryCommand and sends it to the command gateway. See Listing 17-23.

Listing 17-23. OrderDeliverController deliverOrder (ch17\ch17-01\Ax2-Ecom-No-Security\Ecom-delivery\src\main\java\com\acme\ecom\delivery\web\ OrderDeliverController.java)

```java
@RestController
@RequestMapping("/delivery")
public class OrderDeliverController {

    @Autowired
    private CommandGateway commandGateway;

    @RequestMapping(method = RequestMethod.POST)
    @ResponseBody
    public void deliverOrder(@RequestBody DeliveryDTO deliveryDTO) {

        OrderDeliveryCommand orderCommand =
            new OrderDeliveryCommand(deliveryDTO.getOrderId(),
        deliveryDTO.isDelivered(),deliveryDTO.getReasonForFailure());
        commandGateway.send(orderCommand);
    }
}
```

4. The command gateway delivers the OrderDeliveryCommand to the command bus.

5. The OrderDeliveryCommandHandler consumes the OrderDeliveryCommand from the command bus. See Listing 17-24.

Listing 17-24. OrderDeliveryCommandHandler handleOrderDelivery (ch17\ ch17-01\Ax2-Ecom-No-Security\Ecom-delivery\src\main\java\com\acme\ ecom\delivery\command\handler\OrderDeliveryCommandHandler.java)

```java
@Component
public class OrderDeliveryCommandHandler {

    @Autowired
    private EventBus eventBus;

    @CommandHandler
    public void handleOrderDelivery(
            OrderDeliveryCommand orderDeliveryCommand) {

        if(orderDeliveryCommand.isDelivered()){
            eventBus.publish(asEventMessage(
            new OrderDeliveredEvent(orderDeliveryCommand.getOrderId(),
                new Date())));
        }else{
            eventBus.publish(asEventMessage(
                new OrderDeliveryFailedEvent(
                orderDeliveryCommand.getOrderId(),
                orderDeliveryCommand.getReasonForFailure())));
        }
    }
}
```

6. In the current flow, when the back office admin clicks the Delivered button, the check if(orderDeliveryCommand. isDelivered()) is true and hence a new OrderDeliveredEvent is sent to the clustered event bus.

7. The OrderDeliveredEvent registered during Step 6 is consumed by the order process saga.

8. The saga's life cycle is ended after the invocation of the handleOrderCanceledEvent handler since you annotated that Event's handler on the saga with @EndSaga. See Listing 17-25.

Listing 17-25. OrderProcessSaga handleOrderDeliveredEvent (ch17\ch17-01\ Ax2-Ecom-No-Security\Ecom-core\src\main\java\com\acme\ecom\core\ order\saga\handler\OrderProcessSaga.java)

```java
public class OrderProcessSaga extends AbstractAnnotatedSaga {

    private Long orderId;

    @EndSaga
    @SagaEventHandler(associationProperty = "orderId")
    public void handleOrderDeliveredEvent(OrderDeliveredEvent
            orderDeliveredEvent) {

        commandGateway.send(new OrderUpdateCommand(
        orderDeliveredEvent.getOrderId(),OrderStatus.DELIVERED));
    }
}
```

9. The saga sends an OrderUpdateCommand to the command gateway.

10. The command gateway delivers the OrderUpdateCommand to the command bus.

11. The Order Command Handler picks up the OrderUpdateCommand for further processing.

    Refer to Listing 17-21 for a walkthrough of the code showing the Order Command Handler handling the OrderUpdateCommand.

12. The handleOrderUpdate first retrieves the corresponding order and calls updateOrderStatus.

13. The order aggregate sends an OrderUpdatedEvent to the clustered event bus. Listing 17-22 shows this code.

14. The OrderUpdatedEvent is consumed by the Order History Event Handler in the Ecom-history microservice.

15. The Order History Event Handler in the Ecom-history microservice updates the corresponding record of the order in the Order History table.

Listing 17-17 shows the code of the Order History Event Handler handling Order Updates.

This completes the "deliver a shipped order" flow, and you will later look at the execution of the actual use case.

Delivery Failure for a Shipped Order

The example application has a provision to simulate a delivery failure for an already shipped order. This event can happen for many reasons, like unable to locate the delivery address, consignment rejected by the customer, a natural calamity en route the consignment delivery, etc. Whatever the case, once the consignment comes back to the warehouse, there is no need to keep the products within that order in that packed state; instead the products can be released to inventory (if found fit, of course) for sales again. You will look at the flows and state changes when such a scenario is simulated in Figure 17-10.

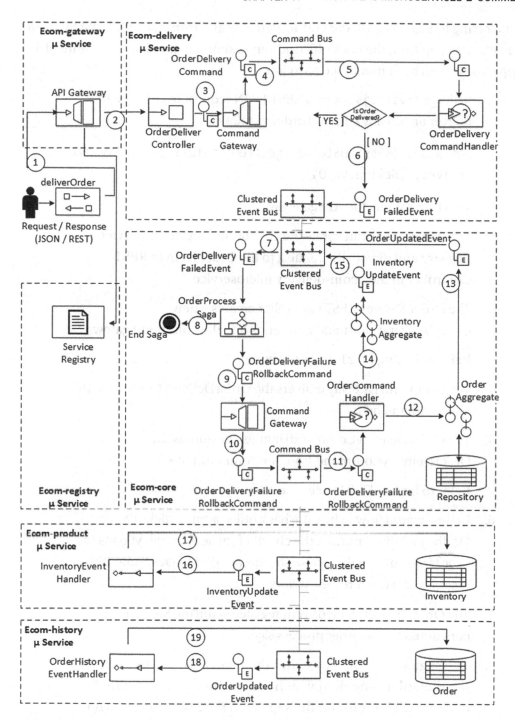

Figure 17-10. *Order delivery failure*

Referring to Figure 17-10, the end-to-end flow as a result of a REST JSON request using the web app from the back office admin to simulate the delivery failure of a shipped order can be summarized as follows:

1. `order_service.js` sends a REST JSON request over HTTP to deliver an already shipped order as follows:

   ```
   $http.post(sessionStorage.getItem('apiUrl')+'/delivery/
   delivery',deliveryDTO)
   ```

   This request hits the API gateway.

2. The API gateway interprets the URL by looking at the Service Registry and directs the request to the Order Deliver REST Controller in the Ecom-delivery microservice.

3. The Order Deliver REST Controller creates a new OrderDeliveryCommand and sends it to the command gateway.

   Refer to Listing 17-21 to see the code.

4. The command gateway delivers the OrderDeliveryCommand to the command bus.

5. The OrderDeliveryCommandHandler consumes the OrderDeliveryCommand from the command bus.

   Refer to Listing 17-24 to see the code.

6. In the current flow, when the back office admin clicks the "Delivery Failed" button, the check `if(orderDeliveryCommand.isDelivered())` will be false so a new OrderDeliveryFailedEvent is sent to the clustered event bus.

7. The OrderDeliveryFailedEvent registered during Step 6 is consumed by the order process saga.

8. The saga's life cycle ends after the invocation of the handleOrderCanceledEvent handler since you annotated that event's handler on the saga with `@EndSaga`, as shown in Listing 17-26.

Listing 17-26. OrderProcessSaga handleOrderDeliveryFailureEvent (ch17\
ch17-01\Ax2-Ecom-No-Security\Ecom-core\src\main\java\com\acme\ecom\
core\order\saga\handler\OrderProcessSaga.java)

```java
public class OrderProcessSaga extends AbstractAnnotatedSaga {

    private Long orderId;

    @EndSaga
    @SagaEventHandler(associationProperty = "orderId")
    public void handleOrderDeliveryFailureEvent(
            OrderDeliveryFailedEvent orderDeliveryFailedEvent) {

        commandGateway.send(new OrderDeliveryFailureRollbackCommand(
            orderDeliveryFailedEvent.getOrderId(),
            orderDeliveryFailedEvent.getFailureReason()));
    }
}
```

9. The Order Process saga sends an
   OrderDeliveryFailureRollbackCommand to the command
   gateway.

10. The command gateway delivers the
    OrderDeliveryFailureRollbackCommand to the command bus.

11. The Order Command Handler picks up the
    OrderDeliveryFailureRollbackCommand for processing. See
    Listing 17-27.

Listing 17-27. OrderCommandHandler handleOrderDeliveryFailure (ch17\
ch17-01\Ax2-Ecom-No-Security\Ecom-core\src\main\java\com\acme\ecom\
core\order\command\handler\OrderCommandHandler.java)

```java
@Component
public class OrderCommandHandler {

    @Autowired
    @Qualifier(value = "inventoryRepository")
    private Repository<Inventory> inventoryRepository;
```

```
@Autowired
@Qualifier(value = "orderRepository")
private Repository<Order> orderRepository;

@CommandHandler
public void handleOrderDeliveryFailure(OrderDeliveryFailureRollbackCommand
        orderDeliveryFailureRollbackCommand) {

    Order order = orderRepository.load(
        orderDeliveryFailureRollbackCommand.getOrderId());
    order.updateOrderStatus(OrderStatus.DELIVERY_FAILED);
    rollbackInventory(order);
}

private void rollbackInventory(Order order){

    for(LineItem lineItem:order.getLineItems()){
        Inventory inventory =
            inventoryRepository.load(lineItem.getInventoryId());
        inventory.updateProductStock(lineItem.getQuantity(),
            ProductStockOperation.ADD);
    }
}
}
```

12. The Order Command Handler loads the respective order
     aggregate entity from the repository and invokes the
     updateOrderStatus method of the order to change the status to
     "Delivery Failed."

     See Listing 17-22 for the code walkthrough of invoking the
     updateOrderStatus method of order to change the status.

13. The order aggregate sends an OrderUpdatedEvent to the clustered
     event bus.

14. In Step 11, the Order Command Handler also retrieves the
     inventory items of all the products associated with the order and
     invokes updateProductStock. The objective is to revert the stock
     to account for the effect of failed delivery of the order so that those

inventories can be made available for sales again.
The rollbackInventory in Listing 17-14 depicts this.

15. While readjusting the stock back, each inventory aggregate
    registers an InventoryUpdateEvent into the clustered event bus.

16. The InventoryUpdateEvent generated in Step 15 is consumed by
    the Inventory Event Handler in the Ecom-product microservice.

17. The InventoryEventHandler in the Ecom-product microservice
    refreshes its own materialized view of the inventory read model.

    Listing 17-11 shows the code of handleInventoryUpdates doing this.

18. The OrderUpdatedEvent is consumed by the Order History Event
    Handler in the Ecom-history microservice.

19. The Order History Event Handler in the Ecom-history
    microservice updates the corresponding record of the order in the
    Order History table.

Listing 17-17 shows the code of the Order History Event Handler handling order updates.
This completes the simulation of "failure of delivery of a shipped order" flow, and
you will later look at the execution of the actual use case.

Retrieve Order History Views

The order history is required to render all orders of a particular user, that too filtered by
status. This is effected by the Order History Mongo Repository. The interesting part is
that there is no REST controller in the Order History microservice; instead you use the
@RepositoryRestResource. See Listing 17-28.

Listing 17-28. OrderHistoryRepository (ch17\ch17-01\Ax2-Ecom-No-Security\
Ecom-history\src\main\java\com\acme\ecom\order\history\repository\
OrderHistoryRepository.java)

```
@RepositoryRestResource(collectionResourceRel = "orderHistory",
    path = "orderHistory")
public interface OrderHistoryRepository extends
        MongoRepository<Order, String> {
```

```
@RestResource(exported = false)
public Order findByOrderId(@Param("orderId") Long orderId);

public List<Order> findByUserId(@Param("userId") String userId);

public List<Order> findByOrderStatus(
    @Param("orderStatus") String orderStatus);

@Override
public Order findOne(String id);

@Override
@RestResource(exported = false)
public Page<Order> findAll(Pageable pageable);
}
```

At runtime, Spring Data REST will create implementations of the above interface automatically. Then it will use the @RepositoryRestResource annotation to direct Spring MVC to create RESTful endpoints at /orderHistory, the details of which you saw in the "Perform Data Operations Using Spring Boot and MongoDB" section in Chapter 7.

Design and Code the E-Commerce Microservice Infrastructure

Apart from the business microservices in the previous section, you also have a set of infrastructure microservices in the example application. The code base for the microservices is straightforward and understandable, and most of them were covered in the "Spring Cloud" section of Chapter 8 so I will not cover them in detail here. You will, however, see how they fit together in the overall architecture.

Config Server

The Config Server microservice hosts the configuration parameters for all the other business microservices and infrastructure microservices. Due to this aspect, a healthy running state of the Config Server microservice is required for the startup of all other microservices. You point to this microservice to find the configuration files for all other microservices from a single location. In a production environment, this location will point to a GIT repository so that the configuration files themselves are version controlled.

Figure 17-11 reflects the above dependency, labelled as 1.

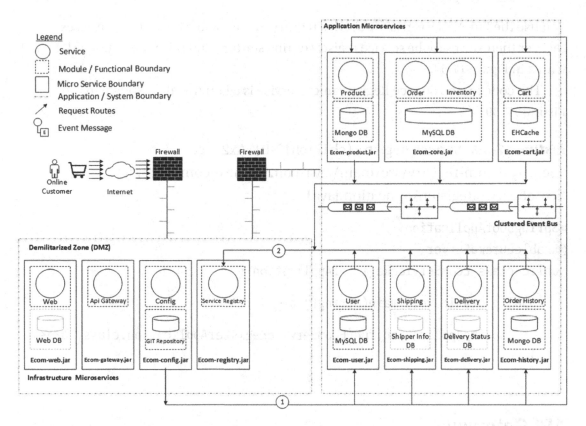

Figure 17-11.   *Config Server and Service Registry*

The code for the Config Server microservice is trivial, as shown in Listing 17-29.

Listing 17-29.   Config Server (ch17\ch17-01\Ax2-Ecom-No-Security\Ecom-config\src\main\java\com\acme\ecom\config\EcomConfigApplication.java)

```java
@SpringBootApplication
@EnableConfigServer
public class EcomConfigApplication {

    public static void main(String[] args) {
        SpringApplication.run(EcomConfigApplication.class, args);
    }
}
```

Service Registry

You use the Eureka server as the service registry. All of the business microservices register themselves to the service registry during startup, and this registration is labelled with 2 in Figure 17-11.

The code for the Service Registry microservice is again trivial, as shown in Listing 17-30.

Listing 17-30. Service Registry (ch17\ch17-01\Ax2-Ecom-No-Security\Ecom-registry\src\main\java\com\acme\ecom\registry\EcomServiceRegisterApplication.java)

```
@SpringBootApplication
@EnableEurekaServer
public class EcomServiceRegisterApplication {

    public static void main(String[] args) {

        SpringApplication.run(EcomServiceRegisterApplication.class, args);
    }
}
```

API Gateway

You enable Zuul as the API gateway. Any requests from the web app will only hit the API gateway and it's up to the API gateway to resolve the request target by contacting the service registry and routing the request to the respective service. See Listing 17-31.

Listing 17-31. Zuul API Gateway (ch17\ch17-01\Ax2-Ecom-No-Security\Ecom-gateway\src\main\java\com\acme\ecom\gateway\EcomApiGatewayApplication.java)

```
@SpringBootApplication
@EnableZuulProxy
@EnableDiscoveryClient
@EnableCircuitBreaker
@EnableHystrix
@EnableHystrixDashboard
```

```java
@EnableFeignClients
public class EcomApiGatewayApplication {

    public static void main(String[] args) {

        SpringApplication.run(EcomApiGatewayApplication.class, args);
    }

    @Bean
    public CorsFilter corsFilter() {

        UrlBasedCorsConfigurationSource source =
            new UrlBasedCorsConfigurationSource();
        CorsConfiguration config = new CorsConfiguration();
        config.setAllowCredentials(true);
        config.addAllowedOrigin("*");
        config.addAllowedHeader("*");
        config.addAllowedMethod("OPTIONS");
        config.addAllowedMethod("HEAD");
        config.addAllowedMethod("GET");
        config.addAllowedMethod("PUT");
        config.addAllowedMethod("POST");
        config.addAllowedMethod("DELETE");
        config.addAllowedMethod("PATCH");
        source.registerCorsConfiguration("/**", config);
        return new CorsFilter(source);
    }
}
```

Figure 17-12 depicts the various interactions of the web app with the server-side microservices.

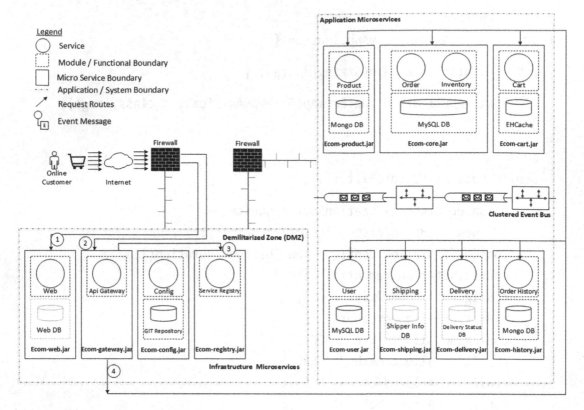

Figure 17-12. *API Gateway*

Referring to Figure 17-12, the various interactions of the web app with the server-side microservices are as follows:

1. The web app is directly accessible from the external network or the Internet. Once entering the home page URL in the browser, the web app will be downloaded into the browser.

2. All subsequent requests from the web app hit the API gateway.

3. When a request from a web app hits the API gateway, the gateway contacts the Service Registry to resolve the IP, port, and service name of the microservice.

4. Subsequently, the request is routed to the microservice.

Table 17-1 provides a complete view of the application and infrastructure components for the microservice sample application. This will be handy when you want to understand the dependency and the flow of various use cases discussed earlier.

Table 17-1. *Complete View of Application and Infrastructure Components*

No	μ ?	Microservice	Component	Stereo Type	Method	Param	Notes
1	μ	Ecom-web	Config Controller	Rest Controller	getAPIGatewayURL		
2	μ	Ecom-user	User Controller	Rest Controller	postCustomer		
3					validateCredential		
4			Customer Service	Service	saveCustomer		
5			Service		findCustomer		
6			User Repository	Crud Repository	findByUserId		
7			Online User Repository	Crud Repository	findByScreenName		
8	μ	Ecom-product	Product Rest Controller	Rest Controller	updateProduct		
9					postProduct		
10					getProduct		
11					getAllProducts		
12					deleteProduct		
13					deleteAllProducts		
14					getAllProductsByCategory		
15					getAllProductsByName		
16			Product Repository	Mongo Repository			
17			Product Category Repository	Mongo Repository			
18			Inventory Event Handler	Event Handler	handleInventoryUpdates	Inventory Update Event	

(*continued*)

Table 17-1. (*continued*)

No	μ ?	Microservice	Component	Stereo Type	Method	Param	Notes
19	μ	Ecom-cart	Customer Cart Application Controller	Rest Controller	getCustomerCartInfo		
20			Customer Cart Controller	Rest Controller	updateCustomerCartToCache		
21					getCustomerCartFromCache		
22			Cart Cache Service	Service	updateUserCartInCache		
23					getUserCartFromCache		
24	μ	Ecom-core	Order Controller	Rest Controller	createOrder		
25					cancelOrder		
26			Order Process Saga	Saga Event Handler	handleOrderCreationEvent	Order Created Event	Start Saga
27					handleOrderShippedEvent	Order Shipped Event	
28					handleOrderCanceledEvent	Order Cancelled Event	End Saga
29					handleOrderDeliveredEvent	Order Delivered Event	End Saga
30					handleOrderDelivery FailureEvent	Order Delivery Failed Event	End Saga

(*continued*)

Table 17-1. (*continued*)

No	μ ?	Microservice	Component	Stereo Type	Method	Param	Notes
31	μ	Ecom-core	Order Command Handler	Command Handler	handleNewOrder	Order Create Command	
32					handleOrderUpdate	Order Update Command	
33					handleOrderCancel	Order Cancel Command	
34					handleOrderDeliveryFailure	Order Delivery Failure Rollback Command	
35			Inventory Creation Command Handler	Command Handler	handleInventoryCreation	Inventory Create Commad	
36			Order	Aggregate Root	notifyOrderCreation		
37					updateOrderStatus		
38					cancelOrder		
39					notifyOrderFailure		
40			Inventory	Aggregate Root	updateProductStock		

(*continued*)

Table 17-1. (*continued*)

No	μ ?	Microservice	Component	Stereo Type	Method	Param	Notes
41	μ	Ecom-shipping	Order Shipping Controller	Rest Controller	shipOrder		
42			Order Shipping Command Handler	Command Handler	handleOrderShipping	Order Shipping Command	
43	μ	Ecom-delivery	Order Deliver Controller	Rest Controller	handleOrder		
44			Order Delivery Command Handler	Command Handler	handleOrderDelivery	Order Delivery Command	
45	μ	Ecom-history	Order History Event Handler	Event Handler	handleOrderCreationEvent	Order Created Event	
46					handleOrderUpdatedEvent	Order Updated Event	
47	μ	Ecom-security		Infra			
48	μ	Ecom-gateway		Infra			
49	μ	Ecom-registry		Infra			
50	μ	Ecom-config		Infra			

(*continued*)

Table 17-1. (*continued*)

No	μ ?	Microservice	Component	Stereo Type	Method	Param	Notes
51	×	Ecom-common		Common Libraries			
52	×	config-repo		Config Files			
53	×	Delivery-setup		Utility Folder			

Configure the E-Commerce Microservice Application

You need to make the required configuration changes in the microservices. You will do so one by one.

1. Microservice 1: Ecom-config. See Listing 17-32.

Listing 17-32. Ecom-config Microservice Configuration (ch17\ch17-01\Ax2-Ecom-No-Security\Ecom-config\src\main\resources\application.yml)

```
spring:
  cloud:
    config:
      server:
        git:
          uri: file://D:/binil/gold/pack03/ch17/ch17-01/Ax2-Ecom-No-
          Security/config-repo
```

Note   Make any changes required for your environment. Ensure that the config URI is proper. You will need to later start the config server before any other server. Further, the retrieval of the configuration parameters for all other microservices will depend on the proper configuration of this Config Server microservice.

2.   Microservice 2: Ecom-registry. See Listing 17-33.

Listing 17-33. Ecom-registry Microservice Configuration (ch17\ch17-01\Ax2-Ecom-No-Security\config-repo\ecom-registry.yml)

```
eureka:
  instance:
    hostname: localhost
  client:
    registerWithEureka: false
    fetchRegistry: false
    serviceUrl.defaultZone: http://${eureka.instance.hostname}:${server.
    port}/eureka/
```

Note   Don't make any changes here.

3.   Microservice 3: Ecom-gateway. See Listing 17-34.

Listing 17-34. Ecom-gateway Microservice Configuration (ch17\ch17-01\Ax2-Ecom-No-Security\config-repo\ecom-gateway.yml)

```
zuul:
  routes:
    ecom-core:
      path: /core/**
      service-id: ecom-core
    ecom-user:
      path: /customer/**
      service-id: ecom-user
    ecom-cart:
      path: /cart/**
      service-id: ecom-cart
    ecom-product:
      path: /product/**
      service-id: ecom-product
```

```
ecom-history:
  path: /orderhistory/**
  service-id: ecom-history
ecom-delivery:
  path: /delivery/**
  service-id: ecom-delivery
ecom-shipping:
  path: /shipping/**
  service-id: ecom-shipping

eureka:
  client:
    serviceUrl:
      defaultZone: http://localhost:8761/eureka/
```

Note   Don't make any changes here.

---

4.   Microservice 4: Ecom-cart. See Listing 17-35.

Listing 17-35. Ecom-cart Microservice Configuration (ch17\ch17-01\Ax2-Ecom-No-Security\config-repo\ecom-cart.yml)

```
eureka:
  client:
    serviceUrl:
      defaultZone: http://localhost:8761/eureka/
```

Note   Don't make any changes here.

---

5.   Microservice 5: Ecom-core. See Listing 17-36.

Listing 17-36. Ecom-core Microservice Configuration (ch17\ch17-01\Ax2-Ecom-No-Security\config-repo\ecom-core.yml)

```
spring:
  data:
```

```
  mongodb:
    uri: mongodb://localhost:27017/ecom
  datasource:
    url: jdbc:mysql://localhost/ecom
    username: root
    password: rootpassword
    driver-class-name: com.mysql.jdbc.Driver

jpa:
database-platform: org.hibernate.dialect.MySQL5InnoDBDialect

eureka:
  client:
    serviceUrl:
      defaultZone: http://localhost:8761/eureka/

ecom:
  amqp:
    rabbit:
      address: localhost:5672
      username: guest
      password: guest
      vhost: /
      exchange: Ecom-exchange
      queue: Ecom-core-queue
```

Note   Make any changes required for your environment.

---

6.   Microservice 6: Ecom-delivery. See Listing 17-37.

Listing 17-37. Ecom-delivery Microservice Configuration (ch17\ch17-01\Ax2-Ecom-No-Security\config-repo\ecom-delivery.yml)

```
eureka:
  client:
    serviceUrl:
      defaultZone: http://localhost:8761/eureka/
```

```
ecom:
  amqp:
    rabbit:
      address: localhost:5672
      username: guest
      password: guest
      vhost: /
      exchange: Ecom-exchange
      queue: Ecom-delivery-queue
```

Note   Make any changes required for your environment.

---

7.   Microservice 7: Ecom-history. See Listing 17-38.

Listing 17-38.   Ecom-history Microservice Configuration (ch17\ch17-01\Ax2-Ecom-No-Security\config-repo\ecom-history.yml)

```
spring:
  data:
    mongodb:
      uri:mongodb://localhost:27017/ecom

eureka:
  client:
    serviceUrl:
      defaultZone: http://localhost:8761/eureka/

ecom:
  amqp:
    rabbit:
      address: localhost:5672
      username: guest
      password: guest
      vhost: /
      exchange: Ecom-exchange
      queue: Ecom-order-histo-queue
```

Note   Make any changes required for your environment.

8.   Microservice 8: Ecom-product. See Listing 17-39.

Listing 17-39. Ecom-product Microservice Configuration (ch17\ch17-01\Ax2-Ecom-No-Security\config-repo\ecom-product.yml)

```
spring:
  data:
    mongodb:
      uri: mongodb://localhost:27017/ecom

eureka:
  client:
    serviceUrl:
      defaultZone: http://localhost:8761/eureka/

ecom:
  amqp:
    rabbit:
      address: localhost:5672
      username: guest
      password: guest
      vhost: /
      exchange: Ecom-exchange
      queue: Ecom-product-queue
  product.img.location: D:/binil/gold/pack03/ch17/ch17-01/Ax2-Ecom-No-
  Security/Ecom-xtra-setup/productImg/
```

Note   Make any changes required for your environment.

9.   Microservice 9: Ecom-shipping. See Listing 17-40.

Listing 17-40. Ecom-shipping Microservice Configuration (ch17\ch17-01\Ax2-Ecom-No-Security\config-repo\ecom-shipping.yml)

```
eureka:
  client:
    serviceUrl:
      defaultZone: http://localhost:8761/eureka/

ecom:
  amqp:
    rabbit:
      address: localhost:5672
      username: guest
      password: guest
      vhost: /
      exchange: Ecom-exchange
      queue: Ecom-shipping-queue
```

Note   Make any changes required for your environment.

---

10.   Microservice 10: Ecom-user. See Listing 17-41.

Listing 17-41. Ecom-user Microservice Configuration (ch17\ch17-01\Ax2-Ecom-No-Security\config-repo\ecom-user.yml)

```
spring:
  datasource:
    url: jdbc:mysql://localhost/ecom
    username: root
    password: rootpassword

eureka:
  client:
    serviceUrl:
      defaultZone: http://localhost:8761/eureka/
```

Note   Make any changes required for your environment.

---

11.   Microservice 11: Ecom-web. See Listing 17-42.

Listing 17-42. Ecom-web (ch17\ch17-01\Ax2-Ecom-No-Security\Ecom-web\ src\main\resources\application.yml)

```
spring:
  application:
    name: ecom-web
  server:
    port: 8080
  ecom:
    apigateway:
    url: http://localhost:9000
```

The web app will make use of the above configured API gateway URL to route all requests to the microservices. Don't make any changes here.

Set Up the Environment Infrastructure for the E-Commerce Microservice Application

Next, you need to set up few infrastructure settings to run the example. Let's do that too one by one.

1.   Set up RabbitMQ Server.

As the first step, you need to bring up RabbitMQ Server. You may want to refer to Appendix B to get started with RabbitMQ server.

D:\Applns\RabbitMQ\rabbitmq_server-3.6.3\sbin>D:\Applns\RabbitMQ\ rabbitmq_server-3.6.3\sbin\rabbitmq-server.bat

2.   Set up MongoDB Server.

Next, make sure MongoDB is up and running. You may want to refer to Appendix A to get started with MongoDB.

```
D:\Applns\MongoDB\Server\3.2.6\bin\mongod.exe --dbpath D:\Applns\
MongoDB\Server\3.2.6\data
```

You can now connect to the above started MongoDB Server using
another Windows command prompt and executing the program

```
D:\Applns\MongoDB\Server\3.2.6\bin>D:\Applns\MongoDB\Server\3.2.6\
bin\mongo
```

```
> use ecom
switched to db ecom
> db.getName()
ecom
```

Here again, one easy way to start with clean collections with data
for your example is to simply drop the database and create it
newly as you create the required collection:

```
> db.dropDatabase();
```

```
> show collections
```

You will create the required collections now. For that, in another
Windows command prompt, you need to use the following
mongoimport tool:

```
cd D:\Applns\MongoDB\Server\3.2.6\bin
```

First, create the ecom database and import the product category
data into a collection named productCategory:

```
D:\Applns\MongoDB\Server\3.2.6\bin>mongoimport --db ecom
--jsonArray --collection productCategory --file D://binil/gold/
shuffle/pack02/ch17/ch17-01/Ax2-Ecom-No-Security/Ecom-xtra-setup/
productCategory.json
2018-05-25T12:11:12.587+0530     connected to: localhost
2018-05-25T12:11:13.032+0530     imported 6 documents
```

Next, do the same for the product and inventory collections:

```
D:\Applns\MongoDB\Server\3.2.6\bin>mongoimport --db ecom
--jsonArray --collection product --file D://binil/gold/shuffle/
pack02/ch17/ch17-01/Ax2-Ecom-No-Security/Ecom-xtra-setup/products.
json
2018-05-25T15:58:44.679+0530    connected to: localhost
2018-05-25T15:58:44.913+0530    imported 34 documents

D:\Applns\MongoDB\Server\3.2.6\bin>mongoimport --db ecom
--jsonArray --collection inventory --file D://binil/gold/shuffle/
pack02/ch17/ch17-01/Ax2-Ecom-No-Security/Ecom-xtra-setup/
inventory.json
2018-05-25T15:59:47.156+0530    connected to: localhost
2018-05-25T15:59:47.502+0530    imported 34 documents

D:\Applns\MongoDB\Server\3.2.6\bin>
```

You can list the newly created collections like so:

```
> show collections
inventory
product
productCategory
>
```

3. Set up MySQL Server.

    Make sure MySQL is up and running. You may want to refer to
    Appendix H to get started with MySQL.

    First, bring up MySQL Server:

    ```
    D:\Applns\MySQL\mysql-5.7.14-winx64\bin>mysqld --console
    ```

    Now open a MySQL prompt:

    ```
    D:\Applns\MySQL\mysql-5.7.14-winx64\bin>mysql -u root -p
    ```

    ```
    mysql> SHOW DATABASES;
    mysql> use ecom;
    Database changed
    ```

To start with clean tables, let's delete all the tables with the names you use for your current example (if they exist) and recreate them automatically later during the microservices start up:

```
mysql> drop table inventory;
mysql> drop table line_item;
mysql> drop table customer_order;
mysql> drop table user_info;
mysql> drop table address;
mysql> drop table user_role;
mysql> drop table user_credential;
```

Build and Run E-Commerce Microservice Application

You have already seen that there are 11 microservices in the application, so you are advised to use an IDE, preferably Eclipse to better manage the build and run complexity.

You need to first set up your 11 microservices projects as Eclipse Projects. Go to the below root folder first:

```
cd ch17\ch17-01\Ax2-Ecom-No-Security
```

To generate the Eclipse project files from your POM, execute the following command:

```
mvn eclipse:eclipse
```

The Maven Eclipse Plugin is used to generate Eclipse IDE files (*.classpath, *.project, *.wtpmodules, and the .settings folder) for use with the project. If your Maven project has dependencies, the eclipse classpath will be synchronized with the current list of Maven dependencies as well as any transitive Maven dependencies.

The Maven project for the sample application consists of a number of aggregated projects with a common root pom, and some of these aggregated projects depend on each other. The eclipse:eclipse goal will configure each dependent project in Eclipse as an Eclipse project dependency, rather than an Eclipse jar dependency. By doing this, changes to code within project A will be available immediately to project B, assuming that project B defines a dependency on project A.

Next, you have to import the project into your Eclipse workspace (from the menu bar, select File ➤ Impor ➤ Existing Projects into Workspace). Here the project (directory) should not be located in your workspace because Eclipse might come into trouble, especially if you want to use Eclipse as the scm client.

1. In Eclipse Project Explorer, import existing projects.

2. Select Maven ➤ Existing Maven Projects ➤ Next.

3. In the "Select Maven projects" Window, click Browse.

4. In the "Select Root Folder," select D:\binil\gold\pack03\ch17\
    ch17-01\Ax2-Ecom-No-Security and click OK, as shown in
    Figure 17-13.

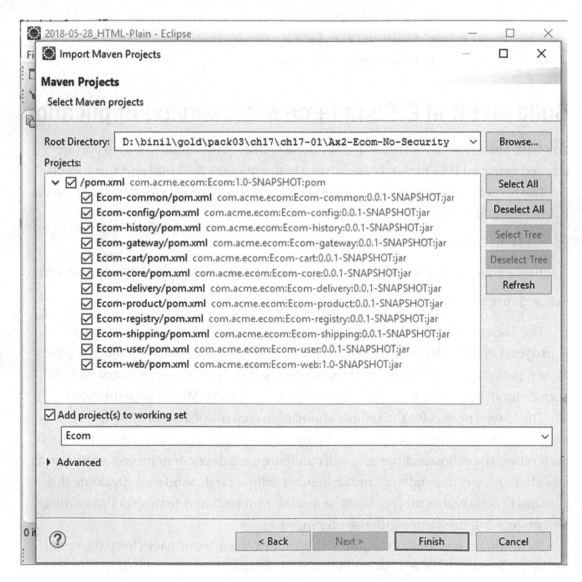

Figure 17-13. *Import the e-commerce microservices Maven projects*

5. Once you make sure the import is complete (by watching the Eclipse status bar), in Java EE Perspective, select all projects (except Ecom).

6. Right-click and select Maven ➤ Update Projects.

7. In the "Update Maven Project" window, click OK.

If everything goes fine, all the projects should get built without any errors. You may ignore any warnings and proceed to bring up the servers one by one. To bring up the servers, you need to follow the below sequence for the first three microservices:

```
Ecom-config
Ecom-registry
Ecom-gateway
```

For the rest of the microservices, you may start them in any order. This flexibility also demonstrates two other aspects:

- **Independence of the microservices**: There is absolutely zero dependency between microservices. This is different from the older CORBA, RMI, IIOP, and SOAP service paradigms where the dependent microservice required the stubs of the independent microservice.

- **Partial failures of the application**: Even if you don't bring up all the microservices, the web app will function by partially consuming available services.

To start a microservice, select the project in Eclipse, right-click and select Run As > Java Application. See Figure 17-14.

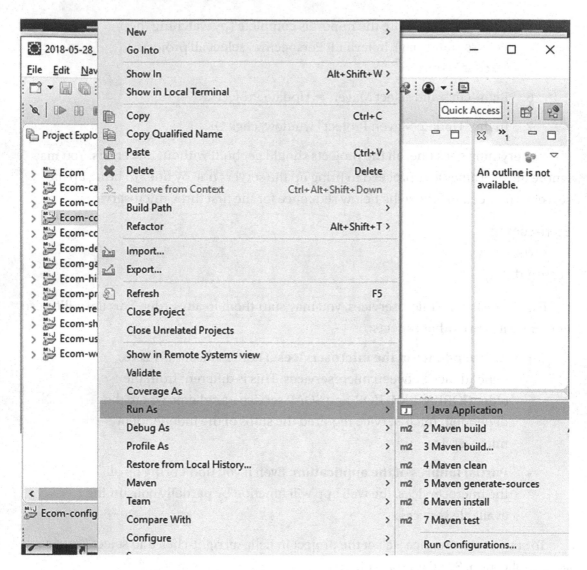

Figure 17-14. *Run each microservice as a Java application*

In the next window, select the Java class with the main method you intend to run. You can type "Ecom*" to list the Java classes with the main method and click OK, as shown in Figure 17-15.

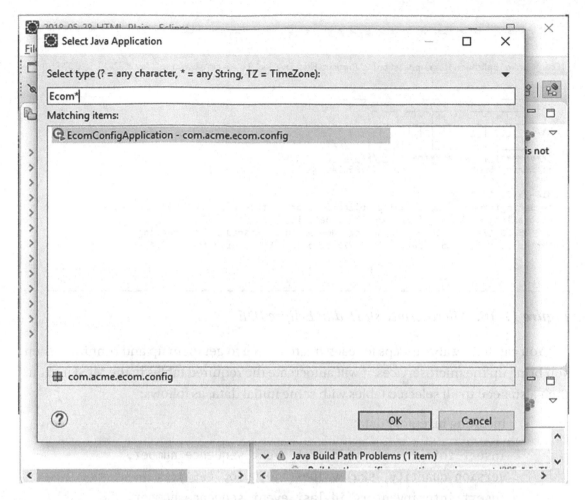

Figure 17-15. *Run the main class of each microservice as an application*

Be patient until the microservice initializes fully. Typically this will be indicated by the console logs within Eclipse, as seen in Figure 17-16.

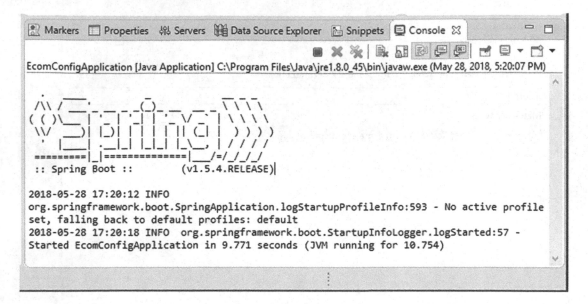

Figure 17-16. *Microservice started in Eclipse IDE*

You can follow above steps for each microservice to get them up and running. When you bring up the microservices, it will autocreate the required tables in the MySQL. You then also need to fill selected tables with some initial data, as follows:

- Inserting inventory data:

```
insert into inventory(id,last_event_sequence_number,
version,quantity, sku) values(1,0,0,10,'LEE');
insert into inventory(id,last_event_sequence_number,
version,quantity, sku) values(2,0,0,10,'ACTION');
insert into inventory(id,last_event_sequence_number,
version,quantity, sku) values(3,0,0,10,'ADDIDAS');
insert into inventory(id,last_event_sequence_number,
version,quantity, sku) values(4,0,0,10,'NIKE');
insert into inventory(id,last_event_sequence_number,
version,quantity, sku) values(5,0,0,10,'LEE_1');
insert into inventory(id,last_event_sequence_number,
version,quantity, sku) values(6,0,0,10,'ACTION_1');
insert into inventory(id,last_event_sequence_number,
version,quantity, sku) values(7,0,0,10,'LAXME');
```

```
insert into inventory(id,last_event_sequence_number,
version,quantity, sku) values(8,0,0,10,'LAXME13');
insert into inventory(id,last_event_sequence_number,
version,quantity, sku) values(9,0,0,10,'ADDIDAS_W');
insert into inventory(id,last_event_sequence_number,
version,quantity, sku) values(10,0,0,10,'WEDGES');
insert into inventory(id,last_event_sequence_number,
version,quantity, sku) values(11,0,0,10,'LEE_2');
insert into inventory(id,last_event_sequence_number,
version,quantity, sku) values(12,0,0,10,'LEE_3');
insert into inventory(id,last_event_sequence_number,
version,quantity, sku) values(13,0,0,10,'RAYBAN1');
insert into inventory(id,last_event_sequence_number,
version,quantity, sku) values(14,0,0,10,'RAYBAN2');
insert into inventory(id,last_event_sequence_number,
version,quantity, sku) values(15,0,0,10,'RAYBAN3');
insert into inventory(id,last_event_sequence_number,
version,quantity, sku) values(16,0,0,10,'FASTTRACK1');
insert into inventory(id,last_event_sequence_number,
version,quantity, sku) values(17,0,0,10,'FASTTRACK2') ;
insert into inventory(id,last_event_sequence_number,
version,quantity, sku) values(18,0,0,10,'FASTTRACK3');
insert into inventory(id,last_event_sequence_number,
version,quantity, sku) values(19,0,0,10,'ARROW1');
insert into inventory(id,last_event_sequence_number,
version,quantity, sku) values(20,0,0,10,'ARROW2');
insert into inventory(id,last_event_sequence_number,
version,quantity, sku) values(21,0,0,10,'ARROW3');
insert into inventory(id,last_event_sequence_number,
version,quantity, sku) values(22,0,0,10,'POLO1');
insert into inventory(id,last_event_sequence_number,
version,quantity, sku) values(23,0,0,10,'POLO2');
insert into inventory(id,last_event_sequence_number,
version,quantity, sku) values(24,0,0,10,'POLO3');
```

```
insert into inventory(id,last_event_sequence_number,
version,quantity, sku) values(25,0,0,10,'DON1');
insert into inventory(id,last_event_sequence_number,
version,quantity, sku) values(26,0,0,10,'DON2');
insert into inventory(id,last_event_sequence_number,
version,quantity, sku) values(27,0,0,10,'DON3');
insert into inventory(id,last_event_sequence_number,
version,quantity, sku) values(28,0,0,10,'DON4');
insert into inventory(id,last_event_sequence_number,
version,quantity, sku) values(29,0,0,10,'X-COTTEN1');
insert into inventory(id,last_event_sequence_number,
version,quantity, sku) values(30,0,0,10,'X-COTTEN2');
insert into inventory(id,last_event_sequence_number,
version,quantity, sku) values(31,0,0,10,'X-COTTEN3');
insert into inventory(id,last_event_sequence_number,
version,quantity, sku) values(32,0,0,10,'X-COTTEN4');
insert into inventory(id,last_event_sequence_number,
version,quantity, sku) values(33,0,0,10,'X-COTTEN5');
insert into inventory(id,last_event_sequence_number,
version,quantity, sku) values(34,0,0,10,'X-COTTEN6') ;
```

- Inserting back office admin:

```
insert into user_credential (id,active,password,user_id) values
(1,1,'admin','admin');
insert into user_role (id,role,user_id) values (1,'ROLE_ADMIN',1);
insert into user_role (id,role,user_id) values (2,'CUSTOMER_READ',1);
insert into user_role (id,role,user_id) values (3,'PRODUCT_WRITE',1);
insert into user_role (id,role,user_id) values (4,'ORDER_READ',1);
insert into user_role (id,role,user_id) values (5,'PRODUCT_WRITE',1);
insert into user_role (id,role,user_id) values (6,'ORDER_WRITE',1);
insert into user_info (id,email,first_name,last_name,phone,user_id)
values(1,'admin@admin','admin','admin',903766787,'admin');
```

Note You won't be utilizing the roles added here until you reach Chapter 18.

Test the E-Commerce Microservice Use Cases

You can test the application using your preferred browser. You can take two browser windows, one for the normal customer or end user and another for the back office admin.

Typing this URL will bring up the end user screen shown in Figure 17-17: `http://localhost:8080/`. (Refresh your browser if the full content is not loaded as shown in Figure 17-17).

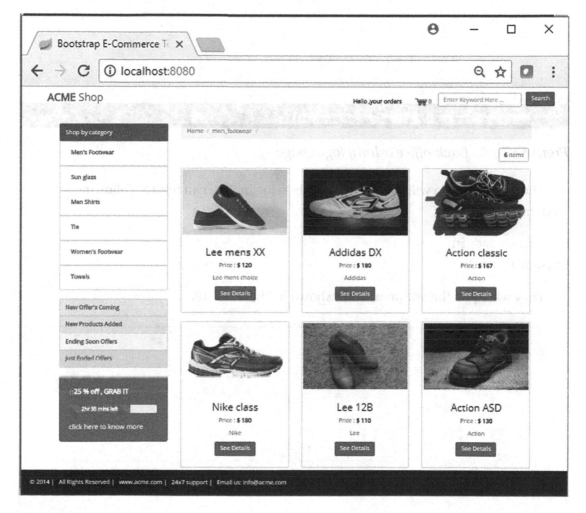

Figure 17-17. *End user home page*

To bring up the back office admin screen, type this URL: `http://localhost:8080/admin.html`. See Figure 17-18.

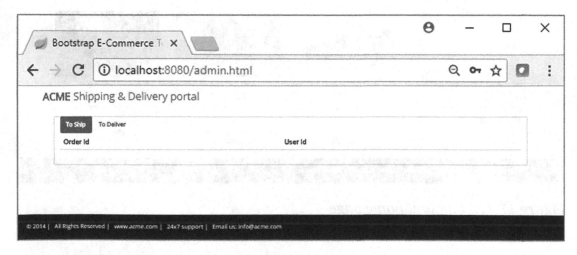

Figure 17-18. *Back-office admin login page*

The admin screen will ask for credentials to log in. You can use the following credentials:

```
User name: admin
Password: admin
```

They will open the admin window shown in Figure 17-19.

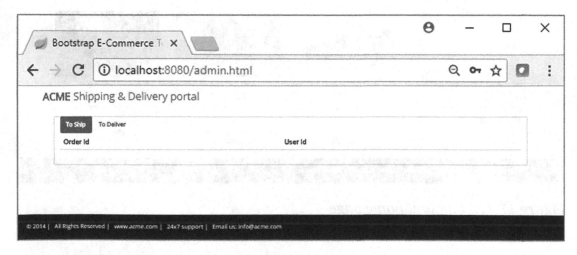

Figure 17-19. *Back-office admin home page*

You can now test the application by executing few use cases. You may want to explicitly refresh your screens to see the effect of your actions using the browser's Refresh button.

View Product Category and Product Details

From the product listing shown in Figure 17-17, select a product to see the product details and available inventory. You can select the required numbers to buy, as shown in Figure 17-20.

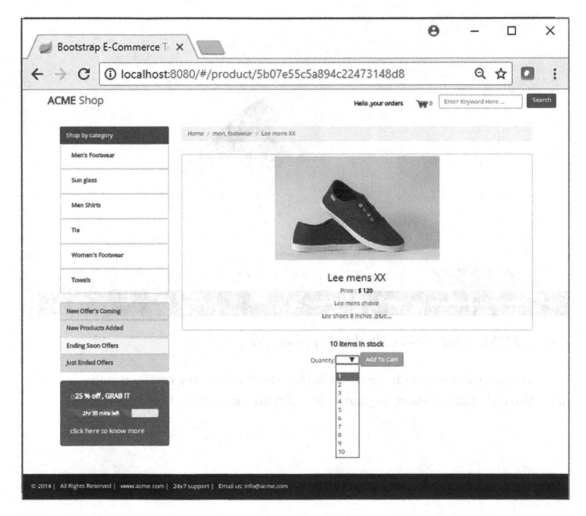

Figure 17-20. *Select the number of items to order*

Add to Cart

In the next step, you can add the selected product and the selected numbers of the product to the cart, as shown in Figure 17-21.

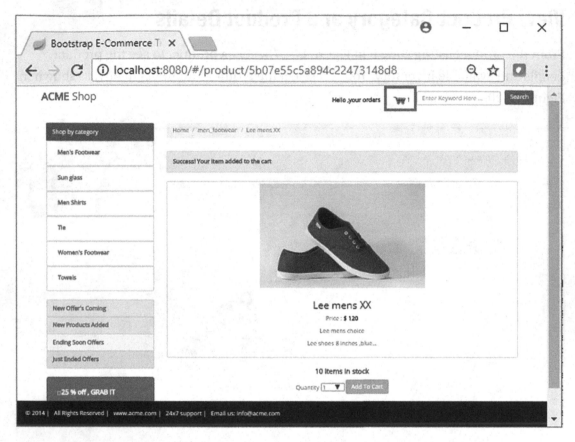

Figure 17-21. Add the item to the shopping cart

You will be able to see the newly added item in the shopping cart icon at the top of the page. You can click the shopping cart icon to display the cart, as shown in Figure 17-22.

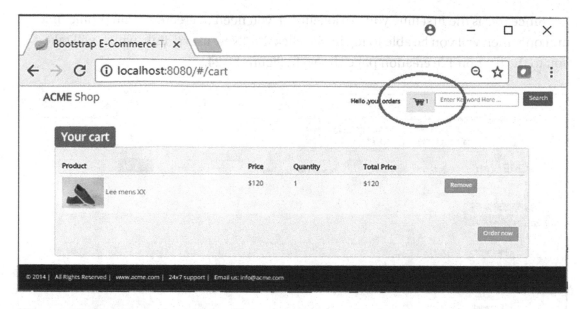

Figure 17-22.   *Shopping cart with items ready to check out*

User Profile Creation

Proceed to order by clicking the "Order now" button in Figure 17-22. It will ask the user to log in, as shown in Figure 17-23.

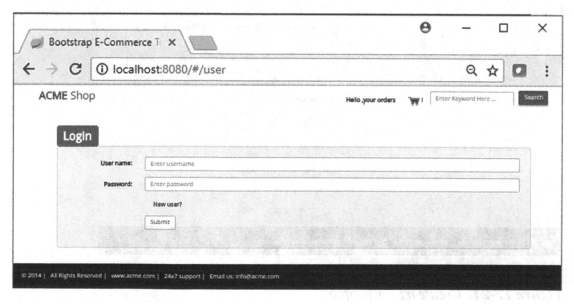

Figure 17-23.   *User login prompt*

Since this is the first time you are logging in, you need to create a login profile first and only then will you be able to log in. So, click the "New user?" link, which will take you to the user profile creation page shown in Figure 17-24.

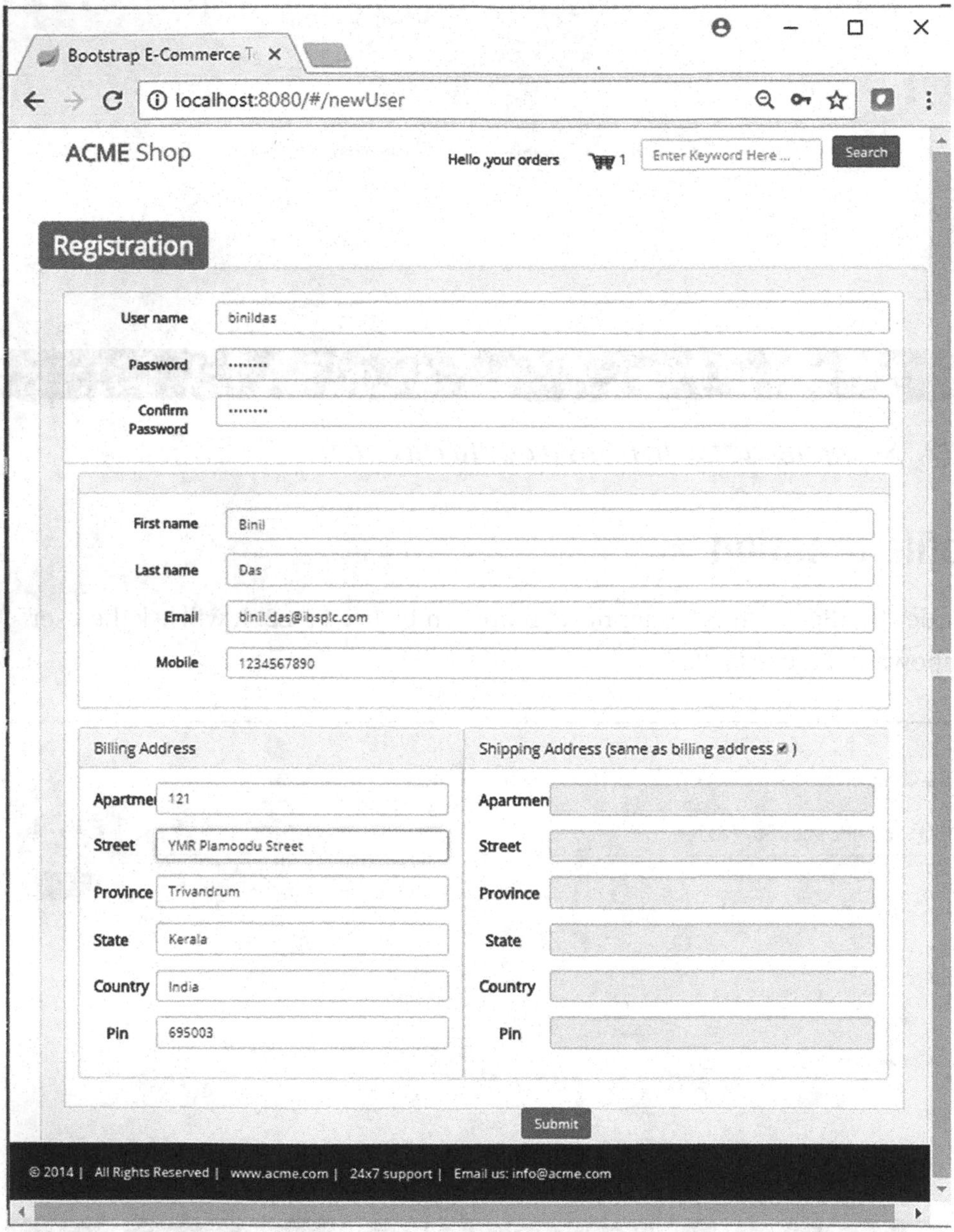

Figure 17-24. *Create a user profile*

Fill in the form to create a user profile, as shown in Figure 17-24, and click "Submit." You can now log into the application (by clicking the shopping cart icon to display the cart, if required), as shown in Figure 17-25.

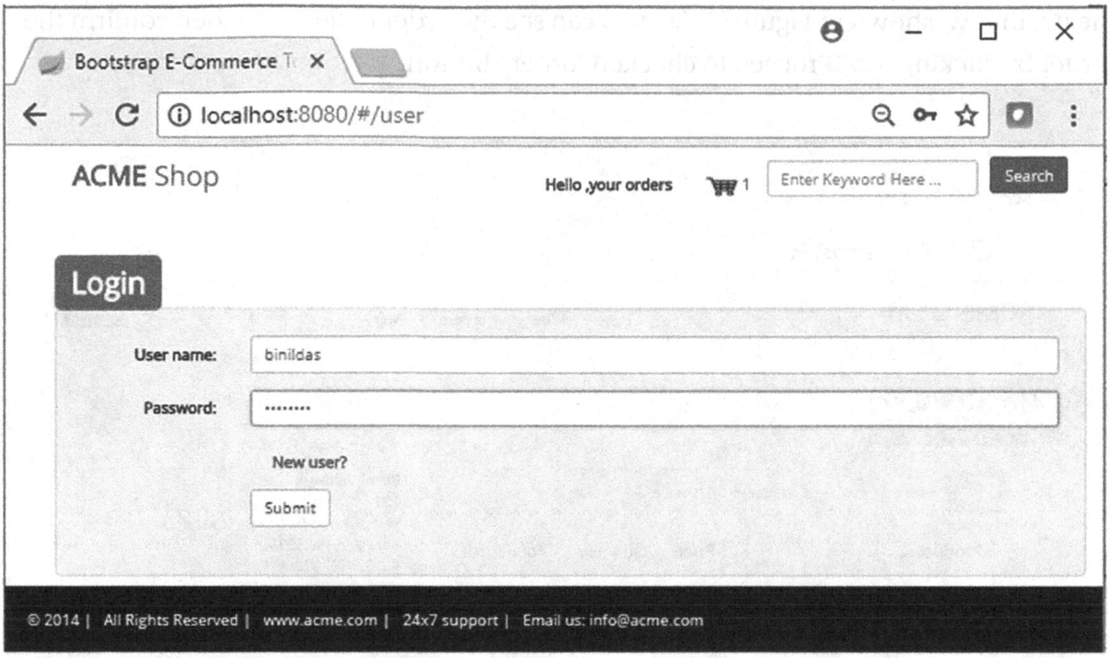

Figure 17-25. User signing in

Create a New Order

After logging in, you can once again click the shopping cart icon to view your cart, as shown in Figure 17-22, and proceed to order by clicking the "Order now" button. In the next window, shown in Figure 17-26, you can see the order details and then confirm the order by clicking the "Proceed to checkout order" button.

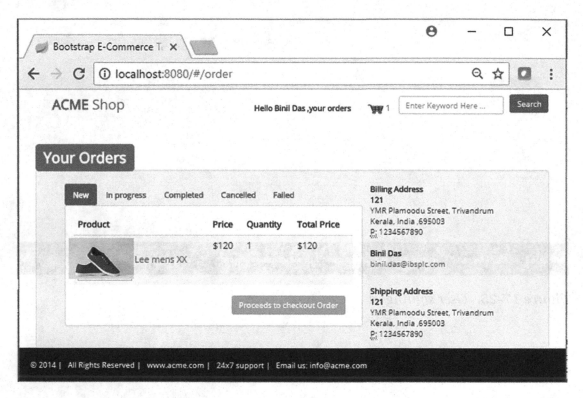

Figure 17-26. *Confirm to create a new order*

If the order creation is successful, it will be displayed in the next window, as shown in Figure 17-27.

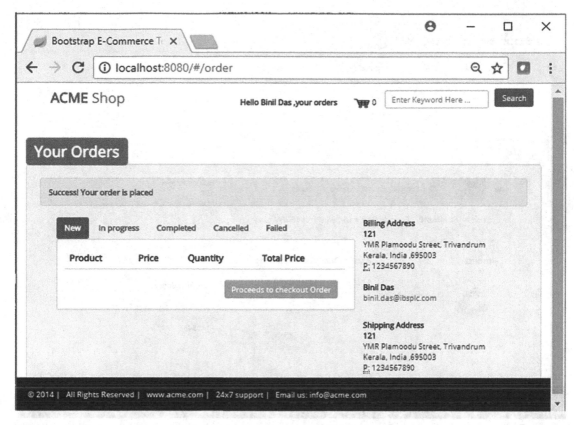

Figure 17-27. New order created

You may view the newly created order by clicking the "In progress" menu (refresh the browser screen to reflect the changes) shown in Figure 17-28.

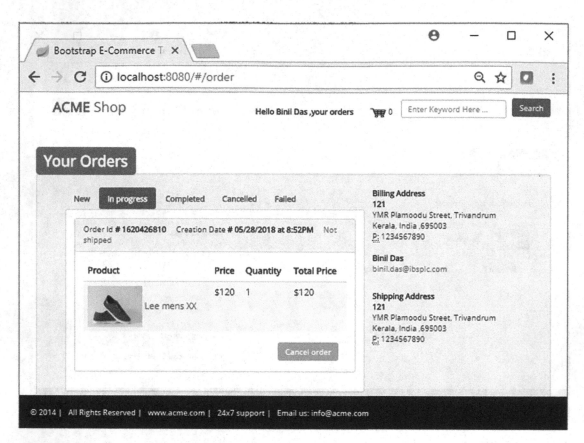

Figure 17-28. *Orders in progress*

Ship a New Order

At the same time, the newly created order will be made available for the back office admin to trigger the fulfilment process. Click the "To Ship" menu (refresh the browser screen to reflect the changes) to see all newly created orders, as shown in Figure 17-29.

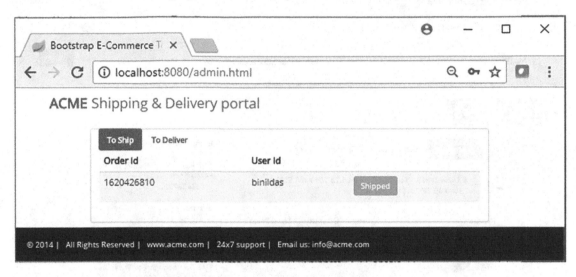

Figure 17-29. *Back office admin to confirm shipment*

The back office admin can simulate the shipping step by clicking the Shipped button in Figure 17-29. Once shipped, the order will get into the next stage of fulfilment; refresh the browser to see it, as show in Figure 17-30.

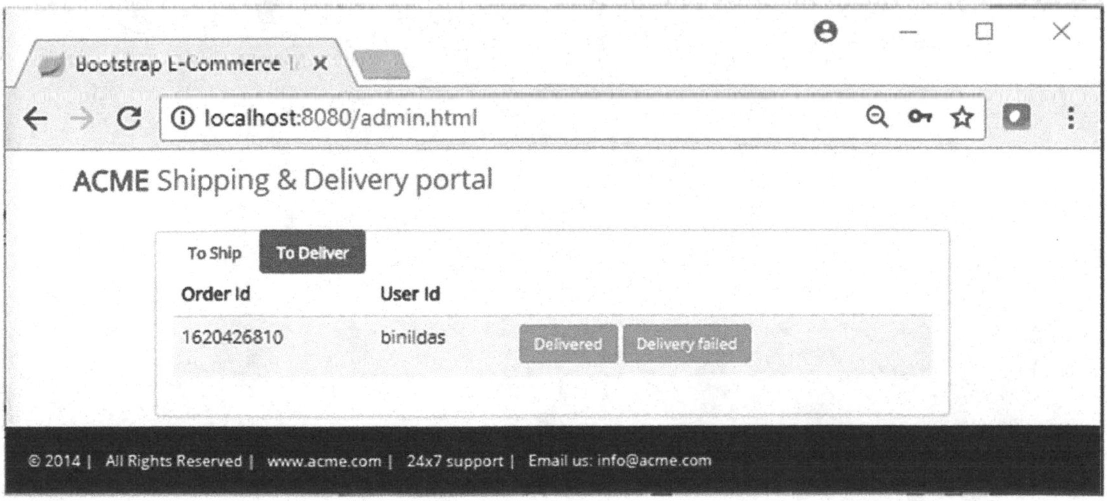

Figure 17-30. *Order shipped, subsequent order delivery in progress*

Once shipped, the customer will also be able to see the status change of the order, as shown in Figure 17-31.

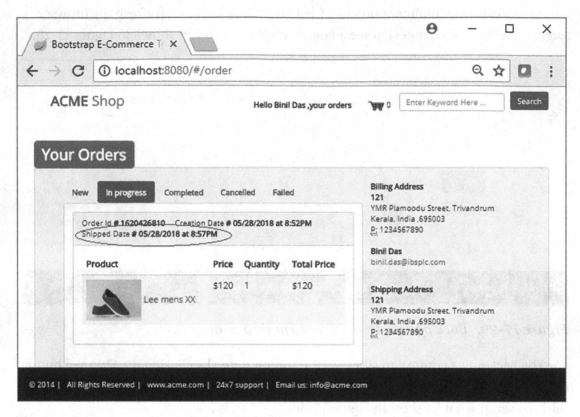

Figure 17-31. *Customer order shipped*

Deliver Successfully the Shipped Order

Next, the back office admin needs to simulate the next step of fulfilment. He needs to click the Delivered button in Figure 17-30. A successful delivery of the order will complete the order process workflow. At this stage, the customer will be able to view his order status in the Completed tab, as shown in Figure 17-32.

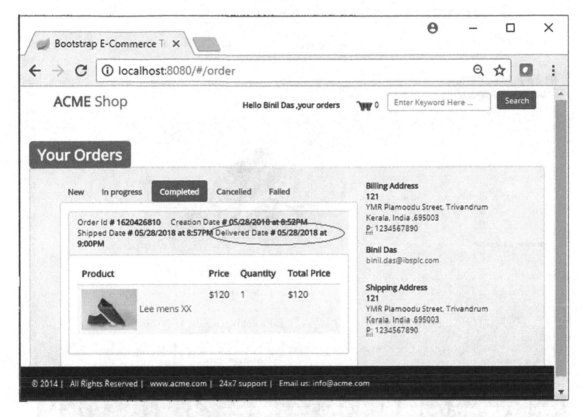

Figure 17-32. *Customer order fulfilled*

When the customer places the order, the inventory of the selected product is reduced and the same is reflected in the product details page of the respective product, as shown in Figure 17-33.

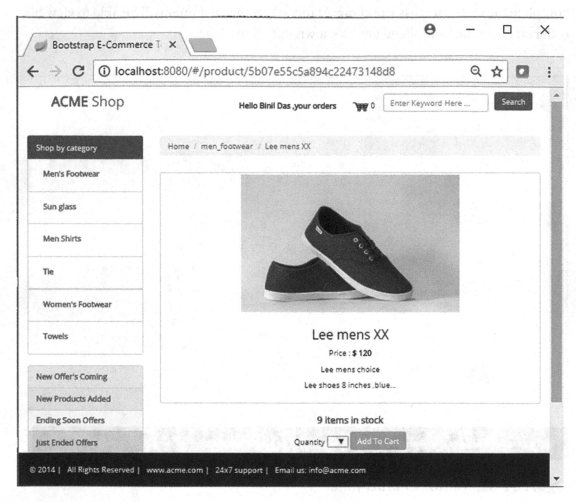

Figure 17-33. *Product inventory gets reduced*

Delivery Failure for the Shipped Order

You will now test the "delivery failure" scenario. Create another order, as shown in Figure 17-34.

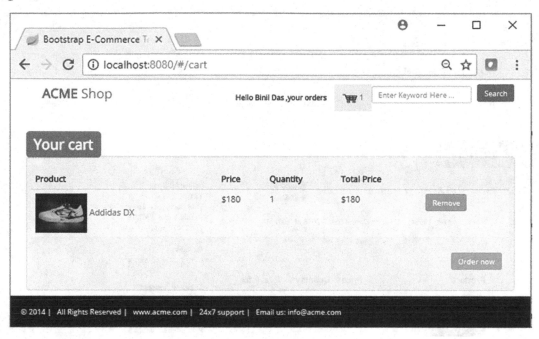

Figure 17-34.   *Create a second order*

Next, use the back office admin screen shown in Figure 17-29 to simulate the shipping. After successful shipping, the order will be available for the next step, as shown in Figure 17-35.

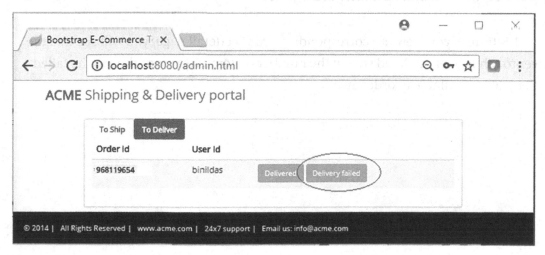

Figure 17-35.   *Second order ready for delivery*

This time, simulate a delivery failure by clicking the "Delivery failed" button shown in Figure 17-35. When the delivery fails, it will again be reflected in the end user screen, as shown in Figure 17-36.

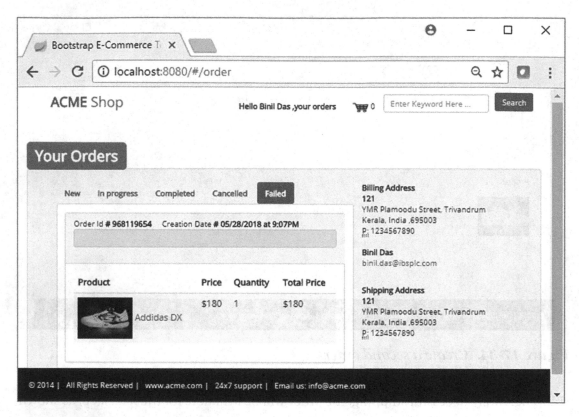

Figure 17-36. *Second customer order failed*

This time, if you view the corresponding product detail page, you will see that the inventory has been updated so that the number of items corresponding to the failed order will be available to order again.

Cancel a New Order

To test the final use case, create a third order, as shown in Figure 17-37.

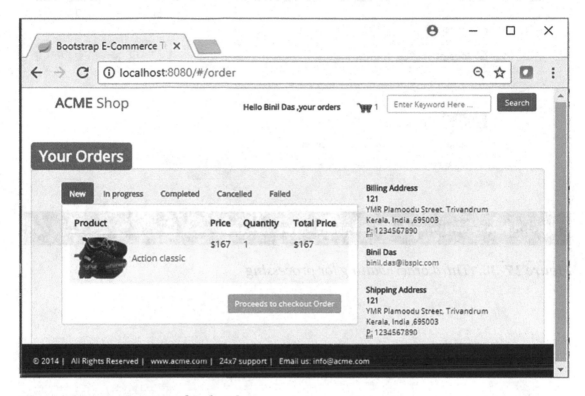

Figure 17-37. *Create a third order*

The new order will be available for the back office admin for further processing, as shown in Figure 17-38.

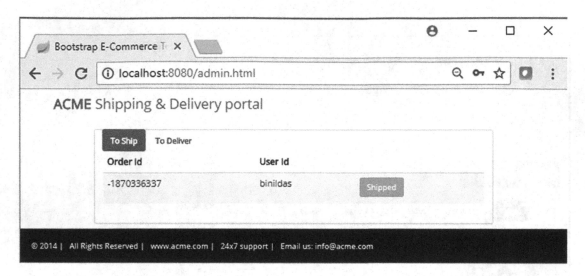

Figure 17-38. *Third order waiting for processing*

However, let the back office admin do nothing this time. If the end user checks the inventory of the product he has newly ordered, he'll see that the inventory has been reduced, as seen in Figure 17-39.

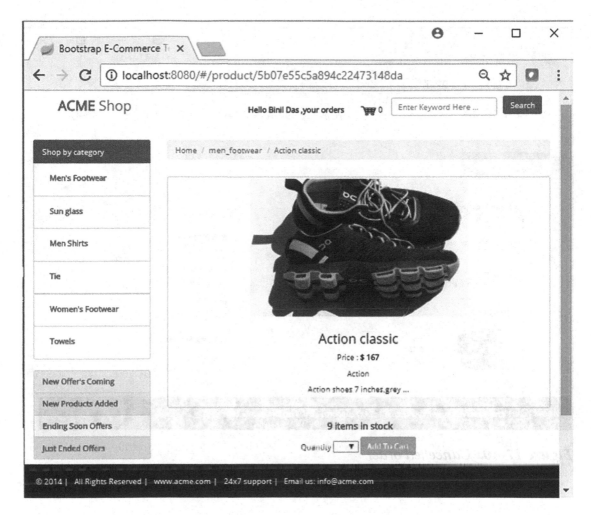

Figure 17-39. *Inventory reduced*

Now, the end user has to cancel the order he just created by clicking the "Cancel order" button next to the order, as seen in Figure 17-28. Once cancelled, the end user can see the order in the "Cancelled" tab under "Your Orders," as seen in Figure 17-40.

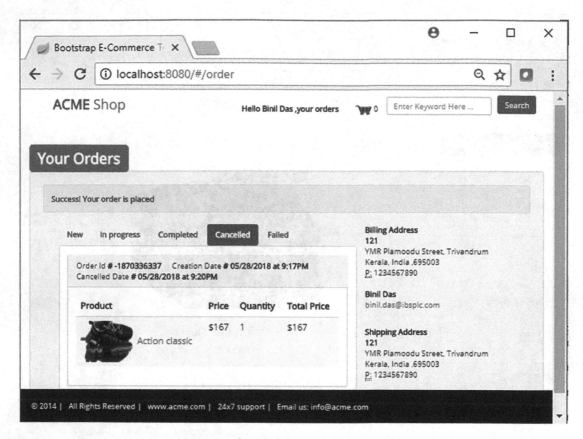

Figure 17-40. *Cancelled order*

Reverting the Inventory

As soon as the order is cancelled, if you view the corresponding product detail page, you will see that the inventory has been reverted so that the number of items corresponding to the cancelled order will be available to order again, as seen in Figure 17-41.

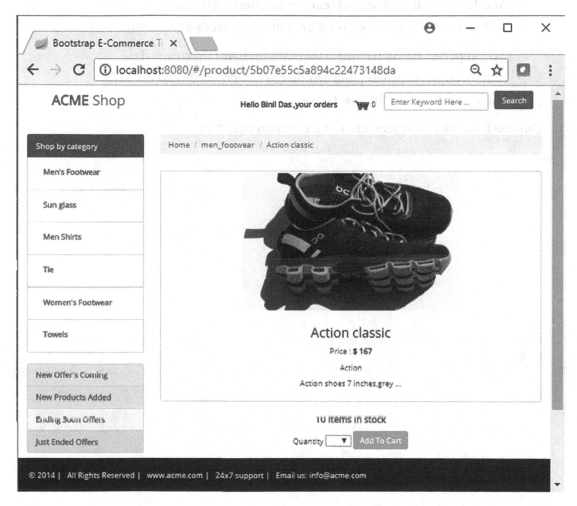

Figure 17-41. *Inventory reverted due to cancellation*

Summary

In this chapter, you made a lot of progress on your CQRS-based microservices journey. You are now armed with all the basic tools to build enterprise-grade applications of any scale using event-driven microservices. However, there are two caveats:

- You have not implemented security (authentication and authorization) in your e-commerce microservices application.

- You kept two domain entities together to maintain strong data consistency; otherwise, they would have been separated out into their own separate microservices.

You will look into these aspects in the next two chapters.

CHAPTER 18

Microservices Security

In the e-commerce microservice application in Chapter 17, you should have noticed that there are few API methods, especially those in the product category and product services which are freely accessible by anyone; however, for accessing all other microservices you need to be logged in either as the back office admin or as a customer who has already created a user profile in the application. So far, so good, but how secure are those microservices even though you need to be logged in?

Quite different from the traditional monolith architecture where all the services are centrally located, in a microservices architecture there are many nodes or processes where the services are distributed. Even if you consider the API gateway as a single, central, front controller where all your requests are initially intercepted, the API gateway has to then route the requests to the respective microservices, all through the internal network. Similarly, intermicroservice communication also happens through the same internal network. Even if you have secured the gateway access, your data is not free from insider attacks. One way to achieve security is to share the user credential data for all services and authenticate the user on each service before access. Even though this is actually a working approach, it would be a weird idea to distribute the credentials in multiple places. You should have a better approach.

You will look at the concern of microservices security in this chapter. You will also build security features for the example from Chapter 17 so that you learn how this functions in a real-world situation.

You will be exploring the following in this chapter:

- OAuth 2.0

- Client types in the context of OAuth 2.0

- Authorization code grant type in OAuth 2.0

- JSON Web Token (JWT)

- Enabling security for the microservices e-commerce application

© Binildas Christudas 2019
B. Christudas, *Practical Microservices Architectural Patterns*, https://doi.org/10.1007/978-1-4842-4501-9_18

OAuth 2.0 and Microservices

With Spring Security and its support for OAuth 2.0, you have everything you need to lock down your API gateway as well as your back-end resource servers. You can set it up to automatically propagate your access tokens from one microservice to the other, ensuring that everything stays secure and encrypted along the way. I won't cover OAuth 2.0 in detail, but I will introduce the minimum aspects required so that you can enable security for your example microservices application.

OAuth 2.0

Internet Engineering Task Force (IETF) Request for Comments (RFC) No. 6749 defines the OAuth 2.0 as an authorization framework that enables a third-party application to obtain limited access to a HTTP service, either on behalf of a resource owner by orchestrating an approval interaction between the resource owner and the HTTP service, or by allowing the third-party application to obtain access on its own behalf. The OAuth2.0 specification replaces and obsoletes the OAuth 1.0 protocol.

OAuth 2.0 Roles

OAuth defines four roles, which are central to the OAuth interactions:

- **Resource owner**: Any entity capable of granting access to a protected resource. When the resource owner is a human, it is referred to as an end user. A resource owner can grant access, and this grant may be used for subsequent and repeated access of the resource.

- **Resource server**: The server hosting the protected resources, capable of accepting and responding to protected resource requests using access tokens. In your microservices scenario, each microservice may become a resource server, if they own protected resources.

- **Client**: This is an application making protected resource requests on behalf of the resource owner and with its authorization. The client, when it makes a request, may do so on behalf of an end user, who may or may not be the resource owner. The term "client" does not imply any particular implementation characteristics (e.g. whether the application executes on a server, a desktop, or other device).

- **Authorization server**: The server issuing access tokens to the client after successfully authenticating the resource owner and obtaining authorization. The authorization server may be the same server as the resource server or a separate entity. A single authorization server may issue access tokens accepted by multiple resource servers.

OAuth 2.0 Client vs. User Agent

Even though OAuth specifies only four roles, you should also note another entity, which is typical in many cases like when you use a browser-based application:

- **User agent**: The user agent is typically the interface with which the end user or the resource owner interfaces with the client program. Sometimes the user agent and the client can be the same.

To understand the last statement, you need to explore a few typical architectures and understand the difference in the level of exposure of the respective client programs to the external world, and you will do so in the next section.

Trusted vs. Untrusted Clients

An OAuth client can be classified under two categories, trusted client or untrusted client. Whether a client falls into the trusted or the untrusted category depends based on whether the client has the ability to securely store and transmit information. The concept can be made clear by revisiting the selected architectural models described below.

Classic Three-Tier Monolith

A three-tier monolith architecture has a presentation tier, a middle tier, and a database tier. A classic three-tier architecture is a multipage architecture (MPA), which means that every time the user interface needs to display the data or submit data back to server, it has to request a new page from the server and then render it in the web browser. Java Server Pages (JSP) technology is used in creating MPA web apps; however, there are many other technologies that can be used to build MPA. Figure 18-1 depicts a three-tier monolith MPA.

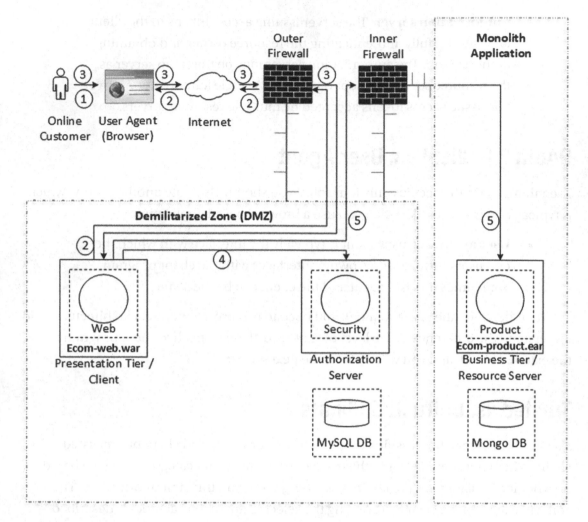

Figure 18-1. *Classic three-tier monolith*

Typical interactions of a three-tier monolith MPA are as follows:

1. The end user types the URL in the browser.

2. The presentation tier component, usually a JSP page, generates the required HTML tags and sends them back to the browser where the HTML content gets rendered.

3. User clicks and actions from the browser get intercepted by the presentation server where the next page needs to be generated.

4. At this stage, if the page requires data from any protected resources, it needs to contact the security server or the authorization server where user authentication and authorization happens.

5. Once authenticated and authorized, the presentation server will contact the business tier to retrieve any back-end data, embed it to the generated HTML content, and push the content back to the browser where the content gets rendered again.

The notable point here is that at the end of Step 3, user authentication and authorization must be orchestrated and the end result of that is sent to the presentation server where it can cache or store the status of the authentication and authorization steps associated with the user (session). From then onwards, for every subsequent click and action of the end user from the browser, if it requires protected resources, the presentation server can retrieve the status of the authentication and authorization steps associated with the user (session) for that request and make decisions or route the request to other back-end servers. The status of the authentication and authorization steps cached or stored in the presentation server is safe since it is stored within the Demilitarized Zone (DMZ).

Classical Three-Tier Monolith with HTTP Front

In a slightly variant architecture, you will place only a HTTP server in the DMZ and all of the other components shown in the DMZ in Figure 18-1 will be moved to within the internal perimeter. Here, the status of the authentication and authorization steps cached or stored in the presentation server is even safer. Figure 18-2 depicts this deployment setup.

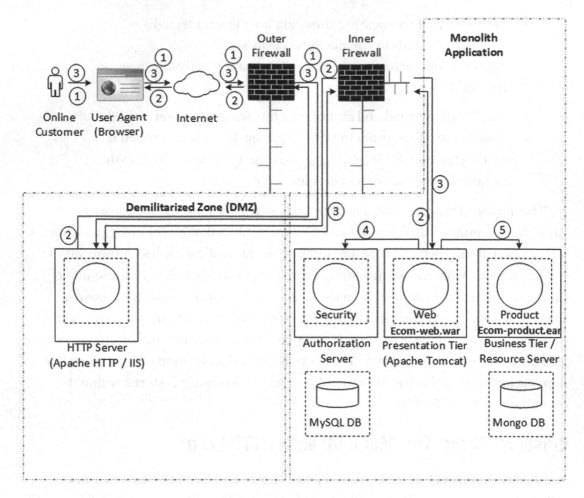

Figure 18-2. *Classic three-tier monolith with HTTP front*

In this architecture, all static content including HTML templates can be served by the HTTP server whereas all dynamic web content and protected resources in the business tier are accessed in a manner similar to that explained below (and shown in Figure 18-2):

1. The end user types the URL in the browser.

2. The presentation tier component, usually a JSP page, will generate the required HTML tags and send them back to the browser where the HTML content gets rendered. All static content including HTML templates can be served by the HTTP server.

738

3. User clicks and actions from the browser again get intercepted by the presentation server where the next page needs to be generated.

4. At this stage, if the page requires data from any protected resources, it first needs to contact the security server or the authorization server where user authentication and authorization happen.

5. Once authenticated and authorized, the presentation server contacts the business tier to retrieve any back-end data, embed it to the generated HTML content, and push the content back to the browser where the content gets rendered again.

Microservices with an API Gateway

Figure 18-3 depicts the API gateway-based microservices architecture. You saw many variants of this in previous chapters; however, it's shown here to emphasize the security flow.

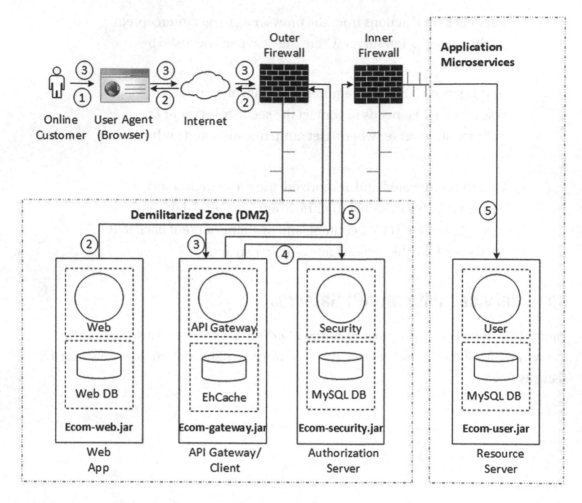

Figure 18-3. *Microservices API architecture*

It is typical for microservices architectures to use single page architecture (SPA), which is essentially an evolution of the MPA + AJAX design pattern. In SPA, only the shell page is generated on the server and the rest of the UI is rendered by browser JavaScript code. SPA requests the markup and data separately, and renders pages directly in the browser. The overall flow is summarized as follows:

1. The end user types the URL in the browser.

2. The presentation tier component, usually a SPA web app, is downloaded into the browser and the first page or the default page is rendered. SPA resources (HTML+CSS+scripts) are loaded only once throughout the lifespan of the application. Further, only data is transmitted back and forth.

3. Further user clicks and actions from the browser get intercepted by the API gateway.

4. At this stage, if the request requires data from any protected resources, the API gateway will first need to contact the security server or the authorization server, where user authentication and authorization happen.

5. Once authenticated and authorized, the API gateway contacts the microservice to retrieve any back-end data and pushes the data alone as a response back to the browser where the content gets rendered again.

Here again, at the end of Step 3 at the API gateway, user authentication and authorization must be orchestrated and the end result of that is sent to the API gateway where it can cache or store the status of the authentication and authorization steps associated with the user. From then onwards, for every subsequent click and action of the end user from the browser, when the request hits the API gateway, if it requires protected resources, the API gateway can retrieve the status of the authentication and authorization steps associated with the user for that request and make decisions or route requests to other back-end resource servers. The status of the authentication and authorization steps cached or stored in the API gateway is safe since it is stored within the DMZ with strict controls enforced by the enterprise in terms of security and access control.

Client App with No Server

Another variant possible is a case where the complete web app (or the SPA), once downloaded, will then continue executing completely from within the browser, in which case there is no presentation tier, or business tier for that matter. In short, there is no server-side counterpart of the web app in the browser. There can be a scenario where the web app will still need to access some protected resource; however, this time it's from a third party, as shown in Figure 18-4.

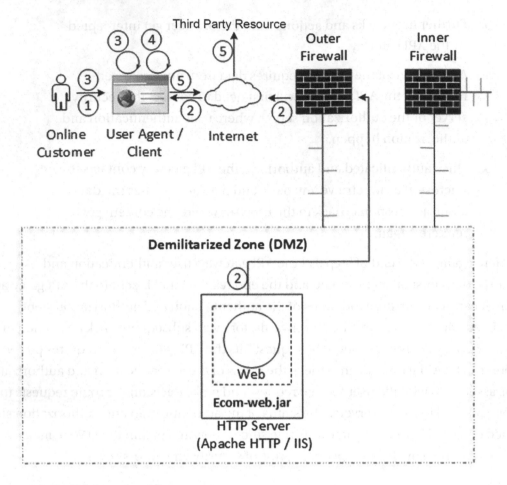

Figure 18-4. *Web app without a server*

There are more variants of deployment options available, but let's stick to the scenarios explained earlier.

The Authorization Code Grand Types

There are several grand types defined by OAuth; however, I will limit this discussion to the authorization code grant type, since it is suitable for OAuth clients that can keep their client credentials confidential when authenticating with the authorization server. For the microservices scenarios, the API gateway is the "client" implemented on a secure server. As a redirection-based flow, this OAuth client must be able to interact with the user agent of the resource owner and also must be able to receive incoming requests through redirection from the authorization server.

Let's look at an authorization code grant type sequence of flows, with the example you are going to visit in the next section in mind. See Figure 18-5.

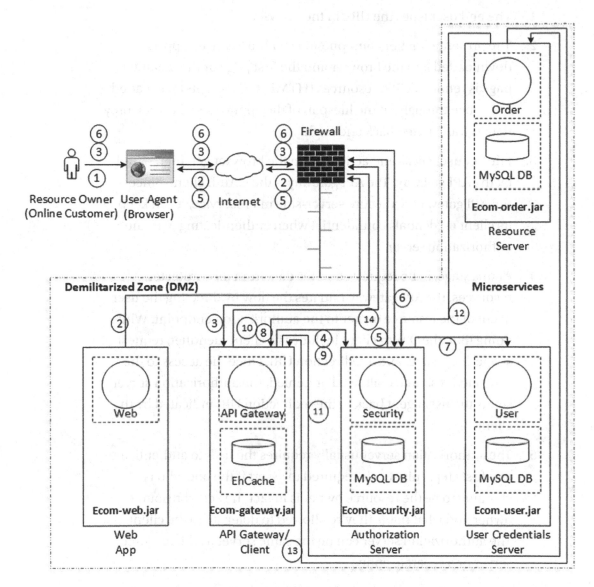

Figure 18-5. *OAuth authorization code grant type*

Referring to Figure 18-5, the typical sequence of interactions for an end-to-end authorization flow in accessing a protected resource can be summarized as follows:

1. The end user types the URL in the browser.

2. The presentation tier component, usually a SPA web app, is downloaded into the browser and the first page or the default page is rendered. SPA resources (HTML+CSS+scripts) are loaded only once throughout the lifespan of the application. Further, only data is transmitted back and forth.

3. Further user clicks and actions from the browser get intercepted by the API gateway. The API gateway is the OAuth client. Since the API gateway is a secure server-side microservice, it can keep its client credentials confidential when authenticating with the authorization server.

4. At this stage, if the request requires data from any protected resources, the API gateway initiates the flow by directing the user agent of the resource owner to the authorization endpoint. While doing that, the OAuth client includes its client identifier, requested scope, local state, and a redirection URI. Once the access to the protected resource is allowed or denied, the authorization server sends the user agent back to the redirection URI indicated by the client.

5. The authorization server usually requires the user to authenticate as a first step. This step is required to assert if the one who is claiming to be the resource owner is in fact the actual resource owner and what rights they're allowed to delegate to the client. The authorization server can be the same server as the resource server or a separate entity.

6. The authorization server authenticates the resource owner through the user agent. The user's authentication passes directly between the user (through the user agent) and the authorization server, so it's never seen by the client.

7. Authentication may be done by looking at an internal authentication server. OAuth doesn't dictate any specific authentication technology, and the authorization server is free to choose methods such as a username/password pair, cryptographic certificates, security tokens, single-sign-on, or any of the other possibilities.

8. Once the resource owner grants access, the OAuth client uses the redirection URI provided in Step 4 to redirect the user agent back to the OAuth client. The redirection URI also includes an authorization code and any local state previously provided by the OAuth client.

9. Now that the client has the authorization code, it can send it back to the authorization server on its token endpoint. The OAuth client also includes the redirection URI used to obtain the authorization code for verification.

10. The authorization server validates the client credentials and the authorization code. The server also ensures that the redirection URI received matches the URI used to redirect the client in Step 3. If the authorization code is valid, has not been used previously, and the client making this request is the same as the client that made the original request, the authorization server generates and returns a new access token for the client. A single authorization server may issue access tokens accepted by multiple resource servers.

11. With the token in hand, the client can present the token to the resource server (protected resource).

12. The resource server can check with the token validation end point of the authorization server.

13. If the token presented in the previous step is valid, the resource server can return the protected resources to the client.

14. The client can return this protected resource back to the SPA web app as a response to the user click in Step 3.

Tokens for Scalable API Invocations

Having looked at the dynamics of a typical authorization grand type OAuth flow, you should now look at some aspects of this security schema with respect to microservices architecture, especially in terms of scalability and security of the token themselves.

Session IDs

Traditionally, authentication has been done as a stateful operation. When the user inputs his or her credentials, the server generates a unique session ID, stores it on the server side, and hands it back to the user as well. Along with each request that needs access to protected resources, this session ID is passed as a request header and the server will always validate the session ID against the actual user credentials on the server side or with the "sessions on play" cache maintained on the server side. This is near to a perfect solution for monolith applications, where for each request response cycle you need no more than one such validation.

For microservices architectures, this can be limiting. Getting data from the central store for every other operation can be troublesome, especially when a single user-side request-response cycle internally spans across a graph or many intermicroservice calls. Even when a single user-side request-response cycle internally gets served by a single microservice, the cumulative process of user authentication and authorization DB (or cache) lookup and validations for all the API methods for a high transactional system is cumbersome, so we need smarter design mechanisms.

You should notice one good thing about session IDs: session IDs are opaque, meaning no easily decipherable data can be extracted from session IDs by third parties. The linkage between the session ID and its inferable data is entirely done server-side.

Tokens

Tokens are an alternative to making session ID-based security design smarter. A token is more than an identifier, with meaningful and inferable data too in it. A token, in addition to the session ID, can also contain less sensitive portions of user credentials, like the user name. In this manner, the user or the service requester detail is already available in the request header, so microservices don't need to do another I/O (input/output) to the database or cache to interpret the requestor. Now you need to look at the authorization part: who has access to what protected resources, and once accessed, what actions can that user execute over the resource. So you could also include information about the types of operations available for the user into the token. You could, for example, add a field named `scope`, which can have values like `user` to represent the authority of a normal end user and `admin`, who will have extra authority to perform critical back-office operations. If so, when a user supplies the token along with the request to perform an operation, say by making a call to an API endpoint, the service handling that endpoint and safeguarding the protected resource can validate the token, look for the right "scopes" in it, and authorize (or deny) the user to perform that operation.

JSON Web Token (JWT)

You may create your own token for the convenience described in the previous section or you can adopt a standard that already exists in the industry called JSON Web Token (JWT).

JWT has three distinct parts that are URL encoded for transport:

- **Header**: The header contains the metadata for the token and at a minimum it contains the type of the signature and/or encryption algorithm.

- **Claims**: The claims contain any information that you want signed.

- **JSON Web Signature (JWS)**: The headers and claims are digitally signed using the algorithm specified in the header.

A JWT encodes a series of claims in a JSON object. Some of these claims have specific meanings, while others are left to be interpreted by the users. Some of the claims you commonly encounter are

- Issuer (iss)

- Subject (sub)

- Audience (aud)

- Expiration time (exp)

- Not before (nbf)

- Issued at (iat)

- JWT ID (jti)

Using a common data format like JWT allows for easy interoperability with established solutions and libraries so that you have tried and tested patterns for common, recurring problems.

A typical JWT payload is as follows:

```
{
  "sub": "1234567890",
  "name": "John Doe",
  "iat": 1516239022
}
```

Such a token provided by server will be sent along with the request by each client application, many times the browser or user agent being this client. This data then is vulnerable for man-in-the-middle kinds of attacks. To make it clear, someone intercepting this token can attempt to replay the request using the same token. There should be a way to prevent this.

Let's look into the three claims listed above.

- **Expiration time (exp)**: UNIX timestamp of when the token will be considered expired, required if iat is not present

- **Issued at (iat)**: UNIX timestamp of when the token was created, required if exp is not present

- **JWT ID (jti)**: A unique token string, effectively a nonce, must be unique to each request, cannot be an empty string

This timestamp information helps to limit the validity of tokens to prevent replay attacks. In one schema, the server can choose not to accept messages that have been sent more than x minutes before the current time. This raises the issue of clock skew between the client and server machines, so you will probably want to build some tolerance into the server to make up for this discrepancy by padding the time frame by n minutes on either side to make up for potential differences in clocks on different machines, assuming you have already taken care synchronizing the clocks of different servers.

The above nonce (as a jti value) helps to prevent replay attacks. A nonce is just an arbitrary set of bytes that you create to help prevent replay attacks. Every request must have a unique payload. The jti value cannot be reused even if the request failed (400-599 HTTP status codes) or was incorrectly sent over HTTP instead of HTTPS. For each request, it is recommended to generate a Global Unique Identifier (GUID) or a sufficiently random string to ensure no two requests have the same jti value within the "x minute" span.

Since JWT is sent along with the request by each client application, many times the browser or user agent being this client, this data then is vulnerable for malicious tampering too. It can be tampered with to add claims for privileges not intended to be available for a user. Hence the token itself should be tamper proof.

When the API authentication scheme uses JWTs in the HTTP authorization header of requests made to it, every request will have the authorization header set with the bearer scheme. The following is an example:

```
Authorization: Bearer eyJhbGciOiJIUzI1NiIsInR5cCI6IkpXVCJ9.
eyJzdWIiOiIxMjM0NTY3ODkwIiwibmFtZSI6IkpvaG4gRG9lIiwiaWF0IjoxNTE2MjM5MDIyfQ.
SflKxwRJSMeKKF2QT4fwpMeJf36POk6yJV_adQssw5c
```

Here, the header and claims are JSON that are base64 encoded for transport. The header, claims, and signature are appended together with a period character (.), thus providing JWT a structure like

```
[Base64Encoded(HEADER)] . [Base64Encoded (PAYLOAD)] . [encoded(SIGNATURE)]
```

Assuming that all of the above has been taken care of, how do you verify that a valid token as complying with all of the above was originally sent from the right partner end point itself? JWT can't be trusted if it's not signed. JWTs allow for different signing and encryption algorithms using the JSON Web Signature (JWS) specs. They are specified in the JWT header. For the most part, JWTs are usually not encrypted, just signed. However, if your token contains data that is sensitive, then encrypting it using JSON Web Encryption (JWE) is a choice. A typical encryption scheme uses an already signed JWT as the payload for encryption. This is known as a nested JWT. It is acceptable to use the same key for encryption and validation also.

Enough is enough; you have scratched the surface of JWT. There are more intricacies and loop holes, but this is enough for you to understand the following example.

Design Security for the Example Microservices Application

You will now secure the microservices application from Chapter 17. The example from Chapter 17 had very basic authentication implemented. This is the reason why you are able to browse through the initial pages starting from the home page of the example application up to the point where you can add items to your shopping cart; however, for the next step of checking out to be permitted, you should have either already been signed in, you should sign in if you already have a profile in the application, or if you do not have a ready profile in the application, you should create one then and sign in. Similarly, for the back-office admin to carry out this functionality in the application, he should also be logged in.

However, this logging-in is only one part of the securing process. For a real microservices application to be properly secured, you should also take care of the authorization part. Without proper authorization, even if your web app functionality is limited with the help of authentication, the individual microservices APIs themselves are not secure. So if someone from within the same network of the individual microservice is able to access the individual microservice, they can execute functionality. Of course this can be permitted, but only after the required authorization. This is what you are going to enable in your example application.

Security Architecture for Microservices

Refer to Figure 17-11 in Chapter 17 for the basic architecture for the example microservices application. Let's enhance it with the extra pieces required to secure the example application end to end. See Figure 18-6.

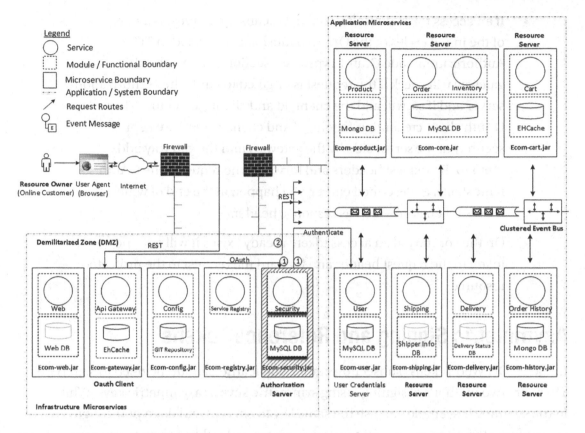

Figure 18-6. *Security architecture for the microservices e-commerce application*

Observe the differences between the architectures shown in Figure 17-11 and Figure 18-6. The latter shows a new Security microservice. This Security microservice is an OAuth authorization server. There is more than one resource server, since each of the application microservices has to secure its own data based on the authorization schema deployed.

You should now refer back to Figure 18-5 where you saw the OAuth dance during the initial authorization code type flow. The same design will be followed in the enhanced security architecture for your example microservice application too. All the requests from the web application in the browser will be first intercepted by the API gateway. It's the API gateway's responsibility to take care of the microservice's security. The API gateway will first check if the incoming REST request has an existing access token for the protected resource, Referring to Figure 18-6,

- If an access token doesn't exist, that means the request is a part of the initial cycles of the OAuth handshake described in "The Authorization Code Grand Types" subsection earlier. If so, the gateway will check if the request is targeted towards the authorization server and if so, will add the client_id and client_secret too. The OAuth client credentials (client_id and client_secret) are kept securely at the server side by the gateway, and the gateway adds them to the request headers and forwards the request. The OAuth handshake, as described earlier, will happen at the end of which an access token is provided as response header.

- On the contrary, if an access token already exists, it will add the token to the request header and forward the request to the protected resource.

Asymmetric Signing and Reference Tokens

In the "JSON Web Tokens" subsection earlier, you learned about the need to sign JWTs. There are two methods of signing, using symmetric keys or asymmetric keys. While in the symmetric scenario you use the same key to encrypt and decrypt the digital signature, in the asymmetric case you use a private and public key combination.

Another concern you face when using tokens is the length of token in complex authorization scenarios. It is quite possible that the size of the JWT can grow to an extent that it will meet technical hurdles to be passed as the header of the request. Moreover, even though you can sign and encrypt a JWT, it is still "sensitive information" and it is best not to make this information float outside your DMZ. Let's consider the notion of a reference token here. A reference token is a reference to the actual JWT, and you will pass only the reference token beyond your DMZ (or OAuth client).

In securing the example microservice application, you will leverage both the above. See Figure 18-7.

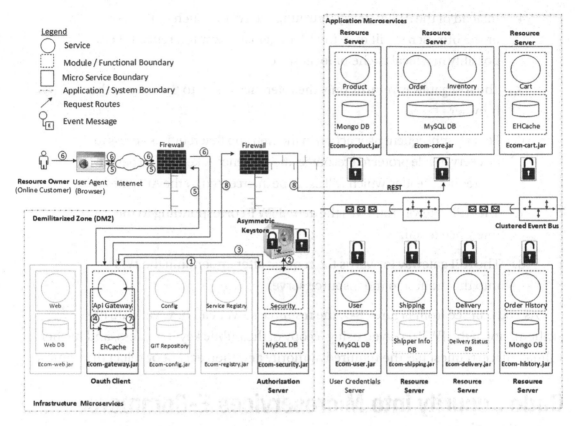

Figure 18-7. *Asymmetric encryption and reference tokens*

Referring back to the subsection titled "The Authorization Code Grand Types", in Step 4 you assume the user request for a protected resource has already reached the API gateway. Now, referring to Figure 18-7,

1. The user request for a protected resource reaches the API gateway.

2. The authorization server, after doing all basic checks and validation for authentication and authorization, will first create a JWT. This JWT is signed and encrypted using asymmetric keys. Asymmetric keys have the notion of a private key, which is accessible only to the authorization server, and its counterpart key, called a public key, which the authorization server will freely distribute to anyone who has a need for it, to all resource servers in your case.

3. The signed and encrypted JWT is returned back to the API gateway.

4. Instead of the API gateway returning the JWT as such to the user
    or the browser, it will map the JWT against a new reference token,
    possibly in a local cache or local store.

5. The API gateway returns only the reference token to the user or the
    browser.

6. For any subsequent user action in the web app that requires access to
    any server-side protected resource, the reference token is also passed as
    the request header, which will again be intercepted by the API gateway.

7. The API gateway retrieves the actual JWT corresponding to the
    reference token.

8. The API gateway forwards the request after appending the JWT
    into the request to the resource server.

As you can see from Figure 18-7, the resource server can now validate the
authenticity of the JWT received using a copy of the public key it possess, and further
validate if the request has the required authority and then accept or reject the request.

Code Security into Microservices E-Commerce Application

This section is a continuation of the code you saw in Chapter 17. You are advised to
go through Chapter 17 before proceeding further with the example application in this
chapter. I will incrementally add and explain the critical code required to establish
OAuth-based security for this example. The complete code required to demonstrate
establishing OAuth security for the example E-Commerce microservices application is in
folder ch18\ch18-01\Ax2-Ecom-With-Security.

Enable the Web App to Handle Security

As you have already experienced by running the application in Chapter 17, there are
many screens in the web app that you can browse through without actually logging into
the system. However, certain actions require the user to be logged in, as follows:

•   The web app will ask you to log in before you confirm your order
    when checking out. See Listing 18-1.

Listing 18-1. Order Now in Web App (ch18\ch18-01\Ax2-Ecom-With-Security\
Ecom-web\src\main\resources\static\cart.html)

```
<!DOCTYPE html>

<div ng-controller="CartController  as cartCtrl" data-ng-init="init()">

    <div class="row">
        <div class="caption col-sm-12 text-right">
            <a class="btn btn-warning" role="button" ng-click="doOrder()">
                Order now
            </a>
        </div>
    </div>
</div>
```

- If you explicitly click the "Hello, My Orders" link towards the middle
  upper portion of the screen, the web app will ask you to log in. See
  Listing 18-2.

Listing 18-2. Your Orders on the Home Page (ch18\ch18-01\Ax2-Ecom-With-
Security\Ecom-web\src\main\resources\static\index.html)

```
<form class="navbar-form navbar-right" role="search">
    <li>
        <a  href=""  ng-click="doOrder()" >
            <span style="color: maroon; ">
                <b>Hello {{screenName}} ,your orders</b>
            </span>
        </a>
    </li>
</form>
```

Both the above actions will be routed by the code in Listing 18-3.

Listing 18-3. Routing the doOrder Action (ch18\ch18-01\Ax2-Ecom-With-Security\Ecom-web\src\main\resources\static\js\controller\application_controller.js)

```
$scope.doOrder = function() {
    if(sessionStorage.getItem('loggedUser')==null){
        $location.url('/user');
    }else{
        $location.url('/order');
    }
};
```

Listing 18-3 shows that if the user is not already logged in, he will be prompted to the login screen.

Listing 18-4 shows other core parts of the code.

Listing 18-4. Route Mappings (ch18\ch18-01\Ax2-Ecom-With-Security\Ecom-web\src\main\resources\static\js\app.js)

```
ecomApp.config(['$routeProvider', function($routeProvider) {
    $routeProvider.
        when('/order', {
            templateUrl:  '/order.html',
            //controller: 'ShowOrdersController'
        }).
        when('/user', {
            templateUrl:  '/user.html',
            //controller: 'ShowOrdersController'
        }).
        when('/newUser', {
            templateUrl:  '/newUser.html',
            //controller: 'ShowOrdersController'
        }).
        otherwise({
            templateUrl:  '/productSearch.html'
        });
    }]).config(['$httpProvider', function($httpProvider) {
```

```
        $httpProvider.defaults.withCredentials = true;
        $httpProvider.interceptors.push('AuthInterceptor');
    }]);

ecomApp.factory('AuthInterceptor', function ($window, $q) {
    return {
        request: function(config) {
            config.headers = config.headers || {};
            if (sessionStorage.getItem('xtoken')) {
                config.headers['x-token'] = sessionStorage.getItem('xtoken');
            }
            return config || $q.when(config);
        },
        response: function(response) {
            if (response.status === 401) {
                alert(response.status);
            }
            return response || $q.when(response);
        }
    };
});
```

If you use the standard $http service to access remote APIs, it will just work as long as the server is configured to allow HTTP requests from your domain and you don't need to store cookies. But for many applications, including yours, you also need to set and store cookie information, especially for logins. By default, this is not allowed in most browsers, and withCredentials is a flag you can set on a low-level XMLHttpRequest (AJAX) object. In Angular JS you can configure the $http requests to set this flag for everything by doing

```
$httpProvider.defaults.withCredentials = true;
```

As a next step, you inject an AuthInterceptor. The AuthInterceptor code is invoked every time a request is fired from the browser. It will retrieve the reference token stored in the session store and append it along with the request header.

user.html will allow a user to log into the application. If the user is a new user, there is an option for him to click the "New user?" button and create a new user profile. Even if you create a new user profile, you will be led to the user login page subsequently. See Listing 18-5.

Listing 18-5. User.html (ch18\ch18-01\Ax2-Ecom-With-Security\Ecom-web\ src\main\resources\static\user.html)

```
<form class="form-horizontal">

    <div class="form-group">
        <label><a href="#newUser"><strong>New user?</strong></a>
    </div>

    <div class="form-group">
        <button type="submit" class="btn btn-default"
            ng-click="loginCtrl.doLogin()">Submit</button>
    </div>
</form>
```

loginCtrl.doLogin() first invokes the UserService to validate the user trying to log in. If successful, it will load the cart for that user and also redirect to /order so that the order widgets can be prepopulated and shown to the user. See Listing 18-6.

Listing 18-6. user_controller.js (ch18\ch18-01\Ax2-Ecom-With-Security\Ecom-web\src\main\resources\static\js\controller\user_controller.js)

```
ecomApp.controller('LoginController',
        ['$scope','$location','UserService','CartService',
    function($scope,$location,UserService,CartService) {

        loginCtrl.doLogin =function(){
            UserService.validateUser($scope.userCredentialDTO)
                .then(
                    function(data) {
                        sessionStorage.setItem('loggedUser',
                            JSON.stringify(data));
                        sessionStorage.setItem('sessionUser',data.userId);
                        $scope.screenName=data.firstName+ ' '+data.lastName;
                        $scope.$emit('userModified', $scope.screenName);
                        if($scope.myCart!=null){
                            $scope.myCart.userId=data.userId;
                        }
```

```
                loginCtrl.loadCart();
                $location.url('/order');
            }
        );
    }
}]);
```

Listing 18-7 shows the UserService.validateUser implementation.

Listing 18-7. Web App-Side User Authentication (ch18\ch18-01\Ax2-Ecom-With-Security\Ecom-web\src\main\resources\static\js\service\user_service.js)

```
'use strict';
ecomApp.factory('UserService', ['$http','$httpParamSerializer',
        '$q','$cookies', function($http, $httpParamSerializer,$q,$cookies){

    return {

        validateUser: function(userCredentialDTO){

            var data = {
                grant_type:"password",
                username: userCredentialDTO.userName,
                password: userCredentialDTO.password,
                client_id: "ecom_app"
            };

            var encodedData = $httpParamSerializer(data);
            var authUrl=sessionStorage.getItem('apiUrl')+
                "/security/oauth/token"
            var req = {
                method: 'POST',
                url: authUrl,
                headers: {
                    "Content-type": "application/x-www-form-urlencoded;
                        charset=utf-8"
                },
                data: encodedData
            };
```

759

```
                return $http(req)
                    .then(
                        function(response){
                            var token=(response.headers()['x-token']);
                            sessionStorage.setItem("xtoken", token);
                            return $http.get(sessionStorage.getItem('apiUrl')+
                                '/customer/customer')
                            .then(
                                function(response){
                                    return response.data;
                                },
                                function(errResponse){
                                    console.error('Error while getting user info'+
                                        errResponse);
                                    return $q.reject(errResponse);
                                }
                            );
                        },
                        function(errResponse){
                            console.error('Error while validating user'+
                                errResponse);
                            return $q.reject(errResponse);
                        }
                    );
            }
        };
}]);
```

The request call will pass through above function once during a user session, when the user wants to log in. You do two things here:

1. First, you invoke the authentication flow, supplying the user credentials and the client_id as a request parameter.

2. If the above authentication request is successful, you first retrieve the reference token from the response and cache it in the session storage so that the same can be supplied along with request

parameters in cases where you need to access any server-side
protected resource. As a next step, you invoke the customer end
point to retrieve the full details of the logged-in user.

This completes the minimal information for you to understand the critical flows
involved on the web app side to implement security.

Zuul, the API Gateway as OAuth Client

Security is handled using Zuul filters. You use both a pre-filter and a post-filter to Zuul.
A Zuul pre-filter is invoked before Zuul delegates the request to the actual resource
server. See Listing 18-8.

Listing 18-8. Zuul Pre-Filter (ch18\ch18-01\Ax2-Ecom-With-Security\
Ecom-gateway\src\main\java\com\acme\ecom\gateway\zuul\auth\filter\
AuthenticationPreFilter.java)

```
@Component
public class AuthenticationPreFilter extends ZuulFilter {

    @Override
    public String filterType() {
        return "pre";
    }

    @Override
    public int filterOrder() {
        return 1;
    }

    @Override
    public boolean shouldFilter() {
        return true;
    }

    @Autowired
    private CacheManager cacheManager;
```

```
@Override
public Object run() {

    RequestContext ctx = RequestContext.getCurrentContext();
    HttpServletRequest request = ctx.getRequest();
    request.getRequestURL().toString()));
    if(request.getRequestURL().indexOf("/oauth/token") > 0 &&
            request.getParameter("grant_type") != null &&  (
        StringUtils.equals(request.getParameter("grant_type"),
            "password"))){
        ctx.addZuulRequestHeader("authorization", "Basic " +
            new String(Base64.getEncoder().
            encode("ecom_app:ecom".getBytes())));
        ctx.addZuulRequestHeader("content-type",
            "application/x-www-form-urlencoded; charset=utf-8");
    }else{
        final String xToken = request.getHeader("x-token");
        if(StringUtils.isNotEmpty(xToken)){
            ValueWrapper value =
                cacheManager.getCache("AUTH_CACHE").get(xToken);

            if(value != null){
                TokenDTO tokenDTO=(TokenDTO) value.get();
                ctx.addZuulRequestHeader("Authorization", "Bearer  " +
                    tokenDTO.getAccess_token());
            }
        }
    }
    return null;
}
```

In the Zuul pre-filter there can be three major scenarios:

- If the request is for authentication, the Zuul pre-filter will add a
  header to denote basic authentication. While it does so, it will also
  add client_id and client_secret along with the header. Note that
  client_secret is a parameter only the Zuul API gateway knows, since
  the Zuul API gateway is the OAuth client.

- If the request is not for authentication, there can be two cases. The first case is when the user has not already logged in. In that case, the Zuul pre-filter will do nothing.

- The second case when the request is not for authentication is when the user has already been authenticated. In that case, the Zuul pre-filter assumes that there is a reference token available in the request header and, using that token, it will do a look-up into its local EHCache for the actual JWT. For the time being, assume that whenever the API gateway receives a JWT for the first time for a user session, it first caches that into the EHCache against a reference token and it's this reference token that is returned to the user. The JWT retrieved is then added to the request header to effect bearer authorization.

A Zuul post-filter is invoked after the Zuul receives the response from the actual resource server. Listing 18-9 shows your Zuul post-filter.

Listing 18-9. Zuul Post-Filter (ch18\ch18-01\Ax2-Ecom-With-Security\ Ecom-gateway\src\main\java\com\acme\ecom\gateway\zuul\auth\filter\ AuthenticationPostFilter.java)

```
@Component
public class AuthenticationPostFilter extends ZuulFilter {

    public static final String MAGIC_KEY = "obfuscate";

    @Autowired
    private CacheManager cacheManager;

    @Override
    public String filterType() {
        return "post";
    }

    @Override
    public int filterOrder() {
        return 1;
    }
```

```java
@Override
public boolean shouldFilter() {

    RequestContext ctx = RequestContext.getCurrentContext();
    HttpServletRequest request = ctx.getRequest();
    return request.getParameter("grant_type") != null &&
        (StringUtils.equals(request.getParameter("grant_type"),
        "password"));
}

@Override
public Object run() {

    RequestContext ctx = RequestContext.getCurrentContext();
    HttpServletRequest request = ctx.getRequest();
    if (request.getRequestURL().indexOf("/oauth/token") > 0 ) {

        HttpServletResponse response = ctx.getResponse();
        if (response.getStatus() == HttpServletResponse.SC_OK) {

            final String responseData = CharStreams.toString(
                new InputStreamReader(responseDataStream,"UTF-8"));
            TokenDTO tokenDTO = new ObjectMapper().readValue(
                responseData, TokenDTO.class);
            long expiryTime = System.currentTimeMillis() +
                ((Integer.valueOf(tokenDTO.getExpires_in()) - 1) * 1000);
            String refToken = expiryTime + ":" + createReferenceToken(
                request.getParameter("username"), expiryTime);
            ctx.addZuulResponseHeader(
                "Access-Control-Expose-Headers", "x-token");
            ctx.addZuulResponseHeader("x-token", refToken);
            cacheManager.getCache("AUTH_CACHE").put(
                refToken, tokenDTO);
        }
    }
    return null;
}
```

```java
private  String createReferenceToken(String username, long expires){
    StringBuilder signatureBuilder = new StringBuilder();
    signatureBuilder.append(username);
    signatureBuilder.append(":");
    signatureBuilder.append(expires);
    signatureBuilder.append(":");
    signatureBuilder.append(MAGIC_KEY);
    MessageDigest digest;
    try {
        digest = MessageDigest.getInstance("MD5");
    } catch (NoSuchAlgorithmException e) {
        throw new IllegalStateException("MD5 algorithm not available!");
    }
    return new String(Hex.encode(digest.digest(
        signatureBuilder.toString().getBytes())));
    }
}
```

The Zuul post-filter will be invoked only during the authentication flow. The main job of Zuul post-filter is, whenever it receives a JWT for the first time for a user session from the authorization server, it first caches that into the EHCache against a reference token and this reference token is returned as a response header.

Authorization Server

The authorization server forms the core of the OAuth process, which will take care of both authentication and authorization.

For authentication, you use Spring Security's web infrastructure, a collection of standard servlet filters. Here's a quick look at Spring's definition of terms:

- **Principal**: A user, device, or a system that performs an action.

- **Authentication**: The process of establishing if a principal's credentials are valid

- **Authorization**: Deciding whether the principal is allowed to perform an action

- **Secured item**: The protected resource

You must enable the security configuration class shown in Listing 18-10 to use the jdbc datasource you defined for authenticating and authorizing users.

Listing 18-10. Spring Security Configuration (ch18\ch18-01\Ax2-Ecom-With-Security\Ecom-security\src\main\java\com\acme\ecom\security\oauth\ WebSecurityConfig.java)

```
@Configuration
class WebSecurityConfig extends WebSecurityConfigurerAdapter {

    @Autowired
    private JdbcTemplate jdbcTemplate;

    @Override
    @Bean
    public AuthenticationManager     authenticationManagerBean()
            throws Exception {
        return super.authenticationManagerBean();
    }

    @Override
    protected void configure(HttpSecurity http) throws Exception {

        http
            .csrf().disable()
            .exceptionHandling()
            .authenticationEntryPoint((request, response, authException) ->
                response.sendError(HttpServletResponse.SC_UNAUTHORIZED))
            .and()
            .authorizeRequests()
            .antMatchers("/**").authenticated()
            .and()
            .httpBasic();
    }
```

```
@Override
protected void configure(AuthenticationManagerBuilder auth)
        throws Exception {

    auth.jdbcAuthentication().dataSource(jdbcTemplate.getDataSource())
    .usersByUsernameQuery("select user_id, password, active from
        user_credential where user_id=?")
    .authoritiesByUsernameQuery(
        "select user.user_id, role.role from user_credential user
            join  user_role role on user.id = role.user_id and
            user.user_id =?");
}
}
```

The Java configuration method creates a servlet filter known as the springSecurityFilterChain (DelegatingFilterProxy and FilterChainProxy) which is responsible for all security (protecting the application URLs, validating username and passwords submitted, redirecting to the login form, etc.) within your application.

You declare the authenticationManagerBean as a bean, which will be injected in the Spring OAuth security configuration later.

WebSecurityConfigurerAdapter provides a default configuration in the configure(HttpSecurity http) method, hence all users require to be authenticated for accessing any URLs of web application. But you can override this method as shown in Listing 18-10.

First, configure HttpSecurity to define what resources must be secured, authorized, not authorized, not secured, login page, logout page, access denied page, etc. One important thing to note here is the order of configuration. Configuration that is specific to certain pages or URLs must be placed first, then configurations that are in common among most URLs.

If the authentication fails, you get back the expected 401 Unauthorized and subsequently the authentication challenge. The browser in a normal web page context will interpret this challenge and prompt you for credentials with a simple dialog. From the browser environment, a login page is no longer a hard requirement since all browsers support basic authentication and can use a standard dialog to prompt the user for credentials. Also, the BasicAuthenticationEntryPoint provisioned by Spring Security by default returns a full page for a 401 Unauthorized response back to the client.

This HTML representation of the error also renders well in a browser, but it's not well-suited for scenarios like yours, such as a REST API or a Zuul API gateway where a JSON representation may be preferred. So you should prevent the authentication dialog by retaining the HTTP Basic but changing the 401 challenge to something other than "Basic." You can do that with a one-line implementation of AuthenticationEntryPoint in the HttpSecurity configuration callback:

```
authenticationEntryPoint((request, response, authException) ->
response.sendError(HttpServletResponse.SC_UNAUTHORIZED))
```

Next is the configuration for authentication. For authentication, Spring Security provides various methods:

- The DAO authentication provider is the Spring's default

  Spring here expects an org.springframework.security.core.
  userdetails.UserDetailsService implementation to provide
  credentials and authorities.

  - Built-in: In-memory (properties), JDBC (database), LDAP

  - Custom

- Custom authentication provider

  Example: To get preauthenticated user details when using single
  sign-on

  - CAS, TAM, SiteMinder

You will use JDBC authentication using a Java configuration where you can customize the default queries. Listing 18-10 shows how to plug in JDBC authentication. You need to configure it by providing a DataSource. Since you are using custom tables, you are also required to provide the select queries to get the user details and its roles. You set up two queries for AuthenticationManagerBuilder, one for authentication in usersByUsernameQuery and the other for authorization in authoritiesByUserNameQuery.

- users-by-username-query: This query will select the username, password, and enabled properties of the user, and will take username as parameter according to your custom tables. In the actual implementation, the search may possibly be case sensitive or case insensitive depending on how the implementation instance is configured.

- authorities-by-username-query: This query will select username and the role of the user and accept username as parameter according to your custom tables.

Once authentication is taken care of, you can start configuring the authorization server responsible for managing the access tokens. Spring Security OAuth2 handles the authorization. To configure and enable the OAuth 2.0 authorization server you have to use the @EnableAuthorizationServer annotation in Listing 18-11.

Listing 18-11. Spring OAuth Security Configuration (ch18\ch18-01\Ax2-Ecom-With-Security\Ecom-security\src\main\java\com\acme\ecom\security\oauth\OAuth2Configuration.java)

```
@Configuration
@EnableAuthorizationServer
public class OAuth2Configuration extends
AuthorizationServerConfigurerAdapter {

    @Autowired
    @Qualifier("authenticationManagerBean")
    private AuthenticationManager authenticationManager;

    @Override
    public void configure(ClientDetailsServiceConfigurer clients)
            throws Exception {

        clients.inMemory()
            .withClient("ecom_app")
            .secret("ecom")
            .scopes("PRODUCT","CUSTOMER","ORDER_HISTO",
                "CORE","SHIPPING","DELIVERY")
            .autoApprove(true)
```

```
            .authorities("PRODUCT_READ", "PRODUCT_WRITE","CUSTOMER_READ",
                "ORDER_READ","ORDER_WRITE")
            .authorizedGrantTypes("implicit","refresh_token",
                "password", "authorization_code");
    }

    @Override
    public void configure(AuthorizationServerEndpointsConfigurer endpoints)
            throws Exception {

        endpoints.tokenStore(tokenStore()).tokenEnhancer(jwtTokenEnhancer()).
            authenticationManager(authenticationManager);
    }

    @Bean
    public TokenStore tokenStore() {

        return new JwtTokenStore(jwtTokenEnhancer());
    }

    @Bean
    protected JwtAccessTokenConverter jwtTokenEnhancer() {

        KeyStoreKeyFactory keyStoreKeyFactory = new KeyStoreKeyFactory(
            new ClassPathResource("jwt.jks"), "mySecretKey".toCharArray());
        JwtAccessTokenConverter converter = new JwtAccessTokenConverter();
        converter.setKeyPair(keyStoreKeyFactory.getKeyPair("jwt"));
        return converter;
    }
}
```

You configure the OAuth 2.0 authorization server by adding
the @EnableAuthorizationServer annotation and implementing
AuthorizationServerConfigurer by using Spring's AuthorizationServerConfigurerAdapter
implementation. You override the empty configure() methods.

AuthorizationServerConfigurerAdapter relies on few methods that can be overridden to set up the configuration. The main methods are

- void configure(AuthorizationServerSecurityConfigurer security): You can configure the security of the authorization server, which means in practical terms the /oauth/token endpoint. The token endpoint (/oauth/token) will be automatically secured using HTTP basic authentication on the client's credentials. The /oauth/authorize endpoint also needs to be secure, but that is a normal user-facing endpoint and should be secured the same way as the rest of your UI. In your case, you leave it as it is.

- void configure(ClientDetailsServiceConfigurer clients): This will configure the ClientDetailsService (the service that provides the details about an OAuth2 client), like declaring individual clients and their properties. Note that password grant is not enabled (even if some clients are allowed it) unless an AuthenticationManager is supplied to the configure method. At least one client or a fully formed custom ClientDetailsService must be declared or the server will not start. You registered another client and authorized the "implicit," "password," "authorization_code," and "refresh_token" grant types. In order to use the "password" grant type, you need to wire in and use the AuthenticationManager bean. The authentication manager will represent the web-security users.

- void configure(AuthorizationServerEndpointsConfigurer endpoints): You can configure the non-security features of the authorization server endpoints, like token store, token customizations, user approvals, and grant types here. You shouldn't need to do anything by default, unless you need password grants, in which case you need to provide an authentication manager.

By default, Spring Security will provide access_token and refresh_token in UUID format which will then get verified by the resource servers. In cases where you have a huge amount of requests for your services, this may turn the authorization server into a bottleneck. Instead, and as per the earlier discussion on tokens and JWT, you make your authorization server issue signed JWTs that contain all the information necessary to validate the user in the token itself. To achieve this, you need JwtTokenStore and

JwtAccessTokenConverter. You use a custom JwtAccessTokenConverter that will use a pregenerated certificate for your JWT signatures. To do this, you must use your keyPair configuration and configure a custom JwtAccessTokenConverter, as seen in Listing 18-11. JwtAccessTokenConverter translates between JWT-encoded token values and OAuth authentication information (bidirectional). It also acts as a TokenEnhancer (a Strategy class for enhancing an access token before it is stored by an AuthorizationServerTokenServices implementation) when tokens are granted. A TokenStore represents the storage mechanism to store the OAuth access token. Spring supports different kind of token store like InMemoryTokenStore, JDBCTokenStore, JwtTokenStore, and so on. You use JwtTokenStore for your case. The JWT version of the store (JwtTokenStore) encodes all the data about the grant into the token itself and it doesn't persist any data. Once you have created the JwtTokenStore and JwtAccessTokenConverter beans, you wire them up to the AuthorizationServerEndpointsConfigurer in the OAuth2Configuration class.

Resource Server

Next, you can enable annotation-based security for your resource servers using the @EnableGlobalMethodSecurity annotation on any @Configuration instance. This enables Spring method-level security. See Listing 18-12.

Listing 18-12. EnableGlobalMethodSecurity (ch18\ch18-01\Ax2-Ecom-With-Security\Ecom-core\src\main\java\com\acme\ecom\core\security\ GlobalMethodSecurityConfiguration.java)

```
@Configuration
@EnableGlobalMethodSecurity(prePostEnabled = true)
public class GlobalMethodSecurityConfiguration   {

}
```

@EnableGlobalMethodSecurity can take several arguments:

- prePostEnabled: Determines whether Spring Security's pre and post annotations (@PreAuthorize,@PostAuthorize,..) should be enabled.

- secureEnabled: Determines if Spring Security's secured annotation (@Secured) should be enabled.

- jsr250Enabled: Determines if JSR-250 annotations (@RolesAllowed, ...) should be enabled.

You should enable only one type of annotation in the same application for any interface or class; otherwise, the behavior will not be well-defined. If two annotations are found that apply to a particular method, only one of them will be applied.

You use prePostEnabled = true and Spring's @PreAuthorize/@PostAuthorize annotations are preferred way for applying method-level security. They support the Spring Expression Language and provide expression-based access control. Let's look at how they are leveraged here:

- @PreAuthorize: This is suitable for validating authorization before entry into a method. @PreAuthorize can take into account the roles/ permissions of a logged-in user, the argument passed to the method, etc.

- @PostAuthorize: This can check for authorization after the method has been executed. It is suitable for verifying authorization on returned values; however, it's not commonly used. Spring EL provides a returnObject that can be accessed in the expression language, which reflects the actual object returned from the method.

Next, you need to configure the resource server. EnableResourceServer is a convenient annotation for OAuth2 resource servers, and it enables a Spring Security filter that authenticates requests via an incoming OAuth2 token. This enables a Spring Security filter named OAuth2AuthenticationProcessingFilter that authenticates requests using a passed-in OAuth2 token. You should add this annotation and provide a @Bean of type ResourceServerConfigurer (e.g. via ResourceServerConfigurerAdapter) that specifies the details of the resource (URL paths and resource ID). You create a bean named CoreResourceServerConfiguration that extends ResourceServerConfigurerAdapter and overrides the configure(HttpSecurity http) method to enable the security of the Ecom-core microservice. See Listing 18-13.

Listing 18-13. Enabling Resource Server (ch18\ch18-01\Ax2-Ecom-With-Security\Ecom-core\src\main\java\com\acme\ecom\core\security\CoreResourceServerConfiguration.java)

```
@Configuration
@EnableResourceServer
public class CoreResourceServerConfiguration extends
ResourceServerConfigurerAdapter{
```

```
@Autowired
TokenStore tokenStore;

@Autowired
JwtAccessTokenConverter tokenConverter;

@Override
public void configure(HttpSecurity http) throws Exception {

    http
        .csrf().disable()
        .authorizeRequests()
        .anyRequest().authenticated()
        .antMatchers(HttpMethod.POST).hasAuthority("ORDER_WRITE")
        .antMatchers(HttpMethod.DELETE).hasAuthority("ORDER_WRITE");
}

@Override
public void configure(ResourceServerSecurityConfigurer resources)
        throws Exception {

    resources.resourceId("CORE").tokenStore(tokenStore);
}
}
```

In the configure method you use the passed-in HttpSecurity instance to secure the POST and DELETE methods and only allow authenticated users with ORDER_WRITE authority to access the resources. Then you use the ResourceServerSecurityConfigurer class to create a resource id with the name CORE. The name of this resource id must match the name used in the authorization server.

Next, you need to read values from the encrypted JWT. As you have already seen, the JwtAccessTokenConverter helps to translate between JWT-encoded token values and OAuth authentication information in a bidirectional manner. Since you use asymmetric encryption and since the token has already been encrypted with the private key by the authorization server, you will now use the public key pair to decrypt and read. See Listing 18-14.

Listing 18-14. Token Decryption (ch18\ch18-01\Ax2-Ecom-With-Security\Ecom-core\src\main\java\com\acme\ecom\core\security\JwtConfiguration.java)

```java
@Configuration
public class JwtConfiguration {

    @Autowired
    JwtAccessTokenConverter jwtAccessTokenConverter;

    @Bean
    @Qualifier("tokenStore")
    public TokenStore tokenStore() {

        return new JwtTokenStore(jwtAccessTokenConverter);
    }

    @Bean
    protected JwtAccessTokenConverter jwtTokenEnhancer() {

        JwtAccessTokenConverter converter =  new JwtAccessTokenConverter();
        Resource resource = new ClassPathResource("public.cert");
        String publicKey = null;
        try {
            publicKey = new String(FileCopyUtils.copyToByteArray(
                resource.getInputStream()));
        } catch (IOException e) {
            throw new RuntimeException(e);
        }
        converter.setVerifierKey(publicKey);
        return converter;
    }
}
```

That completes the resource server setup.

Note   The certificates and keystores are included with the code example downloads. The creation of them is not covered here, since it can be done following any standard literature on the subject. Further, the code for other resource servers (microservices) of the example application is not explained, since it follows a setup similar to that of the Ecom-core microservice, which you saw here.

Set Up the E-Commerce Microservice Application

In this section, you will configure, build, and run the e-commerce microservice application and execute various test cases.

Configure the Application

You need to make the required configuration changes in the microservices. The changes you need to make are similar to what was explained in Chapter 17.

Set Up the Environment Infrastructure

Next, you need to set up a few infrastructure settings to run the example. This again is similar to what was explained in Chapter 17.

Build and Run the Application

There are 12 microservices in the application. The methodology to build and run the application again is similar to what was explained in Chapter 17.

In Chapter 17, you were required to bring up the servers in the below sequence for the first three microservices:

```
Ecom-config
Ecom-registry
Ecom-gateway
```

I advise you to then start the following two microservices:

```
Ecom-security
Ecom-user
```

For the rest of the microservices, you may start them in any order.

Test the Application

You can test the application, preferably in the Chrome browser. Here again, you may refer to the steps described in Chapter 17 to test the complete application end to end.

Summary

You just explored OAuth 2.0 in general and looked into specific aspects of selected grand types relevant to the microservices context. You also plugged in authentication and authorization into the microservices e-commerce application. This is a major step forward since security is a prime concern in any enterprise-grade application. What is left from the discussions through the previous chapters is a deep dive into the necessity of keeping the order and inventory domains close and together, and you will do so in the next chapter.

Test the Application

Summary

CHAPTER 19

Axon Microservices and BASE Transactions

You saw Axon 2 in Chapter 12, and you also saw working examples. As mentioned in that chapter, you will be using multiple versions of Axon in this book. In Chapter 12, you used Axon 2.4.1. It required explicit wiring of components, either through annotations or using XML configurations. Using Axon 2 and demonstrating examples based on it in Chapter 12 was intentional, since I wanted to make the bean wirings explicit so that the concepts were be clear for you as a first time reader of the concepts of CQRS and as a first time user of the Axon framework.

In this chapter, you will look at examples in the later versions of Axon where you will use Spring version 5.0.7.RELEASE, Spring Boot 2.0.3.RELEASE, Axon 3.3.2, or later versions. Here in Axon 3, a lot of explicit bean wirings can be avoided since Axon uses the Spring Application Context to locate specific implementations of building blocks and provide defaults for those that are not there. Axon 3 contains a complete overhaul of the inner workings of Axon mainly because of a lot of new features in Java 7 and 8. To make it clear, if you add a few starter dependencies, that is enough; the Axon Spring Boot components will set up a basic infrastructure for you depending on the other dependencies you have in the project. As an example, if you have JPA, then Axon will automatically configure all the JPA-based components for you. If you have marked @ `Aggregate` or `@Saga` on a class, Axon will automatically configure the components necessary to operate these aggregates and sagas. All of this is going to make your life a lot easier, as you will see shortly in the examples.

Further, if you recollect the discussion in the "The ACID Within the BASE" section in Chapter 17, you kept the order and inventory aggregates together. By using a single resource manager (the MySQL persistence engine) in that case, you avoided distributed transactions. However, you still used ACID-style transactions. Let's find out if it's possible to avoid ACID-style transactions if there is a need to do so.

© Binildas Christudas 2019

B. Christudas, *Practical Microservices Architectural Patterns*, https://doi.org/10.1007/978-1-4842-4501-9_19

Note   You may want to refer to the Axon 3 reference documentation[1] and API documentation[2] while you go through this chapter.

You will be doing the following in this chapter:

- Understanding how Axon 3 differs from Axon 2, by looking at code

- Migrating the Axon 2 command and event handling in the single JVM example from Chapter 12 to Axon 3

- Migrating the Axon 2 distributed command and event handling example from Chapter 12 to Axon 3

- Migrating the microservices e-commerce application from Chapters 17 and 18 to Axon 3

- Removing the ACID-style transactions used in Chapters 17 and 18 across multiple aggregates

- Meeting Axon 4 so that you have a smooth roadmap to continue with your own exploration after finishing this last chapter of the book

Let's straightaway get our hands dirty with Axon 3.

Command and Event Handling in the Same JVM Using Axon 3

You will migrate the example in the "Command and Event Handling in the Same JVM" section in Chapter 12 from Axon 2 to Axon 3. While doing so, I will highlight the main changes.

Design the Example Scenario

Since you are building over the same example, you will follow the same design explained in Chapter 12 for this example in Axon 3. Refer to Figure 12-1.

---

[1]https://docs.axoniq.io/reference-guide/v/3.3/
[2]https://axoniq.io/apidocs/3.3/

Code the Example Scenario

All the code examples for this section are in folder ch19\ch19-01. Visit pom.xml to see the explicit mention of the Axon dependency. See Listing 19-1.

Listing 19-1. Axon 3 Maven Dependency (ch19\ch19-01\Ax3-Commands-Events-Same-JVM\pom.xml)

```
<dependency>
    <groupId>org.axonframework</groupId>
    <artifactId>axon-spring-boot-starter</artifactId>
    <version>3.3.2</version>
</dependency>
```

The most important class of this example, where you do the setup of all Axon components is EcomAppConfiguration. See Listing 19-2.

Listing 19-2. EcomAppConfiguration (ch19\ch19-01\Ax3-Commands-Events-Same-JVM\src\main\java\com\acme\ecom\EcomAppConfiguration.java)

```
@Configuration
public class EcomAppConfiguration {

    @PersistenceContext
    private EntityManager entityManager;

    @Bean
    @Qualifier("productRepository")
    public GenericJpaRepository<Product> productJpaRepository(
            EventBus eventBus) {

        SimpleEntityManagerProvider entityManagerProvider =
            new SimpleEntityManagerProvider(entityManager);
        GenericJpaRepository<Product> genericJpaRepository =
            new GenericJpaRepository<Product>(entityManagerProvider,
            Product.class, eventBus, ((String id) -> Integer.valueOf(id)));
        return genericJpaRepository;
    }
```

```java
@Bean
@Qualifier("orderRepository")
public GenericJpaRepository<Order> orderJpaRepository(EventBus eventBus) {

    SimpleEntityManagerProvider entityManagerProvider =
        new SimpleEntityManagerProvider(entityManager);
    GenericJpaRepository<Order> genericJpaRepository =
        new GenericJpaRepository<Order>(entityManagerProvider,
        Order.class, eventBus, ((String id) -> Integer.valueOf(id)));
    return genericJpaRepository;
}
}
```

Compare this code with the `EcomAppConfiguration.java` code in Listing 12-3 of Chapter 12. You can see that all of the explicit configurations from Chapter 12 have disappeared; however, you get the same utility from the Axon-based architecture in the current example.

The next major change in the code base is for the `OrderCommandHandler`; see Listing 19-3.

Listing 19-3. OrderCommandHandler (ch19\ch19-01\Ax3-Commands-Events-Same-JVM\src\main\java\com\acme\ecom\order\commandhandler\ OrderCommandHandler.java)

```java
@Component
public class OrderCommandHandler {

    @Autowired
    @Qualifier("orderRepository")
    private Repository<Order> orderRepository;

    @Autowired
    @Qualifier("productRepository")
    private Repository<Product> productRepository;

    @CommandHandler
    public void handle(NewOrderCommand newOrderCommand) throws Exception{
```

```
Aggregate<Product>  productAggregate =
    productRepository.load(newOrderCommand.getProductId().
    toString());

Product product =  productAggregate.invoke(
    (Product p)->{p.depreciateStock(newOrderCommand.getNumber());
    return p;}
);

orderRepository.newInstance(()->new Order(new Random().nextInt(),
    newOrderCommand.getPrice(), newOrderCommand.getNumber(),
    OrderStatusEnum.NEW, product));
    }
}
```

The command handler retrieves the order domain object, which is an aggregate from a generic repository implementation that stores JPA-annotated aggregates and executes methods on them to change their state. If you compare the code of the OrderCommandHandler in Listing 19-3 to the code in Listing 12-8 in Chapter 12, you can appreciate the little differences even though functionally you are doing the same thing.

Next, the order aggregate contains the actual business logic of managing the order and is therefore responsible for guarding the invariants. The state changes of the order aggregate result in the generation of domain events, as shown in Listing 19-4. The domain events and the aggregates form the domain model.

Listing 19-4. Order Entity (ch19\ch19-01\Ax3-Commands-Events-Same-JVM\ src\main\java\com\acme\ecom\order\model\Order.java)

```
import  static org.axonframework.commandhandling.model.AggregateLifecycle.
apply;

@Entity
@Table(name="ECOM_ORDER")
public class Order{

    private static final long serialVersionUID = 1L;
```

```java
@Id
private Integer id;

@Column(name="PRICE")
private Double price;

@Column(name="NUMBER")
private Integer number;

@Column(name="ORDER_STATUS")
@Enumerated(EnumType.STRING)
private OrderStatusEnum orderStatus; ;

@ManyToOne(fetch=FetchType.LAZY)
@JoinColumn(name="PRODUCT_ID")
private Product product;

public Order(Integer id, Double price, Integer number,
        OrderStatusEnum orderStatus, Product product){

    super();
    this.id = id;
    this.price = price;
    this.number = number;
    this.orderStatus = orderStatus;
    this.product = product;
    apply(new OrderCreatedEvent(id, price, number,
        product.getDescription(), orderStatus.toString()));
}

public Order() {

}
}
```

Compare the code of the order aggregate in Listing 19-4 with the same in Listing 12-4 in Chapter 12. Axon 2 requires that both order and product aggregates extend AbstractAggregateRoot, a very basic implementation of the AggregateRoot interface, whereas in Axon 3, your aggregates are not required to extend that base class.

AggregateRoot must declare a field that contains the aggregate identifier. This identifier must be initialized at the latest when the first event is published, and this identifier field must be annotated by the @AggregateIdentifier annotation. However, if you use JPA and have JPA annotations on the aggregate, Axon can also use the @Id annotation provided by JPA.

Aggregates use the AggregateLifecycle.apply() method to register events for publication. Applying events means they are immediately applied (published) to the aggregate and scheduled for publication to other event handlers.

The code in all other classes remains the same as is listed in the "Code the Example Scenario" subsection under the "Command and Event Handling in the Same JVM" section in Chapter 12, hence they are not repeated here.

Build and Test the Example Scenario

The complete code required to demonstrate the simple Axon example is in ch19\ch19-01. To build and run this example, refer to the instructions provided in the "Build and Test the Example Scenario" subsection in the "Command and Event Handling in the Same JVM" section in Chapter 12.

The only difference in the process is in the step where you start with clean tables. In the current example, you want to delete any tables with the names you want for your examples, which may be as many as seven:

```
drop table association_value_entry;
drop table domain_event_entry;
drop table ecom_order;
drop table ecom_product;
drop table saga_entry;
drop table snapshot_event_entry;
drop table token_entry;

drop table ecom_order_view;
drop table ecom_product_view;
```

In the corresponding example in Chapter 12, you deleted only four tables, and there ends the difference. For the rest of the build and run of the example, just follow the instructions from Chapter 12.

Distributed Command and Event Handling Using Axon 3

Here again you will refactor the same design from the "Distributed Command and Event Handling" section in Chapter 12 to make it adaptable for Axon 3. However, I will introduce a little change by replacing the JGroups connector with Spring Cloud.

Design Distributed Command Bus with Spring Cloud

As mentioned, refer to the design illustrated in Figure 12-4 in Chapter 12. You should already be familiar with the distributed command bus there. Unlike the other command bus implementations, the distributed command bus does not invoke any handlers at all. All it does is form a "bridge" between the command bus implementations on different JVMs.

The distributed command bus consists of two components: a command bus connector and a command router. A command bus connector implements the communication protocol between the individual JVMs of the microservices whereas the command router chooses a destination for each incoming command. The router defines to which segment of the distributed command bus a command should be routed based on a routing key calculated by a routing strategy. This asserts that two commands with the same routing key will always be routed to the same segment, provided there is no change in the number and configuration of the segments in the runtime.

In the design in Chapter 12, you used a JGroupsConnector which used JGroups as the underlying discovery and dispatching mechanism. The JGroups-specific components for the distributed command bus are in the axon-distributed-commandbus-jgroups module. Since JGroups handles both discovery of microservice nodes and the communication between them, the JGroupsConnector acts as both a command bus connector and a command router. There is another method for the interconnection and routing between command buses using the Spring Cloud. You can use either Eureka or Consul for this. Since you know how Eureka works from the "Eureka, the Service Registry" section in Chapter 8, you will use it in your refactored design for Axon 3.

When you use Spring Cloud, the Spring Cloud command router uses the Spring Cloud-specific ServiceInstance.Metadata field to infer and inform all of the microservice nodes in the system of its message routing information. So, to use it in conjunction with Axon, the Spring Cloud implementation selected should support the usage of the ServiceInstance.Metadata field. In cases where the desired Spring Cloud implementation does not support the modification of the ServiceInstance.Metadata (e.g. Consul), there are other alternate ways, which I will not describe here.

The easiest way for you to use Spring Cloud Eureka is to use the Spring Cloud starters of the Axon distributed command bus modules. Once the starter is included, a single property needs to be added to the application context, to enable the distributed command bus:

```
axon.distributed.enabled=true
```

The next setting to be used independent of the type of connector is

```
axon.distributed.load-factor=100
```

By doing so, Axon will configure a distributed command bus by default when a command router as well as a command bus connector are present in the application context. The Spring Cloud Connector setup is a combination of the Spring Cloud command router and a Spring HTTP command bus connector; they fill the place of the command router and the command bus connector, respectively, for the distributed command bus. The Spring Cloud command router uses Spring Cloud's Discovery Clients to propagate its command message routing information and to discover other Axon microservices nodes and retrieve their message routing information. It does so by utilizing the ServiceInstance.Metadata for storing the message routing information in. For performance reasons, any other nodes discovered through the Discovery Client system that do not contain any of the required message routing information fields will be black-listed, so no unneeded additional checks are performed on that node.

The Spring HTTP command bus connector will send the given command to the node assigned to handle messages with the given routing key. The sender does not expect a reply, so if the send method throws an exception, the sender is guaranteed that the destination of the command did not receive it. If the method returns normally, the concrete implementation of the connector defines the delivery guarantees. Since connectors route the commands based on the given routing key, using the same routing key will result in the command being sent to the same member. Further, each message must be sent to exactly one member.

Another aspect you need to handle while using the Spring Cloud command router is that your Spring application should have heartbeat events enabled. The Spring Cloud command router implementation leverages the heartbeat events published by your Spring Cloud microservices to check whether its knowledge of all the others nodes is up to date. Hence, if heartbeat events are disabled, the microservices within your cluster will not be aware of the entire setup, thus posing issues for correct command routing.

Figure 12-5 thus becomes Figure 19-1.

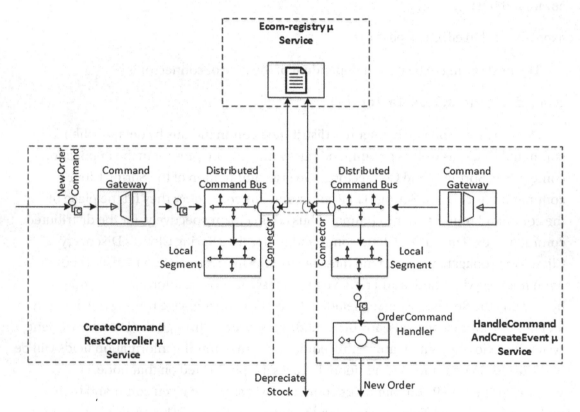

Figure 19-1. *Distributed command bus using Spring Cloud*

You will next look at the code. I will highlight any subtle differences.

Code the Example Scenario

The complete code required to demonstrate the distributed Axon example is in ch19\ ch19-02. There were five microservices in the example code in Chapter 12. You will add a new microservice for the Eureka-based service registry.

Microservice 1: 00-Ecom-registry

This microservice is a typical Spring Cloud Eureka microservice application without any Axon components, which you have already seen in many previous examples, so I will not discuss it further.

Microservice 2: 01-Ecom-web

This microservice is a typical Spring Boot web application, again without any Axon components, so I will not discuss it further.

Microservice 3: 02-Ecom-CreateCommandRestController

Visit pom.xml to see the axon-distributed-commandbus dependency. See Listing 19-5.

Listing 19-5. Distributed Command Bus Maven Dependency (ch19\
ch19-02\Ax3-Commands-Multi-Event-Handler-Distributed\02-Ecom-
CreateCommandRestController\pom.xml)

```
<project>

    <parent>
        <groupId>org.springframework.boot</groupId>
        <artifactId>spring-boot-starter-parent</artifactId>
        <version>2.0.3.RELEASE</version>
        <relativePath/> <!-- lookup parent from repository -->
    </parent>

    <properties>
        <springframework.version>5.0.7.RELEASE</springframework.version>
        <axonVersion>3.3.2</axonVersion>
    </properties>

    <dependencies>

        <dependency>
            <groupId>org.axonframework</groupId>
            <artifactId>axon-spring-boot-starter</artifactId>
            <version>${axonVersion}</version>
        </dependency>
```

789

```
        <dependency>
            <groupId>org.axonframework</groupId>
            <artifactId>axon-distributed-commandbus-springcloud</artifactId>
            <version>${axonVersion}</version>
        </dependency>

        <dependency>
            <groupId>org.springframework.cloud</groupId>
            <artifactId>spring-cloud-starter-netflix-eureka-client</artifactId>
        </dependency>

    </dependencies>

    <dependencyManagement>
        <dependencies>
            <dependency>
                <groupId>org.springframework.cloud</groupId>
                <artifactId>spring-cloud-dependencies</artifactId>
                <version>Finchley.RELEASE</version>
                <type>pom</type>
                <scope>import</scope>
            </dependency>
        </dependencies>
    </dependencyManagement>

</project>
```

You use the axon-distributed-commandbus-springcloud module that contains the Spring Cloud Connector-specific components for the distributed command bus.

The next major update for this microservice is in the main application class. See Listing 19-6.

Listing 19-6. Ecom-CreateCommandRestController Main Class (ch19\
ch19-02\Ax3-Commands-Multi-Event-Handler-Distributed\02-Ecom-
CreateCommandRestController\src\main\java\com\acme\ecom\
EcomCreateCommandAndRestApplication.java)

```
@SpringBootApplication
@EnableDiscoveryClient
public class EcomCreateCommandAndRestApplication {

    public static void main(String[] args) {

        SpringApplication.run(EcomCreateCommandAndRestApplication.class,
        args);
    }
}
```

A Spring Cloud command router has to be created by annotating your Spring Boot application with `@EnableDiscoveryClient`. Once done, it will look for a Spring Cloud implementation on your classpath.

There are few other changes in the code. Let's look into the configuration of the Axon components in Listing 19-7.

Listing 19-7. Ecom-CreateCommandRestController Configuration
(ch19\ch19-02\Ax3-Commands-Multi-Event-Handler-Distributed\02-
Ecom-CreateCommandRestController\src\main\java\com\acme\ecom\
EcomAppConfiguration.java)

```
@Configuration
public class EcomAppConfiguration {

}
```

As you can see, when compared to the code in Listing 12-15 and Listing 12-16, Listing 19-7 contains absolutely no explicit configurations required to configure the Axon 3 components. It's all automatically wired up by Spring!

Microservice 4: 03-Ecom-HandleCommandAndCreateEvent

This microservice has to handle any commands created by the 02-Ecom-CreateCommandRestController microservice and reaching through the distributed command bus from the remote JVM. The only change in code to this microservice from that in Chapter 12 is the introduction of the Spring Cloud command router by annotating the Spring Boot application with @EnableDiscoveryClient as shown in the previous microservice, so I will just display the code here in Listing 19-8 without any detailed explanation.

Listing 19-8. Main Application Class (ch19\ch19-02\Ax3-Commands-Multi-Event-Handler-Distributed\03-Ecom-HandleCommandAndCreateEvent\ src\main\java\com\acme\ecom\EcomHandleCommandAndCreateEvent Application.java)

```
@EnableDiscoveryClient
@SpringBootApplication
public class EcomHandleCommandAndCreateEventApplication {

    public static void main(String[] args) {

        SpringApplication.run(
            EcomHandleCommandAndCreateEventApplication.class, args);
    }
}
```

Microservice 5: 04-Ecom-EventHandleCore

Again, since you have already followed the corresponding example in Chapter 12, there is nothing new in this microservice. So I will not do a detailed code walkthrough. As the name of the microservice hints, it contains the two main event handlers, OrderEventHandler and ProductEventHandler, and the functionality and code snippets are similar to those in the previous example in this chapter. However, a little update needs to be mentioned here.

As you have already seen, all singleton Spring beans components containing @EventHandler annotated methods will be subscribed to the event processor to receive event messages published to the event bus. Event processors can also be configured in application.properties.

```
axon.eventhandling.processors.name.mode=tracking
axon.eventhandling.processors.name.source=eventBus
```

The source attribute here refers to the name of a bean implementing SubscribableMessageSource or StreamableMessageSource that should be used as the source of events for the selected processor, which defaults to the event bus or event store defined in the application context. Next, you can mark to use a so-called tracking processor to process events asynchronously. The processor will tail the events in the event store (or any other source that supports tracking).

To configure a processor to switch to tracking mode, you need to do the following:

1. First, you override the processing group's name. By default, the name of a processing group (and the processor that will process events on behalf of it) is the package name of the event handlers that are assigned to it. You can override it by putting a @ProcessingGroup.

2. Next, in the application.properties, configure the messages processor to be tracking:

   ```
   axon.eventhandling.processors.messages.mode=tracking.
   ```

Here, the messages part is the name of the processor. Inspect application.properties to view this. See Listing 19-9.

Listing 19-9. Ecom-EventHandleCore Configuration (ch19\ch19-02\Ax3-Commands-Multi-Event-Handler-Distributed\04-Ecom-EventHandleCore\src\main\resources\application.properties)

```
axon.eventhandling.processors[ECOM_EVENT_PROCESSOR].mode=tracking
axon.eventhandling.processors[ECOM_EVENT_PROCESSOR].source=eventBus
```

You then attach the processing group to enable it to handle the right event, as shown in Listing 19-10.

Listing 19-10. Order Event Handler (ch19\ch19-02\Ax3-Commands-Multi-Event-Handler-Distributed\04-Ecom-EventHandleCore\src\main\java\com\acme\ecom\order\eventhandler\OrderEventHandler.java)

```
@Component
@ProcessingGroup("ECOM_EVENT_PROCESSOR")
public class OrderEventHandler {

    @EventHandler
    public void handleOrderCreatedEvent(OrderCreatedEvent event) {

        //The code goes here

    }
}
```

Similarly, you attach the processing group to enable it to handle the stock-related events, as shown in Listing 19-11.

Listing 19-11. Product Event Handler (ch19\ch19-02\Ax3-Commands-Multi-Event-Handler-Distributed\04-Ecom-EventHandleCore\src\main\java\com\acme\ecom\product\eventhandler\ProductEventHandler.java)

```
@Component
@ProcessingGroup("ECOM_EVENT_PROCESSOR")
public class ProductEventHandler {

    @EventHandler
    public void handleProductStockUpdatedEvent(StockUpdatedEvent event) {

        //The code goes here

    }
}
```

Microservice 6: 05-Ecom-EventHandlerAudit

The functionality and code for this microservice is the same as what you have already seen for the EventHandlerAudit microservice in Chapter 12. The only change is similar to what was described in the just previous microservice in attaching the processing group, hence I will not repeat that information.

Build and Test the Example Scenario

Follow the instructions in the "Build and Test the Example Scenario" subsection under the "Distributed Command and Event Handling" section in Chapter 12 to build and test the example. The only difference for this example is that you have one additional microservice, the Eureka Registry. You should build and run the Eureka Registry microservice as a first step. Then follow the steps described in Chapter 12.

Axon 3 CQRS Microservices E-Commerce with BASE Transactions

In this section, your primary objective is to migrate the e-commerce example application you built in Chapters 17 and 18 from Axon 2 to Axon 3. There is a secondary objective, which I will define now.

If you recollect the discussion in the "The ACID Within the BASE" section in Chapter 17, you kept the order and inventory aggregates together. This may or may not be the scenario in real life. Order or booking entities are driven by sales channels and end user activities, whereas inventory or stock entities are driven by end user and supply chain activities. As such, applications or systems or microservices responsible for the management of these entities may not be one and the same, and in many cases they will be separate microservices. By using a single resource manager (the MySQL persistence engine) in the examples in Chapters 17 and 18, you avoided distributed transactions. However, you still used ACID-style transactions, since both entities were kept close within a single microservice and you leveraged ACID-style local transactions. But what if you want to keep them separate?

Removing the ACID Knot Between the Order and Inventory Domains

You will first revisit the code from Chapter 17 where you do ACID-style transactions over two aggregate root entities, order and inventory. Listing 17-6 from Chapter 17 is repeated here as Listing 19-12.

Listing 19-12. OrderCommandHandler handleNewOrder (ch17\ch17-01\Ax2-Ecom-No-Security\Ecom-core\src\main\java\com\acme\ecom\core\order\command\handler\OrderCommandHandler.java)

```
@Component
public class OrderCommandHandler {

    @Autowired
    @Qualifier(value = "orderRepository")
    private Repository<Order> orderRepository;

    @CommandHandler
    public void handleNewOrder(OrderCreateCommand orderCreatedCommand) {

        Order order = new Order(Long.valueOf(new Random().nextInt()));
        order.setOrderDate(new Date());
        order.setOrderStatus(OrderStatus.PAID);
        order.setUserId(orderCreatedCommand.getUserId());
        double total = 0;

        if (orderCreatedCommand.getLineItems() != null) {
            for (LineItemDTO lineItemDto :
                orderCreatedCommand.getLineItems()) {
                if (lineItemDto.getInventoryId() != null) {
                    LineItem lineItem = new LineItem(new Random().
                    nextLong(),
                        lineItemDto.getProductId(), lineItemDto.
                        getQuantity(),
                        lineItemDto.getPrice(), lineItemDto.
                        getInventoryId());
                    total = total + lineItemDto.getPrice();
                    order.addLineItem(lineItem);
                    Inventory inventory =
                        inventoryRepository.load(lineItemDto.
                        getInventoryId());
```

```
            inventory.updateProductStock(lineItemDto.getQuantity(),
                ProductStockOperation.DEPRECIATE);
            }
        }
    }
    order.setTotal(total);
    order.notifyOrderCreation();
    orderRepository.add(order);
    }
}
```

You saw in Chapter 12 that a unit of work (UoW) is a set of modifications to be made to aggregates. Execution of a command typically happens within the scope of a UoW. When the command handler method in Listing 19-12 finishes execution, the UoW is committed and all actions are finalized. This means that any repositories are notified of state changes in their aggregates and events scheduled for publication are sent to the event bus. This is a convenient grouping that will help prevent individual events from being published before a number of aggregates have been processed. In the back, it allows repositories to manage resources, such as locks, over an entire transaction. Locks, for example, will only be released when the UoW is either committed or rolled back.

A UoW is not a replacement for traditional ACID-style transactions. It is merely a buffer where changes are grouped and staged. When a UoW is committed, all staged changes are only committed; however, this commit is not atomic. This means if a commit fails, a few changes might have already been persisted, while others not. Axon boot practices dictate to follow the best practice of a command always containing one action.

The UoW in Axon 2 enables a single command to execute logic on more than one aggregate. The UoW has a more central role in managing the work done by command handlers. The UoW currently keeps track of the aggregates that have been loaded by the repositories and persists them when the UoW is committed.

If you have more (than one) actions or more (than one) aggregates in your UoW, then you should consider attaching transactions to the UoW's commit. In Chapter 17, you did so in Listing 17-7, and the specific code is repeated here as Listing 19-13.

Listing 19-13. Bind Transactions to Unit of Work (ch17\ch17-01\Ax2-
Ecom-No-Security\Ecom-core\src\main\java\com\acme\ecom\core\
EcomCoreAppConfiguration.java)

```
@Configuration
@RefreshScope
public class EcomCoreAppConfiguration {

    @Autowired
    @Qualifier("transactionManager")
    protected PlatformTransactionManager txManager;

    @Bean
    public SimpleCommandBus commandBus() {

        SimpleCommandBus simpleCommandBus = new SimpleCommandBus();
        simpleCommandBus.setDispatchInterceptors(
        Arrays.asList(new BeanValidationInterceptor()));
        SpringTransactionManager transcationMgr =
            new SpringTransactionManager(txManager);
        simpleCommandBus.setTransactionManager(transcationMgr);
        return simpleCommandBus;

    }

}
```

Here, SpringTransactionManager is a TransactionManager implementation that uses
a PlatformTransactionManager as underlying transaction manager.

Here you use two aggregate entities, inventory and order, in a single transaction, but
there is no distributed transaction involved since both aggregate entities are managed by
the same resource manager, that too in a single node.

It is possible to bind a transaction to a UoW. Many command bus
implementations, like the SimpleCommandBus and DisruptorCommandBus, allow
you to configure a transaction manager. This transaction manager will then be used
to create the transactions to bind to the UoW that is used to manage the process of
a command. The command handling process can then be considered an atomic
procedure; it should either be processed entirely, or not at all. The Axon framework

uses the UoW to track actions performed by the command handlers. When the command handler completes, Axon will try to commit the actions registered with the UoW. When a UoW is bound to a transaction, it will ensure the bound transaction is committed at the right point in time.

Moving on to Axon 3, there are a few differences.

Note   In the "Distributed Command and Event Handling" example in Chapter 12, you configured the transaction manager whereas in the Axon 3 migrated version of the same example, you haven't configured or used any explicit transaction manager.

Axon 3 will complain if you deal with more than one aggregate root in a transactional command handler. That means the combination of Listing 19-12 and Listing 19-13 is not easy to get working in Axon 3. Let's refactor the design of the e-commerce microservice Ecom-core a little.

Listing 19-14 reveals the minimum configurations you need to do to wire in the command bus and the event bus in a distributed manner. You attach a transaction manager to the command bus as well as a saga event processor to the event queue in the code.

Listing 19-14. EcomCoreAppConfiguration (ch19\ch19-03\Ax3-Ecom-With-Security\Ecom-core\src\main\java\com\acme\ecom\core\EcomCoreApp Configuration.java)

```
@Configuration
public class EcomCoreAppConfiguration {

    @Value("${axon.amqp.exchange}")
    private String rabbitMQExchange;

    @Value("${axon.amqp.queue}")
    private String rabbitMQQueue;

    @Bean
    public FanoutExchange eventBusExchange() {
        return new FanoutExchange(rabbitMQExchange, true, false);
    }
```

```
@Bean
public Queue eventBusQueue() {
    return new Queue(rabbitMQQueue, true, false, false);
}

@Bean
public Binding binding() {
    return BindingBuilder.bind(eventBusQueue()).to(eventBusExchange());
}

@Bean
public SpringAMQPMessageSource ecomCoreEventQueue(
        AMQPMessageConverter         messageConverter) {

    return new SpringAMQPMessageSource(messageConverter) {

        @RabbitListener(queues = "${axon.amqp.queue}")
        @Override
        @Transactional
        public void onMessage(Message message, Channel channel) {
            super.onMessage(message, channel);
        }
    };
}

@Bean
public CommandBus commandBus(org.axonframework.common.transaction.
        TransactionManager transactionManager) {
    SimpleCommandBus commandBus = new AsynchronousCommandBus();
    commandBus.registerHandlerInterceptor(
        new TransactionManagingInterceptor(transactionManager));
    return commandBus;
}
```

```
@Bean("orderSagaConfiguration")
public SagaConfiguration<OrderProcessSaga> orderSagaConfiguration() {
    return SagaConfiguration.trackingSagaManager(
        OrderProcessSaga.class,"ECOM_CORE_EVENT_PROCESSOR");
}
}
```

Listing 19-15 shows configuring the values for the parameters you saw in Listing 19-14.

Listing 19-15. ecom-core.yml (ch19\ch19-03\Ax3-Ecom-With-Security\config-repo\ecom-core.yml)

```
axon:
    amqp:
        exchange: Ecom-axon3-exchange
        queue: Ecom-core-queue
        eventhandling:
            processors:
                ECOM_CORE_EVENT_PROCESSOR:
                    source: ecomCoreEventQueue
```

Next, let's look at the major refactoring to be done to the code of OrderCommandHandler in Listing 19-12. You rewrite the OrderCommandHandler as shown in Listing 19-16.

Listing 19-16. Order Command Handler Refactored for Axon 3 (ch19\ch19-03\Ax3-Ecom-With-Security\Ecom-core\src\main\java\com\acme\ecom\core\order\command\handler\OrderCommandHandler.java)

```
@Component
public class OrderCommandHandler {

    @Autowired
    @Qualifier(value = "orderRepository")
    private GenericJpaRepository<Order> orderRepository;

    @Autowired
    private CommandGateway commandGateway;
```

```java
@Transactional
@CommandHandler
public void handleNewOrder(OrderCreateCommand orderCreatedCommand
        )throws Exception {

    Long orderId = Long.valueOf(new Random().nextInt());
    Order order = new Order(orderId);
    order.setOrderDate(new Date());
    order.setOrderStatus(OrderStatus.PAID);
    order.setUserId(orderCreatedCommand.getUserId());

    double total = 0;
    if (orderCreatedCommand.getLineItems() != null) {
        for (LineItemDTO lineItemDto :
                orderCreatedCommand.getLineItems()) {
            if (lineItemDto.getInventoryId() != null) {
                LineItem lineItem =
                    new LineItem(new Random().nextLong(),
                        lineItemDto.getProductId(),
                        lineItemDto.getQuantity(), lineItemDto.getPrice(),
                        lineItemDto.getInventoryId());
                total = total + lineItemDto.getPrice();
                order.addLineItem(lineItem);
            }
        }
    }
    order.setTotal(total);
    Aggregate<Order> orderAggregate =  orderRepository.newInstance(
        ()->order);
    orderAggregate.invoke((Order orderSaved) ->{
        orderSaved.notifyOrderCreation();
    return orderSaved;});
    }
}
```

You remove all inventory-related operations from the OrderCommandHandler. Instead, you do all validations and calculations required to create a full order along with all line items, as shown in Listing 19-16. The inventory-related operations are moved to another handler, the InventoryCommandHandler, as shown in Listing 19-17.

Listing 19-17. Inventory Command Handler Refactored for Axon 3 (ch19\ch19-03\Ax3-Ecom-With-Security\Ecom-core\src\main\java\com\acme\ecom\core\inventory\command\handler\InventoryCommandHandler.java)

```java
@Component
public class InventoryCommandHandler {

    @Autowired
    @Qualifier(value = "inventoryRepository")
    private GenericJpaRepository<Inventory> inventoryRepository;

    public void setInventoryRepository(GenericJpaRepository<Inventory>
            inventoryRepository) {
        this.inventoryRepository = inventoryRepository;
    }

    @CommandHandler
    @Transactional
    public void handleInventoryCreation(InventoryCreateCommad
            inventoryCreatedCommand)  {

        Integer id = new Random().nextInt();
        try{
            inventoryRepository.newInstance(()->new Inventory(Long.
            valueOf(id),
                inventoryCreatedCommand.getSku(),
                inventoryCreatedCommand.getQuantity()));
        }catch(Exception ex){
            LOGGER.error("InventoryCommandHandler error ", ex);
        }
    }
}
```

```
@CommandHandler
@Transactional
public void handleInventoryUpdation(InventoryUpdateCommand
        inventoryUpdateCommand) {

    Aggregate<Inventory>  inventoryAggregate =
        inventoryRepository.load(inventoryUpdateCommand.
        getLineItemDTO().
        getInventoryId().toString());
    inventoryAggregate.invoke((Inventory inventory) ->
        {inventory.updateProductStock(
            inventoryUpdateCommand.getLineItemDTO().getQuantity(),
            inventoryUpdateCommand.getProductStockOperation());
            return inventory;
        });
    }
}
```

One aspect you need to note in the OrderCommandHandler in Listing 19-16 and the InventoryCommandHandler in Listing 19-17 is that all of the handler methods are executed in transactional context. However, there are no distributed transactions or two-phase commit operations, and also there is no ACID transactions involving more than one aggregate root. There are just local transactions confined to a single aggregate root entity.

So far, so good. Now let's come to the business orchestration part. The orchestration of depreciating inventory and creating a new order will now get moved from OrderCommandHandler in Listing 19-12 to the OrderController REST Controller REST controller in Listing 19-18. The essence is that operations on both entities are to be successful together or all of the actions must be compensated back!

Listing 19-18. Order REST Controller (ch19\ch19-03\Ax3-Ecom-With-Security\ Ecom-core\src\main\java\com\acme\ecom\core\web\OrderController.java)

```
@RestController
@RequestMapping("/order")
public class OrderController {
```

```
@Autowired
private CommandGateway commandGateway;

@RequestMapping(method = RequestMethod.POST)
@ResponseBody
public OrderCreationStatus createOrder(@RequestBody OrderDTO orderDTO) {

    OrderCreationStatus orderCreationStatus = null;

    //Step1 :  depreciating  inventory of products.............
    List<LineItemDTO> inventoryUpdatedList = new ArrayList<>();
    try {
        for (LineItemDTO lineItemDTO : orderDTO.getLineItems()) {
            commandGateway.sendAndWait(new InventoryUpdateCommand(
                lineItemDTO, ProductStockOperation.DEPRECIATE));
            inventoryUpdatedList.add(lineItemDTO);
        }
    } catch (Exception ex) {

        Throwable e = ex.getCause();
        if (e instanceof OutOfStockException) {
            LOGGER.error("Error while creating
                new order due to Out of Stock", e);
            orderCreationStatus = OrderCreationStatus.OUT_OF_STOCK;
        } else {
            LOGGER.error("Unknown Error while updating inventory", e);
            orderCreationStatus = OrderCreationStatus.FAILED;
        }

        //Step2 : Any exception, rollback updated inventory
        for (LineItemDTO lineItemDTO : inventoryUpdatedList) {
            commandGateway.send(new InventoryUpdateCommand(
                lineItemDTO, ProductStockOperation.ADD));
        }
        return orderCreationStatus;
    }

    //Step 3: create new order
```

```
        try {
            OrderCreateCommand orderCommand =
                new OrderCreateCommand(orderDTO.getUserId(),
                    orderDTO.getLineItems());
            commandGateway.sendAndWait(orderCommand);
            orderCreationStatus = OrderCreationStatus.SUCCESS;
        } catch (Exception ex) {

            LOGGER.error("Unknown Error while creating new order", ex);
            orderCreationStatus = OrderCreationStatus.FAILED;

            // Step 4: Any exception, rollback all updated inventory
            for (LineItemDTO lineItemDTO : orderDTO.getLineItems()) {
                commandGateway.send(new InventoryUpdateCommand(lineItemDTO,
                    ProductStockOperation.ADD));
            }
        }
        return orderCreationStatus;
    }

    @RequestMapping(value = "{orderId}", method = RequestMethod.DELETE)
    @ResponseBody
    public void cancelOrder(@PathVariable Long orderId) {

        OrderCancelCommand orderCommand = new OrderCancelCommand(orderId);
        commandGateway.send(orderCommand);
    }
}
```

The first aspect you need to note in Listing 19-18 is that the HTTP POST method createOrder is not within any kind of transaction. This is where you do the orchestration of depreciating inventory and creating a new order. This means that while the aggregate root entity operations happen within local transactions of command handler operations of OrderCommandHandler in Listing 19-16 and that of the InventoryCommandHandler in Listing 19-17, their orchestration is done without any enclosing transaction context, as shown in Listing 19-18. This means exceptions and errors can happen at (or after) any line of code (a.k.a. instructions or operations), in which case the actions done so far must be compensated back too!

Listing 19-18 shows that in Step 1 you sendAndWait as many InventoryUpdateCommands as you have line items in the Order POST request. The sendAndWait dispatches an InventoryUpdateCommand to the command gateway so that the commands will be picked up by the InventoryCommandHandler in Listing 19-17. Further, since both the OrderController and the InventoryCommandHandler are in the same microservice (or partition) and since sendAndWait is a synchronous blocking call, if sendAndWait is successful, you can be sure that the intended operations are executed with certainty. For all line items for which the sendAndWait is success, you keep track of them in an inventoryUpdatedList to do compensating actions later, if required. If you are able to successfully sendAndWait an InventoryUpdateCommand for all of the line items for an order, then you proceed to Step 3, where you start to create an order. In other words, you make sure enough inventory exists and you also depreciate all the required inventory before you proceed to create an order.

While you check for stock or inventory, errors can happen for any of the line items either due to non-availability of enough stock or due to some other failure. Whatever the reason, the complete Order cannot be honored in that case, so you need to compensate for any inventory changes already effected for that Order. This is marked as Step 2 in Listing 19-18.

If Step 1 is fully successful without any errors, it means you have already have enough inventory to fulfil the order, so you start executing Step 3. Here again you create an OrderCreateCommand and sendAndWait to the command gateway. The OrderCommandHandler in Listing 19-16 that handles new order creation is again in the same microservice, so a successful sendAndWait is deterministic enough to assume that order creation is successful. An exception at this stage also means you need to compensate for any inventory changes already effected for that order. This is marked as Step 4 in Listing 19-18.

This is an example of a BASE transaction; however, the overall transaction is not fail safe. What that means is if a microservice crash happens while the createOrder HTTP REST POST method is getting executed, the rest of the instructions within the createOrder will not be executed; there is every chance for the following state to happen:

- Inventory corresponding to line items of an order gets updated; however, the order is not created and inventory is not reinstated.

- Inventory corresponding to all line items of an order gets updated; however, the order is not created and inventory is not reinstated.

- Inventory corresponding to all line items of an order gets updated; however, the order is not created and inventory corresponding to few line items alone gets reinstated.

The system may not become eventually consistent, since the "gravitational force" required to bring back the system to an eventually consistent state disappeared with the microservice crash! To make it clear, the essential state required to bring the system back to a semantically consistent state is lost since you have not made the microservice stack state persistent.

Partitioning the Order and Inventory Domains into Separate Microservices

You saw that the handleNewOrder processing in the OrderCommandHandler shown in Listing 19-12 is equivalent to an ACID-style operation over the order and inventory entities. However, in the refactoring you have done in this chapter, you transitioned the code to the createOrder HTTP POST method in the OrderController shown in Listing 19-18. The processing here is equivalent to BASE style but without any inherent failover characteristics. Having adopted a BASE style transaction across order and inventory aggregate root entities, the order and inventory domains have now become first class citizens to be domain-independent of each other, so they can be separated out into their own microservices too if required.

You won't implement the refactoring shown in Figure 19-2 here. Instead, it's an exercise for later. The next subsection will provide more hints for doing so.

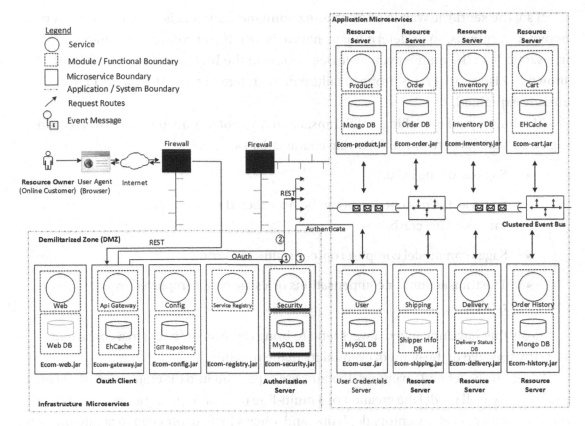

Figure 19-2. *Microservices e-commerce architecture refactored for Axon 3*

Sagas for Deterministic Eventual Consistency

Having adopted a BASE-style transaction across the order and inventory aggregate root entities, the order and inventory domains can now become separate microservices. However, there is a catch! The moment you separate the order and inventory domain into separate microservices, the following are no more collocated:

- OrderCommandHandler, shown in Listing 19-16

- InventoryCommandHandler, shown in Listing 19-17

- OrderController, shown in Listing 19-18

If so, the sendAndWait to one or more command handlers is to be executed across network partitions, so its deterministic nature is lost. If you continue to model BASE transactions in the manner you have been doing in the InventoryCommandHandler shown in Listing 19-17, it's prone to failure in the range of more than what I have already explained.

Manual ways of modelling BASE transactions are not a good idea here. You require saga transactions here due to following characteristics:

- Sagas are long lived.

- Sagas are persistent. Sagas can be resurrected even after a microservice crash.

- Sagas can model complex compensating scenarios.

- The transactions or compensations of a saga can be replayed or retried.

Sagas that have not ended always tend to bring the system (back) to a consistent state irrespective of the point of eventuality in the timeline.

When the order and inventory domains are separated into different microservices, you can very well model the creation of a multi-line item order using a saga. A saga can track the state of each inventory depletion and, once satisfied, proceed to create the new order and then end the saga. In this example, I have not done this since I don't want to make the demonstration overly complex, since it already has one saga.

Configure the E-Commerce Microservice Application

Follow the directions in the "Configure the E-Commerce Microservice Application" and "Set Up the Environment Infrastructure" sections in Chapter 18.

Build and Run the E-Commerce Microservice Application

Here again, you should follow the directions in the "Build and Run the Secure E-Commerce Microservice Application" section in Chapter 18.

Having looked at Axon 3, let's look at Axon 4 in the next section.

Command and Event Handling in the Same JVM Using Axon 4

In this section, you will migrate the code discussed in the "Command and Event Handling in the Same JVM" section in Chapter 12 to Axon 4. The migrated codebase is placed in folder ch19\ch19-04. You may want to refer to the Axon 4 Reference documentation[3] and the Axon 4 API documentation[4] while going through the code.

In fact, this code is a refactoring of the code you saw in the "Command and Event Handling in the Same JVM Using Axon 3" section early in this chapter. To build and execute the example, follow the instructions mentioned there with the exception that you have one additional step to do, which you may do as the first step, and that is to set up the Axon server.

The Axon server complements the Axon framework by having knowledge about the different types of messages that are being exchanged, like events sent from one service to one or many other services, commands that are sent to one service to do something, etc. You can download and expand the Axon server libraries from https://download.axoniq.io/axonserver/AxonServer.zip.

```
cd D:\binil\Study\Sites\axon\AxonQuickStart-4.0.3_2019-02-19\AxonServer
java -jar axonserver-4.0.3.jar
```

This will bring up the Axon server. Subsequently, follow the instructions mentioned in the "Command and Event Handling in the Same JVM Using Axon 3" section earlier in this chapter.

Distributed Command and Event Handling Using Axon 4

In this section, you migrate the code discussed in the "Distributed Command and Event Handling" section in Chapter 12 to Axon 4. The migrated codebase is in folder ch19\ch19-05.

---

[3]https://axoniq.io/docs/axon-4
[4]https://axoniq.io/apidocs/4.0/

In fact, this code is a refactoring of the code you saw in the "Distributed Command and Event Handling Using Axon 3" section earlier in this chapter. To build and execute the example, follow the instructions mentioned here with the exception that you have one additional step to do, which you may do as the first step, and that is to set up the Axon server.

Follow the instructions in the just previous section to bring up the Axon server. Once the Axon server is up, follow the instructions mentioned in the "Distributed Command and Event Handling Using Axon 3" section earlier in this chapter.

Summary

Every end is a new beginning. You have reached the end of this book; however, you have just started your microservices journey. You have demystified few dilemmas around architecture choices and looked into every detail of few concerns, including data consistencies, which you may come across in your everyday life while adopting the microservices architecture. I hope you have liked many parts of this book in the same way I have liked spending the time to get into the intricacies with code to explain them. I have tried to balance the amount of theory and the amount of code to give you a hands-on feel of almost all concepts explained. Last but not least, I have also attempted to cover even the latest release of the Axon CQRS framework through the current chapter. Frameworks will come and go, and specifications will keep evolving, since "change is the only constant thing." However, the architectural foundations discussed throughout the book will still be relevant and valid—at least that is what I have experienced in my 25 years of an IT career. Keep moving, and keep a fast pace.

APPENDIX A

Install, Configure, and Run MongoDB

MongoDB is an open source document database, the server of which is licensed under Free Software Foundation's GNU AGPL v3.0, which provides high performance, high availability, and automatic scaling. MongoDB is available for download from www.mongodb.com/.

You will look at the following in this section:

- An introduction to MongoDB

- How to download, install, and configure MongoDB

- How to start MongoDB Server

- How to connect to MongoDB Server

- How to execute basic operations against MongoDB Server

- How to install and use Robomongo, a UI for MongoDB

Introducing MongoDB

MongoDB is a kind of document database in the sense that a record in MongoDB is a structured document. Since the document is structured, it has a data structure composed of field and value pairs. MongoDB documents follow a structure similar to JSON (JavaScript Object Notation) objects. As values of fields, a MongoDB document may include other documents, arrays, and/or arrays of other documents.

813

© Binildas Christudas 2019
B. Christudas, *Practical Microservices Architectural Patterns*, https://doi.org/10.1007/978-1-4842-4501-9_20

The MongoDB Document

Here is a sample MongoDB document so you can understand what it looks like:

```
{
    name: "bob",
    class: 2,
    division: "B",
    subjects: ["english", "science", "maths"]
}
```

Since a MongoDB document may contain other documents and arrays of other documents, the data structure is extensible. Further, MongoDB documents are synonymous to data types in a programming language

Install and Configure MongoDB

In this section, you will download the community edition of MongoDB. You will also install and configure it and then test the installation

Download MongoDB Community Edition

MongoDB is available for download at www.mongodb.com/download-center. Detailed installation instructions are also available at https://docs.mongodb.com/manual/tutorial/install-mongodb-on-windows/. A MongoDB installation file can be found at www.mongodb.org/downloads.

You must have Windows Server 2008 R2, Windows Vista, or later to install MongoDB Community Edition. The .msi installer includes all the software dependencies required for MongoDB and will also automatically upgrade any older version of MongoDB if found installed in your machine. See Figure A-1.

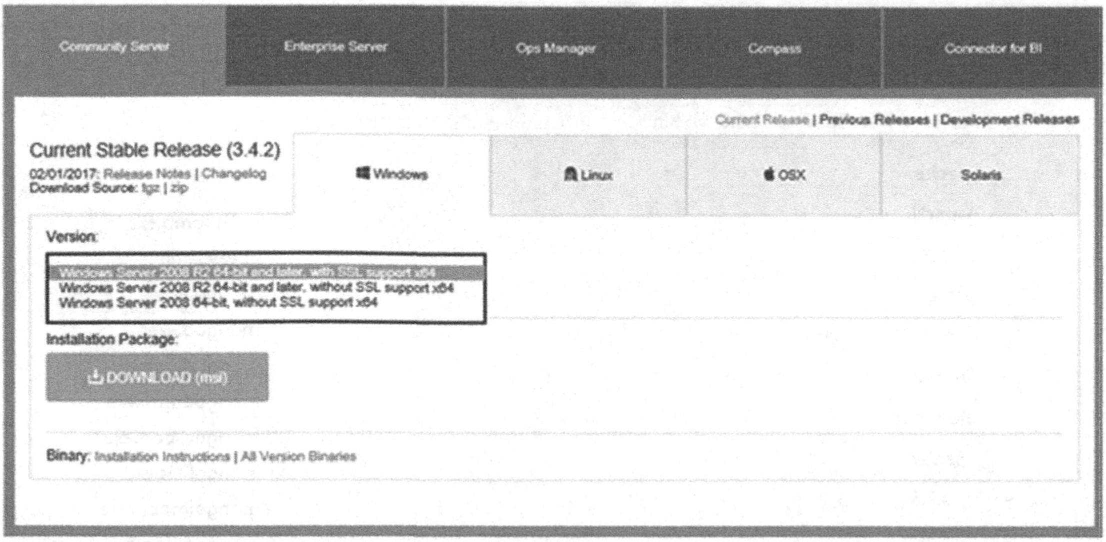

Figure A-1. *MongoDB Community Server Installable*

Install and Configure MongoDB

After you download the MongoDB installation file, locate the downloaded MongoDB .msi file in Windows Explorer, which typically is located in the default Downloads folder. Once you double-click the .msi file, a set of screens will appear to guide you through the installation process. Even though you may choose any location, like

```
C:\Program Files\MongoDB\Server\3.2\
```

I explicitly avoid a location with a space in the path, like the space in Program Files. Hence in my Windows machine, I use the following location:

```
D:\Applns\MongoDB\Server\3.2.6
```

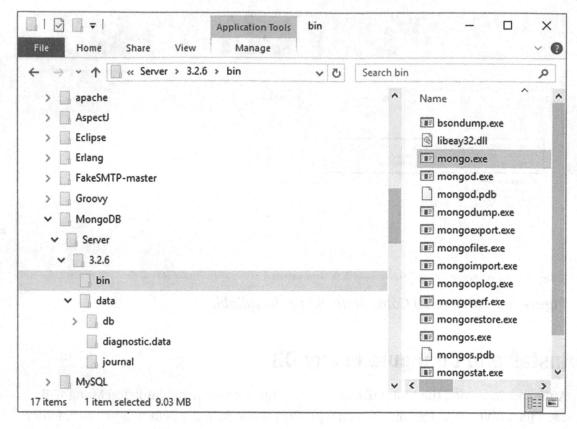

Figure A-2. *MongoDB installation folder*

MongoDB server requires a data directory to store all data (Figure A-2). You may run MongoDB from any folder you choose. MongoDB's default data directory path is the absolute path \data\db on the drive from which you start MongoDB. You can create this folder by running the following command in a Windows command prompt:

```
md D:\Applns\MongoDB\Server\3.2.6\data
```

Start Using MongoDB

In this section, you will connect to the installed MongoDB server and carry out basic data operations.

Start and Connect to MongoDB

You can now start MongoDB by using this command:

```
D:\Applns\MongoDB\Server\3.2.6\bin\mongod.exe --dbpath D:\Applns\MongoDB\
Server\3.2.6\data
```

Listing A-1 shows starting the MongoDB Server.

Listing A-1. Start MongoDB Server

```
D:\Applns\MongoDB\Server\3.2.6\bin>D:\Applns\MongoDB\Server\3.2.6\bin\
mongod.exe --dbpath D:\Applns\MongoDB\Server\3.2.6\data
2019-03-02T19:37:34.958+0530 I CONTROL  [initandlisten] MongoDB starting
: pid=7632 port=27017 dbpath=D:\Applns\MongoDB\Server\3.2.6\data 64-bit
host=tiger
2019-03-02T19:37:34.959+0530 I CONTROL  [initandlisten] targetMinOS:
Windows 7/Windows Server 2008 R2
2019-03-02T19:37:34.959+0530 I CONTROL  [initandlisten] db version v3.2.6
2019-03-02T19:37:34.959+0530 I CONTROL  [initandlisten] git version:
05552b562c7a0b3143a729aaa0838e558dc49b25
2019-03-02T19:37:34.960+0530 I CONTROL  [initandlisten] OpenSSL version:
OpenSSL 1.0.1p-fips 9 Jul 2015
2019-03-02T19:37:34.960+0530 I CONTROL  [initandlisten] allocator: tcmalloc
2019-03-02T19:37:34.960+0530 I CONTROL  [initandlisten] modules: none
2019-03-02T19:37:34.960+0530 I CONTROL  [initandlisten] build environment:
2019-03-02T19:37:34.960+0530 I CONTROL  [initandlisten]     distmod:
2008plus-ssl
2019-03-02T19:37:34.960+0530 I CONTROL  [initandlisten]     distarch: x86_64
2019-03-02T19:37:34.960+0530 I CONTROL  [initandlisten]     target_arch: x86_64
2019-03-02T19:37:34.960+0530 I CONTROL  [initandlisten] options: { storage:
{ dbPath: "D:\Applns\MongoDB\Server\3.2.6\data" } }
2019-03-02T19:37:34.967+0530 I -        [initandlisten] Detected data files
in D:\Applns\MongoDB\Server\3.2.6\data created by the 'wiredTiger' storage
engine, so setting the active storage engine to 'wiredTiger'.
```

```
2019-03-02T19:37:34.968+0530 I STORAGE  [initandlisten] wiredtiger_
open config:create,cache_size=8G,session_max=20000,eviction=(threads_
max=4),config_base=false,statistics=(fast),log=(enabled=true,archive=true,p
ath=journal,compressor=snappy),file_manager=(close_idle_time=100000),checkp
oint=(wait=60,log_size=2GB),statistics_log=(wait=0),
2019-03-02T19:37:36.552+0530 I NETWORK  [HostnameCanonicalizationWorker]
Starting hostname canonicalization worker
2019-03-02T19:37:36.552+0530 I FTDC     [initandlisten] Initializing
full-time diagnostic data capture with directory 'D:/Applns/MongoDB/
Server/3.2.6/data/diagnostic.data'
2019-03-02T19:37:36.583+0530 I NETWORK  [initandlisten] waiting for
connectionson port 27017
```

If your path includes spaces, enclose the entire path in double quotes, like so:

```
D:\Applns\MongoDB\Server\3.2.6\bin>D:\Applns\MongoDB\Server\3.2.6\bin\
mongod.exe --dbpath "D:\Path with space\MongoDB\Server\3.2.6\data"
```

You can now connect to the above started MongoDB Server using another Windows command prompt and executing the program:

```
D:\Applns\MongoDB\Server\3.2.6\bin>D:\Applns\MongoDB\Server\3.2.6\bin\mongo
```

Listing A-2 shows how to connect to the MongoDB.

Listing A-2. Connect to MongoDB Server

```
D:\Applns\MongoDB\Server\3.2.6\bin>D:\Applns\MongoDB\Server\3.2.6\bin\mongo
MongoDB shell version: 3.2.6
connecting to: test
>
```

Execute Basic Data Manipulations with MongoDB

In the Windows command prompt where the mongo shell is connected to a running mongod instance, you can query the currently connected database using this command:

```
db.getName()
```

This command will show all databases:

```
showdbs
```

You can switch to the test database using this command:

```
use test
```

You can then list all the collections available in the current database using this command:

```
show collections
```

Listing A-3 shows how to connect to a specific database in MongoDB.

Listing A-3. Select a Database in MongoDB

```
D:\Applns\MongoDB\Server\3.2.6\bin>D:\Applns\MongoDB\Server\3.2.6\bin\mongo
MongoDB shell version: 3.2.6
connecting to: test
> db.getName()
test
> use test
switched to db test
> show collections
product
productCategory
>
```

You can insert a new document into the students collection using this command:

```
db.students.insert(
    {
        name: "bob",
        class: 2,
        division: "B",
        subjects: ["english", "science", "maths"]
    }
)
```

You can query the just inserted document from the students collection using this command (see also Listing A-4):

```
db.students.find()
```

Listing A-4. Insert Documents into MongoDB Collections and Query

```
> db.students.insert(
... {
... name: "bob",
... class: 2,
... division: "B",
... subjects: ["english", "science", "maths"]
... }
... )
WriteResult({ "nInserted" : 1 })
> db.students.find()
{ "_id" : ObjectId("5c7a9071f2a95d2c70e35476"), "name" : "bob", "class" :
2, "di
vision" : "B", "subjects" : [ "english", "science", "maths" ] }
>
```

You may now update the just inserted document with the name field having a value of bob in the students collection using this command:

```
db.students.update(
        { "name" : "bob" },
        {
        $set: { "division": "C" }
        }
)
```

You can query the just updated document using this command:

```
db.students.find()
```

Listing A-5 shows how to update a document in a collection in MongoDB.

Listing A-5. Update Documents in MongoDB Collections

```
> db.students.update(
... { "name" : "bob" },
... {
... $set: { "division": "C" }
... }
... )
WriteResult({ "nMatched" : 1, "nUpserted" : 0, "nModified" : 1 })
> db.students.find()
{ "_id" : ObjectId("5c7a9071f2a95d2c70e35476"), "name" : "bob", "class" : 2, "di
vision" : "C", "subjects" : [ "english", "science", "maths" ] }
>
```

Note that the value of the division field has changed from B to C.

You may now delete the document with the name field having the value of bob in the students collection using this command (see also Listing A-6):

```
db.students.remove( { "name": "bob" } )
```

Listing A-6. Remove Documents from MongoDB Collections

```
> db.students.remove( { "name": "bob" } )
WriteResult({ "nRemoved" : 1 })
> db.students.find()
>
```

You may remove an entire collection from the database using this command (see also Listing A-7):

```
db.collection.drop()
```

Listing A-7. Remove Collections from MongoDB

```
> show collections
product
productCategory
students
> db.students.drop()
true
> show collections
product
productCategory
>
```

db.dropDatabase() will drop the database you are connected to.

Robomongo, A GUI for MongoDB

Robomongo[1] is a cross-platform MongoDB management tool that is mongo shell-centric. It embeds the actual mongo shell in a tabbed interface. It provides access to a shell command line as well as a GUI.

Download and Install Robomongo Community Edition

The Robomongo community edition is available for download at https://robomongo. org/download. See Figure A-3.

---

[1]Robomongo is now Robo 3T

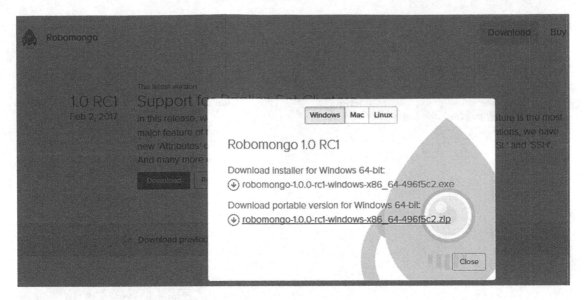

Figure A-3. *Download Robomongo*

You are advised to download the portable version for Windows 64-bit and unzip the archive again to a location of your convenience. In my machine, the location is

`D:\Applns\Robomongo\robomongo-0.9.0-rc9`

Start and Connect to MongoDB Using Robomongo

You can execute this file to bring up the GUI:

`D:\Applns\Robomongo\robomongo-0.9.0-rc9\Robomongo.exe`

Once the GUI is up, you can connect to the MongoDB server by selecting the Connect button shown in Figure A-4.

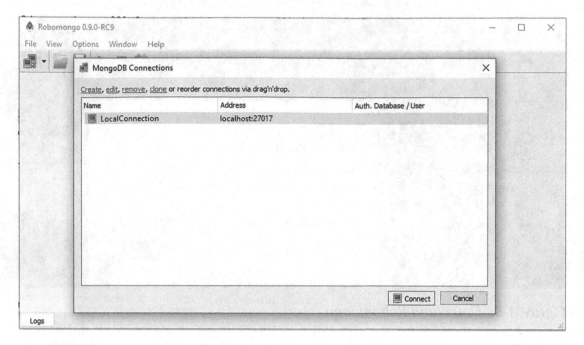

Figure A-4. *Connect to MongoDB using Robomongo*

Execute Basic Data Manipulation with MongoDB

The browser pane allows you to select the required collection in the MongoDB and a
right click provides many options to do basic data operations. See Figure A-5.

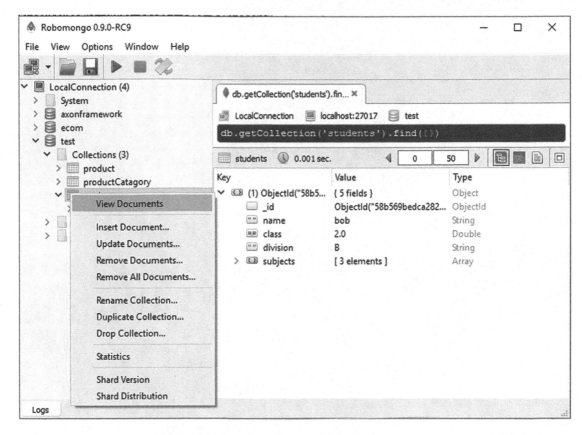

Figure A-5. *Browse MongoDB Collection using Robomongo*

Summary

This appendix walked you through installing and using MongoDB. You will be using MongoDB extensively for the samples in this book. Refer this appendix when you want to do operations against MongoDB.

APPENDIX B

Install, Configure, and Run RabbitMQ Cluster

RabbitMQ is an open source messaging middleware which can run in all major operating systems and with support of development tools for many platforms. Being a message broker, it allows you to send and receive messages, and your messages can be kept in a safe place to live until received by the consumer. RabbitMQ is available for download from www.rabbitmq.com/.

You will explore the following in this appendix:

- How to download and install Erlang, a prerequisite to installing RabbitMQ

- How to install and start RabbitMQ Server

- How to enable RabbitMQ management plugins and view the RabbitMQ management console

- How to set up a RabbitMQ cluster with two nodes

- How to shut down and bring up individual nodes in a RabbitMQ cluster

Introducing RabbitMQ

The main distinguishing feature of message brokers is the ability to decouple the message producers from the message consumers. As such, producers and consumers can publish and consume messages at their own pace and convenience. Some of the features of RabbitMQ are

© Binildas Christudas 2019
B. Christudas, *Practical Microservices Architectural Patterns*, https://doi.org/10.1007/978-1-4842-4501-9_21

- **Reliability:** RabbitMQ trades off performance with reliability. The reliability features include but are not limited to message persistence, delivery acknowledgements, publisher confirms, and high availability.

- **Routing:** RabbitMQ routes messages through exchanges before arriving at queues. Several built-in exchange types are available for typical routing logic. You can also bind exchanges together or even write your own exchange type as plugins for more complex routing.

Set Up RabbitMQ

In this section, you will download and install Erlang and install and configure RabbitMQ and test the installation.

Download and Install Erlang

Erlang is a programming language typically used for building massively real-time and highly available systems. Erlang's runtime has built-in support for concurrency, distribution, and fault tolerance. RabbitMQ requires Erlang to be available in the machine, so you will install Erlang and set it up in this section.

Erlang is available for download at `www.erlang.org/downloads`.

Run the Erlang installation file. Even though you may choose any location, like

```
C:\Program Files\erlx.x.x\
```

I explicitly avoid a location with a space in the path, like the space in `Program Files`. Hence in my Windows machine, I use the following location:

```
D:\Applns\Erlang\erl8.0-otp_win64_19.0
```

Set `ERLANG_HOME` to the location where you actually put your Erlang installation. It's `D:\Applns\Erlang\erl8.0-otp_win64_19.0\erl8.0` in my machine. The RabbitMQ startup files expect to execute `%ERLANG_HOME%\bin\erl.exe`:

```
set ERLANG_HOME=D:\Applns\Erlang\erl8.0-otp_win64_19.0\erl8.0
```

Install and Configure RabbitMQ

RabbitMQ is available for download at www.rabbitmq.com/download.html. Detailed installation instructions are also available at www.rabbitmq.com/install-windows-manual.html.

Download the RabbitMQ installation file named rabbitmq-server-windows-- 3.6.9.zip. From the zip file, extract the folder named rabbitmq_server-3.6.9 into C:\ Program Files\RabbitMQ (or somewhere suitable for application files).

I explicitly avoid a location with a space in the path, like the space in Program Files. Hence in my Windows machine, I use the following location:

D:\Applns\RabbitMQ\rabbitmq_server-3.6.9

By default, the RabbitMQ logs and Mnesia database are stored in the user's application data directory, which is C:\Users\binil\AppData\Roaming\RabbitMQ in my machine.

If you have to run RabbitMQ as a manually installed Windows Service, you need to synchronize the Erlang cookies, too; in other words, the Erlang security cookies used by the service account and the user running rabbitmqctl.bat must be synchronized for rabbitmqctl.bat to function. This can be done by ensuring that the Erlang cookie files contain the same string. To do this, copy the .erlang.cookie file from the Windows directory (C:\WINDOWS\.erlang.cookie in my machine) and replace the user's .erlang. cookie, which can be found in the user's home directory (C:\Users\binil\.erlang. cookie in my machine).

Start Using RabbitMQ

In this section, you will start and connect to the installed RabbitMQ server and carry out basic data operations.

Enable Management Plugin

The Rabbitmq-management plugin exposes an HTTP-based API for management and monitoring of the RabbitMQ server. It also includes a browser-based UI utility by which basic management can be done. You need to first enable the management plugin that is included in the RabbitMQ distribution:

```
D:\Applns\RabbitMQ\rabbitmq_server-3.6.3\sbin>D:\Applns\RabbitMQ\rabbitmq_
server-3.6.3\sbin\rabbitmq-plugins enable rabbitmq_management
```

After starting the RabbitMQ (explained in next section), you can view the Web UI at the default URL of `http://server-name:15672/`.

Start RabbitMQ Server

You can now start RabbitMQ Server by using this command:

```
D:\Applns\RabbitMQ\rabbitmq_server-3.6.3\sbin>D:\Applns\RabbitMQ\rabbitmq_
server-3.6.3\sbin\rabbitmq-server.bat
```

Listing B-1 shows the results.

Listing B-1. Start RabbitMQ Server

```
D:\Applns\RabbitMQ\rabbitmq_server-3.6.3\sbin>D:\Applns\RabbitMQ\rabbitmq_
server-3.6.3\sbin\rabbitmq-server.bat

              RabbitMQ 3.6.3. Copyright (C) 2007-2016 Pivotal Software, Inc.
  ##  ##      Licensed under the MPL.  See http://www.rabbitmq.com/
  ##  ##
  ##########  Logs: C:/Users/binil/AppData/Roaming/RabbitMQ/log/RABBIT~1.LOG
  ######  ##        C:/Users/binil/AppData/Roaming/RabbitMQ/log/RABBIT~2.LOG
  ##########
              Starting broker...
 completed with 6 plugins.
```

View RabbitMQ Management Console

You can now connect to the above started RabbitMQ server using your favorite web browser and view the RabbitMQ management console (see Figure B-1):

http://127.0.0.1:15672

Figure B-1. RabbitMQ management console login

You can log in to the management console using the default credentials

Username: guest
Password: guest

See Figure B-2.

Figure B-2. *RabbitMQ management console*

Set Up a RabbitMQ Cluster

A RabbitMQ cluster is a grouping of one or several Erlang nodes, with each node running the RabbitMQ application instance and sharing users, virtual hosts, queues, exchanges, bindings, and other runtime parameters.

Configure RabbitMQ Cluster

Explained here is how to set up a two-node RabbitMQ cluster quickly. You may want to create two scripts in the sbin folder of your RabbitMQ installation, as shown:

```
D:\Applns\RabbitMQ\rabbitmq_server-3.6.3\sbin\rabbitmq-server1.bat
D:\Applns\RabbitMQ\rabbitmq_server-3.6.3\sbin\rabbitmq-server2.bat
```

The contents of each are as follows:

```
D:\Applns\RabbitMQ\rabbitmq_server-3.6.3\sbin\rabbitmq-server1.bat
set RABBITMQ_NODE_PORT=5672
set RABBITMQ_NODENAME=rabbit1
set RABBITMQ_SERVICE_NAME=rabbit1
set RABBITMQ_SERVER_START_ARGS=-rabbitmq_management listener [{port,15672}]
REM rabbitmq-server -detached
rabbitmq-server
```

The above script will bring up a RabbitMQ instance with a node named rabbit1. The following script will bring up a RabbitMQ instance with a node named rabbit2:

```
D:\Applns\RabbitMQ\rabbitmq_server-3.6.3\sbin\rabbitmq-server2.bat
set RABBITMQ_NODE_PORT=5673
set RABBITMQ_NODENAME=rabbit2
set RABBITMQ_SERVICE_NAME=rabbit2
set RABBITMQ_SERVER_START_ARGS=-rabbitmq_management listener [{port,15673}]
REM call rabbitmq-server -detached
rabbitmq-server
```

You now want to stop rabbit2, ask it to join it into a cluster with the other running node, rabbit1, and then restart rabbit2. The following script will do exactly this:

```
D:\Applns\RabbitMQ\rabbitmq_server-3.6.3\sbin\rabbitmq-cluster2.bat
call rabbitmqctl -n rabbit2 stop_app
call rabbitmqctl -n rabbit2 join_cluster rabbit1@tiger
call rabbitmqctl -n rabbit2 start_app
call rabbitmqctl -n rabbit1 set_policy ha-all "^.*" "{""ha-mode"":""all""}"
```

Note   You may want to replace the hostname, which is `tiger` in the above scripts, with the name of your host.

Bring Up the RabbitMQ Cluster

Assuming you have only created the required scripts mentioned in the previous section, and have not started any server yet, you can now bring up the RabbitMQ cluster by executing following commands in the same order in separate command windows:

```
cd D:\Applns\RabbitMQ\rabbitmq_server-3.6.3\sbin
D:\Applns\RabbitMQ\rabbitmq_server-3.6.3\sbin>rabbitmq-server1
```

Listing B-2 shows the results.

Listing B-2. Start Node 1 of RabbitMQ Cluster

```
D:\Applns\RabbitMQ\rabbitmq_server-3.6.3\sbin>rabbitmq-server1

D:\Applns\RabbitMQ\rabbitmq_server-3.6.3\sbin>set RABBITMQ_NODE_PORT=5672

D:\Applns\RabbitMQ\rabbitmq_server-3.6.3\sbin>set RABBITMQ_NODENAME=rabbit1

D:\Applns\RabbitMQ\rabbitmq_server-3.6.3\sbin>set RABBITMQ_SERVICE_NAME=rabbit1

D:\Applns\RabbitMQ\rabbitmq_server-3.6.3\sbin>set RABBITMQ_SERVER_START_
ARGS=-rabbitmq_management listener [{port,15672}]

D:\Applns\RabbitMQ\rabbitmq_server-3.6.3\sbin>REM rabbitmq-server -detached

D:\Applns\RabbitMQ\rabbitmq_server-3.6.3\sbin>rabbitmq-server

              RabbitMQ 3.6.3. Copyright (C) 2007-2016 Pivotal Software, Inc.
  ##  ##      Licensed under the MPL.  See http://www.rabbitmq.com/
  ##  ##
  ##########  Logs: C:/Users/binil/AppData/Roaming/RabbitMQ/log/rabbit1.log
  ######  ##        C:/Users/binil/AppData/Roaming/RabbitMQ/log/RABBIT~3.
LOG
  ##########
              Starting broker...
 completed with 6 plugins.
```

The management console to instance with name rabbit1 can be viewed pointing your browser to http://127.0.0.1:15672/. See Figure B-3.

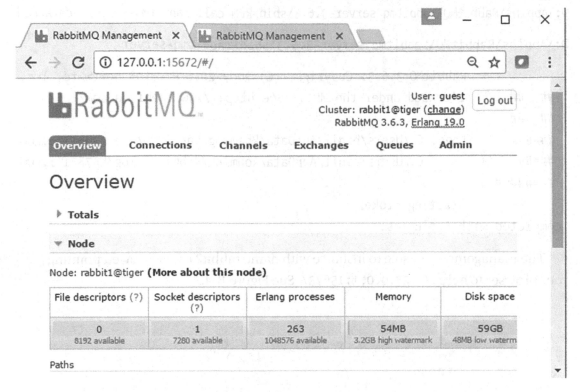

Figure B-3. *Management console for node 1 of RabbitMQ*

In another command window, execute following commands:

```
cd D:\Applns\RabbitMQ\rabbitmq_server-3.6.3\sbin
D:\Applns\RabbitMQ\rabbitmq_server-3.6.3\sbin>rabbitmq-server2
```

Listing B 3 shows the results.

Listing B-3. Start Node 2 of RabbitMQ Cluster

```
D:\Applns\RabbitMQ\rabbitmq_server-3.6.3\sbin>rabbitmq-server2

D:\Applns\RabbitMQ\rabbitmq_server-3.6.3\sbin>set RABBITMQ_NODE_PORT=5673

D:\Applns\RabbitMQ\rabbitmq_server-3.6.3\sbin>set RABBITMQ_NODENAME=rabbit2

D:\Applns\RabbitMQ\rabbitmq_server-3.6.3\sbin>set RABBITMQ_SERVICE_NAME=rabbit2

D:\Applns\RabbitMQ\rabbitmq_server-3.6.3\sbin>set RABBITMQ_SERVER_START_
ARGS=-rabbitmq_management listener [{port,15673}]
```

835

D:\Applns\RabbitMQ\rabbitmq_server-3.6.3\sbin>REM call rabbitmq-server -detached

D:\Applns\RabbitMQ\rabbitmq_server-3.6.3\sbin>rabbitmq-server

```
              RabbitMQ 3.6.3. Copyright (C) 2007-2016 Pivotal Software, Inc.
  ##  ##      Licensed under the MPL.  See http://www.rabbitmq.com/
  ##  ##
##########    Logs: C:/Users/binil/AppData/Roaming/RabbitMQ/log/RABBIT~4.LOG
######  ##          C:/Users/binil/AppData/Roaming/RabbitMQ/log/RA7871~1.LOG
##########
              Starting broker...
completed with 6 plugins.
```

The management console to instance with name rabbit2 can be viewed pointing your browser to http://127.0.0.1:15673/. See Figure B-4.

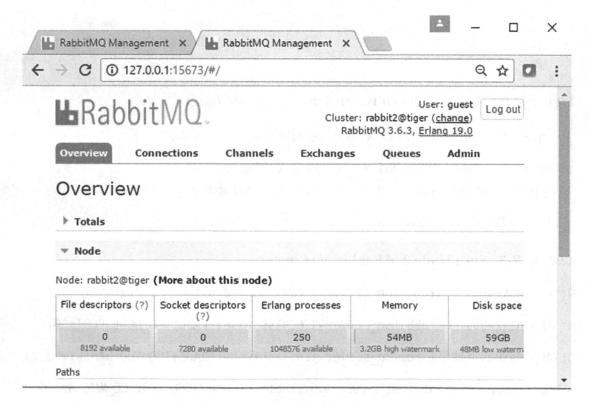

Figure B-4. *Management console for node 2 of RabbitMQ*

Note that the data required by these instances are created in my machine in the path
`C:\Users\binil\AppData\Roaming\RabbitMQ\db`. See Figure B-5.

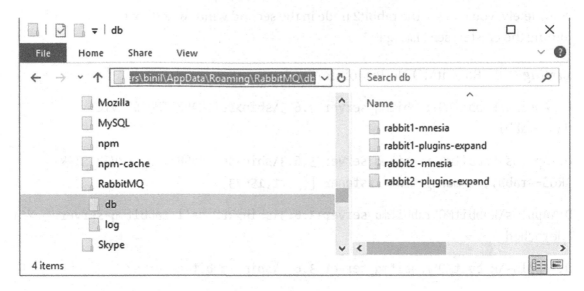

Figure B-5. *RabbitMQ instances data folder*

You now need to ask rabbit2 to join rabbit1 in a cluster mode. For this, execute the
following script in a third command window:

```
cd D:\Applns\RabbitMQ\rabbitmq_server-3.6.3\sbin
D:\Applns\RabbitMQ\rabbitmq_server-3.6.3\sbin>rabbitmq-cluster2
```

Listing B-4 shows the results.

Listing B-4. Creating a Two-Node RabbitMQ Cluster

```
D:\Applns\RabbitMQ\rabbitmq_server-3.6.3\sbin>rabbitmq-cluster2

D:\Applns\RabbitMQ\rabbitmq_server-3.6.3\sbin>call rabbitmqctl -n rabbit2
stop_app
Stopping node rabbit2@tiger ...
Clustering node rabbit2@tiger with rabbit1@tiger ...
Starting node rabbit2@tiger ...
Setting policy "ha-all" for pattern "^^.*" to "{\"ha-mode\":\"all\"}" with
priority "0" ...
```

D:\Applns\RabbitMQ\rabbitmq_server-3.6.3\sbin>

Once you have finished the execution of the `rabbitmq-cluster2` command completely, you can see the rabbit2 node in the second window getting restarted and joining the cluster; see Listing B-5.

Listing B-5. RabbitMQ Nodes Joining a Cluster

```
D:\Applns\RabbitMQ\rabbitmq_server-3.6.3\sbin>set RABBITMQ_SERVICE_
NAME=rabbit2

D:\Applns\RabbitMQ\rabbitmq_server-3.6.3\sbin>set RABBITMQ_SERVER_START_
ARGS=-rabbitmq_management listener [{port,15673}]

D:\Applns\RabbitMQ\rabbitmq_server-3.6.3\sbin>REM call rabbitmq-server
-detached

D:\Applns\RabbitMQ\rabbitmq_server-3.6.3\sbin>rabbitmq-server

              RabbitMQ 3.6.3. Copyright (C) 2007-2016 Pivotal Software, Inc.
  ##  ##      Licensed under the MPL.  See http://www.rabbitmq.com/
  ##  ##
  ##########  Logs: C:/Users/binil/AppData/Roaming/RabbitMQ/log/RABBIT~4.LOG
  ######  ##        C:/Users/binil/AppData/Roaming/RabbitMQ/log/RA7871~1.LOG
  ##########
              Starting broker...
 completed with 6 plugins.

              RabbitMQ 3.6.3. Copyright (C) 2007-2016 Pivotal Software, Inc.
  ##  ##      Licensed under the MPL.  See http://www.rabbitmq.com/
  ##  ##
  ##########  Logs: C:/Users/binil/AppData/Roaming/RabbitMQ/log/RABBIT~4.LOG
  ######  ##        C:/Users/binil/AppData/Roaming/RabbitMQ/log/RA7871~1.LOG
  ##########
              Starting broker...
 completed with 6 plugins.
```

Once you see the above, the cluster is ready and you can open the management consoles to both nodes and verify that they have joined as active participants of a cluster.

The management console of the instance named rabbit1 can be viewed by pointing your browser to http://127.0.0.1:15672/. See Figure B-6.

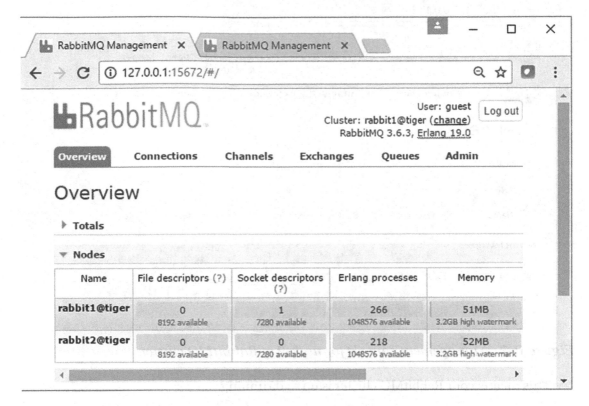

Figure B-6. *Management console for node 1 of RabbitMQ cluster*

You may also open the management console of the instance named rabbit2 by pointing your browser to http://127.0.0.1:15673/. See Figure B-7.

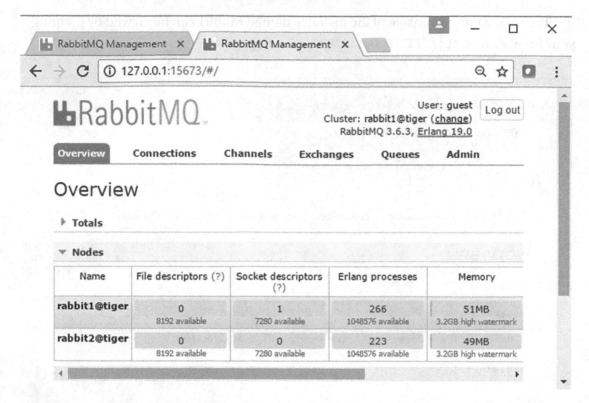

Figure B-7. Management console for node 2 of RabbitMQ cluster

This means your RabbitMQ cluster is up and running.

Restart a RabbitMQ Cluster

When the entire cluster is brought down, the last node to go down must be the first node to be brought online. If this doesn't happen, the nodes will wait 30 seconds for the last disc node to come back online, and fail afterwards. You may refer to RabbitMQ documentation online for further details.

To restart a node (rabbit2) in your cluster, you can use the script named rabbitmq-cluster2.bat, which you have already seen. To restart rabbit1, use rabbitmq-cluster1.bat:

```
D:\Applns\RabbitMQ\rabbitmq_server-3.6.3\sbin\rabbitmq-cluster1.bat
call rabbitmqctl -n rabbit1 stop_app
call rabbitmqctl -n rabbit1 join_cluster rabbit2@tiger
call rabbitmqctl -n rabbit1 start_app
call rabbitmqctl -n rabbit2 set_policy ha-all "^.*" "{""ha-mode"":""all""}"
```

If you mess up with things while you start and restart your clusters, you may want to go to the data folder of RabbitMQ and delete everything and then retry starting and restarting instances and clusters in the right order.

Connect to a RabbitMQ Cluster from a Client

A client can connect to any single node within a cluster. In the event that this node fails and the rest of the cluster survives, then the client should notice the closed connection and should explicitly reconnect to some surviving member of the cluster. I don't advise baking in hostnames or IP addresses into client applications, since this is an inflexible approach. Instead, the recommended approach is to adopt any of the below abstractions:

- Use a dynamic DNS service which has a very short TTL configuration.

- Use a plain TCP load balancer.

- Use some sort of mobile IP achieved with a pacemaker or similar technology.

Refer to Appendix C where I explain how to set up a TCP load balancer with Nginx. If you use such a TCP load balancer in between your RabbitMQ cluster and the client program, in the event that one of the nodes in the cluster fails and the rest of the cluster survives, then the client needn't notice the closed connection and will be routed to any surviving member of the cluster implicitly.

Summary

RabbitMQ is a reliable and persistent message queue server which can be configured in High Availability mode with multiple nodes in a cluster. I use RabbitMQ for many code demonstrations in this book. In some of the code demonstrations, I use RabbitMQ only as a single-node server; however, in all those scenarios RabbitMQ can be configured in a cluster to test the samples.

APPENDIX C

Install, Configure, and Run Nginx Reverse Proxy

Nginx is an HTTP and reverse proxy server which can also play as a mail proxy server or as a generic TCP/UDP proxy server. Basic HTTP server features include serving static and index files. Nginx also supports keep-alive and pipelined connections. TCP/UDP proxy server features include generic proxying of TCP and UDP as well as load balancing and fault tolerance. Go to `https://nginx.org` for more information.

I cover the following in this appendix:

- How to install and start using Nginx

- How to set up Nginx as an HTTP reverse proxy

- How to set up Nginx as a TCP reverse proxy

Install Nginx

In this section, you will download, install, and configure Nginx and test the installation. Nginx is available for download at `https://nginx.org/en/download.html`.

Save the installation archive file to a suitable location in your hard disk first and then extract the archive to a location of your choice. Even though you may choose any location, like

`C:\Program Files\nginx\`

I explicitly avoid a location with a space in the path, like the space in `Program Files`. Hence in my Windows machine, I use the following location:

`D:\Applns\nginx\nginx-1.10.1`

843

© Binildas Christudas 2019
B. Christudas, *Practical Microservices Architectural Patterns*, https://doi.org/10.1007/978-1-4842-4501-9_22

Start Using Nginx

You can now start Nginx Server by using the following command, shown in Figure C-1:

```
D:\Applns\nginx\nginx-1.10.1>nginx
```

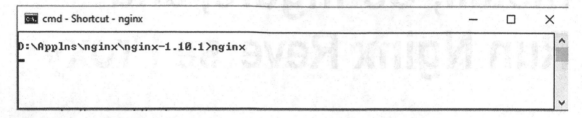

Figure C-1. *Start Nginx Server*

Once Nginx is started, it can be controlled by invoking the executable with the -s parameter, as in

```
nginx -s flag
```

where flag may be one of the following:

- Stop: Forceful shutdown

- Quit: Graceful shutdown

- Reload: Reload the configuration file

- Reopen: Reopen the log files

Start Using Nginx as Reverse Proxy

Nginx is frequently used for setting up as a reverse proxy server. When set as a reverse proxy server, Nginx receives requests, passes them to the proxied servers, retrieves responses from the proxied servers, and sends them back to the clients.

Configurations in Nginx are effected in the nginx.conf file located in the conf path.

Configure HTTP Reverse Proxy

An HTTP reverse proxy can be set up in Nginx to proxy requests with the HTTP protocol. Relevant sections in `nginx.conf` for setting up an HTTP proxy are shown in Listing C-1.

Listing C-1. Nginx HTTP Reverse Proxy Configuration

```
http {

    upstream myapp1 {
        server localhost:8081;
        server localhost:8082;
    }

    server {
        listen        8080;
        server_name  localhost;

        location / {
            proxy_pass http://myapp1;
        }

    }

}
```

Now, an HTTP request similar to URL pattern `http://localhost:8080` will be proxied to both of the following URLs in a load-balanced fashion:

```
http://localhost:8081
http://localhost:8082
```

Configure TCP Reverse Proxy

A TCP reverse proxy can be set up in Nginx to proxy requests with the TCP protocol. Relevant sections in `nginx.conf` for setting up a TCP proxy are shown in Listing C-2.

Listing C-2. *Nginx TCP Reverse Proxy Configuration*

```
stream {

    upstream myapp1 {
        server localhost:5672;
        server localhost:5673;
    }

    server {
        listen      5671;

        proxy_pass myapp1;
    }
}
```

Summary

The reverse proxy setup of Nginx can be really useful in load balancing external requests to microservices. Hence I use Nginx to demonstrate many scenarios in this book.

APPENDIX D

cURL and Postman

cURL is a command line tool for getting or sending files using the URL syntax. cURL supports a range of common Internet protocols like HTTP, HTTPS, FTP, FTPS, SCP, SFTP, TFTP, and LDAP, out of which HTTP is of interest for our discussions in this book.

Postman is a UI-based app that can be used to carry out all HTTP actions in an easier manner. I will introduce this app, too.

The "Performing Data Operations Using Spring Boot and MongoDB" section in Chapter 7 introduced a sample Spring Boot application. You used Spring Data REST there to create implementations of the MongoDB repository interface automatically. Then Spring Boot directed Spring MVC to create RESTful endpoints at /`products` and /`categories`. I will assume that this sample is built and is up and running so that you can perform the basic operations of cURL and Postman using this sample.

I will cover the following in this appendix:

- How to use cURL for HTTP operations

- How to use Postman for HTTP operations

cURL Operations for HTTP

Basic cURL operations involve typing `curl` at the command line, followed by the URL of the output to retrieve. For example, to retrieve the `microservices.io` homepage, type

```
curl www.microservices.io
```

cURL defaults to displaying the output it retrieves from the URL to the standard output specified on the system, normally the terminal window (in Mac). So running the above command will, on most systems, display the `www.microservices.io` source-code web page in the terminal window.

© Binildas Christudas 2019
B. Christudas, *Practical Microservices Architectural Patterns*, https://doi.org/10.1007/978-1-4842-4501-9_23

HTTP GET to Retrieve an Entity

You can use cURL to get a first glimpse of what the server's API endpoint has to offer by issuing the command shown in Listing D-1.

Listing D-1. HTTP GET using cURL

```
binils-MacBook-Pro:~ mike$ curl http://localhost:8080
{
    "_links": {
        "categories": {
            "href": "http://localhost:8080/categories{?page,size,sort}",
            "templated": true
        },
        "products": {
            "href": "http://localhost:8080/products{?page,size,sort}",
            "templated": true
        },
        "profile": {
            "href": "http://localhost:8080/profile"
        }
    }
}
```

The response says there is a products link located at http://localhost:8080/ products. It has some options such as ?page, ?size, and ?sort. You can check other URLs like

```
binils-MacBook-Pro:~ mike$ curl http://localhost:8080/ profile
binils-MacBook-Pro:~ mike$ curl http://localhost:8080/products/search
```

If there is corresponding data available in the backing database, you can also fire custom queries similar to

```
binils-MacBook-Pro:~ mike$ curl http://localhost:8080/products/search/findB
yProductCategoryName?productCategory=Mobile
```

HTTP POST to Create an Entity

You can now create a few product instances, as shown in Listing D-2.

Listing D-2. HTTP POST using cURL

```
binils-MacBook-Pro:~ mike$ curl -i -X POST -H "Content-Type:application/
json" -d '{"name":"Giomi", "code":"GIOME-KL", "title":"Giome 10 inch gold",
"imgUrl":"giome.jpg", "price":11000.0, "productCategoryName":"Mobile"}'
http://localhost:8080/products
HTTP/1.1 201
Location: http://localhost:8080/products/595ce0f073ed92061ca85665
Content-Type: application/hal+json;charset=UTF-8
Transfer-Encoding: chunked
Date: Wed, 05 Jul 2017 12:52:00 GMT

{
  "name" : "Giomi",
  "code" : "GIOME-KL",
  "title" : "Giome 10 inch gold",
  "description" : null,
  "imgUrl" : "giome.jpg",
  "price" : 11000.0,
  "productCategoryName" : "Mobile",
  "_links" : {
    "self" : {
      "href" : "http://localhost:8080/products/595ce0f073ed92061ca85665"
    },
    "product" : {
      "href" : "http://localhost:8080/products/595ce0f073ed92061ca85665"
    }
  }
}
```

Here

- `-i` instructs that you need to see the response message including the headers. The URI of the newly created person is also shown.

- `-X POST` signals that this is a POST used to create a new entry.

- `-H "Content-Type:application/json"` hints at the content type, so the application expects the payload to contain a JSON object.

- `-d '{"name":"Giomi", "code":"GIOME-KL", "title":"Giome 10 inch gold", "imgUrl":"giome.jpg", "price":11000.0, "productCategoryName":"Mobile"}'` is the data being sent, in JSON format in this case.

If you run into trouble when you copy these commands cross platform (from Windows to Linux or Mac, etc.), you may want to carefully type them manually into the terminal window directly. Also note that the entity ID, 595c937473ed9208488808b5, is auto-created and returned by the system. Using this same ID, you can now use the `curl` command to retrieve the above newly created entity, as shown in Listing D-3.

Listing D-3. Using cURL to View the Effect of HTTP POST

```
binils-MacBook-Pro:~ mike$ curl http://localhost:8080/products/595ce0f073ed
92061ca85665
{
  "name" : "Giomi",
  "code" : "GIOME-KL",
  "title" : "Giome 10 inch gold",
  "description" : null,
  "imgUrl" : "giome.jpg",
  "price" : 11000.0,
  "productCategoryName" : "Mobile",
  "_links" : {
    "self" : {
      "href" : "http://localhost:8080/products/595ce0f073ed92061ca85665"
    },
    "product" : {
```

```
      "href" : "http://localhost:8080/products/595ce0f073ed92061ca85665"
    }
  }
}
```

HTTP PUT to Replace an Entity

If you wish to replace an entire group, use HTTP PUT. The server may opt to create a new group and throw the old one out, so the ids may remain the same. But the client should assume that he gets an entirely new item, based on the server's response.

In the case of a PUT request, the client should always send the entire resource, having all the data that is needed to create a new item, as shown in Listing D-4.

Listing D-4. HTTP PUT Using cURL

```
binils-MacBook-Pro:~ mike$ curl -i -X PUT -H "Content-Type:application/
json" -d '{"name":"Giomi-New", "code":"GIOME-KL-NEW", "title":"Giome New 10
inch gold", "imgUrl":"giomenew.jpg", "price":15000.0, "productCategoryName"
:"Mobile"}' http://localhost:8080/products/595ce0f073ed92061ca85665
HTTP/1.1 200
Location: http://localhost:8080/products/595ce0f073ed92061ca85665
Content-Type: application/hal+json;charset=UTF-8
Transfer-Encoding: chunked
Date: Wed, 05 Jul 2017 12:53:27 GMT

{
  "name" : "Giomi-New",
  "code" : "GIOME-KL-NEW",
  "title" : "Giome New 10 inch gold",
  "description" : null,
  "imgUrl" : "giomenew.jpg",
  "price" : 15000.0,
  "productCategoryName" : "Mobile",
  "_links" : {
    "self" : {
      "href" : "http://localhost:8080/products/595ce0f073ed92061ca85665"
    },
```

```
      "product" : {
        "href" : "http://localhost:8080/products/595ce0f073ed92061ca85665"
      }
    }
}
```

You may query and see the changes you made just now via the code in Listing D-5.

Listing D-5. Using cURL to View the Effect of HTTP PUT

```
binils-MacBook-Pro:~ mike$ curl http://localhost:8080/products
{
  "_embedded" : {
    "products" : [ {
      "name" : "Giomi-New",
      "code" : "GIOME-KL-NEW",
      "title" : "Giome New 10 inch gold",
      "description" : null,
      "imgUrl" : "giomenew.jpg",
      "price" : 15000.0,
      "productCategoryName" : "Mobile",
      "_links" : {
        "self" : {
          "href" : "http://localhost:8080/products/595ce0f073ed92061ca85665"
        },
        "product" : {
          "href" : "http://localhost:8080/products/595ce0f073ed92061ca85665"
        }
      }
    } ]
  },
  "_links" : {
    "self" : {
      "href" : "http://localhost:8080/products{?page,size,sort}",
      "templated" : true
```

```
    },
    "profile" : {
      "href" : "http://localhost:8080/profile/products"
    },
    "search" : {
      "href" : "http://localhost:8080/products/search"
    }
  },
  "page" : {
    "size" : 20,
    "totalElements" : 1,
    "totalPages" : 1,
    "number" : 0
  }
}
```

HTTP PATCH to Modify an Entity

If you wish to update an attribute, like the status, which is an attribute of a group that can be set, use PATCH. An attribute such as status is often a good candidate to limit to a whitelist of values, but in Listing D-6 you use PATCH on the price attribute.

Listing D-6. HTTP PATCH Using cURL

```
binils-MacBook-Pro:~ mike$ curl -i -X PATCH -H "Content-Type:application/
json" -d '{"price":15000.50}' http://localhost:8080/products/595cc0f073ed92
061ca85665
HTTP/1.1 200
Content-Type: application/hal+json;charset=UTF-8
Transfer-Encoding: chunked
Date: Wed, 05 Jul 2017 12:54:49 GMT

{
  "name" : "Giomi-New",
  "code" : "GIOME-KL-NEW",
  "title" : "Giome New 10 inch gold",
  "description" : null,
```

```
  "imgUrl" : "giomenew.jpg",
  "price" : 15000.5,
  "productCategoryName" : "Mobile",
  "_links" : {
    "self" : {
      "href" : "http://localhost:8080/products/595ce0f073ed92061ca85665"
    },
    "product" : {
      "href" : "http://localhost:8080/products/595ce0f073ed92061ca85665"
    }
  }
}
```

HTTP DELETE to Delete an Entity

The same entity you can delete using the DELETE command, as shown in Listing D-7.

Listing D-7. HTTP DELETE Using cURL

```
binils-MacBook-Pro:~ mike$ curl -i -X DELETE http://localhost:8080/products
/595ce0f073ed92061ca85665
HTTP/1.1 204
Date: Wed, 05 Jul 2017 12:55:40 GMT
```

Another query will confirm that the entity is in fact deleted! See Listing D-8.

Listing D-8. Using cURL to View the Effect of HTTP PUT

```
binils-MacBook-Pro:~ mike$ curl http://localhost:8080/products
{
  "_embedded" : {
    "products" : [ ]
  },
  "_links" : {
    "self" : {
      "href" : "http://localhost:8080/products{?page,size,sort}",
      "templated" : true
```

```
    },
    "profile" : {
      "href" : "http://localhost:8080/profile/products"
    },
    "search" : {
      "href" : "http://localhost:8080/products/search"
    }
  },
  "page" : {
    "size" : 20,
    "totalElements" : 0,
    "totalPages" : 0,
    "number" : 0
  }
}
```

Postman for HTTP Operations

Postman is a Google Chrome app for interacting with HTTP APIs. It presents you with
a friendly GUI for constructing requests and reading responses. The app is available
from www.getpostman.com/. As of this writing, the Postman app is available for the Mac,
Windows, and Linux platforms.

HTTP GET Using Postman to Retrieve an Entity

Once the app is installed, you will want to test all HTTP actions against it. Here again
I refer back to Chapter 7 where I introduced a sample Spring Boot application. I also
refer to Figure 7-4, which shows the execution of the GET action on the link http://
localhost:8080/profile/products using Postman.

Summary

Both cURL and Postman are great utilities for quickly interacting with REST endpoints
and performing basic HTTP operations. You will be using them extensively while
executing the samples in this book.

APPENDIX E

Apache TCPMon

Apache TCPMon is a utility that allows traffic, especially HTTP traffic messages, to be viewed and resent. It is useful as a debug tool so you can look into what is being passed through the wire between a client and a server, or for that matter even between two microservices. It was originally part of Axis1 and now stands as an independent project. Go to `https://ws.apache.org/tcpmon/` for more information.

I cover the following in this appendix:

- How to install and start TCPMon

- How to set up TCPMon as a proxy

Install TCPMon

In this section, you will download, install, and configure TCPMon and test the installation. TCPMon is available for download at `https://ws.apache.org/tcpmon/download.cgi`.

Save the installation archive file to a suitable location on your hard disk first and then extract the archive to a location of your choice. Even though you may choose any location, like

`C:\Program Files\tcpmon\`

I explicitly avoid a location with a space in the path, like the space in `Program Files`. Hence in my Windows machine, I use the following location:

`D:\Applns\apache\TCPMon\tcpmon-1.0-bin`

© Binildas Christudas 2019

B. Christudas, *Practical Microservices Architectural Patterns*, https://doi.org/10.1007/978-1-4842-4501-9_24

Start Using TCPMon

You can bring up TCPMon by going into the build folder of the TCPMon extracted folder (shown in Figure E-1):

```
cd D:\Applns\apache\TCPMon\tcpmon-1.0-bin\build
D:\Applns\apache\TCPMon\tcpmon-1.0-bin\build>tcpmon
```

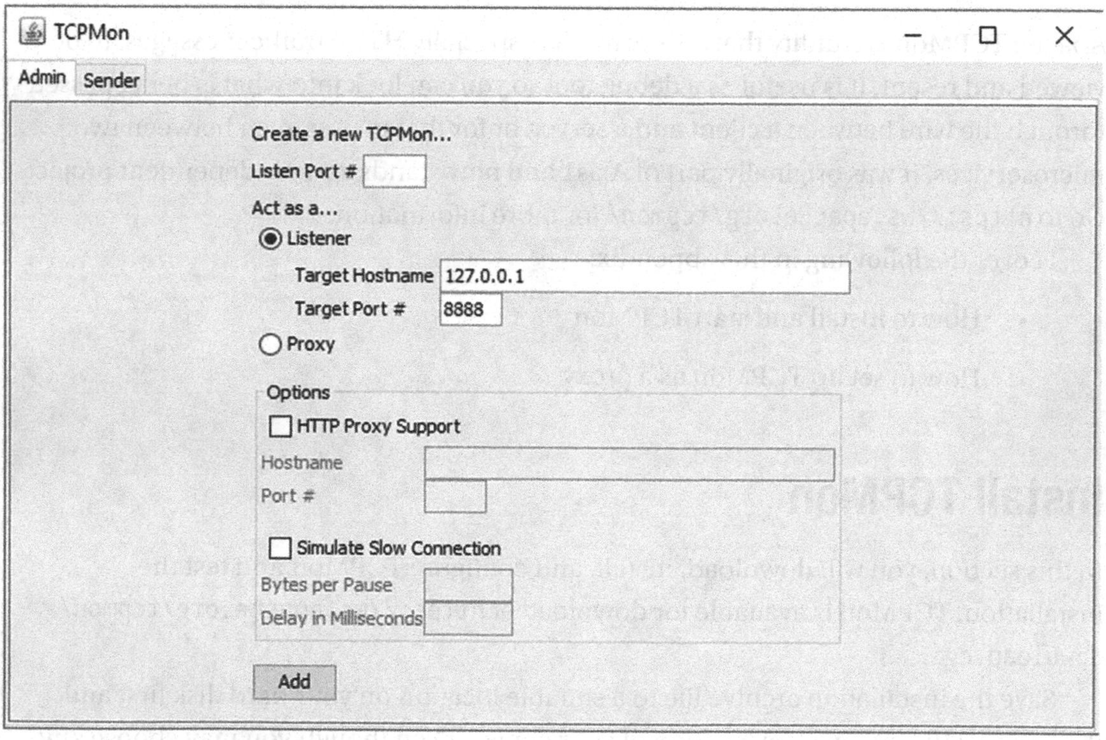

Figure E-1. *Bring up TCPMon*

Set Up TCPMon as a Proxy

TCPMon can act as a proxy. To set TCPMon in proxy mode, just select the proxy option from the radio buttons and configure the host and port towards which the calls are to be proxied.

Alternatively, you can supply the configuration parameters when you start TCPMon itself. The usage pattern is

```
D:\Applns\apache\TCPMon\tcpmon-1.0-bin\build>tcpmon [listenPort targetHost targetPort]
```

You will get the screen shown in Figure E-2 if you start like

```
D:\Applns\apache\TCPMon\tcpmon-1.0-bin\build>tcpmon 8081 127.0.0.1 8080
D:\Applns\apache\TCPMon\tcpmon-1.0-bin\build>java -cp ./tcpmon-1.0.jar org.
apache.ws.commons.tcpmon.TCPMon 8081 127.0.0.1 8080
```

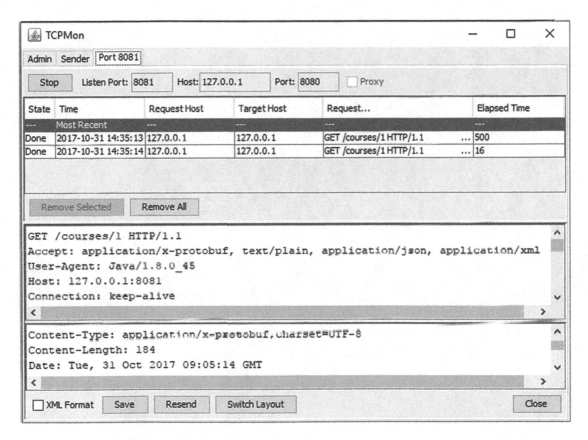

Figure E-2. *TCPMon configured as a proxy*

All requests hitting port 8081 in the host where TCPMon is running will be proxied to port 8080 in host 127.0.0.1 in the above case.

Summary

TCPMon is a nice utility to inspect HTTP requests and responses. You can install and keep it ready on your machine so that it's easy for you to quickly proxy HTTP requests and responses through TCPMon and inspect the contents of the messages.

ActiveMQ

Apache ActiveMQ is an open source messaging and integration patterns server. ActiveMQ is fast and supports many cross-language clients and protocols, and it comes with easy-to-use enterprise integration patterns and many advanced features. ActiveMQ fully supports JMS 1.1 and J2EE 1.4 and is released under the Apache 2.0 License. ActiveMQ is available for download from `http://activemq.apache.org/`.

The main distinguishing feature of ActiveMQ is its support for a variety of cross-language clients and protocols including Java, C, C++, C#, Ruby, Perl, Python, and PHP. ActiveMQ supports the following protocols, among others:

- OpenWire for high performance clients in Java, C, C++, and C#

- Stomp support so clients can be written easily in C, Ruby, Perl, Python, PHP, ActionScript/Flash, and Smalltalk to talk to ActiveMQ as well as any other popular message broker

- AMQP v1.0 support

- MQTT v3.1 support allowing for connections in an IoT environment

Install and Configure ActiveMQ

ActiveMQ is available for download at `http://activemq.apache.org/download.html`. Detailed installation instructions are also available at `http://activemq.apache.org/getting-started.html#GettingStarted-InstallationProcedureforWindows`.

Download the ActiveMQ installation file named `apache-activemq-5.13.3-bin.zip`. From the zip file, extract the folder named `apache-activemq-5.13.3` into `C:\Program Files\ActiveMQ` (or somewhere suitable for application files).

© Binildas Christudas 2019
B. Christudas, *Practical Microservices Architectural Patterns*, https://doi.org/10.1007/978-1-4842-4501-9_25

I explicitly avoid a location with a space in the path, like the space in `Program Files`. Hence in my Windows machine, I use the following location:

```
D:\Applns\apache\ActiveMQ\apache-activemq-5.13.3
```

Start Using ActiveMQ

You can start ActiveMQ Server via the following command:

```
cd D:\Applns\apache\ActiveMQ\apache-activemq-5.13.3\bin
D:\Applns\apache\ActiveMQ\apache-activemq-5.13.3\bin>activemq start
```

Listing F-1 shows ActiveMQ getting started.

Listing F-1. Start ActiveMQ Server

```
D:\Applns\apache\ActiveMQ\apache-activemq-5.13.3\bin>activemq start
Java Runtime: Oracle Corporation 1.8.0_45 D:\Applns\oracle\jdk\jdk1.8.0_45\
jre
...
ACTIVEMQ_HOME: D:\Applns\apache\ActiveMQ\apache-activemq-5.13.3\bin\..
ACTIVEMQ_BASE: D:\Applns\apache\ActiveMQ\apache-activemq-5.13.3\bin\..
ACTIVEMQ_CONF: D:\Applns\apache\ActiveMQ\apache-activemq-5.13.3\bin\..\conf
ACTIVEMQ_DATA: D:\Applns\apache\ActiveMQ\apache-activemq-5.13.3\bin\..\data
Loading message broker from: xbean:activemq.xml
 INFO | Refreshing org.apache.activemq.xbean.XBeanBrokerFactory$1@62ee68d8:
        startup date [Wed Mar 06 13:06:42 IST 2019]; root of context
        hierarchy
 INFO | Using Persistence Adapter: KahaDBPersistenceAdapter[D:\Applns\
        apache\ActiveMQ\apache-activemq-5.13.3\bin\..\data\kahadb]
 INFO | KahaDB is version 6
 INFO | Recovering from the journal @4:13937439
 INFO | Recovery replayed 28377 operations from the journal in 1.604 seconds.
 INFO | PListStore:[D:\Applns\apache\ActiveMQ\apache-activemq-5.13.3\
        bin\..\data\localhost\tmp_storage] started
 INFO | Apache ActiveMQ 5.13.3 (localhost, ID:tiger-61203-
        1551857807769-0:1) isstarting
```

```
INFO | Listening for connections at: tcp://tiger:61616?maximumConnections=
       1000&wireFormat.maxFrameSize=104857600
INFO | Connector openwire started
INFO | Listening for connections at: amqp://tiger:5672?maximumConnections=
       1000&wireFormat.maxFrameSize=104857600
INFO | Connector amqp started
INFO | Listening for connections at: stomp://tiger:61613?maximumConnection
       s=1000&wireFormat.maxFrameSize=104857600
INFO | Connector stomp started
INFO | Listening for connections at: mqtt://tiger:1883?maximumConnections=
       1000&wireFormat.maxFrameSize=104857600
INFO | Connector ws started
INFO | Apache ActiveMQ 5.13.3 (localhost,
       ID:tiger-61203-1551857807769-0:1) started
INFO | For help or more information please see: http://activemq.apache.org
INFO | No Spring WebApplicationInitializer types detected on classpath
INFO | ActiveMQ WebConsole available at http://0.0.0.0:8161/
INFO | ActiveMQ Jolokia REST API available at http://0.0.0.0:8161/api/
       jolokia/
INFO | Initializing Spring FrameworkServlet 'dispatcher'
INFO | No Spring WebApplicationInitializer types detected on classpath
INFO | jolokia-agent: Using policy access restrictor classpath:/jolokia-
       access.xml
```

Working directories get created relative to the current directory. To create the working directories in the proper place, ActiveMQ must be launched from its home/ installation directory.

ActiveMQ's server will be started in the default port, which is 61616. You may verify this by using another window to run netstat and search for port 61616. From a Windows console, type

```
netstat -an|find "61616"
```

See Listing F-2.

Listing F-2. Verify ActiveMQ Listen Port

```
Microsoft Windows [Version 10.0.17134.345]
(c) 2018 Microsoft Corporation. All rights reserved.

C:\Windows\System32>netstat -an|find "61616"
  TCP    0.0.0.0:61616          0.0.0.0:0              LISTENING
  TCP    [::]:61616             [::]:0                 LISTENING

C:\Windows\System32>
```

From a Unix command shell, type

```
netstat -nl|grep 61616
```

View ActiveMQ Management Console

You can now connect to the above started ActiveMQ Server using your favorite web browser:

```
http://127.0.0.1:8161/admin/
```

You can log into the management console using the following default credentials:

```
Username: admin
Password: admin
```

See Figure F-1.

Figure F-1. *ActiveMQ management console*

Configure ActiveMQ

ActiveMQ installation contains a file named `activemq.xml` that can be used to configure ActiveMQ server. This is typically found at `D:\Applns\apache\ActiveMQ\apache-activemq-5.13.3\conf`.

In ActiveMQ, it is not required to explicitly set up/configure the queues you are going to use in your application. When you try to publish or subscribe from any queue or topic, the respective queue or topic will be silently created on the fly. However, if for any reason you want to pre-specify queues and topics, you can do so in the configuration file. For example, do this when you want to put destinations into JNDI so that they can be pulled out by your application without needing to know the real, physical queue/topic name. Listing F-1 provides a sample configuration of a queue and Figure F-2 shows the result.

Listing F-3. Configure a Queue in ActiveMQ

```
<beans>
    <broker>
        <destinations>
            <queue physicalName="notification.queue" />
        </destinations>
    </broker>
</beans>
```

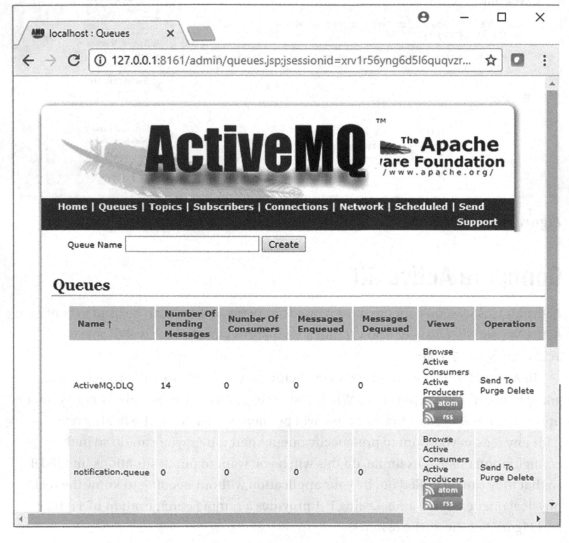

Figure F-2. *Configure ActiveMQ*

Summary

This appendix covered the basic installation and setup of Apache ActiveMQ, the open source messaging and integration patterns server. I use ActiveMQ for the samples in few chapters, so please refer this appendix while going through those samples.

APPENDIX G

Derby

Apache Derby is an open source relational database implemented entirely in Java and available under the Apache License. Derby follows Java, JDBC, and SQL standards and supports the client/server mode operation with the Derby Network Client JDBC driver and Derby Network Server. Go to `https://db.apache.org/derby/` for more information.

I will cover the following on Derby in this appendix:

- How to install and configure a Derby database

- How to start and stop Derby in Network mode

- How to creating a new database in Derby

- How to execute basic table creation and table manipulation commands in a Derby database

Install and Configure Derby

In this section, you will download, install, and configure Derby and test the installation. Derby is available for download at `https://db.apache.org/derby/derby_downloads.html`.

Since I have Java 8 on my machine, I opted for the 10.14.1.0 release of Derby, which is available at `https://db.apache.org/derby/releases/release-10.14.1.0.cgi`.

Save the installation archive file to a suitable location in your hard disk first and then extract the archive to a location of your choice. Even though you may choose any location, like

```
C:\Program Files\Derby\
```

© Binildas Christudas 2019
B. Christudas, *Practical Microservices Architectural Patterns*, https://doi.org/10.1007/978-1-4842-4501-9_26

I explicitly avoid a location with a space in the path, like the space in `Program Files`. Hence in my Windows machine, I use the following location:

`D:\Applns\apache\Derby\db-derby-10.14.1.0-bin`

Set the `DERBY_HOME` environment variable to the location where you extracted the Derby distribution. For example, if you extracted Derby to the `D:\Applns\apache\Derby\` directory, set the environment variable as

`set DERBY_HOME=D:\Applns\apache\Derby\db-derby-10.14.1.0-bin`

If you prefer, you may also add the `DERBY_HOME/bin` directory to the `PATH` environment variable so you can run the Derby scripts from any directory.

Start and Stop Derby Server in Network Mode

Applications can access a Derby database using the familiar client/server mode. This is achieved via a framework that embeds Derby and handles database requests from applications, including applications running in different JVMs on the same machine or on remote machines. The Derby Network Server embeds Derby and manages requests from network clients.

To easily start Derby Network Server, you must first change the working directory to the `bin` folder within `DERBY_HOME` (shown in Figure G-1):

`cd D:\Applns\apache\Derby\db-derby-10.14.1.0-bin`
`D:\Applns\apache\Derby\db-derby-10.14.1.0-bin\bin>startNetworkServer`

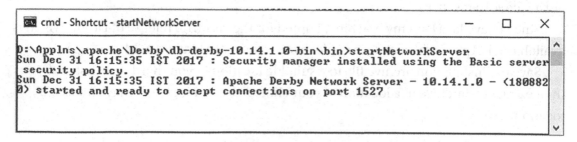

Figure G-1. *Start Derby Server in Network mode*

This will start the Network Server on port 1527 and echo a few startup messages. Further messages will continue to be output to this same window as the Network Server processes connection requests. Since the Network Server also starts Derby, you'll find the derby.log error log in the directory where you start the Network Server.

To maintain the sanity of the databases, it is always advised to properly shut down Network Servers after use. You can do this easily by the following commands:

```
cd D:\Applns\apache\Derby\db-derby-10.14.1.0-bin
D:\Applns\apache\Derby\db-derby-10.14.1.0-bin\bin>stopNetworkServer
```

Create a New Derby Database

It is always good to create and maintain your actual databases in a directory separate from the Derby installation location. In my machine, I created a parent directory to hold all my Derby databases:

```
D:\Applns\apache\Derby\derbydb
```

Change your current directory to that folder:

```
cd D:\Applns\apache\Derby\derbydb
```

You may now use the Derby embedded driver to create and connect to the sampledb database. The Derby ij tool can be used to create and then to load a Derby database. If you included the DERBY_HOME/bin directory in your PATH environment variable, type

```
ij
```

If you have not included the DERBY_HOME/bin directory in your PATH environment variable, type

```
java -jar %DERBY_HOME%\lib\derbyrun.jar ij
```

In my machine, I used the following command:

```
D:\Applns\apache\Derby\derbydb>ij
ij version 10.14
ij>
```

You can now create the database named sampledb and open a connection to the database using the embedded driver using the following command:

```
connect 'jdbc:derby://localhost:1527/D:/Applns/apache/Derby/derbydb/
sampledb;create=true';
```

See Figure G-2.

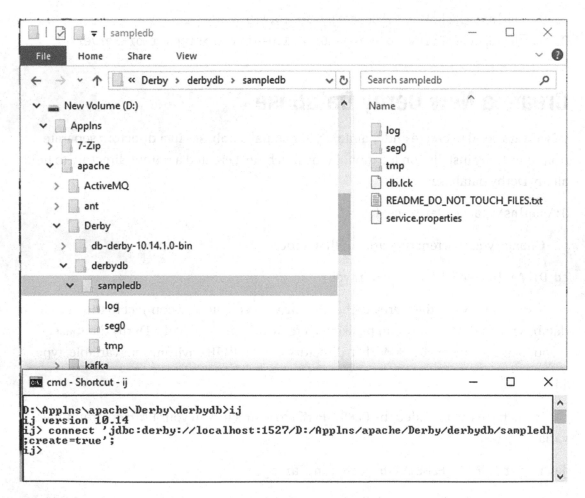

Figure G-2. *Start Derby Server in Network mode*

The above command prompt will also be connected to the newly created database, sampledb. You exit from this window using the following command:

```
exit;
```

Once exited, you can then use the Derby embedded driver again to connect back to the previously created database via the following code:

```
D:\Applns\apache\Derby\ derbydb>ij
ij version 10.14
ij>connect 'jdbc:derby://localhost:1527/D:/Applns/apache/Derby/derbydb/
sampledb;create=false';
```

The following are a handful of helpful commands:

- SHOW CONNECTIONS: If there are no connections, the SHOW CONNECTIONS command returns "No connections available." Otherwise, this command displays a list of connection names and the URLs used to connect to them. The currently active connection, if there is one, will be marked with an ∗ after its name.

- SHOW SCHEMAS displays all of the schemas in the current connection.

- SHOW TABLES displays all of the tables in the current schema. If IN schemaName is specified, the tables in the given schema are displayed.

See Figure G-3.

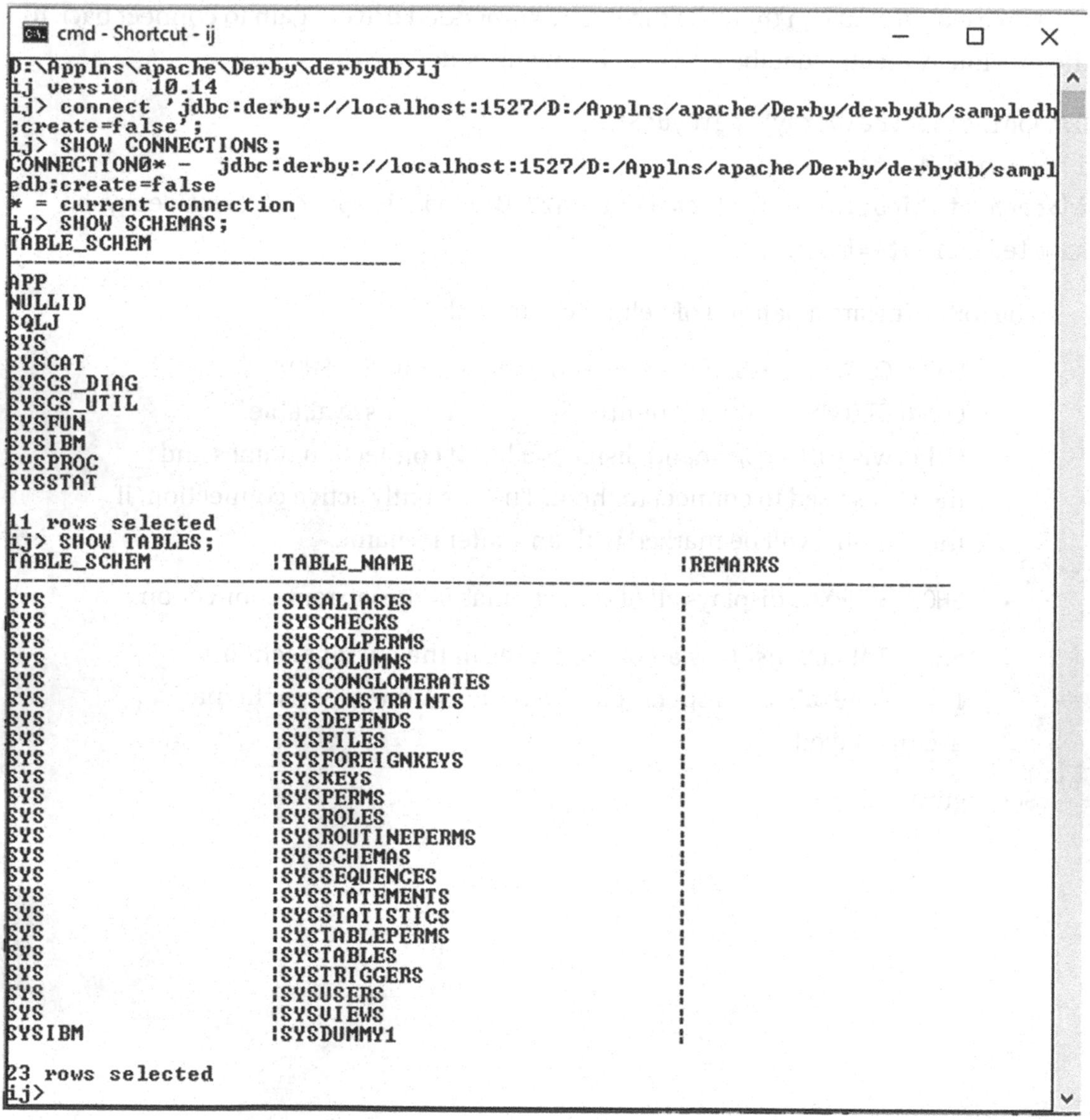

```
cmd - Shortcut - ij                                              —    □    ×

D:\Applns\apache\Derby\derbydb>ij
ij version 10.14
ij> connect 'jdbc:derby://localhost:1527/D:/Applns/apache/Derby/derbydb/sampledb
;create=false';
ij> SHOW CONNECTIONS;
CONNECTION0* -   jdbc:derby://localhost:1527/D:/Applns/apache/Derby/derbydb/sampl
edb;create=false
* = current connection
ij> SHOW SCHEMAS;
TABLE_SCHEM
------------------------------
APP
NULLID
SQLJ
SYS
SYSCAT
SYSCS_DIAG
SYSCS_UTIL
SYSFUN
SYSIBM
SYSPROC
SYSSTAT

11 rows selected
ij> SHOW TABLES;
TABLE_SCHEM             |TABLE_NAME          |REMARKS
------------------------------------------------------------------------------
SYS                    |SYSALIASES          |
SYS                    |SYSCHECKS           |
SYS                    |SYSCOLPERMS         |
SYS                    |SYSCOLUMNS          |
SYS                    |SYSCONGLOMERATES    |
SYS                    |SYSCONSTRAINTS      |
SYS                    |SYSDEPENDS          |
SYS                    |SYSFILES            |
SYS                    |SYSFOREIGNKEYS      |
SYS                    |SYSKEYS             |
SYS                    |SYSPERMS            |
SYS                    |SYSROLES            |
SYS                    |SYSROUTINEPERMS     |
SYS                    |SYSSCHEMAS          |
SYS                    |SYSSEQUENCES        |
SYS                    |SYSSTATEMENTS       |
SYS                    |SYSSTATISTICS       |
SYS                    |SYSTABLEPERMS       |
SYS                    |SYSTABLES           |
SYS                    |SYSTRIGGERS         |
SYS                    |SYSUSERS            |
SYS                    |SYSVIEWS            |
SYSIBM                 |SYSDUMMY1           |

23 rows selected
ij>
```

Figure G-3. *Use the Derby embedded driver ij to interact with the database*

Execute Basic Commands in Derby Database

You can now test your database using the following SQL commands:

```
CREATE TABLE SIMPLETABLE (ID INT PRIMARY KEY, NAME VARCHAR(12));
```

```
DESCRIBE SIMPLETABLE;
```

```
INSERT INTO SIMPLETABLE VALUES (50,'FIFTY'),(60,'SIXTY'),(70,'SEVENTY');

SELECT * FROM SIMPLETABLE;

DELETE FROM SIMPLETABLE;

DROP TABLE SIMPLETABLE;
```

See Figure G-4.

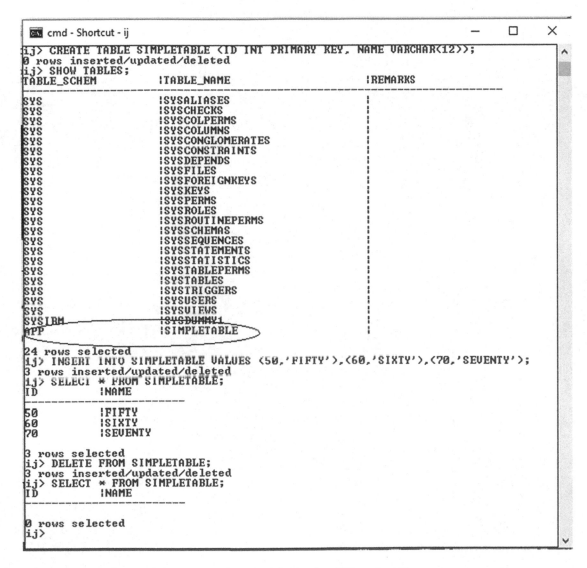

Figure G-4. *Basic SQL operations with Derby DB using ij*

Summary

Derby is a relational database exhibiting strong consistency characteristics, which is why I use Derby to demonstrate the distributed transaction scenarios in this book.

APPENDIX H

MySQL

MySQL is a popular open source SQL database management system that is developed,
distributed, and supported by Oracle Corporation. MySQL manages a structured
collection of data. A MySQL database helps you to add, access, and process the data
stored in the database. MySQL stores data in separate tables. The database structures are
organized into physical files optimized for speed. The logical model, with objects such as
databases, tables, views, rows, and columns, offers a flexible programming environment.
The SQL part of "MySQL" stands for "Structured Query Language," which is the most
common standardized language used to access databases. MySQL software uses the GPL
(GNU General Public) License and is open source software. You can get more details on
MySQL at www.mysql.com/.

I will cover the following on MySQL in this appendix:

- How to download and install MySQL

- How to initialize a data directory for MySQL

- How to start MySQL server and connect to the server

- How to test a connection to MySQL server and disconnect from
  the server

- How to create a database and do basic table operations

- How to add user accounts to the database

Install MySQL

In this section, you will download, install, and configure MySQL and test the installation.
MySQL is available for download at https://dev.mysql.com/downloads/mysql/.

877

© Binildas Christudas 2019
B. Christudas, *Practical Microservices Architectural Patterns*, https://doi.org/10.1007/978-1-4842-4501-9_27

For Microsoft Windows, MySQL is available for 64-bit operating systems only. You may download the following archive:

```
mysql-8.0.14-winx64.zip
```

Extract the above archive to the desired install directory. Even though you may choose any location, like

```
C:\Program Files\MySQL\
```

I explicitly avoid a location with a space in the path, like the space in the `Program Files`. Hence in my Windows machine, I use the following location:

```
D:\Applns\MySQL\mysql-8.0.14-winx64
```

Detailed installation instructions are also available at `https://dev.mysql.com/doc/refman/8.0/en/windows-install-archive.html,`.

Initialize the Data Directory

Since you have installed MySQL using the noinstall package, no data directory, is included. To initialize the data directory, invoke `mysqld` as shown below from the home folder where you unpacked the archive:

```
cd D:\Applns\MySQL\mysql-8.0.14-winx64
D:\Applns\MySQL\mysql-8.0.14-winx64>D:\Applns\MySQL\mysql-8.0.14-winx64\
bin\mysqld --initialize --console
2019-01-22T13:26:05.124628Z 0 [System] [MY-013169] [Server] D:\Applns\
MySQL\mysql-8.0.14-winx64\bin\mysqld (mysqld 8.0.14) initializing of server
in progress as process 14464
2019-01-22T13:26:54.151969Z 5 [Note] [MY-010454] [Server] A temporary
password is generated for root@localhost: S9wdszB#<t.G
2019-01-22T13:27:16.565870Z 0 [System] [MY-013170] [Server] D:\Applns\
MySQL\mysql-8.0.14-winx64\bin\mysqld (mysqld 8.0.14) initializing of server
has completed

D:\Applns\MySQL\mysql-8.0.14-winx64>
```

Detailed instructions to initialize the data directory are also available at https://dev.mysql.com/doc/refman/8.0/en/data-directory-initialization-mysqld.html.

Since you used --initialize for the "secure by default" installation (i.e. including the generation of a random initial root password), the password is marked as expired and you will need to choose a new one. However, you may need to note the above password to be able to use a client to connect to the server, and then to choose a new password,.

Start MySQL Server

To start the server,, enter this command:

```
D:\Applns\MySQL\mysql-8.0.14-winx64\bin>mysqld --console
2019-01-22T13:34:14.562420Z 0 [System] [MY-010116] [Server] D:\Applns\MySQL\
mysql-8.0.14-winx64\bin\mysqld.exe (mysqld 8.0.14) starting as process 22172
2019-01-22T13:34:21.355370Z 0 [Warning] [MY-010068] [Server] CA certificate
ca.pem is self signed.
2019-01-22T13:34:21.605828Z 0 [System] [MY-010931] [Server] D:\Applns\
MySQL\mysql-8.0.14-winx64\bin\mysqld.exe: ready for connections. Version:
'8.0.14'  socket: "  port: 3306  MySQL Community Server - GPL.
2019-01-22T13:34:21.870413Z 0 [System] [MY-011323] [Server] X Plugin ready
for connections. Bind-address: '::' port: 33060
```

The server continues to write to the console any further diagnostic output it produces. You can open a new console window in which you can run client programs.

Detailed instructions to start the server for the first time are available at https://dev.mysql.com/doc/refman/8.0/en/windows-server-first-start.html.

Connect to MySQL Server

Since you used --initialize to initialize the data directory, you connect to the server as root using the random password the server generated during the initialization sequence:

```
D:\Applns\MySQL\mysql-8.0.14-winx64\bin>mysql -u root -p
Enter password: ***********
Welcome to the MySQL monitor.  Commands end with ; or \g.
```

```
Your MySQL connection id is 8
Server version: 8.0.14
```

Copyright (c) 2000, 2019, Oracle and/or its affiliates. All rights reserved.

Oracle is a registered trademark of Oracle Corporation and/or its affiliates. Other names may be trademarks of their respective owners.

```
Type 'help;' or '\h' for help. Type '\c' to clear the current input statement.
mysql>
```

You may next assign a new root password:

```
mysql> ALTER USER 'root'@'localhost' IDENTIFIED BY 'rootpassword';
Query OK, 0 rows affected (0.25 sec)
mysql>
```

While you connect to a MySQL server from your Java programs, you may have to edit the version of the mysql-connector-java maven artefact based on the version of the server you are using in the build script, pom.xml:

```xml
<?xml version="1.0" encoding="UTF-8"?>
<project>
    <properties>
        <mysqljcon.version>8.0.14</mysqljcon.version>
    </properties>
    <dependencies>
        <dependency>
            <groupId>mysql</groupId>
            <artifactId>mysql-connector-java</artifactId>
            <version>${mysqljcon.version}</version>
        </dependency>
    </dependencies>
</project>
```

Test the MySQL Server Installation

You can test whether the MySQL server is working by executing the following
commands:

```
D:\Applns\MySQL\mysql-8.0.14-winx64\bin>mysqlshow -u root -p
Enter password: ***********
+--------------------------------+
|       Databases                |
+--------------------------------+
| information_schema    |
| mysql             |
| performance_schema  |
| sys                       |
+--------------------------------+

D:\Applns\MySQL\mysql-8.0.14-winx64\bin>
```

Disconnect from MySQL Server

If you are connected to the MySQL server using the mysql client, you can disconnect via
the following code:

```
mysql> quit
Bye

D:\Applns\MySQL\mysql-8.0.14-winx64\bin>
```

Create and Select a Database

You can again connect to the database, as mentioned in the "Connect to MySQL Server"
section, by using the new password supplied. Once connected, you can query the
connected user and databases like so:

```
mysql> SELECT USER();
+----------------------+
| USER()               |
+----------------------+
| root@localhost |
+----------------------+
1 row in set (0.00 sec)

mysql> SELECT DATABASE();
+-----------------+
| DATABASE() |
+-----------------+
| NULL            |
+-----------------+
1 row in set (0.00 sec)
```

If you have not yet selected any database, the result is NULL.

You can create a new database using the following code:

```
mysql> create database ecom01;
Query OK, 1 row affected (0.16 sec)

mysql>
```

You can view the newly created database using the following code:

```
mysql> show databases;
+-------------------------------+
| Database                      |
+-------------------------------+
| ecom01                        |
| information_schema   |
| mysql                         |
| performance_schema |
| sys    |
+-------------------------------+
5 rows in set (0.00 sec)

mysql>
```

You need to first select the newly created database, like so:

```
mysql> use ecom01;
Database changed
mysql> SELECT DATABASE();
+-----------------+
| DATABASE() |
+-----------------+
| ecom01         |
+-----------------+
1 row in set (0.00 sec)

mysql>
```

Create Tables

Once you have selected a database, you can create tables in the database selected:

```
mysql> CREATE TABLE pet (name VARCHAR(20), owner VARCHAR(20),
    -> species VARCHAR(20), sex CHAR(1), birth DATE, death DATE);
Query OK, 0 rows affected (0.63 sec)

mysql>
```

Next, you can view the schema for the newly created database:

```
mysql> desc pet;
+---------+-------------+------+-------+---------+--------+
| Field   | Type        | Null | Key   | Default| Extra  |
+---------+-------------+------+-------+---------+--------+
| name    | varchar(20) | YES  |       | NULL    |        |
| owner   | varchar(20) | YES  |       | NULL    |        |
| species | varchar(20) | YES  |       | NULL    |        |
| sex     | char(1)     | YES  |       | NULL    |        |
| birth   | date        | YES  |       | NULL    |        |
| death   | date        | YES  |       | NULL    |        |
+---------+-------------+------+-------+---------+--------+
6 rows in set (0.01 sec)

mysql>
```

Add User Accounts to MySQL Server

You can add new user to access the database server and grant privileges like so:

```
mysql> CREATE USER 'tutorialuser'@'localhost' IDENTIFIED BY
'tutorialmy5ql';
Query OK, 0 rows affected (0.07 sec)
```

```
mysql> GRANT ALL PRIVILEGES ON *.* TO 'tutorialuser'@'localhost' WITH GRANT
OPTION;
Query OK, 0 rows affected (0.03 sec)
```

```
mysql> CREATE USER 'tutorialuser'@'%' IDENTIFIED BY 'tutorialmy5ql';
Query OK, 0 rows affected (0.00 sec)
```

```
mysql> GRANT ALL PRIVILEGES ON *.* TO 'tutorialuser'@'%' WITH GRANT OPTION;
Query OK, 0 rows affected (0.00 sec)
```

https://dev.mysql.com/doc/refman/8.0/en/adding-users.html

Stop MySQL Server

To stop the server, enter this command:

```
D:\Applns\MySQL\mysql-8.0.14-winx64\bin>mysqladmin -u root -p shutdown
Enter password: ***********
D:\Applns\MySQL\mysql-8.0.14-winx64\bin>
```

Summary

MySQL is a relational database that can be used for operations where strong consistency is required like those in ACID transactions. I use MySQL for demonstrating many of the samples in this book.

Index

A

© Binildas Christudas 2019
B. Christudas, *Practical Microservices Architectural Patterns*, https://doi.org/10.1007/978-1-4842-4501-9

B

C

E